THE ENGLISH MEDIAEVAL HOUSE

The first-floor hall, Brinsop Court; *c.* 1340.

THE ENGLISH MEDIAEVAL HOUSE

MARGARET WOOD
M.A., D.LIT., F.S.A.

(MRS E. G. KAINES-THOMAS)

*With frontispiece, 60 pages of half-tone plates, 32 pages of engravings
and 117 illustrations in the text*

Bracken Books
LONDON

This edition published 1983 by Bracken Books,
a division of Bestseller Publications Ltd,
Brent House, 24 Friern Park, North Finchley, London N12.

Copyright © text, Margaret Wood, 1965

Printed and bound in the United States of America

ISBN 0 946495 02 5

TO K-T

Contents

Illustrations

PLATES

Photographs
(Except where otherwise stated, photographs are by the author)

Engravings

TEXT FIGURES

Foreword

By SIR MORTIMER WHEELER

THE making of this important book began with a systematic study of Norman houses and thence proceeded steadily and logically from century to mediaeval century. Here was no floundering amongst a miscellaneous amalgam. In the course of her research, Mrs Kaines-Thomas has herself followed (I had nearly said re-lived) stage by stage the evolutionary sequence represented in successive architectural modes, so that these have been allowed to express themselves as a natural process, with a minimum of applied conjecture. That is as it should be, but has not always been so. Half a century ago, when the scattered material had not been assembled critically and much of it had not even been recognized, wayward theory was rife. The baron then, more often than not, was encased within the iron curtain of his keep and almost went to bed in chain-mail. Now and then, especially if he were King John, he might entrust himself to a hunting lodge. Beyond, the lesser folk lived in huts and barns, save for the occasional Jew who wisely provided himself with a fire-proof stone house and in it, for the most part, lived upstairs. In all this there was not very much of historical science; it was nearer to the world of *Camelot*.

But now Mrs Kaines-Thomas has devoted longer years than I can chivalrously recall to discovering, re-discovering, ferreting out, measuring up, documenting and conferring about the mediaeval houses of England, and here reviews her more detailed essays with the aid of invaluable lists and bibliographies. The result is a clear statement of much that was unclear in the older archaeological or architectural tradition. Her work is timely. Its later phases have coincided with a remarkable and heartening revival of archaeological interest in such things; particularly in the buried vestiges which are year by year being revealed by the aeroplane, the mechanical excavator and the spade. Deserted mediaeval villages, hitherto ignored, are being planned and sampled by excavation. The Ministry of Public Building and Works, through its Ancient Monuments Division, is year by year the patron of widespread salvage-work, sometimes all too close to the devouring machinery of agriculture and 'development' but in the aggregate of high value to more than one aspect of historical study. It would be a pardonable exaggeration to say that we are beginning to know and appreciate our countryside in this new sense precisely at the moment when we are inflicting upon it unprecedented and irredeemable mutilation. The recent excavation (by the Ministry) of the vast timber hall of the royal palace at Cheddar is a dramatic example. Reduced largely to ruts and post-holes, it presents nevertheless a vivid outline of the domestic environment of 12th-century royalty, and adds materially to our picture of the early Middle Ages.

Of all this new exploration in depth, Mrs Kaines-Thomas is of course very fully aware. But her primary contribution is in the field of upstanding architecture, often immured, maybe, within later accretion but at the same time susceptible in a surprising number of instances to skilled interpretation. Her book is itself a monument of persistent and orderly inquiry and of methodical exposition. If, as she sometimes avers, I had some small part in its initiation, I proudly accept her generosity without too close inquiry. (Old men forget.)

MORTIMER WHEELER

1964.

Introduction

The poetry of history lies in the quasi-miraculous fact that once, on this earth, once, on this familiar spot of ground, walked other men and women, as actual as we are today, thinking their own thoughts, swayed by their own passions, but now all gone, one generation vanishing after another, gone as utterly as we ourselves shall shortly be gone, like ghosts at cock-crow.

G. M. Trevelyan: *Autobiography of an Historian.*

THE charm of mediaeval architecture lies not in its intrinsic beauty alone. It is a link with our ancestors. We are looking at buildings which they saw. The essence of the past still lingers like the notes of distant music, faintly heard, and for a while our spirits are in tune. Old buildings mirror the conditions of their time, and the dwelling-house most of all. More than any other form of architecture, the mediaeval house reflects the daily life of a period, and yet, until recently, it has seldom been studied as a whole. There have been good descriptions of individual places, especially of the 15th century,* yet for a general view of the house in the Middle Ages we have to return to J. H. Parker's admirable work of over a hundred years ago. Unlike many architectural writers, who describe the 'typical mediaeval house' as if unchanged for some 450 years, he follows the house from the 12th to the 15th centuries, and gives many examples of each period. Since his day, more houses of these centuries have been discovered and planned, including those of lesser folk, and it is now possible to trace a gradual development in type and design. Much research still is needed, but here it is proposed, from the knowledge now available, to attempt a survey of the mediaeval house, as it evolved, and study its growth as influenced by changing social conditions.

Just as the *Oxford History of English Art* sets out to show the visual arts as part of the general history of England, so this study of the English House endeavours, in a small way, to reflect the social history of England as it develops from the late 11th to early 16th centuries. The picture cannot, however, be complete, because the domestic buildings that remain are from their nature the more permanent homes of the wealthy and not, except in stone areas or where excavated, the flimsy dwellings of ordinary people. But more and more of these are being discovered in this way, through the careful uncovering of the evidence of vanished timbers, which have left their 'ghosts' in the form of different filling in the holes and channels they once occupied. In the country, peasant houses in abandoned mediaeval villages, now in fields, reveal their plans in uneven surfaces on the ground, and

* See Garner and Stratton (1929); also Tipping (1921).

especially to the eye of air photography, thus facilitating the work of the excavator. Much research in this is being conducted by the Deserted Mediaeval Village Research Group, allying excavation to the information obtained from documents, particularly those relating to tax assessment, and a new vista has been opened in our knowledge. In the towns where later buildings occupy the position of the old, evidence must be gained when demolition occurs, and sometimes an ancient structure is found embedded and disguised in the later one being removed. This research must be done immediately and recording made, for 20th-century foundations reach the subsoil, and the bulldozer removes all archaeological evidence. Thus more and more material is being collected and our knowledge is still fluid. Indeed mediaeval archaeology, so long confined chiefly to ecclesiastical building, is now coming into its own with wider scope, and this is signalized by the inauguration, in 1956, of a new Society solely devoted to our mediaeval period in its widest sense. This, summarizing in its journal the discoveries made year by year, is a powerful aid to the excellent work of inventory performed by the Royal Commission on Historical Monuments as well as the excavations now carried out by that body, and the Ancient Monuments Department of the Ministry of Works, whose 'rescue digs' on threatened sites are added to the admirable preservation and report of the important buildings entrusted to it. Also valuable are the guide books published by the National Trust and other bodies with historic houses in their care. The task of recording old buildings small as well as great, throughout the land, is assigned to the investigators of the Ministry of Town and Country Planning, who with those of the Victoria County Histories and the photographers of the National Buildings Record are making a careful advance county by county. However, the impetus of modern demolition is, alas, the speedier, and the recording by local archaeologists of urgent necessity. A number are banded together in the Vernacular Architecture Group, with its emphasis on the homes of ordinary people and research in cruck buildings. The Group links together the work of these archaeologists, and their reports on individual buildings are published by the national and county societies which, together with the local Museums, are associated in the Council for British Archaeology, a co-ordinating body of increasing importance. Indeed mediaeval recording is gathering momentum, the latest step being taken by the School of Architecture of Manchester University, where the late Professor Cordingley and his colleagues inaugurated a series of Studies in Regional Domestic Architecture, 'the investigation and recording of old houses, generally below Great House scale, with a view to extracting the history of their development in terms of architectural character, accommodation and structure, and the difference of practice between one region and another'. This will be a valuable advance in our research, and, concentrating on lesser houses, supplement the information provided by the admirable and well-illustrated articles on greater houses provided by Mr Christopher Hussey and Mr Arthur Oswald in *Country Life*.

Historical research in the documentary sense is now combined with that of the tape and spade, and here too many new discoveries are appearing, as more and more documents, particularly those of local importance, are being deciphered. Archaeology, the study of the material remains of former ages, is now regarded as the ally of documentary research; in fact they are the two paths, both indispensable, to the discovery of the past, which is history.

Here an attempt is made, however inadequate, to summarize the information to date for the benefit of the general reader and student. Almost every month, however, brings fresh discoveries to modify our views. But that only adds to the excitement of the hunt into the past.

Every effort has been made to avoid errors, but these tend to creep in in spite of care, and any corrections will be gratefully received by the author for inclusion in a possible further edition of this book.

In England the Middle Ages are usually dated from the Norman Conquest of 1066 (pre-Conquest and earlier examples are however mentioned where they throw light on mediaeval development). In general this is a convenient term for the late 11th to 15th centuries inclusive. But in text books the period is reckoned as ending with Richard III at Bosworth Field (1485), to class Henry VII with the other Tudors in the 16th century. In domestic architecture there is no such break, and here it is proposed to end the mediaeval period in 1539–40. This is not only the date of Henry VIII's Dissolution of the Monasteries, whose abbots had had a great influence on house design; but it also coincides with the more definite inroad of classical influences via the Continent, which had been infiltrating in court circles, but for a long time affecting only the ornament.

The study of the mediaeval house is focused on the development of the hall, which was the chief room, originally perhaps the only one. In the 12th century a separate building, the hall attached to itself other 'houses', one room deep, added as separately roofed wings; these gradually become incorporated, and by the end of the period the house was something like the compact block usual today, with a number of apartments under a single roof.

The mediaeval hall developed from the barn-like structure of prehistoric and Saxon times, with a central hearth. This mode of heating required a building on ground level and a lofty roof for the escape of smoke: with a low ceiling there could have been risk of fire. One end of the hall became extended to provide service apartments, a buttery for the drinks, a pantry for bread and table utensils, with, between the two, a passage to the kitchen, which until the 15th century was an isolated building as a precaution against fire. Over these service rooms was a bed-sittingroom for the owner and his family. This private room was called the great chamber or solar, the latter term being used in general for any room on an upper level. Here a central hearth would not be practicable and so wall fireplaces with chimneys were used from the late 11th century onwards.

In the earlier Middle Ages the hall itself might be raised to the first floor, and like the great chamber be equipped with a wall fireplace; though occasionally, when particularly lofty, as originally at Ludlow and later Hampton Court, it had a central hearth. These 'first-floor halls' were more defensible, being raised on a stone basement which was often vaulted, and thus could have larger windows; narrow loops widely splayed within sufficed as windows for the storage or servants' quarters in the basement beneath. Such upper halls were in use from the late 11th century, and formed a convenient type for the abbot's house incorporated into the monastic cloister; they continued into the 14th century, especially in areas of possible unrest such as the Marches of Wales and the Scottish Border. New and splendid halls of this nature were built in the bishops' palaces of Pembrokeshire, Lamphey and St David's, in the mid 14th century. But elsewhere they tended to be ousted by the more convenient ground-floor hall.

Important developments were taking place in this barn-like structure. At first the hall was aisled like a church, with two rows of posts or stone pillars, necessary to reduce the span when long timbers were not available for roofing a wide area. But these verticals obstructed the floor space, and towards the end of the 13th century carpenters were experimenting on roofs which would render them unnecessary. Such attempts may be seen at the Old Deanery at Salisbury, and other 'aisled derivatives', raising the triple division to roof level, are found in the early 14th century at Wasperton and West Bromwich. At Stokesay Castle (c. 1285–1305) a form of cruck construction was employed, based on the primitive use of pairs of curved timbers which probably served 12th- and 13th-century halls of lesser span. Gradually only the service end retained its posts, for a while, when these still served as screen divisions in a 'spere truss'.* The arch-braced and hammerbeam roofs, both originating in the earlier 14th century, show their full development in the final period.

The great chamber over the service became inconvenient, being at the opposite end of the hall from the high table. A solar at the upper end gave more convenient access for the owner, who could retire from dinner and ascend to his private room behind, instead of traversing the length of the hall, in the body of which his dependants had their meals. In some cases the solar was already at this end, as at Boothby Pagnell, on one building block with the hall, but often a solar wing was added transversely, a fashion coming in during the 13th century, as we know from the orders of Henry III. This meant that the high table would lose the large window behind it, as was the case in an 'end hall', but a lofty window, sometimes circular, could be placed high up in the gable, where it rose above the separate roof of the chamber block. Below there would be room for a decorated canopy over the owner's seat.

Access was easy where, as at Boothby Pagnell, the great chamber was on the same floor as the hall, but where the hall was at ground level a staircase to the solar must be provided. One rising direct from the hall would impede the high table arrangement. Usually the solar was reached by an outside staircase in a projection off the end of the lateral wall at this point. This mode of ascent was probably the origin of the hall oriel, at first built to house the solar stairs, but later becoming a bay window to give ample light to the high table.

By the 14th century the typical hall was at ground level with a central hearth, and a two-storeyed block at each end, at the upper a great chamber over a store room, which soon became a parlour or withdrawing room for the occupants of the high table, and another bedchamber, perhaps for guests or the eldest son and his family, over the butteries at the lower end. Between these service rooms a passage was normal, leading to the kitchen, which was still set apart for fear of fire, but incorporated in the main building in the 15th century. This is the mediaeval 'H-plan'.

Along with this, however, there was a revival of the first-floor hall, in the tower house, which might also be regarded as a recrudescence of the Norman keep, of which there was continuous development on the unruly Scottish Border. In the later 14th and 15th centuries the tower house appears further south, serving as a strong residence for the lord against lawless neighbours, and even his own retainers, who now were paid mercenaries instead

* A spere is 'a form of screen in a hall, with side-posts forming part of the roof truss (timber framework) above, the middle part being commonly closed by a moveable screen'. (R.C.H.M.)

of trustworthy tenants long associated with the family. This increase in the lord's *entourage* was rendered necessary to maintain his prestige and even security in an age of violence. The retainers might be housed in older buildings round the court adjoining the new tower house, but often further quarters were necessary. The 15th century shows a multiplication of lodgings, each equipped with fireplace and garderobe (latrine), not only for retainers but to meet the increased demand for comfort and privacy, especially by the more important members of the family and staff. The private room, at first the privilege of the owner, was now more general.

In the 15th century a parlour under the great chamber was usual, and the solar staircase tended to lead off it, leaving the oriel projection to serve as its anteroom and a window recess. By the second half of the 15th century this bay window was normal, built in new halls and added to old ones. The wall fireplace, found in some 14th-century halls, was now common, placed on a side wall and occasionally behind the high table. However, the central hearth persisted in some houses into the 16th century, even provided in new buildings such as the great hall of Henry VIII at Hampton Court.

But the more convenient wall fireplace caused the decline of the lofty open hall. With a side chimney to control the smoke, height was no longer necessary, and the hall could safely have a lower ceiling, which made for comfort and warmth, and gave opportunity for another room above. Ashbury Manor (*c.* 1488) has two well-appointed chambers over the hall. This Berkshire house belonged to the Abbey of Glastonbury, and appears to have been built by Somerset masons: this compact form of house seems, from our present state of knowledge, to be a west-country type of building.

Certainly the later 15th century shows houses more akin, in their rectangular plan and uniformity of roof line, to modern buildings. The kitchen was now incorporated into the main oblong block. By now the hall was no longer the centre of the life of the household, but rather a servants' hall, the family normally preferring to dine apart. With the increase of rooms and the development of the parlour, the hall starts on its descent, in size and in social scale, to the mere vestibule of today.

I have many friends to thank for their assistance in the compilation of this book, some of whom have most kindly placed unpublished material at my disposal, as have Mr A. J. Taylor, M.A., F.S.A., with regard to the chimneys found by the Ministry of Works at Conway; Mr R. W. McDowall, F.S.A., and Mr F. Atkinson, B.Sc., F.M.A., concerning the aisled halls found near Halifax; Mr G. C. Dunning, B.Sc., F.S.A., for his mediaeval chimney-pot and ventilator finds; and Mr P. G. M. Dickinson, F.S.A., F.R.Hist.S., who has shown me his discoveries of early date in Suffolk. Mr. J. T. Smith, M.A., F.S.A., has allowed me to draw on his great knowledge of mediaeval roofs, and Mr S. E. Rigold, M.A., has kindly looked through my chapter on timber framing. It should be stressed, however, that I alone am responsible for the conclusions drawn from this material, unless otherwise stated. Mr C. A. Ralegh Radford, M.A., F.B.A., F.S.A., has been generous in his help, and perused my section on pre-Norman houses. Also I am most grateful to Mr L. F. Salzman, M.A., F.S.A., from whose invaluable documentary research on buildings I have drawn much information, as from Mr John Harvey, F.S.A., concerning the architects, and especially to Mr. W. A. Pantin, M.A., F.B.A., F.S.A., and Mr E. T. Long, F.S.A., for sharing with me their extensive discoveries on the houses remaining, and the latter also for reading my 15th-century chapter and others. Mr A. W. Everett, F.S.A., has kindly given me the benefit of his great knowledge of Devon houses and beautiful photographs of them.

Among others who have helped me, I should like to mention Mr Maurice Barley, M.A., F.S.A., Mr Hugh Braun, F.S.A., F.R.I.B.A., Mr Martin Biddle, Mr G. E. Chambers, F.S.A., who has assisted me over Wardour Castle; Mr Norman Drinkwater, F.S.A., A.R.I.B.A., with regard to Norrington Manor and the Old Deanery at Salisbury; Mr A. R. Dufty, F.S.A., A.R.I.B.A., concerning Corfe and Farnham Castles; Mr Gilyard-Beer, M.A., F.S.A., for his aid and fine photographs of Northborough Manor, Mr. J. G. Hurst, M.A., F.S.A., for his introduction to lost peasant houses; Mr S. R. Jones relating to Wasperton; Mr R. T. Mason, F.S.A., for help in Sussex houses; Mr H. de S. Shortt, M.A., F.S.A., at Salisbury and Mr. P. S. Spokes, B.Sc., M.A., F.S.A., for his excellent photographs as well as help with the measuring tape. The late Mr A. W. Vivian-Neal, M.A., F.S.A., and Mr R. C. Sansome, F.S.A.(Scot.) and his colleagues at Taunton Castle gave me much kind assistance over the Somerset houses. The late Mr W. H. Godfrey, F.S.A., F.R.I.B.A., and Mr B. H. St J. O'Neil, F.S.A., also gave me great support and encouragement.

Two American scholars have been most kind and co-operative, Professor U. T. Holmes with his wide knowledge of Old French texts and 12th-century houses in England and France, and Professor Walter Horn who has generously allowed me to use measured drawings made for his research on early aisled buildings.

Nor must I forget Mr M. B. Cookson, to whom I owe any success in photography, and the loyal helpers at the other end of the measuring tape like my friends Miss Alison Cunningham, Miss P. Furness, Dr L. H. Jeffery, F.S.A., and Mrs Averil Hassall. Thanks are also due to Mr Cecil Farthing, B.A., F.S.A., and the staff at the National Buildings Record, the Librarian and staff of the Society of Antiquaries, and to Misses D. Hervey, Claire Lock and Jane Ward, who typed my manuscript. Above all I wish to thank my publishers for their unfailing helpfulness in the production of this book.

Especially fortunate have I been in my parents, who did all they could to encourage me in this chosen work, and a special thanks is due to my husband, E. G. Kaines-Thomas, who has helped me not only with the tape and in other ways but by reading and discussing the chapters, and whom I first met outside a Norman window (at Sherborne Castle) on an archaeological congress.

My very grateful thanks are due to Sir Mortimer Wheeler, who started me off in research on the Norman houses which, as he told me, needed doing, and which he would have embarked on himself if he had the time, and who has so suitably, and kindly, consented to write the preface.

M. E. W.

Donnington Dene,
Newbury, 1964.

To conjure, even for a moment, the wistfulness which is the past is like trying to gather in one's arms the hyacinthine colour of the distance. But if it is once achieved, what sweetness!—like the gentle, fugitive fragrance of spring flowers, dried with bergamot and bay. How the tears will spring in the reading of some old parchment—'to my dear child, my tablets and my ring'—or of yellow letters, with the love still fresh and fair in them though the ink is faded—'and so good night, my dearest heart, and God send you happy'. That vivid present of theirs, how faint it grows. The past is only the present become invisible and mute; and because it is invisible and mute, its memoried glances and its murmurs are infinitely precious. We are tomorrow's past. Even now we slip away like those pictures painted on the moving dials of antique clocks—a ship, a cottage, sun and moon, a nosegay. The dial turns, the ship rides up and sinks again, the yellow painted sun has set, and we that were the new things, gather magic as we go.

Mary Webb in *Precious Bane*.

I

Norman Town Houses; Jews' and Merchants' Houses; 'King John's Houses'

NORMAN domestic architecture has been neglected in the past. The reason is, of course, to be found in a scarcity of recognizable examples, occasioned by the very nature of the dwelling house, more liable to alteration and destruction than any other type of building. Norman houses, being earliest, have naturally suffered most; indeed their only chance of escape lay in a greater sturdiness of wall, sometimes the sole means of recognition. Hence there is even a general ignorance that good 12th-century buildings existed other than castles, churches and monasteries. The Normans are always pictured in these, and in some works on domestic architecture keeps form the illustration for the 12th century, and the reader can even assume that subsequent houses were developed from them. When the author is aware of Romanesque houses—and then it is usually Jew's House, Lincoln, and Boothby Pagnell manor that are known—they are mentioned rather as anomalies.

This may account for the attribution of a Jewish origin to certain houses, all in towns, which derive a local fame from that assumption. For if the Normans lived in castles, then the Jews must be responsible for dwelling houses. There may be some truth in the 'Jewish theory', notably with regard to two of the houses at Lincoln assigned by tradition to such owners. The Jews were accustomed to a higher standard of living than that of their simpler neighbours, many of whom, as in London, were apparently content with timber, wattle-and-daub and the danger of fire. The Jews were rich and had more to lose in a fire; also as money-lenders they were unpopular and so liable to attack by the mob. A stone house was thus preferred for protection and comfort.

The Jews occupied a special position in the early mediaeval economy. Unable to take part in the usual crafts of the time, being prevented through religious reasons from taking the guild oath to the Trinity, they concentrated on finance, and thus filled a definite need in times when no Christian was permitted by canon law to lend money on interest. Indeed they had control of a large proportion of the actual coin of the country,* in days when so much capital was locked up in land.

Barter was of no avail when great projects such as the equipment of armies or the building of cathedrals and monasteries were on hand, and the Jews provided the funds for such enterprises. The most famous of them was Aaron of Lincoln, who flourished from 1166 to 1185, and at his death had no less than one king (of Scotland), five earls, one archbishop, two bishops, nine Cistercian abbeys (including Rievaulx), and the towns of Winchester and Southampton, besides many smaller debtors, on his books. These are recorded on the Pipe Rolls, as his property went to the king, Henry II, in 1185. The Abbey of St Albans owed him much: its chronicler relates how 'Aaron the Jew who held us in his debt coming to the house of St Alban in great pride and boasting, with threats kept on boasting that it was he who made the window for our St Alban, and that he had prepared for the saint a home when he was without one'.† Indeed Bishop Chesney of Lincoln (1148-66) pawned the ornaments of his church, redeemed from Aaron by his successor.‡ Aaron had agents throughout the country, and owned a house in London, in Lothbury near Walbrook, but Lincoln was apparently his headquarters.

The Jewish financiers charged interest of at least 40 per cent, partly, perhaps, because of the great risks involved and the difficulty of getting the money back, in spite of the royal 'exchequer of the Jews' which was supposed to help them. In their stone houses they kept not only gold and silver, like a bank, but also the deeds relative to their loans; hence the need for a very strong fireproof building. The opportunity of seizing these was one of the chief reasons for the hysterical anti-Jewish outbreaks from time to time. At Lincoln, in 1265, the chirograph chest with evidence of the debts was burned,§ but on the whole, unlike the Jews of Lynn, Norwich, and especially York in 1189, and London and Canterbury in 1265, the Jews of Lincoln escaped the worst of the massacres, seeking refuge in the castle when necessary, in spite of the gross charges of ritual murder at the death of 'Little St Hugh' in 1255.

The Jews had come into England with the Conqueror. The king was their protector and they were regarded as his property. This was most profitable to him, for he derived taxation from them when they married, or went into business partnership, and at their death either seized their property or charged their heir a large sum in relief. Aaron was a great source of revenue to Henry II from taxation during his lifetime, and at his death the Exchequer set up a special department, the 'Scaccarium Aaronis', to collect the debts due to him. These

* Salzman (1929), 246.
† Gesta Sancti Albani, ed. H. T. Riley. 'Rolls Series' (1867-9), 193.
‡ Hill (1948), 218.
§ Hill (1948), 209.

amounted to £15,000,* and this sum they, like him, collected with great difficulty, some £12,000 being still owing in 1201.† The Jews have been called 'indirect tax-gatherers for the king',‡ and 'sponges in the king's hand to suck up his subjects' wealth, helpless clients whom he alone protected from popular malice and massacre'.§

But after the death of Henry II (1189) persecution began, and by the end of the 13th century the Jews were impoverished from this as well as from royal restrictions and taxation. Also they had been meeting competition from foreign merchants, Christian money-lenders, the Caorcins (*caursini*),‖ who evaded the church law against usury by a specious form of contract, reported by Matthew Paris, the Chronicler of St Albans Abbey, as early as 1235.¶ They charged as high rates of interest as did the Jews, and Bishop Grosseteste called them less considerate.** They became generally unpopular, and like the Jews were in turn protected and exploited by Henry III, always in need of money for his building schemes.†† His son, Edward I, expelled the Jews in 1290, which he would not have done had they still been of service. Their expulsion had already been effected in Gascony and his dominions on the Continent, and was connected with his forthcoming crusade. It was a very popular act, and resulted in large sums being granted to the king by clergy and laity. Some fifteen or sixteen thousand Jews left that year, and the expulsion was completed in 1358.‡‡ Their race was not to return to England until the mid 17th century, in the time of Cromwell.

But the later 12th century marked the peak of Jewish prosperity in mediaeval England. In 1194 their share in the ransom of Richard Cœur de Lion shows the relative importance of their position in the main cities, London leading the way with twenty-nine contributors, Lincoln next in amount but with forty persons (the great Aaron having already died), followed by Canterbury and, a long way behind, Northampton, Norwich and Winchester. York does not appear on the list, due to the 1189 massacre, but provides double the amount given by London in an 'aid' of 1221, when Winchester came third with Lincoln just below.§§

The stone houses attributed to Jews are of the late 12th century. In London none remain, though originally they must have stood out more prominently than at Lincoln, which is on the limestone belt, for in London all building-stone would have to be imported. We know, however, that the London Jews had stone buildings, for Stow tells us how the Barons of 1215 'repaired the walles and gates of the Citie, with stone taken from the Jewes broken houses'.‖‖

In Lincoln there are three houses associated with the Jews. The best known is Jew's

---

* To be multiplied by at least 40–60 to compare with our money.
† Hill (1948), 220.
‡ Kent (1945).
§ Trevelyan (1945), 33.
‖ Powicke (1947), 313; Salzman (1929), 246.
¶ *Chronica majora*, III, 329.
** Paris, *Chronica majora*, V, 404–5.
†† Powicke (1947), 314–15.
‡‡ Many Jewish bonds are preserved in original presses at Westminster Abbey. Davis (1924), 581.
§§ Hill (1948), 217; J. Jacob (1893), *Jews of Angevin England*, 162, 381.
‖‖ Stow (1598), I, 9; also 30, 38, 280, 283.

House, 15 The Strait, [1]* dated *c.* 1170–80 from stylistic evidence (Fig. 1; Pls. I A and B). Documentary sources agree that here lived the Jewess Belaset of Wallingford, who was hanged in 1290 for clipping the king's coin, but its earlier owners are not known. Certainly the rich decoration points to a wealthy builder, but even richer decoration occurs at St Mary's Guild (Pl. II A), traditionally not Jewish but belonging to a civic guild. Next to Jew's House, on the east, is Jew's Court,[3] which has no datable features and looks later. It used to be considered the place of the (supposed) martyrdom of little St Hugh of Lincoln in 1255. But the well 'in which the body was concealed' was removed in 1928

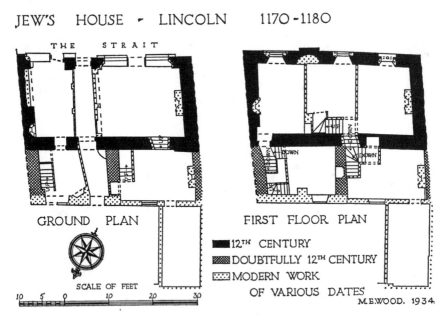

JEW'S HOUSE · LINCOLN 1170-1180

THE STRAIT

GROUND PLAN

FIRST FLOOR PLAN

■ 12TH CENTURY
▨ DOUBTFULLY 12TH CENTURY
▧ MODERN WORK OF VARIOUS DATES

SCALE OF FEET

10　5　0　10　20　30

M.E.WOOD. 1934

Fig. 1.

as a forgery only a few years old, the workman who made it giving evidence. The tradition that this was a synagogue has been accepted by Dr Roth and other Jewish scholars, who have identified the recess in which the scrolls of the law were kept.

Further up Steep Hill to the Cathedral is the so-called Aaron the Jew's House,[2] alike in date and build to Jew's House, and possibly with a similar 12th-century occupant. The owner, however, was definitely not Aaron. The recent 'tradition' connecting the house with that famous Lincoln Jew lately has been proved incorrect. He lived in Lincoln *c.* 1166–85, but in another part of the city, namely the Bail.

Another important Jewish financier, Jacob, is associated with Canterbury. He contributed nearly half the city's share of the 1194 grant, and seems to have been the wealthiest of a colony of Jews who appear in the city *c.* 1180. Here we know exactly where he lived, from documentary evidence, and the County Hotel preserves in its cellar (and above

* For numbered references see list of examples at end of chapter.

•A and B. Jew's House, Lincoln; *c.* 1170–80.

C. 12th-century house with chimney at Cluny (Burgundy). D. 12th-century chimney at Bayeux (Normandy).

Plate I. 12th-century Town Houses.

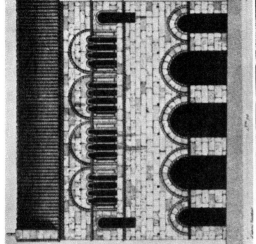

Plate II.

A. St Mary's Guild, Lincoln; *c.* 1180–90. B. 12th-century house at Périgueux (Dordogne). C and D. The 'Gloriet', Corfe Castle, hall range and hall entrance; 1201–2.

ground until 1927) a very thick wall of the 'great stone house' which he built just before 1200.[6] The front of the hotel covers the three plots of ground which he bought for this purpose, and behind, with its frontage to Stour Street, earlier called 'Heathen Man's Lane' (*Hethenmannelane*), was the Synagogue and the house of another Jew, Benedict or Baruch, beyond. Jacob died in or about 1216, and his sons Samuel and Aaron sold his house to the cathedral monks, who by 1230 had let it to another Jew called Cressel, at which time there was a Jew called Aaron living in a smaller property opposite in Stour Street; and in Best Lane there were more stone houses, one of Sampson the Jew, another of Goldwin the Mercer. Thanks to the researches of Dr William Urry into the cathedral

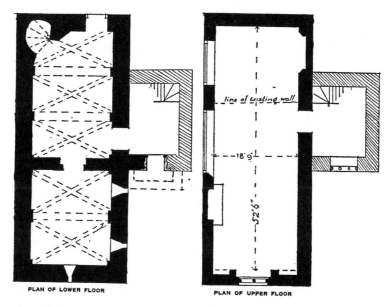

PLAN OF LOWER FLOOR   PLAN OF UPPER FLOOR

Fig. 2. Plan of the 'Music House', Norwich. The existing walls are shown in solid black; the shaded part shows the position of the original entrance forebuilding.

property surveys of *c*. 1200 and *c*. 1230, a plan of early mediaeval Canterbury has been reconstructed which shows that the building sites have hardly changed in dimension, and a number of 12th- and 13th-century cellars on them remain.

In Norwich, the late 12th-century 'Music House' [4] (Figs. 2 and 3) with its vaulted cellars may have been the residence of the great financier Isaac the Jew. He is portrayed in a 13th-century cartoon in the Public Record Office as a three-faced king of Norwich, but he died in 1199, his property passing to King John. From a resemblance in architectural detail to the Priory Infirmary, the house is believed to date from *c*. 1175, thus probably was built by Isaac himself, though his father (Abraham) and grandfather (Moses) seem to have had an earlier house in Conisford on this site, or near by.

A Jewish origin is possible but not proved in the case of Moyses Hall, Bury St Edmunds.[5] The building certainly occurs within the period before the Jews at St Edmundsbury were

Fig. 3. Reconstruction of the 'Music House', Norwich, c. 1175.

expelled, in 1190, much earlier than elsewhere. The name may be Jewish, and is certainly old, first occurring in a document of 1328. Dr Margoliouth considers it was a Jewish house or synagogue, and certainly the subvault is unnecessarily lofty for a space of storage, while traces of a further range to the west might be said to fit in with his view that the whole side of the market place was filled by the Synagogue and its subsidiary buildings, seminary, baptisteries and official residences. On the other hand it may have belonged to the Abbey, being perhaps one of the stone houses which Abbot Samson (1182–1212) bought in the town (c. 1198) to house his scholars; * or even one of the stone houses that the Abbot built himself, and which the Londoners threatened to destroy.† Perhaps it belonged to Jews, and the Abbot acquired it after their expulsion.

To sum up: there is no doubt that the Jews had stone houses for reasons of defence, wealth and importance, but it is unwise to consider that every surviving Norman town house necessarily had a Jewish owner.

There were other persons of wealth in the 12th century besides Jew and baron: people who could afford to build a substantial house, and especially in districts where stone was abundant. In the country stone houses might be feudal, manor houses, or monastic granges, but in the towns the craft and merchant guilds were increasingly active, and guild houses and even solid private houses could be afforded by the members. The question of defence concerned the merchant less than it did the Jew, but he also had valuable stores to protect from fire and theft, and money to build a stone basement for that purpose, with a pleasant hall above to live in.

Very few of these early merchants' houses have survived. But there is documentary evidence that they were in stone, mentioned thus in the records because this was remarkable, a sign of wealth, in days when ordinary people were content with wooden buildings; and a stone house was also a landmark. Near the Jewish houses at Canterbury, Dr Urry has found references to the 'Stone house of Goldwin the Mercer' and others.

At Lincoln, where stone was the local building material, there would be many more, and indeed numbers were left as late as the 18th century. The observant Mr E. King

---

* *Chronicle of Jocelin of Brakelond;* translated by L. C. Jane (1931), 72.
† Ibid. 120.

remarked in 1782 on a 'circumstance almost peculiar to it of all cities in England; which is, the vast number of beautiful Saxon and Norman doorways, constructed in the most finished manner, and to be met with, in every part of the streets; and in the walls of what are now the most private houses'.* But Defoe attributed this wealth of 'Gothic remains' to civic decay.† Since Turner's volume of 1851 more have been abolished.

In his study of Lincoln documents Sir Francis Hill has discovered that in the late 12th century the fashionable quarter for rich merchants was the suburb of Wigford, south of the city, which is now incorporated with it. It is therefore not surprising that here should be found the only mediaeval building left apart from churches, St Mary's Guild (sometimes called erroneously John of Gaunt's Stables),[9] the headquarters of what must have been an important social-religious guild. It was named after Our Lady, patron saint of Lincoln, and its chapel seems to have been the church of St Andrew, which stood nearly opposite. In 1348 property was granted to two chaplains there to celebrate for the grace-man, brothers and sisters of the ancient guild of St Mary, and for the soul of King Henry III, a former brother of the guild; and in a guild return of 1389 an important citizen (bailiff 1386–7), Ralf de Scremby, is styled master and warden of the 'old great gild in honour of God and St Mary'.

According to stylistic evidence St Mary's Guild (Pl. II A) was built c. 1180–90, and there remain its entrance range with great archway, an elaborate string-course (Pl. LI A) and a beautiful capital at the dais end of the hall which was once above (Pl. VIII D). One wing of the courtyard is left, partly rebuilt. Even now there is a certain magnificence about it, and it must have been sumptuous in its prime.

The homes of the great merchants were built around.[10] Next to it was the house where Adam, the first mayor of Lincoln, lived. This is strongly suggested by a charter of c. 1284, in which Peter de Holm, son of Adam's great-nephew and heir, sold the home of his ancestors to Peter of Goxhill. ‡ Adam was the alderman of the guild merchant from c. 1185, and mayor in 1210, probably in 1206, being deprived by King John in 1216. His grandfather is called Eilsi of Wigford. Adam's father Reginald also had a stone house in Hungate, which Adam gave outright to the Cathedral. Neighbours of his in Wigford were Godwin and Reimbald, both called 'the Rich' and both on the long list of ninety-five names of those fined for assaulting the Jews in 1191. Godwin's town house seems to have been here, for his daughter is called Mary of Wigford, but he also traded in Boston, where he had a house c. 1200. He seems first heard of in 1176–7. Reimbald was cited as one of the twenty-four principal citizens in 1206.

The stone vaults remaining at Canterbury [12] must have been the basements of merchants' houses, also that in 24 St Thomas Street in Winchester, and there would have been many others, some awaiting discovery. There were also well-to-do merchants in thriving places like Southampton, one of the chief ports of London, where the so-called

---

* Sequel to observations on Ancient Castles, *Archaeologia*, VI (1782), 261.
† *A Tour through the Whole Island of Great Britain* (1724–6) (Everyman's Library edition), II, 91.
‡ Hill (1948), 164. 'Extending in length from the king's highway to the water called the dyke [*fossatum*] and in width from the hall of the great gild of St Mary in Wigford to the house formerly of Jordan the clerk of Lincoln' (Goxhill Leiger, No. 298).

King John's House [7] (*c.* 1150) and Canute's Palace (*c.* 1180) are two of their houses surviving.

It is interesting to compare our 12th-century town houses with those of France, of which many more examples remain or have been recorded. Professor U. T. Holmes has made a special study of these,* and remarks that although rich in town buildings, France is almost entirely lacking in early mediaeval manor houses. This might be considered due to English depredations during the 'Hundred Years War' (1337–60, 1369–1453), but that did not affect the centre and south of France. Rather does it seem that upper-class Frenchmen concentrated on having a good town residence.

The common feature with England is the raised position of the hall (*salle*). This and the solar occupy the first and second floors of the building, leaving the ground stage for commercial uses. Whether the French houses had their side to the street (like Jew's House, Lincoln), or gable end on, which grew to be the rule, the customary arrangement at street level includes one and often a series of large semicircular or pointed arches. This open ground floor probably contained the owner's shop and working quarters rather than storage space, though that must have been incorporated, perhaps at the back. The simplest houses, as at Cluny (Pl. I c), in rue de la République [16] and rue d'Avril,[17] have one large arch opening into a barrel-vaulted *cave*, and a doorway from the street giving access to the straight staircase up to the dwelling portion above. These living-rooms are distinguished by a row of windows, often most elaborate, an architectural composition with at least a common hoodmould, or arranged as an arcade, like the treforium of a church. These lit the hall and there was frequently a further row above to serve the solar. Le Maison des Plaids, Dol-de-Brétagne [22] is a good example. A variation of this arrangement is found as at Périgueux (Pl. II B) [23] and le Puy, [24] where the ornamental windows are raised high, suggesting a clerestory to a lofty hall, or that there was a low first floor originally unlighted on the front, perhaps used for storage, with the main room on the second floor. Another possibility is that the ground stage was very lofty to allow for furnaces, in a goldsmith's or armourer's shop, thus taking up the equivalent of the first floor. It is difficult to tell, for surviving buildings are usually much altered inside, the French care for external detail and carved ornament, enforced by law, not extending to the interior, which can be changed at will.

Indeed much study is needed, before it is too late, to disentangle the original internal arrangement, such as the staircase access between the floors. Some houses had a corridor and straight steps up, but the better ones were provided with a newel staircase.

Some important French houses had a tower at one end. This supplied a private suite and look-out for the owner, and was also a status symbol, like the seigniorial skyscrapers still remaining at San Gemignano [27] in Italy, or Longthorpe Tower in Northamptonshire later. A fortunate survival of this type can be seen at Saint Antonin (Tarn-et-Garonne), the town house of Archambaud de Saint Antonin, and now a museum.[26] The main block is parallel to the street and of three storeys with a tower attached. On the ground floor

* I am indebted for the generous way in which he has shared his knowledge with me, correlating it with his research in Old French texts.

there are four large open two-centred arches, the first under the tower serving as a roadway, the second with access to the staircase to the tower and hall, the third opening into a court, and the fourth perhaps a shop or store, the opposite wall having two loop windows. The hall windows are separated by shafts and enclosed in one long moulded frame, while those to the solar floor are two-lights with semicircular hoodmoulds linked. The tower is also of three stages externally, but its windows do not correspond to those of the main block, over which it rises considerably, and it is crenellated.

How are these features represented in the 12th-century houses that remain in England? There is evidence of large open arches, here on to a quay, in the lower floor of King John's House, Southampton, and at the Long House ('Canute's Palace') there was once a frontage 111 feet long with a series of windows, some with linked hoodmoulds. The hall windows at Moyses Hall could also be mentioned here. Pudsey's Hall at Durham (Pl. LIII c), with its upper range of chevron window arches, might be compared with the tall house at Saint Antonin, with important rooms on both first and second floor. Professor Holmes considers that the Norman doorway on the top floor at Durham gave access to a balcony; the magnificent main entrance, once with external staircase, served the hall below.

The simpler type of front with two doorways in the end wall to the street, one opening down into a cellar, the other with access to the staircase, is the arrangement found at Marlepins, Shoreham, in Sussex.[13] The front, which has chequer-work (flint and Caen stone), was apparently rebuilt in the early 14th century, but the evidence of a Norman window, now doorway, on the east wall shows that the building dates from the 12th century. The left-hand south doorway still opens on to the stairs to the upper floor, and the larger right-hand one to the basement, here two feet below street level. Between them is a small two-centred 'business window', and there is a larger window, altered, to the floor above. Marlepins was possibly a toll house of the de Braoses, Lords of Shoreham in the 12th and 13th centuries, where their agent collected taxes and harbour dues. In a 14th-century document it is a stone corner tenement which is called Malduppinne, and in the late 15th century 'a certain cellar and a chamber or loft above the cellar built . . . called Malapynnys'.

The fireplace at King John's House (Pl. XLI A) has a corbelled buttress like one which existed at Cluny, but the latter had a chimney with conical cap. Twin shafts with such caps existed at a house at Laon,[20] serving a wide fireplace buttress here extending to ground level; this is unlike any example yet found in England. However, the external staircase of the Tolhouse at Great Yarmouth, and of Aydon Castle, of 13th-century date or restored, are reminiscent of one still remaining in a 12th-century house at Viterbo [25] in Italy, rising to the semicircular first-floor entrance, and supported on an arch which allows access to the basement doorway.

Some of these buildings have been swept away since Verdier's measured drawings of 1855, which provide such an important source of information. The rows of 12th-century houses illustrated at Cluny [18, 19] are now represented by a few examples, the finest being the house on the rue d'Avril [17] and one on the rue de la République [16]; there is a similar house at Chaise-Dieu (Haute-Loire).[21] Yet compared with England France is rich in such buildings, and these survivors, with the illustrations of those now gone, throw light on what Lincoln still looked like in the 18th century. Thus it is to France that we must look for the appearance of our lost 12th-century town houses.

The raised hall persisted in French houses of the 13th century, with open arcades below, and the window treatment became more elaborate with Gothic tracery (*see* Pl. 1 A). Beautiful series of grouped windows embellished the upper floors, each shafted with two trefoiled lights under a trefoil or quatrefoil, like the openings in a cathedral cloister. A fine example may be seen in the Hôtel de Vauluisant at Provins (Seine-et-Marne),[28] and another, of the end of the century, at Cordes (Tarn), 'La Maison du Grand Fauconnier'.[29] An English country house at Ower Moigne perhaps provides the nearest example, but it may be wondered if Bennett's Hall at Shrewsbury (*c.* 1260),[14] with evidence of a finely decorated fireplace,* had such windows to match. This is one of the few English town houses of the 13th century yet discovered, apart from the vaulted cellars of those remaining at Canterbury, Southampton and elsewhere. At Chester, indeed, Mr J. T. Smith believes that concealed contemporary stonework remains above the cellars of the famous Rows, which represent a project of town planning, after the disastrous fire of 1278. In one case, 48–50 Bridge Street, the three arches,[15] at Row level, are akin to the arcading of the Continent, and, if their late 13th-century date is accepted, form 'the only surviving front of a mediaeval town house of stone to survive anywhere in England'. In plan, No. 48 Bridge Street corresponds closely to Bennett's Hall, with undercroft divided by two arches, and the fireplace placed above the pier and having a doorway adjoining in the mid wall; Bennett's Hall however is freestanding.†

But the mercantile element in early building was not recognized by tradition, and when the Jews were not regarded as the builders of stone houses, King John was often selected, this being at variance with his nickname of 'Lackland'. The 'wicked king' seems to have seized the public imagination, and as Grose said in 1777: ‡

> The title of King John's House is an appellation common to many ancient structures in which that king had no concern; King John and the devil being the founders, to whom the vulgar impute most of the ancient buildings, mounds, or entrenchments, for which they cannot assign any other constructor, with this distinction, that to the king are given most of the mansions, castles, and other buildings, whilst the devil is supposed to have amused himself chiefly in earthen works.

Canute (1017–35) is a variant in Southampton where King John already had one house. 'Canute's Palace' in Porter Lane,[8] now more correctly styled The Long House, dates from *c.* 1180, judging from architectural evidence. Its misleading name derives from H. C. Englefield, who 'walked through Southampton' *c.* 1801, and whose 'fond conjecture it was that from this hall Canute with his courtiers viewed the rising tide, and from it descended to the beach to repress by a striking and impressive lesson, their impious flattery'.

* Mr J. T. Smith was the first to realize its character, in 1957.
† Lawson & Smith (1958), 36–7.
‡ Warnford pages.

The other building, King John's House (or Palace), Southampton,[7] was built c. 1150, and obviously not by King John, who was born in 1166, and reigned from 1199 to 1216. It is also extremely doubtful that he even lived there. The building was more probably the house of a merchant with business on the western quay, for the large west arches would give easy means of transport there of goods, possibly wine or wool, stored in the basement. As for the origin of the name here, Professor Hearnshaw gives a complete solution in the guide to the Tudor House Museum, in the garden of which the 12th-century ruins stand. He attributes the rise of the King John idea to J. Duthy's *Sketches of Hampshire* (1839), and agrees with him that neither the castle nor Canute's Palace is meant by the writers of the 13th-century Close Rolls, when they refer to 'the quay in front of our houses'; but disagrees that King John's House was meant instead, as the West Quay opposite it was the town quay, not the king's. The king's houses were outbuildings on the castle quay which belonged to the king. Also, John, when he visited Southampton, would lodge at the Castle, not at an undefended low-lying house near by.

King John's name is commoner, and with greater reason, for houses of the 13th century, these being seldom ascribed to Jews, though they were not expelled from England until 1290. Certainly the king is known, from documentary evidence, to have travelled extensively, being seldom in one place for long, due to hunting, legal and political reasons. There are ruins of a 'King John's Palace' at Clipstone (Edwinstowe, Nottinghamshire), and another has been excavated at Writtle in Essex; there is a 'King John's House' at Warnford, and a 'King John's Hunting Box' at Romsey, both in Hampshire, also 'King John's House' at Tollard Royal (Wiltshire) in Cranborne Chase, where it is known that he frequently hunted. At Warnford [35] the name is derived in error from the St John family, who owned the manor in his reign. Adam de Port, who rebuilt the church, was outlawed for an attempt on the life of Henry II, but restored to the manor c. 1180. His son William, who succeeded in 1213, adopted the name of his maternal grandmother, St John.

At Romsey [36] the king seems nearer. In his guide Mr Andrews gives the evidence for the house having been the hunting box of King John, built c. 1206, and the possible home of his daughter Joanna, who was educated by a governess, Christiana de Romsey. Joanna married the King of Scots in 1221, in which year her brother Henry III granted the house 'which the lord King John our father caused to be made in Romsey' to the Abbess of Romsey as, says Mr Andrews, an 'infirmary guest house' for the Abbey (*ad faciendum inde firmariam suam infra Abbatiam de Rumes*). The incised shields and inscriptions on the walls are believed to have been drawn by the barons or their servants who would be lodged in the guest house when Edward I was entertained at the Abbey in 1306, some of the arms having been identified with those shown on the roll of the Battle of Boroughbridge (1322) and in the Great Roll of c. 1314. Furthermore, there is a doorway in the east wall of the hall, leading out into what may have been the chapel in a vanished block, and this may have been the 'chapel of St Andrew within the Infirmary' mentioned frequently in the abbey records. This chapel was destroyed at the Dissolution, and its chaplain, John Foster, was allowed to continue to use the guest house as a dwelling. He may have added the Tudor wing at his marriage with Jane Walham, ex-nun of Romsey, a niece of Queen Jane Seymour. The fact that John Foster figures in the deeds of King John's Hunting Box, as a predecessor to Miss Moody, the last owner, would seem, as Mr Andrews points out, to prove the identi-fication of the present house with the infirmary.

But on further study of the document some difficulties arise, first as regards his 'infirmary guest house'. According to the late Sir Alfred Clapham, there was no such thing in the monastic plan, and if King John's Hunting Box was the infirmary, it was of unusual type and in the wrong position with regard to the Abbey Church. Also the text might be taken to mean that the Abbess was given permission to remove any material from the house that she wished, for her infirmary, not necessarily using the house as it stood.*

With regard to architectural evidence, fortunately King John's Hunting Box is rich in datable material. The mouldings, however, suggest that it was built later than the death of King John in 1216, certainly after 1206. But may it not be that the house was changed beyond recognition (or even rebuilt—the earlier house may have been of wood) on becoming abbey property? The surviving detail might be as late as 1240.

King John's House at Tollard Royal [37] again is near to justifying the legend, but only as regards the site. John, when Earl of Gloucester, held a knight's fee at Tollard Royal, and is known to have hunted in the surrounding Cranborne Chase. The present house, however, from architectural evidence, cannot be earlier than c. 1240–50.† The 13th-century ruins popularly called 'King John's Palace' in Heaton Park, Newcastle-upon-Tyne, were more probably part of the house of Adam of Jesmond, a devoted supporter of Henry III.[38]

But King John must have stayed at the royal hunting lodges, 'King John's Palaces', at Clipstone and Writtle, both of which have been excavated by Mr P. A. Rahtz for the Ministry of Works. Clipstone [31] was the chief one in Sherwood Forest, and seems to have been an extensive country house. There is a record of building there in 1176–80, and in July 1244 Henry III ordered the Sheriff of Nottingham 'to build at Clipstone, a fair, great and becoming hall of wood, and a kitchen of wood, and a wardrobe for the queen's use'.‡ In 1251–2 there is reference to a chalice, vestments and books for the new chapel, decoration for the queen's chapel, and to the high bench and others in the new hall (apparently of 1244) as well as instructions for fireplaces, windows and privy chambers, and to build a great gate with a chamber over.§ In 1357 a new hall for one of the lodges is ordered, and in 1368 and 1370 repairs and upkeep are mentioned.‖ The ruins still standing,

---

* *Rotuli Litterarum Clausarum* (ed. Sir Thomas Hardy, 1833), I, 479. 9 Nov. 1221. *Et ideo tibi precipimus quod ipsam Abbatissam libere et sine impedimento permittas domum illam quo voluerit abducere.* The Hampshire County Archivist, Mrs E. Cottrill, comments: 'I think the phrase permitting the Abbess *domum illam quo voluerit abducere* can only indicate removal to another site of a prefabricated building. If it had been of stone I think that the materials would have been granted rather than the house itself.' Mrs Cottrill kindly sends the following translation of the whole passage:

'The king to the sheriff of Southampton greeting. Know that we directed by God have given to the Abbess of Romsey our house which the lord John the king our father caused to be made in Romsey, to make from it her infirmary within the Abbey of Romsey. And therefore we order you that you permit the said Abbess to remove that house freely and without hindrance anywhere she wish. Witnessed by Henry, etc. at Westminster, the 9th day of November.'

† The opinion of Sir Alfred Clapham.

‡ Liberate Rolls, 28 Henry III; Turner (1851), 205. In dating it should be remembered that the year of this reign began on 19th October.

§ Liberate Rolls, 36 Henry III; Turner (1851), 235, 236. Close Roll, 36 Henry III; Turner (1851), 262.

‖ Salzman (1952), 99, 157, 201, 252, 254.

A

C

B

D

c. Chepstow Castle, hall of Great Tower, late 11th century with additions of c. 1260–70. D. Kenilworth Castle, hall with remains of vaulted undercroft; 1390–3.

A. Christchurch Castle, hall with chimney; c. 1160. B. Ludlow Castle, hall and solar block, c. 1283–92, with (*right*) great chamber wing, c. 1320.

Plate III. The First-floor Hall.

A and B. Boothby Pagnell Manor House showing three original doorways and solar window, and chimney; c. 1200.

B

C

c. Development of the great hall, Winchester Castle. *Top*, late 11th century; *centre*, 1222–35; *below*, late 14th century.

Plate IV.

of masonry with no datable features, seem to belong to the undercroft of a large building, probably the principal one constructed by Edward I in 1278–80. However, there were at least two earlier periods of building, the first of timber, the second of stone; the latter Mr Rahtz relates to the 1176–80 documents, and among its rubble was found a corbel carving of an English mastiff.

King John's Hunting Lodge at Writtle [34] really seems to have been built by King John in 1211, and to have been repaired in 1223, 1229–30 and 1231–2, often used by his son and grandson. There were a hall, kitchen, chamber, chapel and gaol. It passed to the

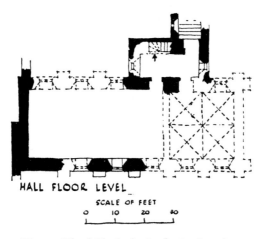

HALL FLOOR LEVEL

SCALE OF FEET

0   10   20   30

Fig. 4. The 'Gloriet', Corfe Castle, plan.

Bohun family in the 14th century, then to the Dukes of Buckingham in the 15th century when extensive building took place. The royal buildings were of wood.

From King John's reign also dates the 'Gloriet' (Fig. 4; Pls. II c and d), the early 13th-century house within Corfe Castle,[32] east of the 12th-century keep. We know that it was built in 1201–2 and cost £275.* Yet this never, apparently, has been called 'King John's House'. In 1209–11 he spent £50 on the royal palace at Cheddar [33], rebuilding the 12th-century aisled (eastern) hall on a shorter plan. The west hall was dismantled and the palace now became hardly more than a hunting box. This was another excavation by Mr Rahtz for the Ministry of Works. Fourteenth-century examples bearing that king's name occur at 21 Church Street, Lacock, Wiltshire,[41] and Cranborne Manor (c. 1300) in Dorset; [39] and, with early roof, at Wraysbury in Buckinghamshire, King John's Hunting Lodge or Place Farm near Magna Carta Island.[40] A King John's tower is incorporated in the manor house of Nevill Holt in Leicestershire.[42]

---

* Multiply by at least 40–60 to get 1965 comparison. The reference of 1215 quoted by Mr Toy, *aula nostra in baillio*, refers not to this building but to the 11th-century hall, the 'herring-bone' building in the West Bailey (information from Mr A. R. Dufty of the Royal Commission on Historical Monuments).

EXAMPLES OF JEWS' HOUSES

		References
(1) *c.* 1170–80	Jew's House, 15 The Strait, Lincoln	Wood (1935), 194–6, fig. 8, pls. V A, XIII A (plans & illus.); Hill (1948), 234–5.
(2) *c.* 1170–80	Aaron the Jew's House, 46–47 Steep Hill, Lincoln	Wood (1935), 197–8, pl. V B (illus.); Hill (1948), 220–3, pl. 17 (drawing & plan of 1800).
(3)	Jew's Court, The Strait, Lincoln	Wood (1935), 196, fig. 9 (plans); C. Roth, 'Medieval Lincoln Jewry and its Synagogue' (Jewish Historical Society), a paper read in 1934 in the room with the recess; Helen Rosenau (1936), *Archaeological Journal*, XCIII, 51 *et seq.*; Hill (1948), 231–2.
(4) *c.* 1175	'Music House' (Isaac's Hall), 167 King St, Norwich	Kent (1945) (plan & illus.); *Country Life* (20) (plan & illus.).
(5) *c.* 1180	Moyses Hall, Bury St Edmunds, Suff.	Wood (1935), 203–5, fig. 12, pls. VII B, X A (plans & illus.); D. S. Margoliouth (1870), *The Vestiges of the Historic Anglo-Hebrews of East Anglia.*
(6) before 1200	Evidence of Jacob the Jew's House in cellar of County Hotel, Canterbury, etc.	Urry (1953) contains translations of the documents of 1190, and site plans.

EXAMPLES OF EARLY MERCHANTS' HOUSES

		References
(7) *c.* 1150	King John's House (or Palace), Southampton, via Tudor House Museum	Wood (1935), 181–4, fig. 3. pls. II, VIII A (plans & illus.); Hearnshaw & Macdonald Lucas (1932), 4–7, 11–15.
(8) *c.* 1180	'Canute's Palace' (the Long House), Porter Lane, Southampton	Wood (1935), 180–1, pl. X B; Englefield (1808), 84 (measured drawings); (1801), 49–54; (1805), 50–4, also 97–104 (one elevation).
(9) *c.* 1180–90	St Mary's Guild, 385 High St, Lincoln	Wood (1935), 191–4, fig. 7, pls. IV A, XII A, XIII B (plan & illus.); Watkins (1913), plans, elevations, etc.; Hill (1948), 162–5, pl. 15.
(10) C 12th	House, at Wigford, Lincoln; documentary evidence	Hill (1948), 164, 194–5, 380, 385–6, 392–3, 397–8.
(11) C 12th	Vault under 24 St Thomas St, Winchester	*V.C.H. Hants*, V, 8, 9 (plan & illus.).
(12) C 12th & C 13th	Cellars at Canterbury; High St, Burgate St, etc.	
(13) C 12th & C 13th	Marlepins, Shoreham, Sus. (? Toll House)	Packham (1924) (plans & illus.).
(14) *c.* 1260	Bennett's Hall, Shrewsbury	J. T. Smith (to be published).
(15) after 1278	48–50 Bridge St (The Three Arches), Chester; and others	Lawson & Smith (1958), 4–5, 29–30, 36–7 (plan, sections, elevation).

SOME EXAMPLES OF EARLY MERCHANTS' HOUSES IN FRANCE AND ITALY

		References
(16) C 12th	Rue de la République, Cluny, Saône-et-Loire	via Professor U. T. Holmes.
(17) C 12th	Rue d'Avril, Cluny	via Professor U. T. Holmes.
(18) C 12th	Rue Dauphine (now Lamartine), Cluny	Evans (1948), pl. 221 for 1838 lithograph by Sagot.
(19) C 12th	Other houses at Cluny; documentary evidence	Verdier & Cattois (1855).
(20) C 12th	House at Laon; documentary evidence	Verdier & Cattois (1855).
(21) C 12th	House at Chaise-Dieu, Haute-Loire	via Professor U. T. Holmes.
(22) C 12th	Maison des Plaids, Dol-de-Brétagne	via Professor U. T. Holmes.
(23) C 12th	Houses at Périgueux	Verdier & Cattois (1855).
(24) C 12th	Houses at Le Puy	Verdier & Cattois (1855).
(25) C 12th	Houses at Viterbo, Italy	Verdier & Cattois (1855).
(26) C 12th	House of Archambaud de Saint Antonin, Saint Antonin, Tarn-et-Garonne	Evans (1948), pl. 145; Verdier & Cattois (1855).
(27) C 12th	Towers at San Gemignano, Italy	Verdier & Cattois (1855).
(28) C 13th	Hôtel de Vauluisant, Provins, Seine-et-Marne	Evans (1948), pl. 224.
(29) end C 13th	La Maison du Grand Fauconnier, Cordes, Tarn	Evans (1948), pl. 225.

EXAMPLES OF 'KING JOHN'S HOUSES'

		References
(30) c. 1150	King John's House (or Palace) Southampton	See reference 7.
(31) 1176–80 1244 1278–80, etc.	King John's Palace, Clipstone, Edwinstowe, Notts. (ruins and excavations)	Rahtz (1957) (plan).
(32) 1201–2	The Gloriet, Corfe Castle, Dor.	R.C.H.M. *Dorset*, II; Toy (1929), 88, pls. XXXVII & XL (plans & illus.).
(33) 1209	Building at Cheddar Palace, Som. (excavated)	Rahtz (1962–3).
(34) 1211 1223, etc., & C 15th	King John's Hunting Lodge, Writtle, Ess. (excavated)	Rahtz (1957) 160; (1958) (plan).
(35) early C 13th	Warnford Manor House ruins ('King John's House') near West Meon, Hants	Nisbett (1906) (plan, section, etc.); *V.C.H. Hants*, III, 269 (plan); Wyndham (1779) (plan, view of interior roofed, etc.); Wood (1950), 27–9 (plan).
(36) c. 1230–40	King John's Hunting Box, Romsey, Hants	Andrews & Atkinson (1929) (plan & illus.); Wood (1950), 24–6, fig. 7, pl. V A (plans & illus.).
(37) c. 1240–50	King John's House, Tollard Royal, Wilts.	Pitt-Rivers (1890) (plans & illus.); Wood (1950), 96–7.
(38) C 13th	'King John's Palace', Heaton Park, Newcastle-upon-Tyne	Knowles (1898) (plan & measured drawings).
(39) end C 13th or beg. C 14th	Cranborne Manor, Dor.	Original house illustrated in Norden's survey; reproduced in Oswald (1935), 63 (plan).
(40) early C 14th	King John's Hunting Lodge (or Place Farm), Wraysbury, Bucks.	Rouse (1927–33) (with drawing).
(41 early C 14th	King John's House, 21 Church St, Lacock, Wilts.	
(42)	King John's Tower incorporated in Nevill Holt Manor House, Leics.	Thompson & Farnham (1923–4) (plan).

2

The First-floor Hall

AT PRESENT we know of over forty examples of Norman domestic architecture, though many are fragmentary or mutilated. Stone being the chief building material to survive, most occur on the rich limestone belt which crosses England from north-east to south-west, the 'Jurassic zone' from Lincolnshire through Northamptonshire and the Cotswolds to Dorset. Not many have been found in the sandstone country west of it, but the millstone grit of Yorkshire provides examples, and, in the chalk and clay lands of the east, flint took the place of building-stone. Indeed, it is the south-eastern half of England that preserves most Norman houses.

Most examples date from the second half of the 12th century. Political unrest discouraged good civil building until the reign of Henry II (1154–89), and before then stone was not in general use for building, even castles being mainly composed of timber, except for special cases such as London, or in places like Richmond in Yorkshire, where stone was abundant and easily worked. Castles would be the first to be translated into less destructible material, beginning at the gatehouse. Earlier dwelling houses would be of wood or mud, and so do not survive.

Even under Henry II the question of defence was important, and it was safer to have the living-rooms raised to first-floor level, a similar arrangement being found in the keeps of mid 12th-century castles. In the 13th century conditions were more secure, and the hall tended to come downstairs. Yet first-floor halls were still built, houses of 'hall and cellar' type, and it was not until the later 14th and 15th centuries that the ground-floor hall was usual.

For this reason, of defence, the first-floor hall * is by far the most common type of surviving Norman house, providing at least half our examples. The aisled hall, probably of older, timber origin, will be considered separately. Although much more prevalent

---

* Or main room, a convenient term frowned on by some architects, to whom the hall is essentially a ground-floor type of building. But to call such rooms the 'chamber' would confuse them with the subsidiary great chamber or 'solar' which adjoins.

16

under Henry II, the raised hall even appears in the late 11th century, in Yorkshire stone country at Richmond Castle, where Scolland's Hall [2] is earlier than, and separate from, the keep. It is contemporary with the Bayeux Tapestry, worked *c.* 1077,* in which the *aula* of King Harold at Bosham [1] is shown as a similar hall but over a vaulted basement. Recent research inclines to the view that the embroidery was worked in England by English people, but even so they may have been depicting the type of house the Normans introduced. Another possible Saxon first-floor hall is mentioned in the *Anglo-Saxon Chronicle* for 978. We read how the Council was held in an upper chamber at Calne (Wiltshire), the floor of which apparently collapsed, casting the *Witan* † into the room below, all save the holy Dunstan who 'alone stood upon a beam'. This is interesting in the light of Mr Rahtz's recent excavations at Cheddar, where in the 9th-century palace of the kings of Wessex an important timber building some 90×18 feet, the 'Long Hall', may have had its main rooms at first-floor level, the inner row of posts sloping to support an upper floor.‡ Otherwise there is as yet no evidence that the first-floor hall occurred in Saxon England, which is to be expected as it was essentially a stone type of building.

It is doubtful whether any Romanesque stone house dates from the pre-Conquest period, although several examples have been claimed as such, largely owing to the presence in them of herring-bone walling, now known to be generally of early Norman, not Saxon, date. Such are Barton Farm, Nytimber (Sussex) and early halls at Corfe (Dorset) and Chilham Castles (Kent). Thus, unless definite proof arises to the contrary, it may be assumed that the Saxons used stone only for churches, and not always for these, while for domestic use they were content to follow the Nordic tradition of building in wood. Indeed, 'to build' in Old English is *timbran*.

Although we should expect a difference in type between town and manor houses, occasioned by considerations of space, the compact first-floor hall is found common to both. But early mediaeval towns were not crowded, as a rule, inside the walls, and there was space for gardens and courts and even farm buildings.

This type is also found in castles, where a hall was often built apart from the keep, and formed a separate house in the bailey, usually against the curtain wall, where an escarpment, as at Richmond, or water defence gave it the most protection. At Framlingham Castle, Suffolk,[10] there are traces of an original stone house of two storeys, with two chimneys (Pl. XLIV B and C), built by Hugh Bigod *c.* 1150 and thus before the curtain wall of 1190–1200 was built against the outside of it, the original defences being of timber. The outer wall of the hall acts as curtain at Christchurch Castle, Hampshire,[11] and is washed by the millstream of the river Avon (Fig. 5; Pl. III A). This is one of the most complete Norman houses left to us, admirably preserved by the Ministry of Works. Architectural evidence suggests a date *c.* 1160; § so it was probably built by Richard de Redvers, second Earl of Devon, who held the castle 1155–62, or by his son Baldwin (d. 1180).

---

* It was made for the Conqueror's half-brother, Odo, when Bishop of Bayeux. He was dedicated in 1077 and disgraced in 1082, which gives a time bracket for the work.
† The wise men of the *Witenagemöt* (council).
‡ Information from Mr P. A. Rahtz of the Ministry of Works.
§ Information from the late Sir Alfred Clapham, F.S.A., who kindly dated the author's early domestic photographs.

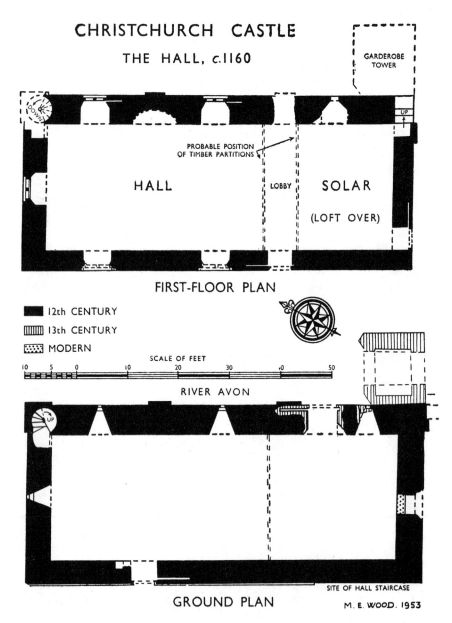

CHRISTCHURCH CASTLE

THE HALL, c.1160

GARDEROBE TOWER

DOWN

UP

PROBABLE POSITION OF TIMBER PARTITIONS

HALL   LOBBY   SOLAR

(LOFT OVER)

FIRST-FLOOR PLAN

■ 12th CENTURY

▥ 13th CENTURY

▦ MODERN

SCALE OF FEET

10   5   0   10   20   30   40   50

RIVER AVON

UP

SITE OF HALL STAIRCASE

GROUND PLAN   M. E. WOOD. 1953

Fig. 5.

Monastic guest houses could be of similar build, like the two adjoining examples built after the fire of 1147 at Fountains Abbey, Yorkshire.[5]

So the first-floor hall is the typical Norman house, of which some twenty examples remain. In it the stone hall is raised on a basement or cellar, in the mediaeval ground or semi-ground floor sense, either vaulted or with a wooden ceiling: hence the term 'hall and cellar house'. This arrangement would provide safe storage accommodation below, and raise the living-rooms to a defensible height above the ground. The hall windows could be large, narrow loops widely splayed internally sufficing for the storage basement, which would be vaulted for extra safety against fire. A simple quadripartite vault occurs under the hall at Boothby Pagnell (c. 1200) [20] (Fig. 6) and in the 'Music House' (Isaac's Hall), (c. 1175) at Norwich,[13] (see Fig. 2) while at Burton Agnes Old Manor House, Yorkshire (c. 1170–80),[14] the undercroft is divided into aisles by a row of cylindrical columns, and the same arrangement is found at Moyses Hall, Bury St Edmunds (c. 1180) [17]

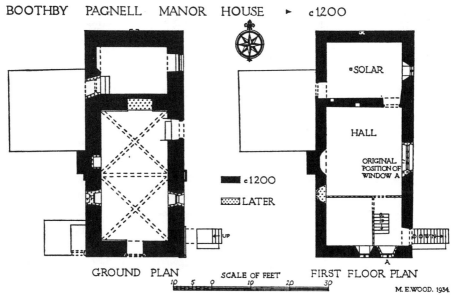

BOOTHBY PAGNELL MANOR HOUSE ▸ c.1200

■ c.1200

▦ LATER

GROUND PLAN   SCALE OF FEET   FIRST FLOOR PLAN

M. E. WOOD. 1934.

Fig. 6.

(see Figs. 32, 33; Pl. XIV A). The basement would be entered, as at Christchurch, by a doorway towards one end of a side wall. On this or the opposite wall, also near the angle, would be the hall entrance, reached by an external staircase in most cases rising parallel to the wall. At the 'Music House' the staircase was enclosed in a forebuilding similar to that of a castle keep, such as the existing one at Castle Rising, Norfolk. At Canterbury an arcaded external staircase remains to the Guest Hall of the Cathedral Priory, but most domestic examples have been destroyed: many may have been of wood. Near this entrance might be the spiral staircase from hall to basement, as at Scolland's Hall and Burton Agnes; at Christchurch the staircase is at the 'high table' or opposite end from the entrance. Occasionally, as at Hemingford Grey Manor, Huntingdonshire (c. 1150),[9] the entrance is in an end wall, but always near the angle.

In a two-storeyed block the wall fireplace was used, and usually placed near the middle of one side, as at Christchurch and Hemingford Grey. At Framlingham the lower storey had a fireplace also, so there may have been an upper and a lower hall, or hall with solar above. There are two cylindrical chimneys here, and one at Christchurch and Boothby Pagnell (Pls. IV B, XLIV B and C).

Such halls were usually lit by two-light windows, perhaps two a side, with one in the end wall and a circular window in the gable, like Christchurch and Fountains Abbey. Window seats occur in late 12th-century examples. The Norman windows would have had shutters and not glass, which was still too expensive except for palaces and churches.

The high table, where the owner and his family would dine, was at the upper end of the hall, furthest from the entrance. Often the lord had his private quarters, or solar, off the end, and at first this may have consisted of a portion of the main block divided off when he retired, perhaps with leather curtains. This probably developed into a separate room, set behind the high table, with a wooden partition, and by the late 12th century, if not earlier, this 'great chamber' might have a more permanent division built in stone. Of this we have a good example at Boothby Pagnell,[20] (Pl. IV A) where the solar is added at the end of a hall apartment of the same build, and has its separate vaulted basement below. The cellar is also in two portions at the 'Music House',[13] but here a timber partition may have existed above, the solar forming the shorter room on the west; indeed the internal measurement of the whole first floor resembles that of Boothby Pagnell, which is subdivided.

At Christchurch [11] one oblong stone compartment on each floor is left, but there is evidence of a wooden subdivision. While the entrance is usually near the end of the hall, here it is a third of the way from the end of the block. It seems to have opened into a transverse passage between wooden partitions, long since perished, through which doors would have opened northwards into the hall, and southwards into the solar or private apartments.* This would make the hall with passage the usual 2 : 1 measurement. Here the solar was at the lower end of the hall, the high table with a specially elaborate window behind it being at the north. There were two windows in the corresponding position at the upper end in the hall at Grosmont Castle (Monmouthshire),[23] on either side of the flue from the end fireplace of the room below. The hall fireplace is in the same position as at Christchurch, between two side windows, and the newel staircase also in the angle near it. Indeed, there is a remarkable similarity between Christchurch and this hall block of c. 1210 at Grosmont, which is on a larger scale, and again with solar beyond the hall entrance, of which the staircase roof creasing remains. The division between these upper rooms has gone, but the stone one in the basement survives: this wall is central and on either side of it is an entrance to each undercroft from the courtyard.

The early hall block at Eynsford Castle † (Kent) [24] may be classed with these. Here the stone division occurs some third of the way along the length of the basement, and the newel staircase adjoins the cross wall on the hall side; the garderobe, or privy chamber,

---

* The discovery of Mr A. J. Taylor, F.S.A., of the Ministry of Works.

† Mr Rigold's recent excavations show that the block dates from the first half of the 12th century, reconstructed in the same form after a fire of c. 1250. The hall undercroft, of wide span, had a row of three arches down the centre to support the floor above. The solar basement, without access to the other rooms, suggests a self-contained apartment for the bailiff. The entrance forebuilding is probably a late 12th-century addition with a timber predecessor.

Plate V. The First-floor Hall in the 14th Century.

A. Meare Manor House, c. 1322–35, showing traceried windows to hall.
B. Brinsop Court, hall of c. 1340 from the courtyard.

Plate VI. The Aisled Hall.

West Bromwich Old Hall, *c.* 1290–1310, before and during restoration; a remarkable rescue by a public-spirited local authority.

was at one angle of the solar, which had a fireplace in the end wall. There are four loops in the other end wall, serving the hall basement, and another near the division wall opposite the staircase doorway; this undercroft had an entrance from the bailey, and the solar basement had one near the north-west angle. In the same county, at Chilham Castle, remains of an 11th-century hall have been found incorporated in the forebuilding of the octagonal keep (1171-4). The basement was divided into two unequal bays by a lofty semicircular arch. Scolland's Hall,[2] of similar date, was once subdivided also, at the upper end. At Merton Hall (the School of Pythagoras), Cambridge (c. 1200),[21] there is another long block almost certainly subdivided, and the position of the fireplace, on the analogy of Boothby Pagnell, bears this out. However, there is also a solar projection making an L-plan at this upper end.

Our knowledge is of course limited to the examples that survive. But increasing excavations may show that the most common type of house in the 12th century was one of timber, with living-rooms on the ground floor and possibly other sleeping accommodation in a loft in the roof. Aisles would only be necessary in the larger buildings. Sometimes such an arrangement may have been translated into the more durable material, which would explain the few stone examples left to us, ground-floor halls as at Pickering Castle and Huttons Ambo (excavated) in Yorkshire and 'Norman Hall' Sutton Courtenay (Berkshire). But it is more probable that where stone could be afforded the builder would choose the compact, defensible, first-floor hall.

A complete first-floor hall in wood is unlikely, for there would be no advantage and only danger in an elevated position when the basement could easily be set alight. The exception would be a hall raised on a motte, as depicted in the Bayeux Tapestry. Here limited space and the need for a look-out would be the important factors. However, although all surviving first-floor halls are in stone, composite examples may have existed; stone may have been used only in the basement to protect valuable stores against fire; the less expensive hall above could have been replaced more easily. None of this kind remain, but it is possible that the Castle hall at Devizes was of such a composite build. The sub-vault that remains at St Thomas Street, Winchester, may have carried an upper storey of timber; also the London crypt, now destroyed, at Corbet Court, and that of the Priors of Lewes at Southwark.

Up to now some hundred surviving 13th-century houses have been recognized. Of this number perhaps a third are very good examples. They are found throughout England, but again chiefly in the south-eastern half, in stone- and flint-working regions. Timber houses in the west have mostly disappeared. Shropshire, however, provides several stone houses of merit, as does Dorset, and there are a number of flint survivals in Hampshire, Kent and Sussex. Again the emphasis is on the second half of the century, and many good buildings date from the reign of Edward I (1272–1307).

In this number, which includes at least sixteen cellars, twenty-four examples with solar or chapel only and seven of doubtful type, there are nine aisled halls, twenty-three ground-floor halls without aisled evidence (now) and twenty-six first-floor halls. The result is approximately 50 : 50 lower to upper halls, showing the latter still popular, although more stone halls were being built at ground level, this being a more convenient type, especially where large numbers had to be accommodated. But the first-floor hall develops along the lines of the previous century. Good examples [25, 35, 39] include King John's House (c. 1240–50) at Tollard Royal (Wiltshire) [29] and Moigne Court, Ower Moigne (Dorset) (c. 1270–80).[33] West Dean Rectory (Sussex) (c. 1270–80) [34] is unusual in having an end fireplace, entrance and newel staircase. The hall of Aydon Castle (Northumberland) (c. 1280)

LITTLE WENHAM HALL _ SUFFOLK _ c 1270-80

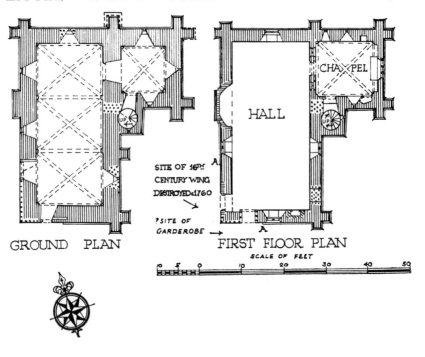

GROUND   PLAN   FIRST FLOOR PLAN

A . STRINGCOURSE ENDS
▥ c1270-80
▨ 15ᵗʰ CENTURY
▤ 16ᵗʰ CENTURY
▦ MODERN

Fig. 7.

retains an outside staircase, but has no sign of a wall fireplace, apparently being heated from the great lateral one of the room below. At Ludlow (c. 1283–92) (Pl. III B) a central hearth was supported on a pier of the undercroft 6 feet square; in the 16th century a wall fireplace was placed in a window embrasure.[38]

The vaulted basement became very popular, built usually with quadripartite bays, like those below the hall at Boothby Pagnell (Pl. XVI A), and now at the Abbot's House at Netley, Hampshire (c. 1250–60),[31] and Little Wenham Hall, Suffolk (c. 1270–80) [32] (Fig. 7). Where greater width was necessary, as at Burton Agnes earlier, double bays of this kind were used, the two aisles separated by a central row of columns. This arrangement is very typical of the first half of the 13th century, and is used in Bishop Poore's Palace of 1221, now the Cathedral School, at Salisbury. A fine example also remains at Nettlestead Place (*c.* 1250–60) (Pl. XIV B) near Mereworth in Kent. Sometimes the entire house was raised on these columned vaults, Bishop Jocelyn's Palace at Wells (*c.* 1230–50) [27] (Fig. 8) being a notable survival, with hall, solar, parallel gallery and garderobe, all on undercrofts. Likewise the Abbot's House at Battle (Sussex) [28] is a fine example of the fully vaulted type, the vaults forming an L-plan below chapel, hall and great chamber; it was built during the abbacy of Ralph of Coventry (1235–61).

Indeed we can learn a great deal about mediaeval houses from monastic architecture, for here may be preserved certain domestic features lost to us elsewhere. Moreover, at the Reformation the domestic parts of monasteries, in particular the abbot's lodgings, often modernized *c.* 1500, were frequently retained as useful to the new secular owner, whereas the church and chapter house would be destroyed. Muchelney Abbey (Somerset) is an important example (Pl. XIII B).

Hospitality being a duty of the monastic houses, accommodation for guests was an essential feature of the plan. In Benedictine abbeys it was usually in the western or cellarer's range of the cloister, nearest to the outer court and gatehouse. The guest house was raised on a vaulted undercroft, and the more important visitors were entertained above, their servants and lesser folk below. Between this range and the church would be the vaulted parlour, with chapel over. This arrangement is to be found in Chester, Castle Acre and Battle Abbeys.

In Cistercian abbeys the lay brethren were accommodated in the western range, and the guest house tended to be a separate building, usually in the outer court, as at Fountains, where two first-floor halls remain. At Kirkstall, also in Yorkshire, it was an aisled hall with cross wings, which finally developed into a self-contained establishment complete with stables.*

At first the abbot had to sleep in the dorter with his monks, but in the 13th century the rule was relaxed and he was given a chamber adjoining the guest hall, in which he had direct responsibility for the more important guests, the poorer ones now being accommodated in a separate building. In Cistercian houses the abbot's lodging was placed near the reredorter, thus technically in touch with the dorter; this was the case at Fountains, where he was quite separate from the guest houses, and at first at Kirkstall. But soon, as at Netley and Croxden (Staffordshire), the abbot had a free-standing house, which by the 14th century at Roche (Yorkshire) had come to resemble a complete manor house of the period, with ground-floor hall, chambers, screens, buttery, pantry and kitchen. South-east of the cloister was the usual position, as found in the detached prior's houses at Kirkham (Yorkshire) and Finchale (County Durham).†

In days before hotels,‡ the abbeys, scattered throughout the country, were of great service to travellers, and these included persons of the highest rank downwards. The king and his *entourage* might be entertained, which meant a heavy expenditure for the convent

---

* R. Gilyard-Beer (1958), 31–4, fig. 22 IV and V (plan).
† Ibid., 33, figs. 22 III, 15, 27.
‡ In our modern sense; the word was first used to denote the town house of a nobleman.

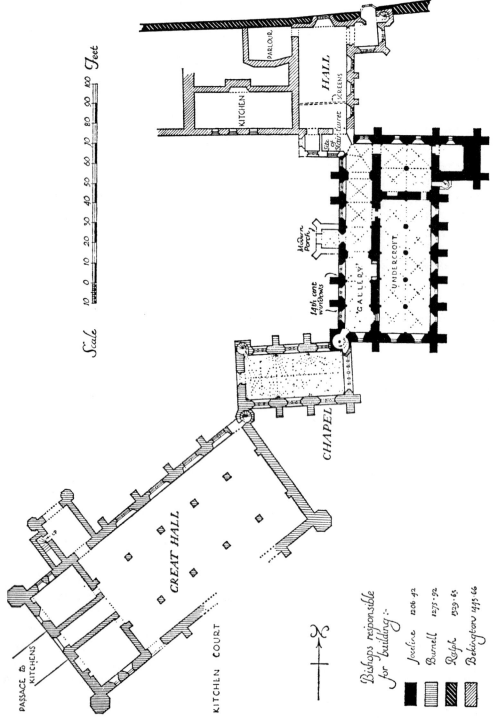

PASSAGE to KITCHENS

KITCHEN COURT

GREAT HALL

CHAPEL

KITCHEN

PARLOUR

HALL

SCREENS

Site of Stair turret

'GALLERY'

UNDERCROFT

Modern Porch

14th cent windows

Scale

10 0 10 20 30 40 50 60 70 80 90 100 Feet

Bishops responsible for building :-

Joceline 1206-42
Burnell 1275-92
Ralph 1329-63
Bekington 1443-66

Fig. 8. The Bishop's Palace, Wells.

unless balanced by munificent gifts to the house. In great Benedictine monasteries the abbot had frequently to act as host in the guest hall, while the cellarer concentrated on the lesser folk, now often accommodated in another part of the precincts. The hall, great chamber and chapel, being so often in use, and becoming state rooms, the abbot tended to have a suite of his own, separate but near by, still near the main entrance of the abbey. Here he could entertain visitors of the highest rank.

At Ely, the seat of a bishop who counted as abbot, the prior was the head of the Benedictine community. Like the abbot elsewhere, he had great responsibilities, not only for the spiritual welfare of the convent but also for the administration of its extensive properties, and he was often used by the king in a political capacity. For these duties he would need privacy from the normal working of the monastery; which in turn must not be interrupted by the pressure of his business. Thus more and more the head of the convent tended to have a private establishment, where he continued to entertain the most important of the monastic guests, and his task required a personal staff. In 1314 the prior's establishment at Ely consisted of seventeen persons, a chaplain-monk who kept his privy seal, two chaplains (not monks), a steward in charge of the household, six esquires (two with horses), a marshal of the household, three valets, cook, porter and watchman. Of the prior's and guest houses there, most of the buildings, mainly of late 13th- and 14th-century date, survive, although later altered for use as canonical dwellings and now the King's School. Owing to the conditions of the site they were not placed in the usual position west of the cloister, but well to the south, beyond the refectory and monastic kitchen.

The second quarter of the 14th century was a time of great building activity at Ely. Not only do the choir (1322–6), Lady Chapel (1321–49) and octagon (1322–46) date from this period, but the prior's and great hall were also being brought up to date, to meet the increased flow of pilgrims to the shrine of St Etheldreda, itself refashioned c. 1330. The result was a cluster of no less than four halls and two kitchens, a chapel (Prior Crauden's, c. 1325–35) and covered galleries, or bridges, these now disappeared. With one exception, the prior's great hall, these halls are raised on undercrofts, which are, however, of earlier date or have been remodelled.

In the great hall [40] on the north-west (Fig. 9), probably the main body of guests was entertained, pilgrims of moderate income, while the more important would be under the special hospitality of the prior, in his own hall, and the poorest were the responsibility of the infirmarer in his separate infirmary block to the east of the monastery. The great hall was a large building of five bays, the normal size for a guest hall adjoining the western range but here lying west to east, and south-west of the monastic kitchen. As usual it had the main room on the first floor, over a vaulted undercroft with central row of columns. Except for the earlier western bays it seems to have been built in the 13th century and reconstructed in the 14th century, the date of the roof with its crouching figure corbels. The porch on the east has access to both storeys, also to the prior's great hall which lies parallel to it but further south and east. This is probably of late 13th-century date, judging from the detail of its south porch, in the surviving end. It was built at ground level, and its width suggests that it may have been aisled. Recent research associates it with the *bougie*, a dining-hall, and it was probably not only the hall of the prior's personal retinue, for the sleeping chamber of his squires and knights once adjoined it, the 'knights' lodging', but also the *misericord* of the convent, where the monks were allowed to eat meat on certain occasions; the northern entrance was for the monks, the southern for the laity.

West of this hall was a kitchen, adjoining the south-eastern angle of the great hall, and probably shared by both, and south of this was the prior's own hall,[46] on a vaulted undercroft of six bays, which date from the early 12th century and must once have supported a first-floor hall of Norman type. It may have been replaced as a hall for the prior's retinue by the more spacious late 13th-century ground-floor hall already mentioned, and been retained as the prior's solar. In the 14th century the upper part was modernized, probably by Prior Crauden (1321–41) or Alan de Walsingham (1341–64), and, the south part of the east wall of the undercroft having settled, and leaning out, the vault at this point was rebuilt. There were rooms projecting at right angles on the corners: at the north-east probably a checker over the south porch of the prior's great hall, and a garderobe which

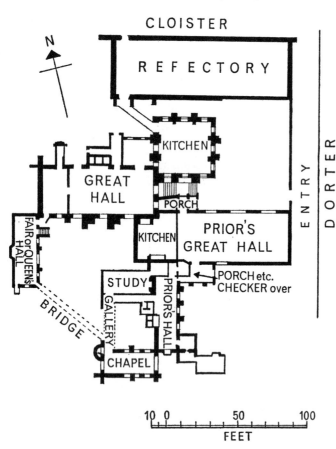

Fig. 9. The Prior's House, Ely, simplified plan.

was once at its south-east. At the north-west was probably the original staircase, and in the same block a wooden room built by Prior Crauden as his study and bedroom, now demolished but of which a fine wooden traceried window is preserved in the cloister and the magnificent stone fireplace has been reset in the hall itself. From the study there was a covered gallery, or bridge, leading south to Prior Crauden's Chapel at the south-western angle of the prior's hall, over a possibly earlier undercroft. From here another bridge ran obliquely north-west to the fourth hall, the Queen's or Fair hall,[47] standing parallel to the prior's hall across the courtyard. It is said to have been built *c.* 1330 by Prior Crauden for the reception of his young friend and patron Queen Philippa, the wife of Edward III. It is also raised on an earlier undercroft, and adjoins the south-west angle of the original great hall.

Westminster is of exceptional interest in the development of the abbot's house. In the 12th century its guèst hall was as usual in the western range, but when the wider 14th-century nave replaced that of the Confessor, the parlour with chapel above had to be moved from the normal position next the church to the other side of the guest hall, in line with the south walk of the cloister.

About this time the convent had a remarkable abbot in Nicholas Litlyngton (c. 1316–1386), a man of tremendous energy, 'a stirring person' 'very useful to the monastery'. After being a monk here for many years, and prior in 1352, in 1362 he became abbot, repaired the monastic buildings which badly needed it, and reconstructed the abbot's lodgings at his own expense. A new suite of apartments was built, further west across a court from the old hall. This comprised a *camera* on the north, overlapping the south-west tower of the abbey church and perhaps incorporating some earlier work; a hall south of it also raised on a basement, and beyond that a kitchen. The *camera* was completed by 1372; named the Jerusalem Chamber from its original Crusader tapestries, it was the scene of the death of Henry IV in 1413, the king being carried here after collapsing with a stroke when praying at the shrine of the Confessor: it had been foretold that he would die 'in Jerusalem'. Abbot Litlyngton's hall [51] also remains, with his initials in some of the glass, and his arms with that of the abbey and the Confessor held, each differently, by the angel-corbels of the roof. This was probably the work of Hugh Herland, as the design of the hall may be attributed to Henry Yevele, and contains his characteristic tracery in the windows; it was nearing completion in 1375–6, when John Payable received £8 for the glass. There was a central hearth until 1850, and its louver remains in part.*

Litlyngton also refashioned the earlier abbot's lodgings on the south, when the parlour was rebuilt, and his arms and mitred initials N.L. appear in the bosses of the vaulting here. From this, and passing along the east side of the court, he built a gallery giving access to his bedchamber on the north side, with its access to the church and Jerusalem Chamber. This northern range was rebuilt by Abbot Islip (1500–32) and the Jericho Parlour is on the first floor of this three-storey block of sunny rooms well lighted towards the south.

After the Dissolution (1538) the abbot's hall became part of Westminster School, and the Jerusalem Chamber and other portions the Deanery. The bombing of 1941, though destroying a great deal of later work on the east of the court, revealed much of 14th-century date, and this has been restored by Lord Mottistone. Over the parlour, of four vaulted bays, are the Langham and Litlyngton Rooms, the latter probably the abbot's chapel, looking east along the south cloister roof. These rooms are reached by a new staircase rising from a restored vaulted bay, in the angle between the west cloister and parlour, once part of the undercroft of the guest hall, but which had become the Deanery scullery.†

The Benedictine abbots' houses, situated in the western range of the cloister, which made compactness needful, may have had some effect on other kinds of domestic architecture. This discipline was necessary, for early mediaeval planning tended to be haphazard.

---

* It is pleasing to think of Abbot Litlyngton presiding in his beautiful hall, or setting out for the chase, of which he was fond. In his account rolls there are many references to dogs and horses; in 1369 a collar was bought for a harrier called Sturdy.

† It is a pleasant conceit that on the new cornice of the Litlyngton Room the general foreman, Mr Markham, has carved small heads representing the Dean and Canons, Abbey surveyor, the Keeper of the Muniments (Mr Lawrence Tanner), the clerk of works, and the architects, builder and others connected with the reconstruction. This is in the mediaeval tradition.

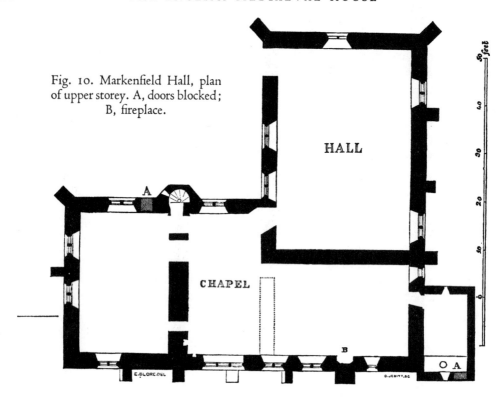

Fig. 10. Markenfield Hall, plan of upper storey. A, doors blocked; B, fireplace.

Even the palaces of Henry III, not only in the portions which he inherited but also in the new parts which he built, were a collection of buildings, one room deep, separately roofed: a group of halls, chambers and wardrobes (then an important room) loosely tacked together and extended when necessary. There is a case of extra accommodation being run up for a special guest: in 1260 a 'penthouse chamber, fifty feet long with chimney [fireplace] and wardrobe' was ordered at Winchester for the Bishop of Laodicea.*

This attitude is shown in Henry III's Liberate Rolls, which contain detailed instructions for alterations and additions to the palaces of Winchester, Westminster, Clarendon and elsewhere. These are never regarded as a whole, but as a collection of houses: the king's hall, chamber and wardrobe; those of the queen, and of the Prince Edward; and frequently there is mentioned a penthouse (pentice), or covered way connecting these buildings and shielding the occupants from the weather as they passed from one to the other; sometimes these passages are in two stages. The internal corridor seldom appears in this century save in the thickness of the wall. The bishops' palaces, such as that of Bishop Jocelyn at Wells, seem more compact than those of the king, who in his attention to detail and comfort might be considered the 'housing expert' of the 13th century.

In the 14th century we find remarkably few first-floor halls except in monastic enclosures. But even there, where room allowed, as in Cistercian houses like Roche, the ground-floor type was preferred. Those that remain, however, are of excellent quality.

* Liberate Roll, 44 Henry III; Turner (1851), 251. Here 'wardrobe' may have meant, or contained, a garderobe.

C

F

A

D

B

E

Plate VII. Detail. Old Soar, c. 1290. A. Respond to vanished arcade; B. Corbel in chapel; C. Crown-post in solar. D. Bennett's Hall, No. 2 Pride Hill, Shrewsbury, c. 1260, capital to fireplace on first floor. E. Prior Crauden's fireplace, Ely, c. 1325, detail of jamb and lamp bracket. F. Camoise Court, Chislehampton, 1318, crown-post in solar.

Plate VIII. A and B. Hereford Bishop's Palace, c. 1160; part of timber arcade with nail-head ornament and scalloped capitals. C. Oakham Castle, hall interior, c. 1190. D. St Mary's Guild, Lincoln, c. 1180–90, capital to dais arcade. E. Ashbury Manor, c. 1488, frieze in roof of porch chamber. F and G. 20 Swan Street, Kingsclere, head carved in central truss of late 14th-century hall.

One of the earliest is Markenfield Hall (Yorkshire) [42] (Fig. 10; Pl. 1 B), licensed in 1310, and like Brinsop Court (Herefordshire) [50] (Pl. V B) situated in potentially unruly country. But the type also occurs in peaceful regions such as Somerset, where at Meare [44] the country house of the Abbot of Glastonbury is of this build (Pl. V A), like the little Fish House [45] which Adam de Sodbury had erected on the shores of the lake near by. Cranborne Manor (Dorset) had a hall of this nature before the Cecil alterations, as Norden's drawing of 1605 reveals.

The Bishop of Winchester's palace at Southwark [43] had the great hall at first-floor level, and of this a shafted entrance remains with moulded arch, two-centred like the three service doorways in the adjoining end wall, and above these a magnificent wheel window, now bricked up; the last suggests a date c. 1320–30, though the doorways could be somewhat earlier. Here William of Wykeham resided in 1376–7, and the palace was the scene of the wedding feast in 1426 of James I of Scotland and Joan, niece of Bishop, later Cardinal, Beaufort. The building now forms part of a warehouse on the south side of Clink Street, Southwark, a hundred yards north-west of the Cathedral. Wykeham's colleges at Oxford (1380–6) [52] and Winchester (1387–94) [53] also had upper halls, like that of c. 1383 at St Cross.[54]

A hall raised on an undercroft with transverse barrel vaults was customary in the palaces of the see of St David's, not only in the smaller 13th-century buildings [37] but in the greater halls of Bishop Henry de Gower (1327–47) added at Lamphey [49] and St David's [48] (Pembrokeshire). The latter retains a beautiful wheel window and an original porch covering the stairs of access; in both the arcaded parapet is a special feature.

At Portchester, where Richard II rebuilt the domestic buildings (1396–9), forming a courtyard house in the inner bailey near the keep, a raised hall [56] was again chosen, reached through a projecting porch with a flight of steps. It was finished in the last year of his reign, for in 1399 glass was being made for the heraldic windows; and the workmen used 26 lb. of candles for work at night. But the beautiful new work was enjoyed by the king's supplanters, and presumably occupied by Henry V when the expedition for France (and Agincourt) was mustered here in 1415.

Often now not defence but convenience dictated the placing of the hall on an upper level. The higher position also allowed for a magnificent staircase of approach, as once at Kenilworth Castle (Fig. 11). This hall [55] (Pl. III D) seems, from documentary evidence, to have been built for John of Gaunt by Robert Skillyngton, mason, between 1390 and 1393, the roof probably designed by Gaunt's chief carpenter, William Wintringham, who died in 1392. Its dimensions (90×45 feet) are approximately the same as a hall here (89×46 feet) ordered in 1347, less than fifty years earlier. That October a contract was signed on behalf of the then owner, Gaunt's father-in-law, Henry, Earl of Lancaster (absent in the French wars), by his council John Buckingham, Bishop of Nicole (Lincoln), Peter de la Mare his seneschal, and Sir Richard de Felstede, citizen and carpenter of London. This hall we know was of stone, because Master Richard was to make a roof for it, as well as for the pantry, buttery and kitchen, as soon as the masonry was ready.*

Could this earlier hall be represented by the present building, perhaps refaced? The

---

* *Duchy of Lancaster, Miscellaneous Books*, II, fol. 52 V (repeated on fol. 6 IV); Salzman (1952), 436.

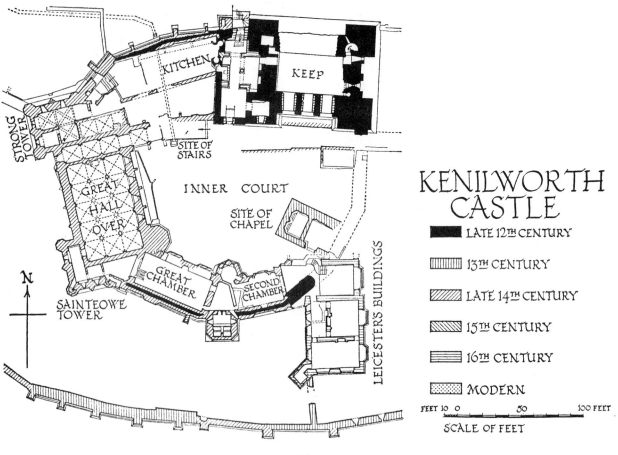

Fig. 11.

dimensions suggest the same site, and a small piece of earlier masonry with a small window is embedded in the lesser oriel facing the court at the end of the east wall.

Now John of Gaunt (1340–99) was an even greater lord than Henry, Earl, later Duke (1351), of Lancaster, whom he succeeded, through his marriage with Henry's daughter and heiress Blanche. After her death (1369) he wed Costanza, a daughter of Pedro the Cruel, in 1371 and became nominal king of Castile and Leon, in 1384 leaving for Spain in pursuance of these claims.

Royal state demanded a suitable environment, and a sumptuous new suite of apartments was planned for Kenilworth, which meant a drastic destruction of the earlier domestic buildings, including the mid 14th-century hall but not of course the massive Norman keep. The hall and its servery were raised on vaulted undercrofts, three aisles wide, the service quarters projecting in the square 'Strong Tower' with angle turrets and chambers, perhaps for important officials, on the top floor. This was balanced at the upper (south) end of the hall by the Sainteowe Tower, similar in shape, containing the oriel chamber which gave access, along the back of the hall, to the duke's private apartments. At the inner angle between these and the hall, on the courtyard side, was a smaller oriel, polygonal in plan, with large windows and a fireplace, this being reached from the opposite end of the high table. The line of the late 12th-century curtain wall dictated the layout of the southern rooms, the duke's great chamber making an obtuse angle with the hall; east of it was a lobby with semi-octagonal turret room, probably once vaulted like its basement, and projecting south a double garderobe tower serving three storeys of apartments, while beyond to the east was another state room, 'the Second Chamber', following the inner curtain almost as far as the earlier chapel.

It is interesting to note that in 1379, some ten years before these new buildings, John of Gaunt had a special floor laid in the Priory hall at Kenilworth, for dancing at Christmas,* which suggests that the castle hall was then not suitable for such festivities. Possibly it was an apartment with the old central hearth (though no louver is mentioned in the 1347 contract) or even aisled, the span being 46 feet. Certainly the new ducal hall must have embodied the latest improvements with two wall fireplaces, probably a hammer-beam roof, splendid entrance and traceried windows; in ruins it is still magnificent.

A dancing chamber (*le daunsyngchambre*) is mentioned at Leicester Castle, another favourite residence of the Dukes of Lancaster.† In 1377–8 a new window was made there, and it was one room away from the *countasse chamber* (later 'queen's chamber'), for in 1433–4 the accounts mention repairs to the *camera inter cameram Regine et le Daunsyng chambre.*‡ Dancing appears to have been a fashionable recreation. In 1385 there is reference to the dancing-room at Clarendon Palace, William Brown, mason, being paid 'for making a great fire-place of 2 hearths [*focis*] made for the dancing room [*camera tripudiant*] and the king's ward-robe.§ At Richard II's great festivities during his short-lived triumph of 1397, 'my lady of Exeter', the wife of his half-brother John Holland, Lancaster's daughter, 'received the prize as the best dancer and the best singer'.‖

John of Gaunt died in 1399, and did not long enjoy the splendid new work at Kenil-worth, but we may picture him there with the beautiful Katharine Swynford, his third wife, mother of Cardinal Beaufort. Gaunt's son by Blanche, Henry IV, was often at Kenil-worth, as was Henry V. Similar great halls raised on an undercroft do not seem to have been built in the 15th century, except where necessitated by the lie of the land, as at South Wingfield (Derbyshire), this being built on a slope. However, Henry VIII's great hall at Hampton Court (*c.* 1531–5) [58] is definitely at first-floor level, approached by a noble staircase, as is the hall at Christ Church (Cardinal College), Oxford.[57]

    * J. H. Harvey (1948), *The Plantagenets*, 98 n. Batsford.
    † Their London house, the Palace of the Savoy, was sacked in the Peasants' Revolt (1381). It has gone except for its name and the 16th-century chapel, perhaps on the site of an earlier consecrated building, and used for the hospital founded here by Henry VII. The name derives from a previous owner, Peter of Savoy, one of the uncles of Henry III's queen, Eleanor of Provence.
    ‡ L. Fox (1944), 19.
    § Exchequer, K. R. Accounts, 473, 2; Salzman (1952), 100.
    ‖ H. F. Hutchinson (1961), *The Hollow Crown*, 187; *Chronique de la Traison et Mort de Richard II*, ed. B. Williams (1846), 11, 140. English Historical Society.

EXAMPLES OF FIRST-FLOOR HALLS

		Internal Measurements	*References*
(1) 1077–82	Harold's hall at Bosham (Bayeux Tapestry)		Stenton (1957); Holmes (1959), (illus.).
(2) late C 11th	Scolland's Hall, Richmond Castle, Yorks.	*c.* 56′ × 26′	M.O.W. Guide (36), 6, 13–14 (ground plan); *V.C.H. Yorkshire*, I, 12–16 (plan at hall level).
(3) *c.* 1130	Sherborne Old Castle	*c.* 72′ × 24′	R.C.H.M. *Dorset*, I, 64–6 (plans & illus.).
(4) *c.* 1140–50	Prebendal House, West Malling, Kent		F. C. Elliston Erwood (unpublished).
(5) after 1147	Guest houses, Fountains Abbey, Yorks.	E. 48′ × 23′ 3″ (whole block 73′) W. 49′ 3″ × 24′ 9″	Hope (1900) (plan).
(6) *c.* 1150	Portslade Manor House, Suss., ruins		Packham (1934) (plan, etc.).
(7) *c.* 1150	King John's House, Southampton, Hants.	? 41′ × 29′	Wood (1935), 181–4, fig. 3, pls. II, VIII A (plan and illus.).
(8) *c.* 1150	Saltford Manor House, Som.	? 38′ 6″ × 19′	Wood (1935), 203, pl. IX D; *Country Life* (24).
(9) *c.* 1150	Hemingford Grey Manor House, Hunts.	*c.* 31′ × 18′	Wood (1935), 188–9, fig. 6, pl. IX A & B (plan & illus.); Dickinson(1946)(plan & illus.).
(10) *c.* 1150–60	Framlingham Castle, Suff., hall	*c.* 64′ × 25′	M.O.W. Guide (17).
(11) *c.* 1160	Christchurch Castle, Hants, hall	*c.* 49′ × 24′ (whole block 68′ long)	M.O.W. Guide (10) (plans).
(12) *c.* 1170	Wolvesey Castle, Winchester, Hants, hall	*c.* 136′ × 30′ (? once subdivided)	Nisbett (1894–7), 207 *et seq.* (plans & illus.).
(13) *c.* 1175	'Music House' (Isaac's Hall), 167 King St, Norwich	Whole block (originally subdivided) 52′ 6″ × 18′ 9″	Kent (1945) (plan & illus.); *Country Life* (20) (plan & illus.).
(14) *c.* 1170–80	Burton Agnes Old Manor, Yorks.	44′ 9″ × 22′ 6″	M.O.W. Guide (6) (plans).
(15) *c.* 1170–80	Jew's House, Lincoln	33′ 6″ × 15′	Wood (1935), 194–6, fig. 8, pls. V A, XIII A (plans & illus.).
(16) *c.* 1170–80	Aaron the Jew's House, Lincoln		Wood (1935), 197–8, pl. V B.
(17) *c.* 1180	Moyses Hall, Bury St Edmunds, Suff.	38′ × *c.* 25′	Wood (1935), 203–5, fig. 12, pls. VII B, X A (plans & illus.).
(18) *c.* 1180	Charleston Manor House, Suss.	37′ × 18′	Godfrey (1932) (plan & illus.).
(19) *c.* 1180–90	St Mary's Guild (John of Gaunt's Stables), Lincoln	42′ + × 18′	Wood (1935), 191–4, fig. 7, pls. IV A, XII A, XIII B (plan & illus.); Watkins (1913) (plans, elevations, etc.).
(20) *c.* 1200	Boothby Pagnell Manor House, near Grantham, Lincs.	35′ × 20′	Wood (1935), 198–200, fig. 10, pls. III B, VI, VII A, VIII B, X C (plans & illus.).
(21) *c.* 1200	Merton Hall (School of Pythagoras), Cambridge	Whole block (originally subdivided) 62′ 3″ × 23′ 3″	R.C.H.M. *Cambridge*, 377–9 (plans).
(22) 1201	Corfe Castle, Dor., 'Gloriet'	45′ 8″ × 21′ 8″	Toy (1929), 88, 96, pls. XXXVII, XXXVIII, XL (plans, section, etc.); Faulkner (1958), 167–8 (plan).
(23) *c.* 1210	Grosmont Castle, Mon.	Whole block (originally subdivided) 96′ × 32′	M.O.W. Guide (19) (plan); Faulkner (1958), 152, 155 (plans); Toy (1953 b),156.
(24)	Eynsford Castle, Kent	*c.* 39′ 2″ × 29′ 3″ (whole block *c.* 62′ long)	E. Cresy (1835), *Archaeologia*, XXVII, 391–7 (plan); Toy (1953 b),155–6(plan); M.O.W. Guide (16).

		Internal Measurements	References
(25) c. 1230–40	King John's Hunting Box, Romsey, Hants	32′ × 17′	Wood (1950), 24–6, fig. 7, pl. V A (plans & illus.); Andrews & Atkinson (1929) (plan & illus.).
(26) c. 1230–40	Tolhouse, Great Yarmouth, Norf.		Wood (1950), 47–8; *Guide to Tolhouse*, published by John Buckle, Great Yarmouth.
(27) c. 1230–50	Bishop Jocelyn's Palace, Wells, Som.	68′ × 28′	Wood (1950), 74–6; Parker (1866) (plan, etc.).
(28) c. 1235–61	Abbot's House, Battle, Suss.		Brakspear (1933a), (plans, etc.).
(29) c. 1240–50	King John's House, Tollard Royal, Wilts.	38′ × 16′	Pitt-Rivers (1890) (plan & illus.); Wood (1950), 96–7.
(30) c. 1250	Temple Manor, Strood, Kent	c. 42′ × 22′ (? subdivided)	Wood (1950), 39–40; Faulkner (1958), 151–3, (plans and section); M.O.W. Guide (39).
(31) c. 1250–60	Abbot's House, Netley, Hants	c. 48′ × 20′	M.O.W. Guide (29), 20 (plan); *V.C.H. Hants.*, III, 472–6 (plan).
(32) c. 1270–80	Little Wenham Hall, Suff.	39′ × 18′ 6″	Wood (1950), 76–81, fig. 15, pls. II A, VII C, VIII A, IX A, B (plans and illus.); Tipping (1921), Vol. I, 92–100 (plan & illus.).
(33) c. 1270–80	Moigne Court, Ower Moigne, Dor.	30′ × 21′	Wood (1950), 16–18, fig. 5, pls. I B, VIII D, XI A (plans & illus.).
(34) c. 1270–80	West Dean Rectory, near Seaford, Suss.	27′ × 17′	Wood (1950), 90–2, fig. 19, pl. V B (plans & illus.).
(35) c. 1280	Donington-le-Heath Manor House Farm, Leics.	41′ × 16′	Wood (1950), 41–3, fig. 10, pl. VI B, C (plans & illus.); Marsden (1962).
(36) c. 1280	Aydon Castle, Northumberland	40′ × 25′	Knowles (1899), 71–88 (plans); Turner (1851), 148–9 (plans, etc.).
(37) c. 1280–93	Bishop's Palace (Thomas Bek), St David's, Pembs.	60′ × 24′	M.O.W. Guide (37), 4, 8, 12–13 (plan).
(38) c. 1283–92	Ludlow Castle, Salop, hall	60′ × 30′ 6″	Hope (1908), figs. 10, 11, 12, pl. XXXVII (plans & illus.).
(39) c. 1290	Moot Hall, Dewsbury, Yorks.	45′ 5″ (W.), 43′ 10″ (E.) × 24′ 3″	Wood (1950), 97; Chadwick (1911) (illus.).
(40) late C 13th & C 14th	Great (guest) hall, Ely Cathedral Abbey, Cambs.	78′ × 33′ 5″	Atkinson (1933), 80–4 (plan & illus.); *V.C.H. Cambs.*, IV, 79 (plan).
(41)	Cranborne Manor, Dor.		Oswald (1935), 63 (John Norden's view & plan).
(42) c. 1310	Markenfield Hall, near Ripon, Yorks.	c. 42′ × 28′	Parker (1853), 231–4 (plans & illus.); *Country Life* (16) (plan & illus.).
(43) ? c. 1320–30	Winchester House, Southwark	c. 79′ × 31′	Toy (1946) (plan & illus.).
(44) c. 1322–35	Manor House, Meare, Som.	c. 60′ × 22′	Parker (1853), 297–300 (plans & illus.).
(45) c. 1322–35	Fish House, Meare, Som.	35′ 6″ × 16′	Parker (1853), 300–1 (illus.); Lloyd (1931), 42, 189, 332, 361, 436 (illus.).
(46) ? c. 1321–41	Prior's Hall, Ely, Cambs.	c. 62′ × 24′	Atkinson (1933), 66–9 (plans, etc.); *V.C.H. Cambs.*, IV, 79 *et seq.*
(47) c. 1330	Queen's (Fair) Hall, Ely, Cambs.	47′ × c. 20′	Atkinson (1933), 87–9 (plans, etc.).

		Internal Measurements	*References*
(48) *c.* 1327–47	Bishop's Palace (Henry de Gower), St Davids, Pembs.	119′ × 31′	M.O.W. Guide (37), 5, 8–9, 15–16 (plan & illus.).
(49) *c.* 1327–47	Bishop's Palace (Henry de Gower), Lamphey, Pembs.	*c.* 73′ × 19′	M.O.W. Guide (26), 2, 6, 8–9 (plan).
(50) *c.* 1340	Brinsop Court, Heref.	42′ × 22′ 3″	R.C.H.M. *Herefordshire*, II, 29–31, pls. 99, 101, 102 (plans & illus.); *Country Life* (5) (plan & illus.).
(51) *c.* 1375–6	Abbot's Hall, Westminster	52′ 6″ × 27′ (4 bays)	R.C.H.M. *London*, I, 86–8, pls. 170, 171 (plan & illus.); Harvey (1954), 319; Harvey (1946), 27–8, 57–8, pl. 20; Tanner & Mottistone (1954), 72–86.
(52) 1380–6	New College, Oxford	*c.* 79′ × 32′ (4 bays)	R.C.H.M. *Oxford*, 86–7, pl. 153 (plan & illus.).
(53) 1387–94	Winchester College, Hants	*c.* 61′ × 25′ (4 bays)	Oakeshott & Harvey (1955) (plan).
(54) ? 1383+	Hospital of St Cross, Winchester	*c.* 45′ × 25′ (4 bays)	Godfrey (1955), fig. 29, pl. 5 B (plan & illus.); Crossley (1951), pl. 160.
(55) 1390–3	Kenilworth Castle, War., hall	90′ × 45′	M.O.W. Guide (23) (plan); Pugin (1839), 19–21, pls. 18–22 (section, details, etc.).
(56) 1396–9	Portchester Castle, Hants, hall	? 52′ × 24′	M.O.W. Guide (34), 4, 9 (plan).
(57) 1525–9	Christ Church, Oxford	114′ 6″ × 29′ 9″	R.C.H.M. *Oxford*, 33–4, pls. 81–3, 85 (plans & illus.).
(58) 1531–5	Hampton Court, Middx, great hall	105′ × 40′	R.C.H.M. *Middlesex*, 34–5, pls. 73, 80 (plans & illus.).

3

The Aisled Hall

MANY early mediaeval halls must have resembled the barns which remain with us today, and which indeed are their descendants. In days when long timbers were not easily obtainable, oak being used exclusively and pine not yet imported,* the problem of roofing a wide building was solved by the erection of an aisled hall. In this the span was subdivided by two lines of posts, or arcades, supporting the roof, and separating the hall, like a church, into nave and aisles. This was a very old method dating from Saxon times and earlier.

There must have been numerous examples of these barn-like halls, probably one at least to every manor and castle in the 12th and 13th centuries, especially where a large assembly had to be accommodated. They were normally built at ground level, and of wood, this being cheaper and easier to work than stone: indeed their construction was in origin one of timber. In view of their material, naturally very few survive, but these give us an idea, reinforced by knowledge of later barns which carry on the same tradition with simpler detail and workmanship (*see* Fig. 12).

Four examples are so far recognized in England of the timber posted hall of the 11th and 12th centuries.

The earliest has been excavated at Cheddar [1] in Somerset, by Mr P. A. Rahtz for the Ministry of Works.† It is the largest timber hall so far known in this country, being 110 × 60 feet in area, of post and timber slot construction, with arcade posts 2 feet square, set in large pits 6 feet deep; this might allow for arcades 50 to 60 feet high. Across the east end was the foundation for a gallery or balcony. It dates from the early 12th century, and was certainly in use when Henry I (1100–35) and Henry II (1154–89) stayed at the palace. Later it was rebuilt with low stone walls and renewed arcade posts, and also reduced in length. This reconstruction probably dates from 1209–11, when King John spent £50 on 'his houses at Cheddar' and had timber (? for the arcade posts) brought over from Wales.

---

* Except as boards of wainscot, from the 13th century onwards, and for scaffolding and ladders in the 14th and 15th centuries. *See* Salzman (1952), 245–8.
† To whom the author is indebted for this new information.

In 1213, however, on his submission to the Pope, the manor was given to the Bishop of Wells.

The hall of the Bishops of Hereford [5] dates from c. 1160, a wooden aisled hall of three, perhaps once five, bays (*see* Figs. 13 and 14). Above an 18th-century ceiling can be seen a moulded semicircular arch of the eastern nave arcade enriched with nail-head ornament. The oak posts are oblong in section with round attached shafts having scalloped capitals, those to the destroyed transverse arches to nave and aisles being on a higher level

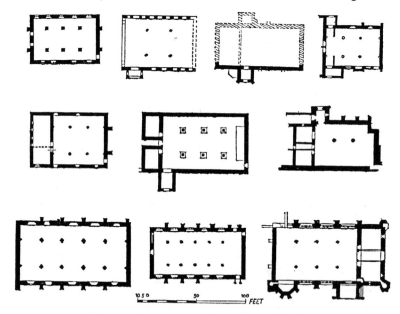

Fig. 12. Comparative plans of aisled halls.
Top, left to right : Oakham, Hereford, Buckden, Ashby de la Zouch.
Centre, left to right : Warnford, Clarendon, Warkworth (one aisle only). *Bottom, left to right :* Winchester, York Guildhall, Lincoln Palace.

than those to the arcades. Three capitals are still visible, and part of a third post remains in a room on the west (Pl. VIII A and B).

Most aisled halls would have had a rubble base, as at Hereford, on which the timber-framed walls could rest, and the type of hall at Leicester and Farnham Castles, where a complete shell of stone encloses the wooden posts (now gone or concealed), may be an elaboration of this. The Leicester hall [3] (now Assize Courts) dates from c. 1150. No capitals remain in position; the detached scalloped one exhibited has no abacus, but the post continuing above it. The oak posts were cut away in the early 19th century, and the remaining woodwork above was regarded as being later owing to the fact that the end tie-beam cuts across the top of the tall chevron decorated windows on the south. In 1957 Professor Horn examined every timber minutely, and was confident that these are of the original Norman work, buckled and driven out of shape. However, other authorities disagree,*

* J. T. Smith follows C. A. Ralegh Radford in considering the roof a reconstruction based on 14th-century work. But Professor Horn believes the reconstruction drawing by T. H. Fosbrooke, exhibited in the hall, is indeed correct.

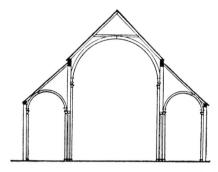

Fig. 13. The Bishop's Palace, Hereford, great hall, *c.* 1160;
transverse section, a reconstruction.

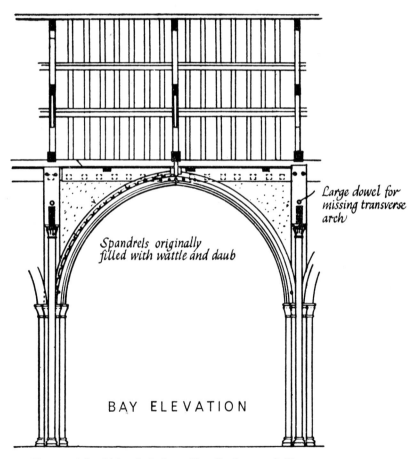

Large dowel for
missing transverse
arch

Spandrels originally
filled with wattle and daub

BAY ELEVATION

Fig. 14. The Bishop's Palace, Hereford, great hall.

and the building needs a detailed survey such as the recent one of the hall at Hereford. A radiocarbon dating test could be decisive.

At Farnham Castle [4] the hall was originally aisled, and built by Henry of Blois, Bishop of Winchester (1129–71), the wealthy brother of King Stephen. Ancient features include a post with scalloped capital, of the destroyed south line, concealed in a cupboard, and three stone service doorways.

But the greatest feudal building must have been the vast hall at Westminster,[2] built for William Rufus in 1097–9 (239 feet 6 inches × 67 feet 6 inches). Its monumental quality was further emphasized in the late 14th century when Hugh Herland's new roof allowed the floor space to be cleared of probably timber posts subdividing the span. Possibly an arcade, like that of Hereford, may be envisaged; however, the arcade is a feature not natural to wood, but influenced by stone construction. It was absent at Leicester and probably Farnham. At Westminster no evidence of the post holes has yet been found, but it is known that the present floor is 3 feet 9 inches higher than the Norman level, and in the repairs of c. 1925 evidence of the original window arrangement was discovered, built up in Yevele's remodelling, which altered the baying. There were twelve bays, each with a window on the side (north and south) walls, these flanked by two minor round-headed arches giving access to a barrel-vaulted passage. The larger window and passage arches were supported on piers formed by four grouped shafts having cushion capitals. Some carved examples of the latter are preserved.* Remains of red and blue paint, with black lines, found in the wall-passages, give us an idea of the brilliant colour which must have embellished the hall of William Rufus.

Thus the hall of the Red King, although on a grand scale, with stone walls, seems to have had its piers in wood, although the evidence is not conclusive. His great-nephew, Henry II, certainly had stone columns in the hall of his palace at Clarendon,[6] for the matrices of their bases have been excavated, and suggest shafts 2 feet in diameter. The stone hall was of four bays, and had a dais at the upper end. It may date from the year 1176–7, when a very large sum was spent on the palace (£268 17s. 9d.), also 2s. 6d. for bringing marble columns to Clarendon. Some idea of its appearance may be obtained from the rather smaller but very elaborate castle hall which remains at Oakham,[8] also of four bays, and dated by its ornament to c. 1190. The stone columns, again 2 feet in diameter, have magnificent Corinthianesque capitals below arches enriched with dog-tooth ornament, and which could have supported a clerestory wall, originally rising clear of the aisles (Pl. VIII c).†

At Bristol part of a late Norman aisled hall was discovered built up in later mediaeval masonry at Colston's House in Small Street. The remains are now incorporated in the Law Library of the Assize Courts.[9] They consist of the east arcade of three pointed arches of two chamfered orders, supported on stone piers with scalloped capitals, much restored.

A remarkable building of about this period is the castle hall, now chapel, at Bishop Auckland.[7] Earlier believed to belong to the first years of the 13th century, it is now

* Exhibited in the Jewel Tower at Westminster.
† C. A. Ralegh Radford (1955). Oakham Castle. *Archaeological Journal*, CXII, 183. J. T. Smith finds no clerestory evidence in surviving aisled halls. At Oakham he believes the original roof was heightened with re-used Norman masonry in the 17th-century alterations. Jones & Smith (1960), 76.

assigned to the episcopate of Hugh Pudsey (1153–95), who introduced the 'Early English' style into County Durham at an exceptionally advanced date. The hall is aisled in four unequal bays with a moulded two-centred arcade. This is supported, not as before on columns, but on piers quatrefoil in plan, made up of four shafts, not unlike the wooden arrangement at Hereford. Frosterley marble, the northern equivalent of Purbeck, is used in the arches and alternate shafts. The western piers have the earlier square abaci and water-leaf capitals, but the eastern have circular abaci and bases and moulded capitals of the newer fashion. There are triple responds, and above the piers are moulded shafts on corbels which supported the original roof, replaced in the 17th century.

Auckland thus foreshadows the type of aisled hall fashionable in the 13th century. It was much more convenient for assemblies than the first-floor hall, and was built when safety and the lie of the land permitted. Many new episcopal halls were built in this manner, to accommodate great gatherings of people, and the earlier halls, often on first-floor level, were retained for the daily, more private use of the bishop.

The circular column, used at Clarendon and Oakham, still occurs in the early 13th-century flint hall of three bays at Warnford in Hampshire.[10] Here the ashlar columns are of exceptional height (25 feet), with moulded capitals and bases with octagonal plinth. One remains, rebuilt in 1910, and halves of two others, as well as tall semicircular responds on the end walls. Wyndham's drawing of 1779 shows all four with two types of capital. They apparently supported tie-beams, for there is no evidence of arcade. The hall has now been preserved by the Ministry of Works.

But usually, as in church naves which they resemble, the aisled halls show a change in their stone piers with the introduction of the 'Early English' style. At Auckland (c. 1195) the piers are quatrefoil, and they were probably of diagonal plan in the 13th-century hall of Canterbury Palace. In the Bishop's hall (c. 1224) at Lincoln,[11] it is known that the columns were circular with four small and four larger attached shafts; the Parliamentary Survey of 1647 speaks of the grey marble pillars. The Palace is now being pre-served by the Ministry of Works, and excavation will doubtless reveal the shape of the pier bases.

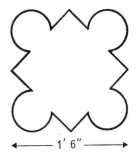

Fig. 15. The Bishop's Palace, Exeter, section of arcade post.

The Bishop's Palace at Exeter,[13] though much altered, retains as nucleus the originally aisled hall of three bays built by Bishop Brewer (1225–45). The chief features remaining are three re-used timber posts, one complete and left exposed, square in section with attached shafts (Fig. 15), the posts with moulded bases and stiff-leafed capitals, coloured,* also a magnificent stone entrance arch, semicircular with a remarkable late variety of chevron ornament.†

Fortunately at Winchester Castle hall [12] the arrangement is, except for the roof, com-plete. The two-centred arcades of five bays, of two chamfered orders separated by mouldings, are supported on piers having four attached shafts, forming an octafoil plan. The finest

* The author is indebted for this information to Mr A. W. Everett, F.S.A., who has also discovered that the 13th-century solar was originally much longer than as given in the 1932 plan. The south wall of the hall was rebuilt 5 feet away (inwards from its original line.
† Similar to that in St Mary's Gate at Gloucester and the chancel of Ozleworth Church (Gloucestershire).

surviving aisled hall of the 13th century, this is important, not only for its association with Henry III and the documentary evidence available, but also for its detail, which is therefore datable. It was begun in 1222 and completed in 1235, as we know from the royal accounts, Master Elias of Dereham being in charge of the works, but Stephen the Mason the actual designer. An earlier building, however, is incorporated, possibly an aisled hall with timber posts, and King Henry's hall seems to be a rebuild and embellishment of a late 11th-century structure, of which some of the walling remains. This in turn was refashioned by Richard II. According to Sir William Portal, there were three stages of development (Pl. IV c): (1) the Norman hall with large round-headed windows; (2) the hall of Henry III with the present windows, but each having a roundel and individual gable between overhanging eaves; and (3) the hall as altered by Richard II with the gables removed, the side walls built up into continuous eaves at the level of the roundels, and the latter reset on the internal face of the raised wall, between the windows. This alteration shows chiefly on the south side, which has been the least restored. Here traces of the first position of the roundels can be seen above the windows, and flanking these some of the angle shafts of the once projecting bays, with the chamfered weathering of the original eaves. The Richard II alterations were perhaps the work of Wynford or Yevele, who in 1390 were appointed, with the carpenter Hugh Herland, for a period of seven years, to see to the repair of the walls, turrets, gates, bridges and houses of Winchester Castle.* The roof seems to have been renewed in the later 15th century, as it bears the badge of Edward IV, the sun in splendour. It is possible that, like other halls with a stone arcade, King Henry's columns supported a range of clerestory windows, the aisles being separately roofed as in a church. The same may have applied to other 13th-century halls where a timber arcade was incorporated. Evidence, however, is so far negative.†

The great hall of the archbishops at Canterbury [14] is incorporated in later buildings, but Sir Alfred Clapham traced the original plan (126 × 62 feet) and excavated the porch. It must have been built before April 1243, when Henry III directed the justices of Ireland 'to cause to be built in Dublin Castle a hall containing one hundred feet in length and eighty feet in width, with sufficient windows and glass casements, after the fashion of the hall at Canterbury'.‡

Similar in dimensions to Winchester is the great hall at Wells Palace which Bishop Burnell had built c. 1274–92.[15] This was also of five bays and measures 115 × 59 feet 6 inches to Winchester's 111 feet 3 inches × 55 feet 9 inches. The columns have gone, but probably reflected, as do the windows, the more delicate treatment of the end of the 13th century.

The aisled hall persisted into the 14th century, after which it tended to be displaced in important buildings owing to more scientific roof construction. Bishop Salmon's hall (c. 1318–25) at Norwich Palace [18] may have been the last example on a grand scale. The porch and newel staircase remain, and enough evidence to show that the hall measured 121 feet 6 inches × 58 feet 6 inches, with piers quatrefoil in plan. In scale close to the Canterbury hall, it was also six bays in length.

---

* Harvey (1954), 317. No great sums were spent, however.
† See Jones & Smith (1960), 76. They cite large French barns with stone arcades and no clerestory.
‡ Close Roll, 27 Henry III; Turner (1851), 259.

Lesser houses continued to have their halls aisled throughout the 14th and even into the ·15th century, and over thirty examples are known, with doubtless more to be revealed in the thorough investigation of roofs, the part of the house normally less prone to alteration, facilitated by the introduction of electric light in remote farmhouses. This has already brought many aisled halls to light, buildings which have lost their timber posts or had them concealed in later subdivisions. Almost all these discoveries are timber halls, with the important exception of Nurstead Court in Kent,[21] where the wooden arcades were from the first enclosed in walls of stone (Fig. 16, Pl. 2). The emphasis of date is still laid on the first half of the century, but the recent discovery of at least five aisled halls around Halifax in Yorkshire suggests—through roof not moulding evidence, these halls retaining no datable detail—that they were built in the late 14th century by prosperous yeomen

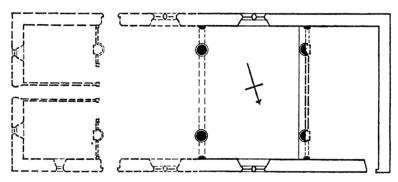

Fig. 16. Nurstead Court, plan.

who combined wool with farming activities. These halls were completely encased in stone in the late 16th and 17th centuries, and only detailed examination, in some cases during demolition, revealed their antiquity.[24, 25, 26, 27, 28]

As Mr J. T. Smith's distribution map* has shown, surviving aisled halls are found predominantly in the lowland half of England, particularly in south-eastern counties, and except for the Halifax houses hardly occur in the highland zone to north and west. This is surprising, for the south-east is regarded as the more advanced region, and spere truss halls, derived from the aisled buildings, are concentrated on the north and west.† However, we are still in the initial stages of the study of vernacular building, and there must be many discoveries yet to be made.

Two bays are common, as at Fyfield Hall, Essex (c. 1300) [16] and Capons Farm, Cowfold in Sussex, also an early 14th-century example; both were apparently separate units originally. But usually, possibly a later development, a third bay formed a two-storeyed solar-service block, as at Stanton's Farm, Black Notley (Essex),[17] High Bentley, Shelf,[25] 47, 49 and 51 Town Gate, Sowerby Town,[27] both near Halifax. Between this block and the hall is the entrance passage divided from the latter by a roof partition or spere truss, which later became the screen. Sometimes this entry with the lower bay equals the size of the upper bay of the hall, as at Lampetts, Fyfield; [22] indeed hall bays of unequal length are

* Smith (1958 a), 133.   † Ibid. 135.

proof of the former existence of this entrance passage. Sometimes it is placed in a separate half bay like the arrangement at Little Chesterford Manor Farm in Essex,[19] and this second method became usual. Less often is there an upper end block for the solar, this probably being a later development; it occurs at Nurstead,[21] and Scout Hall, Shibden Valley near Halifax.[28]

Examples have been found of halls with a single aisle. Warkworth Castle shows evidence of such a semi-aisled hall in the 13th century,[55] and three have been found in Sussex: 38 High Street, East Grinstead,[56] perhaps c. 1325–50; Apple Tree Cottage, Henfield; [57] and Priory Cottage, Bramber.[58] The last, dating from the 15th century, has charming detail: a cinquefoil pierced in the spandrel of the arched brace to the tie-beam, this tracery being continued as a quatrefoil frieze in the strut over the aisle (Fig. 17).

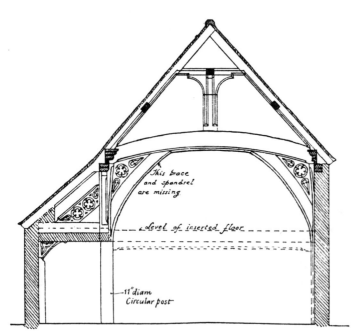

Fig. 17. Priory Cottage, Bramber, section of central truss of hall.

The row of posts was obviously an encumbrance to traffic when many people used the hall, although at Warnford [10] there is evidence of an original cavity in the columns to take the horizontal of a partition or screen, against which, presumably, the side benches could be set.* The aisles may also have been curtained off. However, advance in roof construction enabled the hall to be cleared of posts, and a braced collar beam could be used for the central span, the posts being retained only in the end frames and the truss dividing off the entry, where they remained useful as providing uprights for the 'speres'. This has been called an 'aisled derivative', or 'spere truss hall' † or 'quasi-aisled hall'. Examples include the early 14th-century West Bromwich Old Hall in Staffordshire,[32] a recent discovery of great interest, most carefully restored (Pl. VI), Wasperton Manor Farm,[33] (Fig. 51) which it greatly resembled, Mancetter Hall,[39] also in Warwickshire, c. 1330–40, and the early 14th-century Baguley Hall, Cheshire,[34] where Mr Smith has found Viking influence in the massive timbers and boat-shaped plan. Smithells Hall [35] in Lancashire is a companion building in several ways. In Herefordshire, Amberley Court at Marden [37] is a classic example (Fig. 18). Two and a half bays are usual, as at Sutton Courtenay

* This was pointed out by Dr H. Hubbard, who is making a reconstruction drawing for Professor U. T. Holmes.
† Smith (1955), 76–94.

Abbey [38] and the Old Parsonage at Marlow,[40] of the early to mid 14th century. Such halls are found in great numbers in the north-west, there being many 15th-century examples in Lancashire, such as Ordsall,[46] Denton [47] and Samlesbury Halls,[50] and the notable Rufford Old Hall [51] with its companion late 15th-century building, Adlington Hall in Cheshire.[52]

Mr R. T. Mason's term 'quasi-aisled hall' applies particularly to his early 14th-century

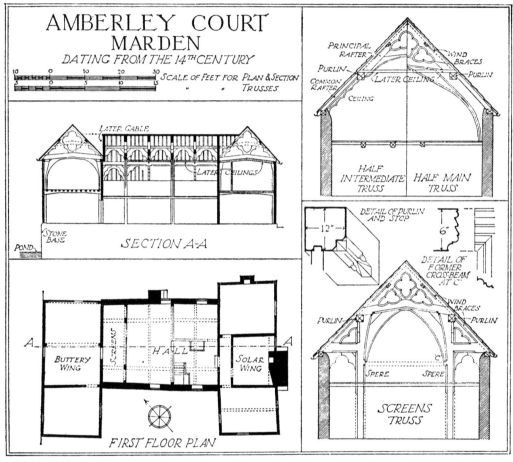

Fig. 18.

discovery Tickerage at West Hoathly in Sussex.[36] This had no spere truss apparently but aisled posts in the end walls of the two-bay hall, which retains a two-storeyed wing at the south end, and evidence of one originally on the north. This would make it comparable in plan, save for the absence of the main pillars, to Nurstead Court. 'Quasi-semi-aisled' halls he has found in Sussex at Homewood House, Bolney,[59] probably of the first half of the 14th century, and Dunster's Mill House, Ticehurst,[60] similarly with one aisle covered by the main truss without a post. Here the mouldings of the arch brace and shaft capital of the cruck-post, which supports it on the unaisled side, suggest a date in the early 15th century; so does the defaced moulded beam with traces of battlements at the south end of the hall.

The advent of the Friars in the early 13th century, particularly the Dominicans, Black or Friars Preachers, gradually exerted a great influence on Church architecture and thence on domestic. Emphasis was not, as earlier, on ritual and the chancel, but on the nave, built so that the whole congregation could see and hear the occupant of the pulpit. One of the first of these 'hall churches' with preaching naves was that of the Austin Friars (later Dutch Church) in London (1354), now rebuilt after the destruction of 1940. The tall clustered columns, as slender as possible so as not to impede the view, were a feature perfected by the coming Perpendicular style, in the wealth of churches built in the 15th century.

Now the aisles were built wider and, instead of the earlier lean-to roof, were given a smaller version of the tie-beam or other form over the nave. As well as width, greater height and larger windows were now possible; there were four-lights in each aisle bay at Austin Friars. Sometimes an additional aisle was provided on each side, as at Great St Helen's Church at Abingdon, Berkshire. This has five aisles and a breadth (104 feet) greater than its length (87 feet).

These hall churches influenced domestic building, and the obsolescent aisled hall seems to have been revived in a new fashion. The York Guildhall [30] (1446), restored after bombing in 1942, was like the nave of a hall church translated into wood, just as its predecessors had resembled the earlier type of church. It is 93 feet long, 43 feet wide and 30 feet high, of six bays. Here the posts* are wide and octagonal, very tall, each hewn from a single tree, with moulded capitals and bases. From these spring curved braces forming semicircular arches in four directions, these ending on wall posts supported on corbels on the outer, stone walls; slightly cambered tie-beams over both nave and aisles produce a low-pitched roof. In St Anthony's Hall at York, [31] however, there is a gabled roof over each portion. A further remarkable building in this city is the Hall of the Merchant Adventurers, [29] said to have been built 1357–68, but more likely an early 15th-century successor. It is of eight bays with a central row of posts forming two 'naves' on each floor, and with a chapel off the east end of the southern nave at undercroft level. This floor served as the Hospital of the Holy Trinity attached to the powerful mercantile fraternity whose hall was above. In the undercroft four great braces spring from each post to hold up the floor of the hall, and in the latter the braces support a tie-beam roof over each portion. The lower part of the walls is of stone, the upper timber-framed.

* The new ones are an exact copy, in a beautiful piece of restoration.

THE AISLED HALL—EXAMPLES

		Internal dimensions (including screens passage)	Bays	References
(1) C 11th	Cheddar Palace, Som., excavations	110′ × 60′		Rahtz (1962–3); *Illustrated London News*, 30 March 1963, 462–5 (plan & illus.).
(2) late C 11th	Westminster Hall	239′ 6″ × 67′ 6″	12	R.C.H.M. *London*, II, 121–3, pls. 177, 179 (plan).
(3) *c.* 1150	Leicester Castle, hall	76′ × 51′	6	Horn (1958), 9; Jones & Smith (1960), 76; Radford in *Archaeological Journal* (1955), CXII, 183 n. i.
(4) *c.* 1150 & 1190	Farnham Castle, Sy., hall	66′ × 44′		*V.C.H. Surrey*, II, 599–602 (plan).
(5) *c.* 1160	Bishop's Palace, Hereford	69′+ × *c.* 48′	3 (5 originally)	Jones & Smith (1960), 69–80 (detailed survey).
(6) *c.* 1176–7	Clarendon Palace	83′ × 51′	4	Borenius & Charlton (1936), 72–3, pl. XIX, i. (plan).
(7) 1153–95	Bishop Auckland Castle, Dur., hall (now chapel)	85′ × 45′	4 unequal	Hodgson (1896), 113–240 (illus. & mouldings); J. Charlton, *Archaeological Journal* (1954), CXI, 222–3.
(8) *c.* 1190	Oakham Castle, Rut., hall	66′ × 44′	4	Turner (1851), 28–31 (plan & illus.); Wood (1935), 201–3 (plan); Radford in *Archaeological Journal* (1955), CXII, 181–4.
(9) 1200+	Law Library, Bristol			E. W. Godwin, *Archaeological Journal* (1866), XXIII, 150.
(10) early C 13th	Warnford Manor House, Hants, ruins	52′ × 48′	3	Wyndham (1779), 357 (plan, view of interior roofed, etc.); Nisbett (1906) (plan, section, etc.); Wood (1950), 27–9 (plan).
(11) *c.* 1224	Bishop's Palace, Lincoln	*c.* 84′ × 58′	4	M.O.W. Guide (to be published); Wood (1951 b) (plan from E. I. Abell & J. D. Chambers (1949), *The Story of Lincoln*).
(12) 1222–35	Winchester Castle, hall (renewal)	111′ 3″ × 55′ 9″	5	Sir William W. Portal (1939), *The Great Hall of Winchester Castle: A Summary* (illus.); *V.C.H. Hants.*, V, 9–12 (plan & illus.); Turner (1851), 175–6 (plan, illus., mouldings).
(13) *c.* 1224–44	Bishop's Palace, Exeter	75′ × 42′ (?47′ originally)	3	Unpublished research by A. W. Everett; J. F. Chanter (1932), *The Bishop's Palace at Exeter*, but hall probably wider than shown in plan.
(14) before 1243	Archbishop's Palace, Canterbury	126′ × 62′	6	A. W. Clapham in *Archaeological Journal* (1929), LXXXVI, pl. II (plan).
(15) 1274–92	Bishop's Palace (Burnell), Wells	115′ × 59′ 6″	5	*Archaeological Journal* (1950), CVII, 109 (plan); Pugin (1839), pls. 53, 54 (plan, elevations, etc.).

		Internal dimensions (including screens passage)	Bays	References
(16) *c.* 1300	Fyfield Hall, Ess.	40′ × 29′ 6″	2	Smith (1955), 77–80, 92 (plan & sections).
(17) early C 14th	Stanton's Farm, Black Notley, Ess.	34′ × 26′ originally	2½	Smith (1955), 81–3, 92 (sections); R.C.H.M. *Essex*, II, 19–20 (plan & section).
(18) 1318–25	Norwich Palace, Bishop Salmon's hall	121′ 6″ × 58′ 6″	6	*Archaeological Journal* (1949), CVI, pl. V (plan by A. B. Whittingham, A.R.I.B.A.).
(19) *c.* 1320–30	Little Chesterford Manor Farm, Ess.	37′ × 29′ originally	2½	R.C.H.M. *Essex*, I, 174–5 (plan, section & details, etc.); Wood (1950), 19–21, pls. XII B, D, XIII A; Smith (1955), 81 (plan & illus.).
(20) early C 14th	The Savoy, Denham, Bucks.	at least 36′ × *c.* 24′ 6″ originally	2	R.C.H.M. *Bucks*, I, 116–18 (plan & illus.); Smith (1955), 81.
(21) mid C 14th	Nurstead Court, Kent	45′ 6″ × 28′ 6″	2	Smith (1955), 82, 84–6, pl. XII (plan & section, etc.); Parker (1853), 281–2 (Blore's drawings exterior and interior).
(22) *c.* 1340–50	Lampetts, Fyfield, Ess.	35′ 6″ + (? 40′ + originally) × *c.* 24′	2	Smith (1955), 78, 80, 84, 88 (plan & sections); *V.C.H. Essex*, IV, 50–2 (plan & sections).
(23) C 14th	St Clair's Hall, St Osyth, Ess.		2	R.C.H.M. *Essex*, III, XXXI, 204–5 (plan).
(24) late C 14th	3, 4 & 5 Sladden St, Boothtown, Halifax, Yorks.		2	Atkinson & McDowall (1959).
(25) late C 14th	High Bentley, Shelf, Halifax, Yorks.		2	Atkinson & McDowall (1959).
(26) late C 14th	Lower Bentley, Royd, Sowerby Bridge, Yorks.			Atkinson & McDowall (1959).
(27) late C 14th	47, 49 & 51 Town Gate, Sowerby Town, Yorks.	32′ wide	2	Atkinson & McDowall (1959).
(28) late C 14th	Scout Hall, Shibden Valley, Yorks.		2	Atkinson & McDowall (1959).

LATE AISLED TYPE

			Bays	References
(29) early C 15th	The Merchant Adventurers' Hall, York		8	Crossley (1951), 151–2, pls. 189, 190.
(30) 1446	The Guildhall, York	93′ × 43′	6	Crossley (1951), 151, pl. 188; Smith (1955), 86; Clapham & Godfrey (1913), 72 (plan).
(31) C 15th	St Anthony's Hall, York			J. S. Purvis & E. A. Gee (1953), *St Anthony's Hall, York.* (St Anthony's Hall Publications No. 1).

AISLED DERIVATIVE (QUASI-AISLED) OR SPERE TRUSS HALLS

		Internal dimensions (including screens passage)	Bays	References
(32) c. 1290–1310	West Bromwich Old Hall, Staffs.	over 32′×26′ 3″	2½	
(33) c. 1300	Wasperton Manor Farm, War.	38′×24′	2½	Jones & Smith (1958) (plans, sections, mouldings, etc.).
(34) early C 14th	Baguley Hall, Ches.	c. 34′×27′ 6″ N. 29′ 3″ mid. 28′ 3″ S.	2½ (boat-shaped plan)	Smith & Stell (1960) (plan, sections, mouldings, etc.).
(35) early C 14th	Smithells Hall, Lancs.	c. 35′×25′	5 uneven	Crossley (1951), 128–9, pls. 137, 147, 152 (sections); Taylor (1884), 60–5, pls. IV, X (2), XII, XIII, XXX (1 & 6), XXXI (2) (plans & illus.).
(36) early C 14th	Tickerage, West Hoathly, Suss. (no spere truss)	29′×23′	2	Mason (1957), 82–5, 91 (plan, sections, mouldings, etc.).
(37) 1st half C 14th	Amberley Court, Marden, Heref.	33′×22′	2½	R.C.H.M. Herefordshire, II, 137, pls. 94, 168, 169 (plan, sections, etc.); III, LXVII (exterior & interior reconstructions); Crossley (1951), 133.
(38) c. 1330	'The Abbey', Sutton Courtenay, Berks.	40′×24′	2½	Parker (1853), 32, 272–4 (plan & illus.).
(39) c. 1330–40	Mancetter Hall, War.	40′×25′	2½	Smith (1955), 80, 89 (section); V.C.H. Warwickshire, IV, 117–119 (plans & sections).
(40) c. 1340	The Old Parsonage, Marlow, Bucks.	36′×24′	2½	Wood (1949), 53–8, pl. XIII (plan & illus.).
(41) mid C 14th	Eaton Hall, Leominster Out, Heref.	38′×23′ 6″	2½	R.C.H.M. Herefordshire, III, 128–9, pl. 39 (plan).
(42) C 14th	Court Farm, Preston Wynne, Heref.	27′ 6″×20′	2½	R.C.H.M. Herefordshire, II, 155, pls. 23, 39.
(43) C 14th	Peg's Farm, Wellington Heath, Heref.		3½	R.C.H.M. Herefordshire, II, 204, pl. 29.
(44) c. 1348	Tiptofts, Wimbish, Ess.	38′×27′ 6″	2½	Smith (1955), 90, 92 (section); R.C.H.M. Essex, I, 351–3 (plan & sections); W. Horn, survey to be published (plan, sections & reconstructed interior view).
(45) late C 14th or early C 15th	Lower Brockhampton House, near Bromyard, Heref.	29′×21′ 6″	2½	R.C.H.M. Herefordshire, II, 32–33, pls. 39, 81 (plan).
(46) mid C 15th	Ordsall Hall, Lancs.	42′×25′	7	Crossley (1951), 131–2; Taylor (1884), 47–53, pls. III, IX (1), XXXI (4) (plan & illus.).
(47) C 15th	Denton Hall, Lancs.	35′×23′	5 of varying width	Taylor (1884), 110–13, pls. XXV, XXXI (3) (plans, sections, etc.).
(48) C 15th	Radcliff Tower, Lancs., (demolished)	43′×28′		Crossley (1951), 132.
(49) C 15th	Little Mytton, Lancs.	33′×24′		Taylor (1884), 94–5.
(50) C 15th	Samlesbury Hall, Lancs.	c. 36′ 6″×26′ 6″	4	Taylor (1884), 89–93, pls. III, XVIII (1), XXIV (1 & 2) (plan, interior view, etc.).

		Internal dimensions *(including screens passage)*	Bays	*References*
(51) *c.* 1500	Rufford Old Hall, Lancs.	47′×23′	7	Crossley (1951), 129, 130, 131, 139, pls. 141, 153 (interiors); Taylor (1884), 77–80, pls. III, XVII, XVIII (2) (plan, interiors, etc.).
(52) *c.* 1500	Adlington Hall, Ches.	45′×*c.* 26′	6	Taylor (1884), 131–5, pls. III, XXIX (plan, etc.); Crossley (1951), 131, pls. 142, 143, 151.
(53) early C 16th	Speke Hall, Ches.	42′×26′		Crossley (1951), 134–5, pls. 154, 155, 156; Taylor (1884), 114–17, pls. III, XXVI (plans & illus.).
(54) 1484–1503	The Commandery, Worcester	47′ 10″×25′ 9″	6	Dollman & Jobbins (1861), pls. 35, 36, 37 (plan & sections).

SEMI-AISLED HALLS *(with one aisle only)*

(55) C 13th	Warkworth Castle, Northumb., hall in bailey	*c.* 57′×41′		M.O.W. Guide (43), 12 (plan).
(56) ? 1325–50	38 High St, East Grinstead, Suss.	24′×20′ 5″	2	Mason (1957), 74, 90–2 (moulding).
(57) C 14th	Apple Tree Cottage, Henfield, Suss.			
(58) C 15th	Priory Cottage, Bramber, Suss.	29′×*c.* 21′	2	Godfrey (1947), 112–17 (plan & sections).

QUASI-SEMI-AISLED HALLS *(one 'aisle' without a post)*

(59) probably 1st half C 14th	Homewood House, Bolney, Suss.	*c.* 26′×22′	2	Mason (1957), 85–92 (plan, sections, mouldings, etc.).
(60) early C 15th	Dunster's Mill House, Ticehurst, Suss.	23′ 6″×16′	2	Mason (1960), 150–5 (plan, section, mouldings, etc.).

4

The Great Hall

WE HAVE noted that the hall in early mediaeval houses tended to be of aisled construction. But gradually, through more scientific roof treatment, the posts which caused obstruction came to be omitted, and a magnificent building type emerged which continued, with slight variations and development, particularly in windows, to the end of the Middle Ages. The great hall met a social need as the central point of the estate, a place of assembly for the tenants, for legal and administrative purposes, as well as being the main living-room for the lord's family and personal staff, where most of them dined and, at first, some of them slept. Indeed the early great hall with its low ancillary buildings, seen in so many villages in mediaeval England, must have formed a chief feature of the landscape, and even when the lesser buildings grew higher and more important, the lofty roof of the great hall could still be distinguished, often towering above the others, to the end of our period. It was the central hearth which necessitated the high roof to accommodate the smoke, and this height persisted a long time, although in the 14th, and especially in the 15th, century a wall fireplace gradually superseded it. Now the hall could be lower and its comfort and warmth increased, with less draught, and space provided for an important room above. It became one of several living-rooms, and finally grew into the mere vestibule that it is today.

THIRTEENTH CENTURY

The 13th century was a period of transition in domestic architecture. Besides the first-floor halls, considered separately, there were as many halls built at ground level wherever it was safe and convenient. Many of the latter were of aisled construction, where a wide span made this necessary. Some nine examples are known of this kind in the period, their width ranging from 62 feet to 33 feet 9 inches.

However, nineteen other 13th-century halls at ground level now show no evidence of having once been aisled.* They may, of course, have been altered later, as is believed by

---

* These approximate figures, changing as more examples are found, give some idea of the development.

49

Fig. 19. The Old Deanery, Salisbury, interior of hall, looking north from the dais.

some to have been the case at Stokesay Castle, though this has been denied in a recent detailed survey. The first view is based on the arrangement on the end walls where two wall-posts on stone corbels support a collar, once a tie-beam, and a purlin, set square like the arcade plate of an aisled hall. It is similar to the scheme in the aisled hall of the late 13th-century St Mary's Hospital at Chichester, but with a nave half the width (some 12 feet) of the latter, yet higher. Similar end wall-posts on corbels occurred in the solar of the prioress at Polsloe Priory, Exeter,* also late 13th century; there were diagonal braces as at

* Everett (1934), 8, Pl. XIX.

Stokesay, and in the other, south, end of the western range (22 feet 6 inches wide) the vertical timbers, braces and collar were recessed into the wall. Here the original roof has gone, but its construction is clear from the evidence of the side walls, in which the posts supporting the principals were recessed, and stood on 'templates' of timber some 4 feet above the floor. At Stokesay similar posts, now encased in cement, stand on moulded corbels, and seem to have supported cruck-like timbers. Indeed one may visualize many early halls with a cruck form of roof construction, if the span allowed, and the late 13th-century carpenters were experimenting in methods which would obviate the necessity of using aisle posts in the wider halls as well.

Except for the 14th-century hall at Nurstead, which is 28 feet 6 inches wide, Stokesay,[8] 31 feet, would have been the narrowest of the aisled halls. But it is more probably an 'aisled hall derivative', with the survival in the end wall of an earlier feature. The great hall of the Knights Templar at Bisham Abbey (c. 1280),[7] almost identical in the measurement, has a trussed rafter roof, repaired in 1859 when smoke-blackened rafters were found. There is no sign of any arcade, which is made most unlikely by the presence of three original graduated lancets, forming an opening 13 feet across in the east end wall.

The Old Deanery at Salisbury (1258–74),[6] recently restored (Fig. 19), contains a hall very like Stokesay in design and measurement, with the same gabled windows. The original roof has been disclosed, showing that it was definitely not an aisled building, but with the arcade plate supported on raking timbers supported on corbels. The hall of the archbishops of Canterbury at Charing [14] is 35 feet wide without the aisled arrangement, great wooden arches over the whole span once being used instead. However, there is evidence of arcades at Old Soar (c. 1290), also in Kent (Pl. VII A), with a hall 33 feet 9 inches in breadth. Other 13th-century halls have had the roof replaced, but the Warden's Lodging built in 1299–1300 at Merton College, Oxford (21 feet wide),[10] has a queen- and king-post roof of a single span.

FOURTEENTH CENTURY

By the 14th century the hall had developed a standard plan. It was usually at ground level, though in less peaceful areas (as at Markenfield) or for special reasons (as at Ely) it could still be built at first-floor level.

As we have noted, the aisled form seems to have been dying out, in the main, after the early 14th century, owing to new methods of roof construction. But examples are still found, such as Nurstead Court, Lampetts and in remote areas, even into the 15th century.

The great royal hall at Westminster [35] was remodelled by Richard II at the close of the century, its floors cleared of timber posts and Herland's magnificent roof erected. It is of exceptional size (239 feet 6 inches × 67 feet 6 inches; 4 : 1); otherwise the proportions were usually 2 : 1 or 3 : 2, the width being approximately half or two-thirds of the length.

One of the largest, earlier, was the hall of Caerphilly Castle,[19] built by the royal craftsmen Thomas Bataile, mason, and William Hurley, carpenter, for Edward II's favourite Hugh le Despenser the Younger who had married the heiress Eleanor de Clare. Hurley was ordered to take carpenters there in 1326, for work in conjunction with Bataile, and

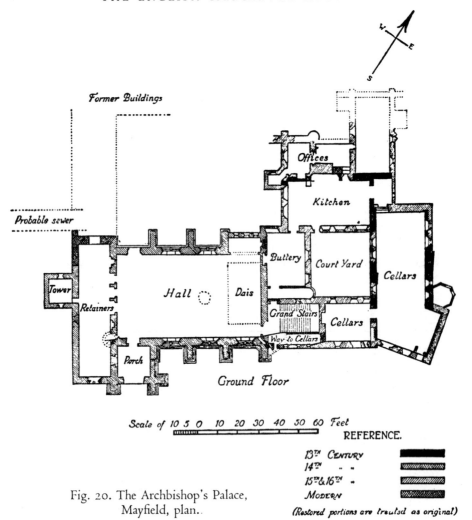

Fig. 20. The Archbishop's Palace,
Mayfield, plan.

REFERENCE.

13ᵀᴴ CENTURY
14ᵀᴴ " "
15ᵀᴴ & 16ᵀᴴ "
MODERN

(Restored portions are treated as original)

his receipt to the Peruzzi, Despenser's bankers, for payment in March 1326 survives. The building must have been in progress when the king sought refuge at Caerphilly that October, but he withdrew after a few days, leaving part of his treasure there in the care of Despenser's son and the constable. These possessions, including armour, the royal bed with his canopy, the king's red retiring robe and pearl decorated cap, 272 silver dishes, together with £13,000 in money, were captured with the Castle by the forces of Queen Isabella. Despenser, captured and executed that November, could not have seen his hall finished. Its ogee-headed windows still remain; they were once of the latest fashion.

Caerphilly is comparable in dimensions to the halls of the Archbishop of Canterbury at Charing (c. 1300) [14] and Mayfield, [15] the latter (Pls. 3, 24; Fig. 20) close to it in date, as well as to the great hall at Dartington, [33] built by Richard II's half brother, John Holland, Duke of Exeter, c. 1388–1400.

William Hurley may also have designed the roof of the hall at Penshurst [24] for the

A. Kingston Seymour Manor House, c. 1470–80, south front.

B. Preston Plucknett Abbey Farm, first half of the 15th century, showing kitchen chimney, porch and hall.

C. Woodlands Manor, Mere, first half of the 15th century. The dais window has been lengthened and the chimney brought from a house in Dorset.

Plate IX. The Great Hall.

Plate X. The Great Hall.

A. South Wraxall Manor, *c.* 1435; hall with two-storeyed oriel block balancing the porch. B. Penshurst Place, *c.* 1341–9; hall with staircase oriel and back porch.

wealthy London merchant Sir John Pulteney in 1341–9 (Pls. X B and XL A). Next in the scale comes the hall of *c.* 1300 at Broughton Castle, [13] which compares in size with Abbot Litlyngton's hall at Westminster (*c.* 1375–6), as Haddon Hall [12] may be compared with that at Clevedon Court (Somerset), *c.* 1320.[17] The hall at Cumnor Place (Fig. 21) is known from illustrations and was similar to the surviving one at Sutton Courtenay 'Abbey' (*c.* 1330),[21] also built by the Abbot of Abingdon. A little smaller is the manor hall of Norrington (Wiltshire) 1377,[32] while another at Northborough (Northampton-shire) [23] closely resembles the hall of the Old Parsonage at Marlow (Buckinghamshire),

Fig. 21. Cumnor Place, a reconstruction based on early 19th-century drawings.

c. 1340 (Fig. 22);[22] the 'Treasurer's House' at Martock (*c.* 1330) [20] was also rectorial. There must have been many of such charming little halls throughout the country, and a number have been surveyed in Westmorland, including Beetham [26] and Middleton Halls,[27] similar in dimensions, and Preston Patrick.[28]

Although the central hearth was normal in a hall at ground level, remains of an original hooded fireplace exist in the side wall at Goodrich Castle (*c.* 1300),[11] and the same is the case at Caerphilly. There is documentary evidence at Hamsey (Sussex) that a fireplace was commissioned in 1321, and apparently not only one in a lateral wall, but another behind the high table as well.* Even earlier, at Peveril Castle (Derbyshire), evidence of a mid 13th-century end-wall fireplace has been found, in a hall also provided with a central hearth. This 'dais fireplace' seems a feature, however, more popular in France and Scotland than in England. But further examples may, of course, come to light, especially as we know it occurred at Dartington Hall in the late 14th century, as well as a number in the 15th century. John of Gaunt's hall at Kenilworth,[34] raised on an undercroft, had two opposite fireplaces in the side walls.

The natural siting of the windows was one in each bay, as at Norrington, except where a doorway or fireplace was needed. Where the dais end wall was also clear of adjoining

---

* *Westminster Abbey Muniments*, 4063; Salzman (1952), 426–7; translated, with ground plan, in Godfrey (1931).

building, as at Martock, a large window over the high table could dominate the hall. At Clevedon Court and Penshurst there are windows of several lights, in two stages, at the ends, above the adjoining buildings, and at Southwark and St David's a great circular 'wheel' window in the gable.

In the first half of the 14th century the hall windows were large two-lights with a transom,

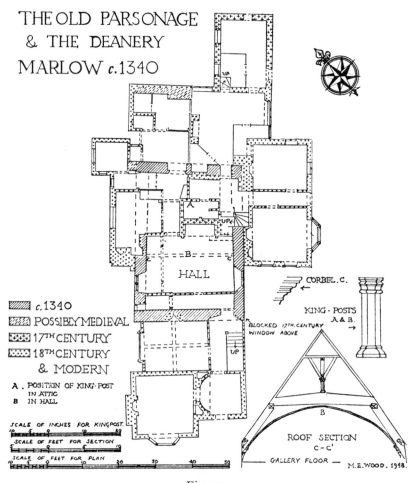

THE OLD PARSONAGE & THE DEANERY MARLOW c.1340

HALL

CORBEL.C.

KING-POSTS A & B.

BLOCKED 17TH CENTURY WINDOW ABOVE

▨ c.1340
▨ POSSIBLY MEDIEVAL
▨ 17TH CENTURY
▨ 18TH CENTURY & MODERN

A . POSITION OF KING-POST IN ATTIC
B IN HALL

SCALE OF INCHES FOR KINGPOST
SCALE OF FEET FOR SECTION
SCALE OF FEET FOR PLAN

ROOF SECTION c-c'
GALLERY FLOOR
M.E.WOOD. 1948.

Fig. 22.

convenient for fixing shutters, the expensive glass probably confined in normal cases to the upper lights, particularly the tracery in the head. Sometimes, as in the 13th century, there were stone seats in the jambs with a foot rest raised above what was mainly a grimy floor level, with rushes to keep down the dust of an earthen floor. Towards the end of the century the windows tended to be set higher, except near the dais, and are shorter, without a transom, in some cases. This may have been to avoid an external penthouse, or it may have been adopted to allow wainscoting or tapestry below and continuous benches to be set against the wall, as in the later example at Ockwells Manor. By now the hall windows were probably glazed entirely, in important houses, and the transom was no longer needed to contain the shutters. Also the long dais window could make further long windows unnecessary for lighting. But transomed windows persisted at Norrington quite late in the period. As yet the bay window had not developed except possibly at the very end of the century, and then more likely as an oriel chamber such as the earlier 14th-century projection at Abbot's Grange, Broadway, to allow room for which one hall window is obliquely set.

At Marlow the walling above the windows is carried up into gables, each with a separate roof, giving a dormer effect to the hall. This was doubtless the arrangement at the very similar house at Northborough, and certainly the case at Sutton Courtenay 'Abbey' originally, and at the destroyed hall at Cumnor, both owned by Abingdon Abbey, and it may have been common. It had already occurred in the Old Deanery at Salisbury (1258–1274), at Stokesay (c. 1285–1305), originally at Winchester Hall, and in 1244 at Woodstock Henry III had ordered three windows of the hall 'to be raised with masonry in the fashion of a porch'.* This may have derived from the need to raise the windows in an aisled hall, and was continued when aisles were no longer in fashion. It seems to have gone out of use by the 15th century.

Where battlements were required and a convenient *alure* (wall walk), the side walls of the hall were thickened by outer arches to the windows, of which Mayfield and Penshurst are examples. The same idea was used at Southampton in the mid 14th century, when after devastation by French raiders the 12th-century town walls (also those of houses) were given battlements, here with machicolation, and this 'arcade' can still be seen on the western shore.

The hall entrance was invariably at the end of a lateral wall, away from the high table, and near the service doorways at the lower end of the hall. All could be screened off by a wooden partition with openings for two-way service traffic, probably developing from two side speres and a movable portion in between. The passage so formed across the service end became known as the 'screens'. If the hall stood clear with a court on either side, as at Haddon [12] and Clevedon, there would be another doorway opposite the main entrance.

By the 14th century it is common to find the H-plan of house, hall and cross-wings. In Westmorland there are many survivals of 14th-century type having this arrangement. The domestic and service wings of the house, often combined in the 13th century, were now kept separate, at least in the larger houses. The domestic or great chamber 'solar block' was set at right angles to the upper end of the hall, with access from the high table. This was the owner's private wing, with the bedchambers (bed-sitting rooms) of his family on the upper floor, sometimes over a vaulted undercroft for special storage, which he could thus control. In the end wall of the hall, as at Penshurst (and Stokesay earlier), there were often small apertures through which from his solar the lord could overlook the activities of his servants below, after he and his family had retired after the common meal. No doubt the great hall was still used for sleeping by many of the servants, though the women would have a separate apartment.

* Liberate Roll, 28 Henry III; Turner (1851), 201.

At the lower end of the hall the service cross-wing normally contained buttery and pantry, with access by a passage in between to the kitchen, still built some distance away. In the end wall of the hall there were thus three doorways, and sometimes a fourth to a staircase leading to other rooms, supplementary bedchambers or guest-rooms above.

FIFTEENTH AND EARLY SIXTEENTH CENTURIES

The 15th century continued along the same lines of development. The aisled hall occurs only in rare or remote examples, although the Guildhall at York (1446), now restored after bombing, shows a variety with transverse arches over aisles as well as nave, comparable to the 'preaching churches' of the period.

The proportions of the hall are still normally 2 : 1 or 3 : 2. The king's hall at Eltham Palace, Kent,[60] is nearly a third longer than the hall of a great noble at South Wingfield [48]

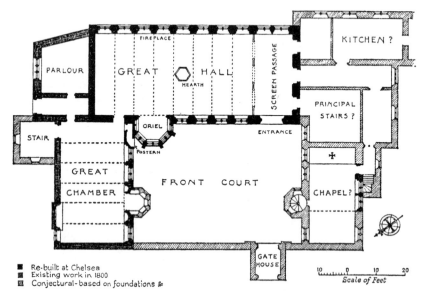

Fig. 23. Crosby Hall, conjectural plan.

and that of a leading merchant at Crosby Hall (Fig. 23).[56] Bishop's Waltham [38] is longer but narrower than the archbishop's hall at Croydon,[49] while the aristocratic Minster Lovell (Fig. 24) [47] is in proportion like Lincoln College, Oxford,[46] in the same county. All very similar in size are the manor halls at Little Sodbury (Gloucestershire),[64] Great Chalfield (Wiltshire) (Pl. 4),[62] Athelhampton (Dorset) [67] and Cothay (Somerset); [63] South Wraxall (Pl. X A) [45] and Woodlands Manor (Pl. XI),[42] both in Wiltshire, are slightly smaller and near in measurement. Of town houses Bowhill (Fig. 25) [41] and the 'Law Library' at Exeter [40] are almost identical in size, their roof design akin; the wooden halls of Rufford (Lancashire) [70] and the Commandery at Worcester [68] are also close in measurement.

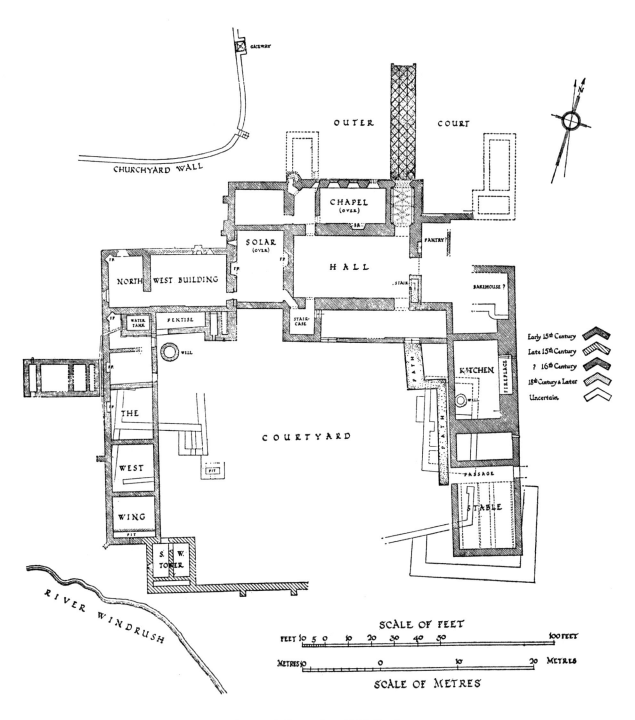

GATEWAY

CHURCHYARD WALL

OUTER COURT

N

CHAPEL
(OVER)

PANTRY?

SOLAR
(OVER)

HALL

NORTH WEST BUILDING

STAIR

BAKEHOUSE?

WATER TANK

PENTISE

STAIR-CASE

STAIR-CASE

WELL

Early 15th Century
Late 15th Century
? 16th Century
18th Century & Later
Uncertain

THE

KITCHEN

FIREPLACE

WEST

COURTYARD

WELL

PIT

WING

PATH

PATH

PIT

PASSAGE

S. W. TOWER

STABLE

RIVER WINDRUSH

SCALE OF FEET

FEET 10 5 0   10   20   30   40   50   100 FEET

METRES 10   0   10   20   METRES

SCALE OF METRES

Fig. 24. Minster Lovell Hall, plan.

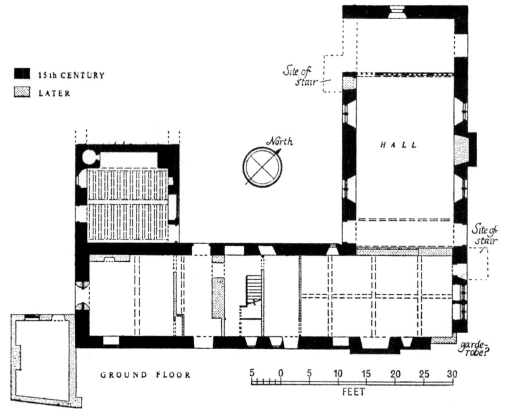

■ 15th CENTURY
▨ LATER

Site of stair

North

HALL

Site of stair

garde-robe?

GROUND FLOOR

5 0 5 10 15 20 25 30
FEET

Fig. 25. Bowhill, Exeter, plan.

In the early 16th century the great collegiate hall of Wolsey at Christ Church, Oxford,[79] is longer than his other work, Hampton Court,[82] completed by Henry VIII; both halls are built on undercrofts, like that at Brasenose College, Oxford.[74] Beddington Hall, Surrey,[86] compares with another aristocratic building at Cowdray,[78] and smaller halls of this period include Corpus Christi College, Oxford,[75] Horham Hall (Essex)[73] and Poundisford Park near Taunton.[83]

Sometimes a hall almost square is encountered, as at Wanswell Court (Gloucestershire) (Pl. 5)[50] and Pykerell's House at Norwich. This indicates a tendency towards a smaller hall, lessening in importance to the advantage of the parlour. Cases are known of an earlier hall being partitioned off to provide a parlour, as at the early 14th-century hall at Wasperton, of which the south bay was subdivided horizontally in the 15th century, the date of the moulded ceiling beams.

The central hearth persists into the 15th century, but is going out of fashion. At Crosby Hall (1466) it occurs together with the wall fireplace. There is a louver showing that a central hearth once existed at Lincoln College, Oxford (c. 1436–7), and Eltham (c. 1479–1480), pictures of a vanished louver turret (c. 1540) at Cowdray and the negative evidence of no wall fireplace at Minster Lovell (probably 1431–42) and Croydon (c. 1443–52).

Usually the central hearths were covered in when later wall fireplaces were added. Original fireplaces in the side wall survive at Ockwells (*c.* 1465) [54] and Fawsley Manor House, Northamptonshire (*c.* 1537–42),[84] and dais-end ones at Woodlands Manor and West Coker.[52]

It is interesting to trace the window development in halls of the 15th century. The 14th-century method was followed at first, and one long transomed window placed in each bay, often of two cinquefoiled lights in a square head. We find this at Bowhill, the Prebendal House at Thame,[43] the Court House at East Meon (Hampshire) [44] and many others. There are tall examples, with early Perpendicular tracery at Hymersford House, East Coker (Somerset) and in Ashleworth Court (Gloucestershire).[53] It will be noticed that all these halls with tall low openings have no bay window. (East) Coker Court [51] and Kingston Seymour (originally) (Pl. IX A), both in Somerset, certainly have an oriel chamber together with long traceried windows in the hall, and indeed very tall windows of three tiers of lights had already been used adjoining oriel chambers in the hall (1390–3) at Kenilworth Castle. But these windows seem to date from the earlier part of the 15th century, before the bay window became fashionable.

Exceptionally high placed windows of the square-headed, two-light (cinquefoiled) transomed type are used as early as *c.* 1431–42 in the south wall at Minster Lovell.[47] The hall here is extremely lofty, and on the north only upper lights are used so as to clear the roof of the adjoining chapel. There is an oriel projection containing the solar staircase.

Transomed windows set high are found in some later buildings such as the Exeter Guildhall (1465) and Cothay Manor (*c.* 1480). At Church House, Salisbury,[59] such windows of four cinquefoiled lights adjoin a bay window. Vertical tracery is used over cinquefoiled ogee lights at Magdalen College (1476), the hall with the earliest bay window in Oxford.* An oriel chamber is present at Great Chalfield (*c.* 1480),[62] where four-centred lights are used throughout. These appear to mark a transitional period in development.

But the short untransomed window, placed high, is typical of the second half of the 15th and early 16th centuries, just as the bay window, developed from earlier oriel chambers, is the significant feature of the period. The latter was one of the two factors which made other low windows unnecessary; the other was the growing popularity of tapestry as a wall treatment. With the bay a range of windows placed high would give ample lighting, and allow room for a continuous row of benches along the side walls, unbroken by window embrasures.

Early examples, perhaps even late 14th century, of the high window can be seen at Tickenham Court in Somerset, which once had a square oriel projection. The longer dais window, a precursor of the bay, accompanies high two-lights at Woodlands Manor and Preston Plucknett (Pl. IX B); at Woodlands the dais window was further lengthened recently, and at Preston it has been restored to its original height. At South Wraxall there are oriel chambers combined with high windows, and at South Wingfield (*c.* 1440–59) [48] with a bay projection, the windows once above tapestry level had their embrasures lengthened when a floor, now removed, was inserted in the 17th century.

Croydon Palace (*c.* 1443–52) [49] is perhaps the earliest surviving hall to have an upper

* Gee (1958).

range of windows forming a continuous band between the buttresses, in each bay a window of three pointed lights in four-centred head, even where there is a low oriel arch beneath. Soon the oriel opening grew higher and its window occupied the whole of one bay. Croydon belonged to the archbishops of Canterbury, Crosby Hall [56] to the wealthy Sir John Crosby, who could also afford wide expanses of tapestry and window glass. He built the hall *c.* 1466+ and gave it a lofty oriel window in the latest fashion, as well as a range of two-light windows, filling each bay at the upper level, their cinquefoiled heads in line with the upper tier of the oriel, their four-centred hoods linked externally without buttresses. King Edward IV's Eltham Palace hall (*c.* 1479–80) [60] has a very similar arrangement. However, there are two double lights in each bay, marked by a buttress, at the level of the arches of the oriel, here square of two tiers, thus ten windows with an oriel on each side. As at Crosby Hall, the lights are cinquefoiled with a small quatrefoil in a four-centred arch with hoods linked in pairs; there is further elaboration in the cusping of the oriel. In the great brick hall built by Cardinal Morton at Hatfield (*c.* 1497) there is one window between each pair of buttresses, and the two lights are now uncusped, within a square head externally; no bay window is present here. There are four uncusped lights in a square head serving the contemporary hall at Athelhampton,[67] and here the dividing buttress is narrowed the width of a mullion at window level. This bears no relationship to the windows of the oriel, which have rudimentary tracery in two-centred heads, on a different plane. The awkward junction of the string-course indeed suggests an adaptation, and perhaps during the course of building.* Fawsley Court, said to be later, has in each bay a square-framed window of three four-centred lights, at the usual higher level, but again not matching the three-tiered oriel.

The high-set window continued in vogue into the early 16th century, and a common form shows this frame of three four-centred lights, as at Horham Hall (1502–5) and Lytes Cary (Somerset). The windows are yet placed high when more elaborate tracery was used, as at Corpus Christi, Oxford (1517), the lights here still cinquefoiled as are those in the great transomed four-light windows, but in an arched frame, at Christchurch (finished in 1529), which so much resembles those in the hall at Hampton Court (1530–5) except that there is no cusping in the latter.

It is noticeable that in the later halls, unlike Crosby Hall and Eltham, no attempt is made to match the heads of the side windows to the tiers of the bay projection. This might be expected at Compton Wynyates (*c.* 1512–20),[77] where Sir William Compton used materials from Henry VIII's gift of the ruinous Fulbroke Castle (Warwickshire). But it even occurs at the king's own palace hall at Hampton Court. It is especially noticeable at Cowdray,[78] where the side windows are tall and transomed with 15th-century type tracery in a two-centred arch, the hood continued as string-course, and the bay has six tiers of four-centred lights. This, however, seems to be an addition, like the porch (*c.* 1537) by the Earl of Southampton to the hall (*c.* 1520–30) of Sir David Owen, bringing it up to date for the visit of Henry VIII in 1538.

Where the hall was built, as often happened, free at gable level from the adjoining wing, there was room for a great end window, set high. At Hampton Court the dais end

* The view of the owner, Mr R. V. Cooke, Ch.M., F.R.C.S.

Plate XI. The Great Hall.
Woodlands Manor, Mere, first half of the 15th century; hall with upper end fireplace.

A. Yardley Hastings Manor House, mid 14th century; solar-service block. B. Goodrich Castle, *c.* 1300; arcade in solar wing.

C. Manorbier Castle, domestic range with staircase to hall entrance (*centre*) solar service (*right*) *c.* 1160, and solar of *c.* 1260 (*left*).
D. Chepstow Castle, part of domestic range, *c.* 1280, in lower bailey, showing east hall with entrance to cross passage, large south window, and private apartments (*right*).

Plate XII. The Solar.

is lit by a window of seven transomed and traceried lights, with twin double-lights above in the gable. At Cowdray the gable was filled with windows, a central five-light flanked and surmounted by twin-lights, other spaces treated as unglazed panels.

Occasionally there are two tiers of side windows. These are possibly original at Compton Wynyates, each of three cinquefoiled lights in a square frame; but definitely not so at Little Sodbury Manor (Gloucestershire),[64] where the lower (modern) windows in Tudor style, matching the old upper row, replace Queen Anne sash insertions.

(For windows *see* Pls. LIII–LVI.)

The oriel, a usual feature of the later 15th- and 16th-century hall, was reached through a great moulded arch near the upper end, but not always in line with the dais. Sometimes, as at Eltham, there was a similar projection opposite. To prevent draught behind the high table, and an interruption of the ornamental hangings on this wall, the doorway to the private wing behind was now often placed in the oriel projection, just within the entrance arch, on its upper side. This gave access not only to a staircase up to the great chamber but to the room beneath, a parlour or withdrawing room for the owner. Here he tended to have his meals away from the noise and hubbub of the great hall. Possibly the first stage was to have them served in the oriel chamber, which was sometimes provided, as at Lytes Cary, with its own fireplace. As early as the later 14th century Piers Plowman had complained of this anti-social habit (*see* page 91).

With high-set windows, window seats were impracticable and no longer needed, the bay giving any private recess that was needed. There is an example in the high table window at Wanswell (*c*. 1450–60), where the windows come down lower.

The entrance doorway, often with another opposite, remained at the lower end of the hall, with the service doorways in the end wall near by. All these were now screened off permanently, as at Haddon and Bisham Halls, but examples of a movable central portion, between the 'speres' at the side, remain at Rufford and Wortham (Devon) of late 15th- and early 16th-century date (Pl. XXV A and D).

The H-plan of hall between cross-wings was fully established, the private and service wings separated by the ground-floor hall. Above the buttery and pantry would be a second chamber of importance, perhaps for guests or the eldest son and his family, and occasionally the lord's great chamber was placed here, as apparently at South Wingfield, where the lie of the land prevented rooms at the bay window end.

The great hall remained important throughout the period, although some late examples, especially in the south-west, were subdivided horizontally. In many cases development came by the extension of the cross-wings, through the increase of rooms at both ends of the hall, these wings being lengthened to form two sides of a courtyard, or two courts with the hall between them. Haddon Hall is an example of the latter, while Bodiam Castle has the hall at the upper end of a single court, and South Wingfield of an inner one. The growth of private rooms for the family and lodgings for guests and retainers was the important factor in plan development, for these apartments could be grouped round a quadrangle, as in monastic and collegiate building, continuing round to join the gatehouse which was often in the side opposite the hall doorway across the court, like Compton Castle (Devon), or sometimes, as at Great Chalfield, placed at right angles to the main block. Of course these lodgings probably replaced timber buildings, for some kind of court, or farmyard, must have been present from the first. Buildings against the perimeter of the site also facilitated the provision of garderobes, which could discharge away from the precincts, into a ditch or moat.

Not only was there an increase of rooms at the solar end of the hall; the buttery wing was also developing, the service departments often pushed out by the presence of a new room, a parlour or dining-room, next the screens, for the family to dine away from the great hall, but conveniently near the kitchen. Great Chalfield has such a dining-room, and probably South Wraxall, though on the whole the parlour for the family tended to be behind the high table, below the solar.

The kitchen might be moved further out beyond the butteries at the side or end of a back court, round which, in a large house, the service departments might be placed together. A small house such as Littlehempston Old Manor (Devon) [36] might have the kitchen opposite the hall, across a small inner courtyard.

THE GREAT HALL (UNAISLED EXAMPLES)

* Raised on an undercroft

		Internal dimensions (including screens passage)	Bays	References
(1) c. 1210	Appleton Manor, Berks.	38′ 6″ × 24′ 6″	2½	Wood (1935), 175–6, fig. 1, pls. I A, XI A (plan & illus.); Wood (1950), 7; *Country Life* (2) (plan & illus.).
(2) early C 13th	The Chantry, Chichester, Suss.	c. 38′ × 31′	2½	*V.C.H. Sussex*, III, 156 (plan & illus.); Hannah (1927), 143–148 (plan & illus.).
(3) 1st half C 13th	The Prebendal Manor House, Nassington, Northants.	c. 37′ × 24′ 6″	2½	Wood (1950), 48–51, fig. 11 (plans).
(4) c. 1250	Cogges Manor, near Witney, Oxon.	c. 35′ × 16′	3	Wood (1950), 56–7, fig. 12, pls. VI A, XI B (plan).
(5) c. 1260	Barnston Manor, Dor.	c. 31′ × 19′	3	Wood (1950), 13–14, fig. 3 (plan).
(6) c. 1258–74	The Old Deanery, Salisbury	50′ × 31′ 6″	4	Drinkwater (1964).
(7) c. 1280	Bisham Abbey, Berks.	52′ 2″ × 33′ 4″	3½	*V.C.H. Berks.*, III, 139–45 (plan, but more service openings (five in all) have been revealed since this plan was made); Long (1939 b) (with *V.C.H.* plan); *Country Life* (3) (with *V.C.H.* plan).
(8) c. 1285–1305	Stokesay Castle, Salop	c. 52′ × 31′	4	Smith (1956), (plan & section, C. F. Stell); Cordingley (1963) (complete survey).
(9) c. 1283–92	Ludlow Castle, Salop, hall	60′ × 30′ 6″	5	Hope (1908), 276 et seq., figs. 10–12, pls. XXXVII, XLI (plans & illus.).
(10) 1299–1300	Warden's Lodging, Merton College, Oxford	28′ 6″ × 21′	2	R.C.H.M. *Oxford*, 26, 76, 77 (plan).

		Internal dimensions (including screens passage)	Bays	References
(11) c. 1300	Goodrich Castle, Heref.			M.O.W. Guide (18), 9, pl. I (plan & illus.).
(12) c. 1300	Haddon Hall, Derbys.	. 42′ × c. 27′	2½	Country Life (10), 1742-6 (plan & illus.); Lloyd (1931), figs. 65-8 (plans).
(13) c. 1300	Broughton Castle, Oxon.	54′ × 30′	? 4 or 5	Parker (1853), 261-7 (plan & illus.).
(14) c. 1300	Charing Palace, Kent	69′ 6″ × 35′	? 4	Kipps (1933), 78-97 (plan. & illus.).
(15) c. 1320-30	Mayfield Palace, Suss.	69′ 5″ × 39′ 3″	4	Bell-Irving, Mayfield (1903), 63-68 (plan); Parker (1853), 290-293 (illus.).
(16) c. 1320-30	Ightham Mote, Kent	31′ × 21′	2	Garner & Stratton (1929), 155-157, figs. 266-7, pl. CXIII (plan & illus.).
(17) c. 1320	Clevedon Court, Som.	c. 40′ × 26′	2½	Country Life (6), 1672-5 (plan), 16-19 (plan without C 19th additions; demolished 1961).
(18) c. 1320	'Abbot's Grange', Broadway, Worcs.	c. 25′ 8″ × 19′ 9″	2½	V.C.H. Worcs., IV, 34-6 (plan).
(19) c. 1326	Caerphilly Castle, Glam.	c. 70′ × 35′	5	Harvey (1954), 142; W. Rees (1937), Caerphilly Castle, 27-31, 51-2 (plan); Thompson (1912), 270-2, 274 (plan & illus.).
(20) c. 1330	'Treasurer's House', Martock, Som.	32′ × 22′	3½	Wood (1950), 72-4, fig. 14 (plan).
(21) c. 1330	The Abbey, Sutton Courtenay, Berks.	40′ × 24′	2½	Parker (1853), 32, 272-4 (plan & illus.).
(22) c. 1340	The Old Parsonage, Marlow, Bucks.	36′ × 24′	2½	Wood (1949), 53-8, pl. XIII (plan & illus.).
(23) c. 1340	Northborough Manor House, Northants.	36′ × 24′	2½	V.C.H. Northants., II, 508-10 (plan & illus.); Parker (1853), 252-7.
(24) c. 1341-9	Penshurst Place, Kent	62′ × 39′	3½	Lloyd (1931), figs. 79-81 (plan & illus.).
(25) mid C 14th	Yardley Hastings Manor, Northants., ruins	45′ × 30′	? 2½	V.C.H. Northants., IV, 296-7 (plan & illus.); Markham (1903-4) 406.
(26) mid C 14th	Beetham Hall, West.	c. 40′ × 24′	2½	R.C.H.M. Westmorland, 40-1, pl. 78 (plan & illus.).
(27) late C 14th	Middleton Hall, West.	c. 40′ × 23′	2½	R.C.H.M. Westmorland, 170-2, pl. 143 (plan & illus.).
(28) late C 14th	Preston Patrick Hall, West.	c. 35′ × 24′	2½	R.C.H.M. Westmorland, 195-6, pl. 148 (plan & illus.).
(29) C 14th	Burneside Hall, Strickland Roger, West.	c. 32′ × 22′	2½	R.C.H.M. Westmorland, 223-4, pls. 154, 155 (plan & illus.).
(30) late C 14th	Selside Hall, West.	c. 29′ × 18′	? 2½	R.C.H.M. Westmorland, 243-4, pl. 158 (plan & illus.).
(31) C 14th	Castle Dairy, Kendal, West.	c. 28′ × 17′	? 2½	R.C.H.M. Westmorland, 125, pl. 114 (plan & illus.).
(32) c. 1377	Norrington Manor House, Alvediston, Wilts.	38′ 6″ × 23′	4	Drinkwater (in press).
(33) c. 1388-1400	Dartington Hall, Devon	69′ 9″ × 37′ 6″	5	Emery (1958), 184-202 (section and illus.).

		Internal dimensions (*including screens passage*)	Bays	*References*
(34) 1390–3	Kenilworth Castle, War., hall *	90′ × 45′	6	M.O.W. Guide (23) (plan); Pugin (1839), 19–21, pls. 18–22 (section, details, etc.).
(35) 1394–1402	Westminster Hall, remodelled	239′ 6″ × 67′ 6″	12	R.C.H.M. *London*, II, 120–3, pls. 174–80 (plan & illus.).
(36) ? c. 1400	Littlehempston Old Manor, Devon			Pevsner (1952 b), 197, pl. 58 (illus.).
(37) c. 1420	Bradley Manor, Newton Abbot, Devon	33′+ × 19′	? 3½	National Trust Guide (1) (plans & illus.).
(38) 1st half C 15th	Bishop's Waltham Palace, Hants	66′ × 27′	4	M.O.W. Guide (4).
(39) 1st half C 15th	'Abbey Farm', Preston Plucknett, Som.	c. 40′ × 21′2″	4	Garner & Stratton (1929), 19–20, fig. 28, pl. III (illus.).
(40) 1st half C 15th	Law Library, Exeter	32′ × 22′	3	*Archaeological Journal*, CXIV (1957), 138–9, fig. 2, pl. XXVII (plan, sections & illus.).
(41) 1st half C 15th	Bowhill, Exeter	33′ × 19′	4	Everett, (1958 b), 203–6 (plan & sections).
(42) 1st half C 15th	Woodlands Manor, Mere, Wilts.	31′ × 21′	3	*Country Life* (31).
(43) 1st half C 15th	Prebendal House, Thame, Oxon.	c. 39′ × 24′	3	*Archaeological Journal*, LXVII (1910), 367–9 (plan).
(44) 1st half C 15th	Court House, East Meon, Hants			*V.C.H. Hants*, III, 65–6 (illus.).
(45) c. 1435	South Wraxall Manor House, Wilts.	31′ 8″ × 19′ 9″	4	Pugin (1840), 16–18, pls. 56–59, 65–70 (plan, sections, etc.); Garner & Stratton (1929), 31–2, fig. 48, pls. XII & XIII.
(46) c. 1436	Lincoln College, Oxford	49′ 9″ × 25′ 9″	4	R.C.H.M. *Oxford*, 65–6, pl. 119 (plan & illus.).
(47) c. 1431–42	Minster Lovell Hall, Oxon.	50′ × 26′	4	M.O.W. Guide (28), 10–13, pls. I, II, IV (plan & illus.).
(48) c. 1440–59	South Wingfield Manor, Derbys.	c. 72′ × c. 37′	6	Ferry (1870) (plans, sections, details, etc.); Thompson (1912), 345–52 (plan & illus.).
(49) 1443–52	Croydon Palace, Sy.	56′ × 37′ 9″		Pugin (1838), 26–9, pls. 38, 39 (plan, sections, etc.); *The History of the Old Palace, Croydon* (1960), Old Palace School, Croydon (illus.).
(50) 1450–60	Wanswell Court, Glos.	c. 26′ × 23′	3	Parker (1859), 77–8, 266–9 (plan & illus.); *Country Life* (28).
(51) mid C 15th	(East) Coker Court, Som.			*Country Life* (7a) (illus.).
(52) after 1457	West Coker Manor, Som.		3	*Country Life* (30) (plan & illus.).
(53) before 1463	Ashleworth Court, Glos.	c. 37′ × 19′	3	National Buildings Record photographs.
(54) c. 1465	Ockwells Manor, Berks.	c. 41′ × 24′	4	*V.C.H. Berks*, III, 93–6, 105 (plan & illus.); Long (1941), 34–5.
(55) c. 1465–75	Great Dixter, Northiam, Suss.			Lloyd (1931), fig. 600 (illus.).
(56) 1466+	Crosby Hall, London	69′ × 27′	8	Clapham & Godfrey (1913), 121–38 (plan & illus.); Garner & Stratton (1929), 206, fig. 379, pl. CLXXV (illus.).

		Internal dimensions (including screens passage)	Bays	References
(57) 1450–80	Llanllechid, Cochwillam, N. Wales	37′×21′	3½ (half bay at dais end)	R.C.H.M. *Caernarvonshire*, I, 134–6, fig. 131, pls. 68, 76–77, 80, 86–7, 91 (plan, sections, etc.).
(58) 1470–83	Hall of John Halle, Salisbury		3	R. L. P. Jowitt, *Salisbury* (1951), 65, 73, fig. 40 (illus.); Collier (1908), *Journal of the British Archaeological Association*, N.S., XIV, 221 et seq.
(59) later C 15th	Church House, Salisbury	*c.* 25′ 6″×20′ 9″	3+	Garner & Stratton (1929), 33, figs. 49, 50 (plan & illus.).
(60) *c.* 1479–80	Eltham Palace, Kent	101′ 4″×36′	6	M.O.W. Guide (15) (plan & illus.); Pugin (1838), 31–42, pls. 43–9 (plan, sections, details, etc.).
(61) between 1470 & 1484	Gainsborough Old Hall, Lincs.	*c.* 56′×28′	6	Brace (1954) (plan); *Country Life* (8) (illus.).
(62) *c.* 1480	Great Chalfield Manor, Wilts.	40′ 2″×20′ 2″	4	Garner & Stratton (1929), 30–31, figs. 45–7, pls. X, XI (plans & illus.); Pugin (1840), 17–23, pls. 29–32 (plans, sections, etc.).
(63) *c.* 1480	Cothay Manor, Som.	*c.* 36′×c. 21′	2½	Garner & Stratton (1929), 21–22, figs. 32–4, pls. IV, CLXXX (plan & illus.); Lloyd (1931), figs. 96–8, 601, 602 (plan & illus.).
(64) *c.* 1485	Little Sodbury Manor, Glos.	*c.* 42′×23′	4	*Archaeological Journal*, LXXXVII (1930), 447–8, 450, fig. 10 (plan); *Country Life* (12).
(65) later C 15th	Wortham Manor, Lifton, Devon	*c.* 34′×22′	4	*Country Life* (32) (sketch plan & illus.).
(66) later C 15th	Weare Giffard, Devon			Garner & Stratton (1929), 213, 215, pls. CLXXX–CLXXXII (illus.).
(67) 1495–1500	Athelhampton Hall, Dor.	38′×21′ 6″	4	Garner & Stratton (1929), 65–67, figs. 106–8, pl. XXXI (plan & illus.); *Country Life* (2b).
(68) *c.* 1484–1503	The Commandery, Worcester	*c.* 47′×26′	5½ (half bay at dais end)	Garner & Stratton (1929), 202–203, figs. 362–4, pl. CLXIX (plan & illus.); Dollman & Jobbins (1861), 35, 36.
(69) *c.* 1498	Milton Abbas, Abbot's Hall, Dor.			*Country Life* (18).
(70) *c.* 1500	Rufford Old Hall, Lancs.	47′×23′	7	Garner & Stratton (1929), 205, 215, pl. CLXXXII (illus.).
(71) *c.* 1500	Adlington Hall, Ches.			Crossley (1951), 140, figs. 142, 143 (illus.).
(72) early C 16th	Speke Hall, Lancs.	42′×25′		Garner & Stratton (1929), 167–169, figs. 286–8, pls. CXXIX & CXXX (plan & illus.).
(73) 1502–5	Horham Hall, Ess.	*c.* 46′×24′	4	Garner & Stratton (1929), 112–114, figs. 194–7, pl. LXXII (plan & illus.).
(74) 1512	Brasenose College, Oxford *	49′×25′	4	R.C.H.M. *Oxford*, 24, 26 (plan).
(75) 1512–17	Corpus Christi College, Oxford	53′×24′	6½	R.C.H.M. *Oxford*, 49–51, pl. 110 (plan & illus.).

		Internal dimensions (including screens passage)	Bays	References
(76) before 1520	Cotehele House, Calstock, Corn.	42′ × 22′	6	Garner & Stratton (1929), 39–41, figs. 59, 60, pls. XVI, XVII (plan & illus.); National Trust Guide (3), 11–12 (illus.).
(77) c. 1512–20	Compton Wynyates, War.	33′ × 23′	4	Garner & Stratton (1929), 117–118, figs. 202–4, pls. LXXVI-LXXXI (plan & illus.).
(78) c. 1520–30+	Cowdray Park, Suss.	c. 59′ 6″ × c. 27′ 6″	4	Garner & Stratton (1929), 49–53, figs. 74–81, pls. XXIII, XXIV (plan & illus., Grimm drawings).
(79) c. 1525–9	Christ Church, Oxford *	114′ 6″ × 39′ 9″	8	R.C.H.M. *Oxford*, 33–4, pls. 81, 82, 83, 85 (plans & illus.).
(80) 1525–38	Hengrave Hall, Suff.	c. 29′ × 16′	4	Garner & Stratton (1929), 138–140, figs. 240–3, pls. XCVII, XCVIII, XCIX (plan & illus.).
(81) c. 1530	Lytes Cary, Som.	c. 33′ × 21′	4	Garner & Stratton (1929), 46–48, figs. 71–3 (plan & illus.); National Trust Guide (4), (illus.).
(82) c. 1530–5	Hampton Court, Middx *	97′ × 40′	7	R.C.H.M. *Middlesex*, 34–5, pls. 73, 80 (plans & illus.).
(83) 1534+	Poundisford Park, Taunton, Som.	28′ × 16′	3	Garner & Stratton (1929), 82–83, figs. 140–3, pl. XLIV (plan & illus.).
(84) c. 1537+	Fawsley Manor House, Northants.	c. 53′ × 25′	5	Garner & Stratton (1929), 59–61, figs. 96, 98 (plan).
(85) c. 1538	Gifford's Hall, Stoke by Nayland, Suff.			Garner & Stratton (1929), 140–141, figs. 244, 245, 386, pl. CI (illus.).
(86) earlier C 16th	Beddington Hall, Sy.	61′ 4″ × c. 33′		Garner & Stratton (1929), 211–212, pl. CLXXXI.

5

The Solar, or Great Chamber

THE solar or great chamber was a private bed-sittingroom of the owner and his family in the early Middle Ages. At this period an individual bedroom was exceptional, and the servants slept in the hall or in a shake-down in the work rooms or between the storage. As time went on, better sleeping accommodation was provided, and in the 15th century, as well as more room for the owner's family, there were many chambers to accommodate the numerous members of a great household. These lodgings seem to have been shared, as were the beds, and the 16th-century 'Great Bed of Ware', 10 feet 9 inches square, used in an inn, cannot have been the exaggeration it appears today.

There is also some evidence of dormitories on the lines of a monastic *dorter*. A long attic room is called the dormitory at Layer Marney in Essex, and the 'barracks' in the east range of the roof at Broughton Castle may have had a similar purpose. A sleeping apartment may be visualized comparable to those in boarding-schools today, and in the 15th century there is evidence that monastic dormitories at least were subdivided into cubicles by curtain and wooden partitions.* But in secular dormitories, where study would not be involved, this would be less likely.

Personal servants often seem to have slept in their master's room, judging from contemporary literature, partly as a protection, using a low truckle bed which could be kept under the large one during the day. Curtained beds gave a certain privacy to their master, as well as a shield from draught when corridors were few, except in the form of an outer gallery; of which evidence has been found at Tretower Court and Abingdon Abbey, this arrangement being perpetuated in surviving examples of inn-yards such as the celebrated New Inn (*c.* 1450) at Gloucester.

'Great chamber' is a better term than the convenient 'solar', which correctly means any room above ground level. This word seems to have been derived from the French *sol* (floor) and *solive* (beam), and was used for an upper floor. In old French texts, the *soler* is the

---

* *Antient Rites of Durham*, quoted in Parker (1859), 98.

upstairs room, the topmost level.* Solars and cellars often appear together in the description of town houses, the cellar at ground or semi-ground level with the solar above it. A modern example is *entresol*,† meaning a stage between two principal floors. There is documentary evidence for the use of 'solar' in the 13th century, but chiefly in its general form, although 'great chamber' figures prominently in Henry III's instructions,‡ also 'chamber' (*camera*),§ and occasionally 'demesne chamber'. In its sense of an upper room 'solar' is found used for the chamber over a gateway, and sometimes 'soleret'. But it is a convenient term for the 'master bedroom', and is now used so generally that it must be accepted. It should, however, not be used for a ground-floor apartment.

In the 12th century, when the hall was at a defensible upper level, the lord's bedchamber adjoined it on the same floor. At Boothby Pagnell (*c.* 1200) this is in the same building block, off the upper end of the hall away from the entrance, and separated by a stone wall with doorway. Indeed this plan was still used in the early hall and solar at St David's, probably the work of Bishop Thomas Bek (1280–93). However, at Christchurch Castle (*c.* 1160), the second chamber was near the entrance, and this allowed an elaborate window to be placed at the high table end of the hall, which thus stood clear. Both rooms were built over a basement, separately vaulted at Boothby Pagnell, but at Christchurch once divided by a timber partition, as was the case on the floor above. At Grosmont Castle the hall of *c.* 1210 is remarkably like the Christchurch arrangement, except that there is an end fireplace to the solar, which was once separated by a wooden partition not apparently resting on the stone division of the basements; there are two windows, not one, in the end wall of the hall.

At Cambridge, Merton Hall (the School of Pythagoras), *c.* 1200, shows a development from the Boothby Pagnell plan. A long domestic block was originally subdivided, here by a timber partition, between hall and solar. Contemporary with this range and opening out of the upper 'solar' part, making an L-plan, is a short northern wing, later extended, called the solar wing in a deed of 1270. We have thus an early building with two solars.

The domestic range at Manorbier Castle is an untouched example of early mediaeval accommodation, and shows the improvement of comfort and increase of privacy from the late 12th to the 13th centuries. Although in Wales (Pembrokeshire)—'the little England beyond Wales'—it had a Norman owner, and may be used to illustrate a development which has been altered by modernization in many English castles. Against the south-west curtain a first-floor hall was constructed, with external staircase and adjoining butteries, over which the solar, with end fireplace, occupied the second floor (Pl. XII c). We thus have an 'end hall' with solar-service block, all raised on semicircular barrel vaults suggesting a date in the latter part of the 12th century.‖ This building was probably seen by the chronicler Giraldus Cambrensis; perhaps his father built it. For Gerald of Cambria was born here *c.* 1146, traditionally in the round tower at the eastern angle of the enclosure, though this tower would seem not earlier than 1200. Gerald was the son of the Norman owner

---

* Latin *solarium*, often over the first-floor hall (*salle*). Information from Professor U. T. Holmes.
† Braun (1940), 18.
‡ e.g. Liberate Roll, 21 Henry III; Turner (1851), 184; Close Roll, 20, 21 Henry III; Turner (1851), 257.
§ Liberate Roll, 30, 34, 36 Henry III; Turner (1851), 212, 225, 240.
‖ Thompson (1912), 207–9.

William de Barri and his Norman-Welsh wife Angharad, and as a boy of seven he saw the garrison 'spring to arms' when the Welsh were attacking Tenby six miles away. He tells how his beloved home, Manorbier, was 'excellently well defended by turrets and bulwarks', and a description of its site and pleasant surroundings is given in *Itinerarium Cambriae*, the most important of his works. He died *c.* 1220 after a stormy career as a churchman, rejected twice in his attempt at the see of St David's.

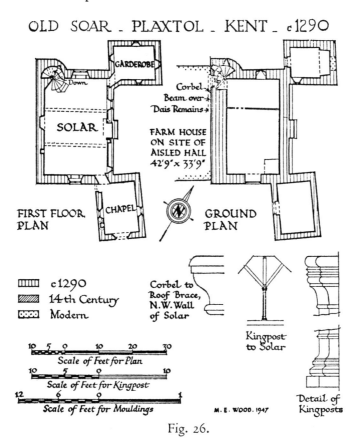

Fig. 26.

About 1260 a second solar was added to the opposite end wall of the hall, in a cross-wing, and off one outer angle of it is the vestibule to a chapel, and off the other, towards the curtain, the passage to a garderobe built over the moat. These are in a kindred position to those off the solar at Old Soar (*c.* 1290) (Fig. 26), and the chapel is also reached from the court by an external staircase.

Ludlow Castle shows a similar development with an earlier and later solar, here of the late 13th and early 14th centuries. The hall was probably built by Peter de Genevill, who held the castle from 1283 to 1292.* It is constructed against the earlier northern curtain,

* Mr A. J. Taylor, F.S.A. (in correspondence with the author), considers it to belong, like Acton Burnell, to the period of quiet immediately following the defeat of the Welsh in 1283. The castle is fully described by W. H. Hope (1908). His plan with Sir Harold Brakspear, F.S.A., makes hall and both solars 14th century, but the text refers to the late 13th century for hall and western block, *c.* 1320 for the eastern. See also plan of the hall level in Toy (1953 b), 76.

and is raised on a cellar, not vaulted, but with a longitudinal beam to carry the hall floor. This beam was supported on two pillars, of which the foundations remain: the western two feet square, the eastern much larger, six feet square, to take the weight of the central hearth of the hall above. Near the main entrance with its external staircase there projects a solar block of similar date in three storeys, the highest level with the upper part of the hall, the parapet of which it shares; the window tracery is also identical.

Peter de Genevill died in 1292, leaving three daughters, two of whom became nuns; the third, Joan, married (before 1308) Roger Mortimer, Lord of Wigmore, who in 1314 became joint Lord of Ludlow with his wife's cousin, Theobald de Verdon. The eastern solar may be assigned to about this period, improvement in accommodation which so often followed the marriage of an heiress. This new chamber block was added at the upper end of the hall, projecting southwards to match the earlier, and also of three storeys, but slightly taller. The window tracery shows the lapse of some thirty years between the two buildings. Now there was ample accommodation for the master of the castle and his family, and the first- and second-floor rooms were each provided with the latest model in hooded fireplaces, complete with light brackets. The lower room has a large 16th-century window inserted in the south wall, replacing an original two-light of which traces remain below, and which probably resembled one near the junction with the hall, of two trefoiled ogee lights in a square head. The room above had a flat open-timbered roof, the wall-post slots and carved corbels for which remain. Here the windows are higher, arched, with signs of excellent tracery, and probably this was the more important chamber, in the same high position as regards the hall as the solar to a ground-floor one. A king's and a queen's head flank the great fireplace. Could they have been carved to represent Edward II and Isabel of France? This would seem ironical in a chamber whose owner was the murderer of one, the paramour of the other. Perhaps Mortimer was there in 1328, when the queen created him Earl of March, in his short ascendancy and period of splendour; in 1330 he was trapped at Nottingham Castle, and executed by command of her son Edward III. Was it here in 1459 that the Duke of York with the king-maker Warwick and the Earl of Salisbury his father, consulted desperately in the face of treachery, before their flight from Ludlow and the sack of the castle that followed?

There is a further development at Ludlow in the early 14th century, a second block adjoining the great chamber on the side furthest from the hall. Its east and south walls were rebuilt in the 16th century, but the earlier existence of rooms here on three floors is proved by the contemporary square tower with garderobes, which is planned in doubled form to serve both these and the great chamber block adjoining, twin passages being contrived in the thick (fireplace) wall, which they share.

In castles such as these the domestic block, sited against the curtain, may have been more compact than in less fortified houses. In the 12th and 13th centuries even palaces seem to have been formed by a series of buildings loosely tacked together by pentices, and it is likely that the ground-floor hall was at first a separate entity,* adjuncts being in the form of lean-to structures. Indeed as late as the 14th and 15th centuries the great hall can be

* Smith (1955), 76-7.

picked out by the height and scale of its roof rising above the surrounding apartments, now usually added as cross-wings to obtain more accommodation.

The service apartments at the entrance end were the first to be incorporated, often with a solar above them. At Clarendon it is interesting that the triple service doorways (excavated) are late 12th-century with diagonal tooling, whereas the butteries to which they lead are structurally later than the hall, apparently Henry III's work replacing earlier ones possibly of wood. A doorway at the dais end leads to the royal apartments by means of a pentice.

The butteries form a long narrow compartment of one bay, in line with the hall, the whole making an oblong plan. The manor ruins at Warnford, c. 1210, show a flint aisled hall with such a two-storeyed end block, retaining doorway evidence of apartments at two levels, as does the end wall at Oakham; in both the solar was reached by steps rising from

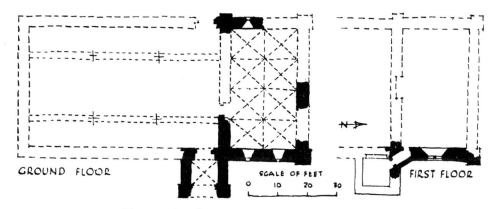

Fig. 27. Crowhurst Manor House, ruins, plans.

inside the hall near the angle opposite the entrance. The chamber block is also included in the (aisled) hall compartment in the palaces at Lincoln (c. 1225) and Wells (c. 1280). These two episcopal halls have much in common; there are octagonal turrets at the angles of the block, and the solar is reached by a staircase approached from within or near the porch. At Crowhurst the solar-service block was wide, the undercroft vaulted in two aisles (Fig. 27).

How was this end bay roofed? A lean-to would only allow for a low upper storey if at all. One of moderate height could be enclosed by the hall roof, if the latter was hipped like that once serving the early 14th-century house at Nurstead. In Mr J. T. Smith's discovery Stanton Farm, Black Notley, the hall gable is also set further on and represented only by a small triangular gablet, serving for a chimney-vent, over the slope of the hipped roof. This was once, no doubt, a very general early arrangement. At Warnford the service floor level is set below that of the hall, probably to make the solar as lofty as possible.

A transverse roof would allow greater height and width to the chamber, and enable the hall to have a gable window clear. At Lincoln Palace, as Mr Faulkner * shows, the hall arcade was continued as a stone arched truss supporting a transverse roof over the solar-service block, and he has found evidence of the same in the wall of the vanished block at Oakham. Perhaps this was the case at Wells and Ashby de la Zouch.

* (1958), 166.

This end now became a cross-wing, roofed separately from the hall, and it could be extended to give additional room. At Gillingham, in July 1250, Henry III ordered 'at the head of our hall there, towards the east a chamber forty feet long and twenty-two feet wide, transversely towards the north with a chimney (fireplace) and privy chamber'.* This suggests an L-plan with the hall, the extension at the north end of the wing. Indeed here 'the head of our hall' indicates that this wing was at the high table, not entrance, end, as it was also to the first-floor hall at Aydon Castle (c. 1280), where the solar (47 feet 6 inches × 18 feet) projects both to north and south, and seems to have contained two rooms originally, the fireplace jamb showing evidence of a timber partition. Three are suggested by the exceptional length (54 × 17 feet) of the early 13th-century solar wing, making a T-plan at the service end of the hall at Ashby de la Zouch. For at first the wing remained narrow, but projected to a greater length.

At Charing Palace there is now a lean-to (51 × 13 feet) of apparently similar date to the hall, c. 1300, but with thinner walls, remaining in part next to three altered service door-ways in the end (south) wall, and projecting on the porch side. Even if rebuilt, it represents an original feature, for no buttresses project southwards, although the porch does, having here a wall staircase leading to an upper chamber in this annexe, as well as to a gallery over the screens, judging from the diagonal projection, corbelled out at the higher level of the south-west angle of the hall on either side. The archbishop's chair back remains at the other end of the hall, where no sign of a solar can be seen. However, west and north of the hall, across the court, are late 13th-century buildings and a chapel, added to considerably by Archbishop Morton (1486–1500), who 'made great building at Charing'. Mayfield Palace, possibly by the same architect, has a long narrow two-storeyed range (c. 67 × 16 feet), projecting especially on the south where it is in line with the porch, and having a tower adjoining. Here the archbishop's private rooms were at the other end of the hall.

But in the 13th and early 14th centuries the master's private room, or *camera*, was often placed over the service apartments, near the entrance of the hall, when the latter was at ground level, making what has been called an 'end hall house'.† The hall thus stood free at the end where the high table was set, with the opportunity of having a great window behind the latter. Bisham Abbey hall (c. 1280) was one of these originally, and triple lancets, blocked by 14th-century work, can still be seen, the 13th-century solar being in a cross-wing near the western end, projecting six feet behind the contemporary porch. The early 14th-century hall at Martock (Fig. 28) has a high table window recently unblocked, with the solar of earlier date near the entry; possibly, as at West Tarring and Little Chester-ford, a first-floor hall re-used. Not many of these end windows remain, for soon cross-wings were added here, although there are a number of examples of this great window lifted up into the hall gable which stood clear, as at Clevedon and Penshurst; and in the later 15th century the high table was lit by a bay window in the lateral wall.

At Chorley Hall in Cheshire (Fig. 29), c. 1330 or later, the solar-service compartment is still in the same building block as the hall, making an oblong plan, but it has a separate transverse roof, of which the original timbers remain.‡ The manor house at Yardley

---

* Liberate Roll, 34 Henry III; Turner (1851), 225.   † Faulkner (1958).
‡ Cordingley & Wood-Jones (1959).

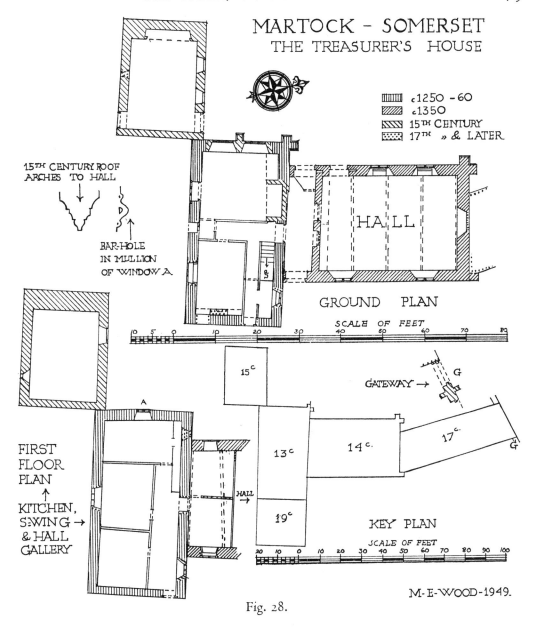

MARTOCK – SOMERSET
THE TREASURER'S HOUSE

|IIII| c1250 – 60
|ZZZ| c1350
|SSSS| 15TH CENTURY
|:::::| 17TH » & LATER

15TH CENTURY ROOF
ARCHES TO HALL

BAR-HOLE
IN MULLION
OF WINDOW A

HALL

GROUND PLAN

SCALE OF FEET

FIRST
FLOOR
PLAN

KITCHEN,
S:WING →
& HALL
GALLERY

15ᶜ

A

13ᶜ

HALL →

19ᶜ

GATEWAY →

14ᶜ

17ᶜ

G

G

KEY PLAN

SCALE OF FEET

M·E·WOOD·1949·

Fig. 28.

Hastings (Fig. 30) was of similar type, the solar-service block alone surviving (Pl. XII A). The next step would be the projection of this wing beyond the hall, which indeed already seems to have occurred in the 13th-century chantry at Chichester, where an additional room to the solar makes an L-plan with the main block, the porch being sited in the re-entrant angle. In the early 14th-century hall excavated at Cefn-y-fan in Caernarvonshire the solar wing projected slightly at both its ends.

It was obviously more convenient for the owner to have his great chamber near the high

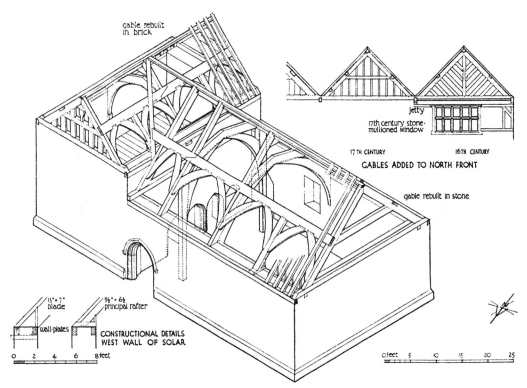

gable rebuilt
in brick

jetty

17th century stone-
mullioned window

17TH CENTURY   16TH CENTURY

GABLES ADDED TO NORTH FRONT

gable rebuilt in stone

13"×7"
blade

9¼"× 6¼
principal rafter

wall-plates

CONSTRUCTIONAL DETAILS
WEST WALL OF SOLAR

0   2   4   6   8 feet

0 feet   5   10   15   20   25

Fig. 29. Chorley Hall, structural evolution.

table, and the upper end solar is found in a number of 13th-century examples. Even some 'end halls' have been found with the chamber block here, and the entrance end free. There is the house of *c.* 1200 next to the infirmary chapel at Peterborough, the abbot's lodgings of *c.* 1220 at Haughmond and the guest house *c.* 1300 at Monk Bretton Priory, Yorkshire.*
In all these (monastic) examples the chamber block does not project, although at Monk Bretton it opens into an annexe (? oriel) overlapping part of the hall as well. Kirkstall Abbey great guest house, dating from the early 13th century, has a block at either end of the hall, with only garderobe projections.

Henry III's transverse chamber block at Gillingham, *c.* 1250, is substantiated by several known examples. At Godmersham Court (*c.* 1250) the solar had gone, but its fireplace corbels remained outside the end wall of the hall, as also the undercroft doorway. The solar does not project at Stokesay (*c.* 1285+),† but at Gillingham it did so, apparently, at one end. At Barnston Manor (*c.* 1260) and the Old Deanery, Salisbury (*c.* 1258–74), it made a T-plan with the hall. Some of these may have been 'end halls', but there is evidence of a service block at Salisbury, Bishop's Cleeve Rectory, Charney Basset (*c.* 1280) and at Stokesay where the earlier north tower was used for this purpose.

In the 14th century it became usual to place a two-storeyed block at each end of the hall,

* Faulkner (1958), 167–9; 169, 171; 170–1 respectively, with plan of each.
† Some experts make the solar later (*c.* 1290–1300 with the south tower) (Smith, 1956). But Professor Cordingley's detailed survey (1963) shows that hall, solar, passage block and south tower are one work (1285–1305).

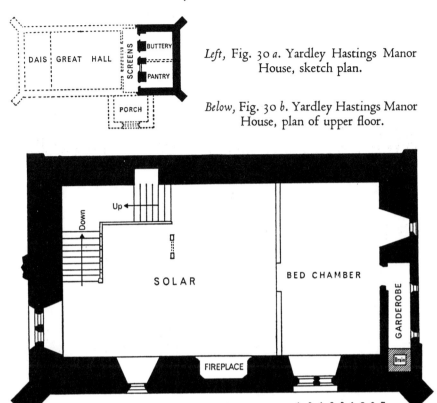

Left, Fig. 30 *a*. Yardley Hastings Manor House, sketch plan.

Below, Fig. 30 *b*. Yardley Hastings Manor House, plan of upper floor.

judging from the buildings that remain. In the 'Abbey' at Sutton Courtenay (*c.* 1330) the cross-wings do not project, except in the case of the solar towards the back, where it was extended probably in the 15th century.* But projecting wings making an H-plan became normal, as in the mid and later 14th-century houses of remote Westmorland surveyed by the Royal Commission, a county remarkable for survivals of this date. At the Castle Dairy, Kendal, the wings project beyond the hall face on one side, but on both at Beetham, Middleton and Preston Patrick halls. A common feature is the provision of a vaulted ground floor to the wing. There are two barrel-vaulted rooms below the solar at Selside Hall, and two vaulted chambers separated by a passage, also barrel-vaulted, in the service block at Preston Patrick, and in Burneside Hall in Strickland Roger.

Sometimes the solar fireplace was sited in the wall common with the hall, and its chimney raised against the end of the latter. The solar chimney at Godmersham was in this position, also one at Aydon Castle, with the fireplace to the solar basement in the opposite wall. Now Preston Patrick has a 14th-century fireplace here. The crocketed chimney at Northborough (*c.* 1340) forms an ornament to the hall gable next to the service over which was an important room, and one may have existed on the rebuilt upper end gable, for a staircase annexe and first-floor doorway survive as evidence of a vanished wing.

* The date of the musician corbels flanking the solar fireplace (Pl. XVII E).

The need for more private accommodation showed itself in the lengthening of the wing at either end. At first in line with the hall, the wing projected first on the entrance, then on the further side, until at least two chambers could be provided at first-floor level. At Mancetter Hall the solar-service wing (c. 41 × 14 feet), like Aydon 3 : 1, must have enclosed two rooms, as did that (38 × 12 feet) at Selside Hall, probably corresponding to the stone cross wall between the vaults below.

In Goodrich Castle (c. 1300) the lord's apartments are sited in a long block making an L-plan with the hall, but separated from it at the dais end by a vestibule with private chapel over. From the vestibule, steps lead down to a large room below what might be called the solar, except that this is at ground level, like the hall. It is certainly the most important chamber, reached from the vestibule, and remarkable for being divided, near the upper end, by a screen of two pointed arches, moulded, springing from a central column carried down to the storey below (Pl. XII b).

Sometimes the extension was upward, providing a third floor, as in both wings at Ludlow; or perhaps in part only, with an attic and gable window over one of the two rooms, which was perhaps the case at Aydon. There were three storeys, once embattled, to both cross-wings at Strickland Roger, the service one forming a tower. Indeed, especially on the border, a semi-fortified wing was popular, usually at the other end of the hall, combining comfort with security. Such 'solar towers' include the south one at Stokesay, c. 1290, well supplied with fireplaces, and the early 14th-century Longthorpe Tower near Peterborough.

The extra room could be obtained by joining an annexe, separately roofed, on to the solar. Sometimes the second chamber, extending the cross-wing, but narrower, was added to the end of it like the chancel to the nave of a church. Indeed it was a favourite position for the domestic chapel, examples being found at Romsey and the Old Deanery (originally), Charney Basset and probably Hambledon Manor (Hampshire) in the 13th century, and Beetham Hall in the 14th century. Sometimes one side wall is in line with the solar, as at Strickland Roger, where the wider solar has a room at either end.

Another method was to place these rooms at the outer angles of the solar, attached like playing-cards to the corners, and reached by diagonal passages. At Old Soar the solar has the chapel at the eastern angle, and a room with garderobe off the north. This is akin to the arrangement in the Prebendal at Thame, where the chapel similarly projects off what was a first-floor hall, later turned solar. Such a plan allowed free walling for windows, but seems to have gone out of use soon after the 13th century, the domestic layout becoming integrated, though the early 14th-century solar block at Southwick (Northamptonshire) seems to have been added to an earlier one in this manner.

More lasting was the scheme whereby the added block was placed at right angles off the outer side wall of the solar, making an L-plan as at Barnston Manor, similar to that formed by chapel and hall at Little Wenham, akin to the arrangement at Markenfield. At Luddes-down Court in Kent the solar itself makes an L-plan with another first-floor hall, and has a further room, narrower and separately roofed, with dovecote, off its extremity. At Aydon Castle the wing joins near the centre of the side wall, making a T-plan with the solar, and has a garderobe at its further end.

The development of the L-plan occurs when a second wing is added, parallel to the solar, off the main block, rather in 'domino' fashion. At Donington-le-Heath (*c.* 1280) (Fig. 31) the hall, on the first floor, has the end east and west walls extended northwards, to contain wings forming a half H-plan. Below there are stone divisions, but above the wings are separated from the hall by timber-framed partitions, in each of which a pointed arch remains. The great chamber was apparently in the north-east wing, and its three windows survive. The other wing, nearer the entrance, has off its north-east angle a further

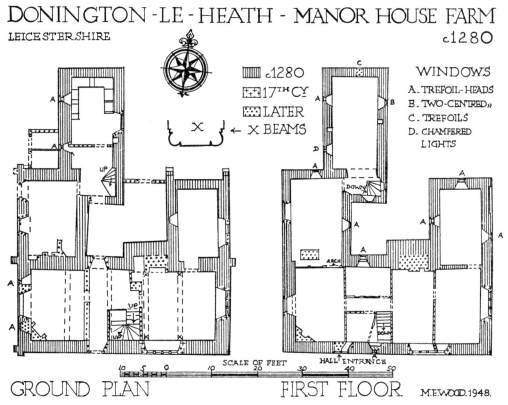

DONINGTON -LE -HEATH - MANOR HOUSE FARM
LEICESTERSHIRE
c1280

WINDOWS

A. TREFOIL-HEADS
B. TWO-CENTRED „
C. TREFOILS
D. CHAMFERED LIGHTS

▥ c1280
⊞ 17TH CY
▦ LATER
← X BEAMS

SCALE OF FEET

GROUND PLAN   FIRST FLOOR   M.E.WOOD.1948.

Fig. 31.

block continuing northwards, and partly projecting into a small court, now completed by a brick wall joining the north and solar wings.

A similar half H-plan on a smaller scale is found in the Abbot's House at Netley, an entirely separate domestic building in the Abbey grounds, providing, although in ruins, an excellent example of the 13th-century house plan. The hall is raised on a ribbed vault of three bays, and off its east wall, at either end, there project, again rather in the manner of dominoes, to the north a solar, over a barrel vault, with a garderobe annexe near its north-east angle; and further south a chapel on a ribbed vault of two bays. Cottisford Manor (Oxfordshire) has a plan resembling these.

At Aston Eyre in Shropshire there are remains of a manor house probably of the 14th century. The upper cross-wing projects beyond the hall on both sides and shared an oriel chamber with it in one angle. From the fireplace position there seems to have been a second room on the upper floor, with access to a garderobe at the opposite end of the block. The lower wing near the entrance did not project on the oriel side of the hall, but extended considerably on the other, having a second room on each floor, with stone division below and apparently a timber one above (*see* Fig. 48, page 133).

The solar also could have parallel wings forming with it a half H-plan. This is the case at Creslow Manor House in Buckinghamshire (*c.* 1330), where the solar itself makes a T-plan with the hall. The western wing of the solar is in the form of a three-storey tower with original moulded parapet and ball-flower ornament; there is a stair turret at its western junction with the solar block.

At Southwick Hall a solar of *c.* 1325, itself an addition, had an extra room built on to it in the later 14th century. Presumably Sir John Knyvet, Lord Chancellor (d. 1381), increased the accommodation built by his father Richard Knyvet, owner *c.* 1320–51.*

Increase in accommodation for the family might be obtained by the addition of a new chamber block to halls, such as Ashby de la Zouch, which had originally a solar-service arrangement. Here the new wing was built in the mid 14th century, the width of the hall, but extended to project beyond the latter in the early 15th century.

Minster Lovell was provided from the start (*c.* 1431–42) with sumptuous private rooms. The solar, at right angles to the hall, had a north-west building of equal length projecting from its further side, making an L-plan with it, while at right angles again from this building ran a long western range of lesser lodgings, flanking the courtyard.

The long solar wing at Tickenham Court (Pl. 6) appears of similar date, judging from the window tracery, which is akin to the enlarged windows in the most important room at Woodsford Castle. Lord Cromwell had a magnificent window to his great chamber at South Wingfield, probably the only source of light since the room was flanked by the hall on one side, and by a parallel wing of chambers over the butteries on the other, while another room occupied the end portion of the solar block. The window below, though smaller, is also traceried, and may have lighted a parlour, with a similar apartment with moulded fireplace at the back, divided from it by the kitchen passage. Owing to the nature of the site, the private block had here to be built at the lower end of the hall. But this was apparently no usual solar over service wing, although it contained the kitchen passage, for the butteries were further west next to the kitchen. There is a cellar beneath, as there is under the hall itself.

Rymans at Apuldram in Sussex shows what solar accommodation might be expected in the 15th-century house of a man of moderate means. William Ryman had his great chamber in a tower with perhaps parlour below, and a further room above, this tower making an L-plan with a two-storey block with a further private room over his office.

This may be compared with a solar tower † at Thame Park, part of an abbot's lodging of three dates in the early 16th century. East of a series of halls at two levels is this square tower with 'Abbot's Parlour' (? solar) on the first floor, added by Robert King, abbot from 1529 to 1539, and retaining linenfold panelling with early Renaissance carved panels and frieze above, all originally coloured, and what may be the earliest surviving example

* *Country Life* (26).   † *See* Solar Towers in Chapter 12.

of the internal porch. Like the room above (? the abbot's bedroom) the parlour has an oriel window, and in the east a polygonal staircase turret gives access between the floors. Robert King was the last abbot, surrendering the abbey, in return for the bishopric of Oxford, to his brother-in-law who became Lord Williams of Thame, and a good friend to Princess (later Queen) Elizabeth.

How attractive these rooms could be may be realized from other late mediaeval solars which remain in use, such as Cothay (Somerset) (Pl. XIII c) and the Suffolk examples at Alston Court in Nayland (*c.* 1472) (Pl. XIII A) and Gifford's Hall, Wickhambrook (*c.* 1500) with their splendid moulded beams and elaborate fireplaces; or with oriels like those of Great Chalfield (*c.* 1480) and the Deanery at Wells (*c.* 1472–98).

EXAMPLES OF THE SOLAR

		Internal Dimensions
c. 1160	Christchurch Castle, Hants, hall	*c.* 24′ × 18′
c. 1200	Boothby Pagnell Manor House, Lincs.	20′ × 14′
c. 1200	Merton Hall, Cambridge	? × 23′ 3″; 17′ × 10′
c. 1200	Little Chesterford Manor Farm, Ess., east wing	37′ 6″ × 18′ 3″
c. 1200	House next infirmary, Peterborough Abbey, Northants.	18′ × *c.* 15′
early C 13th	The Old Palace, West Tarring, Suss.	39′ × 17′ 10″
early C 13th	The Chantry, Chichester	*c.* 30′ × 15′ 6″
early C 13th	Hambledon Manor Farm, Hants	*c.* 36′ × 18′
early C 13th	Kirkstall Abbey, Yorks., great guest house	*c.* 44′ × *c.* 23′
early C 13th	Ashby de la Zouch Castle, Leics., west solar	*c.* 54′ × 17′
c. 1210	Grosmont Castle, Mon.	30′ × *c.* 24′
c. 1210	Warnford Manor House, Hants, ruins	48′ × 18′ 6″
c. 1220	Haughmond Abbey, Salop, foundations	*c.* 36′ × *c.* 19′
c. 1225	Lincoln Palace	*c.* 58′ × 22′
c. 1240	Prebendal House, Thame, Oxon.	*c.* 30′ × 13′ 6″
c. 1250	Gillingham, Dor., documentary evidence	40′ × 22′
c. 1250	Godmersham Court Lodge, Kent, evidence	
c. 1250	Crowhurst Manor, Suss., ruins	40′ 6″ × *c.* 22′
c. 1250–60	Abbot's House, Netley, Hants	*c.* 21′ 3″ × 9′ 6″
c. 1260	Treasurer's House, Martock, Som.	*c.* 38′ × 18′
c. 1260	Barnston Manor, Dor.	30′ 6″ × 15′
late C 12th & *c.* 1260	Manorbier Castle, Pembs.	
c. 1258–74	The Old Deanery, Salisbury	56′ × 22′
c. 1280	Bisham Abbey, Berks.	*c.* 43′ 6″ × *c.* 19′ 6″ (ground meas.)
c. 1280	Charney Basset Manor House, Berks.	*c.* 30′ × 16′
c. 1280	Donington-le-Heath, Leics.	{ 16′ 3″ × 9′ 6″ { 18′ 6″ × 11′
c. 1280	Aydon Castle, Northum.	47′ 6″ × 18′
c. 1280	Wells Palace, Som.	59′ 6″ × 23′
1280–92	Bishop's Palace (Thomas Bek), St David's, Pembs.	28′ × 24′

		Internal Dimensions
c. 1285+	Stokesay Castle, Salop	*c.* 30′ 6″ × 19′ 6″
c. 1283–92 & *c.* 1320	Ludlow Castle, Salop	39′ (& 31′ 6″) × 26′ (irregular plan) & 46′ × 25′ 6″
c. 1290	Old Soar, Plaxtol, Kent	28′ × 18′
c. 1300	Monk Bretton Priory, Yorks., guest house	*c.* 35′ × *c.* 17′ 6″
c. 1300	Longthorpe Tower, near Peterborough, Northants.	16′ sq.
c. 1300	Goodrich Castle, Heref.	*c.* 57′ × 22′
c. 1300	Charing Palace, Kent	51′ × 13′
c. 1320–30	Mayfield Palace, Suss.	*c.* 67′ × 16′
C 14th	Aston Eyre Manor House, Salop	*c.* 38′ × 15′ 6″
c. 1325 & late C 14th	Southwick Hall, Northants.	
c. 1330	The Abbey, Sutton Courtenay, Berks.	*c.* 35′ × 17′
c. 1330	Mancetter Hall, War.	*c.* 41′ × 14′
c. 1330	Creslow Manor House, Bucks.	48′ × 18′
c. 1330+	Chorley Hall, Ches.	24′ 9″ × 16′
c. 1340	Northborough Manor House, Northants., service block	*c.* 36′ × 16′
c. 1340	Stanton's Farm, Black Notley, Ess.	*c.* 25′ 6″ × 11′
mid C 14th	Yardley Hastings Manor, Northants., ruins	30′ × *c.* 16′
mid C 14th	Beetham Hall, West.	*c.* 37′ × 18′
late C 14th	Middleton Hall, West.	*c.* 35′ × 17′
late C 14th	Preston Patrick Hall, West.	*c.* 37′ × 16′
C 14th	Burneside Hall, Strickland Roger, West.	69′ (3 divisions) × 12′ to 17′ *c.* 34′ × 19′ (service north wing, ground meas.)
late C 14th	Selside Hall, West.	*c.* 38′ × 12′ (ground meas.)
C 14th	Castle Dairy, Kendal, West.	*c.* 28′ × 14′
mid C 14th & early C 15th	Ashby de la Zouch Castle, Leics., east solar	*c.* 60′ × 26′
c. 1431–42	Minster Lovell Hall, Oxon.	47′ × *c.* 20′; 51′ × 22′ (NW. building)
early C 15th	Tickenham Court, Som.	*c.* 53′ × 16′
c. 1440–59	South Wingfield Manor, Derbys.	*c.* 64′ × 25′
C 15th	Rymans, Apuldram, Suss.	25′ × 15′
c. 1472	Alston Court, Nayland, Suff.	*c.* 22′ 6″ × 16′ 6″
c. 1472–98	The Deanery, Wells, Som.	*c.* 42′ × 18′ & *c.* 21′ × 16′
c. 1480	Great Chalfield Manor, Wilts.	30′ 6″ × 18′ 10″
c. 1480	Cothay Manor, Som.	*c.* 35′ × 16′
c. 1500	Gifford's Hall, Wickhambrook, Suff.	
c. 1529–39	Abbot's 'Parlour', Thame Park, Oxon.	17′ × 16′

6

Vaulted Cellars; the Cellar under the Solar; the Parlour

THE ground floor of an early mediaeval house was often vaulted in stone, wholly or in part, to provide fireproof storage accommodation. By this means the living-rooms, raised to first-floor level, became more defensible, and this is frequently the arrangement in the first-floor halls and adjoining solar of the Norman period, hence the term 'hall and cellar house'.

Stone basements or 'cellars' in the mediaeval ground- or semi-ground-floor sense remain in many of our towns and cities, such as Canterbury, Chester, Guildford and Southampton. They formed the lower floor of merchants' houses, of which the upper storey, sometimes timber-framed, has been rebuilt. They may have combined the function of workroom and shop, or a safe storage place to a booth or stall in the street in front, the family and apprentices living in the rooms above. These basements are sunk some six to ten feet below street level, though that level tends to rise as the roads are made up through the centuries. They were accessible from the street by steps down from a doorway or hinged flap. The small windows would also be at ground level, placed high in the cellar wall, and splayed within sideways and doorwards. Often a second staircase remains, leading to the destroyed or transformed upper floor.

There were three main types of vault or stone ceiling: the barrel vault like a tunnel, semicircular in the 12th century, developing into the pointed form in the 13th century; the groined vault formed by the intersection of two barrel vaults; and the ribbed vault, where the weak groin intersections were strengthened by stone arches, these taking the place of temporary wooden centering for the vaulting cells. But now came a problem the solution of which had much to do with the introduction of Gothic architecture. To get a uniform height with the round-headed transverse and longitudinal arches, the diagonal ribs on the groins, being wider, could not be true semicircles, and had to be adjusted into an elliptical form. This proved unsatisfactory, for this arch was too flat and its voussoirs tended to sink or fall out, and stilting the other arches to match a semicircular diagonal gave a very ugly appearance to the vault. In the second half of the 12th century, however, the Gothic arch was introduced, perhaps to solve this problem, for the pointed arch can be raised to any height. The diagonals could thus be true semicircles, though later they became pointed like all the others.

In a ribbed vault the four compartments formed a quadripartite bay, typical of many early houses. From the later 13th century, however, a more complex plan was introduced, through the addition to the basic transverse, diagonal and wall ribs of intermediate ones called 'tiercerons'. These met at a ridge rib, and the stone roof was now a framework of arched ribs carrying the thin webbing of the vaulting compartments, and with the intersecting stones usually elaborated into carved bosses. To the quadripartite and tierceron vaults there was added, in the 14th century, the lierne vault, contrived by the addition of short tie or 'lierne' ribs to the main arches, forming an elaborate stellar pattern, and in the later 15th century the multiplication of ribs, rising from the springing, developed into the fan vault of which many examples remain, chiefly in ecclesiastical architecture. Where simpler vaulting was used the ribs now formed four-centred arches and a ridge.

In 12th-century houses the round barrel vaults are plain, as those below the hall and service (c. 1160) at Manorbier,[5] or the solar at Boothby Pagnell [16] (c. 1200), running at right angles to the adjoining ribbed vault below the hall. There are a number at Southampton,[11] a chamfered string-course being the feature of this date, absent in semicircular barrel vaults of the 13th century here. At 58 French Street (c. 1200) the vault with its window has been incorporated into a modern block of flats. Or the barrel vault maybe divided into bays by transverse arches resting on corbels, of which six out of an original sixteen, of waterleaf type, remain in the large vault on the Western Shore at Southampton.[12] At 24 St Thomas Street, Winchester,[3] there is a groined vault of two bays divided by a stone arch supported on responds. Buckler's drawings show the vanished later 12th-century 'Hostelry of the Priors of Lewes' at Southwark,[13] where one groined vault was divided into four bays by transverse arches resting on wall shafts with scalloped capitals.

That the groined vault persisted alongside the ribbed one is evidenced by the 'Music House' at Norwich (c. 1175).[7] It has an undercroft in two sections, divided by a stone wall. The eastern (solar) cellar is a groined vault of three bays separated by transverse bands, and having a newel staircase in the north-east angle, while the western cellar has the same wide arch between its two bays, but here there are diagonal ribs of a bold roll section flanked by hollow chamfers. Two loop windows remain to the south, and on the same wall is evidence of a forebuilding once containing an external staircase to the hall above.

At Boothby Pagnell (Pl. XVI A) [16] the hall basement has a ribbed vault of two quadripartite bays with chamfered transverse and diagonal ribs resting on cushion corbels; and there is another ribbed vault of three bays with moulded corbels at Bury Farm, Redmarley D'Abitôt in Worcestershire.[4]

In a wider undercroft a double aisle of quadripartite bays would be required, and a central row of columns. In Moyses Hall (*c.* 1180), Bury St Edmunds,[8] the hall basement is divided into two aisles, each of three groined vaulted bays, by two cylindrical piers from which spring wide arches, separating the bays (Fig. 32).

At Burton Agnes Manor House in Yorkshire [6] the late 12th-century subvault is concealed, except on the west, behind a skin of 18th-century brickwork (Fig. 33; Pl. XIV A). Stepping into this seemingly Georgian house the visitor is amazed at the sight of a splendid Norman undercroft. It consists of two aisles, each of four quadripartite bays divided by three cylindrical piers with square abaci and waterleaf capitals, the bases moulded with leaf spurs; the east and west responds are half columns of similar design; the transverse,

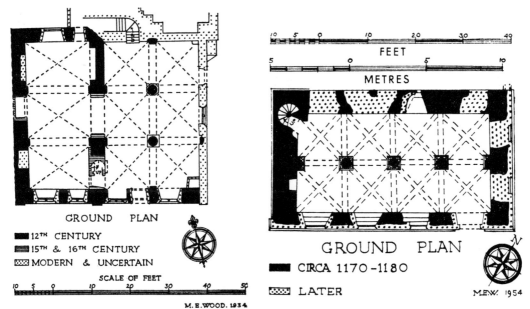

Fig. 32. Moyses Hall.　　　　Fig. 33. Burton Agnes Manor House.

longitudinal and diagonal ribs are of chalk. Another hall undercroft to a Yorkshire manor, of similar date (*c.* 1180–90) has been excavated at Wharram Percy. The walls are 4 feet thick (5 feet at Burton Agnes) and a row of three central pillar bases has been found, but no sign of vaulting otherwise.

Canterbury is rich in 12th-century undercrofts. That at 36 High Street [10] was probably the Mint, and there remains one aisle of a subvault of four quadripartite bays, with evidence of a parallel aisle, divided by square piers with scalloped capitals, of which two survive; the diagonals are chamfered but not the transverse arches. On the site of the Guildhall, [9] in the street of that name, there is a tall column with scalloped capital and square abacus, of *c.* 1180. It has above it the start of keel-moulded ribs rising steeply and suggesting a lofty undercroft of which it was the central feature like that in the keep at Newcastle (1172–7). Ribs also rising vertically over two much lower columns produce a vault 11 feet 6 inches high, and a double aisle, of three quadripartite bays, in a late 12th-century undercroft at Chichester, once serving a guildhall but later incorporated into the Vicars' Hall.[15]

At Lincoln there are extensive late 12th-century remains, much disguised, at Deloraine Court.[14] The chief interest lies in the west range, possibly a storage basement to the domestic block set at right angles to the hall. It is of exceptional length (89 feet 6 inches × 16 feet) and is divided by a thick wall into two compartments. The northern (37 feet long) was probably of four double bays, and retains two central columns, partly built up in later walls. The southern room (50 feet 6 inches) has a free-standing column near the north end, but others may be hidden by later subdivisions, and the spacing suggests a room of five bays, unless the northernmost portion only is original. Certainly the walls, except at the south end, are somewhat less thick than those of the northern apartment. The columns have scalloped capitals with a square abacus, chamfered base and plinth. No sign of the vaulting remains, but there is otherwise a resemblance to a monastic western range.

Indeed the 12th-century guest house, often included in the cellarer's (western) range, was really a domestic building incorporated in the monastic plan, and became the nucleus of the abbot's house. They were first-floor halls raised over vaulted cellarage, the ground floor being used for storage and also as sleeping accommodation for the servants of the richer sort of traveller, who was housed above. The undercroft being wide is usually divided into two aisles by a central line of pillars. At Castle Acre [2] there are six such double bays under the hall, but at Chester [1] the range is subdivided with four double bays below the hall and three below the great chamber. At the end of the block next to the church is the parlour, one double bay in width, with a chapel above, but sometimes the parlour had a barrel vault. There is a slightly later projecting porch to the hall at Castle Acre.

At Peterborough the Abbot's House [22] had all the rooms 'built above stairs, and underneath were very fair vaults, and goodly cellars for several uses'. The hall (96 × 36 feet) was over the west range as usual, with the great chamber (99 × 30 feet) at right angles and at the door of the abbot's chamber a 'great solar' with a cellar beneath it. This last, added by Abbot Alexander (1222–6) is the portion now remaining, the ground floor in five double bays of quadripartite vaulting, with central piers having moulded capitals, and corbels. It now serves as entrance hall to the bishop's palace.

The vaulted ground floor was extremely popular in the first half of the 13th century, and is a feature of the original dwellings in the Close at Salisbury. A vault very similar to that at Peterborough, but of three double bays, remains of Bishop Poore's Palace of 1221, now the Cathedral School,[21] the room above, where Henry III was entertained, being transformed in the 18th century. There is an undercroft of like date at the North Canonry, its upper floor refashioned in the 15th century, as was the case over the fine subvault at Nettlestead Place,[28] c. 1250–60. Here four double bays, quadripartite as usual, have a central row of three sturdy columns with moulded capitals and bases; from these spring the customary chamfered ribs, transverse, longitudinal and diagonal, supported on the walls by moulded corbels terminating in leaf ornament and twists (Pl. XIV B).

Thus the house raised on undercrofts, convenient in the monastic plan, is also found in those outside. Such a large house is Bishop Jocelyn's Palace at Wells,[23] c. 1230–50. Here the hall undercroft of five double bays resembles a cellarer's range, and divided from it by a stone wall is the solar undercroft of two more bays with one central column in line with the others. West of these and a third the width of the building is a vestibule

A. Alston Court, Nayland, interior of solar; c. 1472.

B. Muchelney, Abbot's parlour, c. 1508, with fireplace and benches.

C. Cothay Manor, interior of solar; c. 1480.

Plate XIII. The Solar.

Plate XIV. Vaulted Cellars.

A. Burton Agnes Old Manor House; *c.* 1170–80. B. Nettlestead Place; *c.* 1250–60.

or gallery of seven bays, which may have been subdivided. On the other side, at the north-east angle, is a projection, also vaulted, and containing the solar garderobe. The bishop's chapel is at the south-west angle of the block, transformed in the later 13th century, and reached by a staircase turret.

Comparable to Wells in size and date is the Abbot's House at Battle [24] built by Ralph of Coventry (1235–61)(Fig. 34). It is a superb example, the entire mid 13th-century house, hall, parlour, lobby, porch and great chamber surviving, raised above ribbed vaults. Whereas at Wells the hall and solar are in line, as also at Boothby Pagnell, at Battle they are at right angles, the site being more restricted. The hall subvault is four double bays long, with a double-bayed lobby in line with it on the south, off which projects the solar undercroft, also of four double bays, making an L-plan. The vaulted parlour is at the north end of the hall, as usual next to the monastic church, and it projects westwards by one bay, the end wall in line with a porch vestibule of three and a half bays flanking the hall undercroft on this side, as at Wells, and probably once communicating with that of the solar. Besides his chapel over the parlour, the abbot, as at Peterborough, had a smaller one off his great chamber, towards the west end of its south wall, and its undercroft was later made into a porch for the 15th-century hall adjoining.

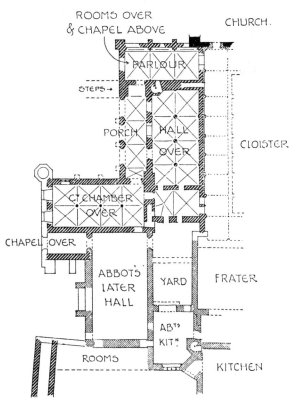

Fig. 34. Battle Abbey, Abbot's House.

At Cakeham near West Wittering [18] in Sussex there are remains of a palace of the bishops of Chichester with 16th-century look-out tower. There was an early 13th-century hall or, more probably, solar, on a subvault of which two quadripartite bays at the west end remain, and one of a line of central columns, with square abacus, now partly embedded in a wall. There are chamfered cross and diagonal ribs, tapering corbels, and others in a garden wall which continues the line east of the building, which was once four times its present size.

The separate Abbot's House at Netley [27] doubtless gives the plan of many smaller 13th-century houses now gone. The hall and chapel undercrofts, ribbed vaults of three and two bays respectively, are set at right angles, while parallel to the latter, off the same side wall of the hall at the other end, is a barrel vault below the solar, with a garderobe near the further angle. The hall cellar may be compared with that at Temple Manor, Strood (c. 1250).[25] Little Wenham Hall [30] (c. 1270–80) resembles Netley, but here there remains only one projection, the chapel, of a single vaulted bay, with a room (possibly the great chamber) above; there are signs that a garderobe may have protruded near the entrance at the further end of the building.

At Corfe Castle in 1201–2 King John built a new house [17] apart from the late 11th-century hall in the bailey, and separate from and east of the keep. It was called the Gloriet in 1278. The remains, though greatly damaged in the Civil War, yet show some beautiful detail and enough evidence for a plan reconstruction. Here the chapel (or presence chamber) * is in the same range as the hall, both raised on vaulted undercrofts, and access to each given from a porch near the north-west angle, forming an L-plan with them. The porch is raised on a barrel vault, and the steps to it on a half one. As at Little Wenham the chapel is vaulted, but in two perhaps double bays, and once had a room above it. The existing barrel vaults off the south (dais) end of the hall probably carried the private chambers of the king and queen; but the rooms beyond the chapel, now represented by low walls, may be connected with Richard II's new Gloriet of 1377–9. From the evidence of a plan of 1586, the house seems to have surrounded a courtyard, with the kitchen, now completely gone, on the north-west.

The chapel at Manorbier [5] added c. 1260 has a pointed segmental vault like the cellar beneath. These might illustrate 'the cellar to hold the king's wines' under the queen's chapel at Freemantle commanded in January 1251. That same June a chamber was ordered 'over the king's wine cellar at Gloucester Castle'.†

Purbeck marble, used in the capitals and bases at Wells Palace, is also a feature of the early 13th-century undercroft to the chapel at Lambeth Palace.[20] The three central Purbeck columns seem slender in comparison with the lofty vault, and the four double bays, still quadripartite, are more oblong than usual. Not far off, probably, in date, is the undercroft of a chapel of the Knights Hospitaller surviving at Widmere Farm near Marlow.[19] The vaulted cellar, here underground, is divided into four double bays by three cylindrical piers with octagonal capitals. They support segmental transverse and longitudinal arches, but the bays are not groined but roughly domical, an arrangement which, if not a rebuild, is remarkable for the period.

A lofty crypt, below ground level, existed until c. 1852 in London at Gerrard's Hall.[41] It dated from the end of the 13th century, and had five double bays, quadripartite, with tall central columns, and ribs now hollow chamfered. The cellar was reached by a staircase in a corner bay, and there was also a wall staircase leading to the upper floor. The house was clear on three sides, judging from window evidence.

When the apartment was square, forming a double aisle of two bays, as in the solar undercroft at Wells, one central column only was necessary. At 13–15 St Mary's Hill, Stamford,[26] there is a fine underground crypt of this nature, with either half-column responds or moulded corbels on the walls to support the other ends of the ribs. The cellar

---

* Mr R. Dufty, of the Royal Commission on Historical Monuments, believes this to have been a presence chamber, not chapel. Mr P. A. Faulkner (1958, 168), says: 'Having an upper storey makes its use as a chapel unlikely.' But there is a chamber over the definite chapels at Little Wenham and Carew Castle.
† Liberate Roll, 35 Henry III; Turner (1851), 228, 229.

was reached by steps from the street, and above there is a stone building of which a portion of round-arched wall arcade is left.

Carved bosses in houses suggest a date from the late 13th century onwards. At Little Wenham (c. 1270–80) the chapel ribs meet in a *vesica* containing foliage, and a figure said to represent St Petronella. At Seaford in Sussex [40] a cellar has bosses of naturalistic leaf carving, grape and fig, resembling the detail at Southwell Chapter House (c. 1293). A date c. 1295–1300 is thus suggested for this cellar of two quadripartite bays, with its damaged upper storey, the sole survivor in a bombed site south-west of the church. At the east end is a narrow two-centred doorway to a staircase built in the thickness of the wall, and having a pointed cupboard on the south, and at the top a two-centred doorway, blocked on the outside.

In town houses a favourite type of undercroft, wholly or partly underground, contained three double quadripartite bays with two central columns. At Guildford there remain two cellars of this sort, identical in size, on opposite sides of the street. The Angel Hotel cellar (Fig. 35) [31] has its chamfered ribs dying into cylindrical piers, but in 115 High Street [32] the ribs are hollow chamfered and the piers have moulded capitals. Here the corbels retain recognizable figure carving, and scroll-mouldings place

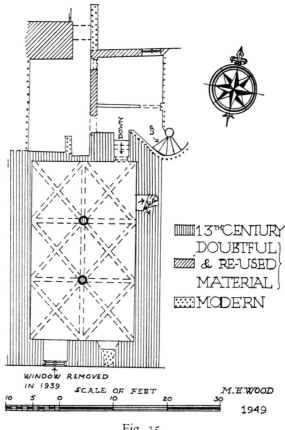

GUILDFORD - ANGEL - CELLAR

13ᵀᴴ CENTURY
DOUBTFUL
& RE-USED
MATERIAL
MODERN

WINDOW REMOVED
IN 1939
SCALE OF FEET
M.E.WOOD
1949

Fig. 35.

them in the later 13th century. Both undercrofts had a wall staircase in the side wall; the Angel one remains, though blocked.

Chester is particularly rich in late 13th-century cellars, the basements of merchants' houses, of which at least one, 48 Bridge Street, retains stonework above and three arches on the Row front.[38] Mr P. H. Lawson's recent drawings include the evidence of others made in 1894 before the parallel wall, at cellar level, lost two pointed arches divided by a central column. In line with these the next house southwards, No. 50, is still spanned by a single segmental arch, also of two chamfered orders, springing from moulded capitals, and above it, at Row level, the stone wall contains a two-centred doorway, of two moulded orders, a segmental-headed recess, also original, with an inner arch and half of another.

In 28–30 Watergate Street [35] the cellar has the unusual arrangement of a longitudinal arcade, the four (once five) arches two-centred with moulded capitals and octagonal piers; the wall they supported carried the beams of the floor above, corbel tables in the side walls taking the other ends. Two contemporary arches span the footwalk of the Row.

At 11 Watergate Street [33] the Old Crypt dates from c. 1270–80, and consists of four double bays with three central octagonal piers having moulded capitals, and shafted responds. In 37 Watergate Street, on the same (south) side, there remain two bays of an undoubtedly similar vault, the chamfered ribs dying into two surviving octagonal piers.

Three other Chester crypts are narrower, and vaulted in oblong compartments. The 'little cellar' at 23 Watergate Street [34] has three wide quadripartite bays and tapering corbels. At 12 Bridge Street [37] the cellar, of six narrow quadripartite bays, has at the west end three graduated round-headed lancets, which might suggest an early 13th-century date,* and are flanked by a square recess, probably a lamp stand; on the south wall a rounded trefoil-headed doorway is reached by three semicircular stone steps. Of the Chester crypts, the latest in development is one in part of 28 Eastgate Row,[39] c. 1290. In this, besides the diagonal each of the narrow bays has a longitudinal and supplementary cross rib, forming as it were a Union Jack in the vaulting plan; the tapering corbels have scroll-moulded abaci.

Other examples have been found by Messrs Lawson and J. T. Smith in their research on the origin of the Rows of Chester. In view of their tendency to a late 13th-century date, Mr Smith believes that these cellars formed part of a rebuilding and attempted town-planning after the great fire of 1278 when 'almost the whole of Chester within the walls of the city was burned down on May 15'. But Mr Lawson has found historical evidence of the existence of stone cellars there before that date. Although agreement is not reached, this is a valuable piece of joint research which should be attempted in other cities with mediaeval cellars both here and on the Continent.

More cellars of this date are found at Canterbury. At Lefevre's store in High Street [42] a pointed barrel vault is set at right angles to another which has two low blocked pointed segmental openings in an end wall, and near the angle a doorway of which the arch is neatly arranged to fit the Caen stone rib setting of the angle. This was Church property and beautifully constructed. At Boots Corner, Mercery Lane,[43] there are two cellars superimposed, the lower with a well in one corner.

The semicircular barrel vault is still popular, divided into bays by hollow-chamfered arches. There are four such bays in the crypt below the Flushing Inn at Rye,[44] and two round arches over original steps to the street. In the Mermaid Inn [45] cellar there are six bays, and a similar doorway in the end wall.

New Winchelsea was being laid out towards the end of the 13th century, Edward I taking a special interest in view of the importance of the wine trade with Gascony, and wine storage seems to have been the reason for the unusual number of vaulted cellars, of which some thirty-four or more remain.[46] A rental of 1292 gives the projected internal

---

* The late Sir Alfred Clapham, commenting on my notes, remarked that the graduated lancets should be early, but the large stones and wide chamfer suggested a later date. The latter was a usual 14th-century form, but might be of the 13th century.

divisions of the town, which was planned on rectangular lines on the model of certain towns in southern France. The main work probably dates from c. 1290–1310, but the early 14th century is stressed by the corbel mouldings of the more elaborate cellars, even as late as c. 1320 in the Salutation Inn [47] and under the Barn in Rectory Lane.[48] Some of the barrel vaults could be earlier, however, and have two-centred, segmental and elliptical cross arches, straight or hollow-chamfered; Little Camber court is typical, of six bays. Other vaults are quadripartite, with cross ribs, some with double aisles; and the Rectory Lane cellar has three compartments, with a barrel, a groined and a ribbed quadripartite vault respectively.

The vaults at Winchelsea are cellars in the modern sense, built below ground, the earthen floor some ten feet below the original street (now raised by five feet), and from which they were reached by a stone staircase, with a hinged flap at the entrance. There were windows at ground level, and cupboards in the cellar walls. The crown of the vault would be one foot above the street, and the floor above raised from it by about two and a half feet. This upper storey may often have been timber-framed, probably burnt by the French later in the 14th century, but in some stone walling can be seen, as in Firebrand and the Armoury.

In the 14th century the use of vaulted undercrofts seems to have become less popular, except in vulnerable areas and in towns. At Southampton several Norman vaults were rebuilt above the original string-course. Where defence was no longer a primary need and space was available, the hall at ground level was more convenient and cheaper to build. However, in the many 14th-century houses found in Westmorland, which is not far from the Scottish border, barrel-vaulted cellars are usual in one or other of the cross-wings, which might be carried up as a tower, as at Burneside Hall, Strickland Roger.[52] Often, as here, this was the service wing, in which case the central passage to the kitchen had a separate vault, a good example being provided by Preston Patrick.[53] The solar wing has an elliptical barrel vault at Selside Hall,[54] and both wings have segmental vaults at Howgill Castle, Milburn.[55]

Subvaults were also useful in providing accommodation in restricted areas, and for fireproof storage in towns. At Norwich brick was now being used for their construction, as (with stone ribs) under part of the Strangers' Hall.[49] The beautiful undercroft of c. 1320 at Southampton,[50] with hooded fireplace, must have been residential; it is of two quadripartite bays with carved bosses.

This is comparable to the arrangement in Chesterton Tower at Cambridge [51] of mid 14th-century date, house of the proctor of the Abbot of Vercelli, owner of Chesterton Church. The main room is raised over an elaborate undercroft with two bays of tierceron vaulting; there are carved bosses at the junction of the hollow-chamfered cross, diagonal, intermediate and ridge ribs, except in the centre where they mitre round a small circle.

There is a fine late 14th-century vault under 20 High Street, Chipping Norton, Oxfordshire.[56] It must also have been at ground level owing to the presence of traceried windows (now blocked), of one and two cinquefoiled lights with cusping in the spandrels. The hollow-chamfered ribs spring from corbels carved with human heads near the angles of the stone floor. The vault is tierceron with ridge ribs.

By now the great hall is usually built at ground level, but there are some notable exceptions, such as that of John of Gaunt (1390–3) at Kenilworth.[57] This was raised on a vaulted undercroft of six triple bays, divided by two rows of piers. The vaulting has been destroyed, but traces of four-centred wall arches give the scale. It is, however, complete in the ground floor of the Strong Tower, which contained storage cellars, the servery (a kind of butler's pantry) at hall level, and private apartments above.

A magnificent crypt of early 15th-century date has been restored recently at the Guildhall in London.[58] It was begun in 1411, but the porch to the hall above not completed until 1425; like Kenilworth it was of three aisles, but of four bays. The three central piers in each row are of Purbeck marble, and have clustered columns with moulded capitals and bases. The main, intermediate and ridge ribs are hollow-chamfered with carved shields and other ornament as bosses at the intersections. There are several original doorways, once reached by steps from the crypt floor level. One at the south-west is especially elaborate, with niches above and alongside. Another, also moulded and shafted, is centrally placed in the east wall; in its jambs are entrances to a wall staircase on either side. The cellar was well lit with windows of three trefoiled lights. The adjoining crypt under the western part of the hall was plainer and altered in the 17th century; there is evidence of octagonal piers without capitals and three aisles of four and a half quadripartite bays with chamfered ribs.

London House in the High Street at Burford [60] retains 15th-century work on three storeys. Below is a crypt of the same date. A central pillar divides it into two aisles of two quadripartite bays, with a further two bays behind one aisle, and a staircase at the side. There was also a staircase, with wide segmental-pointed opening, from the street. The wall arches are four-centred and the chamfered ribs supported on the walls by corbels which have an upper chamfer and ogee-moulded under surface.

At Rectory Farm, Turkdean, Gloucestershire,[61] a 15th-century vaulted undercroft remains which shows the maximum use of ribbing. Sixteen ribs branch out in all directions from a cylindrical pier, the tree effect emphasized by the plain trunk-like character of the latter, its moulded capital and those of the responds suggesting an earlier date; possibly the vault was renewed.

In the 15th century the hall may be raised on an undercroft owing to the lie of the land. This is the case at South Wingfield,[59] where the ground on the north side falls away abruptly. Here the hall cellar remains in perfect condition, with the six double bays divided by a central row of piers; except for the ridge, which is chamfered, the ribs are moulded, with exquisitely carved bosses at the junctions (Pl. XVI B, XVII A). At Hampton Court the early 16th-century hall is also raised, but here supported on two rows of posts, like an aisled hall beneath.

The vault was used in porches (Pl. XV A), again gathering elaboration from the 12th to 16th centuries, and also in the ground floor of gatehouses, such as Donnington Castle, Berkshire, with its unusual cusping (Pl. XV C), and of towers like Henry Yevele's Jewel Tower of 1378, still surviving at Westminster (Pl. XV B), with fine tierceron vault in two bays. Longthorpe Tower (solar), in the early 14th century, has a vault on two floors, like those at Little Wenham earlier, and Beverston Castle (c. 1350–60), the upper storey here containing elaborate chapels. Vaulted passages, found earlier at Swalcliffe and Broughton Castle, are contrived in brick at Tattershall, where the soffits of the window embrasures are also vaulted. There are vaulted oriels to the Angel and Royal at Grantham; in one the central boss depicts 'the pelican in her piety' (Pl. XVII B). A wooden vault over the staircase is preserved at Ashbury Manor (*c.* 1488) (Pl. L D.)

The Cellar under the Solar: Development into the Parlour

In days before the advent of shops easily accessible in country districts, the matter of storing goods of all kinds was of especial importance. Every household had to be self-supporting, and what could not be produced on the manor had to be purchased on certain occasions when there was access to the great annual fairs, and stored until it was needed. These included any dress materials which could not be woven at home, and luxuries such as spices, to enliven the winter diet of salted meat, which also had to be stocked for future use. Storage of special value was doubtless sited under the solar, as it had been earlier below the first-floor hall, hence the fireproof vaulting of stone provided. Placed beneath the owner's chamber, it could thus be kept under his own supervision.

Besides the solar barrel vault at Boothby Pagnell [62] there is a vault of similar type at Old Soar (*c.* 1290).[64] At Crowhurst [63] (*c.* 1250) there were apparently four double bays of quadripartite vaulting, though no central column bases have as yet been excavated.

But in the gradual improvement of accommodation this solar basement, so conveniently placed behind the upper end of the hall, became transformed into a further living-room, the parlour or withdrawing room of the owner and his family. The storage was placed elsewhere, and the room, no longer vaulted, was made into a comfortable apartment into which they could retire from the adjoining high table. In this smaller, less draughty room, with its wall fireplace, the family more and more tended to dine apart from their servants and retainers, leaving the great hall to the latter except on special occasions of festivity, or the entertainment of visiting lords and their retinues; on these occasions the parlour was the place in which special guests would gather before dinner—as indeed is done today at civic functions—and made a suitable withdrawing-room afterwards.

It is interesting to study when this change took place. In the 13th century it was regarded as essential for the lord and lady to dine in hall with their people. We know that the Countess of Leicester, Eleanor de Montfort, sister of Henry III, was scrupulous in obeying this injunction of Bishop Grossteste of Lincoln. But in the 14th century there was a marked tendency to dine apart, as Langland complained in *The Vision of Piers Plowman* (*c.* 1362):

> Wretched is the hall . . . each day in the week
> There the lord and lady liketh not to sit;
> Now have the rich a rule to eat by themselves
> In a privy parlour . . . for poor men's sake,
> Or in a chamber with a chimney [fireplace], and leave the chief hall
> That was made for meals, for men to eat in . . .*

* Early English Society, 1869. Text B. Passus X, 94.

The rich merchant Sir John de Pulteney, four times Lord Mayor of London and financier to Edward III, seems to have been content to dine on the dais of the great hall he built at Penshurst (1341–9). For in the solar basement behind the high table there is vaulted storage still, though only in part, but with access from the dais. Indeed this cellar,[65] incorporated by Sir John, seems earlier in date than his hall, and may have been part of the house of Sir Stephen de Penchester (d. 1299), Warden of the Cinque Ports, whose effigy

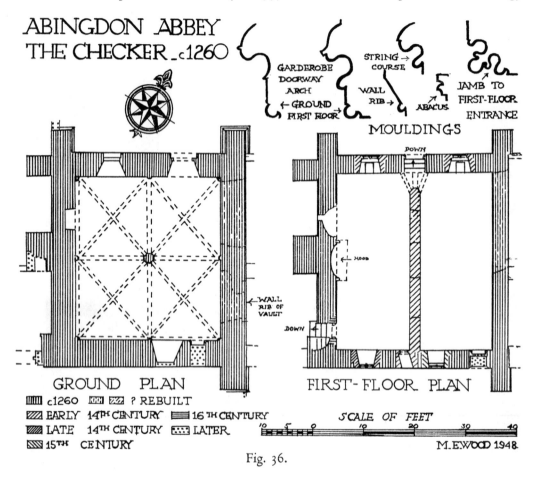

ABINGDON ABBEY
THE CHECKER _ c1260

GARDEROBE
DOORWAY
ARCH
← GROUND
FIRST FLOOR →

STRING →
COURSE

WALL
RIB →

ABACUS

JAMB TO
FIRST-FLOOR
ENTRANCE

MOULDINGS

DOWN

← WALL
RIB OF
VAULT

HOOD

DOWN

GROUND   PLAN

▥ c1260   ▦ ▨ ? REBUILT
▨ EARLY 14ᵀᴴ CENTURY   ▤ 16 ᵀᴴ CENTURY
▨ LATE 14ᵀᴴ CENTURY   ░ LATER
▧ 15ᵀᴴ CENTURY

FIRST- FLOOR PLAN

SCALE OF FEET

M.E.WOOD 1948.

Fig. 36.

lies in Penshurst Church. The vault is almost square (*c.* 30 × 27 feet), divided into four quadripartite bays by a central pier. It closely resembles the Checker vault of *c.* 1260 [29] at Abingdon Abbey (Fig. 36); this (*c.* 31 feet 6 inches × 29 feet) has the same central octagonal column, also without capital, the chamfered ribs dying into the facets of the shaft, as they do in the mid 13th-century cellarium at Fountains, and the hall undercroft at St Cross. Another of these four-bay vaults, perhaps a little later, is found at Swalcliffe Manor, Oxfordshire,[66] below the early 14th-century solar, and associated with a narrow vaulted passage similar to those at Broughton Castle (*c.* 1300). At Swalcliffe, however, the pier is circular, and it has a curious square capital like a Norman base reversed. Thus it is

Plate XV.

A. The Chantry, Chichester, early 13th century porch. B. The Jewel Tower, Westminster, 1378. C. Donnington Castle, gate hall, 1386. D. The King's House, Salisbury, porch; mid 15th century.

C

A

B

Plate XVI.

A. Vaulted cellar at Boothby Pagnell; c. 1200. B. Vaulted cellar at South Wingfield; 1440–59. C. The Treasurer's House, Martock, solar window c. 1250–60, and parlour windows inserted in the 15th century below.

suggested that the Penshurst crypt is that below the solar of an earlier, smaller hall, perhaps of wood, and that Sir John incorporated it, probably rebuilding the south wall, certainly enlarging the windows. His staircase oriel was built in line with this, and like the vault has access from the dais.

Broughton Castle [67] (c. 1300) has an extensive residential portion on three floors at the upper (east) end of the hall. A doorway near the south-east angle opens into a narrow vaulted passage, seven quadripartite bays in length, with windows and a doorway on the south side. On the north it gives access by three arches to the solar undercroft (now dining-room) of three quadripartite bays, with two altered windows, probably loops originally, at the northern end. Then the passage turns at right angles one bay to a straight staircase to the chapel, which mounts between the side wall of the undercroft and that of another basement at the original end of the block. There is a south doorway opposite the staircase, and near it the entrance to a vaulted bay of the end room, which has access to the lowest portion of a projecting garderobe tower. The chapel undercroft, of two bays, is in the original north-east corner, at right angles to the solar subvault, and west of the latter is a smaller chamber surrounded by passages on the other three sides. Indeed this building is of especial interest for its passages, vaulted like most of the ground floor (Pl. 17 A.)

In Devon at Broadclyst [68] Mr Everett has excavated part of the manor house of the Nonants, who died out c. 1340. In an extension of the churchyard one side wall of the solar undercroft is visible, with four corbels for the springing of cross, diagonal and wall ribs. The vault was 31 feet 4 inches × 15 feet 6 inches in extent, of three quadripartite bays, and may have resembled the vault (30 × 17 feet) inserted c. 1275 under the reredorter at Egglestone Abbey in Yorkshire. At Broadclyst there is an unusual double-chamfered abacus to the corbels, and the hollow-chamfered ribs might suggest a date c. 1300. The plain chamfer is more usual in the 13th century, though the hollow chamfer does occur at Little Wenham (c. 1270–80).

In the new solar block of c. 1325 added at Southwick Manor (Northamptonshire) [69] the vault is square with chamfered ribs springing from moulded corbels with carved heads, and meeting in a central boss of equal interest.

A cellar under only part of the solar occurs in several 14th-century houses. Creslow Manor [70] (c. 1330) has one bay of tierceron vaulting with carved bosses at the rib junctions, the kind the Penshurst crypt should have shown, had it been contemporary with Sir John Pulteney's Hall. The Creslow cellar is 14 feet square and 9 feet high, the chamfered ribs springing from near the floor. It is under the eastern third of the solar, but below ground level, the dairy floor being raised to accommodate it. This is reminiscent of Chepstow Castle, where there is a vault of three bays under part of the late 13th-century hall, which is at ground level, though on a slope.

At Norrington Manor [71] (c. 1377) the northern third of the solar undercroft contains two bays of tierceron vaulting, possibly under a chapel subdivision, as it is correctly orientated. The solar has been rebuilt and any upper partition removed. The late 15th-century Great Chalfield Manor [72] also had a vault in part, here under the front portion of the undercroft. Possibly such cases represent a transitional stage between storage basement and parlour.

Certainly in the 15th century the solar basement in earlier houses might be made into a parlour, and a fireplace supplied. At Compton Castle it was heightened two feet, as we know from alterations to the solar fireplace. Larger windows were inserted in the end wall of the undercroft at Martock, here on the service side of an 'end hall', two triple lights with cinquefoiled heads, and a large fireplace was added (Pl. XVI c). A similar three-light was inserted in the solar basement of Sutton Courtenay 'Abbey', and in the side wall a two-light of this nature and another of two trefoiled transomed lights. The replaced windows would have been loops. A window of eight cinquefoiled lights was inserted *c.* 1500 to light the 'parlure' of Sir William Vernon at Haddon Hall.

In new houses large windows were of course provided from the start. At Hampton Court, the Great Watching Chamber [73] is on the same level as the hall, and at its upper end. Unlike the hall, which rests on wooden posts and one cross wall, this chamber is supported on a vaulted wine cellar, of five double bays in brick, with ridge and four-centred diagonal and wall ribs, and a range of octagonal stone columns with moulded capitals.

EXAMPLES OF VAULTED CELLARS

		Type	*Bays*	*Internal Dimensions*	*References*
(1) C 12th	Abbot's House, Chester	hall: quadripartite with central columns / solar: columns	4 double; 3 double originally	60' × c. 28' 6"; 44' × c. 28' 6"	Brakspear (1933 a), 140, pl. XXXI (plan).
(2) mid C 12th	Prior's House, Castle Acre, Norf.	hall: groined with central piers	6 double	80' × 27'	Brakspear (1933 a), 141, pl. XXXI (plan); M.O.W. Guide (8), 12–16 (plan & illus.).
(3) C 12th	24 St Thomas Street, Winchester	groined with transverse arch	2	27' × 17' 6"	V.C.H. Hants, V, 8, 9 (plan & illus.).
(4) late C 12th	Bury Farm, Rednarley D'Abitôt, Worcs.	quadripartite	3	30' × 18'	V.C.H. Worcs., III, 482 (plan & illus.).
(5) c. 1160 / c. 1260	Manorbier Castle, Pemb.	hall: barrel / solar-service: barrel / chapel: pointed segmental barrel	2	c. 18' × c. 12' & c. 18' × c. 12'; c. 22' × 18'; c. 26' × 11'	Royal Archaeological Institute, Tenby programme (1962) (sketch plan).
(6) c. 1170–80	Burton Agnes Manor House, Yorks.	quadripartite with 3 central columns	4 double	40' 6" × 19' 9"	See chapter 2 (14).
(7) c. 1175	'Music House', Norwich	hall: groined with transverse arch / solar: quadripartite with transverse arch	3 + 2	c. 50' 8" × 17' 7" (with cross wall)	See chapter 2 (13).
(8) c. 1180	Moyses Hall, Bury St Edmunds, Suff.	hall: groined with transverse & longitudinal arches. 2 central piers / solar	3 double	37' × 24'	See chapter 2 (17).
(9) c. 1180	Guildhall site, Canterbury		3	37' × c. 16'	Clapham (1948).
(10) c. 1200	36 High St (The Mint), Canterbury				
(11) 1201–2	Southampton; Quilter's Vault; 58 French St, etc.	barrel	4 double	44' × 26' orig.	
(12) late C 12th	Southampton, vault on the western shore	barrel with transverse arches	9+	56' × 19' 6"	Wood (1935), 185, pl. XII B (plan).
(13) late C 12th	'Hostelry of the Priors of Lewes', Southwark (evidence)	groined with transverse arches	4	40' 3" × 16' 6"	J. Gage in Archaeologia, XXIII (1831), 299–308; C. E. Gwilt in Archaeologia, XXV (1834), 604–6; Turner (1851), 47; V.C.H. Surrey, IV, 126–7, 138 (plan & illus.).
(14) late C 12th	Deloraine Court, Lincoln: North apartment / South apartment	2 central columns visible / 1 central column visible	4 double probably / 5 double	37' × 16' / 50' 6" × 16'	Wood (1952) (plan).
(15) late C 12th	The Vicars' Hall, Chichester	ribbed quadripartite	3 double	35' × 25'	Steer (1958) (plan & illus.).
(16) c. 1200	Boothby Pagnell Manor House, Lincs.	hall: quadripartite	2	32' 6" × 17' 6"	See chapter 2 (20).
(17) 1201–2	Corfe Castle, Dor., 'Gloriet'	quadripartite (originally)	2	c. 18' × 12'	See chapter 2 (22).
(18) early C 13th	Cakeham, West Wittering, Suss., palace remains	quadripartite	4 double originally	probably c. 48' × 22' 6" originally	Wood (1950), 93.
(19) early C 13th	Widmere Farm, near Marlow, Bucks., chapel	domical with 3 central columns	4 double	38' × 17'	R.C.H.M. Bucks, I, 169.

		Type	Bays	Internal Dimensions	References
(20) early C 13th	Lambeth Palace, London, chapel undercroft	quadripartite with 3 central columns	4 double	70' 6" × 23' 9"	R.C.H.M. London, II, 79–80, pl. 127.
(21) 1221	Old Palace, Salisbury	quadripartite with 2 central columns	3 double	c. 52' × 23'	J. A. Reeve, The Bishop's Palace at Salisbury. Wiltshire Archaeological & Natural History Magazine, XXV (1891), 181–2, 184 (plans).
(22) 1221–6	Abbot's House part of Bishop's Palace), Peterborough	solar: quadripartite with central piers	5 double		V.C.H. Northants, II, 453 et seq. (plan).
(23) c. 1230–50	Bishop Jocelyn's Palace, Wells, Som.	hall: quadripartite with central columns / solar: quadripartite with central columns	5 double / 2 double	67' × 26' / 24' × 26'	See chapter 2 (27).
(24) c. 1235–61	Abbot's House, Battle, Suss.	hall: quadripartite with 3 central piers / solar: quadripartite with 3 central piers	4 double / 4 double	53' × 27' 6" / 50' × 23'	See chapter 2 (28).
(25) c. 1250	Temple Manor, Strood, Kent	quadripartite	3	41' × 17' 6"	See chapter 2 (30).
(26) mid C 13th	13 & 15 St Mary's Hill, Stamford, Lincs.	quadripartite	2 double		
(27) c. 1250–60	Abbot's House, Netley, Hants	hall: quadripartite / solar: barrel / chapel: quadripartite	3 / / 2	45' 9" × 16' 10" / 21' 3" × 9' 6" / 21' × 12' 3"	See chapter 2 (31).
(28) c. 1250–60	Nettlestead Place, Kent	quadripartite with 3 central columns	4 double		Country Life (19), 887, 889 (plan & illus.).
(29) c. 1260	The Checker, Abingdon Abbey, Berks.	quadripartite with central octagonal pier	2 double	31' 6" × 29'	Wood (1950), 4–6 (plan).
(30) c. 1270–80	Little Wenham Hall, Suff.	hall: quadripartite / chapel: quadripartite	3 / 1	37' 6" × 16' / 10' 6" square	See chapter 2 (32).
(31) late C 13th	Angel Hotel, Guildford, Sy.	quadripartite	3 double	32' 4" × 11' 4"	Wood (1950), 82–3, pl. VIII c (plan & illus.).
(32) late C 13th	115 High Street, Guildford, Sy.	quadripartite	3 double	32' 5" × 19' 4"	Wood (1950), 83–4 (plan).
(33) c. 1270–80	11 Watergate Street, Chester (Quellyn Roberts)	ribbed quadripartite with 3 central octagonal piers	4 double	c. 44' × 23'	Lawson & Smith (1958), 19–20 (plan & section); Wood (1950), 11–12.
(34) C 13th	23 Watergate Street, Chester (under Pointer Dog Inn)	ribbed quadripartite	3	34' × 14'	Lawson & Smith (1958), 20–1 (plan & section); Wood (1950), 12.
(35) C 13th	28–30 Watergate Street, Chester (College of Further Education; Northover; Langley)	longitudinal two-centred arcade	4 (originally 5)	c. 41' × 22'	Lawson & Smith (1958), 15–17 (plan & section).
(36) late C 13th	37 Watergate Street, Chester (St Ursula's Café)	ribbed quadripartite with 2 central octagonal piers	2 double	24' 4" × 16' 2"	Lawson & Smith (1958), 21–2 (plan & sections); Wood (1950), 12.
(37) C 13th	12 Bridge St, Chester (Willerby's)	ribbed quadripartite	6 narrow	42' × 15'	Lawson & Smith (1958), 2–3, 20 (plan); Wood (1950), 12.
(38) late C 13th	48–50 Bridge Street, Chester (Wm. Jones)	No. 48: 2 two-centred arches in transverse wall (originally) / No. 50: 1 segmental transverse arch		c. 37' × 23' / c. 50' × c. 16'	Lawson & Smith (1958), 4–6 (plan & sections).

No.	Date	Building	Vault type	Bays	Dimensions	References
(39)	1290	28 Eastgate Row, Chester (Browns)	quadripartite + intermediate & ridge ribs	4	42' 4" × 13' 9"	Lawson & Smith (1958), 12–13 (plan & sections, etc.); Wood (1950), 11.
(40)	c. 1295–1300	27 Church Street (Crypt House), Seaford, Suss.	quadripartite	2	27' 4" × 13' 4"	Wood (1950), 90, pl. VII A (illus.).
(41)	end C 13th	Gerrard's Hall, London (evidence)	quadripartite with 4 central columns	5 double	49' 3" × 21' 3"	Parker (1853), 185 (plan, illus., mouldings).
(42)		High Street, Canterbury (Lefevre's)	pointed barrel, etc.			
(43)		Mercery Lane, Canterbury (Boots)				
(44)		Flushing Inn, Rye, Suss.	barrel	4		
(45)		Mermaid Inn, Rye, Suss.	barrel	6		
(46)	c. 1290–1310	Cellars at Winchelsea, Suss. Little Camber Court, etc.				Unpublished plans and sections by W. Maclean Homan, deposited in Sussex Record Office at Chichester and available to students; Chambers (1937), 204 (plan of cellar sites).
(47)	c. 1320	Salutation Inn, Winchelsea, Suss.	quadripartite	3	56' × 17'	
(48)	c. 1320	Barn in Rectory Lane, Winchelsea, Suss.	(a) barrel (b) groined (c) ribbed quadripartite			
(49)	early C 14th	Strangers' Hall, Norwich	brick quadripartite	3		Guide to Strangers' Hall Museum (1958); Archaeological Journal, LXXX (1923), 332–3 (plan); CVI (1949), 80–1.
(50)	c. 1320	The Undercroft, Southampton	quadripartite	2		
(51)	mid C 14th	Chesterton Tower, Cambridge	tierceron	2	26' × 15' 9"	R.C.H.M. Cambridge, 381–2, pl. 297 (plans & illus.); Parker (1859), 298 (plan & interior view).
(52)	C 14th	Burneside Hall, Strickland Roger, West.	north wing (service) east vault barrel, west vault south wing (solar) east vault mid. vault west vault		c. 17' × 12' 6" 19' × 12' 23' × 12' 22' 6" × 13–17' c. 17' × 13'	See chapter 4 (29).
(53)	late C 14th	Preston Patrick Hall, West.	barrel, north dairy south dairy		c. 12' 6" × 13' 14' × 13'	See chapter 4 (28).
(54)	late C 14th	Selside Hall, West. (south wing)	elliptical barrel, east dairy west dairy		22' 6" × 12' 14' × 12'	See chapter 4 (30).
(55)	late C 14th	Howgill Castle, Milburn, West.	elliptical barrel north-west wing, segmental barrel south-west wing, segmental barrel		c. 31' × 13' c. 33' × 13'	R.C.H.M. Westmorland, 174 (plan).
(56)	late C 14th	20 High Street, Chipping Norton, Oxon.	quadripartite with 2 rows of piers originally	6 triple	90' × 45'	See chapter 2 (55).
(57)	1390–3	Kenilworth Castle, War., hall	tierceron with 3 central piers	4 triple		
(58)	1411–25	The Guildhall, London	tierceron with 5 central piers	6 double		R.C.H.M. London, IV, 63, 65–67, pl. 132 (plan & illus.).
(59)	1440–59	South Wingfield Manor, Derbys.	quadripartite and central column	2 double + 2		See chapter 4 (48).
(60)	late C 15th	London House, High Street, Burford, Oxon.				M. S. Gretton (1944), Burford Past and Present, 32 (drawing).
(61)	C 15th	Rectory Farm, Turkdean, Glos.	tierceron with 1 central column	2 double	210' × 144'	Country Life, 30 July 1953, 357 (illus.).

THE CELLAR UNDER THE SOLAR

	Type	Bays	Internal Dimensions	References
(62) c. 1200 Boothby Pagnell Manor House, Lincs.	barrel		17' 6" × 12'	See chapter 2 (20).
(63) c. 1250 Crowhurst Manor ruins, Suss.	quadripartite	4 double (originally)	40' 6" × c. 22'	V.C.H. Sussex, IX, 77–8 (plan).
(64) c. 1290 Old Soar, Plaxtol, Kent	pointed barrel		27' × 16'	M.O.W. Guide (33) (plan).
(65) late C 13th Penshurst Place, Kent	ribbed quadripartite and central octagonal pier	2 double	c. 30' × 27'	See chapter 4 (24).
(66) early C 14th Swalcliffe Manor, Oxon.	quadripartite & central column	4 oblong	24' 6" (E.) & 23' 6" (W.) × 16' 6" (N.) & 18' (S.)	Long (1938), 53 (illus.).
(67) c. 1300 Broughton Castle, Oxon, extensive, with passages	quadripartite	3, etc.		Parker (1853), 261–7, 79–80; (1859), 270, 421 (plan, section, etc.).
(68) c. 1300 Broadclyst Manor, Devon, excavations	quadripartite	3	31' 4" × 15' 6"	To be published by A. W. Everett.
(69) c. 1325 Southwick Hall, Northants.	tierceron	1	c. 18' × 16'	Country Life (26), 1236–40 (plan & illus.).
(70) c. 1330 Creslow Manor House, Bucks., under part	tierceron	1	14' square	R.C.H.M. Bucks, II, 94–8 (plan & illus.).
(71) c. 1377 Norrington Manor House, Wilts., under part	tierceron	2	20' × 10'	See chapter 4 (32).
(72) c. 1480 Great Chalfield Manor House, Wilts., under part	quadripartite with ridge ribs	2	c. 18' 6" × 10' 6"	See chapter 4 (62).
(73) c. 1530–5 Hampton Court, Middx., Great Watching Chamber	tierceron with 4 central octagonal piers	5 double	c. 56' 6" × 26'	R.C.H.M. Middlesex, 35, pl. 82 (plan).

7

Oriels

TWELFTH- and especially 13th-century documents frequently mention a mysterious addition called an oriel (oriol), obviously larger than a mere projecting window. In modern use the term 'oriel' is strictly confined to a projection from an upper storey. But in later mediaeval documents this obtrusion might be called a 'bay window', the modern term for an oriel at ground level. The earliest reference so far discovered is one of 1186.* There has been much debate about this word *oriole* (*oriolum*), Parker † deriving it from an oratory or the gallery in a domestic chapel.

However, the term seems to have been used for any projection or built-out gallery, whether external or internal. Mr Hugh Braun ‡ thinks the word may have been coined in recognition of the ear-like appearance of such appendages; and indeed we must visualize the 13th-century house with many such timber excrescences, on the lines of hoards or fighting platforms in military architecture. The oriel was often built as a landing at the head of an external staircase, rather in the nature of a forebuilding, and porch-staircases, of which there is evidence at the Netley Abbot's House, Stokesay and Aydon Castles, and later at Markenfield, would have been called oriels when they were erected. Indeed, as Mr Salzman has shown,§ the word 'orell' survives in Cornwall as the porch at the top of an outside stairway. This seems conclusive evidence, and marches with the references in Henry III's Liberate Rolls,[1] where the oriel was commonly situated at the head of a staircase, presumably as a covered landing outside an upper entrance, and there are many allusions to its position before a doorway. It may be defined as a vestibule or covered entrance, often timber-framed.

Luckily drawings were made before the destruction, in 1823, of such a vestibule, in stone, at Westminster Palace. It was built in 1237–9 for Queen Eleanor of Provence, to give access from her chamber to her chapel. This oriel was sited in the re-entrant angle of these adjoining blocks of building, and had two shafted pointed doorways at right angles.[2] ‖

* Pipe Roll, 32 Henry II. M.O.W. (1963), 122, 178. † (1853), 82.
‡ (1940), 19. § (1952), 95. ‖ M.O.W. (1963), 122, plan III, pls. 28, 29.

99

In December 1237 'a certain oriol at the top of the stair' is ordered for the king's chamber at Clarendon; and in May 1240 'the oriol before the door of our queen's chamber at Woodstock' is to be wainscoted. At Oxford in November 1245 the sheriff is ordered to 'make also a door and windows in the oriol beyond the porch of our hall there'. In March 1246 'the keeper of the manor of Ludgershall is ordered to make an oriol before the door of the king's chamber'; and in April the next year the sheriff of Buckinghamshire is told to 'make an oriol with a stair [*cum stagio*] before the door of the queen's chamber at Brill'. *

At Guildford the oriel seems to have served as porch to an aisled hall on ground level, for in the same paragraph referring to the rebuilding of 'a certain oriel before the door of the king's hall' in May 1256, there is the command to paint the pillars and arches in the same building. Yet in January of the same year the sheriff is to pay for 'making the porch to the hall of stone'. † Perhaps the other was in front of a subsidiary entrance, possibly one near the high table, with access to the king's chamber.

Thus the oriel was often in close proximity to the porch, if it was not the porch itself, as was the case in the guest house at St Albans. In 1235 'at the entrance a splendid porch adjoins it, which is called a portico or an oriel'. ‡

Sometimes the oriel had a room underneath. At Guildford in November 1257 the sheriff of Surrey is ordered 'to block up the outer and inner doorway of the chamber under the oriol, and to make a door from the king's wardrobe into that chamber under the oriol'. § But at Winchester Castle in 1268 'the sheriff of Southampton is directed to build an oriol (*auriolum*) between the new chamber and the queen's chapel of the width of the same chamber', and to build under it 'two walls from the said chamber to the chapel aforesaid, and a gate by which carts can enter and go out'. ‖ This is reminiscent of St Albans in the next century, where Abbot John, *c.* 1396, 'built a beautiful hall called "The Oriole of the Convent" praised even by kings, and under it are buildings made very usefully for a larder and for the keeping of fish and storing other things'. ¶ This suggests a first-floor anteroom, probably projecting from the earlier buildings of the Abbot's House.

The oriel could be associated with a chapel. In September 1233 a large chapel 25 feet long was ordered to be made at the head or end of the oriel (*ad capud oriolli*) of the king's chamber in Hereford Castle. ** Sometimes the chapel, as at Winchester, contained an oriel, †† and sometimes the oriel, as at Geddington, a chapel. At the latter in January 1252 the sheriff of Northampton was ordered to 'make a chapel in the oriol beyond the door of our chamber, and three glass windows in the same chapel'. ‡‡ At Prudhoe Castle, Northumberland, an oriel chapel of 14th-century date remains,[5] which seemed to Parker to confirm his view of the oratory derivation of the term (Fig. 37). It is akin to the oratory recess projecting from the early 14th-century solar at Southwick Hall.[9]

* Liberate Roll, 22, 24, 30, 30, 31 Henry III; Turner (1851), 188, 196, 208, 210, 213. Mr Salzman translates *stagio* as upper storey.
† Liberate Roll, 40 Henry III; Turner (1851), 245–6.
‡ *Gesta Abbatum*, I, 314. 'Rolls Series'; Salzman (1952), 381.
§ Liberate Roll, 42 Henry III; Turner (1851), 249.
‖ Liberate Roll, 53 Henry III; Turner (1851), 256.
¶ *Gesta Abbatum*, III, 441–7; Salzman (1952), 400.
** Liberate Roll, 17 Henry III; Turner (1851), 183–4.
†† Liberate Roll, 35 Henry III; Turner(1851), 228 (December 1250).
‡‡ Liberate Roll, 36 Henry III; Turner (1851), 238.

At Marlborough Castle the oriel was used to lengthen a room. It could be wainscoted, have a tiled floor, and privy chambers attached to it on two floors.* At Winchester the oriel even contained a chimney (fireplace) 'to heat the queen's victuals'.†

The oriel usually had windows. At Rochester in July 1240 the constable is commanded

Fig. 37. Prudhoe Castle, plan and exterior of the oriel chapel.

'to cause the windows in the oriol before the door of our chamber in the castle to be repaired where necessary', and even 'pillared windows' are mentioned at Clarendon (March 1244).‡

The modern use of the word as a projecting window recess is not found in the houses of Henry III, although his oriels commonly contain windows and are on an upper floor. In 1268 the sheriff of Wiltshire was ordered 'to repair without delay the aisles, windows and

* Liberate Roll, 34, 24, 28 Henry III; Turner (1851), 222, 196, 203.
† Liberate Roll, 53 Henry III; Turner (1851), 255–6.
‡ Liberate Roll, 24, 28 Henry III; Turner (1851), 196, 203.

oriols' of the king's hall at Clarendon.* These oriels are unlikely to have been porches, though we know that a porch was ordered for the hall there in 1245. This being a ground-floor hall (aisled), upper projecting windows are not feasible unless from an adjoining room or gallery. Indeed the document could almost be used as evidence, absent elsewhere at this period, except possibly at Nassington, of a ground-floor recess or bay window. But nothing of this sort was found during excavation. Perhaps individual gables over the window were meant.

It has been suggested † that the oriel may have derived from the projecting reader's pulpit which came into use in monastic refectories in the late 12th century, and of which remain a 13th-century example at Beaulieu and 14th-century ones at Shrewsbury and Chester. These may have had some influence, but seem to have been styled *pulpitum*, not 'oriol', in the documents, and were usually of stone, not wood.

The lack of evidence in Henry III's buildings suggests that the oriel in our covered balcony sense dates from the period after his reign (1216–72), and other references place its coming into fashion at the end of the 13th century. One case has existing archaeological evidence to support it. At Conway Castle there are still signs of where a balcony of timber projected, the 'oriol in the middle of the castle' ‡ (wall) for which Master Henry of Oxford was paid in 1286 by Edward I. This, built on the external south wall of the inner ward, was designed with access, via a wall passage off a window embrasure, from the adjoining chambers of the king and queen. It may have been constructed as an afterthought, and reconstructed in stone *c.* 1346–7 with re-used corbels.[4]

At Stirling new apartments included even the construction of an oriel for the Queen (Margaret), the Countesses of Gloucester and Hereford and other ladies to view the siege of the castle by Edward I in 1304.§

Thus, except in one possible case, at Clarendon, the 13th-century oriels do not fit into the modern conception of a bay window, a projecting window embrasure at ground level. However, the term bay window comes into use in the 14th century, chiefly in the latter part, though an apparently early 14th-century document refers to a room to be built at Englefield (Berkshire) which is to have a 'vay' (presumably 'bay') window in the vault.‖ The word seems not to have applied to ground-floor projections only, for in some documents it is used where we should write 'oriel' and vice versa. In 1342 a timber hall, on an upper floor, and bedroom each were to have a bay window flanked by lintelled windows, above a tavern in Paternoster Row.¶ Also in London, in 1369, a range of twenty shops was to be built, having two bay windows as a decorative feature at the corner.** *Bayes fenestres* are also to be made in 1380 at Hertford Castle.††

* Liberate Roll, 53 Henry III; Turner (1851), 255.
† Clapham & Godfrey (1913), 75.
‡ *pro oriol in medio castre.* Exchequer Accounts, 485/28. I am indebted for this information to Mr A. J. Taylor, F.S.A. However, he adds: 'But I am not at all sure whether it may not have been just what you say those of the Liberate Rolls generally were, namely wooden porch at the top of an outside stair. There were two outside stairs in the inner ward.'
§ 'A ringside seat, in fact', as Mr Taylor comments, to whom I am further indebted for this reference. British Museum, Addison MS., 8835, fol. 15b. *Ac eciam pro uno oriolo pro Regina et Comitissa Glove' et Hereford et aliio dominabus et domicellis pro insultu castri predicti videndo.*
‖ Salzman (1952), 417; Ancient Deeds, D, 6548 (Public Record Office).
¶ Salzman (1952), 434; Bridge House Deeds (Guildhall) Portfolio G, no. 17.
** Salzman (1952), 441; St Paul's MSS., no. 1796.
†† Salzman (1952), 459; Duchy of Lancaster, Miscellaneous Books, 14, f. 81. (Public Record Office).

Surviving examples of bay windows, so frequent in the 15th century, are very rare in the 14th century. This might suggest that the fashion came first in wood rather than stone, the more lasting material, and that most early examples have disappeared, except a possible one at Stanton's Farm, Black Notley, c. 1340, where the semi-octagonal bay may be original.[11] Indeed there is a London document of 1308 in which a carpenter agrees to build an 'oriel at the head of the hall beyond the high bench',* as well as 'one step with an oriel' (here probably a porch) 'from the ground to the door of the hall, outside the latter'. An

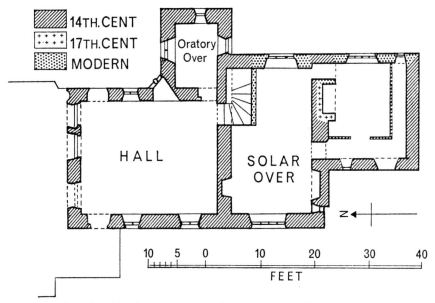

Fig. 38. Abbot's Grange, Broadway, plan. *See also* Pl. LV B.

incipient stone bay window at Nassington [3] has a squint to command the entrance, of 13th-century date, then there seems a dearth of stone examples until the slightly projecting bay window, c. 1400 or later, of Grevil's House, Chipping Campden.[16]

But what we do get in the 14th century are little projecting rooms off the dais end of the hall, which in that protruding sense are the successors of the oriels of Henry III. They do not however, occur in all houses of this period. These small private rooms were reached through a doorway, as at Abbot's Grange, Broadway (c. 1320) [8] (Fig. 38), where there is a two-light window set obliquely in their angle with the hall,[8] or else by a wide and lofty arch as at Clevedon Court, not far off in date.[7] The oriel chambers formed a partially secluded corner for the owner and his family, and the lower storey of his chapel, which could be reached from his great chamber on the first floor beyond the upper end of the hall. At Clevedon the recess gives entry to the room below this solar, and it is suggested that a chief function of such oriels was to give convenient access to the solar block. Certainly at Penshurst [12] the projection, here polygonal and embattled like the hall, contained the

* '*et j oriole in capite aule ultra summum scannum, et j gradum cum oriole a terra usque hostium aule predicte extra illam aulam.*' Salzman (1952), 417; Guildhall Muniments: letter book C, f. 96; translated in Riley (1868), 66.

staircase to the great chamber as well as an entrance to its undercroft. The annexe at Northborough Manor (Pl. XVIII A) once served a staircase also.[10] In the hall c. 1400 * at Tickenham Court, Somerset, a moulded arch, now blocked, led into a square chamber (8 feet 4 inches internally) which can be traced on the adjoining walls outside, and which retains its entrance to the wing (Pls. 6, XVIII D).[15] At Aston Eyre, Shropshire, probably earlier, this is also the case. A great arch, at the upper end of the hall, once led to a small rectangular chamber covering the doorway to a projecting solar undercroft and newel staircase on the angle.[6] (See Fig. 48, page 133.) Such entrances to the solar block persist in later bay windows such as Athelhampton in the 15th century (Pls. XX A, XXII A).

At the end of the 14th century there was a further development. John of Gaunt's great hall at Kenilworth, raised on a vaulted undercroft, has a polygonal oriel chamber at the south-east angle, this having long transomed windows (with seats) (Pls, 28, XVIII C) on four sides, and a fireplace, a new feature, on the other, instead of the usual doorway. Opposite it, also reached through a lofty moulded arch, is another oriel chamber with great windows, but oblong in plan and forming part of the south-west Sainteowe Tower. These are akin to bay windows, but are oriels in the first-floor sense, though not as projecting balconies. The second oriel gives access to a passage behind the end wall of the hall, leading to the Great Chamber off its south-east angle, adjoining the polygonal oriel but without egress to it.[14] There is a somewhat similar arrangement at Wardour Castle, where the plan is also determined by the exigencies of the site.

The simpler little 'oriel chambers' persisted into the 15th century, still at the junction of hall and solar wing, and often balancing the porch projection, as at (East) Coker Court in Somerset (Pl. XXI A). This has a great transomed window like those of the hall, and, as the porch, another room above. Here the solar wing is rebuilt, but there is the usual entrance to it.[27] At Minster Lovell the square oriel chamber projects clear of the solar wing. Like Penshurst earlier, it contains a vaulted staircase up to the solar, and below, in the angle, a diagonal passage to its undercroft. Above the vault a third-storey apartment, reached by a wall staircase from the solar, was probably Lord Lovell's treasury or muniment room. Across the hall a similar doorway opens to an oblong chamber incorporated between the solar and chapel blocks, with access to both and to a newel staircase in its junction with a further apartment, once projecting north.[21] Here, as at Coker Court and West Coker,[28] the access is by a doorway from the hall, but usually, as at Bradley Manor,[18] it is through a lofty chamfered or moulded arch. This is also the case at Ashleworth Court (Pl. XIX B),[29] where the square two-storeyed projection contains a newel staircase in one angle. At Caister Castle (1432–46) the arch has been disguised with cement, but the start of a hoodmould can be seen, carried as a string-course over the adjoining doorway to the north-west tower. The oriel chamber is square with storeys over, but the presence of two large, partly blocked, traceried windows, one on each free wall, shows development towards the true bay window of the later 15th century.[22]

Where there was a back courtyard to the hall, the oriel was repeated at the other end of the dais. Little Sodbury retains the original arches to these.† [46] Bewley Court has two

---

* This hall is difficult to date. The window tracery looks 14th-century, but the doorway mouldings later.
† One oriel has been rebuilt from the old material.

Plate XVII. Detail.

A. South Wingfield, boss in hall cellar; 1440–59. B. The Angel and Royal, Grantham, 'the pelican in her piety', boss in oriel; 15th century. C. Norrington Manor, 'face' boss in porch; early 15th century. D. Gainsborough Old Hall, lion ornament in oriel; c. 1480. E. Sutton Courtenay 'Abbey', musician corbel to solar fireplace; 15th century. F. Norrington Manor, king's head corbel in porch; early 15th century.

A. Northborough Manor House, hall with oriel projection; *c.* 1340.
B. Thornton Abbey gatehouse, oriel chamber, interior; 1382 +.

C. Kenilworth Castle hall, polygonal oriel chamber; 1390–3. D. Tickenham Court, evidence of square oriel chamber in angle between hall and solar; *c.* 1400.

Plate XVIII. Oriels.

A. Bradley Manor, Newton Abbot, east front after *c.* 1495 reconstruction with oriels; chapel (*right*), 1428.

B. Ashleworth Court, hall, oriel projection and solar wing; before 1463.

C. Eltham Palace; great hall, south front; *c.* 1479–80.

Plate XIX. Oriels.

C

D

A

B

Plate XX. Oriels. A. Athelhampton Hall, south front; *c.* 1495–1500. B. South Petherton, late 15th century; the principal front before restoration. C and D. Castle Acre, oriel to Prior's lodging; end of the 15th century.

such opposite arches, though again one chamber has gone. The southernmost has a window, and the usual access to the undercroft, now parlour, while on the other side a four-centred arch opens to a staircase five feet wide, running up parallel to the hall, its outer wall a continuation of that fronting the parlour and oriel. This gives access to the room over the porch, and the great chamber beyond, here over the service apartments.[39]

There is a great similarity in plan between two other Wiltshire houses, South Wraxall Manor, probably dating from the second quarter of the 15th century,[19] and Great Chalfield, built by Thomas Tropenell, steward to Robert Lord Hungerford, who held the property from 1467 until his death in 1490 [45] (Pls. 4, X A). Both halls have a two-storeyed oriel block to balance the porch, with the chimney-breast set in its angle with the hall. There is a similar chamber opposite, also reached through a great archway, and having a doorway to the solar wing, as have the small rooms above. At Great Chalfield the latter have squints into the hall, concealed in masks (Pl. 31 A).

Drawings of Kingston Seymour Manor House (Pl. IX A) show a single oriel projecting further than the porch, each having the front wall in line with that of the adjoining wing (Figs. 39, 40).[43] At Lytes Cary, also in Somerset, John Lyte, who succeeded to the property in 1523, 'newe buylt the Hall oriall', which projects much further than the porch, which he also rebuilt (Pl. XXI B).[67] However, Poundisford Park (c. 1534), near Taunton, has two oriel projections, each with a third storey, exactly balancing the porches, entered from the hall by moulded arches.[69] Speke Hall [71] has not only one of these dining recesses, like Lytes Cary with fireplace, but a bay window opposite as well; however, both may be additions.

With the transformation of the solar undercroft, originally for storage, into the private dining-room or parlour, the small oriel chambers became unnecessary, and it may be now that the bay window developed at the expense of these small secluded rooms. With further advance in glazing, the bay became a great window alone, a frame for the display of the owner's heraldic glass, and as such an embellishment of the great hall, an integral part of it, instead of a separate entity. Polygonal now, to catch the light at various angles, rather than square in plan, these window projections were added to older halls, such as that of the bishops at Lincoln, bringing them up to date. They were not only placed at the dais end of the hall, but also adorned the great chamber wing, often lighting both floors of this, as at South Petherton [48] and Lytes Cary.[67]

As early as the 14th century, indeed, there had been a development towards the bay window in the lowering of the sill of the window at the dais end of the hall. In some great buildings, where the windows came low, as at Mayfield or Penshurst, this was of course unnecessary, but in others the windows were set higher, to allow room for a side bench below, and it was convenient to have a lower window at the dais end. This was not only to give more light to the high table but also, and especially, so that the master of the house could see what was happening in the courtyard. It was realized that a view of the hall entrance was needed, hence the projection with just a small side opening or spyhole, then one similar to the main window, and so to the final development of the great bay window in the late 15th and 16th centuries.

The beginning of this process is seen at Nassington,[3] and there remain many examples

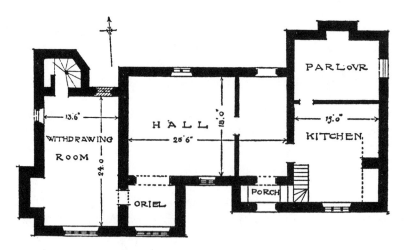

Fig. 39. Kingston Seymour Manor House, plan.

Fig. 40. Kingston Seymour Manor House, *c.* 1470–80, withdrawing-room
(great parlour), interior.

of miniature windows, often re-used elsewhere, as at Burford, which may have served as such squints to control the entrance. At Wanswell Manor, of the mid 15th century, the parlour projects with the original spyhole in position.

There are several mid or late 14th-century halls in which a lengthening of the dais window can be observed, such as Beetham Hall (*c.* 1340). The same arrangement is found at Preston Plucknett * in the early 15th century. In St Cross the hall windows are stepped up in length, but all have a transom, and Grevil's House at Chipping Campden has the tall window in a slight projection. At Woodland's Manor the dais window has been lengthened further recently.

In the hall at Croydon Palace, remodelled by Archbishop Stafford (1443–52), there remains the moulded arch of an oriel, of which the original window has been replaced by a sash. Pugin in 1838 shows it with three pointed lights similar to the others, one of which is set above it, the range of windows here allowing for tapestry below (Pl. 7 A and B). The oriel arch resembles the rear arch of these but is longer, extending to dais level. This 'bay window' seems to have projected beyond the wall thickness, but was of only one storey because of the tier of windows above. Though the end wall of the hall did once project further than the buttresses, an entrance from oriel to solar block was unnecessary, owing to the existing doorway at the other end of the wall. Indeed this oriel may be considered as one of the first bay windows, as distinct from the oriel chambers.[24]

Position

The oriel chambers seem always to have been at the upper end of the hall, one side a continuation of the end wall of the latter, except at Caister where room is left for the entrance to the north-west tower. The bay windows, however, vary considerably in position, and although some are in the usually accepted place in line with the high table in the dais bay, many are found in the second or even third bay from the end wall.

From earlier examples such as Croydon and Ockwells (*c.* 1465) to Hampton Court (1530–5) the bay window lights the dais from the end of a lateral wall. This is approximately the position at Gainsborough,[44] where a stone oriel of particular interest is not the same build as the timber hall it serves, definite proof of its insertion being found in the recent restoration of the latter.† The hall was a rebuild of the earlier house of Sir Thomas de Burgh, a noted Yorkist, which was destroyed by the Lancastrians in 1470. Sir Thomas died in 1480; his son, bearing the same name, was a Knight of the Body to Richard III, and entertained his lord at Gainsborough in 1484. It may be that the fashionable oriel was added then to a rebuilt hall slightly earlier in date. It is of irregular plan, clearly an addition made to fit, and a curious feature is the side doorway, with lion ornament (Pl. XVII D) (re-set), which traditionally should lead into the private wing, but here gives on to the open. Did it once lead to an outside staircase or passage to the solar block? The presence of a window, with sill higher to suit the doorway, seems evidence against its being designed to serve a rebuilt private wing. Professor Hamilton Thompson considered

---

* The dais window has been restored to its original size.
† Information kindly supplied by Mr H. W. Brace, F.R.Hist.S., president of the Friends of the Old Hall Association.

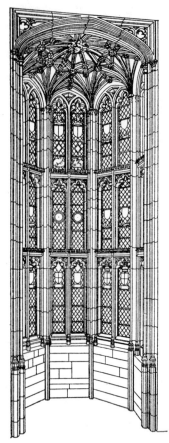

Fig. 41. Crosby Hall (1466 +),
interior of the oriel.

the oriel an addition of *c.* 1500 to a hall of *c.* 1480, and indeed its vault is akin to that of Athelhampton (*c.* 1495–1500), though the sub-cusped windows could be earlier; in which case it might be a remnant of the hall destroyed in 1470, or even brought, for re-use *c.* 1480, from somewhere else, like the bay window at Compton Wynyates, brought from the destroyed house of Fulbroke.

The bay window at South Wingfield (1440–59) is not quite at the end of the hall, so as to allow room for steps down to the undercroft,[23] and at Athelhampton the dais edge is in line with the upper wall of the oriel, continuing as a step to the side doorway of the latter.[51] This is also the position at the Commandery, Worcester: here a dais entrance adjoins the oriel doorway at right angles, both giving access to a lobby and the private apartments.[53] Eltham Palace (*c.* 1479–80) (Pl. XIX c) has two opposite projections in the second bay, with access to a lobby sited in the end one leading to the private rooms.[42] This bay is used at Horham Hall (1502–5) for a similar reason, the first one containing a doorway approaching the private wing by means of a slanting passage, treated like a second bay window.[57] The same position applies at Fawsley (Pl. XXII B),[70] perhaps to give an isolated and more imposing effect externally, for this oriel is tower-like, with an extra storey; like Ockwells it has its own dais within. At Corpus Christi (1517) and Christ Church (1525–9) Oxford, a like position is found, as at Cowdray (*c.* 1525). In Crosby Hall (1466) the oriel is off the third bay from the end, opposite the fireplace, so as to allow access to the parlour, which adjoins the hall at right angles, and is reached by an elaborate entrance.[31]

Plan

The oriel chamber had usually been rectangular, but when emphasis became laid on the window and a large expanse of glass, the plan with canted sides grew popular. One of the earliest remaining is at South Wingfield, and others with three sides * include Queens' College, Cambridge (1448–9),[25] and Magdalen (1476)[37] and Brasenose (1512) Colleges, Oxford.[61] The five-sided oriel, possibly somewhat later in development, is found at Crosby Hall (Fig. 41) and Athelhampton, while an imposing example in two storeys lights the prior's lodging at Watton, Yorkshire;[49] this plan lent itself to the umbrella type of vault with central boss. The rectangular oriel, however, is used in the timber-framed

---

* i.e. the projection beyond the wall thickness. The latter would give the three-sided oriel five sides within.

Fig. 42. Oriels at Thornbury Castle.

Ockwells,[30] Eltham Palace (two oriels each of two vaulted bays) and Corpus Christi, Oxford (1517);[62] at the highest level it seems to have supplanted the polygonal oriel in the early 16th century. Wolsey's great hall at Christ Church (1525–9)[64] and Henry VIII's at Hampton Court (1530–5)[68] were given oblong oriels and two bays of fan vaulting. For the latter this was a more convenient plan.

The early 16th century is noted for several bay windows of great beauty and intricacy. In the Duke of Buckingham's great house, Thornbury Castle (1511–22) there is a remarkable window, which might be called of half-stellar plan, with three angular projections like the cutwaters of a bridge; on the higher stage these are curved to give a fluted or scalloped plan to the window (Fig. 42).[60] This multiangular oriel, or window of 'star polygonal plan',* had already been used in Henry VII's Tower (1498–1500) at Windsor Castle,[52] there angular on both (upper) floors, designed by Robert Janyns, junior. With Robert Vertue and John Lebon, Janyns was also a King's Master Mason concerned with Henry's great chapel at Westminster (1503–19) completed by his son Henry VIII. Here the east windows have the same triangular projections on a semi-octagon, and the side windows three intersecting curves, like both features at Thornbury. There were similar windows at Richmond Palace, built after the destruction by fire in 1497 of the old palace of Shene, and it has been suggested that Janyns was the mason in charge here and that he furnished the design for Thornbury, although we do not hear of him after 1506, when the will of one Robert Janyns of Burford was proved.† Certainly this type of window occurs in buildings associated with him, and as might be expected from its intricacy, it was not easily copied and hence was a short-lived fashion.

The oblong bay window continued into the Elizabethan and Jacobean ‡ periods, and there is a good example of 1562–8 at Loseley Park in Surrey. At Littlecote (Wiltshire), rather earlier in date, one hall window comes down to ground level like the usual bay window, but the recess does not project externally. The three-sided bay window is also popular, and many serve several floors.

Oriel Arches

At Clevedon a two-centred arch of two chamfered orders leads from the hall into the oriel chamber, and similar arches remain at Aston Eyre and Bradley Manor (c. 1419), the latter with moulded imposts carved with foliage. At Bewley Court the arch is hollow chamfered. The arch is moulded and two-centred at Tickenham Court, moulded and segmental at Norrington Manor,[17] at South Wingfield segmental-pointed, heavily moulded, but here the jambs are plain. Gainsborough Old Hall has a moulded arch of elliptical form and hood with out-turned ends. The four-centred arch, steep with traceried panels, at Kenilworth, becomes the form usual in the 15th century, as at South Wraxall and Great Chalfield. There is a wide example at Nevill Holt (Pl. 7 c), with tablet flowers to the hollow chamfer, and three great carved bosses on the arch. At Cowdray the arch rests on moulded corbels.

A square frame to the four-centred arch is often found, with carved spandrels, a quatre-foil at Crosby Hall, Wolsey's arms at Christ Church, and a rose at Hampton Court. This seems a feature of later, more elaborate, houses, continuing to the mid 16th century.

Frequently the jambs are shafted, continuing the mouldings of the head. There may be one slender column a side, like Great Chalfield, or a group of three as at Crosby Hall. At Athelhampton the three shafts are separated, supporting the outer and inner order and a middle rib on the soffit of the arch; an additional column of larger scale serves a covering arch on the hall side.

A feature of the 'Perpendicular period' is the great use of rectangular panels with cusped heads, similar to blind window lights. This stone panelling was much used in the soffits

---

* Harvey (1947), 130, pls. 141, 142.   † Harvey (1954), 147.
‡ 'Jacobethan'—the happy invention of Mr E. T. Long, F.S.A.

and jambs of window arches, particularly those of bay formation, where the deep embrasures offered especial scope, as did the great tower arches of churches. Indeed this method was particularly effective in oriels, as the window lights were thus continued, as blind tracery, round the recess, sometimes part of the window being glazed and the other lights filled in, according to convenience. In Crosby Hall the twin side lights are similar to the main ones, with cinquefoiled heads and two battlemented transoms; at Christ Church, as at Hampton Court, the returns of the oriel have each a three-light, like the part in the main face.

At Horham Hall there is not room for an oriel arch; instead the inner jambs are treated with narrower panels, trefoiled also at the base, otherwise resembling the four tiers in the wall thickness, each of two trefoil-headed panels and like the window lights, with a quatrefoil over the uppermost tier.

But other, later, oriels do not follow the window design so closely, though the same horizontals are used. At Cowdray and Fawsley the arch jambs are cusped, whereas the window tracery is not. The Cowdray arch has an embattled string-course between the five tiers of the jamb, and the panels also trefoiled at the ends of the actual soffit. At Fawsley the head of the upper (third) tier turns into the four-centred arch where similar panels are cusped at both ends.

Indeed the oriel arch to a bay window is becoming a separate entity, as it was to the separate 'oriel chambers'. These still persist, as at Lytes Cary, which has an arrangement similar to that at Fawsley, but lower and with more elaborate tracery. The earlier oriel arches at Little Sodbury also have a stone panelled soffit. By the middle of the 16th century, in the hall of the London Charterhouse [72] the treatment of the soffit, cusped panelling continuing down the jambs, makes no attempt to match the window transoms, and the oriel arch is now an entirely separate composition.

At Fawsley the lofty oriel is vaulted below a turret chamber. But usually where there was another room above, as at Nevill Holt, a flat ceiling would be used. Here there are pairs of quatrefoils in the panels formed by the moulded beams, matching a similar ornament in the windows; the beams have carved bosses at their intersection. The boarded ceiling was also used in wooden oriels such as the Commandery at Worcester, where it is enriched with moulded beams and foliage bosses; at Ordsall Hall in Lancashire it is plainer with a central shield.

The bay window was normally vaulted from the latter part of the 15th century onwards, this being increasingly the case where funds would permit. At Great Chalfield the square oriels are treated like a porch, with an intermediate vault, though there is only a central boss, which is heraldic, instead of the usual ones at each intersection, as in the porch vault here. However, the twin bays to the oblong oriels at Eltham have no less than forty carved bosses to the lierne vault. In Crosby Hall this is further developed into a stellar vault, with converging ribs from the four angles of the oriel, and the apex of each window, two ranges of lierne (linking) ribs forming an umbrella or star shape in the crown. The arrangement of these with their bosses is beginning to form a fan. A large central boss contains Sir John Crosby's helm and crest.

A central pendant with converging ribs, but not producing a fan, is the type used at

Gainsborough. Here, as at Crosby Hall, the ribs rise from the apex and springing of the window arches, but at Athelhampton, otherwise similar, the ribs rise only from between the windows, continuing the line of their shafts, and swell to a lozenge form midway in their curve to meet in a central floral boss.

The fan vault was popular in the late 15th and early 16th centuries. It was used by Dean Gunthorpe (1472–98) at Wells, with a scroll with shields placed longitudinally between the fans, of which the end ones are modified to fit the three-sided plan (Pl. 9).[41] But the oblong oriel was simpler for this fashionable vault, and perhaps influenced the plan at Christ Church and Hampton Court. At Fawsley the fans are fitted into a five-sided bay window.

Sometimes the oriel served a first-floor room, as in the Hall and Great Watching Chamber [68] at Hampton Court, and the Deanery at Wells (Pl. 8). But here it was supported on a basement, and not corbelled out from the wall, as is the case with what we now call the oriel window. These upper oriels, corbelled out, became increasingly popular, not only adding to the light and accommodation of the chamber, but providing an opportunity for decoration, heraldic and otherwise, as a great feature of the Tudor elevation, on both stone and wooden buildings. In later examples the ground-floor windows were similarly treated, each with slight projection and moulded corbel, such as those (restored) at Paycocke's, Coggeshall.

In stone and brick, the oriel might be continued to ground level, as a double composition, to serve the parlour also. This is the centrepiece of an end wall at South Petherton (Pl. XX B) and may be compared with a larger five-sided projection, really an oriel chamber, in the contemporary Old Rectory, Walton, in the same county,[47] or with that at Lytes Cary (c. 1530) on a lateral wall, centrally placed. In later 16th-century houses this was a favourite treatment of the façade, each projection having a separate gable. Earlier that century the oriel became a popular adjunct to the room over a gatehouse arch, as at South Wraxall and, two-storeyed, at Eton College. The same treatment might be used for porches such as the tower-like entrance at Forde (c. 1528) [66] and Cerne (c. 1497–1509) [54] Abbeys in Dorset. Holcombe Court in Devon (c. 1520–30) has three levels of projection, but here the treatment is plainer.

Oriels were sometimes used in churches, not only as a vestry window (Adderbury, Oxfordshire), but even projecting internally as a private pew. At St Bartholomew the Great, Prior Bolton built one filling a treforium arch in the choir, and there is a royal example in a similar position, but on the north side, at St George's Chapel, Windsor. This is of elaborate wooden construction, built to enable Queen Catherine of Aragon to view the Garter service. In the adjoining bay a stone oriel serves the chantry chapel over the tomb of Edward IV.

At first the 'upper' oriels might seem covered balconies or 'ears' stuck on to the external wall, rather as an afterthought. Perhaps one of the earliest surviving occurs on the inner face of the great gatehouse at Thornton Abbey, Lincolnshire, licensed in 1382 (Pls. XVIII B, XXX B). This has the appearance of a separate little attachment, though apparently of similar build. Internally there is a richly moulded wall arch, opening out of an 'oriel chamber' over the main archway, and which itself projects through a great four-centred arch from the main first-floor room of the gatehouse. Thus we have oriel chamber and oriel window combined.[13]

Plate XXI. Oriels.

A. (East) Coker Court, interior of oriel chamber; mid 15th century. B. Lytes Cary, view of hall through oriel arch of c. 1530.

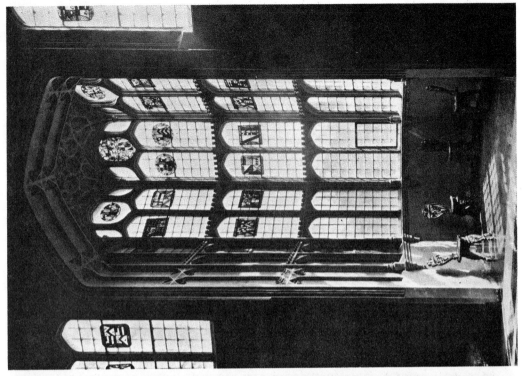

Plate XXII. Oriels. A. Oriel at Athelhampton Hall; *c.* 1495–1500. B. Oriel at Fawsley Manor House; *c.* 1537–42.

A separate roof to the oriel is also present in the mid 15th-century example on the south gable of a vicar's dwelling at Wells, and in two others, one restored, at Great Chalfield, but by now they form an integral part of the structure, as well as an important decorative feature to the wings. In the *c.* 1495 reconstruction at Bradley Manor [18] a central third gable was added to the frontage, incorporating the porch projection. This was embellished with a three-sided oriel, while those of the wings are rectangular (Pl. XIX A). All are traceried, and surmounted by battlements, as in the Gothic revival oriel further south. Later the projections were further absorbed into the main building, and carried up to the parapet of the roof, as at Thornbury Castle. However, separate oriel roofs persisted, as on the bay window of Hengrave Hall (1525–38),[65] which, like Athelhampton, has its own crenellated parapet apart from the main battlement.* At Lytes Cary (*c.* 1530) the parapet of the two-storeyed oriel surmounts the eaves of the main roof; but in a similar projection at Sutton Place in Surrey (1523–7) the parapet, here of terracotta, is one with that of the whole range, this incorporating panels of the same design.

In plan the oriel is generally three-sided like a simple type of bay window, with canting lights similar to those, often more numerous, on the outer face. In smaller projections there may be a single transomed light in each side, as at Bradley Manor, where indeed the other oriels are rectangular projections with a large two-light window only. There are instances of a semicircular plan at Castle Acre (*c.* 1500) (Pl. XX C and D) [50] and the Great Watching Chamber of Hampton Court. At Conway, Buckler illustrated a double oriel of this type, and the half-round plan continued into the early 17th century in houses such as Bramshill (Hampshire) and Chantermarle in Dorset. The fluted outline occurs in the gatehouse to Hengrave Hall,[65] and, accompanied by the stellar plan, at Thornbury Castle.

Except for the corbelling, where present, the treatment of an oriel is akin to that of a bay window in the modern sense, and they may be classed together. The roof may be semi-pyramidal, as at Thornton (where it is ribbed), and the gatehouse at South Wraxall.[20] It may be surmounted by a finial or a heraldic plaque. The parapet may be simply crenellated, but often it is a vehicle for elaborate decoration. There are ornate finials to the miniature buttresses separating the cinquefoiled lights of the oriel at Lincoln Castle. This came from the so-called John of Gaunt's Palace, which was more likely the residence of the de Sutton family.[33] † At Wells the vicar's dwelling [26] has a frieze of tablet flower and crenellation while the solar (eastern) oriel at Great Chalfield has a richly foliated cresting. The Deanery at Wells has a deep parapet with trefoil-headed panels to the merlons, and below four large cinquefoiled panels with shields bearing devices, separated by buttresses which terminate as crenellated finials.[41] At Lytes Cary there is a frieze of quatrefoils below the battlements, as at Brympton D'Evercey, where it is continued round the building. A separate gable is common where the oriel, set laterally, is of wood.

A cornice is less often found in the bay window to the hall, where there is room for the

---

* The Athelhampton bay window does not fit properly and may have been an expensive afterthought during building. This is the opinion of the owner, Mr. R. V. Cooke, Ch.M., F.R.C.S.

† The arms of John of Gaunt on the house were probably placed there by John de Sutton (d. 1391), who held lands from the Duke of Lancaster (who may have been his patron). But most of the house dated, like the oriel, from the 15th century. Hill (1948), 167–8.

window to have arched heads with tracery above the lights. Often they are longer versions, with one or more transoms, of the ordinary windows, as at Crosby Hall, where the upper level of the hood is maintained throughout. At Athelhampton the windows differ, the oriel lights having ogee heads with uncusped tracery, whereas the others are four-centred in a square head; this is one reason for believing the oriel to be of slightly different date.[51]

In the upper oriels the arch is commonly contained in a square head below the cornice. But at South Petherton, where the projection serves two floors, the higher windows have definite arched heads, like those of a hall bay, with elaborate tracery over three cinque-foiled lights on the face, two on each canting side.[48] In the Deanery at Wells there are still separate two-light transomed windows with cinquefoiled lights and tracery, two on the face, one on each side, but each main arch is set in a square frame (Pl. 8). The adjoining oriel, west of this, has one great traceried four-light in the face of each storey. The square frame is emphasized in the eastern oriel at Great Chalfield, where the cusping is confined to the panelling below, and the western oriel is still plainer, without a common arch to the lights. However, there is tracery over the cinquefoiled lights in the straight heads of the oriels at Bradley Manor, as well as in the oriel added by Bishop Rotherham (1471–90) at Newark Castle.[34]

Indeed the square framework encourages the substitution of a horizontal arrangement—tiers of lights instead of the earlier grouping of two- or three-light windows. This is notice-able at Thornton Abbey and might be evidence that this oriel is a 15th-century addition (resembling, indeed, one of that date at West Tanfield Castle, Yorkshire),[35] and having two rows of six cinquefoiled lights with crenellation, grouped equally on each face. In the oriel at Purse Caundle Manor in Dorset, probably dating from the third quarter of the 15th century, there is one row of long cinquefoiled-headed lights, two in the front, one on each side, with panelling below.[32] At Thornbury Castle the scalloped oriel of the great chamber has four tiers of sixteen trefoil-headed lights, and there are three of eight round-headed lights to the star-shaped projection below. Other oriels on the south front have four rows of ten, and three of six lights respectively.[60] There are four tiers of six four-centred lights in the Great Watching Chamber at Hampton Court. One row of eight similar lights serves each floor of the oriel in the parlour wing at Lytes Cary.

This window arrangement in tiers of lights is noticeable in the bay windows of later halls. There are six tiers of eight four-centred lights at Cowdray,[63] and at Horham Hall a row of quatrefoils surmounts four tiers of eight trefoiled lights.[57] In the great hall at Hampton Court there are six tiers, but the four-centred lights are grouped in threes, with a common arch to fit the fan vault within. In the oriel at Raglan Castle,[73] refashioned c. 1570, only the highest tier is trefoiled, the other three having square heads, like the bay windows of late 16th-century houses; another late feature is the narrowness of the face (two lights) to the sides of the oriel, which have three lights in each row.

Unlike the bay window, near ground level, the upper oriel gave opportunity for panelled decoration below the lights. Sometimes the panels were blind versions of lights, with cinquefoiled or trefoiled heads. The South Wraxall panels are trefoiled, a contrast to the cinquefoiled lights above. But they might be square and traceried, like a tomb chest, as in the vicar's dwelling at Wells.

These panels often contained the arms or devices of the owner. The vicar's oriel has a plain shield in each traceried panel, but in the Deanery at Wells a full record is given. Below each coupled window of the oriel there is one wide cinquefoil-headed panel, thus four in all, like those of the cornice. Each contains a shield *à bouche* * of undulating outline, in which is displayed either the rebus (a gun with strap or scroll) of John Gunthorpe (dean 1472–98), or the sun in splendour, badge of Edward IV. Great guns also protrude below the upper panels.[41] At Purse Caundle the shields are also of late type, with concave sides, possibly painted originally; whilst at South Petherton each panel, again cinquefoiled, encloses not only a shield with fluted outline, but one of the earlier 'flat-iron' type below. Small examples of the latter are often used in a quatrefoil frieze, as on each floor of the porch oriel at Cerne Abbas. In such a double oriel serving two storeys, the panels may mark a floor division, as at South Petherton; this is apparently the case at Grevil's House, Chipping Campden, where the cusping is reversed from that of the lights, comparable to the 'inverted bay window' in a 15th-century range at Worcester College, Oxford. There are plain shields in panels dividing off the upper storey of the bay window at Nevill Holt.[36]

An impressive effect is achieved when the portion below the lights, the 'apron wall', is treated as one heraldic composition. This is found in the Warden's Lodgings of the two Cambridge foundations of Henry VII's mother, Lady Margaret Beaufort, Countess of Richmond and Derby: Christ's College (1505–11)[58] and St John's (1511–16).[59] In both, the oriel of the chamber which she occupied on her visits remains and on it her coat of arms is displayed, with its Yale † supporters, on the sides the Tudor rose and portcullis, royally crowned, and the background, as on the gatehouse, adorned with her daisies and germander speedwell (*souvenez-vous-de-moi*), referring to her motto *souvent me souvient*. Perhaps it was from one of these oriels ‡ that she 'saw the dean call a faulty scholar to correction; to whom she said "*Lente, lente* [gently, gently], Mr Dean" as accounting it better to mitigate his punishment than procure his pardon'.

Below, the oriels are often boldly corbelled out with deep mouldings, sometimes with further panelling, which may be gathered into a fan. There was a double fan and oriel, flanked by shields and tracery, in a house at Conway of which the Buckler drawing survives.§ Frequently coving is used with the owner's or patron's arms and devices displayed. An important citizen's house at Thaxted, again in wood, displays the arms of Edward IV, with lion and bull supporters (painted), while at Newport, also in Essex, an early 16th-century house, 'Monk's Barn', has the Coronation of the Virgin with angel musicians carved below the oriel of one jettied wing.

There is the additional support of a flat buttress at Great Chalfield, Bradley Manor and Castle Acre. In some cases this may have been added later.

Bay windows in wood remain in such 15th-century halls as Ockwells, and at Potterne Manor, Wiltshire, there is elaborate tracery.[38] Judging from documents as well as survivals here and there, timber oriels in one or two storeys must have been a feature of the

---

* With carved notch in the dexter chief for the lance to project.
† A heraldic composite animal, like a spotted deer with swivelling horns. She inherited these supporters with the manor of Kendal from her cousin the Duke of Bedford, brother of Henry V.
‡ Or from the window of her chamber overlooking the upper end of the hall. Fuller (1840), *History of Cambridge*, 182.
§ Reproduced in Crossley (1951), fig. 172.

town house from the 14th century onwards. We may visualize streets of 15th- and 16th-century wooden houses with such slightly projecting windows, ornamented with carved frieze and moulded corbelling, buildings of such attraction as Thomas Paycocke's house at Coggeshall or the Guildhall of 1525 at Lavenham. Alston Court, at Nayland in Suffolk, is one of the richest examples, the home of a cloth merchant, and the earliest part, *c*. 1472, has oriels on both storeys, those to the parlour being especially elaborate with tracery also in frieze and transom, and a sill deeply carved with beasts in scrollwork. The courtyard one has, in addition, an ornate bressumer above it, with animals and humorous figures in the running ornament.[40] The Golden Cross at Oxford retains one range of plainer oriel windows dating from the 15th century.

In country houses, too, the oriels were used. Agecroft Hall from Lancashire is now in Richmond, West Virginia. Parker's illustration shows a perfect example dating from the early 16th century (Pl. 10 A). Besides the elaborate oriel of semicircular plan, over the entrance, there were three others on each floor, all crenellated, with various traceried ornament below the lights.[55] Another Lancastrian timbered house of similar period, Ordsall Hall, is preserved by Salford Corporation. The seven-sided hall oriel has tracery on the transom internally, with a band of quatrefoils on the stone base. Another oriel, to an upper floor, has coving enriched with quatrefoil and panelling.[56]

ORIELS

No. / Date	Name	Type	Plan	Position	Storeys	Internal opening	Vault	References (most with illustrations)
(1) C 13th	Documentary evidence in Liberate Rolls	porch to external staircase, etc.			1 & 2		—	see footnotes in text.
(2) 1237–9	Westminster Palace (drawings)	vestibule		angle between solar & chapel		two-centred shafted doorway	—	J. T. Smith (1837) *Antiquities of Westminster*, reproduced in M.O.W. (1963), 122, plan III, pls. 28, 29.
(3) 1st half C 13th	Prebendal Manor House, Nassington, Northants.	slight projection with squint	oblong	3' from end wall	1	segmental-pointed	—	Wood (1950), 49–50 (plan).
(4) 1286	Conway Castle, Caern., evidence	solar oriel			1		—	see footnote ‡, p. 102.
(5) early C 14th	Prudhoe Castle, Northum.	altar recess to chapel over gateway	half-hexagon, irregular	E-end	1	two-centred chancel arch	—	Parker (1853), 206.
(6) C 14th	Aston Eyre Manor House, Salop	oriel chamber with access to staircase	oblong	end bay	1	two-centred arch of two chamfered orders	—	Faulkner (1958), 170–171 (plan).
(7) c. 1320	Clevedon Court, Som.	oriel chamber below chapel	oblong	end bay	2	two-centred arch of two chamfered orders	—	*Country Life* (6), 17, 18.
(8) c. 1320	'Abbot's Grange', Broadway, Worcs.	oriel chamber below chapel	oblong	end bay	2	doorway	—	*V.C.H. Worcs*, IV, 34–36 (plan).
(9) c. 1325	Southwick Hall, Northants.	oratory recess	oblong-slight	gable end	1st floor projection	chamfered two-centred rear arch	—	*Country Life* (26), 1239–1240, figs. 1, 11 (plan).
(10) c. 1340	Northborough Manor, Northants.	staircase oriel	oblong	end wall	2	doorway	—	Parker (1853), 254–5 (plan).
(11) c. 1340	Stanton's Farm, Black Notley, Ess.	hall bay window	three-sided	second bay	1	—	—	Smith (1955), 81; R.C.H.M. *Essex*, II, 19–20 (plan).
(12) c. 1341–8	Penshurst Place, Kent	staircase oriel	polygonal (four-sided)	end bay	2	two-centred doorway	—	Lloyd (1931), 187, 188, 450 (plan).
(13) 1382	Thornton Abbey, Lincs.	gatehouse oriel chamber and oriel	oblong + three-sided	inner face	1	moulded four-centred arch	ribbed barrel	M.O.W. Guide (40), 10–11 (plan); Evans (1949), pl. 59.
(14) 1390–3	Kenilworth Castle, War., hall range	3 oriel chambers	oblong, four-sided, octagonal	end bay, etc.	2	steep four-centred arch with traceried spandrels	below (hall), etc.	Pugin (1839), pls. 16–18, 21; M.O.W. Guide (23) (plan).
(15) c. 1400	Tickenham Court, Som., oriel chamber evidence	oriel chamber	square	end bay	1	moulded arch (blocked)	—	Parker (1859), 344.

		Type	Plan	Position	Storys	Internal opening	Vault	References (most with illustrations)
(16) c. 1400	Grevil's House, Chipping Campden, Glos.	hall bay window	three-sided	end bay	2	—	—	Garner & Stratton (1929), 39, pl. XV.
(17) early C 15th	Norrington Manor, Wilts.	oriel chamber	—	end bay		segmental moulded arch		
(18) c. 1420	Bradley Manor, Devon.	oriel chamber	oblong originally	end bay	1	two-centred arch with carved imposts		National Trust Guide (1); Country Life (4).
(19) c. 1420	South Wraxall Manor, Wilts.	hall 2 oriel chambers	oblong	end bay	2	four-centred moulded arch		Pugin (1840), pls. 57, 68; Garner & Stratton (1929), pl. XII.
(20) early C 16th	South Wraxall Manor, Wilts.	gatehouse oriel						Pugin (1840), pls. 8, 9.
(21) c. 1431–42	Minster Lovell Hall, Oxon.	staircase oriel, etc.	square	end bay	3	doorway		M.O.W. Guide (28) (plan).
(22) 1432–46	Caister Castle, Norf.	oriel chamber	square	not quite at end to leave room for doorway	4	arch		Simpson & Barnes (1952), 39, pl. XX A (plan).
(23) 1440–59	South Wingfield Manor, Derbys.	hall bay window	three-sided	not quite at end to leave room for doorway	1	segmental-pointed moulded arch	—	Thompson (1912), 346 349 (plan).
(24) c. 1443–52	Croydon Palace, Sy.	hall bay window		end bay	1	four-centred arch moulded	—	Pugin (1838), pl. 39.
(25) 1448–9	Queens' College, Cambridge	hall bay window	three-sided	second bay	1	four-centred with moulded head and shafted jambs	lierne	R.C.H.M. Cambridge, 172, pl. 221 (plan).
(26) mid C 15th	Vicar's Close, Wells (south end)	solar oriel	three-sided	gable end		—	panelled soffit	Pugin (1840), pls. 5, 6.
(27) mid C 15th	(East) Coker Court, Som.	oriel chamber	square	end bay	1		—	Country Life (7a).
(28) after 1457	West Coker Manor, Som.	? staircase oriel	square	end bay	1	doorway	—	Country Life (30), 470 (plan).
(29) before 1463	Ashleworth Court, Glos.	oriel chamber including staircase	nearly square	end bay	2	wide arch		
(30) c. 1465	Ockwells Manor, Bray, Berks.	hall bay window	oblong	end bay	1	flat wooden arch	—	Lloyd (1931), fig. 603.
(31) 1466+	Crosby Hall, London	hall bay window	five-sided	third bay opposite fireplace	1	four-centred arch, square frame with shafted jamb	stellar or 'umbrella'	Garner & Stratton (1929), pl. CLXXI.
(32) prob. 3rd quarter C 15th	Purse Caundle Manor, Dor.	solar oriel	five-sided	gable wall	1			Oswald (1935).
(33) C 15th	Lincoln Castle, oriel from 'John of Gaunt's Palace'	solar oriel	five-sided	reset	1			

(No.)	Date	Place	Oriel / Window	Plan	Position	No.	Arch	Vault	Reference
(34)	c. 1471–80	Newark Castle, Notts.	solar oriel	three-sided	lateral wall	1			Lloyd (1931), 334.
(35)	C 15th	West Tanfield Castle, Yorks.	gatehouse oriel	square		1		panelled with quatrefoils	Garner & Stratton (1929), 184, pl. CXLVIII.
(36)	c. 1470	Nevill Holt, Leics.	hall bay window	four-sided		2	four-centred with carved bosses		
(37)	1476	Magdalen College, Oxford	hall bay window	three *-sided	end bay	1	four-centred arch-ribbed on the soffit		R.C.H.M. Oxford, 73, pl. 128.
(38)	later C 15th	Porch House, Potterne, Wilts.	hall bay window	oblong, slight projection	end bay	1			Garner & Stratton (1929), pl. CLXVI
(39)	later C 15th	Bewley Court, Lacock, Wilts. (2 originally)	oriel chamber opening to staircase	square	end bay	1	two-centred arch, hollow chamfered		Brakspear (1912) 391, 396, (plan)
(40)	c. 1472	Alston Court, Nayland, Suff.	oriels to solar & parlour						Country Life (1).
(41)	c. 1472–98	The Deanery, Wells, Som.	oriel to great chamber	three-sided	central in lateral wall	1	four-centred arch	fan	Pugin (1839), pls. 45–48; Godfrey (1950) (plan).
(42)	c. 1479–80	Eltham Palace, Kent	hall 2 bay windows	oblong	4′ 3″ from end wall	1	four-centred moulded arch with shafted jambs	lierne (2 bays)	Pugin (1838), pls. 43, 44, 46, 47 (plan).
(43)	c. 1470–80	Kingston Seymour Manor House, Som., evidence	oriel chamber	square	end bay	2	arch		Garner & Stratton (1929), 27–8.
(44)	c. 1480	Gainsborough Old Hall, Lincs.	hall bay window	irregular five-sided	end bay	1	elliptical moulded arch with hood	stellar or 'umbrella'	Garner & Stratton (1929), pl. IX; Brace (1954) (plan).
(45)	c. 1480	Great Chalfield Manor House, Wilts.	2 oriel chambers	square	end bay	2	four-centred arch moulded and shafted	lierne	Pugin (1840), pls. 31, 32, 36; Garner & Stratton (1929), pl. XI.
			2 chamber oriels	semi-circular, & three-sided	gable walls	1	four-centred arch moulded and shafted	panelled	Pugin (1840), pls. 31, 33–5, 37, 38.
(46)	c. 1485	Little Sodbury Manor, Glos.	2 oriel chambers	square originally	end bay	2	arch		Archaeological Journal, LXXXVII (1930), 448 (plan).
(47)	late C 15th	The Old Rectory, Walton, Som.	oriel to solar & parlour	five-sided	gabled end	2			Pantin (1957), 134, 135–7, pl. XX (plan).
(48)	late C 15th	South Petherton Manor House, Som.	oriel to solar & parlour	three-sided	gabled	2			Garner & Stratton (1929), 29, pl. IX.
(49)	late C 15th	Watton Priory, Yorks., Prior's House	oriel to solar & parlour	five-sided	lateral wall	2			Crossley (1935), fig. 118; R. Gilyard-Beer (1958), fig. 18 (plan).
(50)	end C 15th	Castle Acre Priory, Norf., Prior's lodging		semi-circular (N.), oblong (W.)		1			M.O.W. Guide (8), 14 (plan); Crossley (1935), fig. 119.

* Not counting the wall thickness.

		Type	Plan	Position	Storeys	Internal opening	Vault	References (most with illustrations)
(51) c. 1495–1500	Athelhampton Hall, Dor.	hall bay window	five-sided	second bay	1	four-centred arch	stellar or 'umbrella'	Garner & Stratton (1929), 65–6, pl. XXXI; Country Life (2b), 836, 907.
(52) 1498–1500	Windsor Castle, Henry VII's Tower		star polygonal					Garner & Stratton (1929), 184; Harvey (1947), 130, pls. 141, 142.
(53) c. 1484–1503	The Commandery, Worcester	hall bay window	five-sided	bay next dais recess	1	wooden braces		Dollman & Jobbins (1861), pls. 35, 37 (plan).
(54) c. 1497–1509	Cerne Abbey, Dor.	porch oriel	three-sided	front	2			R.C.H.M. Dorset, I, 77, pl. 105 (plan).
(55) early C 16th	Agecroft Hall, Lancs., now in Richmond, W. Virginia, U.S.A.	entrance oriel and others	semi-circular & oblong					Parker (1859), 24, 213; Taylor (1884), pl. IX.
(56) early C 16th	Ordsall Hall, Lancs.	hall bay window	seven-sided	second bay			boarded ceiling	Garner & Stratton (1929), fig. 322; Taylor (1884), 50–1, pls. III, IX (plan).
(57) 1502–5	Horham Hall, Ess.	hall bay window	three-sided	opposite fireplace	1	panelled jambs		Garner & Stratton (1929), 112–13, pls. LXXII, CL (plan).
(58) 1505–11	Christ's College, Cambridge	warden's lodging oriel	three-sided		1			R.C.H.M. Cambridge, 33, pl. 92.
(59) 1511–16	St John's College, Cambridge	warden's lodging oriel	three-sided		1			R.C.H.M. Cambridge, 200, pl. 92.
(60) 1511–22	Thornbury Castle, Glos.	great chamber, etc. oriel	star polygonal, fluted, etc.	lateral wall	2			Garner & Stratton (1929), pl. XVII; Pugin (1839), pls. 30–2, 40; Parker (1859), 54.
(61) 1512	Brasenose College, Oxford	hall bay window	three-sided	end bay	1			R.C.H.M. Oxford, 24, 26, pl. 80 (plan).
(62) 1517	Corpus Christi College, Oxford	hall bay window	oblong	second bay	1	four-centred arch with panelled soffit		R.C.H.M. Oxford, 49, 51 (plan).
(63) c. 1520–30	Cowdray House, Suss.	hall bay window	oblong	second bay	1	panelled four-centred arch		Garner & Stratton (1929), 49–50, pls. XXIII, XXIV, CL (plan).
(64) 1525–9	Christ Church, Oxford	hall bay window	oblong	second bay	1	four-centred arch within square frame with shafted jambs	fan	R.C.H.M. Oxford, 33–34, pls. 83, 85 (plan).

(65) c. 1525–38	Hengrave Hall, Suff.	hall bay window	three-sided	first bay about 2' from end wall	1	panelled & traceried soffit	fan	Garner & Stratton (1929), 139, pl. XCIX (plan).
		gatehouse oriel	fluted					Garner & Stratton (1929), 139, pl. XCVIII.
(66) c. 1528	Forde Abbey, Dor.	porch oriel	three-sided	front	2	panelled & traceried soffit		R.C.H.M. Dorset, I, 244, pl. 186 (plan).
(67) c. 1530	Lytes Cary Manor House, Som.	2 oriel chambers	oblong	end bay	2	panelled four-centred arch		Garner & Stratton (1929), 47 (plan). Country Life (13).
1533		solar wing	three-sided	lateral wall	2	panelled four-centred arch		Garner & Stratton (1929), 47, pl. CXLIX (plan).
(68) 1530–5	Hampton Court, Middx	hall bay window	oblong	end bay	1	four-centred arch in square frame	fan–2 bays	R.C.H.M. Middlesex, 34, pl. 73; Garner & Stratton (1929). pl. CLXXIV.
1535	Great Watching Chamber		semi-circular	second bay	1		ribbed ceiling with pendants	R.C.H.M. Middlesex, 35, pl. 114; Garner & Stratton(1929),pl. CXLIX.
(69) 1534+	Poundisford Park, Taunton, Som.	2 oriel chambers	square	end bay	3	moulded four-centred arch		Garner & Stratton (1929), 82–3, pl. XLIV (plan).
(70) c. 1537–42	Fawsley Manor House, Northants.	hall bay window	five-sided	second bay opposite fireplace	2	panelled four-centred arch	stellar or 'umbrella'	Garner & Stratton (1929), 60 (plan); Braun (1940), pls. 19, 20.
(71) C 16th	Speke Hall, Lancs.	hall bay window & oriel chamber	five-sided rectangular	end bay				Garner & Stratton (1929), 167–8, pl. CXXX; Crossley (1951), 134–5, pls. 155, 156; Taylor (1884), 115, pl. XXXVI.
(72) mid C 16th	Charterhouse, London	hall bay window	oblong	end bay	1	panelled four-centred arch in square head		R.C.H.M. London, II, 23, 24, pl. 44 (plan).
(73) Refashioned c. 1570	Raglan Castle, Mon.	hall bay window	three-sided	end bay	1	moulded segmental		M.O.W. Guide (35), pl. VI; Pugin (1839), pl. 24.

8

Doorway Arrangement; the High Seat; the Chamber over the Service

Entrance Doorways

IN SAXON halls the main entrance might be sited on an end wall, or centrally in a side wall facing another doorway.* But by the 12th century it was normally placed in a side wall at the lower end of the hall, whether this was at ground- or first-floor level. It gave convenient access to service doorways sited in the end wall, and the high table could be far away at the other end, free from the bustle and traffic or even danger. Evidence of early date may be shown when the entrance is not at the extremity of a lateral wall, but several feet from the end as at Swanborough Manor House in Sussex (*c.* 1200).† Horton Court (*c.* 1140) is another case, but this was a prebendal house with its entrance in line with the priest's door in the church. From the latter part of the 12th century it was usually near the angle, and where this seems not to be the case, as at Christchurch and Godlingston Manor, Dorset, it is evidence that the hall block was subdivided, a timber partition once providing the end wall of the hall here and separating it from an adjoining apartment. In this corner position the end wall could provide one jamb of the doorway, or contain a recess into which the entrance door could be swung back, as at West Dean Rectory. At Jew's House, Lincoln (Pl. I B), the recess is segmental, at Little Wenham it has a quarter round head, chamfered. These recesses occur in other rooms as well.

* In the thegn's hall of *c.* 1010 excavated at Sulgrave Mr B. K. Davison has found lower end facing doorways with a screen between, and servery beyond. There was a raised dais, benches along the side walls and a central hearth.
  † Godfrey (1936) (plan).

Where there were no service quarters adjoining the hall, as in some halls of first-floor type, the entrance was in a similar position but occasionally placed in the end, not side, wall, though still near the angle. Hemingford Grey and King John's Hunting Box at Romsey are examples of this.

An unusual arrangement is found at the Jew's House and Aaron the Jew's House, both first-floor halls, at Lincoln. Here the main entrance is on the ground floor near the centre of the side wall facing the street, the hall chimney buttress being supported on the hood-mould of this doorway. This neat arrangement was possibly designed to do away with the need for an outside stair, at least on the street front. In Jew's House the present brick-lined passage denotes the site of earlier wooden partitions, as it leads to another and loftier round-headed doorway in the back wall. This is rebated internally, indicating the existence of an original wing, probably represented by the present annexe.* The family doubtless entered from the street by the elaborate ground-floor doorway, proceeded along a narrow passage between store or business rooms, and after leaving the main block by the north door entered an annexe from which wooden stairs led up to the north-east doorway of the hall above. A rebate in the east annexe wall suggests that this staircase mounted at right angles to the hall, on the lines of the present steps, otherwise it might have interfered with the round-headed doorway to the eastern part of the basement; this doorway is, unlike the hall entrance, several feet clear of the angle. Aaron's House, probably built by the same mason, has opposite the entrance a similar doorway, opening into a back portion, which is contemporary.

The single-storey hall was often built free on both sides to allow the maximum light, and set between two courts. Thus a second entrance would be necessary, opposite the main one, at the end of the 'entry', which became the screens passage. This lesser opening would give access to the stock and service department, the barn and brew house, and in some cases the kitchen court. As in the main entrance, the door-check would be external, unlike the opposite doorway at the Jews' Houses, which led into an annexe. The extra entrance would not suit a first-floor hall, as necessitating a second external staircase, and of course would be unnecessary in halls built, like Stokesay and Ludlow, against the curtain wall.

Such opposing doorways occur at Horton Court. Sutton Courtenay Norman hall has two doorways, but these are not in line. Among 13th-century houses opposite entrances are found at the Nassington Prebendal Manor House and in Barnston Manor, in the latter now formed into windows and not at the extreme end.

Some early halls, such as Oakham (c. 1190) and Warnford (c. 1210), could have no opposite entrance, owing to the siting of the staircase to the solar. Later this was adjusted. It is remarkable that an original window faces the hall entrance at Lincoln Palace (c. 1225), also at Ightham Mote (c. 1330), especially as this is in line with the postern, for at Bodiam the back doorway opens into the postern tower.

In the 14th century opposing entrances were normal, there being often, as at Haddon Hall, an upper and lower court. At Clevedon both entrances retain an original porch. Other examples include Northborough and Norrington Manors.

---

* At first-floor level the east wall of the annexe, which is crumbling, has either fallen inwards or is built against the east chamfer of the hall doorway in a manner suggesting its being of later build.

In the 15th century two entrances continue to be the custom, the back one often giving access to the kitchen situated at one side or across a court, as at Bowhill, where the kitchen entrance faces the back doorway of the hall.

South Wingfield has an unusual arrangement. The ground slopes down steeply beyond the hall, which is at the top of the second court, and its back entrance leads to a lobby which served as an oriel chamber, with access to the solar staircase, here at the service end, and also had steps down into the garden.

Service Doorways

The lower end wall is the position for service doorways opening out to the buttery and pantry adjoining. They have the door-check (are 'rebated') internally, and are at first usually two in number, set near the centre of the wall, in the 'nave' portion of an aisled hall, more and more close together until, as in the 13th-century building in Wenlock Priory, there is only room for a wooden partition between them on the service side. At Swalcliffe Manor the twin doorways are only one foot apart.

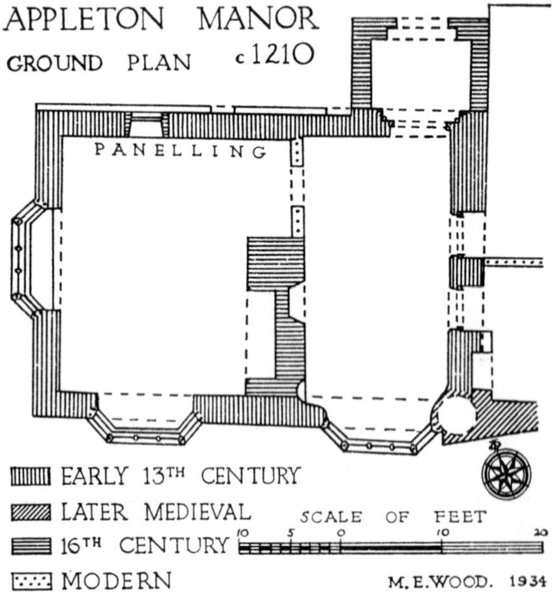

APPLETON MANOR
GROUND PLAN   c 1210

PANELLING

EARLY 13TH CENTURY
LATER MEDIEVAL   SCALE   OF   FEET
16TH CENTURY
MODERN   M.E.WOOD. 1934

Fig. 43.

Normally the two openings are treated in a similar fashion. At Appleton (c. 1210) (Pl. XXIII A; Fig. 43) they have roll-moulded hoods, at Little Chesterford roll-moulded orders with capitals, at Swalcliffe with head-stops to each hood. Double doorways are also found in the 14th century, as at Marlow Old Parsonage, and in the 15th century at South Wraxall.

Triple doorways, however, soon became fashionable, the central one giving on to a passage to the kitchen, a separate building as yet, owing to fear of fire. There were three service openings at Clarendon Palace, where the hall was built probably in 1176–7. The lower portions of these doorways have been excavated, and they show diagonal tooling, unlike the later vertically tooled ashlar of the porch added by Henry III in 1244. They are thus of the original period, though the butteries are structurally later, perhaps replacing earlier wooden buildings.* In Henry III's time the passage led to a cloister giving access to great kitchens to north and west and salsary to the south. So we can consider the triple service doorway as a late 12th-century arrangement in a hall of importance, which became normal.

At Hambledon Manor Farm, Hampshire, in the side wall of a block 36 × 18 feet, are two

* Borenius & Charlton (1936), 73, pl. XV, i.

arches and part of a third, apparently service doorways leading from a vanished hall to the butteries, with solar above. They appear to date from the late 12th or early 13th century.

At Lincoln Palace the central passage led over a bridge to the kitchen, necessitated by the fall of the ground (Fig. 44). Indeed here the solar-service block has a third, vaulted storey

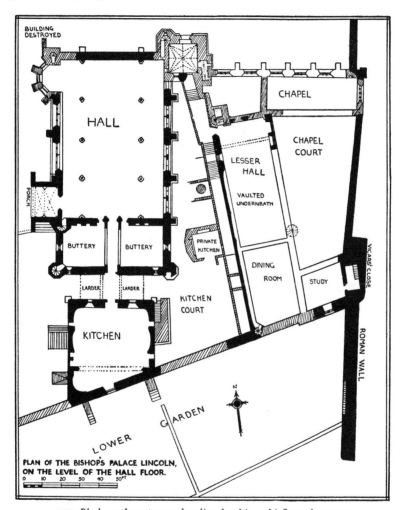

KEY: Black, 13th century and earlier; hatching, chiefly 15th century.

Fig. 44. This plan is subject to correction after work in progress by the Ministry of Works (1965).

below, and the kitchen is also raised on a subvault. Particularly attractive is the triple doorway arrangement here. Set in a square frame the doors form an architectural composition visible, between the speres, from the high table, evidence that the screen was not yet in being (Pl. XXIII B). Probably there was a similar triple centre-piece to another aisled hall of the bishops, at Wells.

There is an ingenious piece of planning at Chepstow Castle, where the service block in the lower bailey is arranged to serve two separate halls (*c.* 1280) (Fig. 45). The western hall, of which one good window survives to the court, has at its lower (porch) end the usual triple doorways, the southern buttery having a newel staircase in its angle with the porch, leading to a room with fireplace above the latter. The chamber over the whole wing was reached by a staircase blocking the entry (screens passage) at the back; being the edge of a cliff, no opposite doorway was needed. The garderobe opened opposite the staircase, situated in the angle with the other hall. The central passage here is a staircase down to the cross passage of the eastern hall, which is on a lower level, and has its own pantry and

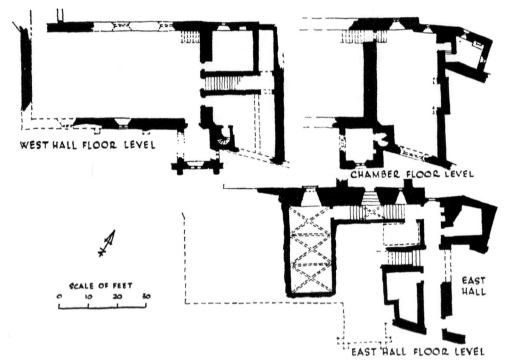

Fig. 45. Chepstow Castle, halls in lower bailey, plans. *See also* Pl. XII D.

buttery below those of the other. The southern buttery is reached direct from the entry as before, but the northern room opens into a corridor leading from the passage at right angles down to a vaulted cellar for storage running north–south under part of the western hall. The eastern hall has its private apartments in a three-storey block at the further end towards the gatehouse; there is evidence of external staircases to their doorways on the courtyard side.* The kitchen serving this domestic block must have been in the courtyard, and service would proceed to both halls through the cross passage of the eastern one. The porch of the western hall opened from its further (western) side. Mr Faulkner is to be congratulated for having disentangled this intricate plan.†

* Plan in M.O.W. Guide (9). Here the kitchen idea for the eastern hall will doubtless be revised in the light of Mr Faulkner's research.
† (1958), 175–6 (plan).

Another unusual plan is found at the Prebendal Manor House, Nassington (Fig. 46). Here the hall is built at ground level, apparently dating from the early 13th century with a two-storeyed cross-wing at the south end; this is recessed 3 feet 3 inches on the east, but projects west to form an L-plan, and comprising a solar-service block. The screens passage has an original entrance at either end, but only one doorway into the wing is visible. This is immediately to the right, south of the west entrance, and in the cross wall next to its

NASSINGTON - PREBENDAL MANOR-HOUSE
NORTHAMPTONSHIRE

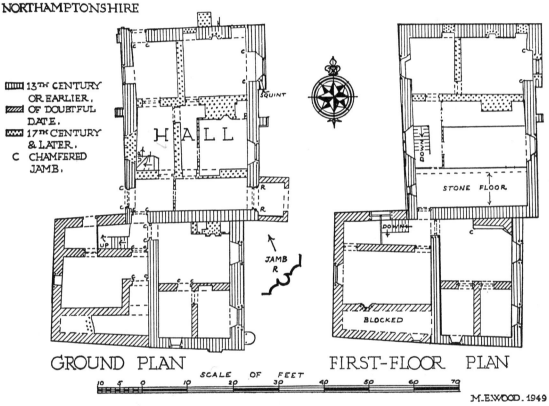

13TH CENTURY OR EARLIER.
OF DOUBTFUL DATE.
17TH CENTURY & LATER.
C CHAMFERED JAMB.

HALL

SQUINT

STONE FLOOR

DOWN

JAMB R

UP

BLOCKED

GROUND PLAN   FIRST-FLOOR PLAN

SCALE OF FEET

10 5 0 10 20 30 40 50 60 70

M.E.WOOD. 1949

Fig. 46.

eastern jamb is a doorway to the east portion of the solar undercroft. The three doorways have chamfered round or segmental heads, two with leaf-and-fillet stops; they are arranged step-wise in plan, and opposite the second two other chamfered doorways form a passage. Indeed the uncommon service doorway arrangement forms the chief item of interest here.

In the 14th century triple doorways form the usual arrangement, though there are twin service doorways at Compton Castle and the Old Parsonage at Marlow, where the kitchen was apparently reached from the back entrance of the hall. Normally they were set close together, centrally in the end wall, for convenient service between the speres into the main portion of the hall, and it was customary to link them in one composition, the three arches attached by their hoods, as at Clevedon and Penshurst (Pl. XXIII c). At Nurstead, according to Blore's drawing of c. 1837, the three pointed arches were linked by shafts in a timber partition. The central arch is slightly higher than the others at Dartington.

The arches are usually two-centred or segmental-pointed, but there are shouldered lintels, grouped, in the late 14th-century hall at Preston Patrick. They may be simply chamfered, this in two orders at Amberley Castle, or moulded. There are two wave-moulded orders at the Provost's House at Edgmond (Shropshire) and at Fyfield Manor (Berkshire). But the most elaborate arrangement occurs at Northborough Manor. Here there are three linked ogee hoods with finials (one left) over individual arches of the same form, enriched with ball-flower ornament and finials. This must have been visible from the high table (Pl. XXIV A and B).

At Amberley there are segmental rear arches towards the service, the further jamb on each side being splayed to allow for easier access into pantry and buttery.

Sometimes the third arch was further away, as at Edgmond, probably opening to a staircase to the room over the butteries. At Yardley Hastings the hall ruins show two linked doorways in the centre for pantry and buttery and a plainer arch at each end of the wall, leading down to a cellar, up to the solar respectively. The kitchen may have been in the back court. At Haddon and Preston Patrick a fourth opening in such a position leads up to the chamber over the service, as does a similar one at Dartington Hall.

In Chorley Hall, Cheshire, the doorway arrangement also survives complete, with the two opposite entrances, three service doorways and buttery hatch, all with moulded two-centred arches.

In the 15th century a number of houses retain the triple arrangement. At South Wingfield (c. 1440–59) the doorways are set close, the central largest and highest, all moulded and two-centred, one with a wall staircase off its northern jamb (Pl. XXIII D). Here they lead through the lower storey of the great chamber, to the butteries set beyond, with a passage between them to the kitchen at the extreme end of the range. A fourth and plainer recess near the entrance was possibly a laver. Here the solar block is of three storeys, the lowest at the level of the hall undercroft; the floors have gone and the service doorways now open into space.

There were three grouped doorways in the hall at Croydon Palace, built, according to heraldic evidence, by Archbishop Stafford (1443–52). This end of the hall may, however, have incorporated part of an earlier building, but was destroyed in 1830, when the whole (west) wall collapsed. Fortunately the doorways are known from Pugin's drawings.* They had two-centred arches, the central wider and slightly higher; the rather small voussoirs might place them in the 13th century, but the mouldings, ogee with hollow chamfer, suggest a later date.

The triple doorways occur in wood at Gainsborough Old Hall, with central passage to a near-detached kitchen, and at Cowdray (c. 1520–30) the central doorway leads to an open court with hexagonal kitchen beyond. At Horham Hall (c. 1502–5) the triple doorways with central passage were placed towards the rear, to allow for a parlour in front.

At Hams Barton, Devon, there are three openings; but the one nearest the front leads

* (1838), pl. 38.

Plate XXIII. Service Doorways. A. Appleton Manor, c. 1210. B. Lincoln Palace, c. 1224. C. Penshurst Place, c. 1341–9.
D. South Wingfield, 1440–59.

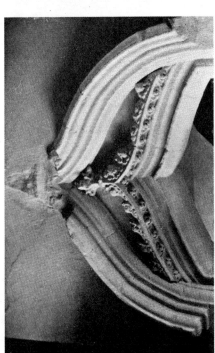

Plate XXIV.

A and B. Service doorways at Northborough Manor, c. 1340.
c. Little Mytton Hall, interior looking towards the high seat; 15th century.

A

B

C

to a staircase, at the base of which is the entrance to the kitchen wing at right angles to the main block. The kitchen at Icomb Place, Gloucestershire,* is in this position, but here, as in other cases where the kitchen was set further away, two screens doorways alone are provided, as in the early 15th-century Court House at East Meon, and Poundisford Park in the 16th century.

For the triple service doorways gradually went out of fashion during the later mediaeval period. One reason was the changed position of the kitchen. At first detached (unless, as in smaller houses, it was one with the hall), it later became incorporated, behind the butteries. But with the development of a second court it grew more convenient to site it at right angles to the service quarters, with access from these or from the back entrance of the hall. A position parallel with the hall across a court is found in other houses such as Bowhill and Littlehempston. The third doorway in the entry thus became unnecessary.

Another tendency was for the buttery position to become a parlour, with the service pushed into the back court. A single doorway would thus suffice in the end wall of the hall. At Great Chalfield this parlour or dining-room is reached from the screens by a lobby with access to a staircase to the room above.

One doorway alone would be needed in smaller houses where buttery and kitchen were combined, such as Stanton Drew Rectory Farm in Somerset (c. 1443–64), though a second doorway might lead to the stairs to the chamber above, as probably was the case at Priesthill, Kentisbeare, in Devon.

At Cotehele (a large house built before 1520) the hall entrance was set further in to face the gateway, and here one service doorway leads to the buttery, thence to the cellarage wing, the other to a right-angular passage leading to the kitchen at the north-eastern angle of the hall.

The Private Doorway

When the great chamber adjoined an upper hall, access was by a doorway in the partition, placed as usual near the angle, where it would interfere as little as possible with the high table at this end. Boothby Pagnell shows a good example.

The arrangement was less easy when the hall and chamber were on different levels. The doorway was in the same position near the angle, at the end of an aisle, at Clarendon Palace (c. 1176–7), thus avoiding the dais; and here the king reached his chamber by means of a pentice flanking an intermediate apartment, perhaps the lodging of his knights.† So far there is not much evidence of an internal staircase rising against the side wall of the hall, and giving access to an upper doorway, as occurs with regard to a chamber at the lower end, as at Oakham, Warnford and the access to the north tower at Stokesay. However, there are some examples. In Bishop's Cleeve Rectory, Gloucestershire, at the upper end of the hall, visible from the solar cross-wing, there is a doorway at first-floor level with two-centred door arch and segmental-pointed rear arch to the solar. It seems to have occurred

---

* Plan in Garner & Stratton (1929), 38.
† At Goodrich (c. 1300) there is also an intermediate 'vestibule', but here it opened into a main chamber at ground level.

too in the great guest house at Kirkstall Abbey; * here a staircase in the north aisle led to the upper chamber, of which the doorway remains in the end wall of the hall, and to allow for these steps the undercroft entrance is here further from the angle. The later staircase in the hall at St Cross gives such access to the master's lodging, doubtless preserving an original arrangement. But normally the fact that squints are found in the partition wall at chamber level, whereby the lord could control conditions in the hall after his departure from it, seems evidence that it was not usual to have a doorway at this level with stairs down into the hall.

There was a complicated arrangement at the upper end of Stokesay. After dinner the owner's family left their high table by a doorway in the usual end position, opening into the solar basement, through the outer door of which they ascended by an external covered staircase to the solar, which by the same means had direct access to the courtyard. This is similar to the staircase of an upper hall, like that in Aydon Castle. At Haughmond in the Abbot's Lodging of *c.* 1220 the solar had an external staircase off its end wall, but, unlike Stokesay, this staircase (foundations) overlaps the side wall of the hall.† There were similar steps in a lodging of *c.* 1200 at Peterborough Abbey.‡

Unfortunately Godmersham Court (*c.* 1250), with its valuable evidence of plan development, has been destroyed. The solar was at the north end, away from the entrance, for the outline of its hooded fireplace could be seen in the common wall with the hall, in which wall, near the north-east angle, a doorway opened outwards to the solar undercroft. Adjoining the doorway was another, at the extremity of the side wall, also with two-centred arch, but this is at a higher level. It may once have led to a staircase oriel, the first steps being in the wall thickness. However, this doorway, in its congested position, may be a 15th-century insertion.

At Old Soar (*c.* 1290) a doorway in the once north aisle of the hall similarly gives access to the solar basement, but in its northernmost jamb opens to a newel staircase housed in a curved projection of this angle of the solar, and rising into the floor of the latter. At Barnston (*c.* 1260) the hall doorway leads in the same way to the solar basement, but the angle staircase arrangement is less neat, apparently altered with 16th-century additions.

The position of a doorway in the end wall could be draughty unless the dais did not extend so far, probably occupying the nave only in an aisled hall, or given side curtains or speres, as were provided to shield later high tables from the parlour doorways. Where the solar projected as a cross-wing beyond the hall, its entrance could be placed in the extension of the end wall of the latter, reached by an external staircase in the re-entrant angle made by the two blocks of building. The lord's exit from the hall could be made in a side wall near the high table.

Such an arrangement came into being at West Tarring Palace, though not from the start. Here a mid 13th-century first-floor hall became solar to a ground-floor one built later in the century, but which was altered *c.* 1400 as regards the windows.§ The staircase in one flight, doubtless of wood, from hall to solar has now disappeared, but the doorways

* Faulkner 1958), 170–1 (plan).
† Faulkner (1958), 171, fig. 24 (plan).
‡ Faulkner (1958), 169, fig. 19 (plan).
§ A. B. Packham (1923), 140–79.

it served and the loops that lit it remain, the annexe being transformed into a porch in the 16th century. The stairs must have been steep with a landing (or winders) at the top, for there is little room though the solar entrance is placed, as usual, at the extreme end of the wall.

The plan at the Old Deanery, Salisbury (c. 1258–74), was better and the hall doorway was placed further from the angle, though still off the dais. This allowed for an easier external staircase, now gone, following the line of the hall, evidence being provided by the raising of the hall window over it. It led up to a solar entrance, recently discovered, near the junction of the hall and projecting solar block. When the 15th-century tower was built, against the north wall of the solar but not directly linked to the hall owing to the penticed

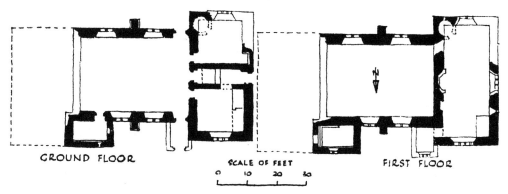

Fig. 47. Northborough Manor House, plans.

stairway, a new doorway was built at first-floor level linking the solar to the tower, and another at ground-floor level linking the tower to the hall.*

Another method seems to have been used in the mid 14th-century Northborough Manor (Fig. 47). The hall doorway is again further from the angle (north-east) leaving room for a wider annexe, and the solar doorway is in the same position, where the cross-wing projected beyond the hall.† But the stairs here were not against the hall but at right angles to it, probably rising from the hall doorway against the west, then the north, wall of the annexe. At ground-floor level the walling of this 'oriel' is original, and contains a cross-loop on the west, a rectangular loop at the west end of the north wall. The oblong chamber excavated in the angle of the mid 14th-century hall with solar at Kirby Muxloe was probably a similar staircase annexe. At Penshurst the elaborate staircase oriel is in the same position. From the dais one doorway leads to the solar steps, and adjoining it, near the south-west angle of the hall; another opens down to the vaulted undercroft. The steps on the opposite side of the dais were formed to give access to the early 15th-century addition, and a doorway was placed in a partially blocked window embrasure. Evidence of a staircase oriel has been found at Compton Castle and the newel turret rebuilt. It was entered from

* Information kindly provided by Mr Norman Drinkwater, F.S.A., A.R.I.B.A., of the Royal Commission on Historical Monuments office at Salisbury.

† The end wall between hall and solar has been rebuilt, but was once in line with the east wall of the annexe containing the solar doorway.

the lateral wall of the hall next the angle beyond which the undercroft doorway opened from it, probably a simplified version of the Penshurst arrangement.

A stair turret remains in the corresponding re-entrant angle between hall and solar in the mid 14th-century Beetham Hall, while at Kirkby Thore Hall the undercroft doorway is in the end wall, which is thickened to contain a wall staircase rising to the angle of hall with solar. Later at Bowhill, Exeter, there is evidence of a stair projection entered through a small doorway, now blocked, at the end of the side wall adjoining the entrance to the narrow solar undercroft. At Mayfield (*c.* 1325) there is a square projection off the north-west end of the dais bay: this also might be significant. An annexe of this nature, in timber with a staircase, seems to have been added at West Bromwich Manor.

It seems as if the hall oriel originated from the need to enclose the solar entrance with its staircase, or at any rate the doorway to the solar undercroft, thus sited conveniently near the high table but without being draughty for its occupants. That the second function continued into the later bay windows is apparent from the fact that most contain, when in line with the hall end wall or near it, a doorway with access to the great chamber or solar block.

At Clevedon Court, indeed, the southern oriel has no staircase, except for one in a turret corbelled out from the first-floor chapel and leading to the battlements. Across the hall another original projection (reached by a doorway, not a great arch) possibly contained a staircase, as now, but there is evidence of a newel serving its upper floor and the solar, in the north-west angle of the hall. However, the solar doorway on the north wall, now giving on to a passage, must have had external steps originally. But at Aston Eyre, not far off in date, the oriel projection contained a newel staircase to the solar as well as an entrance to its undercroft (Fig. 48).

Minster Lovell has two private doorways off the side walls of the hall in line with the high table. The northern opens into a lobby with access eastwards to the chapel undercroft, possibly a withdrawing-room (judging from the elaborate tracery), and on the west to the smaller chamber below the solar, the larger room here being reached from the southern doorway and oriel chamber, which like Penshurst contains the solar staircase. This is again the case at Ashleworth Court.

The whole oriel is a staircase at West Coker Manor which was built *c.* 1473 after the destruction, in 1453, of an earlier house. The present newel, however, may be modern, and the position of a transomed window makes the original interior of the oriel uncertain. The window faces the entrance sideways, which is unusual in a single window of this size, and the oriel in which it is placed has a balustraded roof, unlike other portions of the building. The window tracery could be earlier 15th century, and adds to the possibility that the oriel is a remnant of the earlier house, re-used facing a different way. However, a trefoil-headed squint into the hall seems original, housed in a small chamber in the upper wall thickness, and approached from the first-floor landing of the staircase. As at Minster Lovell the oriel is reached from the hall by a doorway, here moulded and four-centred.*

On the whole, by the late 15th century the staircase seems to have left the oriel, but the doorway into the solar undercroft (now parlour) was still needed. In halls with two oriels,

---

* Care is necessary as this house was restored 1830–40 with contemporary material found elsewhere.

like South Wraxall, there is double access to the private wing, though Poundisford Park (1534) shows a doorway off the front oriel chamber only. At Lytes Cary the back oriel (*c.* 1530) also leads into the great parlour, and so to the little parlour adjoining, but it still contains the staircase to the great chamber above the first.

In this period there are instances, like the earlier arrangement, of the private entrance in one of the main walls of the hall. At Croydon Palace (*c.* 1443–52), as at Stokesay, it was convenient to place what might be called the dais doorway in the end wall near the angle. Crosby Hall (1466) has the great parlour at right angles, and access is not by the oriel but by a doorway on the same wall nearer the upper end. At Horham Hall the dais doorway just avoids a bay window, and leads to a passage externally treated like another oriel, round the angle of the building.

Normally the private staircase is now further from the hall. At Tickenham and Cothay Manor it is in a turret on the opposite wall of the private wing, and at Kingston Seymour in a projection off its end wall at the back. The solar undercroft having now become a private dining-room or parlour, the family would retire to their great chamber from there,

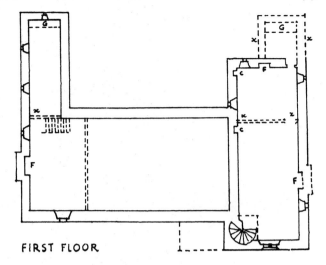

FIRST FLOOR

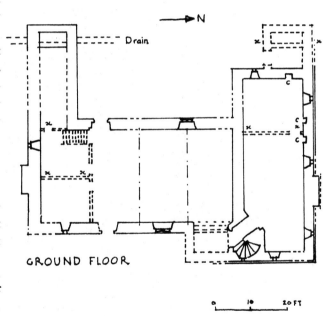

N

Drain

GROUND FLOOR

Fig. 48. Aston Eyre Manor House, plans.

C, cupboard   G, garderobe

F, fireplace   xx, conjectural

not directly from the hall as formerly, so the staircase was sited accordingly. This is shown at Compton Castle, where the transformation of solar basement into parlour (*c.* 1450–75) included the provision of a newel staircase in the south-western angle of the room; earlier the solar was reached by means of a staircase oriel off the hall.*

* National Trust Guide (2) (plan); Everett (1956).

As we have already noted, the parlour could be reached from the hall through one oriel or both. There might be a side doorway between the bay window and the end wall, or one opposite the bay window as at Wythenshawe Hall, Lancashire. But usually, now, access was more direct, through doorways in the end wall, set as near the angle as possible to clear the high table. There is one of such openings at Croydon Palace, and Great Dixter, Northiam (c. 1465–75), two doorways at Cothay Manor, and a number of 15th- and 16th-century halls remaining in Lancashire and Cheshire. The last provide much of the evidence of the means whereby, at least in the north-west, the occupants of the high table were protected from the draughts caused by such openings.

One method was to place the table in a recess, and this is shown in Buckler's drawing of Mytton (Little Mitton) Hall, Lancashire, before it was altered (Pl. XXIV c). The whole recess was panelled, probably in the 16th century, and made one architectural feature with the adjoining carved doorways, set in the same moulded framework. A table recess also existed at Samlesbury Hall in the same county, but here there was a canopy with moulded ribs curved up to a crenellated and traceried cornice in line with the cusped parlour door-ways.* Such a coving was often extended along the whole end wall, as in the Commandery at Worcester. There is evidence of this at Denton Hall,† again without speres near the openings, the second of which is placed in the oriel; and at Smithells Old Hall, also in Lancashire, the framework remains.‡ In the hall at Henbras, the vanished Beaumaris house of which drawings survive, the end coving contained two rows of seven latticed panels.

A magnificent canopy survives at Rufford Old Hall (Fig. 49), the coving with moulded ribs forming thirty-six panels, rising to a battlemented and moulded beam with scalloped soffit; above this the gable has lattice work with quatrefoiled panels; moulded speres of slight projection shield the dais seat from the usual end doorways.§ Even more ornate is the tester (c. 1505) over the high table at Adlington Hall, the coving again twelve panels in length but now five in height (thus sixty in all) and the containing beams rich in orna-ment, the bressumer carved and crenellated, with in addition a drop tester of fourteen pendants with arches between.‖ The present heraldic decoration in the panels dates from 1744, but there is earlier evidence of such treatment behind the present shields in the gable. The parlour here was reached through one of the bays which have later arches. Canopies also remain at Chetham Hospital and Ordsall Hall, and a 16th-century example in the form of a plaster cove with renewed heraldic ornament may be seen at Gloddaeth, Penrhyn in Caernarvonshire; it rises from the crested cornice of a trefoil-panelled partition containing one parlour doorway.¶

Such elaboration above the high table seems less a protection against draught than in the nature of a canopy of honour, a form of crowning, special treatment of the important end of the hall, akin to the cellure, the adornment of the roof over the altar in a church. From the start the dais position had been emphasized, with arcading, of which portions remain

---

* H. Taylor (1884), 90, pls. III, XXIV (plan).
† Taylor (1884), pl. XXV (elevation and plan).
‡ Taylor (1884), pl. XIII (plan).
§ Crossley (1951), fig. 153.
‖ Crossley (1951), 131, fig. 143.
¶ R.C.H.M. *Caernarvonshire*, I, 178, pl. 93.

Fig. 49. Rufford Old Hall, *c.* 1500, the dais end.

at St Mary's Guild and Wolvesley Palace, of 12th-century date, or special wainscoting and painting as favoured by Henry III, or a backing of embroidery and later tapestry, heightened into a heraldic tester over the seal of an important owner. Illustrated documents provide evidence of these.

When an embattled rail is found at the upper end of the hall it may mark the springing of a former curved canopy or coving over the high table. One was found at West Bromwich Old Hall, and as the beam does not extend to the side walls it is believed that speres formerly projected forwards as draught shields from the adjacent doorways. Was this an early 15th-century addition with the present north solar wing, or even dating from the 16th century, when the two-storey bay was added to the west of the 14th-century hall? If original, it must be one of the earliest examples. Another seems to have been provided in the aisled hall, possibly of 14th-century date, at High Bentley, Shelf, near Halifax. Here a moulded and embattled rail was fixed to the end wall, from which must have sprung a canopy extending inwards four feet to the closed king-post truss which marked the end of the hall roof.* This arrangement can still be seen in the Commandery at Worcester.

* Information kindly put at my disposal by the authors before publication in Atkinson & McDowall (1967).

Crenellated beams at the upper end are a feature of many Kentish halls of the 15th and 16th centuries, as in the Town House (*c.* 1480) at Ightham. As it sometimes occurs at the screens end also, it does not necessarily mean that a canopy existed. In a 15th-century house formerly at Benenden, the embattled wainscot at the upper end has a return to shield the high table from the parlour doorway.*

THE HIGH SEAT

A fixed seat for the high table remains in several of the north-western halls, this 'bench of state' being a narrow oak plank some 11 inches wide and 2 feet high. At Rufford it is about 14 feet long and 22 inches high. There are remains of one at Denton, and evidence at Mytton and Chetham Hospital. At Bramhall, Cheshire, there is a moulded bench but no canopy, this being a later hall 12 feet high with a chamber over. The seat at Gawthorpe, Lancashire, is backed by a seven-light window, as this is an end hall without a parlour behind.†

In the centre of this bench could be placed the owner's seat, in the form of a chair with back and arms; for originally only the most important person had a chair, hence the term 'chair man' still in use, other people being content with a bench or stool. Royal chairs would of course be more elaborate, a separate structure, enriched with paint and gilding. At Westminster Palace, his chief residence, Henry III had one of special beauty made. We have his own instructions on 11 March 1245: 'Edward of Westminster is ordered to have the king's marble seat in the great hall at Westminster . . . ready before Easter', and two days later: 'The king to Edward of Westminster. As we remember you said to us that it would be a little more expensive to make two brass leopards to be placed on each side of our seat at Westminster, than to make them of incised or sculptured marble, we command you to make them of metal as you said, and make the steps before the seat aforesaid of carved stone.' ‡ We must visualize one like the Coronation Chair made in 1299 for his son Edward I, to hold the Stone of Destiny, and also as the seat of the Abbot of Westminster. Walter of Durham, the king's Sergeant Painter since 1270, perhaps Edward of Westminster's successor, was paid 100*s.* for the chair; 13*s.* 4*d.* for carving and painting two small leopards in wood, and £1 19*s.* 7*d.* for making and painting a step and case for the chair.§ The present four lions supporting the chair are considered of early Tudor date,‖ regilded in the reign of George IV. Walter's leopards or lions ¶ were apparently separate, for the king's feet to rest on, as shown in seals from the reigns of Henry III to Edward III, and associated with the regal lions of Solomon's throne.

---

* Lloyd (1931), figs. 101, 608.

† Taylor (1884), 13, 78, 148, 105, pl. IV.

‡ Close Roll, 29 Henry III; Turner (1851), 261.

§ Wardrobe Accounts of 1300. See W. Palmer (1953), *The Coronation Chair* (Ministry of Works), based on report and examination of the chair by W. Percival-Prescott.

‖ The back ones are slightly different, perhaps Jacobean copies.

¶ In early heraldry a lion *passant gardant* (walking and looking at the spectator) was depicted as a leopard without spots, a stylized lion (*Boutell's Heraldry*, ed. C. W. Scott-Giles (1950), 65).

THE CHAMBER OVER THE SERVICE

In houses larger or later, when the lord's solar, the great chamber, was moved to the upper end of the hall, the room over the butteries was still important, perhaps for guests, the eldest son and his family, or even for the steward or seneschal of the household. Indeed this room was convenient for supervision of the service, with an opening into the great hall from the adjoining gallery over the screens passage, or even from the apartment itself in cases, as at Little Sodbury, where it included the portion over this 'entry' where a gallery was usual in later houses. Sometimes this service accommodation was more extensive, as in the double cross-wing at East Meon (Pl. XXVI B), where over the buttery, pantry and dairy are the 'lodgings' with garderobe, presumably for the Bishop of Winchester's staff.

We will now consider how these rooms, whether great or secondary chamber, were reached from below. A staircase across the end of the screens passage, impeding any back entrance, provided access from the early halls at Oakham and Warnford, and somewhat later at Stokesay Castle. But it was obviously more convenient to have this staircase off the end wall, and at Haddon (c. 1310) the fourth service doorway, near the back entrance, met this need. At Yardley Hastings in the late 14th century the staircase up to the solar was balanced by steps down to the cellar, from doorways at each end of the service wall. Such steps would normally end in the actual floor of the chamber, and a wall staircase would be a neater arrangement. In the late 14th-century Preston Patrick Hall this is contrived in the thick wall between hall and service; entered by a doorway in the normal position, it rises up at right angles and turns again into the 'courtroom' at the top.

More usual perhaps was the newel staircase, as at Old Soar, here in a thickened angle of the wing. In Northborough Manor the staircase only projected within, where there was once a doorway to it from the service undercroft and not, as usual, from the entrance passage.

The angle with the porch is another position for the staircase to this wing. At Lincoln Palace (c. 1225) it was entered from just inside the entry, and served both the great chamber and the room over the porch. There is a similar arrangement at Clevedon, but here the newel is entered from the porch, and the back porch has a similar staircase to its upper room, in the opposite angle with the hall. The palace at Wells (c. 1280) had a wall staircase in the porch, now gone, leading up to the solar entrance which still remains. At Crowhurst there survives a diagonal passage from the great chamber through its angle to the upper room of the porch, but it was itself entered by a means now lost.

Penshurst (c. 1341–9) has a good newel stair turret on the entrance side between the hall and porch; it opens out of the latter, and gives access to the porch room and chamber over the service, both of which were important, having traceried windows. A larger newel is included in a porch tower at the back. At Dartington Hall (c. 1388–1400) there is also a tall stair turret in the angle of the porch, but here on the service side and opening from the screens. It gives access to both chambers over the butteries.

Buck's view of Minster Lovell in 1729 shows a large five-light transomed window in the end of the room over the service. This was reached from the screens through a small arch with wall staircase. At South Wingfield access to the great chamber, here at the service end, was by means of a newel projection off the back lobby or porch on the garden side. The staircase at South Wraxall was placed inside the lower room (parlour or buttery) in the angle adjoining the back entrance of the hall. It was in a similar position at Great Chalfield, but enclosed in a lobby or internal porch with doorways from both parlour and screens passage.

9

Development of the Screen;

Internal Partitions

The Spere Truss.

THE lower part of the hall often contained as many as five doorways, three service ones in the end wall, the entrance nearby on a side wall, and usually a back door opposite. There was constant traffic here, and to lessen the draught from these openings this portion tended more and more to be screened off. The screens passage, or 'entry', was thus formed, at last entirely partitioned from the main body of the hall and given a gallery above.

At first the separation was only partial. The initial stage was to form 'speres' (barriers) or short screens projecting from each lateral wall on the hall side of the outer doorway. In an aisled hall these would be the width of the aisle, the central (nave) arch being left open, hung with a curtain or given a movable screen like the later example at Rufford Old Hall. An extra roof truss (the spere truss) facilitated this arrangement, for the speres could be contained by the aisle posts, and the screens passage become a separate bay, half the size of each main bay of equal length (a common practice), or making with the lower bay the size of the upper one.

When the aisled hall was supplanted, and the floor cleared of posts, those in the screens truss were retained as a fixed point for the speres, and this aisled survival or spere truss persisted for another century and more, particularly in the north-west. It is strange, however, that distribution maps show many spere truss but only one aisled hall here, contrasted with few spere truss and more aisled halls in the south-eastern region.*

In surviving examples the spere truss appears in the early 14th century, when also there remain several halls without it, such as Fyfield Hall and Black Notley. There is evidence

* Smith (1958 a), 133-6, figs. 13 and 14.

of it in other Essex aisled halls, Little Chesterford and possibly Lampetts, but most examples occur in 'aisled hall derivatives'.

A good idea of the spere truss in its essential framework is seen in the drawing in Parker * showing the early 14th-century hall at Sutton Courtenay. From two spere posts with moulded capitals there spring arched braces to form a two-centred arch under a cambered collar-beam, which has crown-post and trussed rafter roof above. From post to wall on either side there are cross-bars in connection with earlier speres, not with the later screen depicted below.

A similar arrangement must have existed at Little Chesterford. One spere post and mortices of the curved braces remain. The post is double chamfered to the nave, but the slot towards the aisle is evidence for a solid screen from post to wall. This aisled hall has been dated *c.* 1275, but more recently called *c.* 1320–50.†

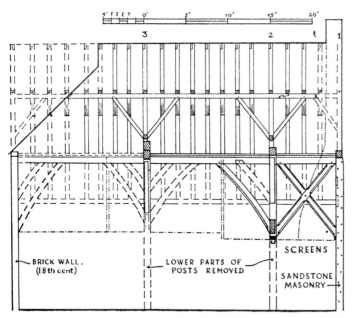

Fig. 50. Manor Farm, Wasperton, longitudinal section of hall.

The halls at Wasperton (Figs. 50 and 51) and West Bromwich are very similar in detail, and it has been suggested that *c.* 1300 they came from the same carpenter's yard. Here is the early feature of double braces below the collar, and at Wasperton the capitals are moulded, with a scalloped middle order. At Mancetter Hall (*c.* 1330–40) the spere posts are chamfered with moulded capitals, and here a great trefoil arch spans the nave under a cambered collar beam.

In the early 14th-century Baguley Hall in Cheshire ‡ the great pointed arch has cross-pieces in its spandrels with the collar, while at Smithells Hall (Lancashire) the spere posts rise little above their moulded capitals, which are more finished than those at Baguley, and the curved braces forming the arch also support the rafters. In each case the apex of the two-centred arch cuts into the cambered collar.

There are a number of 14th-century spere trusses surviving in Herefordshire. The best is at Amberley Court, Marden, dating from the first half of the 14th century. Curved braces form a two-centred arch below the cambered collar, above which is a pointed quatre-foil flanked by trefoils, and the triangles above the cross-beams are also cusped. Such foiled

* Parker (1853), 32.   † Smith (1955), 83.
‡ For references to examples of the spere truss see list at the end of Chapter 3.

openings are a feature in this county, and occur in the other examples. At Eaton Hall, Leominster (mid 14th century) the arch cuts into the beam above. There are moulded posts and braces at Peg's Farm, Wellington Heath, and at Court Farm, Preston Wynne,

Fig. 51. Manor Farm, Wasperton, *c.* 1300, reconstruction of hall looking towards the service end.

the next truss to the spere is one of cruck construction, as it is at Yew Tree Cottage, Dilwyn. Another spere truss, with lofty nave arch, can be seen at Lower Brockhampton House, near Bromyard, which dates from *c.* 1400. Other spere trusses of the 14th century have been found in Wales.*

* Crossley (1951), 133–4; Hemp (1942–3).

By the mid 15th century the arch seems no longer to have been raised above the height of the speres, but is at the same level, the tie-beam (at wall-plate level) terminating the spere arrangement across the hall, instead of the arch rising to the collar as before. The arch now becomes less pointed. At Ordsall Hall it is four-centred, moulded as are the posts, while at Denton Hall, somewhat later, chamfered posts support a semicircular arch. The four-centred form also appears at Little Mytton, where the moulded posts have stone bases. The same arch occurs at Rufford Old Hall and Adlington, while in the Commandery at Worcester (c. 1484–1503) the heavy braces, with tracery in the spandrels, do not even make an arch. There is now no distinction in height between nave and aisles, and the aisled hall idiom is being lost. The spere truss has developed into a screen.

It is interesting to study the development of the speres or side screens. At Little Chesterford the existing slots indicate that they were solid, six feet high. Baguley Hall has three cross-bars in each side, beneath the lowest of which there are oblong panels to shield those seated at tables along the walls, while the two upper tiers have trefoil-headed openings. At Smithells, a smaller hall, the cross-bars contain two tiers of quatrefoiled panels. Amberley retains one cross-rail to the wall plate, on each side, and below evidence of trefoil heads. It is uncertain whether the aisles were screened here, or possibly had a curtain; at the springing of the central arch the mouldings of the spere posts are returned as if for a beam across the nave. Sutton Courtenay has cross-bars, but below wall plate level, above the top of the screen depicted in the Parker drawing, which appears to be later. The cross-bars remain at Little Brockhampton, but there is a modern partition and gallery.

In the 15th century the speres are lengthened to match the arch, and are of equal height below the sometimes cambered tie-beam. There is panelling in two tiers at Ordsall Hall, and square and oblong timber-framing, possibly left open at Denton Hall. At Mytton there are cross-bars, the top one forming three arches. Rufford Old Hall has five cross-rails a side, the lowest panelled, the others with quatrefoil bracing. This might be regarded as a sophisticated version of the spere truss, rich in quatrefoils, at the collapsed Stand Old Hall (c. 1400) near Whitefield in the same county.*

But the greatest feature of interest at Rufford is one of the very rare surviving examples of a movable screen, which dates from the early 16th century (Pl. XXV D). The solid frame (7 feet 6 inches × 7 feet) encloses two rows of four traceried panels containing quatrefoils with *paterae*, and a richly ornamented cornice supports three lofty and elaborate finials†. There was an even richer standard screen at Samlesbury Hall, also in Lancashire, which was cut up in 1835 to form a gallery, but its form is known from illustrations.‡ Here there were six traceried panels in each range, and equally magnificent finials. It bore the date 1532 and name of the owner Thomas Southworth, knight, whose name and the date 1545 also appear on a fireplace in the south-east wing.

Reminiscent of these is the surviving screen at Wortham Manor, Devon (Pl. XXV A).§ This 15th-century hall had an upper floor inserted in the first quarter of the 16th century, which is apparently the date of the elaborate screen, although evidence exists of an earlier

---

* *Transactions of the Ancient Monuments Society* (1961), N.S. IX, frontispiece.
† Taylor (1884), pl. XVIII.
‡ Taylor (1884), 90–1, pl. XVIII.
§ *Country Life* (32), 1228–9.

arrangement with gallery. Here the side speres and middle portion are similar, each with two long linenfold panels, and moulded posts terminating in carved finials which reach the cross-beam above. There is the usual gap but not doorway between the three speres, which are completely separate. This seems a transitional form between the movable central portion of Rufford, and the usual continuous screen with two doorways. There are no projecting feet to support the standard as at Rufford and Samlesbury, whereas these are represented at Hampton Court by the projecting bases of the terminal columns, this being another transitional example.

The Screen

Judging from the few examples known, as at Rufford and originally Samlesbury Old Halls, the movable screen or standard would rely on its own weight to keep vertical, aided by right-angled foot projections which doubtless were awkward and caused tripping.

The heavy movable screen would tend to be left in the same position, and it must have been realized by degrees how much more convenient it would be to incorporate it into one work with the side screens, tying the whole together by a cross-beam, thus forming three solid pieces and two openings.

A transitional example is supplied by the magnificent screen in the hall at Milton Abbas, Dorset.[8] The traceried speres and standard, in two tiers (the lower restored), have their heavy columned side-posts set diagonally, these providing weight without undue projection. The three portions are linked by ornate sub-cusped ogee arches with finials, these being repeated over the solid portions. This enrichment is apparently contemporary work, though perhaps placed in this position in the late 18th century, when the hall was incorporated in Lord Milton's mansion. There are quatrefoils in the friezes continued over the side-posts, and with miniature two-lights in the panels; a central device is the rebus of Abbot Middleton (or Milton), with the date 1498. The speres have the same type of treatment but, being wider, have additional panels (Pl. XXV c).

For some time, indeed, the screen continued to have the threefold aspect, each portion being separately based and moulded, and with no other connection than the horizontal above. This is noticeable in almost every mediaeval example, from Haddon Hall (c. 1475), the late 15th-century screens of Great Chalfield, Cothay and Little Sodbury Manors, the Commandery at Worcester, even into the 16th century at Hampton Court and Cowdray. At Bisham Abbey and Penshurst, however, flat four-centred arches span the openings, and the Ockwells screen is the most compact, with shorter panels continuing over square apertures.

Another factor was the growing popularity of the gallery, which, of course, needed to be supported. It not only gave access to bedrooms over the service quarters, but also accommodation for musicians performing in a suitable place opposite the high table.

It would be interesting to know when the musicians' gallery became fashionable. It was certainly so by the 16th century and, judging from surviving examples, it would be safe to assume its existence by the second half of the 15th century. The evidence of church architecture bears this out, for there was a great development of the 'rood loft' at that very period. This was really a musicians' gallery and received its name from its position under the Great Rood, while having a subsidiary purpose in giving access to the Rood for veiling in Lent, and the placing of candles.*

However, these later 15th-century domestic screens may have been replacements, for in several 14th-century houses, Haddon Hall, Clevedon Court and Penshurst, an original newel staircase leads up to the gallery position.

But for two notable 13th-century survivals, at Great Bricett (Suffolk) and Polsloe Priory, Exeter, which are more service partitions than screens, one of the earliest examples seems to be that of c. 1475 at Haddon Hall.[2] Here each of the three parts has long panels, three each in the sides, four in the central portion, the upper tier being the longer and retaining traceried heads.

As might be expected from the later 15th-century date, the cinquefoiled head to the panel is popular, sometimes in an ogee, usually with tracery above. At Haddon the central part has two cinquefoils in each, with Perpendicular tracery. Two side panels retain cinquefoils in the lower tier as well, which suggests that in some cases it may have existed there originally but been worn off. The Haddon gallery is structurally separate, with different tracery in the parapet, which may be slightly later.

At Bisham Abbey [3] the large gallery front projects over the screen but is apparently of similar, late 15th-century date. The panels have quatrefoils and other tracery in the spandrels of flattened cinquefoil heads, and in the screen the upper tiers are left open.

Ockwells Manor [1] screen resembles a partition with openings in it, and there is no division from the gallery, the longer panels going straight up, and the whole finished with a battlemented cornice. The sills and rails are plain, and there are cinquefoil heads only to the lower panels on the entry side.

At Cothay Manor [5] there are two long panels without subdivision in each section, and a moulded cornice. Above this the projecting gallery is timber-framed with a filling of lath and plaster.

In the hall at Little Sodbury,[6] however, there is no gallery but a close-studded partition up to the roof, the portion above the screen being part of a large room. Below, the eastern section is original, and retains cinquefoil-headed panels in the upper tier. Lytes Cary has an excellent screen and gallery in the mediaeval manner.

Of the screen at Great Chalfield [4] only drawings remain (Pl. 26). It was as elaborate as a church example, each section having two tiers of traceried panels, four in the sides, three in the central portion, with sub-cusped trefoils, the uppermost with Perpendicular tracery above. Each section was a separate entity with moulded cornice and pinnacled buttresses to the front and flanking the openings. The gallery front had already gone before Walker's drawings of 1836.

The Commandery at Worcester [7] is of special interest, for it combines a screen with a contemporary spere truss. Now the two openings are closed and there is a central doorway, but Dollman's elevation of 1863 shows elaborate tracery nearly half way down each of the tiers of (four) panels in the central portion; the side ones, moulded only, have three. There was a moulded, mitred frame to the openings.

* Aymer Vallance (1936), *English Church Screens*, 68, Batsford.

A most interesting discovery was made by Mr A. W. Everett. In a deserted building, Marshall's Farm, Ide (Devon),[9] under lath and plaster he found the original early 16th-century screen; carved on two of the posts was a small trefoiled panel with the rebus, the 'rise' or birchy broom, of John Ryse, Treasurer of Exeter Cathedral, to whom is attributed the fireplace in the Deanery and who presumably owned the house. His screen is now placed in the hall at Bindon.

At Hampton Court [10] (1530–5) there is still Gothic tracery in the upper panels, with the initials of Henry VIII and Anne Boleyn. The three sections of the screen are quite definite, the sides with five panels, the central block with six, and as at Great Chalfield each section has an independent cornice. Here each has a separate moulded base as well, projecting almost in the manner of a standard. Renaissance influence is apparent in the round posts flanking the openings, of which the capitals and bases form portions of the cornice and plinth.* The Great Chalfield uprights were still Gothic, octagonal with pinnacled buttresses. The Milton [8] screen (1498) has clustered shafts and much elaboration, but is otherwise akin to Hampton Court.

The Buck Hall at Cowdray,[11] slightly later, had definitely classical columns and entablature, but still had tracery upper and lower on each section of four panels.

The screen at Penshurst [12] is believed to be later 16th century, as it contains in a frieze the badge of the Bear and Ragged Staff which was adopted by Sir Henry Sidney on his marriage in 1551 to Mary Dudley, heiress of the Beauchamps. Otherwise the screen has a definite look of the Middle Ages, with charming tracery in both tiers of the three sections (of six, eight and six panels respectively) and in the battlemented gallery above. The Renaissance element, however, enters with the classical columns, with capitals and entablature, and there is development in the way the three sections are joined by flat four-centred, slightly cusped, arches over the openings. It has been restored.

Chapel Screens

Although chapel screens are known from the 13th century, surviving domestic examples are considerably later. There is a fine 15th-century one in the Chancery at Lincoln,[13] having elaborate cusping to the open panels, traceried cornice, and crenellated transom dividing off the closed lower portion (Pl. XXV B). In Ashbury Manor [14] there is a screen between the great chamber and the oratory over the porch; it has six panels with trefoiled heads and quatrefoils in the spandrels, similar to the treatment of the doorway. The screen at Cotehele [15] also has cusped and traceried openings, here with a cresting. At Bindon [16] the screen panels are ramped to fit the adjoining staircase. Champ's Chapel at East Hendred [17] once possessed a screen the height of the two western storeys of the chapel.

* The gallery front is modern.

INTERNAL PARTITIONS

Mr Rigold has found horizontal edge-to-edge planks used for internal partitions, especially in prison cells, such as in Milton Regis Court Hall, Kent, and strong-rooms. The use of horizontal boards made for toughness, but they were not watertight and so not used externally. There are some at Chesil Rectory, Winchester.

But the familiar mediaeval partitions that remain are of clapboarding or the more finished plank and muntin type.

In clapboarding * a series of vertical boards were set up on a sill, each tongued on one edge and grooved on the other to fit into its neighbour. Thus it is unlike weatherboarding, where the boards merely overlap. In the partition so formed, the better side is flush, with fine jointing, the other shows overlapping boards. This was probably the kind of wainscot used, often painted, by Henry III, including the fir boards from Norway which he ordered in 1253 for the chamber of Prince Edward at Winchester.† There are cases of thefts of such boarding from unoccupied houses in 1297. The Court Rolls of the Manor of Wakefield relate that at Holne 'a certain house has been left empty by William Yoil, the boards of the inner walls [de parietibus] have been carried away by persons unknown. An inquisition is to be held thereon at the next court'; then 'it is found by the inquisition that Robert de Harop carried away [boards] from the inner wall of a certain house . . . to the value of 2d. He is therefore fined 2d.' ‡

A 15th-century example survives in a house in Church Square, Rye.§ At Compton Wynyates, in the early 16th century, the Council Chamber has the clapboarding in two lengths, and carved decoration masking the horizontal joint.‖

In other partitions, and in screens, the plank and muntin method was used. The muntins, intermediate vertical posts, tenoned into sill and moulded beam, formed a framework into which long panels were set, the edges of these being tapered to fit into a groove (or rebate) in the muntin. The central, wider, portion of the panel might be moulded into a vertical rib, and when this was multiplied and each moulding terminated with a 'stop', at first semicircular, then diversified, what we call 'linenfold' panelling or what the makers called *lignum undulatum* (wavy woodwork) developed. This is a feature of the early 16th century, and is seen in the Guildhall at Lavenham and the screen at Compton Wynyates.¶ The kindred parchemin (parchment) panel** has the central rib branching to the four corners, stopped by ogival curves.

Fifteenth-century examples of plank and muntin partitions are found at Ashbury Manor, the Chantry at Combe Raleigh and, with intermediate rail, in the Chantry at Ilminster, where one panel contains a quatrefoil squint.

* A term still used in the U.S.A., but there the boards are set horizontally.
† Liberate Roll, 37 Henry III; Turner (1851), 241.
‡ Lloyd (1931), 73.
§ Lloyd (1931), fig. 673.
‖ Lloyd (1931), fig. 674.
¶ Lloyd (1931), figs. 679, 680.
** A recent name. See Lloyd (1931), 73–6.

EXAMPLES OF THE HALL SCREEN

For speres see Spere Truss Hall references in Chapter 3

		References
(1) *c.* 1465	Ockwells Manor, Berks.	Lloyd (1931), figs. 356, 604.
(2) *c.* 1475	Haddon Hall, Derbys.	*Country Life* (10), 1742-3.
(3) late C 15th	Bisham Abbey, Berks.	
(4) *c.* 1480	Great Chalfield Manor, Wilts.	Pugin (1840), pls. 43, 44; Parker (1859), 60.
(5) *c.* 1480	Cothay Manor, Som.	Lloyd (1931), fig. 602.
(6) *c.* 1485	Little Sodbury Manor, Glos.	Braun (1940), pl. 22.
(7) *c.* 1484–1503	The Commandery, Worcester	Dollman & Jobbins (1861), 37; Garner & Stratton (1929), 202-3, pl. CLXIX.
(8) 1498	Milton Abbas, Dor., Abbot's Hall	*Country Life* (18), 735, 737.
(9) early C 16th	Marshall's Farm, Ide, Devon, now at Bindon, Axmouth, Devon	Research by A. W. Everett, F.S.A.
(10) *c.* 1530-5	Hampton Court, Middx	R.C.H.M. *Middlesex*, pl. 83.
(11) *c.* 1540	Cowdray, Suss., evidence	Garner & Stratton (1929), 52 (drawing by S. H. Grimm).
(12) after 1551	Penshurst Place, Kent	Hussey (1951), 41.

CHAPEL SCREENS

(13) C 15th	The Chancery, Lincoln	
(14) *c.* 1488	Ashbury Manor, Berks.	
(15) *c.* 1485-9	Cotehele, Corn.	
(16) early C 16th	Bindon, Axmouth, Devon	Research by A. W. Everett, F.S.A.
(17) early C 16th	Champ's Chapel, East Hendred, Berks.	Parker (1859), 177.

10

The Porch

TWELFTH CENTURY

IN DOMESTIC buildings the porch does not seem to have become popular until the late 12th or 13th century. In churches also a few of 12th-century date remain, but it was not until the 13th century that they became common. Perhaps the earliest domestic porch surviving is that added in the late 12th century on the west side of the prior's hall at Castle Acre. This was placed centrally, with access to the undercroft, of one storey vaulted in two oblong bays, but heightened and extended westwards in the 15th century. Its developed plan, akin to the early 13th-century example at Lincoln Palace, suggests that earlier examples must have existed.

There were also porches in the sense of forebuildings containing the external staircase to an upper hall, as in the keeps of 12th-century castles. There is evidence of one at the 'Music House' (*c.* 1175) at Norwich, where the lower portion of one columned jamb of the lower entrance remains. At Canterbury the famous Norman covered staircase, with its columns, still leads up, here at right angles, to the Great Guesthouse of the Poor, now part of the King's School, on its undercroft; and in Durham Castle there must have been an imposing staircase porch to the magnificent first-floor entrance of Bishop Pudsey's Hall (*c.* 1170), this staircase being replaced by a two-storeyed gallery in the early 16th century.

THIRTEENTH CENTURY

A porch would be especially necessary to the great hall, to control the draught from the entrance doorway. For even with speres or screen the lofty room with its central hearth must have been an extremely draughty place.

Henry III's hall at Winchester Castle (1222–35) seems to have had a porch from the first, for on 14 November 1238 the king ordered to be made 'two posts before the porch of our hall, and a certain chain for the same post',* possibly as a protection from traffic,

* Liberate Roll, 23 Henry III; Turner (1851), 189.

and ten days later a chimney (fireplace) for 'our chamber above the porch of the great hall',* which must therefore have been an annexe of some size. At Woodstock in February 1244 he commanded 'a great and decent porch' to be added to the aisle of the hall, near the south angle,† and at Clarendon a 'great and becoming porch' to the king's hall in February 1245: ‡ this has been excavated. At Westminster in the same year a great porch 'which is

to be such as may become so great a palace' is 'to be made between the lavatorium [in the court] before the king's kitchens and the door entering into the smaller hall: so that the king may dismount from his palfrey in it at a handsome front [ad honestam frontem]; and walk under it between the aforesaid door and the lavatorium aforesaid; and also from the king's kitchen and the chamber of the knights'.§ Edward Fitz-Otho is to cover it with lead, and see to its speedy completion before the king's arrival. A porch seems therefore to have been a necessity for an important building in the mid 13th century.

Of existing porches the nearest to that at Westminster is found at the Deanery (once priory) at Winchester (Fig. 52), with its elaborate earlier 13th-century frontage showing three steeply pointed arches with lancet niches. The inner arches have shafts grouped with those of the vault within, which is of three narrow bays set at right angles to the entrance wall, and flanked by a further vaulted passage. On the side opposite this is a trefoiled wall arcade, and this feature is also found at Lincoln Palace, where the porch (of two

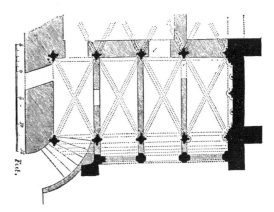

Fig. 52. The Deanery, Winchester, 13th-century porch, exterior and plan.

bays) is complicated by wing walls at the entrance, and the steep arches seem akin to those of the Galilee Porch (c. 1235–40) of the Cathedral.

But usually the porch was simpler, vaulted in one quadripartite bay, with shafted entrance and a chamber above. There is a good example at Bisham Abbey (c. 1280) and an earlier one of two bays at the Chantry, Chichester (Pl. XV A). In the ruined Crowhurst Manor, Sussex (c. 1250), the upper chamber, now gone, was reached by an angle passage from the

* Liberate Roll, 23 Henry III; Turner (1851), 193.
† Liberate Roll, 28 Henry III; Turner (1851), 201.
‡ Liberate Roll, 29 Henry III; Turner (1851), 207. Borenius & Charlton (1936), 72.
§ Close Roll, 29 Henry III; Turner (1851), 206.

solar, for here, as at the Chantry, the porch was set in the re-entrant angle with the solar-service block (*see* Fig. 27). There is a newel staircase in the angle of porch and hall at Canterbury, where the palace entrance has been excavated. Unlike most examples the porch is not against the end bay of the hall but in the next but one, as in the great hall of Winchester Castle.

At Lodsworth Manor (Sussex) the porch is found beneath the chimney breast corbels of an upper hall; this is of unusual type and the entrance had no door, this being also found at Swingfield Preceptory in Kent, as well as Shuthanger (Northamptonshire) early in the 14th century.

A porch in the form of a projecting oriel with external staircase must have served halls built at first-floor level, and there are traces at Netley Abbot's House, Aydon Castle, and Stokesay (solar), where the weathering of the gabled porch-staircase roof can be seen. Similarly the original entrance position in the slightly later hall at Markenfield (*c.* 1310) can be detected by the sloping mark of its staircase roof. These must represent a chief form of the 'oriel' so often mentioned in the Liberate Rolls. A more elaborate example occurs in the house built in 1200 by King John at Corfe Castle. This 'Gloriet' has an external staircase leading up to a porch or vestibule to two chambers at first-floor level, a chapel or audience chamber * to the north, a larger hall to the south. The vestibule was oblong in plan, and probably had windows on the shorter north and south walls. Of the two eastern doorways, that to the hall remains complete. Opposite it is a wall staircase, and north of that the entrance from the main staircase, which extends westward at right angles to the porch.

At Great Yarmouth the Tolhouse retains an external staircase or forebuilding on 13th-century lines if not incorporating early work. The first-floor hall has doorways with dog-tooth ornament that appears to date from *c.* 1230–40, and a newel staircase projection to the front, of which a straight joint with the forebuilding suggests that the latter is an addition perhaps of the late 13th or early 14th century, the rebuild of an earlier external staircase in wood.

FOURTEENTH CENTURY

In the 14th century the porch was a normal adjunct to the hall, sited as before against the last bay of its lateral wall, and now sometimes repeated at the other end of the screens passage. It was often vaulted, usually in one bay, and had a chamber over, which may have led to a gallery over the screens passage.

At Charing (*c.* 1300) (Pl. XXVII A) the south wall of the porch is thickened to contain a wall staircase, supplanted by a 16th-century brick turret on the other side. But usually the upper room is reached by a newel staircase at the angle of porch with hall or butteries; this may, as at Norwich Palace, open out of the hall itself. Clevedon Court (*c.* 1320) provides a useful example, one newel in the angle with the butteries, but opening from the south porch, while there is a second staircase opening from the north porch at its (opposite) angle with the hall. Penshurst also has two porches each with a staircase, the main one in a

* The view of Mr A. R. Dufty, F.S.A., A.R.I.B.A., of the Royal Commission on Historical Monuments.

lofty turret projection in the angle made by the front porch with the hall. Here the porch with upper chamber is the height of the hall and service, with continuous battlements. But the tendency was for the porch projection to become a tower, and at Dartington (c. 1388–1400) the porch of three storeys is loftier than the hall, with a stair turret of additional height, giving access to the leads. It is possible that the upper chamber of the porch may have been used for muniments. At New College, Oxford, though not at Winchester, the entrance staircase to the hall is contained in the Muniment Tower. However, such a document store would have been more properly sited at the lord's end of the building, as possibly was the case at Minster Lovell, in a room over the oriel staircase projection.

Bishop de Gower's porch at St David's (c. 1327–47) (Pl. XXVII c) has no upper chamber, the entrance being itself at first-floor level, with staircase, over a vaulted undercroft. The entrance is not central, to give room for a narrow window, and the hall doorway is nearer the opposite angle to allow access to an angle staircase. Traces remain of a splendid porch at the head of the staircase to John of Gaunt's hall at Kenilworth (c. 1390–3), also raised on a basement. So is Richard II's hall at Portchester (1396–9), but here the porch, entered below, contained all the steps up to the hall doorway; whereas in St David's these are chiefly outside.

The Prior's House at Ely, with its four great 13th- and 14th-century halls, had notable porches of complicated plan. The queen's hall and the prior's hall had covered external staircases, now gone. But the great, or guest, hall on the north, also raised on a vaulted undercroft, retains its open porch containing a straight flight of stone steps. This porch is threefold, for its southern portion, vaulted, gives access to the hall basement as well as to the northern entrance (for the monks) of the prior's great hall to the south, at ground level. The latter hall has a southern entrance (for the laity) almost opposite, which is also provided with a vaulted porch.

A two-centred entrance is the usual type, with moulded jambs and hood. The Mayfield entrance is shafted, but otherwise very similar to that of the Provost's House, Edgmond (Shropshire). At St David's, Gower's porch has a wide ogee doorway, flanked by canopied niches, while at Portchester the arch has a square frame with lantern brackets as stops.

The plain arch at Charing is flanked by trefoiled lancets, but the lower windows are usually placed at the sides, as at Meare, though a front window is normal in the chamber above, the Penshurst example, of two trefoiled lights with quatrefoil tracery in a segmental head, being especially elaborate. At Fyfield Manor, Berkshire (c. 1335–40) (Pl. XXVIII A), the window is of rather similar tracery, but with shields in the spandrels of a square head.*
It is, moreover, of wood, for the upper chamber here is timber-framed, like Sir John Golafré's solar adjoining; the porch itself is of stone, like his hall, which was lengthened in the late 16th century.

Earlier there were right-angled buttresses, but diagonal ones were usual in this century. There are both types at Clevedon Court.

The porch is sometimes vaulted, usually in one bay, but at Norwich there remains that

---

* This window may be reset; no opening shows in the photograph taken before James Parker's restoration of 1868. *Berks., Bucks., and Oxon. Archaeological Journal* (1917), XXIII, fig. 1.

of Bishop Salmon's Hall (*c.* 1318–25), with two oblong bays, more like the arrangement
at Lincoln, but with ridge and intermediate ribs as well as diagonals. Shuthanger, perhaps
contemporary, has one oblong bay with transverse and diagonal ribs only, and a vine decorated boss. Mayfield (*c.* 1325) is more typical, with one square quadripartite bay with wall
and diagonal ribs and massive central boss. Penshurst, some years later, has also tiercerons
(intermediate) with ridge ribs and additional bosses. Dartington Hall is similar, and on its
central boss John Holland placed the badge of his half-brother Richard II, a crowned and
chained white hart, set on a heraldic rose. This porch retains its original wooden benches.

FIFTEENTH CENTURY

The 15th-century porch remains in the traditional position against the end bay of the
hall. Sometimes it projects clear, at others it is placed in the angle of hall and butteries.
When these are in one line of building the porch, wider than the screens passage, tends to
overlap them both. At St Cross and Little Sodbury (Gloucestershire) it contains the stairs
up to the hall. In some halls the porch balances the oriel chamber at the other end, and at
Bewley Court (Wiltshire) it projects into line with the butteries, the upper stage reached
by a straight staircase rising from the oriel, across the front of the hall. This is unusual,
but this porch chamber also has the normal access to the room over the butteries. At
Ashbury Manor (*c.* 1488) it is entered through a screen from the great chamber, which
in this case was over part of the hall, and it perhaps served as an oratory, as at Lower
March Manor, Dunster (Somerset), Coombe Raleigh (Devon) and the shallow porch at
Bridport Chantry earlier. But where, as in some later examples such as Nevill Holt
(Leicestershire) and Seymour Court (Wiltshire) and in churches, a fireplace was provided,
the porch served a domestic function.

The entrance may be two-centred, elaborately moulded or with at least a moulded hood.
The doorway at South Wingfield (*c.* 1440–59) (Pl. XXVII B) is decorated with carved
paterae, and the curves of the hood are repeated in the string-course above. At Salisbury the
mid 15th-century King's House porch has openings with panelled reveals, to both north
and east. But the four-centred entrance soon becomes popular, and there are many examples,
some later arches approaching the semicircular.

The front window varies in size, a two-light being the most usual. An elaborate traceried
and transomed three-light window, like that of an oriel, forms one composition with the
entrance of the House of the Choir Master (*c.* 1480) at Wells. At Nevill Holt there is a
blank space over the entrance, for an armorial never executed. Perhaps Thomas Palmer
Esquire died (in 1474) before it was completed, or it may have been intended for the arms
of the Nevills, into which family his daughter Katherine married, and who became owners
of the property, hence the name. This shows an earlier hall made fashionable in the 1470's,
oriel and porch being added. The battlements of the porch are at a higher level than those
of the hall and bay, but they have a similar carved string-course which is carried over the
fireplace buttress and angle windows and cambered with the battlements on the entrance
front. At South Wraxall earlier both porch and oriel continue the parapet of the hall
roof (Pl. XXVIII C), and at South Wingfield the Lord Treasurer's porch has battlements

A

B

C

D

A. Early 16th-century hall screen at Wortham Manor.
B. Chapel screen at The Chancery, Lincoln; 15th century.
C. Hall screen, Milton Abbey; 1498.
D. Standard at Rufford Old Hall; c. 1500.

Plate XXV. Development of the Screen.

C

A

B

Plate XXVI.

A. Ashleworth Court, hall entrance and service end; before 1463.

B. East Meon Court House, service end gables and long window to hall; first half of the 15th century.

C. Minster Lovell Hall, c. 1431–42, cobbled path to porch; to right, with-drawing-room once with chapel over, and hall window showing above.

C

A

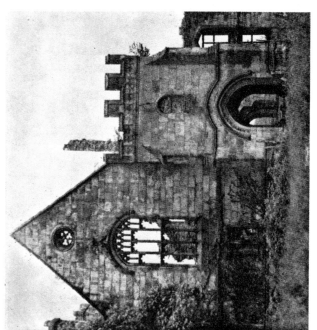

B

Plate XXVII. Porches.

A. Charing Palace, *c.* 1300.
B. South Wingfield, 1440–59, with window of great chamber.
C. Bishop Henry of Gower's Hall, St David's, *c.* 1327–47.

Plate XXVIII. Porches.

A. Fyfield Manor, Berkshire, c. 1335–40, with timber upper storey and solar wing.

B. Norrington Manor, early 15th century.

C. South Wraxall Manor, c. 1435.

over a traceried cornice; a treatment once carried along the walls of the great hall for it appears again over the oriel. But the gabled porch tended to be normal in manor houses as times became more settled, especially at the end of the 15th century, to which so many of our examples belong, and it is notable that the Wiltshire manor houses of South Wraxall (*c.* 1435) and Great Chalfield (*c.* 1480)—so alike in plan and twin porch and oriel —differ in this respect. However, Athelhampton Hall (*c.* 1495–1500) and Horham Hall (*c.* 1502–5) have the more spectacular battlements again. The Athelhampton porch, of bevelled plan, also has shafts or pilasters on the angles instead of the usual diagonal buttresses.

Sometimes the porch is vaulted, possibly less than in the 14th century. There is a lierne (stellar) vault in the porch added to Norrington Manor in the early 15th century (Pls. XVII c, f, XXVIII b), and a tierceron vault with carved bosses at St Cross, the London Guildhall (1411, of two bays) and Great Chalfield (Pl. 10 b). At the King's House, Salisbury, there is a fan vault, probably of the mid 15th century (Pl. XV d). One bay seems to have been usual, but Minster Lovell Hall has a porch of two double quadripartite bays, the ribs in each forming a lozenge at the ridge, and springing from attached shafts; the floriated bosses are weathered. The plan here shows an interesting development, the porch being enclosed in a range parallel with the hall and containing a chapel overhead, with the east end above the porch (Pl. XXVI c). Such an arrangement is also found at Bradley Manor (Devon) *c.* 1420, but the porch originally stood free except on the butteries side, and later in the 15th century was incorporated in a wing built in line with it.

Of timber-framed houses, Ockwells Manor (*c.* 1465) has an original porch with four-centred entrance in a square frame, with carved spandrels. There is a room over and a traceried gable to match the oriel projection at the other end of the hall.

EXAMPLES OF THE PORCH

c. 1175	'Music House' (Isaac's Hall), Norwich: evidence of forebuilding	*c.* 1280	Bisham Abbey, Berks.
		later C 13th	Exeter Palace
later C 12th	Canterbury, covered staircase to the great guest house	later C 13th	Lodsworth Manor House, Suss.
		?*c.* 1300	The Tolhouse, Great Yarmouth, Norf.
late C 12th	Prior's Hall, Castle Acre, Norf.	*c.* 1300	Charing Palace, Kent
c. 1200	Gloriet, Corfe Castle, Dor.	1318–25	Bishop Salmon's Hall, Norwich
early C 13th	The Chantry, Chichester	*c.* 1320	Clevedon Court, Som. (two)
earlier C 13th	Lincoln Palace	early C 14th	Shuthanger, Northants.
earlier C 13th	The Deanery, Winchester	early C 14th	The Provost's House, Edgmond, Salop
c. 1250	Crowhurst Manor, Suss., ruins	*c.* 1320–30	Mayfield Palace, Suss.

early C 14th	Great guest hall, Ely (three-fold)
c. 1322–35	Meare Manor House, Som.
c. 1327–47	Bishop Henry de Gower's Hall, St David's, Pembs.
c. 1335–40	Fyfield Manor, Berks.
c. 1341–9	Penshurst, Kent (two)
c. 1388–99	Dartington Hall, Devon (3 storeys)
1390–3	Kenilworth Castle, War., hall
1396–9	Portchester Castle, Hants, hall
c. 1400	The Chantry, South St, Bridport, Dor.
early C 15th	Norrington Manor, Alvediston, Wilts.
1411	The Guildhall, London
c. 1420	Bradley Manor, Devon
c. 1435	South Wraxall Manor, Wilts.
c. 1431–42	Minster Lovell Hall, Oxon.
c. 1440–59	South Wingfield, Derbys.
1445	Hospital of St Cross, Winchester
mid C 15th	The King's House, Salisbury
c. 1443–64+	The Old Vicarage, Congresbury, Som.
1465	Ockwells Manor, Bray, Berks.
c. 1470's	Nevill Holt, Leics.
later C 15th	Bewley Court, Lacock, Wilts.
later C 15th	Seymour Court, Wilts., (with fireplace)
c. 1480	House of the Choir Master, Wells
c. 1480	Great Chalfield Manor, Wilts.
c. 1480	Little Sodbury Manor, Glos.
c. 1488	Ashbury Manor, Berks.
c. 1495–1500	Athelhampton Hall, Dor.
c. 1502–5	Horham Hall, Ess.

II

The Gatehouse

AT ST MARY'S GUILD, Lincoln [1] (*c.* 1180–90), the entrance (Pl. LI A) serves as the gateway to a court, though it forms part of a range containing the hall at first-floor level. But otherwise surviving examples suggest that the domestic gatehouse was a feature rather of the later Middle Ages, a defensive measure partly explained by the unsettled condition of the times, still more by the improvement of protective measures, earlier houses having to rely on a moat, bank and palisade. Indeed the sites of many vanished 12th- and 13th-century manor houses are known from their moats, the only remaining evidence above ground of their existence. Excavation of these 'homestead moats', just beginning, should show that the buildings in these enclosures were of timber, sometimes later replaced by stone, like Ightham Mote in Kent.

In the 14th century there was growing social and economic unrest. It flared up as early as 1327, when the Abbey of Bury St Edmunds was stormed, and culminated in the widespread Peasants' Revolt of 1381. Also Edward III's wars brought the danger of French raiding on the coast, then an aftermath of restless unemployed soldiery ready for any violence to property; and their services were used by the great lords against their neighbours in the 15th century.

In castles, when the keep was supplanted in the 13th century by lofty curtain walls, the gatehouse became of prime importance, and notable examples remain at White Castle (Monmouthshire) (*c.* 1220-40), Pevensey (Sussex) (*c.* 1250) and Goodrich in Herefordshire (*c.* 1300), as well as in the famous Edwardian castles of Caernarvon (1283-1325), Conway (1283-9) and Harlech (1283-90).

Such defences were extended to non-military enclosures, such as cathedral closes, many of which received licences to erect stronger walls and gates during the last quarter of the 13th century. At Norwich the close wall was fortified *c.* 1276, following on disputes between the cathedral priory and the citizens. Lincoln, York and St Paul's were licensed in 1285, Exeter and Wells in 1286, Lichfield in 1299 and Canterbury in 1309.* At

* Thompson (1912), 298, 301.

155

Lincoln the first licence permitted a precinct wall 12 feet high, but apparently the work was delayed and in 1318 a licence of Edward II allowed greater height and also permission to crenellate the walls and provide them with embattled turrets. Much of the close wall remains. This and other licences show the need, owing to homicide and other crimes being perpetrated in the close at night, for walls and gates to be closed from twilight to sunrise, 'for the security of the canons and other ministers of the church passing by night between their lodgings and the church through the streets and lanes for celebration of the various services'.*

More widespread dangers are suggested at Lichfield in the unsettled reign of Edward II, and in a document of 1321–2 eight Lichfield masons swore an oath to defend the close.† At Salisbury Edward III's licence of 1327 permitted a close wall to be built and crenellated, and in 1331 the dean and chapter were allowed to remove and use the stones of the former cathedral and houses at Old Sarum.‡ Hereford was the last to be protected against malefactors by night, in 1389.

The episcopal palaces soon followed in this development. Indeed, the bishops were especially vulnerable in the 14th century, often an object of particular hatred to the mob, owing to their political power. Bishop Stapleton of Exeter was murdered outside his London house in 1326; Sudbury, Archbishop of Canterbury, Chancellor of Richard II, was dragged from the chapel of the White Tower of London in 1381; later, Bishop Ayscough of Salisbury, secretary to Henry VI, was seized in the Priory Church at Edington and stoned on a nearby hill, after which his palace was plundered. In 1329 Bishop Burghersh was permitted to repair, raise, crenellate and turrellate the walls of his palace at Lincoln,§ and in 1336 his Lincolnshire manors. Like Lincoln, at Wells the palace is outside the close, and in 1340 the Bishop, Ralph of Shrewsbury, obtained licence to crenellate its precinct, and his walls and gatehouse [13] remain; the moat is possibly earlier.

Many of the finest surviving 14th-century gatehouses are monastic, for abbeys and priories were also adopting defensive measures, with at least a strong gateway in the precinct wall. Good examples remain at Butley Priory, Suffolk [3] (c. 1311–32), with notable heraldic ornament, Beaulieu Abbey, and Bury St Edmunds,[4] built after 1327 when an earlier gate was destroyed, and rivalling the Norman gate tower to the south. These were followed by those at Battle Abbey,[5] a rebuild of 1339, probably in view of the French danger, St Albans [6] (c. 1361) and Ely (Great Gatehouse) [8] 1396–c. 1400, and the most magnificent of all, Thornton Abbey in Lincolnshire,[7] where in August 1382, the year after the Peasants' Revolt, the abbot and convent were granted a licence to 'build and crenellate a new house over and beside the abbey gate'. It is interesting to compare these with the more truly domestic gatehouses left, such as those at Charing Palace, Northborough Manor, and Tisbury Place in Wiltshire.

The domestic gatehouse was not, as a rule, defensive in a military sense, but it gave sufficient protection against bands of marauders or discontented peasantry. The manorial

* Hill (1948), 121.
† Harvey (1947), 159, 172.
‡ K. Edwards (1939). The Houses of Salisbury Close in the Fourteenth Century. *Journal of the British Archaeological Association*, 3rd S., IV, 62–3.
§ Calendar of Patent Rolls (1327–30), 453; Hill (1948) 129. The palace was already partly enclosed and crenellated.

buildings often contained the home farm, as at Markenfield, or at least, like the abbeys, a court, and a favourite type of gatehouse provided two passageways, a larger opening for horses and vehicles and a smaller doorway, more easily opened, for pedestrian traffic. Chichester Bishop's Palace [10] supplies an early 14th-century example. The external face of the outer gateway at Tisbury [14] has the same two arches, the larger segmental pointed, but on the inner face both arches are large. At Northborough Manor [12] (c. 1340) the twofold division is only in an intermediate wall, there being one fine moulded arch in each external face (Fig. 53). At Charing [11] (c. 1333–48) there is another, two-centred, arch in the wall between the gateway passages (Pl. XXIX D).

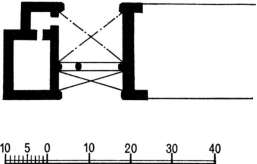

Fig. 53. Northborough Manor House, gateway.

The typical 14th-century gatehouse was an oblong block, like that at Northborough or Tisbury, sometimes part of a range of buildings as at Charing, and of two storeys with porter's lodge adjoining the double passageway, which often had a ribbed vault. The upper room, reached by a newel staircase, was usually the lodging of some important official; a hooded fireplace remains in that at Charing, and there are chimneys in the Tisbury gateways. The room could also be a courtroom or a chapel.

Width gave place to height in many later gatehouses, Maxstoke Castle (1346) and especially Thornton Abbey [7] (1382) providing a link. At the latter there is a great three-storeyed block, with octagonal turrets flanking the gate, as well as corner ones on each wide frontage (Fig. 54; Pl. XXX B). If the side portions were removed, leaving the central arch with its turrets, the result would be a tall gatehouse typical of the late 14th and especially of the 15th century.

The octagonal turret had now become an important feature. It had appeared at the end of the 13th century, at the angles of Burnell's hall at Wells (c. 1285–90), and chiefly used for staircases, as at Markenfield (1309).

At the early example of the tall gatehouse at Maxstoke Castle (Warwickshire) [15] the twin towers are narrow and octagonal and there is a single gate arch with two storeys above. The gatehouse at Wingfield in Suffolk [16] (1384) is similar, but here the octagonal towers are lower and wider, containing lodgings with traceried windows on the two upper floors; there is a single storey above the gate, and a marked resemblance to the gateway (c. 1350) leading to the keep at Alnwick Castle.

At Canterbury the West Gate (1378) clearly had Henry Yevele as designer.* Here the external towers are circular in plan, and it was probably Yevele who added similar towers and vault, in 1385, to the earlier gatehouse at Saltwood Castle in Kent.[17] This is very like the arrangement, on a smaller scale, at Donnington Castle (Berkshire) [18] (Pl. XXX A), where in the next year Sir Richard Abberbury received a licence to crenellate, and added a

* Harvey (1954), 315; (1946), figs. 26, 27, 32 (plan).

gatehouse to what seems to have been a fortified manor. At Donnington one tall circular tower contains a staircase, the other a storeroom with a garderobe off the passage to it from the chamber, on two floors, above the arch. The vault, here of two bays, has analogies not

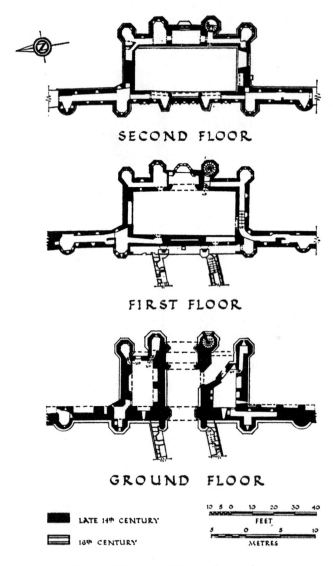

Fig. 54. Thornton Abbey, the gatehouse.

with those of the Kent examples, but with that over the chantry of Bishop William of Wykeham, designed by Yevele's friend William of Wynford, in Winchester Cathedral. Octagonal turrets flanking the entrance are used at Lumley Castle, Co. Durham, c. 1392, the work probably of John Lewyn, the great contemporary mason of the north. At West Bower (Somerset) [21] (Pl. XXIX A and B) the low gate is flanked by octagonal turrets with windows set lantern-wise round the upper part, resembling Yevele's water tower at Canterbury (*c.* 1396 over 12th-century arches).

William of Wynford favoured clear surfaces with the restrained use of ornament, and this is seen in his gatehouses at the two colleges he built for William of Wykeham. They are rectangular in plan with a vaulted gate passage, three bays at New College, Oxford [19] (1380–6), one in the outer and middle gates at Winchester (1387–1401),[20] and a newel staircase at one inner angle, which becomes an octagonal turret above the moulded parapet. A similar arrangement occurs at St Cross,[24] probably by Wynford's successor Robert Hulle, and which shows the arms of Cardinal Beaufort, who followed Wykeham as Bishop of Winchester (1404–47) and refounded the Hospital in 1445. This plain gatehouse tower with one staircase turret is found in other Oxford colleges, All Souls (1438–42) and Magdalen Founder's Tower (1475). At Cambridge, however, the more usual 15th-century domestic gatehouse is adopted, with an octagonal turret at each angle. Smaller gatehouses, as earlier, formed a tower over the passageway, like those built at Michelham Priory (Sussex) [22] and Broughton Castle [23] in 1405, both of two storeys over the gate hall, and Tretower Court [25] (*c.* 1480) where the upper storey has gone; these towers were embattled. The Cothay gatehouse [26] incorporates a small tower. This was probably the last portion of the house to be built, after 1481 when Richard Bluett succeeded to the property; his arms impaling those of his wife Alice Verney were reset on the gatehouse in the 1926–7 restoration.

The founder of Magdalen College, Oxford, was Beaufort's successor at Winchester, Bishop William Waynflete (1447–86), executor to Lord Cromwell, whose great tower at Tattershall Castle (1433–55) had such an influence on later 15th-century building. This is shown in the so-called Fox's Tower at Farnham Castle, which Waynflete is now known to have added in 1470–5 'at the door of the hall', his bricklayer being John Cole. This contains a porch but is on the scale of a gatehouse; it could be classed as a solar tower had it been at the bishop's end of the great hall. Waynflete has been unfortunate in having his work ascribed to others: the new brick gate tower of his palace at Esher (*c.* 1475–80) is known as 'Wolsey's Tower'.[31] It was probably designed by John Cowper, associated with Waynflete in his building operations at Eton College, where Waynflete was the

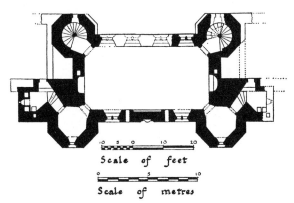

Fig. 55. Kirby Muxloe, gatehouse, plan of first floor.

first provost in 1441, after being headmaster at Winchester College, on which Henry VI modelled his new foundation. Cowper was also connected with Tattershall, having worked on the church tower (*c.* 1465–85), and was in charge of the works at Kirby Muxloe Castle [32] for Lord Hastings, these being left incomplete soon after the execution of the latter in 1483.

The gatehouse at Kirby Muxloe (Fig. 55, Pl. XXX D), like the rest of the castle, is of brick. It has the normal octagonal turrets at each angle, but the main block is wider than usual, with a porter's lodge or guardroom on either side of the gate passage. Above is one long room with transomed two-light windows, and a fireplace at each end; off each outer angle is a turret chamber with access to a garderobe on either side of the gatehouse; the inner turrets contain staircases. The third storey was never completed. It might be considered a simplified version of the Thornton Abbey layout without the oriel projection, wall passages and turrets flanking the entrance.

There is a closer resemblance in plan between Kirby Muxloe and the Great Tower, also in brick, at the Bishop of Lincoln's Palace at Buckden (Huntingdonshire), built by Bishop Rotherham (1472–80) according to Leland, but probably completed by his successor, since the arms of Bishop Russell (1480–94) are known to have appeared in the woodwork. Cowper thus seems to have been the designer, probably influenced by Tattershall Castle.

Like Kirby Muxloe, Thornbury Castle [42] was left unfinished owing to the execution of its owner, in this case Edward Stafford, third Duke of Buckingham (1521). The gatehouse (Pl. 11), begun in 1511, may be considered earlier in type, having deep projections flanking the entrance externally, though the outer angles of these are treated somewhat in the manner of a turret. An octagonal stair turret projects on either side of the inner opening, which is single, but the vaulted gatehall is entered from outside by a wide arch flanked by a smaller one for foot passengers, an early feature not usual in the later Middle Ages, but occurring also in the Deanery at Wells (1472–98). A wicket or small door, cut in the larger gate, normally sufficed for foot passengers, like the entrance to Haddon Hall.

At Hampton Court the Great Gatehouse [43] (1515–25) is like Kirby Muxloe in its long rectangular plan with octagonal angle turrets,* the lodges not projecting on either side of the gate passage, but here half octagonal turret-like buttresses flank the main arch, and with the oriel over the latter are reminiscent of the western face at Thornton Abbey. The architect for Cardinal Wolsey was Henry Redman, who excelled in the pleasant Tudor balance between horizontal and vertical, his string-courses controlling the upward, Gothic lines of the turrets.

Opposite is Anne Boleyn's Gatehouse,[37] Redman's earlier work for Wolsey (1514) but altered by Henry VIII, and containing the great astronomical clock of 1540. It is square, three storeys high, with octagonal corner turrets, the staircases on the inner side, and shows the more usual late mediaeval type, with height preferred to breadth. This tall gatehouse bears a strong resemblance to 'Lupton's Tower' (1516–20) at Eton,[39] also in brick but of four storeys with octagonal turrets of five stages on the front; in this Redman collaborated with his friend and partner William Vertue, with whom jointly in 1519 he became the King's Master Mason.† A third brick gatehouse of this type is the Clock Tower at St James's Palace; [40] this was built c. 1533 for Henry VIII by John Molton, Redman's

---

* The inner (east) front is less restored, but the stair turrets were rebuilt in 1566.
† William Vertue is famous for the fan vaults of St George's Chapel, Windsor, and Henry VII's Chapel at Westminster Abbey. Henry Redman was master mason also at Westminster Abbey, concerned in the rebuilding of St Margaret's Church for Abbot Islip. He was architect for Wolsey at York Palace and Hampton Court, collaborating with John Lebon in the design of the Great Gate (1525–9) of Cardinal College, later Christ Church, Oxford, to which in the next century Wren added the superstructure of 'Tom Tower'. St Stephen's Cloister at Westminster Palace was the joint work of Vertue and Redman. Vertue died in 1527, and next year 'the king is sorry for the death of Mr Redman, his mason' (Letter from Thomas Hensage to Wolsey; quoted in Harvey (1954), 220).

C

E

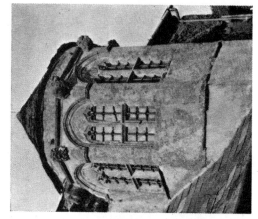

B

A

D

Plate XXIX. The Gatehouse.

A and B. West Bower Farm, Durleigh. Gatehouse turrets of the first half of the 15th century. C. Range of timber windows over an archway, 26 East St Helen's, Abingdon; late 15th century. D. Charing Palace, gatehouse, c. 1333–48. E. Compton Wynyates, c. 1515–20, arms of Henry VIII over entrance.

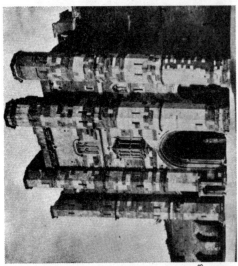

Plate XXX. The Gatehouse.

A. Donnington Castle, 1386. B. Thornton Abbey, 1382, inner side. C South Wraxall Manor, ?c. 1510. D. Kirby Muxloe Castle, c. 1483. E. Lower Brockhampton Hall, 15th century.

successor. The stone gateway *c.* 1540 at Cowdray [41] is similar, but of three storeys instead of four.

Thus the great gatehouse of brick is a particular feature of the late 15th and early 16th centuries. Brick used earlier with stone dressings at Thornton Abbey is the main material at Herstmonceux Castle, Sussex (1441), and found especially in the stoneless districts of the east of England. A number of these gatehouses survive, perhaps because brick is less valuable and more difficult to re-use than stone. The cheaper material may also have influenced the height. Certainly the turrets grew higher and higher, with seven stages at Oxburgh Hall in Norfolk (*c.* 1482), six at Hadleigh (Suffolk) in the Deanery Tower [30] (*c.* 1495) and eight at Layer Marney Towers in Essex (*c.* 1520), where the effect is almost overwhelming. The height may not have been due only to the desire for pomp and the display of power. In flat country such as East Anglia the lofty turret would serve as a landmark and look-out over miles of country. There were still only two storeys above the gatehouse passage, forming loftier rooms than the chambers in the towers.

Oxburgh Hall (Pl. 12) [29] was built by Sir Edmund Bedingfield, who received licence to crenellate in 1482. Of the tall octagonal turrets flanking the gate, the western contains the staircase, and in the eastern the lowest of the seven stages has gun loops and arrow-slits. On the courtyard side there are corner watch turrets at parapet level only, but attached half-octagon turrets flank the main arch; they are of three window stages, finished with battlements below the main parapet of the gatehouse. An 18th-century bridge replaces the original drawbridge over the moat.

At Layer Marney [38] the gatehouse appears loftier than it would have seemed had the proposed main courtyard been completed. The work was stopped at the deaths of Henry, first Lord Marney, in 1523, and of his son in the following year. His was an ambitious scheme worthy of Hampton Court, which Cardinal Wolsey was building about the same time. The gatehouse itself contains no fewer than thirty-nine rooms and is a combination of tower house and gateway. There are the usual two lofty storeys over the gate passage, each 15 feet high with large windows to front and back, and on either side are long, lower rooms 7 feet 6 inches high lit by bay windows formed by three sides of the octagonal turret in the front, and with access to closets in a flanking turret, similar but one storey lower. The courtyard elevation is flat, with the angles carried up as turrets, one containing the staircase.

As in brick castles, such as Herstmonceux, [28] a battlemented parapet is usual, with separate crenellation to the turrets, and this is found as late as 1536 at Little Leez in Essex. But it is now a decorative element entirely. A stepped merlon is a variation at Oxburgh, with the addition of crocketed brick pinnacles at Gifford's Hall in Suffolk. East Barsham, Norfolk [34] (*c.* 1535), is especially elaborate with traceried crenellation. At Layer Marney, however, the merlons are replaced by semicircular pediments of terracotta, flanked by dolphins, a conceit also used on the tomb of Henry, first Lord Marney, in the church.* These are the work of Italian craftsmen, perhaps of Girolamo da Trevizi, who had entered this country in Henry VIII's service, and would have come to Lord Marney's notice at court.†

---

* As in the tombs at Oxburgh, commissioned by his daughter Grace, the wife of Sir Edmund Bedingfield.
† Trevizi, or Trevisano, was probably also used by his friend Lord Sutton at Sutton Place near Guildford. Lloyd (1934), 27–9.

Brick tracery in the form of a trefoil-arched corbel table frequently supports the parapet, as at Oxburgh, or divides up the turret stages. At Farnham this is combined with decorative machicolation. Cinquefoiled heads with traceried spandrels are used at Faulkbourne Hall, Essex (built prior to 1494).*

Sometimes the turrets are crowned, above the battlements, by pinnacles in cut or moulded brick. These are especially elaborate at East Barsham, and at West Stow (Suffolk), c. 1520–1533, are in the form of cupolas, with terracotta figures above.†

The four-centred arch is general, moulded and set in a square frame, often with quatrefoils in the spandrels. Sometimes the outer curve continues to form a decorative ogee arch with finial, which may carry a coat of arms, with supporters and other devices in the square panel above the gate. This is a feature of the two Cambridge gatehouses designed by William Swayn, Christ's College [35] (1505–11) and St John's [36] (1511–26), of both of which the foundress was Henry VII's mother, the Lady Margaret Beaufort, Countess of Richmond and Derby, a great patroness of learning. She died in 1509, but her executor, Bishop Fisher of Rochester, obtained the charter of foundation. In both gateways the four-centred arch, enriched with *paterae*, has this ogee label with rose and portcullis in the spandrel, carrying at the apex the arms of the foundress with Yale supporters, flanked by the coroneted portcullis, badge of the Beauforts, and the red rose of Lancaster, on a bush, royally crowned; the field is strewn with daisy plants (marguerites) and germander speedwell. The St John's panel is the more elaborate, and includes in the field, rabbits, fox and goose, while there is a frieze of daisies and string-course of vine, portcullis and Lancastrian roses.‡ The same craftsman obviously did the work of both. The arms on Henry VIII are carved in brick over the outer ogee arch at East Barsham,[34] and those of the Fermors adorn the courtyard side. This dates from c. 1535; the hall and porch are some ten years earlier.

For the gatehouse was a suitable place for the emblems of the owner, founder or patron, on which the heraldic symbols of their power and dignity could be displayed. There are ten shields in the spandrels of the arcading at Kirkham Priory, Yorkshire [2] (1289–96), and Prior William Geyton's gateway at Butley Priory [3] (1311–32) is a valuable example of an armorial, thirty-five shields in five rows of seven, carved in stone, a pictorial list of important subscribers to the building. The spandrels of the entrance arch are used for the arms of Cardinal Beaufort at St Cross, over which a moulded cornice includes, with *paterae*, four heads said to depict Henry IV, his half brother, John of Gaunt, Duke of Lancaster, their father, Beaufort himself, and his mother Katherine Swynford.

At Thornbury [42] the gateway is decorated over the arch with the arms of the builder enclosed in the Garter. Flanking it are other shields with the badges of his family including the Stafford knot and Bohun swan, and below a scroll with inscription:

Thys Gate was begon in the yere of owre Lorde Gode MCCCCCXI. The ii yere of the reyne of Kynge Henri the VIII by me Ediv Duc of Bukkyngha. Erlle of Herforde Stafforde and Northampto.

The fatal motto 'Doresenavant' * is on a separate scroll below, with a blank one to balance it on the other side of the main arch.

A statue of the patron came to be an important part of the design. Wykeham's two colleges are dedicated to the Virgin Mary, and at Winchester College there is the original figure of Our Lady, of great beauty, in a cusped and canopied niche over the outer gate. There is another, with the kneeling figure of the founder, on both faces of the middle gate, here at second-floor level to allow for larger windows to the rooms below. There is the same arrangement, on both sides of the gate, at this level, at New College, Oxford, and in Beaufort's gate tower at St Cross, where the single figure of the Madonna is renewed on the south side; on the north the figures have gone except that of the cardinal; possibly the companion statue was of Bishop Henry of Blois, the earlier founder.

The room over the gate passage was an important one, well lit to front and back. At Kirby Muxloe Castle provision was still made for the apparatus of a drawbridge, flanked by windows, but in colleges this was unnecessary, and in most other cases out of date, so a large window could take the place of the raising equipment. It was a good place to have an oriel to give as much outlook as possible for arrivals, as well as a decorative feature. This was very popular in the 16th century, as at South Wraxall (Pl. XXX c) [33] and Coughton Court (c. 1530) in Warwickshire.

There must have been many gatehouses of timber such as the little 15th-century one at Lower Brockhampton (Pl. XXX E), [27] with its jettied upper part and close timbering. Of gatehouses with arch and lower portion in stone, and timber work above, examples remain at Wigmore Abbey, [9] also in Herefordshire, and at Bromfield Abbey, Shropshire. At Wigmore the upper part is original 14th-century work.

* *Doresenavant, Dorénavant,* or *Dores-en-avant* (Old French): henceforward or hereafter.

EXAMPLES OF GATEHOUSES

	12TH CENTURY	*References*
(1) c. 1190	St Mary's Guild, Lincoln	Wood (1935), 191–4, pls. IV A, XII A, XIII B (plan).

	13TH CENTURY, MONASTIC	
(2) 1289–96	Kirkham Priory, Yorks.	

	14TH CENTURY, MONASTIC	
(3) c. 1311–32	Butley Priory, Suff.	Evans (1949), 59, 114, pl. 35 B.
(4) after 1327	Bury St Edmunds Abbey, Suff.	
(5) 1339 & earlier	Battle Abbey, Suss.	H. Brakspear, plan in Guide (1934).
(6) c. 1361	St Alban's Abbey, Herts.	
(7) c. 1382	Thornton Abbey, Lincs.	M.O.W. Guide (40), 4, 9–13 (plans & illus.); Thompson (1912), 303 (plan).
(8) 1396–c. 1400	Ely, great gatehouse	
(9)	Wigmore Abbey, Heref.	R.C.H.M. *Herefordshire,* III, 2–3, pl. 28 (plans & illus.); Brakspear (1933 b), 38–9, pls. I & V (plans & illus.).

14TH CENTURY, DOMESTIC, ETC.		*References*
(10) early C 14th	Bishop's Palace, Chichester	*Archaeological Journal*, XCII (1935), 390, pl. I[I] (plan).
(11) *c.* 1333–48	Charing Palace, Kent	Kipps (1933) 81–4, 92–3, pls. I–IV (plan & illus.).
(12) *c.* 1340	Northborough Manor, Northants.	Parker (1853), 254 (plan).
(13) *c.* 1340	Bishop's Palace, Wells, Som.	*Archaeological Journal*, CVII (1950), 103 (plan).
(14)	Tisbury Manor, Wilts.	Dufty (1947), 168, fig. 1, pl. XVII (plan & illus.).
(15) *c.* 1348	Maxstoke Castle, War.	Harvey (1947), fig. 62.
(16) *c.* 1384	Wingfield Castle, Suff.	Harvey (1947), fig. 61.
(17) 1385	Saltwood Castle, Kent	
(18) 1386	Donnington Castle, Berks.	M.O.W. Guide (14) (plans); *V.C.H. Berks.*, IV, 93 (plan).
(19) 1380–6	New College, Oxford	R.C.H.M. *Oxford*, 85, pl. 160 (plan & illus.).
(20) 1387–1401	St Mary's College, Winchester (2)	Oakeshott & Harvey (1955) (plan).

15TH CENTURY

Smaller Gatehouses

(21) first half C 15th	West Bower Farm, Durleigh, Som.	R.C.H.M. (1963) 56 (illus.).
(22) 1405 or earlier	Michelham Priory, Suss.	
(23) 1405	Broughton Castle, Oxon.	
(24) 1404–47	Hospital of St Cross, Winchester	Godfrey (1955), fig. 29, pl. 5 *b* (plan & illus.).
(25) *c.* 1480	Tretower Court, Brecon.	M.O.W. Guide (41), 7–8 (plan & illus.).
(26) after 1481	Cothay Manor, Som.	Garner & Stratton (1929) 21, pl. IV; *Archaeological Journal*, CVII (1950), pl. XX; Lloyd (1931), figs. 96, 98 (plan).
(27)	Lower Brockhampton, Heref.	R.C.H.M. *Herefordshire*, II, 32–3 (plan & illus.).

Tall Brick Gatehouses

(28) 1441	Herstmonceux Castle, Suss.	Pugin (1839), 11–13, pls. 9–14 (plan, etc.).
(29) *c.* 1482	Oxburgh Hall, Norf.	Pugin (1838), 45–9, pls. 54–8 (plan, etc.); Garner & Stratton (1929), pls. CXL, CLIX.
(30) *c.* 1495	'Deanery Tower', Hadleigh, Suff.	Garner & Stratton (1929), pls. CXL, CLVIII.

Long Rectangular Brick Gatehouses

(31) *c.* 1475–80	Esher Palace ('Wolsey's Tower'), Sy.	
(32) *c.* 1483	Kirby Muxloe Castle, Leics.	M.O.W. Guide (24), 12–17 (plans).

16TH CENTURY

Smaller Gatehouses

(33) ?*c.* 1510	South Wraxall Manor House, Wilts.	Pugin (1840), pls. 60–3 (plan, etc.).
(34) *c.* 1535	East Barsham Manor House, Norf. (brick)	Pugin (1838), 50–2, pls. 59–61; Garner & Stratton (1929), 124–5 (plan & illus.).

Tall Brick Gatehouses

(35) 1505–11	Christ's College, Cambridge (refaced in stone 1714)	R.C.H.M. *Cambridge*, 27, pls. 93 & 94 (plan & illus.).
(36) 1511–16	St John's College, Cambridge	R.C.H.M. *Cambridge*, 189, pls. 93 & 94 (plan & illus.).

16TH CENTURY: continued		*References*
(37) 1514+	Hampton Court, Middx, Anne Boleyn's gatehouse	R.C.H.M. *Middlesex*, 33, frontispiece (plan & illus.).
(38) *c.* 1520	Layer Marney Towers, Ess.	R.C.H.M. *Essex*, III, 157–9 (plan & illus.); Tipping (1921), 165 (illus.); Garner & Stratton (1929), 126, pl. LXXXV (plan & illus.).
(39) 1516–20	Eton College, Bucks., Lupton's Tower	
(40) *c.* 1533	St James's Palace, London, Clock Tower	R.C.H.M. *London*, II, 128–9, pl. 200 (plan & illus.).

Tall Stone Gatehouses

(41) *c.* 1540	Cowdray House, Suss.	Garner & Stratton (1929), 50, figs. 74, 75, 77, pl. CXL (plan & illus.).

Long Rectangular Gatehouses

(42) 1511–21	Thornbury Castle, Glos.	Pugin (1839), 35–6, pls. 37–9 (plan, etc.).
(43) 1515–25	Hampton Court, Middx, Great Gatehouse	R.C.H.M. *Middlesex*, 32, pl. 74 (plans & illus.).

12

Tower Houses

THE great residential tower, or 'keep', of the Norman castle became out of date in the 13th century, at least in the south, owing to the growth in defensiveness of the curtain walls, which could guard less confined and more comfortable quarters within. But the idea of a tower house persisted, and continued to the end of the mediaeval period in areas of especial danger, such as the Scottish Border.

The late 11th-century hall at Chepstow Castle (Pl. III c),[1] reorganized in the 13th century, is closer to the later tower house than to the keep. Its dimensions—90 (c. 88 at the south)× 30 feet, internal measurements—the length so much greater than the width, are quite unlike those of the normal square keep, and when a later storey was added over the original first-floor hall, the resemblance to the tower house is striking, except in the lack of corner turrets.

In unfortified buildings, however, there was a tendency towards what might be called the 'solar tower', in which the great chamber, on its upper floor adjoining the hall, might be given a defensive form, the loftiness of which supplied an appearance of authority. It could also serve as a look-out. This is seen in episcopal palaces of the 12th century. Bishop Roger of Salisbury (1107–39) placed a great tower next to the hall in his courtyard 'castle' at Sherborne.[26] Like his other building, at Old Sarum, this is more domestic than military. At Sarum,[27] the strong tower (now called Postern Tower) was added rather later, but corresponds to that at Sherborne. Similarly, Henry of Blois (1129–71) added a tower in his Winchester residence, Wolvesey Castle.[28] There is a 12th-century tower, later heightened, in his palace at Bishop's Waltham,[29] here separated by an ante-chamber from the hall. A low D-shaped tower, with small windows, is attached to the 13th-century hall at Godlingston Manor in Dorset,[30] and Little Wenham [31] might be considered in this tower category, as also the Castle House at Deddington, Oxfordshire, though this contained the chapel.

But the ideal example of the solar tower is found at Longthorpe in Northamptonshire,[32] where a square tower was added to a hall of c. 1260 in the early 14th century (Pl. XXXI e). Here was a suitable chamber for a rising man, Robert Thorpe, Steward of Peterborough

Abbey, decorated in the latest fashion, with fireplace and garderobe, and combining privacy, comfort and defence. It is reached from the first floor of the earlier building, and a mural staircase leads to a room above; there is no direct outside access to the vaulted storage space below. At Creslow Manor House, Buckinghamshire [33] (c. 1330), a three-storeyed tower is added to the solar, with a stair turret at the junction.

Chesterton Tower, Cambridge,[34] is only two storeys in height (Pl. 13; Pl. XXXI A). It dates from the mid 14th century, but the oblong plan * with octagonal turrets, here on two corners only, seems a forerunner of the common 15th-century arrangement. The north turret contained a newel staircase, the west is corbelled out like a 'bartizan' turret to give an octagonal chamber above. Originally a hall may have been attached, perhaps at the eastern angle. This unusual little building was the residence of a proctor representing the owner of Chesterton Church, the Abbey of St Andrew at Vercelli in Italy, to which the founder, Cardinal Gualo, the Papal Legate, gave it, having received it from Henry III. The proctor had a delightful solar with every convenience, and a room below, not only for storage, but perhaps in the nature of an audience chamber, as there are traceried windows and the vault is enriched with carved bosses.

A tower-like building containing the entire accommodation is the late 13th-century mansion Acton Burnell 'Castle' in Shropshire (Pl. XXXI B).[4] The builder was Edward I's trusted friend and secretary, Robert Burnell, who became his Chancellor in 1274 and Bishop of Bath and Wells the following year. In January 1284 he obtained a licence for the mansion at his birthplace, and in July permission to take timber from the royal forests in Shropshire for it.† That month Burnell was here to see the progress of the work, but judging from the late character of the window tracery his new house was probably unfinished at his death in 1292. Yet there is a striking resemblance to the Bishop's other palace at Wells, where his great hall dates from c. 1275–92.

The Shropshire house consists of an oblong block (68 feet × 46 feet 9 inches) two rooms deep, in this nearer the 12th-century hall keep than the 13th-century house plan. There are square towers at three angles, an originally longer tower at the north-east, and a larger annexe off the centre of each shorter side, the eastern destroyed to ground level. Three of the towers retain their battlements, as does the north wall. The main building was divided into four ground-floor rooms, the larger two on the east, and window evidence shows that these rooms were not storage basements but living-rooms, doubtless for the Chancellor's household. The great hall was on the first floor, and may have occupied the three double eastern bays, with a longitudinal arcade to support the twin roofs necessary over so large a span (47 feet). The western bays, over the two lower rooms, would be the Bishop's great chamber, with a further storey at this end to provide him with a private chamber above, with wardrobe ‡ in the western block, and access to a garderobe in the north-west tower. The roof here probably ran at right angles to those of the hall. The corner towers provided lodgings for chaplains and secretaries, a vaulted strong room (south-west), porch (south-east) with a chapel in the north-east tower and priest's room above.

---

* Ground floor 26 feet × 15 feet 9 inches, first floor 27 feet 6 inches × 17 feet 3 inches (internal).
† Calendar of Patent Rolls (1281–92), 110, 126.
‡ Mr Radford thinks that this was his bedchamber.

Another Shropshire tower house, on a much smaller scale, remains at Upper Millichope [3] near Wenlock Edge, the Forester's Lodge (c. 1280). The oblong block (42 feet × 29 feet 3 inches) * has walls some 6 feet thick on both floors, the upper of which was the hall, with shafted two-light windows with seats, raised over an undercroft with loop openings; the angle staircase is partially blocked. †

Millichope resembles the 'pele towers' ‡ like small keeps on the Northern Border, where Scottish raids made the fortification of the whole house essential. Many examples remain, especially from the 14th century onwards. Three storeys are usual: a storage basement vaulted against fire; a hall on the first floor, and the great chamber or sleeping apartment above. In such regions even vicarages needed to be small fortresses, into which the parishioners with their cattle could be crowded when the alarm was given. Of such vicars' peles the best known is at Corbridge in Northumberland [6] (c. 1300), a rectangle 19 × 12 feet with a ground-floor entrance, in one jamb of which rises the wall staircase to the principal room equipped with fireplace, sitting-windows, garderobe and sink, and a mural staircase up to the priest's bedchamber, which has no fireplace but a lectern and may have served as his oratory as well.

Edlingham Castle [10] (c. 1350) in the same county is a similar oblong block only much larger. Above a vaulted basement, now completely buried, is a magnificent hall two storeys in height, vaulted, with clerestory windows and fireplace.

Often wings were added to the main rectangle to give extra accommodation. There is one at Chipchase (Northumberland) [8] (c. 1340) containing the entrance, newel staircase and a chamber on each of the three upper floors. As there is an extra (fourth) storey to this tower, the hall § is raised to the second-floor level. Full use is made of the thick walls to accommodate mural chambers and an oratory. Another splendid Northumbrian tower, similar but of three storeys, stands at Belsay, [9] also c. 1340, perhaps by the same mason. Here there are two wings off the west side, the northern of four stages, the southern containing the staircase and six storeys of small chambers, the highest above roof level. The main body contains a vaulted kitchen, first-floor hall with traceried windows (its chapel adjoining) and great chamber over.

In larger houses angle towers, often projecting to flank the main walls, gave extra accommodation. At Dacre Castle, Cumberland (Pl. 14), [7] begun in 1307, there is the unusual plan of larger square towers to the eastern and western corners of the block, smaller ones set diagonally to north and south. Langley Castle, Northumberland (Pl. 15), [11] is another larger scale tower house, comparable to the massive buildings of Scotland, such as

* External measurements. The upper part of the building is later, and the south-eastern extension is late 17th or 18th century.
† The ground-floor entrance has been rebuilt with ball-flower ornament flanked by roll-and-fillet re-used to form a semi-circular arch. This has caused confusion and suggested a Norman origin. It is also strange to find 12th-century nail-head and early 14th-century ball-flower in the same building, both combined with 13th-century mouldings.
‡ An inaccurate term in current use. The research of Dr R. W. Brunskill has shown that the 'pele tower' never existed. 'Peles', as distinct from palisades, are mentioned in late 13th- and early 14th-century documents, when erected as temporary fortifications as the English army moved against the Scots. Many carpenters and daubers were employed, and the pele seems to have been constructed like a colonial blockhouse, of heavy timbers laid horizontally, jointed at the angles, and made fireproof with earth and clay. 'Tower house' is the correct term for the stone towers of three (or four) storeys, and 'Bastel house' for the longer house of two storeys, the lower for horses and cattle, the upper of two rooms for domestic use. With a tower house a barmkin, a fortified yard, was needed for the cattle. (Information from a lecture 'Towers and Fortified Manor Houses of Cumberland' given to the British Archaeological Association, 13 November 1964.)
§ c. 36 feet 6 inches × 18 feet.

Borthwick Castle, with their great sheer walls and corbelled bartizans. A square tower projects off each end of the lateral walls of the main rectangle, but flush with the end walls, east and west of the building.* At Haughton Castle [12] in the same county, the angle towers do not project and a fifth (higher) one is added midway on the south front. The great block measures 49×107 feet, and Dr Douglas Simpson has discovered that here is the transformation, soon after 1373, of an earlier hall house, of which the 13th-century door-way remains, into a tower house, the heightened walls being carried by a great arcade, its five arches now filled in, to north and south.

Where the tower was particularly great, a central courtyard could be included, as in the magnificent Bolton Castle [14] of the Scropes in Yorkshire, built by John Lewyn c. 1378. Though tower-like in appearance, this is partly akin to the quadrangular mansions of the south. But the main rooms, as in the smaller tower houses, are all at first-floor level and over.

As we have seen, the tower house continued the Norman keep tradition in the turbulent north. Further south it returned in the 14th and 15th centuries to a lesser extent, owing to military necessity. The lord now had a standing army of professional soldiers, found more reliable in attendance than the old feudal levies with their limited forty-day obligation, and for these he had to provide regular quarters.† For convenience these lodgings needed to be separate from those of the owner, his family and immediate household, to ensure privacy and also protection against possible treachery and mutiny in his stronghold. For mercenaries, secured by money and not by traditional devotion to the family, were liable to be bought over by a rival with more pay and to turn against their master. This led to what Dr Douglas Simpson has called 'the Castle of Livery and Maintenance', and it concerns us from the domestic aspect. At first the lord sited his private accommodation in a strong gatehouse, which thus had a strategic position for defence from attack within or without. Such an arrangement can be seen at Tonbridge (c. 1300); and in some of the Edwardian castles such as Denbigh and Harlech. But this proved inconvenient because of the need to devote some of the first floor to drawbridge and portcullis tackle, and to raise the hall to the second floor.

More suitable was a lofty building akin to the tall 'tower keeps' of the 12th century, which gave the lord a strong and commanding position as well as privacy from his mer-cenaries, to whom the earlier old-fashioned domestic buildings against the curtain could be assigned. Apart from the example excavated at Tarset Castle, Northumberland, licensed in 1267, which shows an oblong plan with projecting angle turrets, the earliest tower house of this kind seems to be that at Dudley Castle,[5] built by the notorious Sir John de Somery, who held the lordship from 1300 to 1321. Dudley tower is of two storeys, but raised on an earlier motte. It is oblong in plan ‡ with half-round towers at the angles. Indeed it might be considered an elongated version of the mid 13th-century Clifford's Tower at York,[2] a quatrefoil building once completely roofed, which with Pontefract (c. 1230), of similar shape, is perhaps a link between the earlier keep and later tower house.

---

* The main block is c. 80×24 feet internally. The floors were replaced and the castle restored by Cadwallader Bates early this century.
† Dr Douglas Simpson calls this 'bastard feudalism'.
‡ 70×48 feet externally, with walls 10 feet and over.

Very similar is Nunney Castle,[13] which was built by Sir John de la Mare by licence of 1373. There is no motte here but two extra storeys to the tower, which is an oblong with large drum towers at the angles, a development from Dudley. The kitchen is on the ground floor, and in the jamb of the vaulted entrance a wall staircase gave access to what may have been a guardroom above. From this a newel staircase led to the more important room, with traceried windows with seats, which must have been the hall, and above was the great chamber, also with sitting-windows, a richly moulded fireplace, and the chapel leading off it in the south-west tower. There were supplementary chambers in the towers, some with garderobe.

The great tower house on the motte at Warkworth Castle (Fig. 56) [15] was built by the first Earl of Northumberland between 1377 and 1390, soon after c. 1380 judging from the heraldic evidence.* John Lewyn, architect of Bolton, being the outstanding northern architect at that time, was probably the designer.† It is a square of c. 65 feet in plan, with a projecting bay on each side, giving a cruciform effect; all the angles are chamfered. The ground floor is vaulted and contains storerooms; the main rooms, the hall, chapel and kitchen, are on the first floor, and rise to the height of two storeys, with buttery, pantry and chambers on the first and chambers on the second floor. In the centre is a square light-well rising the whole height of the building.

The light-well is enlarged into a central court in Wardour Old Castle,[17] for which John, fifth Lord Lovell, received a licence to build in February 1393: this was possibly designed by William of Wynford.‡

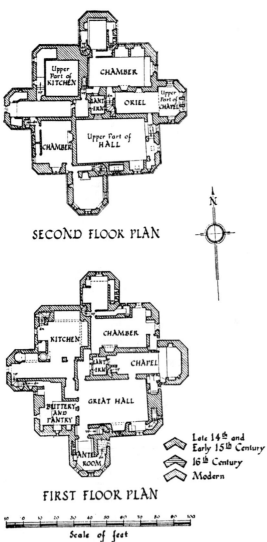

SECOND FLOOR PLAN

FIRST FLOOR PLAN

Late 14th and Early 15th Century
16th Century
Modern

Scale of feet

Fig. 56. Warkworth Castle, the Keep.

It is a remarkable building of hexagonal plan, with projecting square towers on either side of the entrance, and around the court, also hexagonal, the hall and kitchen are arranged on the first floor, rising through the second floor.

* Simpson (1938), 115, and (1941), 93.   † Ibid., and Harvey (1954), 168.
‡ Harvey (1954), 310.

The kitchen with its great end fireplace is set below the hall in the Devon tower house of Shute (Pl. XXXI c).[16] This seems to have been built c. 1380 by Sir William Bonville, sheriff of Dorset and Somerset in 1381–2, and of Devonshire in 1390. A block was added at right angles in the last quarter of the 15th century by Cicely, Marchioness of Dorset, the last of the Bonvilles. The hall they knew is less lofty now, for in the 19th century an intermediate storey was made between hall and kitchen, lessening the height of both, and the windows were altered or re-used. It is interesting to compare Shute with the other Devonshire tower house, Bindon, near Axmouth. The latter presumably dates from the 15th century, but was much altered in the early 16th and 17th centuries. Here there are two parallel rooms on each floor with original fireplaces in the end walls. The house owes much for its restoration to Colonel R. L. Broad, aided by the research of Mr A. W. Everett, F.S.A. A smaller tower house of c. 1400 can be seen at 'The Chantry', South Street, Bridport (Dorset); [18] it has a two-storeyed porch.

A hexagonal building like Wardour, but without court or projecting towers, is the Yellow Tower of Gwent (c. 1430–45) at Raglan Castle,[19] built by an 'overmighty subject' in the south-eastern march, Sir William ap Thomas, who did not scruple to use violence in his rise to power. To protect himself also from his own men, if necessary, his great tower (surrounded by a low outer hexagon, slightly later (c. 1450–69) with corner turrets) is isolated within its moat, alongside the main castle, once reached from it by elaborate drawbridge arrangements. The kitchen with well is on the ground level of the tower, the hall on the first floor, great chamber on the second, and bedchambers on the third and possibly on a fourth floor which has now gone.

Strong residential towers of exceptional height are a feature of the late 14th and early 15th centuries. At Warwick Castle the south-east domestic block over vaults was supplemented by lofty towers on the north and west angles of the curtain wall. We know that Guy's Tower was completed in 1394, at the cost of £395 5s. 2d.,* and Thomas Beauchamp, Earl of Warwick (d. 1401) probably built Caesar's Tower as well. Guy's Tower [40] to the north is 128 feet high, of twelve-sided plan with five storeys all vaulted, four residential, each containing an oblong room with fireplace, mural chamber and garderobe, and an octagonal guardroom at the top. Caesar's Tower [41] is 133 feet in height, tri-lobed in plan, and contains six storeys, all vaulted except the fifth, which was an ammunition store below the hexagonal guardroom. The lowest is a prison, the next three residential, with rooms similar to those in Guy's Tower, comfortable quarters probably for the use of important officials of the earl's household, secure against attack from within or without the castle. In both towers the storeys above the basement are entered from the wall walk at third-floor level and a newel staircase gives access to rooms above and below. A staircase on the further side gives direct access from battlements to the wall walk.

These lofty towers are regarded as French rather than English in character, their great height being more usual in France; likewise a double tier of battlements in Caesar's Tower, with a central turret rising above rampart level, is rare in England but common in French castles. It is also found in the brick towers of Herstmonceux (1441).

Akin to the Warwick buildings is the tall, slender solar tower at Caister, in Norfolk,[42]

* Warwick Castle Guide (1949), 12. This would represent perhaps £40,000 or more today.

the castle built between 1432 and 1446 by Sir John Fastolf, veteran of the wars of Henry V. This is of great interest for its close affinity to the 'Wasserburg' type of the Lower Rhineland, e.g. Schloss Kempen, Krothorf and Hardenburg. These were also built of brick, on a low site, relying on ample water defences and again having a tall, slender look-out tower. Fastolf's tower is *c.* 90 feet high, circular externally, hexagonal internally, in plan. There are five storeys with a single room, each having a fireplace except the topmost, which was probably his look-out and muniment room, perhaps treasure chamber, the *garderoba in domo superiori* of the inventory, a special 'wardrobe' above Sir John's bedchamber and closet, the three upper storeys of the tower forming his private suite, with anterooms below having access also to the great chamber over the dais end of the hall.*

A square garderobe projection ascends up four storeys in the east angle with the curtain wall and there is an octagonal turret with newel staircase on the south.

A friend of Sir John Fastolf was Ralph Lord Cromwell, the builder of Tattershall in Lincolnshire, with Caister and Herstmonceux the third important brick castle of the early 15th century. Another man of great wealth, he was Lord Treasurer of the Exchequer (1433–43) to Henry VI, and the badge of his office, the Double Purse, can be seen carved on the fireplaces here, and on the inner gateway of South Wingfield Manor [35] (*c.* 1440–1459),† which he also built, and in which a strong tower of four storeys is incorporated.

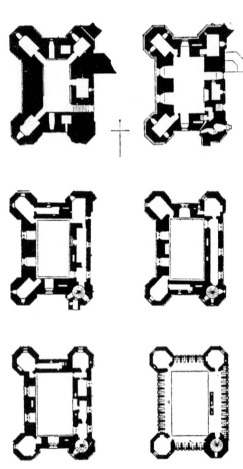

Fig. 57. Tattershall Castle, plans.

Top, basement (*left*), and ground floor.
Centre, first floor (*left*), and second floor.
Bottom, third floor (*left*), and fourth floor.

At Tattershall (Fig. 57; Pl. XXXI D),[20] Lord Cromwell built a brick solar tower of great magnificence, six storeys high.‡ The building accounts show it in active progress in 1445–6, when 322,000 'large tiles' were supplied for 'le Dongeon', the making of these bricks or 'wall tiles' being supervised by Baldwin Dutchman, who probably came from the

* The theory of Mr C. A. Ralegh Radford, in correspondence with the author.
† It was unfinished at his death in January 1456, but completed by John Talbot, Earl of Shrewsbury.
‡ 62 × 48 feet externally (excluding the angle projections), 38 × 22 feet internally, increasing 3 feet each way on each upper floor. Smaller Lincolnshire copies are at Hussey Tower and Rochford Tower near Boston and Tower on the Moor near Woodhall Spa (M. W. Barley (1952), *Lincolnshire and the Fens,* 79–80).

brick-building areas in the Low Countries or the Baltic coast of Germany. There was an earlier and much lower hall on the east of it, reconstructed in 1434–5, presumably used by the garrison, which also had access to the two lower floors of the tower. From these there was no entry to the rest of the building, which formed a private mansion, reached by a newel staircase in the south-eastern turret, entered from outside. There was apparently no kitchen in the tower, which was not really self-contained, but access to an outside kitchen was perhaps *via* the curtain wall walk from a doorway in the staircase turret. The first floor was Lord Cromwell's hall, with a magnificent fireplace, and there is another in his great chamber above, which has a vaulted passage with heraldic bosses in the thickness of the eastern wall. Above this passage, on the third floor, are two vaulted mural chambers for the use of the ladies of the household, to whom, with the children, this floor was probably assigned. On all stages there are mural chambers, with garderobes in the corner turrets, which rise above the covered gallery at roof level. The battlements and heavy machicolation give a sense of dominance and power. However, the militant aspect seems chiefly decorative, for there are two-light windows on even the lower floors. Tattershall escaped the customary treatment of great towers by Parliament, and was not slighted after the Civil War. The work of one Cromwell was not spoilt by another. Thanks to Lord Curzon of Kedleston, in 1912 the tower was rescued from neglect, re-roofed, re-floored, and the heraldic fireplaces just prevented from being shipped to America; they had already been taken out. Buck's view of 1726 shows pyramidal roofs on the turrets.

A similar great tower house, but more self-contained and built in stone, is found at Ashby de la Zouch.[21] Blasted by Parliament in 1649, with one side completely gone, it is still magnificent. The builder, Lord Hastings, was also a man of great wealth and a loyal official of the king, in this case Lord Chamberlain to Edward IV and his dearest friend. Licensed in 1474, the Hastings Tower is 90 feet high and approximately square in plan (46 × 41 feet), with a smaller rectangle (*c.* 14 feet 6 inches × 31 feet) on the east side; it had tall octagonal turrets corbelled out at third-floor level. There are four storeys in the main portion; seven contrived in the smaller part, which is, however, of equal height. The ground floor is vaulted and was apparently used for storage. Above is a vaulted kitchen, with the hall and turret oratory on the second floor, and great chamber with elaborate fireplace remaining above. A well is provided, also two just outside, and garderobes. Although the tower is self-contained, there is an underground passage to the great kitchen across the court.

The south-west tower at Minster Lovell (Oxfordshire) [24] resembles this somewhat on a smaller scale (*c.* 15 feet 6 inches × 18 feet); only its eastern half remains. It was square in plan and has one angle staircase turret, reminiscent of the gatehouse at Magdalen College, Oxford, and 'Pope's Tower' at Stanton Harcourt; perhaps William Orchard was the architect here, for Francis, Viscount Lovell, the friend of Richard III, during the period 1477–83. There were four storeys, the second floor very low and probably not the hall. The fine uppermost room must have been Lord Lovell's great chamber, and part of its oriel window remains overlooking the River Windrush. He cannot have enjoyed this delightful view for long; he was involved in Richard III's downfall, escaped to Flanders after Bosworth, and died in or after the battle of Stoke (1487). His may have been the skeleton found in 1728 in an underground vault at Minster Lovell. Henry VII's uncle, Jasper Tudor, Duke of Bedford, had the house 1486–95.

Tattershall must have had a major influence on the brick towers of the late 15th century. There is a striking likeness in the great tower at Buckden Palace in Huntingdonshire. [23] It was begun by Bishop Rotherham of Lincoln (1472–80), later Archbishop of York, and completed by his successor at Lincoln, Bishop Russell (1480–94), who also followed him as Lord Privy Seal and Chancellor. This tower with its oblong plan (44 × 21 feet) and octagonal corner turrets bears a great resemblance to the gatehouse (41 × 20 feet) being built in 1480–4 by John Cowper for Lord Hastings at Kirby Muxloe Castle. These are akin to the large tower on the north-west curtain at Warwick Castle,[22] which had the same oblong plan and corner turrets; of the latter the two remaining are called the Bear and Clarence Towers. The builder was probably George, Duke of Clarence, brother to Edward IV, son-in-law to 'Warwick the Kingmaker' and who after the latter's death at Barnet (1471) succeeded to his castle, until his own mysterious execution in 1478.

Smaller residential towers must have been frequent in great houses to provide lodgings for the lord's *entourage*. One remains at Stanton Harcourt, 'Pope's Tower' [43] built *c.* 1470, although its name derives from a later and poetic occupant (1717–18). The architect was apparently William Orchard, who probably designed the Harcourt aisle in the church, for Sir Robert Harcourt, high steward of Oxford University from 1446 to 1471.* The vaulted chapel is on the ground floor, and there are a further three storeys above, one probably used by the chaplain.

At Rymans, Apuldram, in Sussex [36] there is a solar tower of three storeys dating from the 15th century, with octagonal stair turret near its junction with a contemporary two-storeyed wing on the south, which makes an L-plan with it. On the east a wall staircase gives further access between the upper floors of the tower, next to the site of the rebuilt hall. The smaller room opening out of the great chamber was another private room, with fireplace and garderobe. The lower room of this wing, similarly provided, was probably William Ryman's office, with access from outside, and where he conducted his legal business and interviewed his bailiff. The adjoining room of the tower, though (now) poorly lit, was probably his parlour; there was further sleeping accommodation on the second floor.

In the early 16th century the solar towers still remained fashionable. The abbot's tower at Thame Park [37] (*c.* 1529–39) contains rooms admirably equipped for comfort. There is another at Compton Wynyates. [38]

A final great tower house, an anachronism, is at Bolsover Castle in Derbyshire.[25] † Here in the early 17th century, on the old foundations, Huntingdon Smithson built a keep-like structure for Sir Charles Cavendish, a son of the notable builder, 'Bess of Hard-wick'. This 'keep' is square with three small angle turrets and one larger staircase pro-jection. Of its four storeys the two lower are vaulted, and there are remarkable hooded fireplaces in many of the rooms. This Jacobean tower house was the last of the series, and the most elaborate internally. The solar towers are represented by the one added in 1627 at Cotehele.[39]

* Harvey (1954), 201.   † In the care of the Ministry of Works.

EXAMPLES OF TOWER HOUSES

		11TH CENTURY	*References*
(1)		Chepstow Castle, Mon., keep	M.O.W. Guide (9), 5, 7, 22–3 (plan & illus.).

		13TH CENTURY	
(2)	1245+	Clifford's Tower, York	M.O.W. Guide (11).
(3)	*c.* 1280	Forester's Lodge, Upper Millichope, Salop	Wood & Salmon (1949); Wood (1950), 70–2 (plan).
(4)	1284–92+	Acton Burnell Castle, Salop	M.O.W. Guide (1); Radford (1962), 94–103, (plan).

		14TH CENTURY	
(5)	*c.* 1300–21	Dudley Castle, keep	Simpson (1939), 151.
(6)	*c.* 1300	Corbridge, Vicars' Pele, Northumb.	Toy (1953 b), 191 (plans).
(7)	1307+	Dacre Castle, Cumb.	Parker (1853), 11, 214 (plan & illus.).
(8)	*c.* 1340	Chipchase Castle, Northumb.	Pevsner (1957), 126, pl. 42; Toy (1953 b), 193, pl. 192 *a* (plans & section).
(9)	*c.* 1340	Belsay Castle, Northumb.	Pevsner (1957), 43, 85–6; Parker (1853), 17, 205–6 (illus.).
(10)	*c.* 1350	Edlingham Castle, Northumb.	Pevsner (1957), 43–4, 143–4; Toy (1953 b), 207.
(11)		Langley Castle, Northumb.	Lloyd (1931), fig. 88; Parker (1853), 332–4 (plan & illus.).
(12)	1373	Haughton Castle, Northumb. (transformed)	Pevsner (1957), 39, 44, 165–6, pl. 40 *b*.
(13)	*c.* 1373	Nunney Castle, Som.	M.O.W. Guide (30) (plan).
(14)	*c.* 1378	Bolton Castle, Yorks.	Jackson (1956) (plans).
(15)	*c.* 1380+	Warkworth Castle, Northumb., keep	M.O.W. Guide (43) (plans).
(16)	*c.* 1380	Shute Barton, Devon	*Country Life* (25) (plans & illus.).
(17)	*c.* 1393	Wardour Old Castle	M.O.W. Guide in preparation.

		15TH CENTURY	
(18)	*c.* 1400	The Chantry, South St, Bridport, Dor.	R.C.H.M. *Dorset*, I, 48–9 (plan).
(19)	*c.* 1430–45	Raglan Castle, Mon., 'Yellow Tower of Gwent'	M.O.W. Guide (35) (plan & illus.).
(20)	*c.* 1433–55	Tattershall Castle, Lincs., solar tower	Thompson (1912), 357 (plans); National Trust Guide (5); Simpson (1935); (1937), 121–7; Tipping (1921), vol. i, 284–307, figs. 319–38 (plans & illus.).
(21)	*c.* 1474	Ashby de la Zouch Castle, Leics., 'Hastings' Tower'	M.O.W. Guide (2) (plan).
(22)	*c.* 1471–8	Warwick Castle, tower on north-west curtain	Toy (1953 b), 55 (plan).
(23)	*c.* 1472–80+	Buckden Palace, Hunts.	R.C.H.M. *Hunts.*, 34–41 (plan); Simpson (1937) (plan).
(24)	*c.* 1477–83	Minster Lovell Hall, Oxon., south-west tower	M.O.W. Guide (28) (plan).

		17TH CENTURY	
(25)	1608–17	Bolsover Castle, Derbys.	Faulkner (1961); M.O.W. Guide in preparation.

SOLAR TOWERS

	12TH CENTURY	*References*
(26) *c.* 1107–39	Sherborne Old Castle, Dor.	R.C.H.M. *Dorset*, 64–6 (plan & illus.).
(27) *c.* 1107–39 and later	Old Sarum	A. W. Clapham, Old Sarum Castle; *Archaeological Journal*, CIV (1947), 139–40; M.O.W. Guide (32) (plan).
(28) *c.* 1129–71	Wolvesey Castle, Winchester	Nisbett (1894–7), 207 (plan).
(29) *c.* 1129–71	Bishop's Waltham, Hants	M.O.W. Guide (4).

	13TH CENTURY	
(30)	Godlingston Manor, Dor.	Wood (1950), 15, pl. III c (plan & illus.).
(31) *c.* 1270–80	Little Wenham Hall, Suff.	Wood (1950), 76–81, pls. II A, IX A (plan & illus.).

	14TH CENTURY	
(32) *c.* 1300+	Longthorpe Tower, near Peterborough	M.O.W. Guide (27) (plans); Rouse & Baker (1955), 1–34 (plans).
(33) *c.* 1330	Creslow Manor House, Bucks.	R.C.H.M. *Bucks.*, II, 94–8 (plan).
(34) mid C 14th	Chesterton Tower, Cambridge	R.C.H.M. *Cambridge*, lxviii, 290, 381–2, pls. 296–7 (plans & illus.); Parker (1859), 12, 298 (plans & illus.).

	15TH CENTURY	
(35) 1440–59	South Wingfield Manor, Derbys.	Thompson (1912), 345–53 (plans & illus.).
(36)	Rymans, Apuldram, Suss.	Peckham (1939), 148–64, (plans & mouldings).

	16TH CENTURY	
(37) *c.* 1529–39	Thame Park, Oxon.	Godfrey (1929), 59–68 (plans & illus.); *Country Life* (27) (W. H. Godfrey, plan).
(38)	Compton Wynyates, War.	Garner & Stratton (1929), 118, pl. LXXVIII (plan & illus.).

	17TH CENTURY	
(39) 1627	Cotehele, Corn.	National Trust Guide (3).

LOFTY RESIDENTIAL TOWERS

	14TH CENTURY	
(40) 1394	Warwick Castle, Guy's Tower	Toy (1953 b), 55, 205 (plan); Pugin (1839), 14–15, pl. 15 (plan, etc.).
(41)	Warwick Castle, Caesar's Tower	Toy (1953 b), 204–6 (plans & illus.).

	15TH CENTURY	
(42) 1432–46	Caister Castle, Norf.	Simpson & Barnes (1952); Simpson & Barnes (1951).
(43) *c.* 1470	Stanton Harcourt, Oxon., Pope's Tower	

Plate XXXI. Tower Houses.

A. Chesterton Tower, Cambridge, mid 14th century.
B. Acton Burnell Castle, 1284–92 +.
C. Shute, Devon, *c.* 1380, east exterior.
D. Tattershall Castle, *c.* 1445–6.
E. Longthorpe Tower, before restoration; *c.* 1300 +.

Plate XXXII. Lodgings.

A. 3 Vicars' Court, Lincoln. South side with garderobe projections; c. 1310. B. Amberley Castle, 1377. C. Winchester College, Chamber Court, north-west corner; 1387–1400. D. Dartington Hall, c. 1388–1400.

13

Lodgings

PRESTIGE in the Middle Ages necessitated the upkeep of a large body of retainers. Indeed a big staff was needed for the management of the great estates of the nobility, for by the latter part of our period vast if scattered properties had become concentrated in a relatively few hands, built up by the politic marriage of heiresses. Many of their owners were related to the royal house, through the sons of Edward III.

These magnates with their great possessions held semi-royal state, and made progresses around their lands, in a similar fashion to the king, travelling with their household, showing themselves to their tenants, settling disputes, supervising their properties, and using, as they proceeded, the produce of their manors.

The royal administration was thus reflected, on a smaller scale, in the households of the great nobles. They had their own executive departments, akin to those of the State, with steward, chamberlain, controller, treasurer, cofferer of the household, keeper of the wardrobe, marshal of the hall, butler and all the clerks under them. These formed a vast personnel.*

The steward or seneschal was responsible for the management of the estate, and had judicial duties representing the lord in the manorial courts. Under him in charge of each manor was the bailiff or reeve. The chamberlain was in charge of the household, assisted by the controller, who checked expenditure, the treasurer with his clerks, who supervised accounts and allowances, and the cofferer, responsible for the money chests. The keeper of the wardrobe was head of the clothing department, which dealt with materials, from the robes of the noble owner down to the livery of his retainers; the officers of the wardrobe, its yeomen, grooms and pages, were concerned with purchases of materials and the making, repair, cleaning and fumigation (by aromatic herbs) of apparel. The marshal of the hall supervised the entry of persons into the latter, and the order and procedure therein; he was

---

* A. R. Myers (1959). The king's efforts against waste and corruption, and to provide a well-regulated household more imposing than those of the great lords, are embodied in the *Black Book* (c. 1471) and *Ordinance* of 1478, which give a good picture of the royal household of this time. *See also* M. Wade Labarge (1962), *Simon de Montfort*, chapter 6; W. L. Warren, (1961), *King John*, 136–7.

assisted by the ushers of the hall, while the butler and sergeant pantler had their own department and staff, as did the clerk of the kitchen with his master cooks and ushers.

There was the important branch of the chaplains and 'children of the Chapel', the secretary, squires of the body and of the chamber, gentlemen ushers, yeomen, grooms and pages of the chamber. The most important of these had their meals in the chamber, under the supervision of the gentlemen ushers. This was becoming subdivided into a series of rooms of increasing privacy for the magnate: great chamber, privy chamber and bed-chamber in fact and later in name; * the lesser folk had their places in the hall, which by the time of Edward IV, if not earlier, was developing into the 'servants' hall' of later times. On state occasions, such as the five great feasts of the year, All Hallows, Christmas, Easter, St George's Day (23 April) and Whitsun, the king dined in hall with his household, attended by his kings of arms, heralds and pursuivants, who accompanied every course which was served. The great lords had similar heraldic splendours.

Music played an important part in the mediaeval household, even in the ordinary activities of the day, such as the announcement ('blowinges and pipinges') of meals, and the summoning of the *meinie* (body of attendants) when the lord rode forth. There was also a *wayte* that nightly piped the watch, four times in winter, three in summer, and made regular perambulations to see that all was well. Like the king, the great lords would have harbingers sent on ahead to provide lodgings for the household in its travels. †

It was the custom for the sons of knightly and noble families to be educated in another similar household, or that of a superior. At the king's court such squires or pages of honour were in the charge of the Master of the Henxmen, who instructed them in courtesy and correct behaviour, riding and how 'to wear their harness', also languages and other 'virtuous learning', and probably after supper, at four or five o'clock, how to harp, pipe, sing and dance. Richard III himself had been brought up, with his friend Francis, later Lord Lovell, in the household of the great Earl of Warwick at Middleham Castle, and he had a full day's activities from dinner at 9.30 a.m. in the great hall to the bedtime 'livery' of bread and ale in the boys' chamber (probably in one of the towers).‡ John Paston the Younger seems to have had a similar education in the household of John Mowbray, fourth Duke of Norfolk, later the chief enemy of his family.

A numerous household was necessary for the upkeep of the lord's property, but it was also an urgent matter of policy, even of safety. To the mediaeval mind a man's position and importance had to be shown by his appearance, his rich costume and surroundings. Clothing was a matter of degree, and there were even sumptuary laws, in 1463 and 1483, to prevent persons from arraying themselves above their rank, as some of the rising middle class tended to do. Ostentation was important to a great lord, he must make an outward show of his power to impress, as of his generosity to win popularity, and Richard Neville, Earl of Warwick, the Kingmaker (1428–71) was a supreme exponent. His magnificence, his four hundred men at arms, all in red with his badge of the Bear and Ragged Staff,

* Myers (1959), 237.
† Myers (1959), 278–9, 132.
‡ P. M. Kendall (1955), *King Richard the Third*, 46–7. Allen & Unwin.

his princely hospitality and sumptuous feasts with more courses than the royal table—all was done for effect. As the *Great Chronicle of London* relates in 1468, 'the which Earle was ever had in favour of the commons of this land, by reason of the exceeding household which hee daily kept in all countries where ever he soiournied, or lay; and when hee came to London, hee held such an house, that sixe Oxen were eaten at a breakfast, and every Taverne was full of his meate, for who that had any acquaintance in that house, hee should have had as much sodden and rost, as he might carry upon a long dagger'.

In the 15th century it was dangerous for a lord not to be magnificent, just as in Henry VIII's reign it meant death to rival the king in splendour, as Buckingham found to his cost. Before the strengthening of the monarchy, begun by Edward IV and continued by the Tudors, and when the crown under Henry VI (1421–61) was politically and financially weak, the great nobles competed for power and men's support. As Professor Myers has said: 'If a lord did not ceaselessly strive to maintain and to enlarge his affinity, he might find himself in the position of a modern bank if the rumour should begin to spread that its finances were no longer sound.' *

A large body of attendants was now a defensive measure, and not only prestige but the safety of the lord's own property was involved. The crown, the prey of rival factions, was unable to enforce law and order, and this situation was intensified by the collapse of the war with France (finally in 1453), and the return of large numbers of undisciplined soldiers accustomed to pillage and loot, and eager to sell their services to the highest bidder. In these lawless years the rule of force prevailed, and a landowner had to increase the number of his retainers, otherwise his property would be in jeopardy. Lesser landowners like the Pastons were victims of greedy neighbours, and it will be remembered how difficult John Paston found it to retain the manors inherited from Sir John Fastolf, in the face of rivals like John Mowbray, fourth Duke of Norfolk, who had private armies to implement their claims, and overcome the courts of law. In 1450 Margaret Paston was carried out from her chamber at Gresham by the hirelings of Lord Moleyns; the Duke of Suffolk's men in 1465 sacked Hellesdon like a French village, and Caister Castle was captured by Norfolk in 1469.† There was no legal redress against such violence until the strengthening of the central government under Edward IV and the Tudors, the rescue of the lawcourts from blackmail and the enforcements of the edict of Livery and Maintenance which controlled the numbers of retainers.

Where were these retainers lodged in the great houses of the 14th and 15th centuries? This aspect of domestic architecture has been neglected, but recent research ‡ is making the picture clearer. We have also a clue to the arrangement in certain buildings which had the same problem of accommodating a number of individuals, such as vicars' closes and collegiate institutions. Houses of chantry priests reveal a similar basic resemblance.

In the early Middle Ages the retainer problem was less acute. The castles had no large

* Myers (1959), 2.
† *The Paston Letters*, II, 4, 30, 31, 47, 82–6.
‡ Emery (1958), 192.

permanent garrison, and it was only in time of war that the lord called out his tenants in chief to man the walls and towers, each being responsible for a particular section, in which his own men at arms were stationed. Scolland's Hall at Richmond Castle, Yorkshire, is named after the Lord of Bedale, seneschal to Alan, Earl of Brittany (1137–46), and who was apparently entrusted with its 'castleguard', although it was probably built by the earl's predecessor and namesake (1071–89). Scolland's successors, the Fitz Alans of Bedale, performed their castleguard here in the mid 14th century, of which time we have the fortunate survival of a drawing of the castle made as a diagram to show the parts where the tenants of the Earl of Richmond did this service, and including their banners and legends, such as 'the place of the Chamberlain in the east of Scoulandhall next the oven', and 'the place of Brian FitzAlan in the Great Hall of Scoulande'.

In normal times these tenants lived at home. For it was the policy of the Norman kings, copied by their barons, to plant their feudal tenants on their own estates, which they held on military service, including castleguard. In periods of quiet they would inhabit such houses as Little Wenham Hall. Meanwhile, the small permanent garrisons of the castle, like the staff of the manor houses, would sleep in towers or basements in the domestic range, in the great hall, or perhaps in wooden lean-to structures. It was probably not until the need arose for a large body of retainers that special quarters were provided.

Thus few examples of service accommodation have been recognized for the 13th and early 14th centuries. The more important officials may have slept in the towers of castles like Conway and Caernarvon, or above the gate. At Conway doubtless Edward I's personal attendants were housed in the rooms below his own hall and chambers in the inner ward. His chancellor built the mansion at Acton Burnell [1] with well-lit rooms below the main hall to accommodate his numerous staff. At Aydon Castle [2] (c. 1280) the basement, with fireplace, of the hall may have been used by the men at arms, but in the 14th century there are signs of separate accommodation, west of the hall block, in a second court where the south wall retains shouldered windows and a doorway. At Meare, [5] when the abbot visited his country manor his train may also have slept below the hall, which is again at first-floor level; if the basement was the original kitchen it could serve as sleeping-place as well. But again there is evidence of at least one other range beside the two surviving round the court; and beyond the house, buildings in the present farmyard retain some original door-ways, heavily moulded, their size suggesting that they once served a higher block, later reduced to one storey, or were re-used. At Markenfield [6] there are two-storeyed ranges of later buildings, lower than the main block of c. 1310, round the court. One to the east has a doorway of 15th-century type with a probably re-used early 14th-century trefoiled head to the window above.

An idea of such accommodation in the early 14th century may be gained from the arrange-ment for the vicars at Lincoln. Here the south range (No. 3) of Vicars' Court (see Fig. 58; Pl. XXXII A) [4] is complete enough for the original layout to be traced. It seems to date from c. 1310, judging from documentary and window evidence. This side would have contained the lodgings or bed-sittingrooms of at least six vicars, three on the ground floor, three on the first, with access to separate garderobes in blocks projecting to the south. On the analogy of Wells, there would be only three vicars, each with a room on both floors,

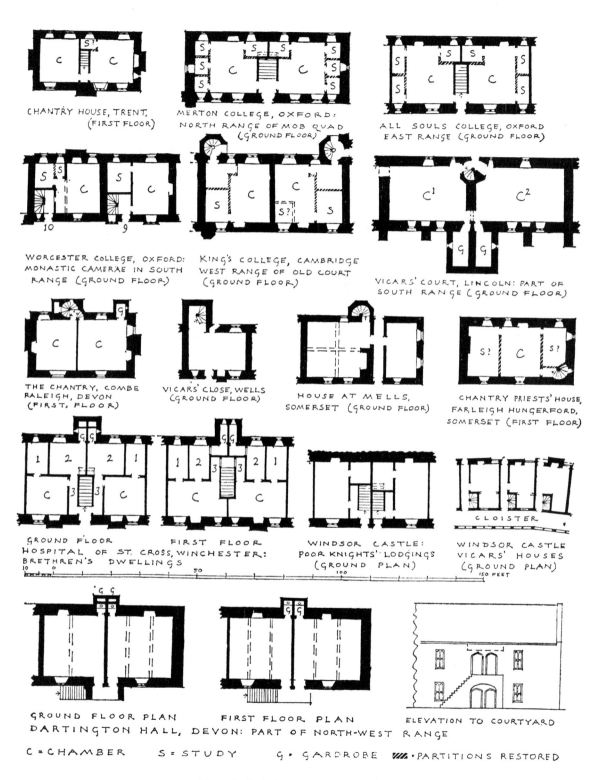

CHANTRY HOUSE, TRENT, (FIRST FLOOR)

MERTON COLLEGE, OXFORD: NORTH RANGE OF MOB QUAD (GROUND FLOOR)

ALL SOULS COLLEGE, OXFORD EAST RANGE (GROUND FLOOR)

WORCESTER COLLEGE, OXFORD: MONASTIC CAMERAE IN SOUTH RANGE (GROUND FLOOR)

KING'S COLLEGE, CAMBRIDGE WEST RANGE OF OLD COURT (GROUND FLOOR)

VICARS' COURT, LINCOLN: PART OF SOUTH RANGE (GROUND FLOOR)

THE CHANTRY, COMBE RALEIGH, DEVON (FIRST FLOOR)

VICARS' CLOSE, WELLS (GROUND FLOOR)

HOUSE AT MELLS, SOMERSET (GROUND FLOOR)

CHANTRY PRIESTS' HOUSE, FARLEIGH HUNGERFORD, SOMERSET (FIRST FLOOR)

GROUND FLOOR

FIRST FLOOR

HOSPITAL OF ST. CROSS, WINCHESTER: BRETHREN'S DWELLINGS

WINDSOR CASTLE: POOR KNIGHTS' LODGINGS (GROUND PLAN)

CLOISTER

WINDSOR CASTLE VICARS' HOUSES (GROUND PLAN)

10 0   50   100   150 FEET

GROUND FLOOR PLAN

FIRST FLOOR PLAN

ELEVATION TO COURTYARD

DARTINGTON HALL, DEVON: PART OF NORTH-WEST RANGE

C = CHAMBER   S = STUDY   G = GARDROBE   ▨ = PARTITIONS RESTORED

Fig. 58. Lodgings, comparative plans.

but at Wells the rooms are smaller. The six here suggested would fit the earlier number of twenty-five for the whole court. The means of access has been altered; originally it was by a round-headed entrance, now blocked, towards the centre of the north wall. This gave entry, east and west, into two large rooms, and also to a newel staircase which led to similar rooms above. A third chamber to the west, divided by a stone wall, was apparently reached through a northern entrance, now altered, near the angle of the court. This last has a window towards the west, blocked but still showing a two-centred arch with remains of two trefoiled lights with quatrefoil above, similar to those still left, one to each of the other rooms, facing north. In most of the southern windows, two to each chamber, the trefoiled heads of each light remain, with lobed trefoil above, although modern sashes have replaced the mullion, except for a Tudor insertion in the eastern room.

For the end of the 14th century, certain evidence of service lodgings has been found at Dartington Hall (*see* Fig. 58; Pl. XXXII D),[12] built *c.* 1388–1400 to house his retainers by Richard II's half-brother, John Holland, Duke of Exeter, and it seems appropriate that the first lodgings of 'livery and maintenance' should appear in the mansion of this turbulent character. The service quarters once lined two sides of the main court, but are best preserved on the west side. This range contains two floors of eight rooms each, these arranged in pairs. Characteristic of the elevation is a 'cluster of doorways'. Access to the ground floor was by twin doorways, set together, separated by a thin partition wall, at the opposite end of which were once twin garderobes. These served two square chambers each once with its own fireplace in the back wall, and a window looking into the court. Above were two similar rooms, the upper entrances reached by an external staircase at the front, which must have had arches over the lower doorways. At least thirty-two of such chambers would be provided by the two sides of the court.*

Having now a clue as to the kind of building to look for, and where, more no doubt will be recognized. At Bodiam Castle,[9] licensed in 1385, a mess hall for the retainers and separate kitchen have been located. The growth of 'livery and maintenance' which led to the multiplication of lodgings made it desirable for the lord to keep aloof from his mercenaries. At Bodiam the owner, Sir Edward Dalyngrigge, and his family had the south and east sides of the court, the retainers the west and north ranges. The retainers' messroom on the west was quite separate from the great hall at the east end of the south range. The main kitchen was at the south-west angle of the castle, but another room with fireplace near the central (west) tower may have served the messroom.

Amberley Castle in Sussex (Pl. XXXII B) [7] represents the enlarging and fortification, in 1377, by William Rede, Bishop of Chichester, of a 13th-century house, which remains in the south-eastern angle of the enclosure. Besides the new hall at ground level, well-appointed lodgings were built in two storeys along the northern curtain of the lower court. Although, as at Bodiam, the courtyard sides have gone, the layout of the rooms can be seen in the arrangement of fireplaces and windows on the outer walls, and a double garderobe tower, which fortunately remains complete. There were further rooms adjoining the gatehouse in the southern range.

---

* One of the retainers was Thomas Proudfoot, an esquire retained in 1399 for life.—Emery (1958), 192; Calendar of Patent Rolls (1399–1401), 244.

The College at Arundel [8] founded by Richard, the sixth FitzAlan Earl, c. 1381, retains its outer wall with windows, and must represent a similar two-storeyed range. As it was for secular canons and not part of a castle, the lower windows, like the upper ones, are traceried two-lights, whereas those at Amberley Castle are defensive loops.

Indeed the collegiate plan has much in common with household accommodation, comprising a two-storeyed range flanking a court, as we have already seen at Lincoln in the early 14th century. The chief difference rises from the provision, in secular colleges, of a number of small studies contrived within the main apartment, which was used as a bed-sittingroom for several students. In most cases the study partitions have gone, but the small window which once lit them gives a clue to their former existence. There were three in each of the fellows' rooms on the upper floor of Chamber Court, Winchester College (Pl. XXXII c) [11] (1387–1400): one in each corner except at the entrance, the end ones comfortably flanking the fireplace. At Wynford's other building, New College, Oxford, [10] the arrangement resembled the later All Souls (see Fig. 58) [15] (c. 1438–42) with a back fireplace and three studies; unless the small window flanking the entrance proves there to have been a vestibule or a further study on either side. But at Merton College, where the north range of Mob Quad (see Fig. 58), [3] c. 1304–7, is near Lincoln in date, a third study was placed against the end wall, the studies being smaller than at All Souls, the fireplace sited at the back; thus four studies could be fitted in. A recent discovery at Magdalene (formerly Buckingham) College, Cambridge, [21] on the south side of First Court, has revealed the original partitions intact; these date from the second half of the 15th century, probably during the rule at Croyland of Abbot John de Wisbech (1470–6), who 'erected chambers convenient for rest and study in the monks' college of Buckingham' at Cambridge, other Benedictine abbeys of Ely, Ramsey and Walden following his example. At Magdalene College, as at All Souls, the room has three corner studies, and in the back wall the original fireplace has a lavabo between it and the doorway to a garderobe, adjoining the room entrance. In the north-eastern study, mediaeval writing scratched on the soft clunch of window jamb gives the Latin names or remarks of some of the 15th-century occupants. Thomas Highfield (Campo de Celso) is a good man (bonus est vir), and a friend chaffs Robert Cave, presumably the absent owner of the study, on his good looks and perhaps vanity:

> O quam formosum Robertus est lepus Antrum
> Omnibus in rebus nullus ei similis.

> (Oh what a handsome charmer is Robert Cave,
> In everything there is no one to touch him.)

Worcester, originally Gloucester, College, Oxford, [20] (see Fig. 58), had similar Benedictine connections. Here several monastic houses built a separate block, known as a camera or mansio, for their own students, and the south ranges of these remain, of 15th-century date. The arms of Pershore, Glastonbury, Malmesbury and St Augustine's, Canterbury, may be seen above the doorways. These form a series of attached houses more like those of the vicars at Wells, except that the staircases (rebuilt) were internal and the fireplaces set at the back. In each *mansio* the whole floor probably formed a single chamber, with one or perhaps two studies in one corner.

Such comfortable quarters were built by certain abbeys for their monastic scholars, but not every student had such good accommodation. Most were lodged in academic halls outside the college, such as the 14th-century Tackley's Inn at Oxford, and on the whole only a privileged minority, mostly graduate fellows (as even yet at All Souls) were housed in the mediaeval college. The plan of Chamber Court (1387–1400) at Winchester already had been used at Wykeham's other foundation, New College, Oxford (1380–6), this now serving for a school and the rooms being increased in size. Fellows occupied the first floor, with studies indicated by the alternating one- and two-light windows, while the boys were lodged below, seventy in the six chambers. Perhaps the lesser retainers in great houses, the boys and pages, were likewise accommodated.

Such shared chambers, but without the studies, were suitable for the lord's *entourage*, though the more important members of the household, the chaplain, chamberlain, steward, butler and marshal of the hall, would require a room to themselves also serving as an office, and their quarters would compare with those of the Lincoln vicars. The doorway arrangement at Vicars' Court is similar to that of the scholastic ranges, one entrance giving access left and right to an adjoining chamber, while a newel staircase next to these openings mounts to similar rooms above. This is like the plan at Winchester, except that a straight staircase between the two rooms there replaces the newel, but like it rises from near the entrance, and in both the garderobes are placed in the back wall opposite. At Vicars' Court there is access to the latter by two doorways on both floors, but at Winchester a common doorway serves near the staircase and upper chamber doorway. Merton College had the same entrance and mid staircase arrangement as at All Souls, both without evidence of garderobes; two of the small studies on the ground floor, lit by small windows, were fitted under the staircase at the back, where the garderobes would be elsewhere. The fireplaces are commonly on the back wall too, except, as we have seen, at Winchester, where they are on the cross wall, and in Cardinal Beaufort's buildings (*c.* 1445) at St Cross (*see* Fig. 58),[18] where the range of chimneys is on the front. This is due to a new feature, a range two rooms deep, each brother having a large chamber, with fireplace, in front and two smaller ones at the back. There is the usual central entrance and straight staircase, here with garderobes behind over a stream, but the chambers open out of a small passage on either side of the staircase, on each floor.

For ordinary retainers, not the great household officials, easy exit from their quarters was desirable to allow quick mustering in the court in front of their dwellings. This was provided in the plan as far off as Viking days, revealed by the excavation of the boat dwellings at Trelleborg (*c.* 1000) in Denmark, where each block has its doorway diametrically opposite to the other, so that the lines of emerging men should not become confused. At Dartington, unlike the collegiate chambers, each room has a separate outer entrance, the upper pair reached by an external staircase arched over the lower doorways.

At Ewelme Manor,[19] home of William de la Pole, Duke of Suffolk (d. 1450), the retainers had, according to Buck's view of 1729, a similar long two-storey range with chimneys at the back, and alternate doors and windows for six chambers on each floor.

Here the upper entrances were reached by a covered gallery, of which post holes are shown in the drawing. Such a gallery, like those of later mediaeval inns, has been restored at the contemporary Tretower Court (Breconshire), and occurs in the Checker range at Abingdon Abbey,[22] and (in stone) at Wenlock Priory. Already at Vicars' Court, Lincoln, there is evidence of a ground-floor pentice, and indeed these were much used in the 13th century, even in palaces.

Another great Oxfordshire house, still remaining though in ruins, Minster Lovell Hall [13] (1431–42), is noted for what may be called solar accommodation, and below these rooms are others furnished with fireplaces, which may have housed Lord Lovell's personal staff. Other members of his household probably used the west wing, parallel to the kitchen range across the wide court. There were five rooms on the ground floor, three with fireplaces on the outer side, and probably the same above.

In the brick castle built in 1432–46 at Caister [14] by Sir John Fastolf, there is a main court lying north-east to south-west with the lofty circular tower at the western angle. The enclosure was separated by its moat from two forecourts, one at the north-east * outside the main entrance, the other to the south-west beyond a postern which was later made into a further gatehouse. Near this was the barge yard, and the arch still remains for the lord's barge to pass along the Barge Ditch from the river Bure, an easier communication from Yarmouth than by road, especially in the winter. The building containing this arch, still called the 'barge house' in the 18th century, makes an L-plan with another wing, now a residence, and there is a 15th-century drum tower at the eastern angle. Perhaps Sir John lodged some of his retainers here,† others, possibly over stables, in the north-eastern forecourt, where they could command the outer (north-west) gate. But it would be reasonable to place those people concerned with household duties in the main court, probably in the north-west range over the wine cellars.

The almost contemporary brick castle of Herstmonceux,[17] licensed in 1441, was begun by Sir Roger Fiennes, Treasurer of the Household to Henry VI. The exterior, beautifully restored by the late W. H. Godfrey, again looks 'as perfect as the first day'—Horace Walpole's comment when he visited the castle in 1752. But in 1777 Samuel Wyatt, the architect, found the timber of the roof much decayed, after being neglected for many years, and the interior was gutted that year by the owner, Rev. Robert Hare, prebendary of Winchester, the material being used to build Herstmonceux Place. In 1948 the castle became the Royal Observatory, removed from Greenwich. But for the interior we have to rely on 18th-century descriptions and illustrations by Grose of what it looked like before it was dismantled in 1777. There were three courts, the largest in the south-east being surrounded by cloisters—'very like Eton College', said Walpole. From this, access was gained to the great hall, and he comments that in the windows of the gallery over the cloisters, which led all round to the apartments, was the device of the Fiennes—a wolf holding a baton, with a scroll le roy le veut ('the King wills it'). Grose writes, following a description of the east corner tower with its octagonal room, that 'above stairs is a suite

---

* The north-eastern court, which has loops of early type, may have been adapted from part of the earlier manor house, which extended further south-east, judging from foundations which prevent ploughing in this area.
† Mr Ralegh Radford's suggestion, in correspondence.

of rooms similar to those of the best apartments over which it stands. The chambers on this floor are sufficient to lodge a garrison, and one is bewildered in the different galleries that lead to them, in everyone of the windows of which is painted on glass the alant or wolf-dog, the ancient supporters of the family of Fynes; many private winding staircases, curiously constructed in brick-work, without any timber, communicate with these galleries.' There must have been many lodgings round the courts and in the seven towers of Herstmonceux Castle.

At South Wingfield Manor [16] (c. 1440–59), with its important owner, we should expect accommodation for a large number of retainers. William of Worcester * relates that Lord Cromwell had at least a hundred people in his household at Tattershall, his other great property, and many of these would travel with him and need lodgings. At South Wingfield the presence of two great courtyards seems to bear this out. The outer, south, or base, court may have contained some farm buildings, and there is an 'ancient barn' on the east end of the south wall, but the remains of a western outer wall with windows and garderobe projections suggest a suite of lodgings here, the width being known by a small portion of the inner wall nearly in line with a similar length of wall on the west side of the inner quadrangle. On the east side of the base court, north of the outer gateway, the inner wall of a somewhat similar range survives, and this is pierced by ten small windows and supported by buttresses; the one doorway is at the northern end. There seems also to have been a range on the south side, continuing the line of the barn, which is in the same relative position as the barn at Dartington Hall, and also next a gateway. More definitive evidence is provided by the west wall of the inner court, containing garderobes and fireplaces of a range of buildings, obviously more important, and said to have been occupied later by Mary Queen of Scots. The eastern wall has gone, but is known to have had two polygonal oriels, or staircase projections, perhaps added in the 16th century.

Thus the increase of lodgings for the lord's retainers, as for the trains of visiting guests, was an important factor in the development of large houses newly built in the later Middle Ages. Chiefly, this appears in the growth of the courtyard plan, the lodgings being arranged round a series of courts, two at Haddon and South Wingfield, three at Caister and Herstmonceux Castles. At Cotehele,[24] besides the 'Retainers' Court' on the west, there were probably other, more important, lodgings in the main court adjoining, the north and possibly east side of which were used by Sir Richard Edgcumbe and his family. But at Dartington, judging from the recent excavations, a second, private, court south of the hall was added c. 1500. The arrangement is well shown in Mr Godfrey's plan of Eltham Palace,[23] based on the original of John Thorpe. There are no less than five courts in the complex containing the Great Hall, other lodgings with pentice round the Great Court south of it, and further buildings including 'My Lord Chancellor his Lodgings', a separate little house with hall, parlour, screens, great chamber and kitchen in the north-west, and opposite 'decayed lodgings' in the outer Green Court across the moat.

Hampton Court [26] shows this complication of lodgings, with access from the Lord Chamberlain's Court, Master Carpenter's Court, Chapel Court and others. Thornbury Castle [25] had three quadrangles, the Base, Inner and Principal Courts (Privy Garden with

* (1415–82?). Secretary to Sir John Fastolf, who disputed the latter's will with John Paston in 1459.

gallery) as well as a kitchen court, but building stopped when Henry VIII executed his supposed rival and feared 'over-mighty subject', the innocent but tactless Edward Stafford, third Duke of Buckingham (1478–1521). Other large houses had the simpler arrangement of fewer larger quadrangles, more like collegiate establishments. Cowdray [27] (c. 1540), Sussex, has a single large court once with lodgings under long galleries, in the side ranges. The courtyard plan for a great house persisted into the later 16th and 17th centuries, but there was a growing tendency to leave one side open to obtain as much light as possible for the wings.

EXAMPLES OF LODGINGS

		Type	Internal * Dimensions	Reference
(1) 1284+	Acton Burnell Castle, Salop	Bishop's staff		Radford (1962), 94–103; M.O.W. Guide (1) (plans & illus.).
(2) c. 1280 & later	Aydon Castle, Northumb.	Men at arms		Knowles (1899), 71–88 (plans, etc.).
(3) c. 1304–7	Merton College, Oxford, Mob Quad	Scholars	22′ × 17′	Pantin (1959), 244–6 (plan); R. C. H. M. Oxford, 81 – 2 (plan).
(4) c. 1310	3 Vicars' Court, Lincoln	Vicars	27–33′ × 18′	Wood (1951 c), 281–6 (plans & illus.); Pantin (1959), 247–8, fig. 88 (plan).
(5) c. 1322–35	Meare Manor House, Som.	Abbot's attendants		
(6) 1310 & later	Markenfield Hall, Yorks.	Servants		
(7) c. 1377	Amberley Castle, Suss.	Bishop's men at arms		Peckham (1921) (plan).
(8) c. 1381	Arundel College, Suss.	Secular canons		
(9) 1385	Bodiam Castle, Suss.	Retainers		Tipping (1921), vol. I, 239–246 (plan).
(10) 1380–6	New College, Oxford	Scholars		R.C.H.M. Oxford, 85 (plan).
(11) 1387–1400	Winchester College, Hants, Chamber Court	Scholars	30–35′ × 20′	Pantin (1959), 247, fig. 88 (plan).
(12) c. 1388–1400	Dartington Hall, Devon	Retainers	22′ × 21′	Emery (1958), 190–3 (plans); Pantin (1959), 251–3 (plans, etc.); S. & N. Buck, Views (1734), X, pl. 19; Platt (1962) (plan, etc.).
(13) c. 1431–42	Minster Lovell Hall, Oxon.	Retainers		M.O.W. Guide (28).
(14) c. 1432–46	Caister Castle, Norf.	Retainers		Simpson & Barnes (1952), 35–51 (plan).
(15) 1438–42	All Souls, Oxford	Scholars	22′ × 20′	Pantin (1959), 246, figs. 85, 86, 88.
(16) c. 1440–58	South Wingfield Manor, Derbys.	Retainers		Garner & Stratton (1929), fig. 6 (plan); Thompson (1912), 346 (plan).
(17) c. 1441	Herstmonceux Castle, Suss., evidence	Retainers		Pugin (1839), 5–13, pls. 9–14; Horace Walpole, Works, V, 264; Grose (1777), 158.

* Chiefly via Pantin (1959), 258. The scholastic chamber measurements include studies. Dimensions are given only with more definite examples.

		Type	Internal Dimensions	Reference
(18) *c.* 1445	Hospital of St Cross, Winchester (Beaufort's work)	Bedesmen	18′ × 24′	Pantin (1959), 249, fig. 88 (plan).
(19) before 1450	Ewelme Manor, Oxon., evidence	Retainers		Pantin (1959), 254; S. & N. Buck, (1729), *Views*, V, pl. 6.
(20)	Worcester (Gloucester) College, Oxford	Monastic scholars	21–22′ × 17′	Pantin (1959), 246–7, fig. 88 (plan); R.C.H.M. *Oxford*, 124–5 (plan & illus.).
(21) prob. 1470–6	Magdalene (Buckingham) College, Cambridge	Monastic scholars	31′ × 20′ *	*Country Life* (14), 1486–7 (illus.); R.C.H.M. *Cambridge*, 137, 144–5 (plan).
(22)	Abingdon Abbey, Berks., Long Gallery	Monastic officials		
(23)	Eltham Palace, Kent, evidence	Courtiers		Pantin (1959), 254; Lloyd (1931), fig. 94 (plan by W. H. Godfrey).
(24)	Cotehele House, Corn.	Retainers		Garner & Stratton (1929), 40 (plan); National Trust Guide (3).
(25) before 1521	Thornbury Castle, Glos.	Retainers	21′ × 23′	Pantin (1959), 254, fig. 89 (plan); Pugin (1839), 28–38, pls. 30–44.
(26)	Hampton Court, Middx	Courtiers		R.C.H.M. *Middlesex*, 30–6 (plans).
(27) *c.* 1540	Cowdray, Suss.	Retainers		Garner & Stratton (1929), 49 (plan); Trotter (1934), 26–31, 47–51 (plan).

* The common room here is 18′ × 20′.

14

Domestic Plans of the Later Middle Ages

MANY houses of 15th- and early 16th-century date remain, particularly in country towns and villages, but the study of them has only just begun. There is no lack of material, particularly in houses of *c.* 1500. In Lavenham, Suffolk, many buildings are of this date or earlier—the heyday of the great mediaeval clothiers. Weobley in Herefordshire is also full of timber-framed houses, some even of the 14th century, and King's Lynn is, among other towns, rich in early domestic structures.

With a few possible exceptions the mediaeval town was not cramped, and there was plenty of room for gardens, even in London, and in some cases farms, within the walls. The town house of a nobleman or the residence of a merchant was usually provided with a court, large or small, reached by a gateway from the street, in a range of which the ground floor was often let out as shops. This gate was closed at night and in periods of disorder. On entering, the hall would either face or be at right angles to the entrance block, along one side of the courtyard, with service rooms at one end, and the best chambers at the other, these sometimes extending into the upper floor of the street range, over the shops. Further lodgings would occupy the other side of the court, and the stabling would be at the back, perhaps adjoining a means of access from the rear.

A large train of retainers would ride into London with their lord and need to be housed. As William Botoner wrote to Sir John Fastolf in 1458: 'The King came the last week to Westminster, and the Duke of York came to London with his own household only to the number of 140 horse, as it is said; the Earl of Salisbury with 400 horse in his company, fourscore knights and squires. The Duke of Somerset came to London last day of January with 200 horse, and lodgeth without Temple Bar, and the Duke of Exeter shall be here this week with a great fellowship and strong, as it is said. The Earl of Warwick is not yet come, because the wind is not yet for him.' *

* He was at Calais. *The Paston Letters*, I, 129.

The same accommodation was necessary in a hostelry, and there is a close likeness between the courtyard type of inn and the town house of a nobleman. Indeed, there are cases when parts of the latter were used as an inn in seasons when it was not required by the owner, and the hotel (hostel) derives from the name, *hôtel*, given to such a town house in France and England.

Mr Pantin * has published a valuable survey on 'Mediaeval English town-house plans'. He distinguishes two main groups according to the placing of the hall, parallel or at right angles to the street. In the *parallel* type the plan may be (1) *extended* in a continuous range along the street, like the house of the wool merchant, John Webbe (now Church House), at Salisbury, where the hall adjoins a wide entry with archway into Crane Street. When the site is narrower the plan is (2) *contracted*, with the solar either 'perched' on the top of the screens passage and partly overhanging the hall, as in the academic Beam Hall (*c.* 1500) at Oxford, or placed behind it, as in other examples. The plan is (3) *double-ranged* where there are two parallel ranges, the hall at the back, a row of shops in the front, as at Tackley's Inn (*c.* 1300+) at Oxford. At Spicer's Hall, Bristol, burnt in 1942, the hall occupied the whole width of the narrow site, with the solar over the shops or parlour on the street. Colston's Hall, Bristol, of which drawings remain, had the hall as the central of three parallel ranges. For larger houses the (4) *courtyard* plan was used, with the hall range still parallel but placed at the back across a court, the frontage being occupied by a row of shops. There was often a second courtyard or garden behind the hall; Strangers' Hall at Norwich is an example.

For more restricted sites, the *right-angle* type was used from earliest times, as shown by the 12th- and 13th-century hall undercrofts remaining. It might be (1) *narrow*, with the hall the entire width of the tenement, as once at Canynge's House, Bristol; or (2) *broad*, where the hall flanks a courtyard, to facilitate its lighting, and forms part of an L-plan with shops in the cross range parallel to the street; the Hall of John Halle at Salisbury is of this nature.

The 'two-part plan' with hall and solar-over-service is fairly usual, especially in the parallel type of town house, while in right-angled examples a common arrangement is the 'three-part plan', with a central hall between two-storey blocks, the solar over shops next to the street, the service (or parlour/counting house) at the other end, with access to a detached kitchen.

The Strangers' Hall, Norwich (Fig. 59), shows the growth of a merchant's house during four centuries. The first known use of the name 'Strangers' Hall' seems to have been in 1841, and may refer to foreign tenants of the Roman Catholic owners of the early 19th century. The building was saved from destruction in 1899 by L. G. Bolingbroke, who made it a folk museum and gave it to the city in 1922. Of the original building there remains a vaulted undercroft of three quadripartite bays, lying north to south, with a passage on the east dividing it from further cellars. This was probably built by Nicholas de Middilton *c.* 1325.† His hall was above it, making an L-shaped plan with his solar to

---

* 1962–3 a. With many plans.
† The considered view of Mr A. B. Whittingham, M.A., A.R.I.B.A. (in correspondence with the author), from architectural details, although a house was probably built in 1286–9 when the site boundaries were settled. See *Archaeological Journal* (1949), CVI, 80; (1923), LXXX, 332–3 (plan including undercroft); *Guide to Strangers' Hall Museum* (1958), (plan); Pantin (1962–3 a), 225–6.

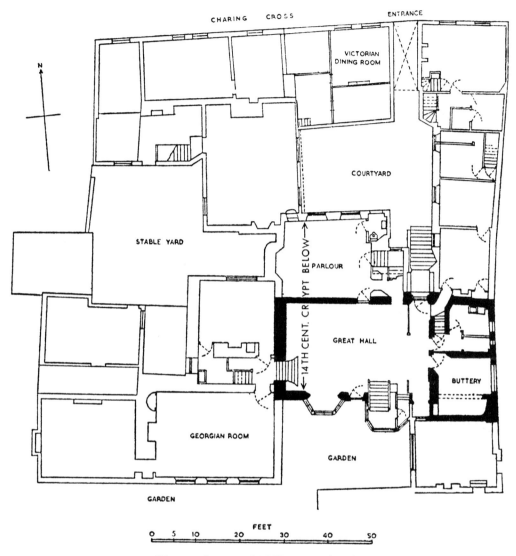

Fig. 59. Strangers' Hall, Norwich, plan.

the east; it was replaced in the 15th century, however. In 1332 he acquired an additional strip of land to the south-west on which a detached bakehouse was built either by him or by his successor Roger Hardegray (1348–98), an M.P., and bailiff of Norwich in 1360. The present hall was probably built *c.* 1450 by William Barley, mercer and alderman, sheriff and M.P. It was placed transversely to the earlier undercroft, the southern part of which lies under the upper (western) portion of the hall, the northern under the adjoining parlour, which has a chamber over. At the lower end of the hall two four-centred doorways lead to buttery and pantry, which have a solar above, and contemporary cellars underneath which project south under a one-storey kitchen. Before 1491 Thomas Cawse, mercer,

M.P., and later mayor,. was in possession, and acquiring an adjoining property added the west wing and stable court. He died in 1509 and his brass may be seen in the church of St John Maddermarket, where is also the brass of Nicholas Sotherton, another mayor (1539), who acquired the house c. 1525; he was a grocer with his shop on the street front. The present roof bears his merchant's mark and the screen his arms. He added the vaulted bay and porch, though the latter probably was not complete at his death in 1540 as it bears a widow's head; it is reached by a staircase from the courtyard. Sotherton also altered Cawse's west wing, making it L-shaped and higher. Another grocer and mayor, Francis Cook, added the staircase bay of the hall (dated 1627) to give access to his new rooms at the south-east corner; he also rebuilt the shop and street front in 1621–2. A still later mayor, the hosier Sir Joseph Paine, enlarged and rebuilt the parlour (dining-room) in 1659, and c. 1748 William Wicks adapted the house to form the Judge's Lodgings and converted Sotherton's great parlour (west wing) into a drawing-room (the 'Georgian' or 'Judge's Room').

Many inns seem to have been built by the monasteries. For by the late 14th century the demands on them for hospitality had become financially crippling, although grateful guests no doubt contributed to the fabric where they could. In the late 15th century we even read of a part charge for hospitality, as when John Howard, Duke of Norfolk, with a train of sixty-five men, stayed at Thetford and his household accounts show the 'bill of the Prior'.*

Now the monasteries started to build large inns as an investment. Not only would this relieve their guest house, but would also become a steady source of income.† One of the earliest is at Norton St Philip in Somerset. To cater for the merchants who attended its two annual fairs, the George Inn was built by Hinton Charterhouse, who owned the manor, in the later 14th century.

Gloucester Abbey, with its tomb of Edward II, drew a multitude of pilgrims and the Abbey built the New Inn c. 1450 to accommodate some two hundred people at a time. This timber-framed building, still in use, must have been one of the largest inns in the country, and it became of 'great advantage and profit' (magnum emoleumentium ac proficium), as intended. Glastonbury also was a centre of pilgrimage, and Abbot Selwood (1457–93), a great builder of houses, gave the George Inn to endow the office of monastic chamberlain. It bears his initials and the arms of Edward IV (1460–83), the tracery suggesting a date of c. 1480. Other inns built by abbeys include the New Inn (destroyed c. 1845) at Sherborne and the George at Winchcombe, Gloucestershire.

The 'Cardinal's Hat' at Lincoln, revealed in 1952 as a late 15th-century building, was built or early adapted as an inn by the dean and chapter. Other corporate bodies adopted this form of investment: Winchester College built the Angel at Alresford (Hampshire) in 1418, and the warden signed a contract in 1445 with two carpenters to construct a large timber-framed inn at Andover. The sister foundation, New College, was responsible for the Golden Cross at Oxford, of which the north range of c. 1490 and gateway survive. The Star Inn here was an investment of Oseney Abbey.

* *Household Books of John, Duke of Norfolk*, Roxburghe Club (1844), 434.
† Pantin (1961), 166–91, with plans and illustrations of the examples quoted.

Pl. 1 A. 13th-century windows at Beauvais (upper floor). *Turner (1851).*

Pl. 1 B. Markenfield Hall; view from the courtyard. *Parker (1853).*

Pl. 2. Nurstead Court; interior before the alterations of *c.* 1837. *Parker* (1853).

Pl. 3. Mayfield Palace; the hall in the mid 19th century. *Parker* (*1853*).

Pl. 4. Great Chalfield Manor; north front. *Parker* (1859).

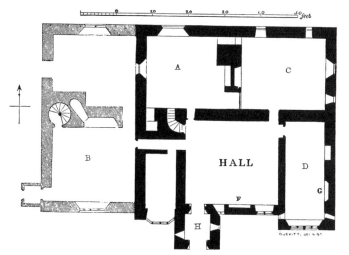

KEY:

A, old kitchen   D, parlour
B, present kitchen   F, G, fireplaces
C, cellar   H, porch

HALL

Pl. 5 A and B. Wanswell Court; plan, and interior of the hall in the 19th century. *Parker* (*1859*).

Pl. 6. Tickenham Court; *above*, hall and solar wing, with arches of the vanished oriel chamber; *below*, solar wing with staircase projection. *Parker* (1859).

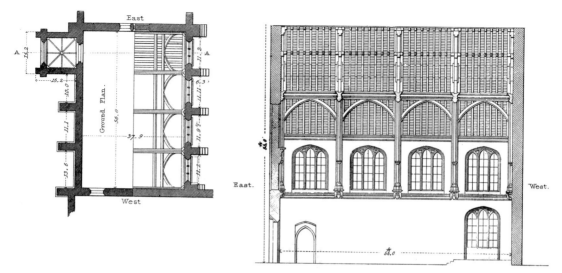

Pl. 7 A and B. Croydon Palace; plan and longitudinal section of the hall. *Pugin (1838).*

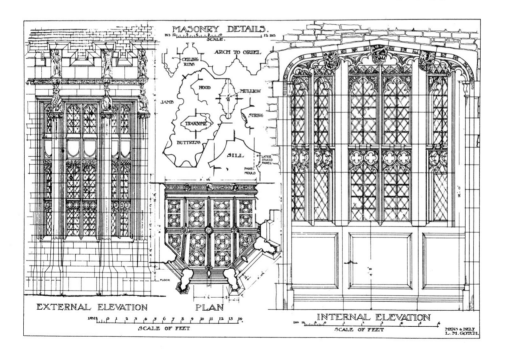

Pl. 7 C. Nevill Holt, oriel; elevations and plan. *Garner & Stratton (1929).*

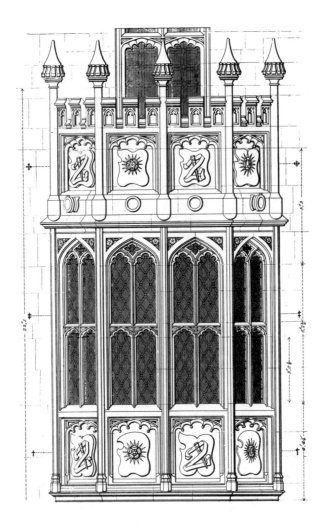

Pl. 8. The Deanery, Wells; elevation of bay window on the
north front. *Pugin* (1839).

looking towards Room.   Nº 1.   looking towards Window.

Plan at ‡·‡

Pl. 9. The Deanery, Wells; plan and section of fan vault, bay window on the north front.
Pugin (1839).

Pl. 10 A. Oriel window at Agecroft Hall, now in Richmond, West Virginia. *Parker (1859)*.

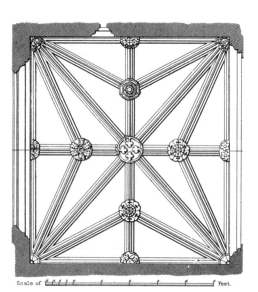

Pl. 10 B. Great Chalfield Manor; vault of porch. *Pugin (1840)*.

Scale of .... Feet.

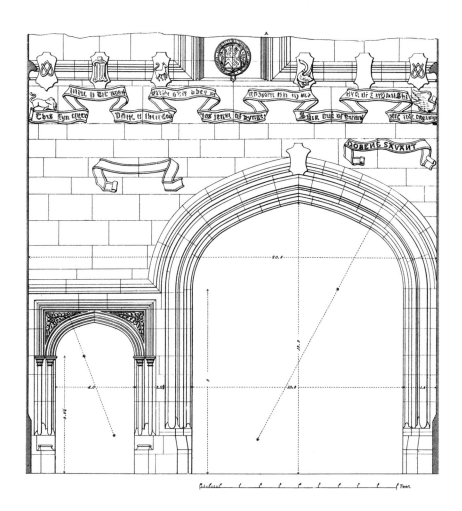

Pl. 11. Thornbury Castle, entrance gateway. *Pugin* (1839).

Section through modern Bridge.

Bottom of the Moat.

Line of.
Water

A.Pugin Arch! direx!

| 5 | 10 | 20 | 30 Feet |

Pl. 12. Oxburgh Hall, north front of gatehouse. *Pugin.* (1839).

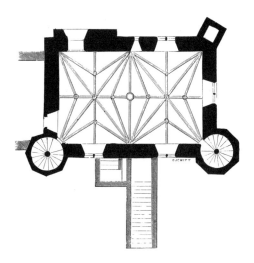

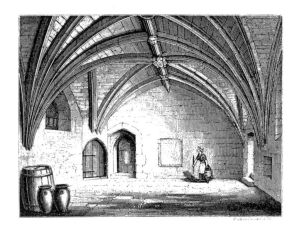

Pl. 13. Chesterton Tower, Cambridge; plan and interior. *Parker* (1859).

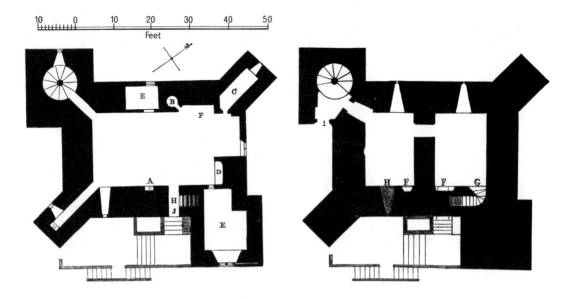

Pl. 14 A and B. Dacre Castle; plan of middle storey (*left*) and basement. *Parker* (1853).

KEY:

A, drain	D, bed recess	G, H, stairs to and from basement
B, oven	E, bedroom	I, original entrance
C, pantry	F, fireplace	J, modern entrance

Pl. 14 C. Dacre Castle; exterior from the south. *Parker* (1853).

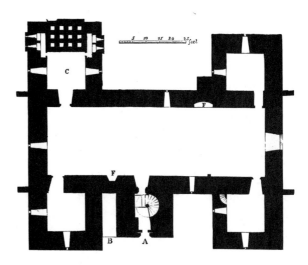

KEY:

A, doorway (the only external entrance)
B, vaulted chamber, or stable?
C, garderobe tower
F, fireplace

Pl. 15. Langley Castle; ground plan (south at top), and exterior from the north. *Parker* (*1853*).

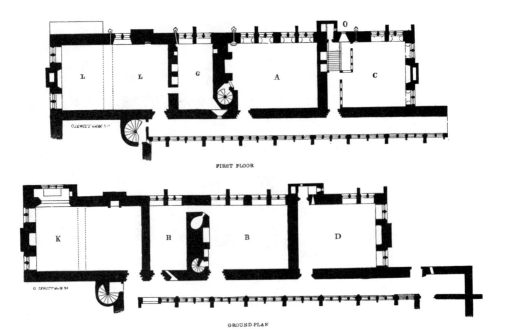

FIRST FLOOR

GROUND-PLAN

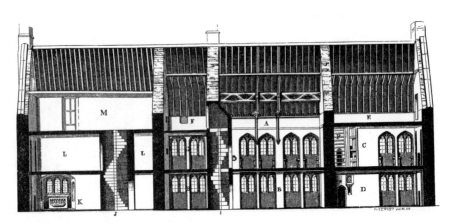

Pl. 16. Prior's House, Wenlock; plans (east at top), and longitudinal section. *Parker (1859).*

KEY:

A, hall, or refectory
B, kitchen
C, Abbot's parlour
D, brewhouse
E, dormitory
F, dormitory in roof

G, H, apartments
I, staircase to all three
   storeys
J, staircase to gallery
   and principal rooms
K, oratory

L, M, apartments (modernized)
N, O, garderobes
P, staircase to Abbot's dormitory

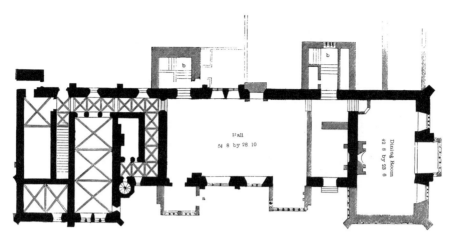

Pl. 17 A. Broughton Castle; plan (south at top). *Parker (1853)*.
KEY:

a, principal entrance   b, staircases

Pl. 17 B. Broughton Castle; east window of chapel, *c.* 1300. *Parker (1853)*.

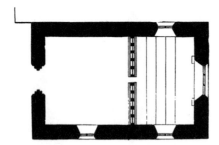

Pl. 18. Champ's Chapel, East Hendred; plan and longitudinal section. *Parker* (1859).

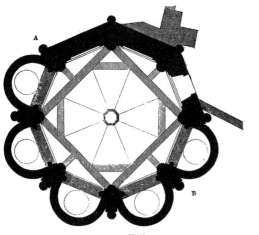

PLAN.

Scale, 20 feet to an inch. A. B. line of section.

Pl. 19. Abbey of Fontevrault; kitchen, c. 1195,
plan, section and exterior. *Turner (1851)*.

Pl. 20 A. Stanton Harcourt; interior of 15th-century kitchen. *Parker* (1859).

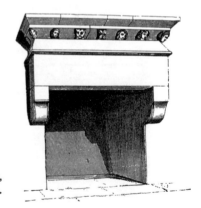

Pl. 20 B. Aydon Castle; fireplace in solar basement, *c.* 1280. *Turner* (1851).

Left, Pl. 21 A. Westminster Hall, louver (exact copy of original). *Parker (1853). Right,* Pl. 21 B. Abbot's Hall, Westminster, before removal of the brazier after 1850. *Parker (1859).*

Pl. 21 C. Bishop's Palace, Wells; late 15th-century fireplace. *Pugin (1839).*

A

B

C

D

E

Pl. 22

A. Chimney at Woodstock, *c.* 1290. *Parker* (*1853*).

B. Chimney of *c.* 1340 at Northborough Manor House. *Parker* (*1853*).

C. Chimney of *c.* 1320, recorded at Chepstow Castle. *Parker* (*1869*).

D. Late 13th-century chimney at Motcombe. *Parker* (*1853*).

E. 14th-century chimney with Constable's Horn, St Briavels Castle. *Archaeologia Cambrensis* (*1858*).

Pl. 23 A and B. Sutton Courtenay 'Abbey', *c.* 1330; *right*, solar before insertion of the ceiling; *below*, interior of hall looking towards screen and spere truss.
Parker (1853).

Pl. 24. Mayfield Palace, interior of the hall in the mid 19th century. *Parker* (1853).

Pl. 25 A. Great Malvern Priory, *c.* 1340; Guesten Hall (demolished). *Parker (1853)*.

Pl. 25 B. Eltham Palace; hall wind-braces, *c.* 1479–80. *Pugin (1838)*.

Pl. 26. Great Chalfield Manor, *c.* 1480; hall with original screen and ceiling bosses. *Parker (1859).*

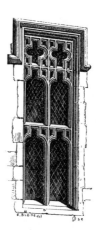

Left, Pl. 27 A. Acton Burnell Castle, *c.* 1284–92 +; hall window exterior. *Turner* (1851). *Right,* Pl. 27 B. Market Deeping Rectory; hall window exterior, mid 14th century. *Parker* (1853).

Pl. 27 C. Battle Abbey; window of Abbot Adam de Katling (1324–51). *Brakspear* (1933a).

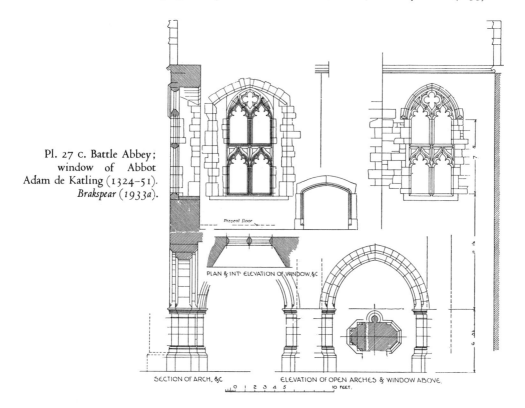

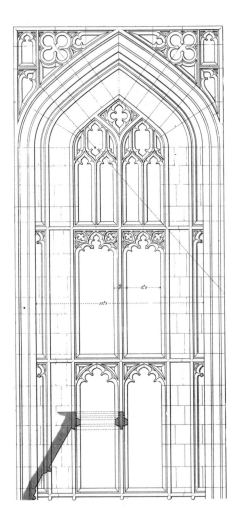

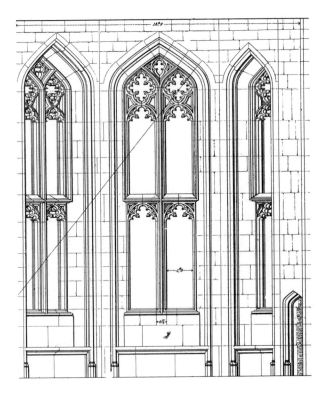

Pl. 28. Kenilworth Castle; *above*, hall window
interior; *right*, windows in polygonal oriel
chamber. *Pugin (1839)*.

Pl. 29. Raglan Castle; window in the State Apartments,
Fountain Court, c. 1450–69. *Pugin* (1839).

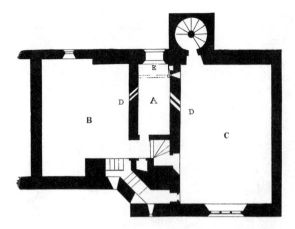

SECOND FLOOR

KEY:

KEY:
A, oratory
B, priest's room
C, lord's bed-chamber
D, squints
E, altar
F, parlour
G, chapel

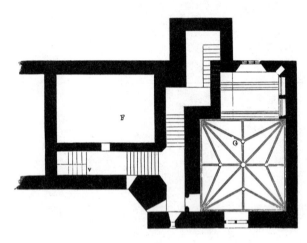

FIRST FLOOR

Pl. 30. Beverston Castle, plans. *Parker* (*1859*).

Pl. 31 A. Squints in the hall, Great Chalfield Manor, c. 1480. *Parker (1859).*

Pl. 31 B. Squint from the parlour, Wanswell Court. *Parker (1859).*

Pl. 31 D. Dacre Castle; 14th-century laver. *Parker (1853).*

Pl. 31 C. Battle Hall; cistern and laver, c. 1330. *Parker (1853).*

Pl. 32 A. Little Wenham Hall; early 15th-century laver with iron bar, probably the support for a lead pipe of a cistern. *Parker (1859)*.

Pl. 32 B. Late mediaeval settle once at Combe St Nicholas, Somerset. *Parker (1859)*.

Mediaeval inns fall into two classes, the courtyard and the gatehouse plan. The court-yard inn, closely resembling a large town house with its court and fringe of shops, most often consists of timber-framed buildings, like the New Inn at Gloucester and the George at Dorchester (Oxfordshire). The second type bears a strong likeness to a mediaeval gate-house, such as the great 14th-century entrances to the abbeys of Battle, Thornton and St Albans. It consists of a rectangular block of two or three storeys, incorporating a gateway, with the main rooms concentrated on the street front, the court behind containing only offices and stabling. This monumental treatment is more usual in stone-built inns, although one of the main examples, Norton St Philip, had its upper storey rebuilt in timber in the 15th century. Other notable gatehouse inns are the Angel and Royal at Grantham, and the George at Glastonbury.

Just as the courtyard inn resembles a great town house, so the gatehouse type seems to reflect a second kind of 15th-century domestic building, a compact rectangular block of usually two storeys, a type that has persisted with modifications up to the present day. As we have seen, the earlier mediaeval house had been composed of a series of buildings tacked together, the hall with its great roof dominating the rest, and its end blocks separately roofed at right angles to it. By the later 14th and early 15th centuries a typical house plan had emerged, with chamber block (and garderobe), hall, butteries beyond the screens, then a kitchen, usually now in line. In smaller houses the kitchen might be combined with the hall or with the buttery, or the solar be placed over the latter. In the 15th century the hall was gradually becoming less important and, with a room above it, was integrated with the end portions so that a uniform roof-line became possible. Sometimes only the jettied upper storeys of the end rooms served as a reminder of the former projecting wings. Indeed, a return to the compact 12th-century house block on a larger scale with additional rooms and the hall below is suggested by some 15th- and early 16th-century houses.

With the development of the parlour or withdrawing room below the solar at the upper end, the hall was starting on its downward grade of importance, leading to the small vesti-bule of today. In the 15th- and early 16th-century houses of magnates, lay and clerical, the great hall needed to be spacious to accommodate large numbers of retainers and for the sake of prestige. Croydon and Crosby Halls are still on a sumptuous scale. But in lesser houses the hall tended to shrink (to the advantage of the parlour), becoming shortened, often square in plan, apart from the screens passage. At Norwich the mercer Thomas Pykerell's House in St Mary's Plain [3] has a hall only a few feet longer than the parlour. The house was saved from demolition in 1931 by the Ministry of Works and the Norfolk Archaeological Trust, the present owners. Thomas Pykerell was mayor of Norwich in 1525, 1533 and 1538.

The Chantry at Mere [2, 28] has a hall, also once open, nearly square; it is of three bays, the solar block of two, but there is a much larger service block of six bays, occupying practically half the building. This house dates from the middle or second half of the 15th century, as do a number of surviving priest's houses. That at Muchelney in Somerset [6] (see Figs. 60 a and b) seems earlier, judging from the 14th-century mouldings of the doorways at either end of the screens passage. However, it was brought up to date, according to window evidence, in the late 15th century, and the tracery matches the new work within the Abbot's

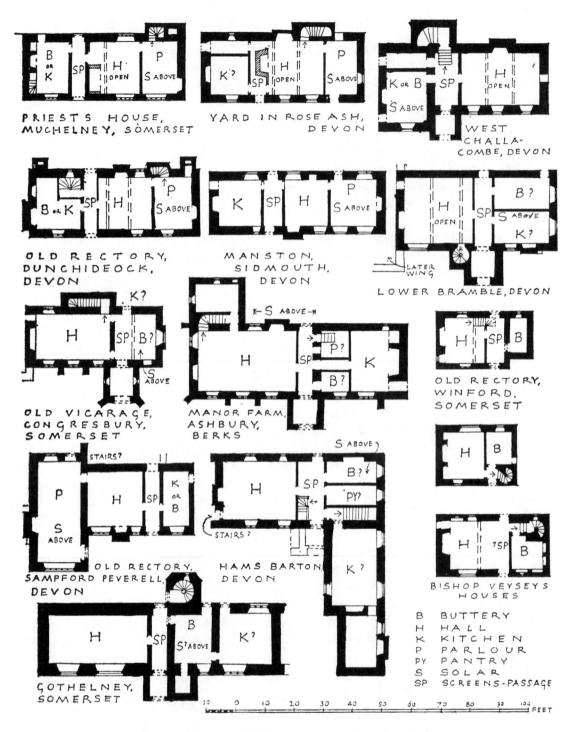

PRIESTS HOUSE, MUCHELNEY, SOMERSET

YARD IN ROSE ASH, DEVON

WEST CHALLACOMBE, DEVON

OLD RECTORY, DUNCHIDEOCK, DEVON

MANSTON, SIDMOUTH, DEVON

LOWER BRAMBLE, DEVON

OLD VICARAGE, CONGRESBURY, SOMERSET

MANOR FARM, ASHBURY, BERKS

OLD RECTORY, WINFORD, SOMERSET

OLD RECTORY, SAMPFORD PEVERELL, DEVON

HAMS BARTON, DEVON

BISHOP VEYSEYS HOUSES

GOTHELNEY, SOMERSET

B BUTTERY
H HALL
K KITCHEN
P PARLOUR
PY PANTRY
S SOLAR
SP SCREENS-PASSAGE

Fig. 60 a. Priests' and lay houses, comparative ground plans.

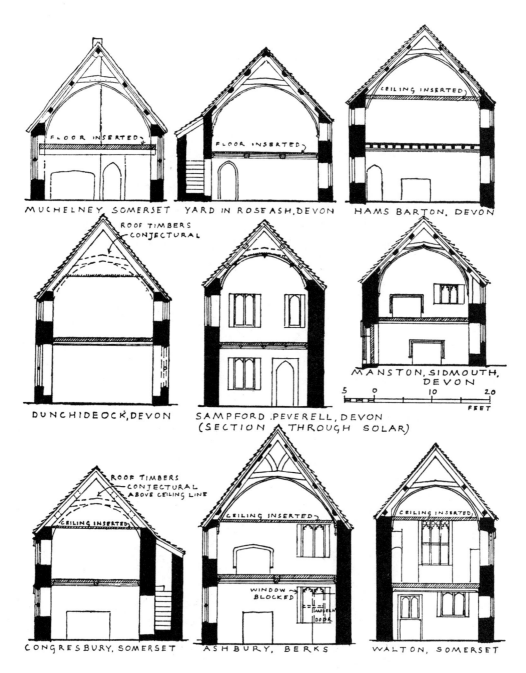

MUCHELNEY, SOMERSET YARD IN ROSE ASH, DEVON HAMS BARTON, DEVON

FLOOR INSERTED FLOOR INSERTED CEILING INSERTED

ROOF TIMBERS CONJECTURAL

DUNCHIDEOCK, DEVON

SAMPFORD PEVERELL, DEVON
(SECTION THROUGH SOLAR)

MANSTON, SIDMOUTH, DEVON

5 0 10 20 FEET

ROOF TIMBERS CONJECTURAL ABOVE CEILING LINE

CEILING INSERTED CEILING INSERTED CEILING INSERTED

WINDOW BLOCKED

MODERN DOOR

CONGRESBURY, SOMERSET ASHBURY, BERKS WALTON, SOMERSET

Fig. 60 b. Priests' and lay houses, comparative sections.

Parlour near by. The hall was originally open to the roof, apparently with central hearth, the floor above and large fireplace backing on the screens being of 16th-century date; apart from that passage it is an exact square. Other examples of halls square or approximately so include the once open one of the 15th-century vicarage Priesthill, Kentisbeare (Devon),[5] and the low hall of the Chantry at Ilminster, Somerset; there are also secular examples.[4, 7, 8, 17]

But the longer hall continues approximately on a 3 : 2 proportion in other 15th-century houses, such as the open hall at Stoke-sub-Hamdon 'Priory', Somerset, [21] and 27–28 George Street, St Albans [20] and the low one at Ashbury Manor, Berkshire. This proportion seems usual in East Anglia.

The use of the wall fireplace, already common in other rooms, in the 15th century tended to oust the central hearth in the hall, and made the lofty roof for smoke there no longer necessary. A low ceiling provided warmth and comfort and also allowed a large room to be placed above. In the 16th century it was normal for houses to be built with this lower hall, and there are countless cases of the insertion of an upper floor into an earlier hall built two storeys in height.

However, there are certain houses of 15th-century date which suggest that an upper and a lower hall were intended from the start. Cases have been found in Somerset and Devon where the upper room was apparently a second hall of equal importance.* The most spectacular is Gothelney Manor (Somerset) [22] (see Fig. 60 a), where the lower hall is the height of an open hall but ceiled, and above is a lofty room, open to a fine arch-braced roof. Each of these corresponds to two storeys of the adjoining portion of the two-part plan. There is a projecting garderobe block next to the porch, and in the opposite wall a staircase turret with a chapel at the top.

Blackmoor (Somerset) [25] and Hams Barton (Devon) [26] (see Figs. 60 a and b) also show the double hall arrangement, and it seems to occur in several parsonages and chantry houses of similar date. At Combe Raleigh Chantry (Devon) [14] the two halls correspond to three storeys of the service block (see Fig. 58, p. 181). Dunchideock Old Rectory (Devon) [11] (see Figs. 60 a and b) had an upper hall from the first, for the chimney stack is staggered to serve two lateral fireplaces; on the same wall a staircase projection gives access between the floors, which again do not correspond, those of the end chambers being lower. The floors are in line in the two-part plan of the vicarage at Congresbury (Somerset) [24] (see Figs. 60 a and b), a particularly fine example, as is Ashbury Manor (Berkshire) [23] (see Figs. 60 a and b; Pl. XXXV c and d), a 'Somerset' house connected with Glastonbury Abbey and Abbot Selwood. Here the lower hall, subdivided later, has two fine rooms above, separated by an original plank-and-muntin partition, perhaps an upper hall with more elaborately roofed solar, with its access through a traceried screen to a small room, probably oratory, over the porch. At the Ilminster Chantry [18] the upper room may have been the principal chamber, as it has squints into a chapel (with fireplace) beyond.

In most cases the windows of both upper and lower hall are similar, often with cinquefoiled heads, as at Ashbury and Congresbury, the lower ones being longer and having a

* W. A. Pantin, lecture on 'Upper and Lower Halls in Priests' and some Lay Houses in Somerset and Devon', given to the conference of the Vernacular Architecture Group on 17 December 1961.

transom, which is not provided above as a rule, as it would make the openings inordinately high. However, transomed lights at both levels are found in the Chantry House at Trent (Dorset).[13]

What was the reason for this 'duplex' system? Could it be that the lower hall served the official business of the estate, or in a parsonage was in the nature of a parish hall, while the upper room was a more private apartment for the family or the priest? It may of course have served as a solar. However, such an upper room could give access from both solar and service blocks on the same floor, instead of these being separated by a great two-storey hall, which made access across possible only at ground level.

Whether it was the old-fashioned 'hall house' with lofty central hall and two-storeyed private and service ends, or the new low hall with chamber or another hall above, the 15th-century domestic building tended towards a compact rectangular plan. In the present state of our knowledge, the more advanced types seem to come from the south-west of England, but this may be due to intensive research in that area, by W. A. Pantin, E. T. Long, A. W. Everett and Dr W. G. Hoskins. Certainly great builders are known there at this period, particularly Abbot Selwood of Glastonbury (1457–93), who was responsible for houses on the vast estates of the Abbey, many houses at Mells,[9] perhaps the Old Rectory at Walton,[46] and possibly Ashbury Manor, which, though in Berkshire, belonged to his abbey and was built during his tenure of office. Thomas Beckington, Bishop of Bath and Wells (1443–65), and his executors can be traced from heraldic evidence as the builders of other 15th-century houses in this region, not only the small ones in the Vicars' Close at Wells, but parsonages such as Stanton Drew (Rectory Farm) [12, 34] and Congresbury.

These rectangular blocks usually contained three rooms on each floor, parlour, hall with screens passage, and buttery-kitchen, with three chambers, or two and the upper part of the hall, above.* The Chantry at Mere [2, 28] is an elaborate version of this plan, with an additional room to the service end.

In West Dorset there are three 15th-century houses [29, 30, 31] of this triple-part plan, which have the feature of diagonal buttresses at one end of the long rectangular block. One of them, at Whitchurch Canonicorum, has the original entrance to a small hall, centrally placed. The others probably contained a screens passage, but being much altered internally, the clue to their original arrangement is given by the early 16th-century Queen's Arms Hotel at Charmouth,[32] where the evidence is complete. The block contains a kitchen with great fireplace, once reached by a passage between butteries from the screens of a square 'low hall', which has a lateral fireplace and a parlour, with end fireplace, beyond. At Charmouth no butteries are provided, but these are present at Naish Priory at East Coker (Somerset), this end having apparently three storeys; at the other, which has a long traceried and transomed solar or chapel window, one buttress is a projection of the lateral, the other of the end wall.

Sometimes the rectangular block is joined to a cross-wing to form an L-plan. This is the case at Ashbury Manor [43] (c. 1488), with Ockwells the most important 15th-century house in Berkshire. The ground plan is typically mediaeval, except for the absence of a private chamber beyond the hall; the latter and the screens passage, butteries and kitchen

---

* Mr Pantin's 'three-part plan, straight'.

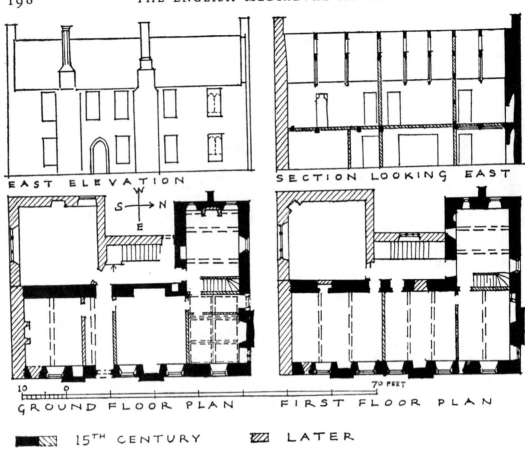

EAST ELEVATION

SECTION LOOKING EAST

GROUND FLOOR PLAN

FIRST FLOOR PLAN

10   0   70 FEET

15TH CENTURY   LATER

Fig. 61. The Chantry, Ilminster, *c.* 1480.

are in line, although the service part is separately roofed. Near the upper end of the low hall, making a right angle with it, is an extension of the lateral 'wall' staircase projection. This provides a small chamber on each floor and contains a garderobe in the further wall.

The Chantry at Ilminster [18] (Fig. 61) has a similar L-plan, the wing again projecting at the upper end, here off the parlour; it possibly contained the kitchen, as now, with a fireplace in the back wall. The room above may be regarded as a 'wardrobe': it has a shallow recess, perhaps for washing purposes, and there was probably a garderobe with its pit in the thickness of the chimney stack. Here the main block contains buttery, screens position, hall and parlour, with three rooms over, the northernmost a chapel yet provided with a fireplace. The chapel retains an image bracket in the form of a miniature column, and next to the piscina on the east wall a small slit window, looking across the church 'close' to the north transept, in which St Catherine's Chantry, founded by John Wadham, was placed. This was built to house the tomb of Sir William Wadham (d. 1452). In it is also the tomb of his great-great-grandson Nicholas (d. 1609) and Dorothy his wife (d. 1618), founders of Wadham College, Oxford (1613). In the partition in the house between

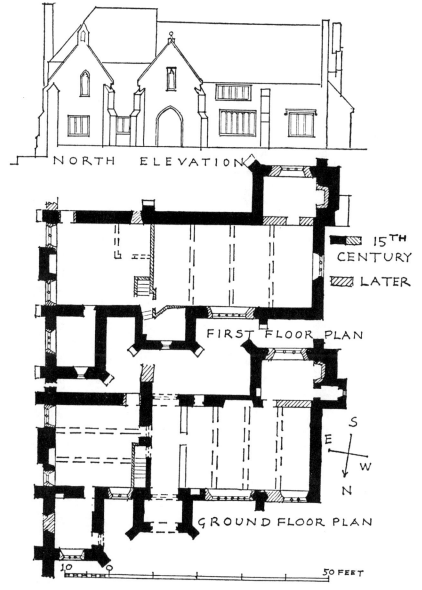

Fig. 62. The 'Priory', 1450–60, Stoke-sub-Hamdon.

the chapel and the central chamber is a squint in the form of a quatrefoil, with a view, at kneeling level, of an altar (Pl. LVII A). The house preserved an original entrance doorway, chimney and two windows (north end) but is especially noteworthy for its chapel and several original fireplaces.

Also in Somerset, at Stoke-sub-Hamdon (Fig. 62), is the 'Priory',[45] more likely the residence of a small college of chantry priests, reorganized c. 1450–60. The main block is of two-part plan, with long, originally open hall, and beyond the screens a buttery or parlour with solar above. The hall has a porch, and a further small block makes a right angle on the other side at the upper end, apparently an 'oriel chamber' with fireplace (perhaps later) and small garderobe. The service (or parlour) has a small room projecting in the same manner, on the porch side; unlike the other it was two-storeyed from the first, and was possibly an oratory, although there is no evidence except a bellcote on the gable. On the other side there was probably a detached kitchen later incorporated.

At Hams Barton [44] the wing lies at right angles to the service rooms near the entrance. But in the Old Rectory at Sampford Peverell, [10] (*see* Figs. 60 *a* and *b*) in the same county, the cross-wing projects on both sides off the upper end of the low hall, making an unequal T-plan reminiscent of some 13th-century houses, and containing the solar over a parlour with fireplaces on the further side from the hall. This house dates from the beginning of the 16th century and was a residence of the Lady Margaret Beaufort, Countess of Richmond. The Old Rectory at Walton (Somerset) (Fig. 63) has the unusual plan of a parallel wing attached in the 13th-century manner at the angle of the (low) hall, with access only to the rooms over the latter; the two blocks had no internal communication at ground level, the common angle here blocked by a newel staircase with external doorway.

Smaller houses of the 15th century are even more like those usual today. The compact rectangular block * contained two compartments on each floor. There was either an open hall, equivalent to a double storey, with solar over service apartment at its lower end, such as the late 15th-century house at Lower Bramble (Devon) [1] (*see* Fig. 60 *a*), or two rooms on each level, the low hall having a chamber over as in the Old Vicarage, Congresbury, [24] which is also provided with a porch † and wall staircase projection. Like Ashbury, this house is remarkably unspoilt, and has many original windows.

The two-part plan is found in three 15th-century houses of chantry priests, at Farleigh Hungerford (Somerset), Trent (Dorset) and Coombe Raleigh (Devon) (*see* Fig. 58, p. 181). These little houses are very similar in dimensions, and all have low halls, approximately square, with end fireplaces, except at Trent where the ground-floor one is in a lateral wall. Farleigh Hungerford Chantry [39] was built *c.* 1440 by Sir William (later Lord) Hungerford for two chantry priests; hence probably the adjoining entrances to the ground-floor apartments, and three rooms, perhaps common room with fireplace, and two bedchambers, or studies, above. The Chantry at Trent [42] is the best preserved of the three, with original windows, doorways and chimneys. It was probably built in the middle or latter part of the 15th century. The upper rooms have the staircase between like a college arrangement; one room was perhaps for the curate. The Chantry at Coombe Raleigh [41] was also built for one priest after 1463, with room for a servant or a lodger. The Devon house differs in having three storeys in the service half of the building; the newel staircase serving all levels projects at the back as in the houses of the vicars at Wells.

Close examples are given by the little houses built in two rows for clothiers by Abbot Selwood at Mells (Somerset) [38] in the late 15th century. A typical house shows a two-part plan (*see* Fig. 58) with a screens passage between a larger and smaller room and a projecting staircase. Some larger ones have a parlour beyond the hall, and a third room

---

* Mr Pantin's 'two-part plan'.
† With the arms of Bishop Beckington (1443–65).

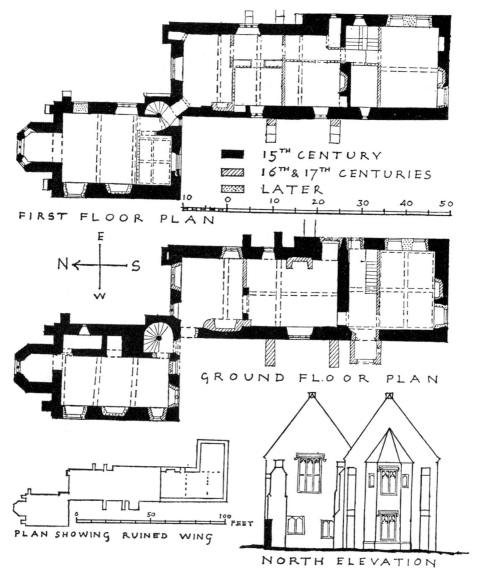

FIRST FLOOR PLAN

15TH CENTURY
16TH & 17TH CENTURIES
LATER

GROUND FLOOR PLAN

PLAN SHOWING RUINED WING

NORTH ELEVATION

Fig. 63. The Old Rectory, Walton.

above. They may be compared with the small houses built by John Vesey, Bishop of Exeter (1519–54), near his birthplace, Sutton Coldfield (Warwickshire) [40] (see Fig. 60 a). Again there are usually two rooms, but the newel staircase here is enclosed in one angle of the building, and the hall fireplace placed in an end wall: at Mells it might be set against the screens passage. The Old Rectory at Winford (Somerset) [48] (see Fig. 60 a) shows the smallest and simplest type, with one room above and below, the hall-kitchen with a lean-to buttery, and single chamber above. Again the chimney is in the gable end.

It has been shown that many of our 15th-century domestic examples are of ecclesiastical origin, which is in some cases the reason for their survival. There was widespread building of houses for chantry priests at this date, when the predominating religious outlet was the establishment of chantry chapels, usually in part of the parish church, where prayers for the souls of the founders and his kin could be said. If there were one, two or three chantry priests, their dwelling would resemble a normal house of the period, such as those we have studied. But if six or more were involved, a collegiate plan was necessary, having a close or quadrangle with the hall one side, and two floors of separate chambers, as was originally the case at Cobham in Kent, the college for six priests founded in 1362 and 're-edified' for twenty almsfolk in 1598.

The foundation might include almspeople, 'bedesmen', to add their prayers to those of the priests. The building of hospitals was a pious act from the 12th century and before, and it is interesting to note how the standard mediaeval form of hospital, like a monastic infirmary, with chapel as chancel to aisled nave for the beds, developed in the 15th century into a set of residential almshouses arranged like a collegiate establishment round a court, each bedesman or bedeswoman having his or her own little lodging but with a room on each floor. From that period onward the naves of early hospitals, such as that of St Mary at Chichester, were, like the monastic dormitories at this time, divided off into separate rooms or cubicles. At St Mary Magdalene, Glastonbury, the 14th-century infirmary hall retains its outer walls, inside which 16th-century almshouses were built in two rows where the hospital beds once stood, and resemble a vicars' close.*

In the 15th century there came into fashion for such communities the plan of a row of individual two-storey houses, attached like a modern terrace. In vicars' closes these are set in two parallel ranges, separated by a long narrow court or path between gardens, and having the common hall and chapel at the ends. At Wells [49] (see Fig. 58, p. 181) the houses appear to have been built or renovated by Bishop Beckington (1443–63) or his executors, for his arms are placed on them; but the hall is earlier, c. 1347. Each of the forty-two vicars had his own little house of two rooms, one on each floor, and a small yard or garden in front. The ground-floor chamber had a four-centred entrance arch and fireplace in the front wall, together with a large transomed window of two trefoiled lights in a square head, and a loop fitted in on the other side of the doorway. There was another two-light opposite, an opening to the garderobe, and a square newel staircase projection. The upper room had a two-light, small fireplace and a loop on the front wall.† At Chichester there is a similar parallel arrangement.

Perhaps closer to the Wells layout are the ranges of monastic *camerae* at Worcester College, Oxford,[47] notably the six buildings in the south range of the main courtyard, one of which has a two-storeyed 'bay window' on each side of the entrance. There are further 15th-century lodgings in the east and south sides of Pump Quadrangle. The twenty-one Vicars' Houses at Windsor Castle [50] (see Fig. 58, p. 181) come into this class of separate two-storey houses, here timber-framed, built c. 1478–81. These, with the

---

* Godfrey (1955), 26.
† The houses have been much altered, but we know the original arrangement from Pugin's drawings and Parker's restoration of one of them.

Old Rectory at Winford, represent the smallest type of 15th-century house, and may be compared with the lodgings of guests and retainers flanking the courtyards of noble mansions.

The rectangular block with uniform roof line is found in the Prior's House at Wenlock in Shropshire [27] (Pl. 16). This dates from the end of the 15th century, a period of improved accommodation for the heads of monastic establishments, and is comparable to the works at Cleeve and Muchelney Abbeys in Somerset. Probably it was Prior Richard Singer (1486–1521) who built the new range running north to south, facing the now vanished dorter across an inner courtyard south-east of the chapter house and cloister. This included not only magnificent new apartments for himself, but also new rooms with a chapel for the farmery (infirmary), forming an extension of the 12th-century infirmary hall on the north side of the court.

This new infirmary portion forms the northern end of the new range. The purely chapel part or chancel is contained in a small gabled eastern projection with triplet windows, original altar and piscina; the rest of the ground-floor room was more secular and contains a fireplace to the north, and a garderobe at the end of a screened-off entrance passage. Above this room, but not over the chancel, is a large apartment, also with fireplace, with access from both the old farmery and the gallery on the western side of the new range. South of these a two-storeyed set of chambers formed the apartments of the infirmarer in charge of the sick, with recesses for medical stores and herbs. The thick south wall contained the infirmarer's staircase, and another, quite independent, leading to the room over his, but from the prior's apartments; this wall divided the farmery department from the prior's half of the range. A well-lit lower room was probably for administrative purposes, and above it the superb hall, open to an elaborate roof, has similar pairs of two-light windows but here with low pedestals in the embrasures, perhaps to support tables, since they appear too high for seats. The roof has a smaller central bay which, with the absence of a moulded collar purlin, here suggests the presence originally of a louver over an open hearth. This is borne out by the presence in the room below of a vast oaken pillar, perhaps to support the hearth? * Yet the fireplace in the north wall looks original. †

The final southern room on this hall floor was the prior's great chamber, reached not from the hall but from the western gallery serving all the range. The moulded entrance probably led to a screened-off passage containing a staircase to the attic, and a garderobe in an eastern projection. A small window and water drain served this entry. In the main portion of the room the two pairs of east windows are set nearer the end (south) wall, which contains a fireplace flanked by similar windows, alike with pilasters in the jambs. The room below was perhaps for a guest or important official; it has no communication with the one above. Only the hall was open to the roof. The other first-floor rooms had a ceiling, with attic room and plainer roof above; they may have served as dormitories for the servants of the prior.

This is a building of the greatest interest, especially since it contains the unusual medi-aeval feature of an internal corridor of two storeys, not a pentice but included under the

---

* However, this is not quite in line, and does not appear in Parker's plan.
† Although Parker believed it to be a later insertion.

main roof. From the two galleries, superimposed, access to the rooms is obtained as in the arrangement in a courtyard inn.

Another modern feature is the symmetry of the fenestration. On the west there is the double range of gallery windows, originally unglazed, as may be observed from the weathering of the lower portions less protected by the low eaves. On the east, owing to the projections and the blank spaces caused by the division walls, the windows cannot be continuous. But otherwise the regularity is stressed, the lower windows placed beneath the upper, which have panels of masonry in line.

Rectangular blocks arranged round a court are seen in the Deanery at Wells,[51] which, in spite of later alterations, remains a fine example of the residence of a man of substance in the late 15th century. It was rebuilt by John Gunthorpe, who was dean in 1472–98, a man greatly esteemed by Edward IV, and his royal patron's badge of the *rose en soleil* is combined with Gunthorpe's rebus of a gun in the decoration of the oriel window.

The gateway from the north side of the close opens into an outer court, and on the west side of this is a square building of four ranges overlooking an inner court, now built over. The eastern range, with porch and screens, must have been the hall, situated next to the outer courtyard. It was made into separate rooms during the Commonwealth but retains on the ground floor the fine late 15th-century hall fireplace. The southern block overlooking the close contained two storeys from the first, the uppermost the more important, as the windows are longer (and transomed) at this level; the square-headed windows, now sashed, would have had twin cinquefoiled lights originally. At each end is a newel staircase housed in a turret with octagonal traceried 'lantern', cornice and spire. There is another range of rooms on the west. But, judging from the ornament, Dean Gunthorpe's personal suite was on the north side, on the first floor reached by a straight staircase enclosed at the western end. It contained a vestibule with laver, screened from a great chamber where the dean and special guests might dine, and a retiring room, perhaps a bedchamber beyond. This room has on the north a projecting window with wide embrasure and a pair of traceried and transomed coupled lights. The great chamber has another slight projection and a richer four-light window with perpendicular tracery, but its great feature is the elaborate oriel which forms a centrepiece to the block, and there is another to the south. On the west side the vestibule is spanned by a great arch supporting an enclosed stone gallery with traceried two-light openings looking into the great chamber over the vestibule screen. This gallery is approached by a newel staircase on the south, which gives access to the second-floor chambers and terminates in a square tower. On the upper floor, besides a closet near the staircase, there were three rooms of importance, judging by the windows, and the westernmost, with a fine traceried four-light window, may have been used by the dean himself. The service department may have been on the ground floor of this range, with the kitchen on the east, to serve both hall and great chamber.

EXAMPLES OF HOUSES IN THE LATE 15TH & EARLY 16TH CENTURIES

OPEN HALLS (*or originally so*) APPROXIMATELY SQUARE IN PLAN (*apart from the screens passage; length including this in brackets*)

		Internal Dimensions	*References*
(1) late C 15th	Lower Bramble, Devon	23′ 3″ (30′) × 22′	Pantin (1957), 141, 146, fig. 30 (plan).
(2) mid C 15th	The Chantry, Mere, Wilts.	21′ (26′) × 22′	Pantin (1959), 224–31, figs. 81–82, pl. XX (plans, sections, etc.).
(3) *c.* 1520–30	Pykerell's House, St Mary's Plain, Norwich	20′ × 16′	J. F. Williams (1949). Pykerell's House, St Mary's Plain. *Archaeological Journal*, CVI, 82–3, (plan).
(4) C 15th	Yard, Rose Ash, Devon	19′ (25′) × 18′	Pantin (1957), 141, 146, figs. 30, 31 (plan, section).
(5) C 15th	Priesthill, Kentisbeare, Devon	19′ (24′ 6″) × 18′	Pantin (1957), 127–9, fig. 24 (plans, sections).
(6) C 14th & late C 15th	Priest's House, Muchelney, Som.	18′ (24′) × 18′	Pantin (1957), 121–4, fig. 22, pl. XVII A–C (plans, section, etc.).
(7) C 15th	Bury Court Farm, Donhead, Wilts.	18′ (23′) × 18′	Pantin (1957), 141, 146.
(8) C 15th	Badlake, Devon	17′ (22′ 6″) × 16′ 6″	Pantin (1957), 146.

LOW HALLS APPROXIMATELY SQUARE IN PLAN

(9) late C 15th	Abbot Selwood's houses at Mells, Som.	*c.* 22′ × 18′	Pantin (1959), 250, fig. 88 (plan); *Country Life* (17).
(10) early C 16th	Old Rectory, Sampford Peverell, Devon	19′ (25′ 6″) × 18′ 6″	Pantin (1957), 139, figs. 29, 30, 31 (plans, sections, etc.).
(11) early C 15th	Old Rectory, Dunchideock, Devon	19′ (24′) × 17′	Pantin (1957), 124–7, 146, figs. 23, 30, 31 (plans, sections, etc.).
(12) *c.* 1443–64	Rectory Farm, Stanton Drew, Som.	18′ 8″ (24′ 8″) × 18′ 3″	Pantin (1957), 131–2, fig. 26 (plan, section, etc.).
(13) mid to late C 15th	The Chantry, Trent, Dor.	18′ 6″ (23′) × 15′	Pantin (1959), 237–40, figs. 85, 86, 88, pl. XX A–C (plans, section, etc.).
(14) after 1463	The Chantry, Coombe Raleigh, Devon	*c.* 17′ square	Pantin (1959), 241–3, fig. 87, pl. XIX E (plans, section, etc.).
(15) *c.* 1440	The Chantry, Farleigh Hungerford, Som.	(17′) × 16′ 6″	Pantin (1959), 234–7, fig. 84, pl. XXI A, B (plan, section, etc.).
(16) early C 16th	Bishop Vesey's houses at Sutton Coldfield, War.	17′ × 16′	Pantin (1957), 144, fig. 30 (plans); Chatwind & Harcourt (1941–2).
(17) late C 15th	Manston, Sidmouth, Devon	15′? (22′) × 15′ 6″	Pantin (1957), 141, 146, figs. 30, 31 (plan, section).
(18) late C 15th	The Chantry, Ilminster, Som.	15′ sq.	Pantin (1959), 231–4, fig. 83, pl. XXI C, D, E (plans, section, etc.).
(19) late C 15th	Old Rectory, Winford, Som.	14′ (20′) × 15′	Pantin (1957), 138, figs. 26, 30, pl. XIX C (plans, sections, etc.).

OPEN HALLS (*or originally so*) APPROXIMATELY 3 : 2

		Internal Dimensions	References
(20) c. 1500	27–28 George St, St Albans, Herts.	c. 28′ (31′) × 22′	Wood (1937), 99–104 (plan & illus.).
(21) c. 1450–60	The 'Priory', Stoke-sub-Hamdon, Som.	28′ (36′) × 18′	Pantin (1959), 219–24, figs. 79–80, pls. XVII, XVIII, XIX A (plans & sections).

LOW HALLS, RECTANGULAR

(22) early C 15th	Gothelney Manor near Bridgwater, Som.	35′ (41′) × 16′	Pantin (1957), 141, 146, fig. 30 (plan).
(23) c. 1488	Ashbury Manor, Berks.	34′ (40′) × 20′	Pantin (1957), 144, 146, figs. 30, 31 (plan & section).
(24) c. 1443–64+	The Old Vicarage, Congresbury, Som.	25′ × 15′	Pantin (1957), 128, 131, 144, 146, figs. 25, 30, 31 (plans & sections).
(25) C 15th	Blackmoor, Som.	24′ (32′) × 18′ 4″	Pantin (1957), 141, 146.

UPPER AND LOWER HALLS

See references 11, 13, 14, 18, 22, 23, 24, 25 above.

(26) late C 15th	Hams Barton, Devon		Pantin (1957), 141, 146, figs. 30, 31 (plan & section).

FOUR-PART PLAN IN LINE (*four compartments on each floor*)

		External Dimensions	References
(27) late C 15th	Prior's House, Wenlock, Salop	113′ × 34′. Upper hall.	*Country Life* (29), 1432–5, 1492–1495 (with plan, illus., including Buckler drawing); Parker (1859), 145, 366–71 (plan & section).
(28) mid C 15th	The Chantry, Mere, Wilts.	89′ 6″ × 27′. Open hall.	See reference 2.

THREE-PART PLAN IN LINE (*three compartments on each floor*)

(29) C 15th	Pickett Farm, South Perrott, Dor.	67′ × 21′. Low hall.	R.C.H.M. *Dorset.* I, XXXVIII–XXXIX (plan).
(30) c. C 15th	Toller Whelme Manor House, Corscombe, Dor.	c. 55′ × 21′. Low hall.	R.C.H.M. *Dorset.* I, XXXVIII–XXXIX (plan).
(31) C 15th	Higher Abbotts Wootton Farm, Whitchurch Canonicorum, Dor.	54′ × 23′. Low hall.	R.C.H.M. *Dorset.* I, XXXVIII–XXXIX (plan).

The above three houses have diagonal buttresses at one end.

(32) early C 16th	Queen's Arms Hotel, Charmouth, Dor.	64′ × 23′. Low hall.	R.C.H.M. *Dorset.* I, XXXVIII–XXXIX (plan).
(33) late C 15th	Manston, Sidmouth, Devon	61′ × 20′. Low hall.	See reference 17.
(34) c. 1443–64	Rectory Farm, Stanton Drew, Som.	60′ × 25–28′. Low hall.	See reference 12.

THREE-PART PLAN IN LINE *with wing making* L-PLAN

See reference 18 above.

TWO-PART PLAN IN LINE (*two compartments on each floor*)

		External Dimensions	References
(35) early C 15th	Gothelney Manor, Som.	84+'×24'. Low hall.	See reference 22.
(36) late C 15th	Lower Bramble, Devon	55'×*c.* 25'. Open hall.	See reference 1.
(37) *c.* 1443–64+	Old Vicarage, Congresbury, Som.	48'×20'. Low hall.	See reference 24.
(38) late C 15th	Abbot Selwood's houses at Mells, Som.	42'×22'. Low hall.	See reference 9.
(39) *c.* 1440	The Chantry, Farleigh Hunger-ford, Som.	*c.* 40'×22'. Low hall.	See reference 15.
(40) early C 16th	Bishop Vesey's houses at Sutton Coldfield, War.	*c.* 38'×20'. Low hall. *c.* 27'×20'	See reference 16.
(41) after 1463	The Chantry, Coombe Raleigh, Devon	37'×22'. Low hall.	See reference 14.
(42) mid to late C 15th	The Chantry, Trent, Dor.	*c.* 37'×20'. Low hall.	See reference 13.

TWO-PART PLAN IN LINE *with wing making* L-PLAN

(43) *c.* 1488	Ashbury Manor, Berks.	74'×25' & 15'×19'. Low hall.	See reference 23.
(44) late C 15th	Hams Barton, Devon	58'×24' & 48'×*c.* 20'. Low hall.	See reference 26.

TWO-PART PLAN IN LINE *with wings making* L-PLAN AT EACH END

(45) 1450–60	The 'Priory', Stoke-sub-Hamdon, Som.	62'×24' & 14'×13' & 11'×19'. Open hall.	See reference 21.

TWO(?)-PART PLAN IN LINE *with* PARALLEL WING ATTACHED AT ANGLE

(46) C 15th	Old Rectory, Walton, Som.	62'×*c.* 22' & 29'×21'. Low hall.	Pantin (1957), 132, 134–8, 146 (plans & sections, etc.).

ONE-PART PLAN (*one compartment on each floor*)

(47) C 15th	Worcester (Gloucester) College, Oxford (monastic *camera*)	26–7'×23'. Low hall.	Pantin (1959), 246–7, fig. 88 (plan); R.C.H.M. *Oxford*, 124–125 (plan & illus.).
(48) late C 15th	Old Rectory, Winford, Som.	25'×19' (excluding outshut). Low hall.	See reference 19.
(49) *c.* 1443–65+	Vicars' Close, Wells, Som.	24'×19' (excluding staircase projection). Low hall.	Pantin (1959), 248, figs. 85–6, 88; Pugin (1840), pls. 2 & 3 (plans & section, etc.); Parker (1866), pls. XXIV–XXVI.
(50) *c.* 1478–81	Vicars' Houses, Hounslow Cloister, Windsor Castle, Berks.	*c.* 14'×17'. Low hall.	Pantin (1959), 248, fig. 88 (plan).

RECTANGULAR BLOCKS ROUND A COURT

(51) *c.* 1472–98	The Deanery, Wells, Som.	North range 81'×23' (whole quadrangle 81–84'×79–85')	Godfrey (1950) (plan); Pugin (1839), pls. 45–52; Parker (1866), 17–20, pls. XVIII–XX.

15

Timber Houses

IT MUST be remembered that most mediaeval houses were of wood, and of these only the better built, especially those in remoter areas and usually of the later centuries, survive. For the earlier ones we must rely on documentary evidence, descriptions and illustrations in contemporary manuscripts, and in the information increasingly provided by archaeology, revealing what the framework was like from the excavated plan, presented by the holes of vanished uprights and sills.

Much research is now being undertaken on the subject of the Anglo-Saxon house, and here we can attempt little more than an interim report. It seems to have been normally of wood, like many of their churches. The picture of the Saxon homestead which is gradually emerging is that of a series of quite separate rectangular buildings, halls and *burs* (bowers or sleeping chambers) in a palisaded enclosure.

Illustrations in manuscripts do not help us over Saxon houses, though churches are often depicted. Indeed they may not be trustworthy, for the artist was often conservative and bound by a drawing tradition not always native to him: thus it is possible that the building he depicts may be of a type standardized elsewhere.* Descriptions in writing are probably more reliable, and recent scholarship has shown that the epic *Beowulf*, although its characters are Scandinavian, gives in its atmosphere an impression of 7th- and 8th-century Northumbria.†

What sort of hall, then, is depicted in *Beowulf*? It is a timber building, at or near ground level, containing one main apartment and a vestibule. The great royal hall of Hroðgar, Heorot, is described as having lofty gables, a golden roof, perhaps of gilded shingles, wooden walls strengthened with bands of iron.‡ No mention is made of timber posts forming aisles, but the impression given is that of a highly ornamental barn.

How does this fit in with the evidence of the spade? Until recently there was nothing comparable, at least in this country, but in 1953–6 Mr Brian Hope-Taylor excavated the

---

* Lloyd (1931), 3 *et seq.*
† *Beowulf* was probably written *c.* 730, but the earliest extant manuscript dates from *c.* 1000.
‡ *Beowulf*, lines 82, 166–7, 484–5, 773–5, 998. *See* R. W. Chambers (1932), *Beowulf, an Introduction*, 361–2; and Cramp (1957).

Plate XXXIII. Timber Houses.

A. Model of a house at Trelleborg, Denmark; c. 1000. B. 39–43 The Causeway, Steventon, showing cruck hall with solar wing having cross-braces and cusped barge-boards; mid 14th century. C. 29 Bridge Street, Leominster, showing trefoil-headed panels and cusped and traceried barge-boards; late 14th or early 15th century. The jettied upper floor was underbuilt in the 18th century. D. House in Bell Square, Weobley; 14th-century hall with jettied cross-wings, having foiled struts and traceried barge-boards. E. Red Lion Hotel, Broad Street, Weobley. East cross-wing, 14th century, jettied, with ogee-headed doorway and blocked windows of three trefoiled ogee lights.

A

B

Plate XXXIV.

A. The Wool Hall, Lady Street, Lavenham, *c.* 1500. Here tension braces show outside the close studding. B. House in Lady Street, Lavenham, showing arched shop windows of *c.* 1500.

palace of the Kings of Northumbria at Yeavering, the Gefrim or *villa regia* of Bede. Here the main periods are the reigns of Æthelfrith (593–617), Edwin (617–33), and Oswald (635–42). Mr Hope-Taylor says:

> The focus of the township was the great hall of the palace. We have not found one such building but a great complex of seven structures, representing different phases. The most impressive are four halls each nearly a hundred feet long; two with a porch at each end; the others of a simpler plan but elaborately buttressed. Set about these main palace buildings were eleven smaller halls. Most were the private halls of noble retainers; but one appears to have been a native servant's house, and another a pagan temple later put to Christian purposes.*

The porches at each end of the two larger halls have a similarity to the vestibule at Heorot.

In his summary of conclusions † the excavator distinguishes a Yeavering style with two main characteristics. The double-square plan, length twice the width, was carefully set out, the unit of measurement being, it was discovered, the door posts. The second feature was the jointed wall construction, of uniform thickness, each squared timber mortised into its neighbour, and every second one sunk well down into the foundation trench. This was a method unparalleled in Europe at this period. Although evidence of aisle posts was found within, these vertical wall timbers were set deep to take much of the weight of the roof in an area of intense gales, and there were also external posts inclined towards the wall. In Æthelfrith's period there were separate posts at each end for the support of the roof ridge, but these were absent in the time of Edwin. However, in Oswald's reign central posts to support the roof ridge were used. A model of the chief 7th-century hall shows a hipped gable at one end, a plain one at the other. Opposed doorways were found in the centre of the long sides, and also at the ends of the buildings.

Such aisled halls with inclined external posts have been found in a number of early sites in northern Germany and Holland, such as Einswarden of the 1st and 2nd centuries A.D., and Ezinge in Friesland as early as the 4th century B.C. This suggests an area of search between the Weser and Zuider Zee for the derivation of the basic type of Yeavering. For the aisled hall has an ancestry dating from prehistoric times, and buildings with internal rows of posts, once supporting the roof, have been excavated at Jemgum near Emden in Germany, which belonged to the 7th and 6th centuries B.C.‡ At Tofting in Holstein, Denmark,§ a continental Saxon village, the aisled long house was normal from the 2nd to 5th centuries A.D. One end was the dwelling portion with central hearth, the other the cow house, all in line. Here the outer walls were of wattlework, strengthened externally with turves, but at Vallhager in Gotland, Sweden, stone and earth were used in long houses dating from the 2nd century A.D. to *c.* 500–50. These buildings have rounded corners and entrances in the end wall; the living portion with its finer entrance, clay floor and pottery

---

* From a talk published in the *Listener* (25 October 1956), 650, quoted in Cramp (1957), 71. The full report is to be published shortly.

† 'Yeavering in Perspective', communicated to the Society of Antiquaries, 28 November 1963.

‡ Professor Walter Horn (1958), 5–7, 21 (Jemgum); 7, figs. 12, 13 (Ezinge), summarizes the evidence and gives a bibliography.

§ Radford (1957), 33.

finds is distinct from the byre in the other half of the structure.* This type of long house is being excavated all over England in mediaeval villages,† and later survivals with house and byre combined may still be seen in Friesland.‡ Among other early examples of aisled buildings is the house of c. 700–c. 1000 uncovered at Leens in Holland, in 7th-, 8th-, 9th- and 10th-century settlements discovered at Wilhelmshaven-Hessens, and those of the 11th to 13th centuries at Emden.§

Akin to Yeavering as regards the inclined external posts, but without the aisles (the span being narrower), or the double-square plan and wall construction, is Warendorf in Germany, a continental Saxon village of c. 650–800. Seventy-five wooden houses were completely excavated, including eleven large long houses. These ranged from 14 to 29 metres (approximately 45 feet 6 inches to 94 feet 6 inches) long to 4·50 to 6·7 metres (14 feet 6 inches to 21 feet 9 inches) wide, and were roughly oblong, outlined by a double row of posts, the inner representing a wall, the outer, set at a raking angle, being supports or buttresses to them.‖ Some had opposite entrances near the centre of the long sides, with projecting porches like those of a barn.

In a gravel pit at Maxey in Northamptonshire, in 1960, Mr Addyman excavated some rectangular buildings associated with Anglo-Saxon pottery. One building was 47× probably 20 feet, with the entrance, 10 feet wide, in the middle of the long side. In another c. 50×23 feet the doorway may have been in a corner.¶ But much more Saxon excavation needs to be done in this country. The flimsy rectangular huts with wattle walls, excavated by the late E. Thurlow Leeds at Sutton Courtenay, are now believed to have been sheds for weaving or pottery working, not dwelling houses. Others have been found at St Neots (Huntingdonshire) with 9th- and 10th-century pottery, and at Bourton on the Water in Gloucestershire.

In 1961–2 the palace of the Kings of Wessex was excavated at Cheddar in Somerset, and a great 9th-century hall was uncovered, probably that of King Alfred himself. This 'Long Hall' was a boat-shaped building, rather wider in the middle than at the ends, about 80 feet long and 18 feet wide,** and of post and trench construction. In a continuous trench small posts at the outer vertical edge probably had planking in between, while an inner row of posts sloping inwards may have formed struts to support an upper floor. This would be an arrangement unparalleled elsewhere at this date, but fitting in with documentary evidence of the meeting of the Witan in 978 at Calne where the floor collapsed. The hall of the Witan had to be large to accommodate the West Saxon council, with representatives from many areas. This building was abandoned in the 10th century, probably in the period after 930, which included the reign of Athelstan (925–40), a widely travelled king, who perhaps brought in a new architectural technique from abroad. A chapel, altered later, was built across its site, and a new 'West Hall' constructed further south. This was more rectangular (60×26 feet) with doorways in the ends, and an internal

---

* Stenberger & Klindt-Jansen (1955), *Vallhagar*, 142, 1000 et seq., figs. 42, 44 (Copenhagen); Radford (1957), fig. 17.
† Jope & Threlfall (1958), 112 et seq.   ‡ Lloyd (1931), fig. 5.
§ Horn (1958), fig. 15 (Leens), fig. 14; also Radford (1957), fig. 8 (Wilhelmshaven-Hessens).
‖ Discussed by Radford (1957), 30–3, with illustrations and references from continental journals; see also pp. 68–9.
¶ I am indebted to Mr P. V. Addyman for permission to refer to his as yet unpublished material.
** This compares with the thegn's hall of c. 1010 (75 × 20 feet) excavated in 1963 at Sulgrave. It was of timber, unaisled.

porch at the west end. It was again of wood, but with massive posts set in pits at intervals of 8 feet, presumably linked by horizontal timbers into which planks were slotted. A well-made post outside the palace entrance is interpreted as the position of a flagstaff with the royal device of Wessex. This would be the hall in which the Witan met in 941, 956, and 968, and perhaps was the scene of King Edmund's reconciliation with St Dunstan, after his miraculous escape from death in Cheddar Gorge (941). This building was in turn superseded by the great aisled 'East Hall' of the 12th century.[*]

Thus the evidence suggests that the larger Saxon house was a long rectangular building, either aisled or with buttressed walls like those at Warendorf, which in reconstruction has the effect of a modern marquee (as the circular hut resembles a tent), or both as at Yeavering. A possible variant is the ancient cruck construction with curved principals supporting the ridge pole: Mr James Walton has found early examples suggesting this.[†] A cruck construction may have been used for the 'nave' of the Vallhager house.[‡]

At Warendorf the older buildings were rectangular with straight sides, while the later ones had the long sides bowed, producing a boat shape, which also occurs at Yeavering (a hint) and at Cheddar. This type of plan shows a resemblance to the celebrated Viking stronghold of c. 1000 excavated at Trelleborg in Denmark (Pl. XXXIII A), where such buildings, each to take one ship's crew, were arranged with military precision in four blocks of four, in a circular enclosure. The latter was divided into four equal sections by two streets, crossing at the centre, leading from gateways in the earthen rampart at the cardinal points. In each quarter the four houses were arranged each on one side of a square court. Each house was about 29·5 metres (96 feet) long and contained a large hall approximately 18 metres (58 feet 6 inches) long by 8 metres (26 feet) at its widest; with a smaller room at each end. Many doors were provided, and where one house faced another across the street the lateral entrances were sited diagonally, not opposite, so as to ensure a quick turn-out without crowding when the alarum was given. A row of fifteen similar boat-shaped houses, slightly shorter, 26–33 metres (approximately 85 feet 6 inches) were set radially in the outer ward.[§] Boat-shaped houses have also been excavated at Thetford in Norfolk, by G. M. Knocker, F.S.A.

What was the reason for this boat-shaped plan? At Trelleborg the hearth is central and the bulged-out walls may have been contrived to give extra space, and safety, on each side of it. However, at Warendorf some buildings of this type show the hearth placed towards one end of the central area. It may be that the convex wall was chosen as a stronger timber construction against the high winds in the same way as a tie-beam which is cambered takes more securely the thrust of the crown post placed upon it.[||]

The boat-shaped plan used in these timber structures also occurs in early Norse houses found in Iceland, Orkney and Shetland, where stone was abundant for building material. At Birsay in Orkney it was used as a revetment for turf, and a typical 9th-century farm-house excavated had a drystone revetment on the inside, and flat stones alternating with

[*] Information kindly given by Mr P. A. Rahtz, excavating for the Ministry of Works. See his article with Alan Sorrell's reconstruction of Athelstan's hall in the *Illustrated London News*, 30 March 1963, 462–5.
[†] Walton (1948).
[‡] Stenberger & Klindt-Jansen (1955), *Vallhager*, 1021.
[§] P. Norlund (1956), *Trelleborg* (Copenhagen).
[||] I owe this idea to my husband, E. G. Kaines-Thomas.

turf originally on the exterior. This house, described by Mr Ralegh Radford, was at first 56 feet long with 15 feet as the maximum width. It was a long house with bowed sides and curved ends, one part forming the living quarters with a central fire position on the natural clay, but no built-up hearth, the other the byre with a central drain. Later in the Norse period it was rebuilt with entirely stone faced walls externally, and shortened by 16 feet. There was an entrance at the byre end, and two opposite doorways on the long sides below the centre.*

Similar stone houses of the early Norse colonial period have been excavated at Jarlshof in Shetland. One of the oldest dates from the beginning of the 9th century, thus even earlier than similar houses yet discovered in Iceland. There is the same rectangular bow-shaped plan in a building 70 feet long originally. The kitchen (*eldhús*), with end-wall fireplace and oven, was in the western portion; then beyond the main entrance, with bar-hole, on the north wall, came the living-room (*stofa*) with the dais (*pallr*) for tables and beds remaining on the north side, and evidence of a similar kerbed platform or 'sleeping bench' on the south; between these in the centre of the floor was originally a stone-lined hearth. In the 11th century a byre was added to the east, with curved cattle road (*fé-gata*) leading to it, and the house was reorganized and extended westwards.† This building is part of a complex Viking settlement of the greatest interest.

Such boat-shaped houses seem to be reflected in the 'hogback' tombstones of the Viking period, particularly the 10th century in northern England, of which Mr James Walton has made a special study.‡ An early 9th-century example at Dewsbury has shingled ornament on the roof, and shingles are also carved on the late 10th- or early 11th-century tomb slab at Brompton, also in Yorkshire, where each end is finished with the forequarters of a bear, his muzzle receiving the ridge of the roof.§ The latter is arched, as was probably the case in the Trelleborg houses.

To return to wooden buildings, how were the walls constructed in the Saxon and Viking houses? Wattle and daub seems to have been common, a hurdle or wattle-work covered on both sides with daub, a mixture of clay, chopped straw or cow-hair, and cow-dung. It was used in the 9th-century boat-shaped houses excavated at Thetford, and is mentioned by King Alfred in his preface to *St Augustine's Soliloquies*.‖ But a more advanced plank construction was being employed in the more important buildings, the halls, at Yeavering as early as the 7th century and Cheddar in the 10th century as we have noted. This is the type used for the main walls in the Trelleborg houses. They are represented by a long unbroken runnel containing oblong post holes. The latter contained the thicker uprights, slightly curved externally, which had a groove or slot on each edge to take the tongue or tapered edge of a thinner alternate plank which need not be set so deeply. Such a stave wall is known from the oldest part (*c.* 1050) of the Norwegian stave church of Urnes, but in such true stave buildings the planks were normally set into the groove on the upper side of a horizontal sill laid on the ground. At Trelleborg no special strengthening at the corners of the building was found, unlike the construction in the remarkable Saxon survival in the nave of Greensted by Ongar church in Essex. Here the uprights are split oak logs,

* M.O.W. Guide (3), 21–2.   † M.O.W. Guide (21), 10, 26–7; also Hamilton (1956), 102–9, 129–30.
‡ Walton (1954).   § Clapham (1930), 140, pl. 58 A.   ‖ Cramp (1957), 68.

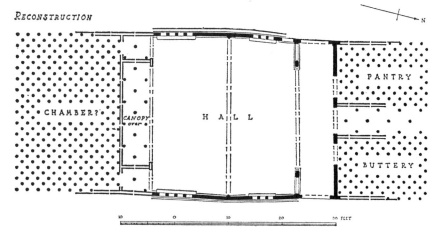

RECONSTRUCTION

CHAMBER?

CANOPY over

H A L L

PANTRY

BUTTERY

N

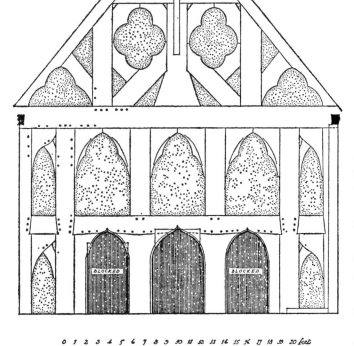

Fig. 64 *a. Above*, Baguley Hall, plan.
Fig. 64 *b. Left*, Baguley Hall, service end
of early 14th-century hall.

again with the curved portion outside, and the corners are formed by a three-quarter log cut to give an internal right angle. Unlike Trelleborg, the timbers were let into a wooden sill, which has had to be renewed; at the restoration the uprights were said to be 'grooved with tongues of oak let in between them'.* This may be the *lignea capella* near Ongar in which the body of St Edmund, King and Martyr, rested on its way back from London to Bury St Edmunds, after the defeat of the Danish invasion of East Anglia in 1013. Such 'log hut' buildings must have been common.

Recently at Baguley Hall in Cheshire there has been found evidence of a 14th-century survival, not only of this primitive plank construction but also of the boat-shaped plan (Figs. 64 *a* and *b*), in an area associated with the Viking invasions of the 10th century. The

* P. W. Ray (1869). *History of Greensted Church*; Lloyd (1931), 6–7, figs. 7 & 8.

massive timbers used are really planks cut to a uniform thickness of 7 inches, with unnecessarily deep grooves on the edges, a survival from the time when, as at Trelleborg, the walls were entirely constructed of such upright planks. The great diagonal cross-braces are another early feature, found in the stave churches of Norway, and the bowed outline of the hall is undoubtedly akin to Trelleborg. The destroyed hall of Radcliffe Tower, Smithells Hall in Lancashire and Tabley Old Hall in Cheshire are other possible buildings of boat-shaped plan and plank construction, as well as Amberley Court in Herefordshire, which lies outside the area of Viking settlement.*

No Norman houses of timber have been recognized so far, above ground, except for the wooden arcade of the aisled hall at Hereford, and the posts at Farnham and Leicester Castles. Yet documentary evidence suggests that late 11th- and 12th-century wooden buildings could be elaborate. It is useful to quote the description left us by Lambert of Ardres in Flanders, of the tower house built † on top of the mound there by the carpenter Louis de Bourbourg:

> Arnold, lord of Ardres, built on the motte of Ardres a wooden house, excelling all the houses of Flanders of that period both in material and in carpenter's work. The first storey was on the surface of the ground, where were cellars and granaries, and great boxes, tuns, casks and other domestic utensils. In the storey above were the dwelling- and common living-rooms of the residents, in which were the larders, the rooms of the bakers and butlers, and the great chamber in which the lord and his wife slept. Adjoining this was a private room, the dormitory of the waiting maids and children. In the inner part of the great chamber was a certain private room, where at early dawn or in the evening or during sickness or at time of blood-letting or for warming the maids and weaned children, they used to have a fire. In the upper storey of the house were garret rooms, in which on the one side the sons (when they wished it), on the other side the daughters (because they were obliged), of the lord of the house used to sleep. In this storey also the watchman, and the servants appointed to keep the house, took their sleep at some time or other. High up on the east side of the house, in a convenient place, was the chapel, which was made like the tabernacle of Solomon in its ceiling and painting. There were stairs and passages from storey to storey, from the house into the kitchen, from room to room, and again from the house into the loggia, where they used to sit in conversation for recreation; and again from the loggia into the oratory.‡

This great three-storeyed wooden structure was built on the limited area on top of the castle mound, which rose in the middle of a marsh converted by Arnold into a lake. The building seems to have resembled a 'hall keep', but in timber, with the usual storage basement, hall and service above with great chamber probably parallel, and further sleeping rooms in the attics.§ The kitchen seems to have been a separate annexe, in the usual early precaution against fire. An interesting feature is the 'loggia', possibly under the projecting chapel.

Such a tall structure in wood brings to mind the lofty stave churches of Norway. Remains of some thirty survive, a few being preserved in Norwegian museums. These are

* Smith & Stell (1960), 130–51.
† In 1099, according to A. H. Thompson (1912), 54, 55.
‡ R. A. Brown (1954), 31–2, who gives the date 1117.
§ Braun (1936), 78–9.

mostly of 12th-century date, the chief examples being at Hoprekstad (*c.* 1135–50), Borgund (*c.* 1150), Urnes (with re-used portions of an earlier building), Torpe, Lydvaloft, Fortun, Gol and the 14th-century Sodrarada in Sweden. Some are also termed 'mast churches' from their four great structural masts on which the whole framework is based, a lofty 'four poster',* set on horizontal sills or sleepers forming a central square in plan. All have scissor trusses, which, with the cross bracing in the framework, show apparent kinship to early mediaeval timber construction in England. Many had low walls of screen-work to protect the base of the main walls from the weather, thus forming porticoes or loggias, like the outer galleries at Trelleborg and another point of resemblance to the castle tower at Ardres.

All these would be more elaborate structures than the watch tower of which Mr Brian Hope-Taylor (1950) has found evidence in the motte at Abinger in Surrey. But further excavation on 11th- and 12th-century castle mounds may confirm the documentary evidence.

The 1964 excavations at Winchester † are of paramount importance in filling in the large gap in our knowledge of early mediaeval wooden town houses. The great project of exploration in Lower Brook Street is revealing a sequence of development which may have analogies elsewhere. The earliest buildings date back to the 11th century, and are approximately square in plan, of which the details are at present lacking. These buildings were succeeded, probably in the first half of the 13th century, by square to rectangular houses represented by their floors and post holes, one uncovered being a small hall. Built on top of these 'post-hole houses' were 'wall-trench buildings', perhaps of the later 13th century. Here the wall trench makes a square to rectangular plan, and in it were set great posts, of which the lower parts survive. These were followed in the late 13th or 14th century by houses with stone ground walls, which were sometimes enlarged by the addition of stone halls built back over the gardens. One excavated in 1964 shows an entrance doorway well cut with a roll-moulded stop chamfer of the second half of the 13th century. Near by a house of *c.* 1125 was uncovered in 1962, this having a fireplace and loop windows on the ground floor and the entrance in the end wall; a projection adjoining this suggests the support for a staircase against the internal wall, and the building may have been a first-floor hall. Because of the mass of documentary evidence relating to these structures it will be possible to date stages of their construction with remarkable accuracy.

The sequence of wooden houses succeeded by timber structures on stone ground walls was also found by Mr Martin Biddle in his earlier excavations at Seacourt in north Berkshire, and this change from timber to stone ground walls in the later 13th and perhaps earlier 14th centuries has also been noted as far apart as Dorset and Lincolnshire.

This is a convenient place to consider the mediaeval peasant's house, of which more and more information is coming to light through the Deserted Village Research Group. In stone country these would be more substantial, and stone foundations, in some cases once with timber work above, show up better from the air than post houses, but the evidence is suggesting that whether of stone or wood, chalk, mud or even turf, the peasants' houses

---

* Term used by Braun (1951), 76.
† Information kindly given me by Mr Martin Biddle, F.S.A., director of the Winchester excavations.

were fairly uniform in plan, though the material might improve and the number of rooms increase. Indeed, excavations show that a village house might be rebuilt about every generation, probably when the son took over from his father. At Wharram Percy in Yorkshire one house excavated (No. 10) included nine periods in 325 years, from the late 12th-century to a little after 1500. Yet the rectangular plans remain, each distinct, for the buildings are not exactly superimposed.*

What clearly emerges is that the long house, with living rooms at one end, byre at the other, is the typical villein's house of the Middle Ages. Examples are coming in fast, as more and more discoveries are made in these abandoned or shrunken settlements. Excavations at Seacourt, as already noted, have revealed a 12th-century timber house, and stone replacements later. At Riseholme in Lincolnshire one excavated 13th-century stone house lies sideways to the village street, being set in one angle of its attached toft (backyard); the larger (living) room has a mortar floor and central hearth, the smaller, part floored with stone slabs, was probably for the cattle. On Bodmin Moor in Cornwall, in a village site south-east of Garrow Tor, one of several buildings has been excavated; dating from c. 1200 it is a granite long house 48 × 20 feet with the usual two divisions, and a manger in the byre end. The 13th-century house with low stone walls uncovered at Beere at North Tawton in Devon had three parts, there being a further living-room at the upper end.†

It may be wondered if there is any connection with the 15th-century manor house, such as Ashleworth Court, long and rectangular, with hall, service, and kitchen in line, and whether this derives from the earlier long house in which the cattle had been ousted and the byre become the service quarters. But we are only at the beginning of this research.

The evidence so far suggests that the farmhouse with separate buildings for the animals is a comparatively recent development in a village, except in so far as the manor house was one. When Wharram Percy was deserted c. 1500, it had only long houses or lesser structures, but by 1550 the long houses appear to have vanished, and from that great rebuilding period in English history seems to date the change-over from long house to farm.

Smaller houses are also being found in the villages, containing one room with a hearth, and possibly once having a sleeping loft over part of it. These would house the lower degree of villager, the cottar, who like the villein held land from his lord. Examples have been found at Seacourt and elsewhere.

Timber-framed Houses

The date of a timber house may often be detected by its general appearance, especially as regards the roof line. But such observation must be allied to a knowledge of domestic development; this will enable the student to unmask and separate the original building from its later alterations and accretions.‡

The simplest plan is revealed at Fyfield Hall in Essex, one of the earliest known examples

---

* Hurst (1957).
† Biddle (1961–2) (Seacourt); F. H. Thompson (1960) (Riseholme); *Medieval Archaeology* (1960), IV, 159–60 (Bodmin Moor); Jope & Threlfall (1958) (Beere).
‡ The author acknowledges information from the late Sir Alfred Clapham in R.C.H.M. *Essex*, IV, XXXV (diagrams); Forrester (1959), 1–16 (diagrams); Braun (1940), 79–81, figs. 10–13.

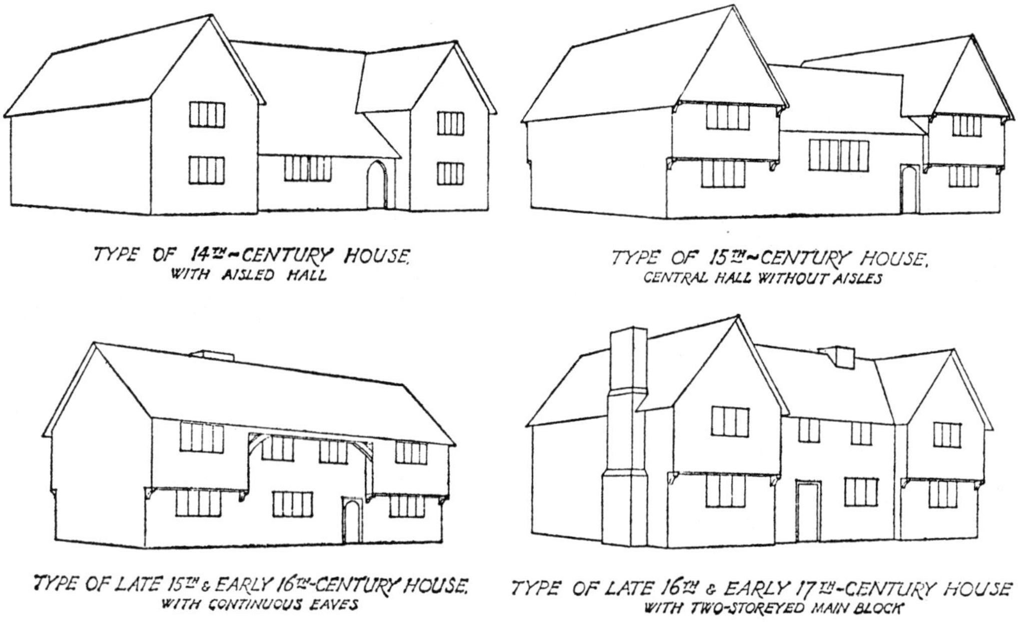

TYPE OF 14TH-CENTURY HOUSE,
WITH AISLED HALL

TYPE OF 15TH-CENTURY HOUSE,
CENTRAL HALL WITHOUT AISLES

TYPE OF LATE 15TH & EARLY 16TH-CENTURY HOUSE,
WITH CONTINUOUS EAVES

TYPE OF LATE 16TH & EARLY 17TH-CENTURY HOUSE
WITH TWO-STOREYED MAIN BLOCK

Fig. 65. Types of timber houses.

surviving above ground and dating from the end of the 13th century. It was merely a hall of two bays, aisled, without wings.*

One or two cross-wings were usual in 14th-century houses. At 39–43 The Causeway, Steventon (Berkshire) (Pl. XXXIII B), there is one at the end of the hall, which is here of primitive cruck construction; for this important survival of cruck hall and contemporary wing a date not later than the mid 14th century is suggested.† In larger houses in most parts of the country, however, the hall is aisled, a lofty apartment the equivalent of two storeys, and a distinctive feature is provided by the great sweep of its roof over the aisles to within 6 or 8 feet of the ground. Base-crucks with massive square-section wind-braces occur in the same context. Such a 'catslide' roof may be seen over the surviving aisle of the hall (c. 1320) at Little Chesterford. The cross-wings are roofed at right angles, and have high-pitched gables, often unjettied in the country. As in stone houses the cross-wing near the hall entrance contained butteries with a chamber over, balancing the parlour with solar above at the other end. In an L- or T-plan, with one wing, often earlier in date, the solar was placed over the service end.

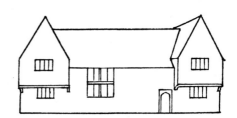

Fig. 66. Central hall type of timber house.

By the 15th century the hall had lost its aisles, and had thus higher walls and roof, the eaves nearer those of the wings (*see* Fig. 66). The wings might not project, except on the

* Smith (1955), 77–9, figs. 1, 2 & 5.
† S. E. Rigold (1958), 8–10 (plan, etc.).

upper storey, which was now usually jettied at one or both ends like some 14th-century houses in towns, such as Weobley in Herefordshire (Pl. XXXIII D and E). The house with one wing is still common.*

As we have seen, many late 15th- and 16th-century houses are similar, except that the hall block was increasingly divided horizontally, providing a low hall with an important room above. This was due to the advent of the brick fireplace, added on the back wall, which supplanted the old central hearth, and made a lofty hall for the escape of smoke no longer necessary. Many earlier halls were brought up to date, divided horizontally along the middle plate of the timbered walls, and had lateral fireplaces added. This alteration can be detected by the difference in floor level between the central and end portions of the building.

There are also many examples, particularly in Kent and its borders and the south-western 'forest' part of Essex, of the house with continuous eaves, the deeper projection of the roof over the hall block being supported by curved braces from the jettied end chambers. The roof is thus in one piece and hipped at both ends. Even where occasionally gables occur, they are incorporated in the overall hipped roof. The type, commonly known as the Wealden House, probably originated in Kent, where the hipped roof is attested from the 13th century, and where a date of c. 1370 has been claimed for the example at Wardes, Otham, but most of the numerous surviving examples are of the later 15th or early 16th centuries.† Recently, however, 'Wealden houses' have been found in West Midland towns such as Warwick, Stratford-on-Avon and Henley-in-Arden. At Coventry in Spon Street a late 14th-century range of six small houses, a variant of this type, implies speculative building. Each unit comprises a single bay hall with solar jettied out over the service, the range having a continuous roof with eaves in line with the solar wall and supported on a plate in front of that of the hall. Other houses at Coventry were built in pairs, as at Weobley.‡ Such regional research as this, by Mr S. R. Jones, may revolutionize our ideas on timber house development.

Other houses of the later 15th and early 16th centuries, often with close studding, have one hall with its chamber over included in a continuous jetty with the wings. Paycocke's at Coggeshall is a classic example. An unusual building, the 16th-century manor house at Bramley (Hampshire) has the hall block jettied, but not the cross-wings.

But the less compact H-plan house, with two-storeyed hall and jettied cross-wings, continued into the late 16th and early 17th centuries. It may be distinguished from 15th-century examples by the lower roof pitch and general maintenance, throughout, of a uniform eaves level, except where thatch demands a high pitch, or stone flags a low one, at all periods. As we shall see, the panes are generally square, nearer the 14th-century size, as distinct from the close studding, the vertical timbers separated by panels of equal width, of the late 15th and early 16th centuries. For new timber was getting scarcer and more expensive, and in the 17th century jetties, forbidden in the towns through fire danger,

---

* In Essex at least small houses did not have two cross-wings at first, the second usually being added later. The remarkably accurate drawings in Walker's maps show that the open hall and single two-storeyed cross-wing was the common type as late as c. 1600. (Information from Mr A. C. Edwards, M.A., of the Essex Record Office.)

† Oswald (1933).

‡ Medieval Archaeology (1960), IV, 156; (1962-3), VI-VII, 215-16.

were being less used in the country. Inbuilt central stacks, with fireplaces back to back, serving hall and parlour, displaced the lateral fireplace in the main rooms. This made jettying of the upper chamber more difficult, for the joists which supported the upper floor had to be cut and rested on the stack. Without jetties the tall side walls had to be most carefully framed for strength, and tied together with wooden 'girders' across the building.

It will be helpful to carry our study of mediaeval timber houses to their logical conclusion in the late 17th and 18th centuries when they were largely displaced by brickwork. This will enable post-Reformation houses and alterations to be distinguished from earlier work. However, often a Georgian front made fashionable an earlier building, of which the disguised timber-framing can be seen inside and at the back.

By the later 16th and especially the 17th century, the farmhouse had become a rectangular block normally of two or three bays with a lean-to 'outshut' at the back. The central stack is the dominant feature, with back-to-back fireplace serving hall and parlour, and smaller ones to the rooms above. The entrance was now near the upper end of the hall or farmhouse kitchen, opening into a lobby, filling the space on one side of the central stack, giving independent access left and right to hall and parlour. This 'baffle entrance', facing the stack,* is a new, unmediaeval position for the entrance doorway, but in some houses the entrance was in the old position, especially if there were a buttery, dairy, or second parlour at the non-fireplace end of the hall. On the further side of the stack a wooden newel staircase was often fitted, but where the stack was less centrally placed it was sometimes off the lobby. The outshut or lean-to service aisle is a regular feature of small 16th- or 17th-century houses. It was sometimes off the end of the hall, but usually at the back, often under a long 'catslide' roof, which may cause confusion with the much earlier aisled buildings.

Often the upper end contained an attic room with a separate gable, the last vestige of the mediaeval cross-wing. Elizabethan and Jacobean houses, with their many chimneys, are also notable for their numerous gables, serving attic bedrooms, and providing a decorative external feature. Indeed the three-storey house, though occurring earlier, is particularly common in the late 16th and early 17th centuries, when more private bedchambers were usual.

It will be noticed that the house is generally one room in thickness, though there may be a parallel range separately roofed. In the 18th century the double-span roof was introduced, covering a building two or three rooms in width, and hipped at both ends.†

Jetties

The jetty, or overhang, is a great feature of buildings of the 15th and 16th centuries. However, it is known to have occurred in the 13th century, especially in towns, and there is even evidence of an early timber building of three storeys, two of them projecting. This was the Benedictine guest house at Coventry which existed until 1820 outside the Close

---

* Spokes & Jope (1959), 86–8. † (Braun 1940), 88, fig. 14.

at the corner of Palmer Lane. The upper floors were jettied on curved braces, and each had pointed trefoil-headed windows in groups of four, of late 13th- or early 14th-century date. Portions of these windows were re-used in the public house which was erected on the site, and stood until 1930 when Trinity Street was constructed. Portions of these windows are preserved at St Mary's Hall.* Part of a town house, jettied on two sides, with archaic, probably late 13th-century, framing, is visible at Friern Bridge, Salisbury.†

Fig. 67. House in Newgate, York, c. 1340, with cross-bracing.

Overhanging storeys were employed in 14th-century towns. Some survive at York, a two-storeyed block c. 1320, Lady Row, Goodramgate, the upper floor jettied to the street, and another row of houses in Newgate c. 1340, much altered, but with similar details (Fig. 67). There is also a three-storeyed building, possibly of the late 14th century, 43 Low Petergate, which is jettied to the street. A York contract of 1335 concerns the building of a row of six timber houses having jetties (jacturas) on both sides ‡ in St Martin's Lane; these were mostly burnt down and rebuilt in the 16th or 17th centuries, but some 14th-century jettying survived until demolition recently.§

In London (Paternoster Row) a carpenter in 1342 agreed to build (on stone-vaulted cellars) a house of two jutting storeys with two gables to the street, the ground floor partly used as a tavern and provided with seats; as also on the first floor; the hall was on the second floor under one gable, and a garret room under the other; both hall and bedroom were to have bay windows and others.‖ In Southwark in 1373 two rows of shops were to be constructed next to the gatehouse of the Prior of Lewes, each with a jutting upper storey (*chescum Schoppe oue une estage oue getteiz*).‖

Jettied storeys are also mentioned in two contracts for the building of inns for the Warden of Winchester College, as an investment: the Angel at Alresford (1418) ‖ and another inn at Andover (1444–5),‖ both in Hampshire. At Alresford the jetty projects 2 feet 6 inches; 18 and 22 inches are also found in 15th-century documents.‖ In the west the overhang is

* Drawings and photographs in possession of the Coventry Corporation. W. G. Fretton (1880), *Antiquarian Houses in Coventry during a century and a half*, 317.
    † Information from Mr S. E. Rigold, M.A.
    ‡ Salzman (1952), 430.
    § For this information I am indebted to Mr T. W. French, F.S.A., of the Royal Commission on Historical Monuments.
    ‖ Salzman (1952), 432–4 (Paternoster Row); 447 (Southwark); 494 (Alresford); 517–18 ('with a joty') (Andover); 551 ('jutty the seid chambers') (1491); 583 ('with a joteye a boue of XXII inche') (1436).

bolder than in the south-east, with heavier timbering.* At Canterbury in 1438 the Guildhall is to have 'dubble stage geteyyd', two projecting storeys,† like the existing Moot Hall at Thaxted, the Bird Cage Inn at Thame (Pl. XXXV A), or the likewise tall 15th-century house from Frog Street, Exeter, moved in 1962 to West Street.‡ This preserves original

Fig. 68. Late 15th-century shop in Butchers' Row, Shrewsbury.

shop fronts, as does Butchers' Row at Shrewsbury (Fig. 68) and other contemporary buildings at Lavenham (Pl. XXXIV B) and Saffron Walden.

The jetty was probably first used in towns where building space was more limited than in the country, and the overhang provided a larger room in the upper storey. Indeed in the late 16th century the tendency to increase the size of the building upwards resulted in

---

* Crossley (1951), 117.   † Salzman (1952), 511.
‡ Isometric representation in R.C.H.M. (1963), *Monuments Threatened or Destroyed*, 30–1.

rows of top-heavy looking structures, timber 'skyscrapers',[*] of which examples remain in towns such as Chester and Shrewsbury (Fig. 68), and more in France and Germany. Jetties darkened the narrow mediaeval streets, of which the flanking buildings might almost meet overhead, allowing persons in the upper storeys to shake hands! They certainly helped to protect the lower storeys from the weather. This practical use is one of several explanations given for the use of jettying, besides the obvious one of additional accommodation. Another, equally probable, is the fact that long timbers, the full height of a house, were difficult to obtain. Shorter posts, superimposed, would make a weak junction at floor level with the horizontal plates. But with projecting storeys these shorter posts could be used satisfactorily, the plate mortised to one set alone, and the fact that one storey overhung the lower meant that the floor joists also would not be weakened by mortices and fixing all at the same point, those of the upper storey being at the end of the horizontal timber, those for the lower some 18 inches to 2 feet in.

The above seems more likely than another explanation put forward for the jetty, one associated with the mediaeval way of constructing an upper floor. Before the 17th century (when indeed the jetty went out of use) carpenters laid the joists flat like planks to cover as much floor space as possible, whereas later it was realized that to place them on edge is a stronger construction. It is believed by some that in the earlier type the floors tended to be 'whippy' (springy) and the whole building might 'dance' when there was movement or heavy weight placed on the floor, unless there were a counterweight at the ends of the joists. This was provided by the sill and vertical timbers of the next floor, placed on these extremities, the joists being strengthened by their projection beyond the supporting wall of the storey below.[†] However, mediaeval oak floor joists are usually thick and strong and not likely to 'whip', and jetties did not always make for stability; as a 17th-century writer, Horman, remarked: 'Buyldynge chargydde with iotyes is parellous when it is very olde.' [‡]

The overhang might be continuous right round the building, as in the 15th-century Guildhall at Thaxted. Where they joined at the corners the projections were supported on a diagonal 'dragon' (perhaps originally 'dragging') beam,[§] into which the ends of each series of joists, graduated in length, were housed. It was held on a braced corner post, originally a tree reversed. This was given a cap and base in the 14th century, as at Weobley, small attached shafts c. 1500, e.g. Lavenham (Pl. XXXIV A), or might be elaborately carved, especially in East Anglia: there are several in Ipswich.

Mr S. E. Rigold [||] is doing valuable research into the development of timber buildings, particularly on the kind of framing, which throws considerable light on their date. He finds six types, these varying in time and popularity in different parts of the country. These are: (1) the archaic framing of the 13th century; (2) the arch-braced open framing from the 14th century onwards; (3) the tension-braced open framing of the first three quarters of the 15th century; followed in the last quarter by (4) close studding which lasted until the third quarter of the 16th century. Then came (5) the eclectic framing of

---

[*] Braun (1940), 82.   [†] Braun (1940), 45–6.
[‡] Salzman (1952), 205.   [§] Forrester (1959), 29.
        [||] This section is based on Rigold (1958).

the late Elizabethan and Jacobean periods, and (6) the plainer framing of the later 17th century.

(1) The *archaic framing*, prevalent in the 13th century, now very rare, is known from contemporary illustrations. The timbers were generally straight, and cross-bracing or 'scissor-bracing' is a feature, corresponding to the 'scissor' truss in the roof. Cross-bracing is characteristic of the Norwegian mast churches of the 12th century, and survives, if only as a decorative feature, in France until the 15th century. The multiple, straight scissor-braces in the house at Friern Bridge, Salisbury, give it a strangely French appearance.

The cross-bracing element occurs in the most valuable survival, 39–43 The Causeway, Steventon, in the end wall of the cross-wing to the contemporary cruck hall. This house, probably dating from the mid 14th century, retains its original ogee-cusped barge (? parge)-boards. It is a very rare example of the house of a small freeman or yeoman of the period. Another 14th-century house with cross-wing to a cruck hall is found at Weobley, in Meadow Street.*

A further characteristic of 'archaic framing' is a tendency to halving rather than mortising made necessary by the relative thickness of the braces. A tell-tale feature is provided by the horizontal angle braces, joining the upper plates on two adjoining walls. This occurs at Stokesay, Chennels Brook near Horsham, the Old Deanery and Friern Bridge, Salisbury, all *c.* 1270, as at Steventon later.

The jetty did occur, and even doubled, as in the late 13th-century house mentioned at Coventry. Its immature form was shown by the excessive number of brackets used, occasionally one under each upright of the projection, more often under every other one.

(2) In the 14th century *arch-braced framing* is characteristic, the upper beam (plate) braced down by a curved timber to a point some way up the vertical post (as always in open trusses with tie-beams). These arch-braces are often short and sometimes cusped, especially in the west. As in the first type the panels (panes) of the framework, when unbraced, are normally quadrilateral. Both arch-braces and quadrilateral panes persist much later in Wessex.

Weobley in Herefordshire is particularly rich in timber houses, with some ten dating from the 14th century (Pl. XXXIII D and E). They show this type of framing, the curved braces forming a pointed arch on either side of the upper window position of the cross-wing, combined with large square panels. There is one arch in the transverse wing of the Red Lion, but two in that of the house opposite in Broad Street. Another late 14th-century house, further down the street on the east side, has similar arches in the end of one cross-wing (north) and two cusped arches in the other; while a house in Chamber Walk combines curved and cusped panels in the same gable end. Such trefoiled arches are found in Leominster, 29 Bridge Street, in a late 14th- or early 15th-century cross-wing, beneath a fine barge-board with cusped and traceried ornament (Pl. XXXIII c). Sometimes the cusped brace passes diagonally across the pane, and forms a pattern with the adjoining one. This is a feature of the front (underbuilt) of Grafton House, 9 Burgess Street, Leominster; at the back another cusped brace can be seen, also an ogee-headed panel which may have been a window; this house probably dates from the late 14th century. Similar one-cusped

* R.C.H.M. *Herefordshire*, III, 197 (No. 14).

braces or foiled struts are found in the cross-wings of a 14th-century house in Bell Square, Weobley; there are also the remains of trefoiled panes or windows in the return of the east wing next the main block.*

In these Herefordshire houses the upper storey of the cross-wing normally projected (sometimes underbuilt later), supported on curved brackets springing from shafts attached to the corner posts. This is shown at the Red Lion, Weobley, which also retains two original windows, each of three trefoiled ogee lights with tracery, now blocked and without their mullions (Pl. XXXIII E).

(3) In *tension-braced framing* long curved braces are characteristic. The vertical posts are now braced from a point near their top down to the lower plate. Whereas in arch-framing the braces rise to the upper plate, in tension-bracing they descend to the lower, and are longer but still curved. This type usually marks the first three quarters of the 15th century, but comes in earlier in some places, such as Winchester and Salisbury. As Mr Rigold remarks: 'Arch-braced *v.* tension-braced may be a long-term contest. In the East and Midlands tension bracing wins an early victory, in the Marches [of Wales] only a partial one, while in Wessex, where tension-bracing occurs early, arch-bracing stages such a widespread revival that the normal order appears to be reversed.' An interesting example remains at 23–4 St John's Street, Winchester, where the mouldings of a string-course and the window of four trefoiled lights to the jettied upper storey suggest a date in the 14th century. Very similar lights occur in a house by the Butter Cross in the same city, which still retains scissor-braces.

(4) *Close studding*, 'Perpendicular' in feeling, is surprisingly late in date, considering how prodigal it is of timber. It is typical of the last quarter of the 15th century until the third quarter of the 16th century, a predominantly 'Tudor' form. Its absence at Ockwells, a major building dated 1465, shows that it was not yet in fashion, at least in Berkshire. However, this is on the fringe of Wessex, so its absence may not be so significant. The hall, partly stone, at Wye College, *c.* 1440, is one of the earliest examples, but cases without Tudor or similar detail are very rare. The term 'half-timber' (though meaning halved-timber) could indeed be used here, for the narrow panes are the width of the vertical studs, and make for a very firm structure. In the south-east the braces, where present, are halved into the studs internally, so do not disturb the parallel patterning of the walls. The bressumer (beam supporting the superstructure) is often moulded with heavy rolls and hollows, and slender wall-shafts are used at the angles.

This type probably arose in the south-east or in East Anglia, where it is especially popular (Pl. XXXV B). It was more slowly adopted in the north-east, late in the west, and is infrequent in Wessex.

The last forms do not concern our period, but may be mentioned. (5) The *eclectic framing* of the later Elizabethan and Jacobean periods is an untidy mixture of types with fussy, over-elaborate ornament, diagonal studding, and panes circled and cusped for decorative, not structural, requirements. It is, however, picturesque and now often preferred

---

* R.C.H.M. *Herefordshire*, III, 199, pl. 180 (No. 22) (Red Lion); 199, pl. 180 (No. 23) and 200 (No. 32) (Broad St); 202, pl. 181 (No. 54) (Chamber Walk), Weobley; 117, pl. 141 (No. 13) (29 Bridge St); 121, pl. 143 (No. 76) (Grafton House), Leominster; 199, pl. 180 (No. 21) (Bell Square), Weobley.

C

D

A

B

Plate XXXV. 15th-century Houses.

A. The Bird Cage Inn, Thame. B. Alston Court, Nayland, *c.* 1472. C and D. Ashbury Manor, Berkshire, *c.* 1488.

Plate XXXVI. The Domestic Chapel: East Windows.

A. Shalford Farm (Commandery), Brimpton; 14th century. B. Bishop's Palace, Chichester, 14th-century window replacing lancets of *c.* 1200. C. Prebendal House, Thame, *c.* 1200. D. Membury Court, *c,* 1290–1300.

to the better mediaeval buildings. The (6) class, of the later 17th century, showed a return to purer forms, with plainer ornaments, the large quadrilateral panes being predominant, though close-studding stages a come-back in places.

For the filling of the panes *wattle and daub* was in general use. The wattle or hurdlework was formed by vertical stakes, each fitted into a hole or slot in one horizontal and sprung into a groove or another hole in the other member of the framework. With these were interwoven pliable material, such as hazel rods, osiers, reeds * or thin strips of oak. In the interstices of this wickerwork and on both faces of it, in several layers, the daub was now applied, being a mixture of clay strengthened with the binding fibrous element of chopped straw, hay, cow-hair and perhaps cow-dung.† The final outer surface was usually treated with plaster (lime, sand and cow-hair) and a coat of white or colour wash. A hair-plaster finish, resistant to the elements, protected the daub from shrinking in dry and swelling in wet weather.

Pargeting was allied to daubing, with mortar or a coarse plaster used instead of clay, and is referred to in 14th-century accounts.‡ But the highly ornate pargeting and modelling figure work of East Anglia, due to improved quality in plaster, tougher and thickened, dates from the late 17th century.

Many old houses have been plastered all over subsequently, to preserve them from the weather, but some more recent and inferior timber buildings, especially of the 18th century, were intended to be covered from the start. In Essex the earlier work has the plastered panel recessed about half an inch, next brought flush with the studding, and finally a plaster covering over the timbers as well.§

With close studding uprights only might be used in the panels, sometimes tied to short cross-strips, or, in East Anglia, with short horizontal slats pegged into one side and grooved into the next.‖ Later, when the panels grew wide again, stout cross-pieces were grooved into the side of the studs, and the wattles, set close, were woven or tied to these. This became a common method.¶

There is also evidence, even in the 14th century, for** the use of laths rather than wattles, and this became usual later. They have been found in 23–24 St John's Street, Winchester, and in the partitions of the late 14th- or early 15th-century Kirkham House at Paignton. Early lathing was possibly a Wessex practice. Mr Rigold thinks that ordinary wattle is found in most places, but it is the alternatives that vary. Much research, however, needs to be done in local methods of building.

Brick nogging is late: so far there are no proven cases before the 17th century, but it might occur *c.* 1550. Bricks, set diagonally for strength as well as effect, replaced decayed wattle-work in an earlier framing (Pl. XXXV B); the original presence of wattle and daub can be detected by the V-groove or holes left in the horizontal timbering. But some late houses

---

* Salzman (1952), 188. To build a barn at Uffington in 1454, five score sheaves of reeds called 'thackrade' were provided for the 'watlyng' under the plaster. R. C. Dudding, *Lincolnshire Notes & Queries*, XIX, 15.
† Forrester (1959), 35.
‡ Salzman (1952), 192.
§ Forrester (1959), 36–7.
‖ Information from Mr S. E. Rigold, who has kindly read this chapter.
¶ Forrester (1959), 35.
** Salzman (1952), 188; at Clare in 1347; 'lathing and daubing' at Sutton in 1402.

may have had brick panels from the first, through conservatism in practice,* and perhaps bricks were still expensive. However, it must soon have been realized that bricks do not need any timber, but on their own are a sound and fireproof method of construction.

Another late method is the use of slate or stone flag infills grooved into the studs, as at Burnley (Elizabethan), a northern and possibly western variety.†

Stud and panel external walls are important. Although surviving examples are late (as in the 16th century at Penshurst), Mr Rigold suggests that the method may have a long history possibly stemming from the stave walls of early times. They appeared in the second phase of the Cherhill barn, recently collapsed. Stud and panel screens are common in Wessex, and he suspects that such walls were once commoner there.

Boarding in an external rebate cut into the frame may have been in general use. Such *rebated boards* occur in the spandrels of the 13th-century north tower-hoards with angle braces at Stokesay, now known to be original.‡

Weather-boarding may be older than is usually supposed; it was used in roofs as early as the 13th century, and therefore possibly in barns and belfries. Kentish barns may have been weather-boarded from the start. A kitchen excavated at Weoley Castle, Birmingham, shows that horizontal weather-boarding was used in the early, vertical in the mid, 13th century.§

* At Donnington, Berkshire, one late 17th-century cottage is timber-framed with brick panels, the bricks laid in horizontal courses, and the adjoining cottage, later and entirely of brick, is painted with black 'framing' to match. The few timber houses that remain in the village (with square panes) must date from after the Civil War, when the village was fired to remove cover for the forces besieging Donnington Castle.
† Rigold (1958).
‡ Cordingley (1963).
§ Oswald (1962–3), 109–23.

16

The Domestic Chapel

RELIGION played an important part in the daily life of our mediaeval ancestors. Every lord would have a chapel or oratory in his house, in which to hear morning mass, and his chaplain, being an educated man, would be in demand as a secretary in days when the owner of the house might not be able to write or, in earlier times, to read.

Many early chapels must have been of wood. In the great wooden house built *c.* 1099 for Arnold, Lord of Ardres, the elaborate chapel was described as high up on the eastern side. It is believed that in a timber castle the chapel and gatehouse were often the first structures to be rebuilt in stone, but even King John built a wooden chapel, within the castle of Sauvey in Leicestershire.*

ELEVENTH AND TWELFTH CENTURIES

Most surviving examples of the 11th and 12th centuries are found in castles, several dating from soon after the Conquest, such as those at Durham (*c.* 1072) [1] and Oxford (1074).[2] These are both aisled structures, having two arcades of three columns dividing the rectangle into nave and aisles almost equal in width. There are groined vaults with cross arches, rebuilt at Oxford, where the columns are very short and may have belonged to a crypt; at Durham they are much taller. The dimensions are remarkably close, Durham being 32 feet 3 inches × 25 feet 9 inches and Oxford 32 feet × 24 feet 6 inches.

Another aisled structure was the Bishop's Chapel at Hereford (44 × 40 feet),[3] known to have been built by Robert of Lorraine (1079–95) 'after the fashion of Charlemagne's minster at Aachen'. Only one wall remains, but 18th-century drawings show its construction. It was almost square, of two vaulted storeys with a central open space and clerestory; the latter was supported on four columns in the upper chapel, with corresponding square piers in the lower. The upper chapel was probably for the bishop, the lower for

---

* Braun (1936), 85.

his servants. Similar chapels remain at the episcopal palaces of Laon and Maintz, and other *Doppel-Kapellen* occur in castles of this district of the Rhineland, and north-east France from which the bishop came.

Another early chapel, mentioned in 1085, survives at Richmond Castle.[4] The chapel of St Nicholas forms the ground floor of a wall tower (Robin Hood's) and has a barrel vault like the room above. At Pevensey Castle [6] the chapel perhaps made use of the upper part of an apsidal Roman bastion, the keep of *c.* 1130 being built against a wall of that period.

Most Norman examples are found in the keeps of castles, usually on the first or second floor. Parts of two floors, the second and third, are used in the White Tower of London, where a superb example remains in the chapel of St John (*c.* 1086–97).[5] It forms a complete little church built in the south-east angle of the tower, its apsidal end projecting eastwards. The semicircular chancel is continuous with the nave of four bays, the aisles also continued as an ambulatory, with treforium passage over on the level of similar wall passages to hall and chamber at third-floor level. Here the apse determined the plan of the tower in its south-east portion, in days before the curved angle was adopted for defensive purposes. There was probably a similar arrangement at Colchester. In the keep at Norwich (*c.* 1130) [10] the apse is placed in the wall thickness of the south-east angle, and at Guildford [13] the little oratory, also at first-floor level, is sited in two adjoining mural chambers at right angles. Indeed the favourite position for the chapel was near a corner of the keep, to allow for east and side windows. There is indication of one in the south-east angle of the third floor at Rochester (1126–39); and at Castle Rising (*c.* 1141–76) [12] the vaulted chancel was constructed in the thickness of the east wall at first-floor level, the east window overlooking the forebuilding. On the third floor of the circular keep at Conisborough (*c.* 1185–90) [16] the hexagonal chapel is fitted into the wall thickness with its east end using a buttress.

It is believed that there was a rule to have no secular room above the chapel, but we have already seen this broken at Richmond, and it was certainly not always in force in the later Middle Ages. It may have been disregarded earlier at Castle Rising, where there seems to have been another room over the chapel, possibly an oratory or the priest's chamber. This difficulty would be obviated by a position in the forebuilding, covering the entrance staircase and not as high as the main body of the keep, and indeed the chapel was sited here in at least four major 'tower keeps'.* At Rochester [9] all the forebuilding stages are vaulted, and a second chapel may have occupied the topmost (second) floor, with access by mural passage from the main building. The two keeps built for Henry II by Maurice the Engineer (*ingeniator*),† Newcastle (1171–5) [14] and Dover (1180–6),[15] alike in so many particulars, differ a great deal as regards the position of the chapel. In both it is placed in the forebuilding, but at Newcastle at basement level, an unusual position, without original access from the main building, but entered through a passage off the foot

---

* Mr Hugh Braun (1936), 40 *et seq.*, has distinguished between the earlier 'hall keep' with hall beside chamber in a large lower building, and the later 12th-century tower keep where the chamber was placed above the hall in a narrower, taller and probably less expensive and more defensible building. Examples of the hall keep include London, Colchester, Corfe, Canterbury, Rising and Middleham; of the tower keep, Hedingham, Guildford, Goodrich and Brougham; Portchester was transformed from one to the other.

† Harvey (1954), 184.

of the external stair; there may have been an oratory (the present 'guardroom') over the chancel. At Dover there were two elaborate chapels in the lower tower of the forebuilding: the lesser on the first floor with access through a vestibule from the great staircase; the more important above with chancel and nave, reached from the main rooms originally by a narrow vaulted passage off a large south-east mural chamber.

The larger chapels were divided into nave and chancel, these often cleverly contrived in the angles of the keep or in the forebuilding. By the second half of the 12th century the apse was no longer fashionable, and this made planning easier. As early as *c.* 1140 the old chapel at Farnham Castle [11] was built with a rectangular chancel (*c.* 8 × 16 feet) separated from the nave (*c.* 24 × 16 feet) by a transitional-pointed arch of two orders. A fine chancel arch divided the two compartments at Newcastle and Dover, and at the latter there was also an elaborate arch between the lower chapel and its vestibule. At Newcastle an L-plan is formed by the addition of a narrow bay to the west of the chancel, facing the east window, here on a side wall, while at Dover the altar is in line with the main axis of the chapel.

Vaulting

The barrel vault is common in the earlier chapels, as at Richmond. At Guildford there is a barrel vault to the nave of the little oratory, and a half barrel over the chancel recess. In the White Tower there are barrel vaults over the treforium and the main one ends in a semi-dome over the apse. The groined vault is without ribs but has wide semicircular transverse and longitudinal arches often supported on cylindrical piers. It is used at Durham and in the ambulatory of St John's Chapel, the arches here stilted across the aisle. At Sherborne Castle (*c.* 1107–35) [7] the chapel undercroft had a groined rubble vault under the three eastern bays and a barrel vault under the western compartment. The ribbed vault, used earlier in church building, appears richly moulded and with chevron ornament at Newcastle, and dog-tooth at Dover Castle. At Rising the ribs meet in a four-headed decoration with hole for the suspended light over the chancel.

Wall Arcading

The wall arcade was a typical decorative feature, and also gave seating facilities. At Richmond the arcade is plain with semicircular arches supported on shafts with cushion capitals. It is found at Ludlow Castle [8] round the circular nave of the detached early 12th-century St Mary Magdalene's Chapel, with chevroned and moulded arches alternating and flanking the loftier chancel arch. At Sherborne Castle the round arches intersect, the capitals scalloped or enriched, as at Ludlow, the decoration remaining in stretches not only inside but also externally. There is a wall arcade in the 'nave' recess at Guildford and Castle Rising. It is especially elaborate in the sister keeps of Newcastle and Dover. At Newcastle each bay has a large semicircular arch with chevron ornament, akin to the chancel arch, with foliated capitals. Both chapels at Dover have wall arcades. In the main one there are two bays of arcading to the side walls of both compartments, but, unlike

Newcastle, only one vaulting bay to each pair. The Gothic dog-tooth is now used with the Romanesque chevron ornament and stiff foliated capitals.

The castle chapel often, but not always, had easy access from the lord's apartment, adjoining the chamber at Guildford and Castle Rising, and in a range parallel to it in the courtyard house of Sherborne. In castles there was often another chapel in the bailey for the use of the garrison.

THIRTEENTH CENTURY

The proximity of the chapel to the main apartments, particularly the hall and solar, becomes very apparent in 13th-century examples. The owner would need his chapel near his chamber and high table, to have his chaplain at hand for religious and secretarial duties, and for both purposes the priest's room, where it remains (chiefly in later houses) usually adjoins the chapel. As the hall was earlier, and the solar invariably, placed on the first floor, the chapel was normally also at that level, making an L-plan with the main building, or attached at the angle and approached diagonally. Sometimes it was placed near the upper end of the first-floor hall, a block projecting east, while the solar was sited off the opposite, western, angle, both with easy access from the high table. This was the original arrangement, c. 1240, in the Prebendal House at Thame.[22] Here the first-floor hall, lying north to south, had a solar off the south end of the west wall, and a chapel at the south-east angle of the hall, reached by a diagonal passage. In the Abbot's House at Netley, [27] probably built c. 1250–60, the two blocks are parallel, projecting off the east side of the hall on north and south, all being at first-floor level. Here the chapel was near the lower, entrance end of the hall, as it may have been in the early 13th-century house in Corfe Castle [17] associated with King John. His son Henry III had a chapel near the entrance of several of his buildings in connection with the oriel or entrance porch at the head of an external staircase.* At Clarendon he had apparently four chapels: the king's demesne chapel, the chapel opposite the corner of the old hall, the king's chapel over the Antioch chamber and the king's new chapel, beside the king's great chamber and over the queen's wardrobe. In Little Wenham (c. 1270–80) the chapel makes an L-plan at the upper end of the hall, with possibly the solar over it, and there is a room over the chapel in the contemporary work at Carew Castle.

The angle approach off the solar was used in the mid 13th-century addition at Manorbier,[34] where the chapel with vestibule projects off one angle furthest from the hall, and the garderobe passage off the other. This is like the arrangement, but without passage, at Old Soar (c. 1290),[38] and both chapels were provided with an outside staircase giving separate access, so as not to disturb the solar occupants.

Occasionally the chapel was placed against the gable wall, as chancel to nave. This was originally the case at King John's Hunting Box at Romsey (c. 1230–40),[20] where a doorway remains to a chapel of which there is documentary evidence. The chapel survives in a similar position, but off the solar, at Charney Basset (c. 1280),[36] placed with its entrance

* See Chapter 7, and Turner (1851), 183–4, 238.

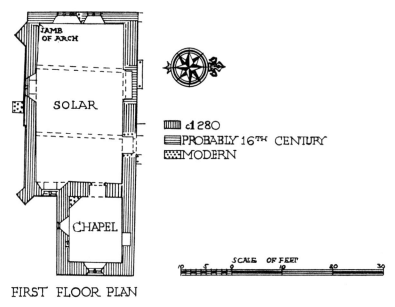

CHARNEY BASSET MANOR-HOUSE. c.1280.

JAMB OF ARCH

SOLAR

IIIIII c.1280
≡PROBABLY 16ᵀᴴ CENTURY
▦MODERN

CHAPEL

SCALE OF FEET

FIRST FLOOR PLAN

Fig. 69.

towards the north end of the solar east wall, to allow an east window to the latter (Fig. 69). These may have resembled the chapel ordered by Henry III in 1251 at Freemantle: 'A certain chamber with an upper storey, with a chapel at the end of the same chamber, for the queen's use; under which chapel he [the sheriff] is to make a cellar to hold the king's wines.' *

At Swainston Hall, Calbourne,[32] in the Isle of Wight, it was included in the east end of the hall range, with only a curtain or timber partition in between. This dates from the mid 12th century, and was still on the first floor, but it foreshadows a 13th-century development which became very popular in the later Middle Ages. This was to have the chapel with a tall chancel the height of two storeys, and the nave divided horizontally by a floor so that the upper part could serve as a private pew or gallery for the lord and his family, reached from their apartments, the lower portion for the servants, with an external doorway. There would be a screen or grille dividing the east and west parts vertically.

We get a hint of such an arrangement in the Liberate Rolls.† In April 1237 the king commanded 'to be made at Kennington, on the spot where our chapel which is roofed with thatch is situated, a chapel with a staircase of plaster, which shall be thirty feet long and twelve feet wide; in such a manner that in the upper part there be made a chapel for the use of our queen, so that she may enter that chapel from her own chamber; and in the

* Liberate Roll, 35 Henry III; Turner (1851), 228.
† Liberate Roll, 21 & 22 Henry III; Turner (1851), 185, 188.

lower part let there be a chapel for the use of our *familia* [household]'. That December Walter de Burgh, keeper of the manor, is further 'commanded to wainscot as well the upper as the lower chapel of the queen at Kennington'.

A few surviving houses show this plan in the 13th century. One occurs at Rockbourne Manor in Hampshire,[31] where the earliest range (now farm buildings) probably had a chapel at ground level, while the western part appears to have had a second floor originally, with two rows of windows, instead of the longer lancets further east. At Uploman Manor in Devon [33] there may have been a similar arrangement. The chapel projects at right angles to the solar block, from which it is divided on the ground floor by an original stone wall, but on the first by a wall introduced later and not tied in, suggesting that there was originally an open screen between solar and chapel. Of this destroyed screen a tracery bar or mullion can be detected in the 16th-century floor, which seems to have been inserted in the chapel itself, as the sill of its east window now reaches the level of the upper floor. This window has two lights with a circle in the head.

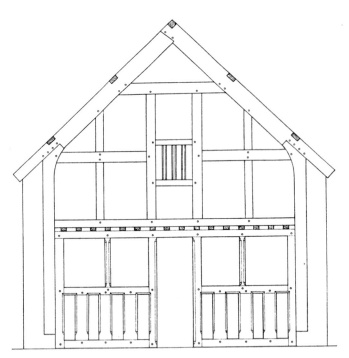

Fig. 70. Membury Court, elevation of the chapel screen, reconstruction.

But the best example remains at the chapel, now part of a barn, at Membury Court in Devon (*c.* 1290–1300).[41] An inserted floor now divides the east window (Pl. XXXVI D), which once lit a 'chancel' the height of the two storeys at the western end, divided off by a timber screen and partition, of which enough remains to allow a reconstruction. The ground-floor screen was panelled in the lower part with plain oaken bars, without tracery, and had a central entrance, while the partition above has a central four-light squint, obviously serving a private pew once with access from the solar (Fig. 70).

A late 13th-century aisled hall, St Mary's Hospital at Chichester, has a chapel in the position of chancel to domestic nave, but both are at ground level, and this is a specialized plan akin to that used in monastic infirmaries such as those at Ely and Peterborough.

Several 13th-century chapels remain, especially in Kent, which belonged to houses of the military orders, the preceptories of the Knights Templar, the commanderies of the Knights Hospitaller. These were centres of estate management, to administer local properties given to the Order, and were small houses including a hall and chapel, if the parish church was not adjacent. The Hospitallers also cared for travellers to a limited extent.*

On the analogy of Chibburn, Northumberland, [67] † of 14th-century date, the plan of which is valuable as showing the complete buildings of a commandery (Fig. 71), the surviving hospitaller chapels may have formed one range of a quadrangular plan. There may have been a two-storeyed block west of the ground-floor chapels of Sutton-at-Hone (c. 1234) [18] and Swingfield [21] in Kent, but these are long buildings apparently not subdivided originally, having long lancets, three or more on each side wall. An L-plan is more likely.

There is a cellar under the east end at Swingfield, but some commandery chapels are placed, like typical 13th-century examples, at first-floor level, approached originally by an external staircase. Such was the case at the recently destroyed Moor Hall chapel, Harefield (Middlesex) [23] and remains at Widmere Farm near Marlow,[24] both of early 13th-century date. The latter is placed over a vaulted undercroft, as is that at Temple Manor,

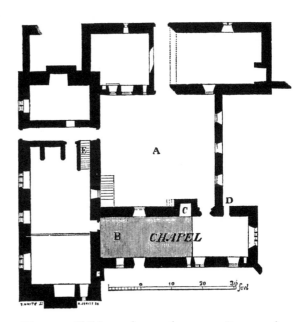

Fig. 71. Chibburn, late 14th-century Commandery chapel and ground plan.

A, Courtyard; B, Shaded portion showing extent of room above; C, Fireplace; D, Doorway to apartments now destroyed; E, Staircase

Strood (c. 1250),[25] which was perhaps only a manor belonging to the Templars, although its once arcaded chapel ‡ speaks of a building of importance.

* D. Knowles and R. Neville Hadcock (1953), *Medieval Religious Houses in England and Wales*, 27. Longmans.

† Chibburn 'Preceptory' was strictly speaking a commandery, but the term was often used for houses of the Hospitallers as well as of the Templars. The head in each was known as a preceptor. At the abolition of the Order of Knights Templar in 1312, most of their properties passed to the Hospitallers.

‡ As this building is correctly orientated, and the wall arcade stops at the east end, the late Sir Alfred Clapham thought it was probably a chapel. However, there is no sign of a piscina, and it may have been a first-floor hall.

Wall Arcading

Although the evidence of Bennett's Hall, Shrewsbury, which has wall arches associated with a fireplace, shows that these were used in a secular chamber, the blind arcade seems chiefly connected with chapel ornamentation, and would produce convenient seating, as in a chapter house.

Included in the rectorial manor house (Castle House) at Deddington in Oxfordshire [26] there is a square tower, of which the two lower floors date from the 13th century. On the first floor there is an arcaded chamber (c. 10 × 11 feet) said to have been a chapel, and although there is a later fireplace the piscina exists with mouldings suggesting a date c. 1250. This is on the north wall, however, and on the east wall there are three chamfered two-centred arches recessed for seats, and also in the south where the central arch has been pierced for a window.* Some elaborate wall arcading, with floral ornament, was made for the chapel of 1258 over the forebuilding of Henry III's ('Clifford's') Tower at York Castle; it was reset when the chapel was re-roofed in 1312.

More definite evidence remains at Conway and Beaumaris Castles, where the royal chapels are situated on the first floor of a tower. At Conway (1283–7) [37] the latter is circular in plan, and a beautiful little apsidal-ended chancel is contrived in the thickness of the wall. In Beaumaris (c. 1295+) [40] the whole chapel is apsidal, and there is a semi-octagonal east end internally. In both there is trefoil-headed wall arcading: at Conway one panel in each of the seven bays, with an uncusped pointed arch above, pierced by lancets in the three eastern bays; Beaumaris has three trefoiled panels in each bay of the apse, with a lancet placed centrally above, three at the east end, one in each side wall. Between the arches are shafts, at Conway with two sets of foliated capitals, and these carry the ribs of the vaulted roof.

Vaulting

At Manorbier Castle the chapel (c. 1260) has a pointed barrel vault, while at Little Wenham (c. 1270–80) [35] there is a quadripartite brick vault with stone ribs, resting on corbels, carved at the east, moulded at the west end; a central boss has a vesica containing a figure said to represent St Petronella, after whom the builder's daughter was named. This chapel perhaps comes nearest to that of the queen of Henry III at Woodstock, in 1244, which was to have vaulting above and beneath.†

Indeed the undercroft of an upper chapel was often vaulted. The barrel vault may have been less used, but it appears at Ledstone Hall chapel, Yorkshire (c. 1236) and, pointed, at Manorbier. There are ribbed vaults at Little Wenham (one bay) and Netley (two bays). Central columns make two arches of four bays (domical) at Widmere Farm and at Lambeth Palace.[28] Other undercrofts, however, were not vaulted, e.g. Charney Basset, and at Old Soar great blocks of stone supported the floor above.

---

* Sir Alfred Clapham was doubtful as to its having been a chapel.
† Liberate Roll, 28 Henry III; Turner (1851), 201.

Thirteenth-century chapels at ground level remain at (East) Hendred House [30] and Petworth,[29] and until 1951 at Tyting House, Chilworth (Surrey).

Glass was used in churches and chapels earlier than in domestic buildings, and was extremely expensive. Henry III made use of it in both, as we know from many entries in the Rolls. In 1268 he ordered at Guildford 'a certain chapel at the head of the same chamber with an upper storey' and glass windows befitting the same chamber and chapel, for the use of Eleanor, the consort of Edward the king's eldest son.* Glazing grooves were found when the Old Soar chapel window was unblocked, and can be seen at Membury Court, both dating from the end of the 13th century.

FOURTEENTH CENTURY

In 14th-century examples, the domestic chapel is in most cases still at first-floor level, often placed at an angle to the main building. At Markenfield (c. 1310) [46] it lies off the upper, south-east, angle of the hall, projecting parallel to it, making an L-plan with the solar (Pl. XXXVII A). At Ely, Prior Crauden's Chapel (1324–5) [50] is placed off the upper end of the Prior's Hall, at right angles to it, and attached only at the corner; it is parallel to 'Prior Crauden's Study', off the lower end of the hall, and was once connected with it by a gallery over a small court. The chapel is also reached by a bridge from the Queen's Hall, across a larger courtyard.

In Abbot's Grange, Broadway,[49] and at Clevedon Court (c. 1320) [48] the chapel is placed on the first floor of an oriel-like projection off the upper end of the hall and adjoining angle of the solar (Pl. XXXVII c). At Prudhoe Castle [45] the gatehouse contains an oratory sited in an oriel, half hexagonal with three lancets and piscina, temp. Edward II. This is comparable to a recess with east window and piscina projecting off the solar at Southwick Manor (c. 1325).[51]

At Woodsford (c. 1337) [53] and Maxstoke Castles (1346) [58] the chapel does not project, but is placed in the main range between hall and chamber, and hall and kitchen respectively. It lies also between the hall and solar at Berkeley Castle (1364),[62] placed in an angle of the domestic block because of the layout of the curtain; and at Warkworth (c. 1377–90) [64] (Fig. 72) is again between these two apartments, but projects beyond them, in the eastern arm of the great tower house. In the mid 14th-century tower at Beverston Castle (Gloucester shire) [61] the chapel is situated on the first floor below the great chamber, and the latter has an oratory adjoining, not directly over the chapel. Beetham Hall [60] has the chapel projecting south-south-east of the solar, sharing a common east wall as at Charney Basset earlier.

Sometimes the chapel is the height of two storeys, with visual access from adjoining chambers at first-floor level. At Broughton Castle [42] (c. 1300) (Pl. 17) there is a two-light opening in the west wall of the great chamber, and another 'squint' in the form of five small graduated lancets on the south, as well as a grille look-out from a staircase. At Maxstoke the chapel was the full height of the building, with access from both hall and

* Liberate Roll, 52 Henry III; Turner (1851), 255.

undercroft, and the sloping west window-sill suggests a flight of steps across that end leading up from the kitchen to the hall. Berkeley Castle had its chapel renovated in 1364, and more than a hundred years later a traceried pew oriel, now in the Long Drawing-room, was placed at the west end with access from the solar. In Warkworth keep corbels remain which supported the western gallery or 'oriel' leading from the hall gallery, and which overlooked a lofty chancel occupying the whole height of the first and second floors (Fig. 72). There seems to have been such a gallery approached from the solar at Bodiam.[66] The Bolton Castle chapel,[65] dedicated in 1399, has a wide semicircular arch at the west end supporting 'the Lady's Gallery'. In the Hospitallers' house at Chibburn the arrangement is akin to that of the 13th-century Rockbourne, the east end being the equivalent of two storeys in height, the west originally floored for two-thirds of the length of the range, and apparently containing the chamber with fireplace and a screen overlooking the chancel.

Fig. 72. Warkworth Castle, chapel in the keep, c. 1377–90.

The oblong plan is now usual, with a square head, though Berkeley and Warkworth have a semi-octagonal east end. At Beverston the square nave has a tierceron vault with carved bosses, the chancel a separate pointed ribbed barrel vault, like the larger one in the common basement. Under these first-floor chapels the undercroft is sometimes vaulted as at Broughton (two quadripartite bays), Woodsford (segmental barrel), and Warkworth (segmental pointed bays), which was a storeroom, perhaps the wine cellar.

There is a fine straight staircase to the chapel at Broughton, and external steps remain to the early 14th-century first-floor chapels at Inceworth [43] and Earth [44] in Cornwall. At Warton Old Rectory (Lancashire) [47] (Fig. 73) the steps to the undercroft entrance are continued as an outer staircase up to the chapel. The latter contains a fireplace, but this was probably added when the room below became the 'Old Kitchen' (by 1678). It was almost certainly a chapel, being so strictly orientated as to make an awkward relation, less than a right angle, with the hall, the upper doorway of which lies some six feet off the east end with its traceried window. It is now attached to a modern vicarage, but its west wall, pulled down in 1905, contained a doorway, which perhaps connected it to a priest's chamber. In Clevedon access to the chapel is from the solar, and a corbelled out newel staircase rises from the chapel to the leads, not downwards to hall level.

At Goxhill Priory in Littleworth (Lincolnshire) [63] there is a 14th-century chapel with good tracery, on the first floor. This was probably part of a hermitage, for in the Lincoln

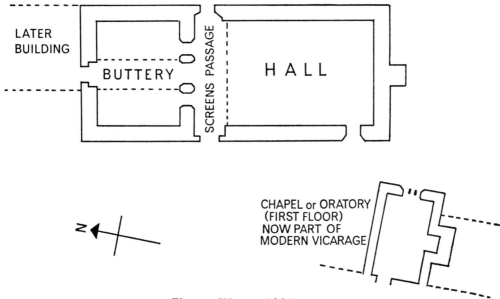

Fig. 73. Warton Old Rectory.

episcopal register of 1369 there is the entry: 'Thomas de Tykhill, hermit, clerk, presented by Philip Despenser to the chapel of St Andrew, in the parish of Goxhill, on the death of Thomas, the last hermit.'

Detached chapels are also found, built at ground level, such as the early 14th-century one at Liscombe Park, Soulbury (Buckinghamshire).[52] That at Lytes Cary,[56] dedicated in 1343, was also originally a separate building, and the squint from the Chapel Room is apparently later. The restored chapel at Stonor,[59] still in use, also dates from this period.

FIFTEENTH CENTURY

In the 15th century the ground-floor chapel seems to have become the fashionable type, with a tall chancel the height of two floors containing a great traceried east window, such as those at Bradley Manor (dedicated in 1428) [68] (Pl. XXXVIII B) and Compton Castle (c. 1450–75). The two-storeyed west end was normal, with at least a gallery adjoining the great chamber, and at Ashby de la Zouch (c. 1470) [78] there was even a third floor at the west end, with rooms apparently looking into the chancel, and approached by means of a turret staircase.

As in churches the chancel was the part regarded as sacred, the *sacrarium*, the special province of the priest, the nave and western portion as more secular, indeed the equivalent of our parish hall, where non-religious activities could be housed. Today the division is still emphasized in the office of churchwarden, where the 'vicar's warden' is responsible for the chancel, the 'people's warden' for the nave. In a chapel then the western portion would have been envisaged as a private pew in the upper part (like the comfortable squire's pew with fireplace in the Georgian period, this often at ground level), reached from the owner's apartments on the first floor, while his servants would assemble below this gallery, entering by a doorway off the courtyard.

Parker's classic example of the two-storeyed west end is the Champ's Chapel * at East Hendred (Pl. 18).[72] This was built by the Carthusian monks of Sheen in the middle of the 15th century, and dedicated to Jesus of Bethlehem. Adjoining it is the Priest's House of the late 15th or early 16th century, lengthened eastwards c. 1690. The west end of two stages is divided from the chancel by a screen rising to roof level. The screen has round-headed not cinquefoiled panels, which suggest a date similar to that of the priest's house to which the gallery gives first-floor access. But the absence of windows at the west end of the side walls indicates that such a division was intended originally, and perhaps at first the priest lived on the gallery level.

Similar in appearance as well as arrangement is the domestic chapel at Trecarrel Hall in Cornwall.[85] The west end was divided by a partition from the well-lit 'chancel' and subdivided horizontally, the upper chamber, presumably the chaplain's room, being provided with a fireplace, garderobe and staircase projections. The roof is plain to the west, more elaborate over the chapel proper. This building is detached from the contemporary hall, but near its lower end.

This arrangement is akin to, and possibly influenced by, the planning of a mediaeval hospital. We have seen how the chapel as chancel to hall as nave appears in the late 13th-century Hospital of St Mary at Chichester, as also in monastic infirmaries. In the Alms-house of SS. John the Baptist and John the Evangelist at Sherborne,† the chapel, completed in 1442, is still at ground level, short in length but lofty, and now the hall has two floors, the upper originally occupied by the women, the lower by men, overlooking the chapel at each level. A similar building is Browne's Hospital, Stamford,‡ founded before 1485, where the upper floor was used as a council chamber, with the almsfolk below. Blackmoor Farm, Cannington, near Bridgwater,[80] has the same tall chapel and two-floored ante-chapel, with evidence of a screen between them. The chapel at Compton Castle, re-windowed c. 1450–75, has visual access from both floors at its lower end, and at Compton Wynyates (c. 1515–20) [86] also, the service in the chapel below could be followed from openings, now glazed, in the chapel drawing-room (with fireplace) at first-floor level.

Mediaeval buildings are usually one room in thickness so that there could be windows on both sides. This was probably derived from the time when the use of glass was limited and windows had shutters which could be open on one side of the room or the other to give

* A late name, from an 18th-century owner.
† R.C.H.M. *Dorset*, I, 211–12, pls. 180 & 181; Godfrey (1955), 17, 39–40, fig. 22., pl. 12.
‡ Rebuilt with very slight change. Godfrey (1955), 41, figs. 23 & 24.

light away from the prevailing wind and weather. But in the 15th century, when glass was more plentiful, glazed windows on one side would suffice, and there developed a tendency to have a building two rooms in thickness, as in modern architecture. At Minster Lovell [69] the chapel is placed alongside the hall, and parallel to it. The hall is lofty and the chapel is at first-floor level, but had a low-pitched roof so as not to block the hall windows, which were placed high on this side. It was reached from the hall by a lobby and spiral staircase, and had an antechapel at the western end. Raglan Castle gives another example of a chapel (c. 1450–69) parallel to the hall, but here the former was apparently at ground level. At Trelawney House, Cornwall, the chapel is in an unusual position, beyond the screens passage.

Occasionally the chapel was placed in a tower. At Stanton Harcourt (c. 1470) [77] there is a vaulted one on the ground level of 'Pope's Tower'. It has three storeys over it, with probably rooms for the priest, and the uppermost used in the 18th century by the poet, who has given his name to the building. At Ilsham Manor, Torquay,[76] the chapel is on the first floor of a tower, again with a priest's room over; it closely resembles the gabled towers of Compton Castle and was probably by the same master mason. There is also a room over the chapel at Guerney Street Farm, Cannington (Somerset),[79] as at Beverston earlier. At Gothelney (Somerset) [70] the little chapel, yet with large east window and angle corbels, is at the top of a circular staircase.

The smaller chapel, or oratory, may be situated over the porch, and adjoining the great chamber. This was probably the case at Congresbury Vicarage,[74] which has the arms of Bishop Beckington of Wells (1443–65) and so was built, like Banwell Court,[73] with another Somerset chapel, by the Bishop or his executors. There is another possible porch oratory at Ashbury Manor [83] divided from the great chamber by an original screen. In these the altar must have faced a side wall as at Clevedon, to get correct orientation. Further porch examples include the Chantry at Bridport (Dorset), Place Court, Collaton Raleigh and Combe Raleigh in Devon, and Lower March Manor, Dunster (Somerset). The last, of the late 15th century, retains its wagon roof and image bracket.

The chapel in the form of an oratory may be found as part of a room in which the presence of a fireplace denotes a secular use. We have noted the 14th-century oriel recess in the solar at Southwick Hall. At Ilminster [81] there is such a chamber on the first floor of the Chantry (late 15th-century), with contemporary fireplace in the north wall. Near the altered east window is an image bracket (Pl. LVII D), and further south a piscina and loop window, the latter overlooking the north transept of the church, where the St Catherine (or Wadham) chantry was sited. Further evidence of the oratory is given by the squints pierced in the plank-and-muntin partition to the larger chamber on the south. Was the north room a bedroom or study with oratory for one chantry priest?

At Wenlock the late 15th-century Prior's House [84] has a somewhat similar arrangement. The northern room, here at ground level, has a fireplace and window on the north, and on the east a projecting recess separately roofed, with a three-light window, stone altar, and a piscina on the south. This is believed to be the chapel which the prior shared with the infirmary adjoining on the west. The southern third of the room, with garderobe projection, was previously partitioned off.

Early Sixteenth Century

The chapel at the Vyne in Hampshire [87] was built by Sir William, later Lord, Sandys, loyal friend and servant of Henry VIII. From the glass it is dated between 1518 and 1527. It has a three-sided apse, which plan is also used in the chapel at Cowdray, [88] suggesting a similar date, though the Cowdray tracery, and hood continued as string-course (like Crosby Hall), could be even earlier. St Hope John believed that the bay was added to an originally square-headed chapel. However, the tracery is akin to that of the hall, the windows of which have the same hood string-course, and which is believed to date from *c.* 1520–1530, which would suit the evidence of the Vyne. A crenellated parapet surmounts both chapels, that of the Vyne being enriched with heraldic ornament. The plainer battlements over the chapel at Cowdray were doubtless added by Sir William Fitzwilliam, later the Earl of Southampton, in connection with the licence of 1522–3.

A beautiful little chapel of *c.* 1520–30 survives at Ightham Mote,[89] reached by an outer staircase from the court. It is called the New Chapel, the older disused chapel remaining on its vaulted crypt in the eastern range. The four-centred barrel roof, painted with Tudor badges, is of especial interest and may be compared with the earlier one, with carved bosses, at Bradley Manor [68] and that at Cotehele,[82] with its carved Tudor roses.

Windows

The east window grew in size throughout the mediaeval period, as in churches, with the greater use of glass and relatively settled conditions. Thus earlier chapels often had their windows enlarged later. But in Richmond Castle the late 11th-century arrangement is still preserved: a small central window on the east wall, with a circular double-splayed opening on either side. The round-headed east window, with chevron ornament, survives at Sherborne Castle, and a more elaborate northern window preserving two orders of chevron.

In the first half of the 13th century the usual eastern arrangement was a triplet of lancets, graduated as at the Thame Prebendal (*c.* 1240) (Pl. XXXVI c). At Tyting Manor, Chilworth, the lancets were short. Sometimes there is a circle over each, as at Swingfield (*c.* 1240), but one, often cusped, in the gable, persisted longer in popularity; at Rockbourne there is evidence of a quatrefoil in this position.

During the latter half of the century the lancets became grouped into a three-light window, and the circles combined in the head to form an earlier type of bar tracery, such as the east window at Swainston Hall. However, single lancets are set in the arcading of the apse at Conway and Beaumaris, which date from the end of the century.

There were usually single lancets in the side and west walls except in more ornate chapels such as that of the archbishops at Lambeth, of mid 13th-century date, where the east and west ends have five graduated lancets; the side walls have four windows each, with the usual eastern triple arrangement. This scheme, but in more advanced type, applies to Bishop Burnell's chapel at Wells (*c.* 1290). [39] Here the east window is of six pointed cinquefoiled lights in a two-centred arch; the west of five, and the side windows of three, with sex-foiled circles or a large lobed trefoil in the head. A magnificent east

Plate XXXVII. The Domestic Chapel.

A. Markenfield Hall, exterior with east window, 1310.
B. Prior Crauden's east window at Ely, 1324–5. C and
D. Clevedon Court, c. 1320.

Plate XXXVIII. The Domestic Chapel.

A. 'Champ's Chapel', Chapel of Jesus of Bethlehem, East Hendred, mid 15th century. B. Chapel at Bradley Manor, Newton Abbot, 1428. C and D. Woodlands Manor, Mere: north window of chapel, mid 14th century; interior of chapel, with 15th-century tracery in east window.

window, now in a dangerous condition, is to be seen inside a barn at Membury Court (Pl. XXXVI D); its great sex-foiled circle with blunt cusps resembles those in the cloister at Salisbury (c. 1263–84). However, here the three lights are trefoiled, with soffit cusps, and above each side one is a lobed trefoil which tends to place the window after 1290. The scroll-moulded hood terminates in the carved heads of a priest and a bishop. This window calls for careful preservation.

In the 14th century the three-light east window was normal, with two-lights in smaller buildings. As in the narrower side windows, the lights usually had trefoiled heads, these at first being steep. Warton Old Rectory [47] has an east window of two such lights with a kite-shaped aperture in bar tracery above, resembling that in the late 13th-century east window at Charney Basset, which, however, has uncusped lancet lights. A quatrefoil above trefoil-headed lights, so popular in houses, was also used in smaller chapels such as Abbot's Grange at Broadway. The trefoiled-ogee light now became the fashionable form, used triple, graduated, at Brimpton (Berkshire), [54] (Pl. XXXVI A) in a square head at Beetham Hall, or elaborated with net tracery at Lytes Cary (Pl. LV D), where the side windows are two-light versions of the eastern one, or in the more developed south window of three lights at Woodlands Manor, Mere [57] (Pl. XXXVIII D).

The larger window had tracery above the lights, at first the 'Geometric' type of the late 13th and very early 14th centuries, of which Broughton Castle [42] has a fine example. Here the lights are cinquefoil-headed, equal in height; there is a rounded trefoil over each side, and a large circle containing three cinquefoiled circles above the central light. At Markenfield (c. 1310) the centre trefoiled light is slightly taller, which allows for a quatre-foiled circle over the head of each, again framed by the two-centred arch (Pl. XXXVII A).

The 'Geometric' was followed by 'Decorated' tracery, of which there are excellent examples with leaf-like tracery, over two trefoiled lights, in the side windows of Prior Crauden's Chapel (1324–5). Its great east window of five cinquefoil-headed lights has elaborate tracery still with slight elements of the Geometric (Pl. XXXVII B). Reticulated tracery seems especially popular in the second quarter of the 14th century. At Clevedon Court the chapel windows (Pl. XXXVII D) are completely formed of this network, without the trefoil-headed lights used below at Lytes Cary or Woodlands Manor; of the two windows the southern is longer than the eastern, which was over the altar. The east window at Chichester Palace [55] was renewed at this period, a three-light with net tracery (Pl. XXXVI B) replacing the 13th-century lancet triplet, remains of which are visible on either side.

At Maxstoke a large western window remains, of six lights, more like three two-light windows combined under a great semicircular covering arch. The heads are all cinquefoiled, the side couples very steep with a cusped kite-shaped opening above, the two central taller in an ogee frame, the point of which reaches the apex of the main arch. There is a similarity between the side lights here and the three-light east window at Beverston Castle, with its fellow, more complete, in the neighbouring church; there is the same narrow pointed cinquefoil-head, and here three cusped kite-shaped apertures above. The central portion of the Maxstoke window is also akin to the design at Warkworth. Here there were three two-light windows in the east wall, and another to north and south, the lights now trefoiled but in a similar ogee arch with kite or diamond tracery. These windows had transoms, both trefoiled. Other tall windows of this period are found in the side windows of the chapel at Bolton Castle, here narrow and cinquefoiled with one transom. Bodiam Castle chapel has the three pointed lights of the east window partly restored; their plain heads are unusual at this date (1385) unless the cusps have fallen and not been replaced.

In earlier 14th-century houses the foiled circles or geometrical gable apertures persist. There are quatrefoils in both gables at Inceworth, and a foiled circle (east) at Liscombe Park. This is also an early house, judging from the lobed trefoils in the (restored) tracery. *

The great east window is the main feature of the 15th century, with vertical or Perpendicular tracery. In the first half of the period, before they became stereotyped, the designs are particularly pleasing. The trefoil-headed light may be a somewhat early feature, for later the cinquefoiled head was normal, the rounded type especially. The east window at Woodlands Manor [57] provides a good example of the earlier scheme in a three-light window. The perpendicular bars rise from the apex of the lights, here with trefoil heads, to form two hexagonal panels or miniature two-lights, also trefoiled, separated by a bar following the division of the main lights, and with a small lozenge in the head; there is a larger kite or diamond, quatrefoiled, in the apex of the arch. A similar window, with cinquefoiled main lights, is found in the tower chapel at Gothelney, at Champ's Chapel (Pl. XXXVIII A) and in the almshouse at Sherborne (1442), but the windows at Trecarrel have rather plainer tracery. In the delightful east window (1428) at Bradley Manor (Pl. XXXVIII B), the hexagons show a development, the panels now trefoiled at both ends, with a lower diamond fitted neatly between the cinquefoiled ogee heads of the lights. The three lights at Stanton Harcourt chapel (c. 1470) are similar, but here the verticals between them and at their apex are all carried up to the main arch, to form six graduated panels, trefoiled at the head.

In a four-light window, such as those at Compton Castle, there is a main central division, forming as it were two separate double-light (cinquefoiled) windows with their hexagon under a pointed arch; and between them in the head is a large kite containing similar trefoiled panels and a transverse bar.

Parallel vertical tracery, according to Buck's engravings, occurred in the chapel windows at Minster Lovell and Ashby de la Zouch. Fortunately the detached chapel at Rycote (Oxfordshire) [71] (1446) survives in good condition, and is being restored by the Ministry of Works. There is a magnificent east window with parallel tracery, cusped, over five cinquefoiled lights, and over the west doorway is a window of three graduated trefoiled lights in a flat four-centred hood, similar to that over the cinquefoiled two-lights on the side walls. A five-light transomed east window of 15th-century date probably came to the chapel at Compton Wynyates from the demolished Fulbroke Castle.

The early 16th-century chapels at Cowdray and the Vyne have a window in each facet of the three-sided apse, and also, originally at Cowdray, in the side walls. At Cowdray they are of three lights, trefoiled below the transom and above, with Perpendicular tracery in a four-centred head, of which the hood continues as a string-course. At the Vyne these arches are not connected, and the lights are cinquefoiled above, but merely curved below the transom.

* The Royal Commission on Historical Monuments dates it *c.* 1350, but the tracery suggests the early part of the 14th century.

EXAMPLES OF THE DOMESTIC CHAPEL

LATE 11TH & 12TH CENTURIES

		Floor	*References (mostly with plan)*
(1) *c.* 1072	Durham Castle	ground	Toy (1953 b), 57; B. Colgrave, *Durham Castle* (English Life Publications), pls. 29, 30.
(2) 1074	Oxford Castle, Chapel of St George	crypt	R.C.H.M. *Oxford*, 156–8, pl. 213.
(3) *c.* 1079–95	Bishop's Palace, Hereford, evidence	ground & first	Drinkwater (1954), *Archaeological Journal*, CXI, 129–37; Clapham (1934), 112, fig. 38.
(4) —1085	Richmond Castle, Yorks., Chapel of St Nicholas	ground	Toy (1953 b), 95
(5) *c.* 1086–97	Tower of London, Chapel of St John	second & third	R.C.H.M. *London*, V, 87, 89, pls. 153–6.
(6) by 1130	? Pevensey Castle, Suss.	first	M.O.W. Guide (1951).
(7) *c.* 1107–35	Sherborne Old Castle, Dor.	first	R.C.H.M. *Dorset*, I, 73, pl. 91.
(8) early C 12th	Ludlow Castle, Salop, St Mary Magdalene's Chapel	ground	Clapham (1934), 111; Toy (1953 b), 76; Thompson (1912), 108.
(9) 1126–39	Rochester Castle, Kent, keep	second (forebuilding)	Thompson (1912), 150.
(10) *c.* 1130	Norwich Castle, Norf., keep	first	A. B. Whittingham (1949). *Archaeological Journal*, CVI, 77.
(11) *c.* 1140	Farnham Castle, Sy.	first	
(12) *c.* 1141–76	Castle Rising, Norf., keep	first	*Journal of the British Archaeological Association* (1934), N.S. XL, 62–3, 64; Godfrey (1911), fig. 2.
(13) *c.* 1150	Guildford Castle, Sy., keep	first	
(14) 1171–5	Newcastle keep	ground (forebuilding)	Toy (1953 b), 97; Parker Brewis, (1947), *Newcastle Keep*, guide, 6, 7, 18.
(15) 1180–6	Dover Castle, Kent, keep; lower chapel, greater chapel	first / second	Toy (1953 b), 101; *Archaeological Journal* (1929), LXXXVI, pl. V.
(16) 1185–90	Conisborough Castle, Yorks., keep	third	A. H. Thompson (1912), 167, 170.

13TH CENTURY

(17) doct. 1200–1	Corfe Castle, Gloriet, ? chapel	first	Toy (1929), pls. XXXVII, XXXVIII.
(18) doct. *c.* 1234	Sutton-at-Hone, Kent, Commandery	ground	Wadmore (1897), 255–60; Kipps (1935).
(19) doct. *c.* 1236	Ledstone Hall, near Pontefract, Yorks.	first	S. D. Kitson (1911), *Yorkshire Archaeological & Topographical Journal*, XXI, 210–13.
(20) *c.* 1230–40	King John's Hunting Box, Romsey, Hants, evidence	first	Andrews & Atkinson (1929); Wood (1950), 24–6, pl. V A.
(21) *c.* 1240	Swingfield, Kent, Commandery	ground with cellar under E. part	Wadmore (1897), 260–4.
(22) *c.* 1240	Prebendal House, Thame, Oxon.	first	*Archaeological Journal* (1910), LXVII, 367–9; Wood (1950), 60, pl. IV c.

			Floor	References (mostly with plan)
(23)	early C 13th	Moor Hall chapel, Harefield, Middx, evidence	first	R.C.H.M. *Middlesex*, 55–6, pl. 131.
(24)	early C 13th & C 14th	Widmere Farm, Marlow, Bucks., Commandery	first	Wood (1950), 11; R.C.H.M. *Bucks*, I, 169.
(25)	c. 1250	? Temple Manor, Strood, Kent, Preceptory	first	Wood (1950), 39–40; Wadmore (1897), 251–5.
(26)	c. 1250	Castle House, Deddington, Oxon.	first	Wood (1950), 58.
(27)	c. 1250–60	Abbot's House, Netley, Hants.	first	M.O.W. Guide (29); *V.C.H. Hants*, III, 472–6 (first-floor plan).
(28)	mid C 13th	Lambeth Palace, London	first	R.C.H.M. *London*, II, 79, 80, pl. 130.
(29)	C 13th	Petworth, Suss.	ground	
(30)	C 13th	(East) Hendred House	ground	Long (1940), 107–8.
(31)	mid C 13th	Rockbourne Manor, Hants	ground	*V.C.H. Hants*, IV, 581–2.
(32)	mid C 13th	Swainston Hall, Calbourne, I.O.W.	first	*V.C.H. Hants*, V, 217–18; Stone (1891), 127–9.
(33)	2nd half C 13th	Uploman Manor, Devon	ground	Research by A. W. Everett, F.S.A.
(34)	c. 1260	Manorbier Castle, Pembs.	first	*Country Life* (15), 311, figs. 3, 10.
(35)	c. 1270–80	Little Wenham, Hall, Suff.	first	Wood (1950), 77–8, pls. VII C, IX A.
(36)	c. 1280	Charney Basset Manor House, Berks.	first	Wood (1950), 8–10, pl. III A.
(37)	1283–7	Conway Castle, Caer.	first	Toy (1937), 192; M.O.W. Guide (12); R.C.H.M. *Caernarvonshire*, I, 51–3, fig. 61, pl. 54.
(38)	c. 1290	Old Soar, Plaxtol, Kent	first	Wood (1950), 36–8, pl. III B.
(39)	c. 1290	Wells Palace, Som. (Bishop Burnell)	first	Parker (1866), pls. X, XIII.
(40)	c. 1295+	Beaumaris Castle, Ang.	first	M.O.W. Guide (1936); R.C.H.M. *Anglesey*, 9, 11–12, pl. 143.
(41)	c. 1290–1300	Membury Court, Devon	ground	Research by A. W. Everett, F.S.A.

14TH CENTURY

(42)	c. 1300	Broughton Castle, Oxon.	first (& second)	Parker (1853), 79–80, 262.
(43)	*temp.* Ed. I	Inceworth, Corn.	first	Parker (1853), 304–5.
(44)	early C 14th	Earth, Corn.	first	Parker (1853), 305.
(45)	*temp.* Ed. II	Prudhoe Castle, Northumb.	first (over gateway)	Parker (1853), 206–7.
(46)	c. 1310	Markenfield Hall, Yorks.	first	Parker (1853), 233–4.
(47)	early C 14th	Warton Old Rectory, Lancs.	first	*V.C.H. Lancs.*, VIII, 156–7; J. K. Floyer (1905), *Transactions of the Lancashire & Cheshire Historical Society*, N.S. XXI, 28–47.
(48)	c. 1320	Clevedon Court, Som.	first (in oriel)	*Country Life* (6), 1672–5, figs. 4–5; 16–19, fig. 8.
(49)	c. 1320	Abbot's Grange, Broadway, Worcs.	first (in oriel)	*V.C.H. Worcestershire*, IV, 34–6.
(50)	doct. 1324–5	Prior Crauden's Chapel, Ely	first	Atkinson (1933), 70, and plans.
(51)	c. 1325	Southwick Manor, Northants.	first (in oriel)	*Country Life* (26), 1239–40.
(52)	early C 14th	Liscombe Park, Soulbury, Bucks.	ground	R.C.H.M. *Bucks*, II, 268–9.
(53)	1337	Woodsford Castle, Dor.	first	

		Floor	References (mostly with plan)
(54) C 12th & C 14th	Shalford Farm, Brimpton, Berks., Commandery	ground	Long (1940), 105–6.
(55) c. 1200 & C 14th	Bishop's Palace, Chichester	ground	*Archaeological Journal* (1935), XCII, 389, pls. II, III A.
(56) doct. 1343	Lytes Cary, Som.	ground	
(57) mid C 14th & C 15th	Woodlands Manor, Mere, Wilts.	first	*Country Life* (31), 732–8, pls. **5**, 6; 776–83, pls. 3, 5.
(58) 1346	Maxstoke Castle, War.	ground	Parker (1853), 246–7.
(59) c. 1349	Stonor, Oxon.	ground	
(60) mid. C 14th	Beetham Hall, West.	first	R.C.H.M. *Westmorland*, 41.
(61) 1356–61	Beverston Castle, Glos.	chapel: first oratory: second	Parker (1859), 181; *Archaeological Journal* (1930), LXXXVII, 454–455.
(62) doct. 1364	Berkeley Castle, Glos.	first	Parker (1859), 178.
(63) before 1369	Goxhill Priory, Littleworth, Lincs.	first	*Lincolnshire Little Guide*, revised A. H. Thompson (1924), 139–140.
(64) c. 1377–90	Warkworth Keep, Northumb.	first & second (with two-storeyed west end)	M.O.W. Guide (43), 17·18; Evans (1949), 123.
(65) c. 1378–99	Bolton Castle, Yorks.	first	Jackson (1956), 9–10.
(66) 1385	Bodiam Castle	ground	
(67) end C 14th	Chibburn 'Preceptory', Northumb.	ground (with two-storeyed W. end)	Parker (1853), 197–8.

15TH CENTURY

(68) dedicated 1428	Bradley Manor, Devon	ground	National Trust Guide (1), 5–6.
(69) prob. 1431–42	Minster Lovell Hall, Oxon.	first	M.O.W. Guide (28), 10, 15, pl. I.
(70) early C 15th	Gothelney Manor, near Bridgwater, Som.	top of staircase	Research by W. A. Pantin, F.S.A.
(71) 1446	Rycote, Oxon.	ground	
(72) mid C 15th	'Champ's Chapel' (Chapel of Jesus of Bethlehem), East Hendred, Berks.	ground (with two-storeyed W. end)	Parker (1859), 177–8.
(73) c. 1443–65	Banwell Court, Som.		
(74) c. 1443–65	Congresbury Vicarage, Som.	over porch	Pantin (1957), 128, 131, fig. 25, pls. XIX A, B.
(75) c. 1450–75 & earlier	Compton Castle, Devon	ground	Parker (1859), 148; National Trust Guide (2), 6.
(76) C 15th	Ilsham Manor, Torquay, Devon	first (in tower)	
(77) c. 1470	Stanton Harcourt, Oxon.	ground	Parker (1859), 175.
(78) c. 1470	Ashby de la Zouch, Leics.	ground	M.O.W. Guide (2), 19.
(79) later C 15th	Guerney Street Farm, Cannington, Som.		
(80) later C 15th	Blackmoor Farm, Cannington, Som.	ground (with two-storeyed W. end)	Research by E. T. Long, F.S.A.
(81) c. 1480	The Chantry, Ilminster, Som.	first	Pantin (1959), 232, 233.
(82) c. 1485–9	Cotehele, Corn.	ground	National Trust Guide (3), 16; Garner & Stratton (1929), 40 (plan).
(83) c. 1488	Ashbury Manor, Berks.	over porch	
(84) late C 15th	Prior's House, Wenlock, Salop	ground	*Country Life* (29), 1284, 1434.

16TH CENTURY

		Floor	References (*mostly with plan*)
(85) early C 16th	Trecarrel Hall, Corn.	ground	Research by A. W. Everett, F.S.A.
(86) *c.* 1515–20	Compton Wynyates, War.	ground	Garner & Stratton (1929), 117–118.
(87) 1518–27	The Vyne, Hants	ground	National Trust Guide, (6), 19-21.
(88) *c.* 1520–30	Cowdray, Suss.	ground	Trotter (1934), 39–41 (with Grimm's drawing of 1786).
(89) *c.* 1520–30	Ightham Mote, Kent	first	Fletcher (1946), 400.

17

The Kitchen

IN SOME small houses the kitchen and hall may have been one. But in many others the kitchen seems to have been a detached building at first, like the other 'houses' which formed the early mediaeval residence. This was the case not only in the greater establishments where a large kitchen was in constant use, but also, as records are revealing, in homes quite humble and early in date. In Essex, where an intensive study of these village buildings is being made, 1292 is the earliest reference found so far to such an outside kitchen. The widow Margery de la Strete, marrying a freeholder, pays a fee to retain the customary lands for life, and agrees with her son that he shall have the house she occupied, but she is to have access for brewing and other necessary things, 'in that house [*domo*] which is called the kitchen'. This is obviously an outside 'house', otherwise it would be called *camera*, not *domo*. There are many other such references.* Only gradually did the kitchen become an integral part of the main building and not fully so until the 15th and 16th centuries. This may have been partly through fear of fire, intensified by the flimsy material, plastered wood, of some early kitchens. Even royalty had such buildings: in July 1244 the sheriff of Nottingham was ordered to build at Clipstone a kitchen in wood for Henry III; and in 1285 a kitchen of plastered wood, with a wooden hall, was built at Woolmer in Hampshire for Edward I; at Oxford in 1232 the royal kitchen was blown down in a gale.†
Temporary kitchens were also erected for great occasions, like those made in 1273 at Westminster for the coronation feast of Edward I.‡

All such ephemeral buildings have of course disappeared, but excavation is throwing more and more light upon them. A 13th-century detached kitchen (41 feet 3 inches × 22 feet 6 inches) with great hearth has been found by Mr Adrian Oswald at Weoley Castle, Birmingham,§ the waterlogged site preserving some of the weather-boarded walls up to 3 feet high. It had a reed-thatched roof, and a pentise gave access to a stone hall which was

* For this information I am grateful to Mr T. Newton and Mr A. C. Edwards of the Essex Record Office at Chelmsford.
† Liberate Roll, 28 Henry III; Pipe Roll, 13 Edward I; Liberate Roll, 17 Henry III; Turner (1851), 205 (Clipstone), 60–2 (Woolmer), 67 (Oxford).
‡ *Liber de Antiquis Legibus* (ed. T. Stapleton, Camden Society), 172; Turner (1851), 65.
§ Oswald (1962–3), 109–23.

burnt down *c.* 1260. The wooden building was reconstructed six times during the period *c.* 1200–60, and *c.* 1230 it was converted into an aisled hall, which implies a change of purpose. Other recent work of great importance has been that of Mr J. G. Hurst at Northolt Manor in Middlesex. The kitchen of *c.* 1300–50 was a detached timber-framed building 30 feet square, with a central hearth and a post hole for a spit or a firehood; the western quadrant had a roughly tiled floor. But most of the cooking seems to have been done outside in an extensive pebbled area with many hearths. The kitchen was retiled and improved in the period 1350–70, but in the late 15th century it was demolished.* Apart from documentary and excavation evidence we must judge from a number of surviving examples in stone. In these the detachment of the kitchen comes out in a striking manner.

The kitchen had nevertheless to be sited not far from the hall, and at Gillingham in 1261 there is to be made 'a certain bench [*scabellium*] between the king's hall and kitchen, to arrange the king's dinner on'. It could be situated a short distance away from the end wall of the hall, with a passage leading to it between the pantry and buttery, and this was the usual mediaeval position. Or it might be reached by a covered way from the back door of the hall, which suggests a position not far from that side wall; this seems to have been the case at Woodstock in 1244. At Ludgershall Henry III ordered the removal of 'the old kitchen to beside the new kitchen behind the king's hall there' (1251). In Guildford, however, there was a stable between the king's hall and kitchen (1257).†

Matters are complicated by the fact that the king's kitchen could be separate from that of his household, and the queen might have her own as well. There were two kitchens at Windsor *c.* 1234, near the great hall, inside a palisade, and at Winchester there is reference to 'two furnaces in the greater kitchen' (1238).‡

In 1244 the sheriff of Wiltshire received orders relating to Clarendon Palace: [4] 'Nigh the king's kitchen he is to make another great, and square kitchen, which is to be every way within the walls forty feet; and a salsary between the wall of the said kitchen and the wall of the hall. And he is to make a *herlebecheria* [scullery] on the outside, beside the wall of the kitchen.'§ The palace was excavated in 1933–5, and two kitchens were found, both square. One which they called the 'Household Kitchen' was built beyond the west end wall of the hall, and reached from the latter by a passage between butteries and the south wall of a small cloister. North of this court is the 'King's Kitchen', *c.* 39 feet square internally, buttressed on its outer angles because of the sloping ground. Its south-west angle almost touches the north-east corner of the western kitchen, and built between them is the small square room which was probably the *herlebecheria*. The excavators believed that the western kitchen (42 feet square internally) was the one ordered in 1244, and that the southern building of the little court was the 'salsary'. Otherwise the more convenient position of the western kitchen would suggest it to be of an earlier date than the other.

It may have resembled the surviving kitchen at Lincoln Palace,[3] built *c.* 1224, which

* Hurst (1961), 214–15, 239–41.
† Liberate Roll, 45, 28, 35, 42 Henry III; Turner (1851), 253 (Gillingham), 201 (Woodstock), 230 (Ludgershall), 249 (Guildford).
‡ Pipe Roll, 18, Liberate Roll, 23 Henry III; Turner (1851), 67 (Windsor), 193 (Winchester).
§ Liberate Roll, 28 Henry III; Turner (1851), 202.

is nearly square, the south (curtain) wall being at an angle, the north wall *c.* 40 feet, and the west 44 feet. Owing to the lie of the land, it is raised on a vaulted basement, and is reached from the hall by a passage between butteries, as at Clarendon, then an arched bridge, flanked by larders, above a quadripartite vault.

There are remains of a square 12th-century kitchen at Ely,[1] serving the monastery, as well as a later one for the prior's hall. One of the 13th century, *c.* 34 feet across, can be seen in the Bishop's Palace at Chichester,[7] the fine oak roof being perhaps somewhat later; it is still nearly free on three sides. At Kersey (Suffolk) [6] Mr P. G. M. Dickinson has found a similar square kitchen, less developed, probably dating from the 13th century.

At Furness Abbey (Lancashire) [9] the 13th-century kitchen was octagonal, and this shape was found also at Charing Palace. One hexagonal in plan was built in 1287–91, costing £414, at St Augustine's Abbey, Canterbury; [10] this also has been excavated. It measures 40 feet across, and has angle buttresses, their line continuing inwards to form the jambs of wedge-shaped fireplaces in the sides.

Also hexagonal, but irregular, is the kitchen of *c.* 1326–61 at Berkeley Castle.[13] It is contained within the main range, however, with a passage from the nearby hall, yet still maintains a certain independence and forms the entire height of the building.

The kitchen at Farnham Castle [5] presents a problem. It was said to be Norman, and is situated within the acute south-west angle of the curtain wall, strengthened by a turret 10 feet square. The apartment is thus rhomboidal with one very pointed corner, and its thinner east wall is separated from the hall by a passage. Thus it appears nearer the hall than usual, but the passage is wide and must have been partitioned for butteries, each served by one small service doorway flanking the tall central one which gave access to the kitchen beyond. Further service accommodation may have been provided by the undercroft of the 12th-century chapel, which lies north of the kitchen, once separated from it by a small open court. This present kitchen is now believed * to be a 13th-century remodelling, possibly of a timber kitchen contained in the angle of the defensive wall, of which the great thickness (and double-splay windows) was needed to carry a wall walk, now obscured except in the south-west angle turret. The latter may have contained a bread oven. The only old fireplace now showing seems to be of 14th-century date, sited on the west wall where it blocks two original windows, a further one to the south being filled with a 14th-century loop. Five windows, double-splayed with slightly pointed heads, are still in use on the south wall, discounting an original fireplace there, but there is the matrix of a great fireplace on the north wall towards the court, probably flanked by windows at one time. The kitchen is said to have had eleven windows originally.

The most beautiful mediaeval kitchen left to us is the famous Abbot's Kitchen at Glastonbury,[14] dating from the mid 14th century (Fig. 74). It is square externally, octagonal within, measuring 33 feet 6 inches across and, like most examples, occupies the whole

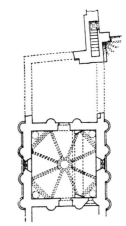

Fig. 74. The Abbot's Kitchen, Glastonbury, plan.

* I am indebted to Mr A. R. Dufty, F.S.A., A.R.I.B.A., for this solution.

height of the building. Here the fireplaces are set in the angles, and have segmental-pointed arches. This kitchen served the abbot's household, which at one stage numbered three hundred persons, not counting numerous guests; it is the sole survival from his extensive lodgings. There was a conventual kitchen as well.

The monastic kitchen at Durham [17] was built by John Lewyn in 1366–71 (Figs. 75 *a, b* and *c*). It is octagonal, 36 feet across, with lateral fireplaces, and rises to a lofty stone vault. The same builder is probably responsible for the great kitchen at Raby Castle (Co. Durham), [19] *c.* 1378, a distinct building forming a square tower beyond the north end of the hall. It is

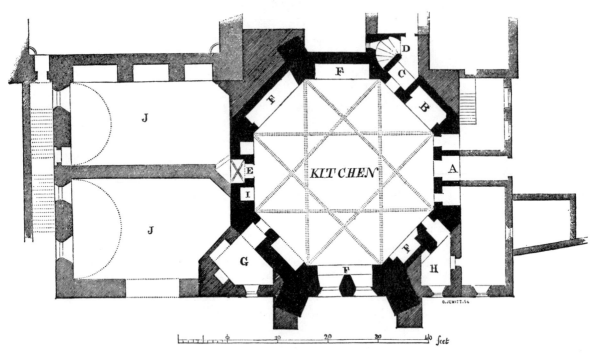

Fig. 75 *a.* Durham, monastic kitchen, 1366–71, plan.

built on a vaulted cellar with central pillar, and is square below, octagonal above, with wall passages.

A fine example, rather earlier, remains at Haddon Hall. [12] It is almost square (24 × 28 feet) and was once loftier, the present ceiling (supported by a post) probably being inserted with another storey in the 16th century. The south wall was also altered then, but in the main a good picture is provided of a 14th-century kitchen, with great fireplaces on two adjoining walls. Especially typical is the access to it from the central service doorway of the hall entry, by a stone-walled passage between butteries, now continued by studded partitions across what was originally an open court. Thus the kitchen was in line with the hall but still a separate building. So was the mid 14th-century 'John of Gaunt's Kitchen' at Canford Magna in Dorset, [15] and the fine one, *c.* 1388–1400, at Dartington, [23] 35 feet square, with lofty windows, the great arched fireplaces over 14 feet high, once with

Fig. 75 *b* and *c*. Durham, monastic kitchen, 1366–71, interior and exterior.

wooden hoods, on two adjoining walls, and approached from the screens passage by a covered way.

Kitchens of the later Middle Ages seem to have been square or oblong in plan. As they were becoming integrated into the main building, as at South Wingfield (1440–59),[32] this would be a convenient shape. But they might still be of tower form and almost detached, such as the magnificent stone kitchen remaining at Stanton Harcourt (Oxfordshire),[35] built in the reign of Edward IV; this is 25 feet square, but has squinch arches to support an octagonal timber roof (Pl. 20 A). At Gainsborough Old Hall,[36] *c.* 1480 (Pl. XXXIX D), the great square kitchen is of brick, projecting west at the end of the main range, and connected to the timber hall by a servery portion and passage between butteries. Of special interest are the scullions' rooms in three corners, each with another chamber above.

A position in line beyond the butteries had now become the normal site for the kitchen, and in 15th-century manor houses the great fireplace is placed in the end wall of the range. At Preston Plucknett [29] this arch can still be seen, blocked by a modern grate, with the

fine louver-like chimney above; there is another arch, probably once a fireplace, in the adjoining wall. A similar chimney remains at West Coker,[34] and here the great fireplace is still open, the upper part of the flue large enough to form a modern bathroom. This kitchen seems to have opened direct from the screens passage, but at Ashbury Manor [37] it is reached by the traditional passage between butteries.

The final development, continuing into the 16th century, was to place the kitchen in an extension of the butteries at right angles to the hall block, forming an L-plan. It was reached through a side door from the butteries, as at Hams Barton (Devon), or, more usually, had access from the back entrance of the hall, as at Woodlands Manor and Corpus Christi College, Oxford.[28] At South Wraxall the kitchen door adjoins the hall doorway at right angles, and the present covered way along this side of the back courtyard no doubt represents an original feature. Such an arrangement was probably more usual in the larger houses where a base court would have the food storage departments, brewhouse and bakery grouped around it. Bowhill [30] has a square kitchen (16 feet 6 inches $\times$ c. 14 feet) in a range parallel to the hall, their doorways facing across the court, the two blocks being joined at this entrance end by a long range containing parlour, butteries, and great and lesser chambers over.

At Martock [31] a 15th-century kitchen (21 $\times$ 16 feet) was added off the south-west angle of the solar buttery block, with a great fireplace occupying most of the west wall, and two opposite doorways near the other end.

Wolsey's and Henry VIII's kitchens at Hampton Court [40] are part of a main range, with great stack projections on to Tennis Court Lane, though reached from the great hall by a cloister and court. But about the same period the Cowdray kitchen [41] was constructed, of earlier type, perhaps a brick rebuild on a 14th-century plan. However, it has a feature unusual in the detached kind—a room above.

Some kitchens seem to have been placed under the hall. Certainly large fireplaces exist in this position at Aydon Castle (c. 1280+) and Meare Manor in the early 14th century, but these may have warmed a lower hall for retainers; at Aydon, indeed, a kitchen wing was added some fifty years later. Shute Barton in Devon [21] had the kitchen with great end fireplace below the hall in the late 14th century. In Warwick Castle, about that period, the kitchen seems to have been housed in a vaulted undercroft with a row of central pillars. At Ashby de la Zouch [16] the great oblong kitchen of c. 1350–1400 had a lofty vault of three bays in the tall ground storey and, in the 15th century at least, a chamber above; at this period all its windows were remodelled. It was connected by an underground passage to the cellar below the kitchen of the later 15th-century Hastings Tower. Thornbury Castle [39] had, besides the great kitchen, a privy kitchen with lodging over it for the cooks.

The original detachment, or near detachment, of the kitchen can be seen in mediaeval survivals at the universities. At Cambridge the Royal Commission has found evidence of three early kitchens, all square, one-storeyed and separate originally. That at Jesus College [8] dates from the 13th century, though much altered, and lies off the north-west of a first-floor hall of similar date, once the refectory of the nunnery of St Radegund. At Trinity Hall [18] the kitchen was built as part of a contract of 1374, and that at Peterhouse [33] dates from the 15th century. Both are in line with the structural unit of hall and buttery, but definitely separated from the lower end of this by an enclosed space some 14 feet wide, perhaps a servery.

In Oxford six mediaeval kitchens remain, of one tall storey and mostly oblong in plan. With one exception (New College) they are not in line with the (present) hall. At Magdalen [11] the kitchen dates from the late 13th century, and seems to have been part of the Hospital of St John; it lies north-east of the 15th-century hall. The kitchen was part of the original late 14th-century work at New College [22] and is the eastern one-storey portion of an oblong block containing the buttery on the level of the first-floor hall west of it; access to this hall was by a staircase up to the screens. The kitchen is almost square at Lincoln College [27] and was built, like the hall, *c.* 1436–7, but lies north-east of it, originally detached. But at Corpus Christi [28] the kitchen is much nearer the buttery and makes a right angle with the 16th-century hall block, with access from the back doorway of the screens passage. Here, as at Brasenose, the kitchen antedates the rest of the college and formed part of the 15th-century Urban Hall. At Christ Church [42] the kitchen (1526) is nearly contemporary with Wolsey's Hall, and lies almost detached to the south of it, having a scullery of similar date beyond.

The siting of the fireplaces is of interest, and depended on the type of plan. Early wooden kitchens probably had a central hearth. In the square 13th-century kitchen at Lincoln there were five fireplaces: three in the angles, the south-west being the largest, and two lateral ones. At Glastonbury an internal octagon was formed by the four angle fireplaces. The hexagonal kitchens at Canterbury and Berkeley Castle had lateral fireplaces, wedge-shaped at the former; and there were four lateral fireplaces in the octagon at Durham, also a kiln for smoking bacon. The square kitchen at Raby had three great fireplaces originally, and Haddon and Dartington retain one large one in each of two adjoining walls; at St Mary's Guildhall, Coventry,[25] there are two, each 9 feet wide, on south and east. Two side by side, also 9 feet wide, were excavated in one wall of the square kitchen, dating probably from the late 14th century, at Sonning Palace, Berkshire.[20] Two fireplaces, adjoining at right angles, often occur, as in the oblong kitchens at Canford and South Wingfield (Pl. XXXIX A), but one large fireplace in the end wall is also found frequently, as at Shute Barton (*c.* 1380), West Coker, Martock, Bowhill, and in many smaller 15th-century houses. At Stanton Harcourt, which is square, instead of fireplace recesses there are screen walls some six feet high, and ovens in the opposite walls. But in another square building, at Durham Castle,[38] used by Bishop Fox (1494–1501) for his new kitchen, two great fireplaces face the buttery hatches, and there is another in the adjoining wall. The fireplaces are also in pairs at Hampton Court (Pl. XXXIX B), with most of their great stacks next to the service lane. But the Cowdray kitchen, of earlier type, has three lateral fireplaces instead of the more 'modern' twin ones.

A fireproof roof of stone was probably built where funds allowed. Superb 14th-century examples remain at Glastonbury and Durham Abbeys, and a rare earlier survival in France, at the Abbey of Fontevrault,[2] should be mentioned for comparison (Pl. 19). It also has a connection with this country, being built *c.* 1195 by a Queen of England, Eleanor of Aquitaine (d. 1204) and endowed by her daughter Joanna Plantagenet (d. 1199). Almost detached, it is of octagonal plan with five apses containing fireplaces, between which are buttresses with columns inside and out. The internal design is fully developed, suggesting many earlier experiments. The fireplaces have pointed arches carried on shafts with foliated capitals, and the larger columns in line with the buttresses face inwards. Four of these support wide pointed arches forming a square plan above, while four even taller columns, in the alternate angles, carry a short rib connected to the apex of each arch, and act as a buttress to it. Across every angle of the square is a squinch arch to form an octagonal base to the spire. Chimney shafts to the apses have been restored since Turner's illustration of *c.* 1851, and others added on the upper line of the buttresses, forming a cluster round the steep upper pyramid, which is completed by an octagonal ventilator, with trefoil-headed apertures, perhaps renewed in the 14th century.

The Glastonbury kitchen [14] is simpler in plan. From each angle of the internal octagon there rises an arched rib, these meeting in a circle to support a central cylindrical shaft, constructed within an outer octagonal casing, both pierced by apertures. This arrangement may be due to structural reasons, but, as Mr Shuffrey pointed out, the cylinder being thus protected from outer air and wind would be a more efficient ventilator. The main smoke from the angle fireplaces would escape from individual chimneys, now destroyed, and the restored shafts at Fontevrault give some idea of how the Glastonbury kitchen looked when complete. However, instead of two, the Glastonbury roof is in three stages, divided by a greater and a lesser lantern (Pl. XXXIX c), represented by the outer and inner ducts. The result is an octagonal truncated pyramid and lantern, crenellated with trefoil-headed vents, both repeated on a smaller scale with slight variations under the final pyramidal cap.

At Durham [17] the vaulting is more complicated. Again the plan is an octagon, with arched ribs, here two from each angle as well as pointed wall ribs. But now they span the space, intersecting, to form a stellar vault with central octagonal opening for the louver.

Raby kitchen [19] also has a massive stone vault, and a louver in the form of a turret, square and containing a loftier octagon, both crenellated.

Timber roofs were built in somewhat similar form. Lincoln Palace seems to have had an octagonal pyramidal roof of timber covered with lead, and there may have been something similar at Chichester, where longitudinal and transverse trusses form a square roof plan, springing from trussed brackets of hammerbeam form across the angles of the room; a central gabled louver can be seen outside, but is ceiled off within. Kersey is a simpler example. St Mary's Guildhall, Coventry, preserves its kitchen louver.

At Stanton Harcourt [35] the square interior has squinch arches of stone across the angles to form an octagonal plan at roof level. From the springing of these arches there rise eight wooden arched ribs meeting at the apex. Instead of a central louver there are, in the vertical portion of the roof, between the wooden spandrels of the ribs, two rows of six pointed vents in each bay. These could be regulated from an alure or passage behind the battlements, reached by a newel staircase at the north-west angle. There are three tiers of pointed wind-braces, and wooden traceried spandrels to the squinch arches and to the timber ones adjoining (Pl. 20 A).

In many later kitchens, which are square or oblong, the roof is not of specialist type, but conforms more to the kind used in other contemporary buildings. Arch-braced collar-beam roofs are used at New College, Lincoln, and Corpus Christi Colleges, and arch-braced tie-beams at Christ Church and Hampton Court. Now great external chimney stacks served the fireplaces, and a central louver was no longer necessary.

The windows could be traceried, as at Glastonbury, and were often set high above the fireplace level, as at Durham [17] and Ashby de la Zouch. At Wardour they are tall and narrow.[24]

Serving hatches still exist at Durham Castle [38] and Hampton Court, and one with the remains of a stone table in it at Ashby de la Zouch, where there is also a serving-room off the south-east angle, with steps down to a cellar and garderobes fitted ingeniously into the chimney stacks. The Merchant Taylors' kitchen in London [26] (37 feet 6 inches square), rebuilt *c.* 1425–32, is entered by three four-centred arches.

KITCHEN EXAMPLES

12TH CENTURY

		References (usually with plan)
(1)	Monastic kitchen at Ely	
(2) *c.* 1195	Abbey of Fontevrault, France	A. Kelly (Cassell, 1952), *Eleanor of Aquitaine and the Four Kings*, XII; Turner (1851), 272 (external view, plan & section).

13TH CENTURY

(3) *c.* 1224	Lincoln Palace	E. I. Abell & J. D. Chambers (1949), *The Story of Lincoln*, 65; plan reproduced in Wood (1951 a), 274.
(4) 1244 & earlier	Clarendon Palace, Wilts., 2 excavated	Borenius & Charlton (1936), 74–5, pl. XVI.
(5) remodelled C 13th	Farnham Castle, Sy.	*V.C.H. Surrey*, II, 616; plan reproduced in A. G. Wade (1956), *Farnham Castle*, 37.
(6)	Kersey Priory, Suff.	To be published by P. G. M. Dickinson in *Suffolk Archaeology*.
(7)	Bishop's Palace, Chichester	*Archaeological Journal* (1935), XCII, 390 & plan.
(8)	Jesus College, Cambridge	R.C.H.M. *Cambridge*, LXXXI.
(9)	Furness Abbey, Lancs., excavated	M.O.W. Guide (S. J. Garton) (1957).
(10) 1287–91	St Augustine's Abbey, Canterbury, excavated	M.O.W. Guide (Sir A. Clapham) (1955), 22.
(11) late C 13th or 14th	Magdalen College, Oxford	R.C.H.M. *Oxford*, 74 & plan.

14TH CENTURY

(12) early C 14th	Haddon Hall, Derbys.	*Country Life* (10), 1745, figs. 6, 7, 11.
(13) *c.* 1326–61	Berkeley Castle, Glos.	Parker (1859), 255.
(14) mid C 14th	Abbot's Kitchen, Glastonbury	Pugin (1839), 50, pls. 61–4; *Archaeological Journal* (1930), LXXXVII, pl. X.
(15) mid C 14th	'John of Gaunt's Kitchen', Canford Manor (School), Dor.	R.C.H.M. *Dorset*, II.
(16) *c.* 1350–1400 & later	Ashby de la Zouch Castle, Leics.	M.O.W. Guide (2), 12–13 & plan.

14TH CENTURY: continued		References (usually with plan)
(17) 1366–71	Monastic kitchen, Durham	Pantin (1948), pl. 26; Parker (1853), 120.
(18) 1374	Trinity Hall, Cambridge	R.C.H.M. *Cambridge*, LXXXI.
(19) *c.* 1378	Raby Castle, Durham.	Parker (1853), 208; O. S. Scott (revised Harrison) (1953), *Raby, its Castle and its Lords*, 12.
(20) late C 14th	Sonning Palace, Berks., excavated	Brakspear (1916), 17 & plan.
(21) *c.* 1380	Shute Barton, Devon	*Country Life* (25), 400.
(22) *c.* 1386	New College, Oxford	R.C.H.M. *Oxford*, 90 & plan.
(23) *c.* 1388–1400	Dartington Hall, Devon	A. Emery, *Archaeological Journal* (1958), CXV, 197–8.
(24) *c.* 1393	Wardour Castle, Wilts.	M.O.W. Guide in preparation.

15TH CENTURY

(25) *c.* 1414	St Mary's Guildhall, Coventry	Shuffrey (1912), 57, fig. 64; Parker (1859), 239–40.
(26) *c.* 1425–32	Merchant Taylors' Hall, London	R.C.H.M. *London*, IV, 34–6.
(27) *c.* 1436–7	Lincoln College, Oxford	R.C.H.M. *Oxford*, 63, 65.
(28)	Corpus Christi College, Oxford	R.C.H.M. *Oxford*, 49, 59.
(29) 1st half C 15th	'Abbey Farm', Preston Plucknett, Som.	
(30) 1st half C 15th	Bowhill, Exeter	Everett (1958 b), 204.
(31)	The Treasurer's House, Martock, Som.	
(32) 1440–59	South Wingfield Manor, Derbys.	Garner & Stratton (1929), fig. 6.
(33) 1450	Peterhouse, Cambridge	R.C.H.M. *Cambridge*, LXXXI, 161.
(34) after 1457	West Coker Manor, Som.	
(35) *c.* 1460–83	Stanton Harcourt, Oxon.	Parker (1859), 151.
(36) *c.* 1480	Gainsborough Old Hall, Lincs.	Brace (1954); Garner & Stratton (1929), 119.
(37) *c.* 1488	Ashbury Manor, Berks.	Pantin (1957), fig. 30.
(38) *c.* 1494–1501	Durham Castle	

16TH CENTURY

(39)	Thornbury Castle, Glos. 2	Pugin (1839), 31, pl. 37.
(40) 1514–29+	Hampton Court, Middx	R.C.H.M. *Middlesex*, 43–4, pls. 118–19 & plan.
(41) *c.* 1520–30	Cowdray, Suss.	Garner & Stratton (1929), 49, 53 (Grimm's drawing of 1786).
(42) 1526	Christ Church, Oxford	R.C.H.M. *Oxford*, 29 & plan.

Plate XXXIX. Kitchens.

A. South Wingfield Manor, *c.* 1440–59. B. Henry VIII's kitchen at Hampton Court, *c.* 1529–40.
C. Lantern roof, Abbot's Kitchen, Glastonbury, mid 14th century. D. Kitchen roof, Gainsborough Old Hall, *c.* 1480.

Plate XL.

A. Penshurst Place, interior of hall showing central hearth; *c.* 1341–9. B. Manor of the More, Hertfordshire, excavated central hearth, *c.* 1364. C. Clevedon Court, *c.* 1320; smoke-hole in soffit of east end window of hall. D. Model of 13th-century hall with louver and solar-service wing. E. 14th-century roof tile from Lincoln.

18

The Central Hearth

THE great hall, equivalent of two storeys in height, was heated until the end of our period by a central hearth, with an opening or louver in the roof for the escape of smoke. There is plenty of proof, documentary and archaeological, for such an arrangement; but later floors have obscured the evidence in most existing houses, this being obtainable only by excavation, for the central hearth was gradually superseded by the wall fireplace, and surface indications were removed. Surviving examples suggest that the change took place, on the whole, in the early 15th century. However, the evidence of an original hooded fireplace in the hall (*c.* 1300) at Goodrich Castle is supplemented by the 1321 document concerning a hall to be built at Hamsey (Sussex) with not one wall fireplace but two. At Crosby Hall (*c.* 1466) both forms of heating were used, apparently contemporary.

The central hearth was certainly usual in the aisled halls of the 13th century. Although Henry III had wall fireplaces elsewhere, he retained the doubtless earlier arrangement in his lofty halls. The hall floor at Clarendon Palace, probably of tiles, has completely gone, but documentary references to the louver show that a central hearth existed here, as also at Nottingham Castle hall and elsewhere.* The hearth would be placed conveniently below the high table and dais, and away from the service traffic at the lower end of the hall. Thus, although on the central line of the hall, it is usually nearer the upper end.

There are some instances of a central hearth at first-floor level where the hall, otherwise of lofty ground-floor type, is for some reason raised on a stone cellar. This is the case at the Hospital of St Cross and in Portchester Castle hall, built by Richard II just before his deposition (1399). As late as 1535 Henry VIII's great hall at Hampton Court had a central hearth raised on a pier of the undercroft. This pier is octagonal, partly embedded in a brick wall of similar date, and it shows four brick ribs on either side, branching out to support a square hearth, now renewed.†

* Borenius & Charlton (1936), 73; Liberate Roll, 35 & 36 Henry III (October & December 1251); Turner (1851), 234 (Clarendon), 235 (Nottingham).

† R.C.H.M. *Middlesex*, pl. 80.

Cases are known of a central hearth in a room other than the hall. In September 1248 the keeper of the manor of Woodstock is ordered 'to make a hearth [*astrum*] of free-stone, high and good, in the chamber above the wine cellar in the great court, and a great louver over the said hearth'.* There was one to the kitchen at Portchester (1396-9).

At ground level the earliest floor would be of rammed earth or chalk, except for a paved dais for the high table, and there would be a stone or tile surround confining the hearth. The shape of the latter could be square, circular or octagonal. Three hearths, superimposed, *c.* 5 feet 9 inches square, of tiles set on edge, have been discovered at the Old Deanery, Salisbury (*c.* 1258-74). At Stokesay Castle (*c.* 1285 +) the hearth is octagonal, formed of stone slabs, and there is a similar plan at Penshurst (*c.* 1341-9) with a hearth of tiles (quarries) within a low stone curb (Pl. XL A); the present andirons ('fire-dogs') are Tudor, but must represent an earlier arrangement for the support of logs. In the Abbot's Hall at Westminster the hearth was octagonal also, known from the sketch Jewitt made before its removal *c.* 1850 (Pl. 21 B).† At Padley Hall (Derbyshire) (*c.* 1350-1400) a circular hearth of stone has been uncovered.

In the excavations at the More in Hertfordshire, by Mr Martin Biddle and the Merchant Taylors' School, the hall floor showed the use and disuse of a series of central hearths, and one excellent survival. This is square in plan, of roof tiles set on edge, with a border of vertical tiles (Pl. XL B). It seems to date from the *c.* 1364 period of the manor house,‡ and may be compared with the contemporary hearth at Northolt Manor, which is 9 feet square and has the tiles set on edge in a diagonal pattern.§ The square form also occurs in the hall at St Cross, where it is of tiles slightly raised in a frame, and, also renewed, at Hampton Court.

Indirect evidence of the former presence of a central hearth is found in soot-blackened timbers where the roof is original, although these might also result from the use of torches for illumination.‖ But certain early roofs are remarkably clean, such as Baguley and Smithells Halls, and recent discoveries in Yorkshire have supplied the reason: in three of the timber aisled halls probably of the later 14th century found near Halifax evidence remains of a canopy over the central hearth. At Towngate, Sowerby Town, the cross-beam which carried the hood survives. It is connected by a central octagonal post to the main tie-beam of a roof of two bays, and has mortices for the raking struts of a timber-framed smoke hood. There is also evidence of such a cross-beam some eight feet above the floor at High Bentley, Shelf, and also at Scout Hall Farm in the Shibden Valley.¶ These canopies seem akin to the great funnels over a central fireplace, which still exist in Brittany.**

Nathaniel Lloyd gives an illustration of a flue of mediaeval type found at Marley Farm, Smarden, Kent. It is constructed of timber and clay 'pug' over an open fireplace in the

---

* Liberate Roll, 32 Henry III; Turner (1851), 217.
† Turner (1851), 49, 58.
‡ Biddle, Barfield & Millard (1959), 146, 148, pl. XIX A.
§ Hurst (1961), 215-16.
‖ As Mr Radford suggests in his M.O.W. Guide (41), 14.
¶ Information kindly provided by the authors before publication in Atkinson & McDowall (1967).
** Illustrated in P. Drobecq (1942), *La Cheminée dans l'habitation*, 119.

middle of the house. In 1931 it was still in daily use, and was swept like an ordinary chimney.* Another flue of timber posts and rails existed until recently at Darwen in Lancashire. The filling was intertwined branches like hurdles, coated with clay plaster locally called raddle and daub.†

There is further evidence of an ancient practice at Chithurst Abbey, Sussex, dating from the 16th century. Here two trusses form a narrow bay, plastered and covered with soot, which made a funnel or canopy to trap the smoke into a louver above.‡ Fireplaces with evidence of a plaster hood, as at Stokesay, also show this arrangement set back into a wall for safety against fire, and served by a stone chimney.

The Halifax halls also provide a clue to the reredos (from the French *l'arrière-dos*) mentioned in mediaeval and 16th-century manuscripts in connection with domestic build-ings. In the early 14th century an ordinance of the City of London forbade the placing of the reredos of the fire for cookery near partition walls of lath or boards because of the danger of conflagration.§ The term is, however, also found later in that century for the back of a fireplace not built against the wall, but set back into it. In 1397 at Portchester 'white tiles of Flaundres [were] bought in London for the reredoses of fireplaces' and cost eight shillings.‖ In the 16th century the term apparently was used for the open hearth in contrast to the wall fireplace. William Harrison, whose *Description of England* was published in 1577, stresses the modern increase in chimney construction, whereas in the old days 'each man made his fire against a reredosse in the hall, where he dined and dressed his meat'. This, as Mr Salzman points out and as we shall see from surviving examples, was true only as it concerned the lesser houses.¶ Thus while in churches the reredos meant the back of an altar, in houses it was the fireback, to which could be fixed a horizontal bar from which a cooking pot could be suspended. In the Shetlands a primitive backing to the central hearth can still be seen in the crofters' cottages.** Such a reredos survives at Town Gate, Sowerby; for below the site of the canopy is a blackened wall contemporary with it, and later heightened and provided with a chimney when a fireplace supplanted the original central hearth; the two periods of construction are clear. This wall backs on to the cross passage ('screens') in a way reminiscent of the end fireplace which replaces the older hearth in Monmouthshire houses.††

The central hearth, thus often called the reredos, remained in use in the college halls of Oxford and Cambridge until the 18th and 19th centuries. At Trinity College, Cambridge, there still remains the iron brazier bought in 1702–3 for £12 and discarded in 1866.‡‡ In 1754 Dr Johnson remarked to Boswell that 'in these halls the fireplace was anciently in the middle of the room, till the Whigs removed it to one side'.

In days before matches it was easier to keep the fire alight continuously, but this was not

* Lloyd (1931), fig. 559.
† Lloyd (1931), fig. 558.
‡ W. H. Godfrey (1930–1). A lead fret in Chithurst Abbey. *Sussex Notes and Queries*, III, 92.
§ *Liber Albus*, ed. H. T. Riley, 288; Salzman (1952), 99.
‖ Exchequer, King's Remembrancer Accounts, 479, 23; Salzman (1952), 141.
¶ Salzman (1952), 97.
** Shuffrey (1912), figs. 10, 11.
†† Fox & Raglan (1951), 31–4, 45–6.
‡‡ R.C.H.M. *Cambridge*, CXXVII, 226, pl. 273.

a safe procedure in a central hearth at night without some protection. This was provided by the fire-cover or curfew (*couvre-feu*) placed on the fire at the ringing of a bell of that name (the curfew is still rung at 8 p.m. from St Mary's Church at Wallingford). Many of these covers would be of pottery, a circular lid with holes for ventilation, and examples of such colander-like objects survive. There is a good one dating from the 13th century in the Museum at Salisbury.*

* Hurst (1961), 265.

19

Fireplaces

ALTHOUGH the great hall was often heated by a central hearth, a method gradually displaced but persisting to the early 16th century, for a two-storeyed block the wall fireplace was used as early as the Norman period. A central hearth would have been inconvenient except in a lofty hall with room for the smoke to escape, unless a funnel was used, while on an upper level it would have been dangerous without a solid floor of stone except above a pier of the vaulted undercroft. However, a portable iron brazier may have been generally used for heating.

Just as the central hearth derives from the earliest type of fireplace which warmed the caves and huts of primitive man, so the wall fireplace was the next development where it was found useful to build the fire against a wall or shorter reredos, and thus enable a pot to be hung from a horizontal bar attached to the back. Then a funnel or hood was invented to collect and control the smoke, and the next stage was to set the hearth back into a stone wall, in which the funnel was incorporated.

The earliest Norman fireplaces were arched, such as the round-headed ones in the keeps at Colchester (*c.* 1090+),[1] Rochester (1126–39)[2] and Castle Hedingham (*c.* 1130),[3] while at King John's House, Southampton (*c.* 1150)[4] (Pl. XLI A) springers remain to show that the head was segmental, a shape used in the two warming-house fireplaces, of the end of the 12th century, at Rievaulx Abbey.[6] Chevron was a favourite ornament for the arch; it is combined with mouldings at Rochester, and doubled at Hedingham. The supporting jamb-shafts had cushion or scalloped capitals, which also survive at Hemingford Grey (*c.* 1150)[5] and King John's House. The semicircular plan is usual, and the fireplace might be set in a slight projection, the walls being also thickened by means of an external buttress which supported the chimney. At Hedingham the cone-shaped flue discharged through two rectangular openings (now closed) like the vents at Colchester and Canterbury keeps.

Towards the end of the 12th century the hooded fireplace appears, an improvement for

261

the discharge of smoke, the hood projecting into the room and allowing for a shallower recess. It has been shown * that the two earliest known examples of a hooded fireplace, at Conisborough keep (c. 1185) [7] in Yorkshire (Pl. XLI D), occur where the circular plan of the room made an arched fireplace difficult to construct. Here a lintel was formed along a chord of the circumference, and the resulting filling above assumed a hooded form.

The hooded fireplace is the predominant type of the 13th century, and continued in fashion, gathering refinement, into the early 14th century. The hood, pyramidal in shape, has a moulded string-course and rests on a joggled lintel, the stones thus stepped to prevent slipping. At Conisborough these are supported by triple clustered shafts, but corbels often occur, as in the fine example, c. 1200, at Boothby Pagnell,[8] the hood here vertical but sloping back near its summit (Pl. XLI B). At Lodsworth Manor Farm [9] in Sussex the sturdy hood rests on bold double-curved corbels, and these are also double, but concave, in the elegant fireplace in the Salt Tower (c. 1230–40) [10] in the Tower of London, where the hood most nearly approaches a pyramid. The hood at Luddesdown Court in (Kent) [11] seems to have been rebuilt, but the joggled lintel places it among the earlier examples.

At Shrewsbury in 1957 a remarkable fireplace was discovered, at first-floor level, in Bennett's Hall (the Old Mint) behind 2 Pride Hill.[14] The hood was exceptionally tall, tapering into a chimney in the mid wall; it was of wood or plaster, with stone frame, top and jamb-shafts, of which the beautifully carved capitals suggest a date 1250–60 (Pl. VII D). It was probably designed for a wealthy merchant, and is a revelation of what exquisite workmanship there must have been in the fireplaces of the rich, from King Henry III downwards, which have entirely disappeared.

Hoods or mantels of plaster must have been greatly used, and the shape of one can be seen in the warming-house of Beaulieu Abbey. At Stokesay (North Tower) [22] the pyramidal recess for it remains, and there are holes for attachment at the summit, and a moulded wooden lintel; the double convex corbels, however, are of stone, as are the shafts beneath, with fillets and moulded capitals.

In stone hoods, after the joggled construction the next step was to have a large central stone to the lintel, joggled only at the ends, and this was probably the case in the hoods of Abingdon [15] and Netley Abbeys,[16] in the checker and infirmary respectively. These must have been magnificent examples. Of the checker hood only the shape is left, but engaged octagonal shafts, with stiff leaf capitals, and the ends of the elaborate lintel remain. More of the hood survives at Netley, with concave corbels and shafts with moulded capitals. Both hoods, like that at Boothby Pagnell, have a crest moulding, and Netley retains lamp brackets, one of the earliest surviving examples. A date of c. 1260 is suggested for these fireplaces.

There are moulded lamp brackets to a stone hooded fireplace in the Jury Room at St Briavels Castle (Gloucestershire).[12] This has been assigned to the royal work of c. 1276,

---

* Shuffrey (1912), 16. In his M.O.W. Guide (31) Mr Ralegh Radford suggested that the curved hood to the hall fireplace in the 'keep' at Ogmore (Glamorgan) might be earlier, the heavy cubical capitals of the columns supporting it indicating a date in the early 12th century. But in his recent survey Mr D. F. Renn considers that the upper portion of the building, with its ashlar detail, is a later addition, the multiple smoke-holes of the hooded chimney, like those of Portchester, suggesting the late 12th century (The Anglo-Norman Keep, *Journal of the British Archaeological Association* (1960), 3rd S., XXIII, 15). New research, however, shows that Portchester was built c. 1135.

but the stiff-stalk capitals with small leaves suggest a date of c. 1240.* The triple shafts used below these single capitals obviously do not belong to them, being 13th-century work re-used from elsewhere. The fireplace has a chimney crowned by the Constable's Horn, moved from elsewhere in the castle.

On the whole, corbels rather than shafting are used to support the hood in later work, as in the fireplace c. 1279 at the Byward Tower, Tower of London.[18] At West Dean Rectory (c. 1270–80) [17] the hood is of chalk, with roll-moulded string-course, lintel and corbels. In Conway Castle (1283–7) [21] the hall has two fireplaces, but the south one had its hood rebuilt to rise vertically, in the 14th century. The west end one is still pyramidal and elaborate with mouldings. The Dewsbury Moot Hall (c. 1290) [23] had a restored hood of which the tapering corbels appeared to be original.

But the most elaborate late 13th-century fireplaces occur at Aydon Castle (c. 1280) [20] (Pl. 20 B), where there are three excellent and unusual examples. In the Lower Hall a great block of stone forms the lintel, with scroll-moulded string-course and curved (convex) corbels. In the solar basement the fireplace has another large block, ogee corbels, but the hood almost concealed by an elaborate cornice carved with a row of heads, and dog-tooth with foliage on the lower chamfer. In the solar the hood is of curved form, without a string-course, the lintel one with the hood, supported on curved and moulded (convex) corbels and jamb-shafts with moulded capitals.

Angle Brackets

The second half of the 13th century sees the development of angle brackets—moulded shelves which served as stands for lights but had a structural function in that, cut out of the side stones supporting the hood, their added weight helped to tie it into the walls, as any side movement would cause the collapse of the front.† We have seen examples of c. 1260 at Netley. An early one associated with lancet windows exists in the infirmary, later abbot's lodging, at Furness Abbey (Lancashire); it is moulded and adjoins the remains of a massive corbel once supporting a hood. There are two at St Briavels, and a plain one at Aydon (Lower Hall). At Conway,[21] in the western fireplace of the hall, the angle brackets are elaborately moulded as a projecting end of the lintel (now dropped), the string-course of which they shared, whereas in earlier examples they are below the latter. In the southern fireplace the corbels taper in a manner resembling that at Dewsbury.

These brackets are a normal feature of early 14th-century fireplaces. In the great chamber at Ludlow (c. 1320) [28] they have carved heads below the circular abacus, while the contemporary hood in the Southampton Undercroft [29] has ball-flower ornament, under a moulded capital, which shares the scroll-and-beaded string-course of the lintel (Pl. XLI C). At Meare Manor House (1322–35),[33], as at Michelham Priory, Sussex,[30] the moulded brackets are sited midway between string-course and corbel. In the elaborate Prior Crauden's fireplace (c. 1325) [35] at Ely, the carved bracket shares the mouldings and crenellation of the corbel and not the string-course (Pls. VII E & XLI F).

---

* The opinion of Dr P. Wynn-Reeves (Tudor-Craig), F.S.A.
† Shuffrey (1912), 21.

Fig. 76. Early 14th-century fireplace at the Old Deanery, Lincoln.

The brackets may be the *canstykes* to which reference is made, with the fireplace, in mediaeval documents.* A list of 1361 concerning Leeds Castle gives the separate parts of the 'apparelling' or framework of a 14th-century fireplace. There is the *linthel* of 9 feet (mantel-stone), two great *coygnestons* (angle-stones), six corbels, *scheu* (stone cut with a bevel), *lermer* (projecting moulding) and *parpaynassheler* (stones worked on two parallel faces) for the hood, and three *chapitrelles* (? central and angle light brackets) as well as *tuell* (flues).†

In the early 14th century the hoods persist. There is one in five of the tower chambers at Goodrich Castle (Herefordshire) [25] and evidence in the great hall; the corbel shafts die into the jambs, and in several the top and sides of the stone hood are in position. The hood is complete at Bampton Castle [27] (licensed in 1315); it has a large block for lintel, secured by joggled end stones; there is a scroll-moulded string-course, and double curved corbels, the upper with a 'T' ending to the fillet resembling that used at Luddesdown and Byward Tower in the previous century. More pyramidal is the Old Deanery fireplace at Lincoln [26] (Fig. 76), of which the narrow head of the hood, as at Shrewsbury, may have served as chimney; here the lintel of one large stone is supported on double ogee-curved corbels. The Ludlow (Great Chamber) and Southampton hoods (*c.* 1320) are much lower, the latter a very perfect example except for the lintel, which has been cut about. At Ludlow [28] the centre of the hood and lintel have fallen, but the wave-moulded jambs and angle-brackets, and four tiers of curved corbels to support the hearth remain. The fireplace on the next floor is more complete, a great hood, rather flat, with scroll-moulded string-course, massive lintel, and roll-and-fillet mouldings to the jambs. To this group belongs the prior's fireplace at Michelham,[30] with its wide hood and scroll-moulded string; the corner-stones of the lintel are again supported by corbels formed by the swelling-out of moulded jambs. A low hood, of similar date, restored with fine head carvings, is found at Southwick Manor, Northamptonshire.[31]

At Edlingham Castle (Northumberland) [32] (Fig. 77) the low hood has a great scallop-joggled lintel, and head carvings in the corbels with roll-and-fillet moulded jambs. But perhaps the most beautiful of the hoods remains in the Manor House at Meare [33] (Pl. XLI E).

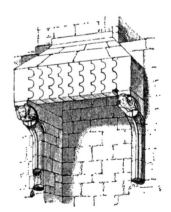

Fig. 77. Early 14th-century fireplace at Edlingham Castle.

* e.g. 1511 at Great Sherston Church House, Wiltshire; Salzman (1952), 101, 561.
† Salzman (1952), 101.

Here the tall slender hood is ridged, semi-octagonal, with scroll-and-bead mouldings in the string-course and partly joggled lintel; the jambs swell to a 'T' corbel as at Luddesdown, and there are angle brackets. This fireplace of Abbot Adam of Sodbury compares favourably with that of Prior Crauden at Ely,[35] where the jambs swell out to carved corbels which, like the moulded brackets and lintel, are battlemented, as are the traceried angle-shafts; the latter stand on the corbels and flank the lintel, a new feature reminiscent of continental work.

The second half of the 14th century shows no remaining examples of the pyramidal hood, which seems to have passed out of fashion in England, remaining much longer in France. The arched fireplace of the 12th century had no doubt persisted alongside the fashionable hoods, being used in the kitchens at Markenfield[104] and Meare,[33] and there is a similar one on the ground floor of the Angel and Royal at Grantham.[105] We have isolated examples in living-rooms earlier, such as the segmental-headed fireplaces in the solar and south tower at Stokesay,[22] * and the segmental-pointed ones in Clifford's Tower at York (1245–62+)[13].

A number of late 14th-century buildings show us the arched type. The segmental head is used at Strickland Roger,[37] Amberley[39] and Bodiam Castles,[41] one at the last being joggled. It also appears moulded in the early 15th-century hall at Woodlands Manor,[44] and cut in a great stone, part of the late hood with double convex corbels, at Kirkham House in Paignton.[45] The square head, moulded, also appears at Nunney (1373)[38] and Donnington[42] Castles; at the latter some have a large block of stone above the lintel or as part of it. All these fireplaces are built with a relieving arch above, triangular at Nunney, segmental elsewhere.

The shouldered lintel, or 'Caernarvon arch', had appeared in doorways towards the end of the 13th century, and was sometimes used in fireplaces, judging from a survivor at Woodstock (c. 1290)[24] with scroll-moulded mantelpiece; and a double-shouldered form in the solar undercroft at Charney Basset (c. 1280).[19] Now it appears in the hall (c. 1340) at Brinsop Court,[36] moulded, and there is an angular version at the Fish House, Meare (c. 1322–35).[34] At Kenilworth (1390–3)[43] the spandrels of the shoulders are pierced, and the jambs splayed to a traceried panel. John of Gaunt would have the latest fashion here, and a fireplace at Burford (Red Lion House)[69] (Pl. XLII D) shows that this form persisted into the 15th century, the quatrefoil frieze on the lintel suggesting a date after c. 1466. A fireplace from Wanswell Court (c. 1450–60),[53] now at Berkeley Castle, comes in this group; it has a trefoil-headed splayed panel, this time on the jambs of a depressed or three-centred arch. Such trefoiled panels are found in the Parliament House at Gloucester,[64] and at Fawsley Manor[100] later.

A favourite type in the 15th century for the plainer fireplace was what might be called the 'shouldered hood'. Here the great oblong hood and lintel were combined, usually rising straight up, like the rebuilt south fireplace to the hall at Conway.[21] This was supported on curved corbels, the swelling of the jambs into 'elbows' not unlike the swollen jambs of certain 13th-century fireplaces, such as that at West Dean. Four examples at Bolton Castle,[40] dating from around the contract of 1378, already show this new form of hood.

* Professor Cordingley believed that these replaced the hooded type.

As before, the great central block of the lintel is joggled into the angle stones. In one the head is straight, in two others there is a flat arch curving at the ends to give a shouldered effect with the corbels. There is a moulded string-course, segmental rear arch, and lamp brackets which are an integral part of the structure, forming an extra order to jamb and corbel. A plainer example, in the priest's room off the chapel, is more akin to the 'elbow' fireplaces of the 15th century; again the great oblong stone of the lintel is joggled into the elbow pieces. A shouldered lintel is produced where the corbels curve in as well as outwards, as at the Bird Cage Inn at Thame,[63] where the great hood rises vertically and then slopes back, a 15th-century example.

At Vale Crucis Abbey (Denbighshire) [75] there are two examples of the 'elbow-corbelled' hood, a plain one from the abbot's *camera*, now reset in the attic, and in his hall, part of the old dorter, another late 15th-century fireplace, with head moulded with the elbow corbels and jambs, and the lintel extending beyond them, in one large stone, to be joggled into the angle pieces. A similar example, without the side extension, can be seen at the Red Lion House, Burford (Pl. XLII A).[69]

The four-centred arch is used in the Long Gallery at Abingdon Abbey [76] supported by curved 'elbows', also moulded, which give it a shouldered effect. The arch has sunk spandrels in a square head, and with the lintel is formed from two large pieces of stone. At Ludlow Castle [77] there is another 15th-century fireplace similar in form, with a relieving arch above, and over the great lintel which forms the remnant of the hood is a mantelshelf, a new feature except for the Woodstock example earlier. In the 15th-century fireplace added to the hall at Cobham College[78] the shelf is more an integral part of the composition, and the four-centred arch still has a shouldered effect, here with 'double-elbowed' corbels. The same type of opening, but moulded with a single elbow, without spandrels, is found in a fireplace of *c.* 1500 at Muchelney Abbey; [93] the shelf surmounts a great lintel in which the arch is cut.

In the priest's house [95] near by the fireplace has a longer lintel (9 feet 6 inches × 2 feet 10 inches) and moulded shelf; the head is square, moulded with the jambs and corbels, the latter hardly projecting at all, a typological vestige only, and bearing out Mr Pantin's view that the fireplace is probably a later insertion, perhaps of the 16th century.

However, the 'elbow type' fireplace persists longer; one at Marcham Priory, Berkshire,[101] is associated with a classical cornice not earlier than 1570, and a central stack. Some of the finest examples occur in Plas Mawr at Conway (1576–80).[102] These have stone lintels with moulded soffit, the jambs corbelled out and extended as pilasters to support the moulded shelf or cornice, projecting at the ends, and in one case with a central projection also. The conical angle brackets are quite separate from the main design.

The four-centred arch, coming into fashion in the late 14th century, was the dominant type of the 15th century. It was a favourite shape for the fireplace, giving the necessary width with opportunity for decoration in the spandrels, and remained popular, somewhat flattened, well into the 17th century. There are four magnificent examples at Tattershall Castle (1433–43) [47] which, but for the speedy action of Lord Curzon in 1912, were nearly lost to us; they had already been removed for shipment to America. The moulded stone arch, in its square frame with carved spandrels, is surmounted by an elaborate frieze of traceried panels or circles with heraldic devices, crowned by a moulded cornice with *paterae* and crenellated top, the whole composition contained within flanking columns, the capitals continuing the decoration of the cornice. The ground-floor fireplace differs somewhat in its central ogee *motif*, which rises to a finial at the level of the cornice, against a background of heraldic shields in two courses. All have segmental relieving arches in brick. South Wingfield Manor [48] was built slightly later (*c.* 1440–58) for the same man, Ralph Lord Cromwell, though he died in 1456, shortly before its completion. In his great chamber is an elegant, less elaborate fireplace of the same four-centred form, but rather flatter, with moulded jambs and head, the latter formed out of two large stones, with a segmental relieving arch above (Pl. XLIII A). The plain chamfered fireplace in the hall at Preston Plucknett [46] is of similar date.

Where a cornice was present flanking columns were usual, sharing the same mouldings in their capitals. This is found at Ockwells Manor (*c.* 1465),[58] where the arch has plain spandrels and the frieze was perhaps once painted; at Church House, Salisbury (hall fireplace); [65] and at the Glastonbury Tribunal,[96] where the arch is simply chamfered. In the solar fireplace at Preston Plucknett (before 1438) [46] two shorter shafts divide off the central panel in addition. But the shafts seem to have gone out of fashion in the later 15th century. There are none in the solar fireplace at Gifford's Hall, Wickhambrook (Suffolk),[82] where the cornice is crenellated, with *paterae* in the moulding as in that of the four-centred opening. At Fawsley Manor (1537–42) [100] the columns are merely represented by small turrets on the frieze, panelled and crenellated like the central projection.

The square frame confining the four-centred arch was most popular, with decoration, often foliage, in the spandrels. At Crosby Hall the fine wall fireplace (*c.* 1466) [59] has moulded bases to the jambs, but usually the mouldings are stopped several inches up the floor, and higher in the 16th and 17th centuries, sometimes some half way up. There is a good example of this kind at Sudeley Castle (Gloucestershire),[60] where the 'banqueting hall' ruins may date from *c.* 1469–78, and a similar fireplace with quatrefoils in the spandrels occurs at the Bede House, Lyddington (Rutland).[83]

The same arch, unframed, is cut out of one large stone at Ashbury Manor; [86] very like it are the fireplaces, again with relieving arch, at Tickenham (chamber block) (Pl.XLII C), [49] one at the Greyfriars, Worcester (*c.* 1480),[80] and another recently discovered in the gatehouse range at Taunton Castle.[79] But in the last, two large stones are used for the arch, and this example is of especial interest for the remains of painting found at the sides of the fireback, and which is apparently original.

Another type is the cambered head, a flat, almost triangular arch which may have developed from the four-centred, the corners being squared instead of rounded. The Chantry at Ilminster [81] has several examples (Pl. XLII B), and the type continued into the 16th century, with instances at Haughmond Abbey and one dating from as late as 1563–87 at Helmsley Castle.

The square-headed fireplace familiar in the late 14th century persisted throughout the 15th century. Often there are continuous mouldings to the jambs and head. There is a good example at Frampton Manor Farm, Gloucestershire,[50] with tracery above and carved flowers in the cornice. The type occurs in a number of fireplaces with quatrefoil frieze, such as the splendid one of John Halle at Salisbury (*c.* 1470+) [61] (Pl. XLII E) and at Bindon House, Axmouth,[73] where square tablet flowers are contained in the cavetto mouldings of the fireplace opening (Pl. XLII F).

An intermediate type, a straight head with rounded corners, is also found, as in the Crypt House at Burford,[70] while the depressed three-centred arch seems to have been fashionable in the mid 15th century, being used widely for fireplaces and other purposes in the House of Jacques Cœur (1443–53) at Bourges. It occurs in the fireplace from Wanswell Court,[53] dated from the head-dresses of the roof corbels to *c.* 1450–60, and in the Hastings Tower (*c.* 1474) at Ashby de la Zouch.[62] These two fireplaces are also akin in the traceried frieze to the lintel, ten trefoiled panels at Wanswell, with a moulded cornice with *paterae*, and nine cinquefoiled at Ashby, flanked by helmet and shield, with richly carved and crested cornice. A similar range of ten cinquefoiled panels remains at the Archbishop's Palace at Southwell,[54] but here over a four-centred arch with base stops and a crenellated cornice (Fig. 78). A square-headed fireplace with a frieze with eleven trefoiled panels has been uncovered at 26 East St Helen's, Abingdon; [87] these match the heads of the window lights (Pl. XXIX c), and date from the late 15th century.

Fig. 78. Mid 15th-century fireplace at the Archbishop's Palace, Southwell.

In the last third of the 15th century there was a great revival of the quatrefoil in ornament, and this continued until the 1530s. It is also found on tomb chests, and may have started *c.* 1466 with Sir John Crosby's hall at Bishopsgate,[59] doubtless built in the height of fashion, which is rich in quatrefoils especially in the cornice of the roof. In fireplaces the ornament was especially effective in the frieze, where the quatrefoil could contain *paterae*, or a shield associated with the owner.

An earlier, less definite quatrefoil had occurred, with other tracery, in the third-floor fireplace at Tattershall, and at Bridport Museum [56] a mantel is preserved showing quatrefoils bearing shields in reticulated tracery, with cinquefoiled panels below. Three quatrefoils, again of pointed type, are set in lozenges with traceried spandrels above a fireplace at Cerne Abbas.[57] Here, as in the cornice, there are *paterae*, not shields, in each panel, the central one containing the initials of Abbot John Vanne (1458–70). At Ashby de la Zouch the solar fireplace [51] has seven incised quatrefoils with shields and diaper pattern, akin to the bolder six-quatrefoiled mantel, reset, at East Meon Court House; [52] these may date from the first half of the 15th century.

The usual, bolder type can be seen at Red Lion House, Burford, [69] with five quatrefoils in circles, and a smaller one in each shoulder of the traceried jambs. In the Hall of John Halle [61] there are trefoiled panels to the jambs, the six quatrefoils have shields, merchant's mark and other ornaments, and are associated with flanking columns which are becoming supplementary roll-mouldings, matched by a central capital also supporting the cornice. Four plain quatrefoils, with shields and without circles, are used at Acacia House, Putson, near Hereford, [68] and seven quatrefoils in circles with *paterae* in Crypt House, Burford. [70] Similar friezes with six or seven quatrefoils adorn the fireplaces at Standlake (Oxfordshire) [71] and East Hendred (Berkshire) [72]; one Bindon fireplace [73] is in this group. At the Chantry at Trent, [90] a fireplace of *c.* 1500 has three quatrefoils, with shields and *paterae*, and there is a similar one at Church House, Salisbury, [65] with *paterae* only, and lancet panels between the quatrefoils. Later the quatrefoils may be sub-cusped as at Hooke Court (Dorset), *c.* 1500, [90] and the Almonry at Evesham. [92] At Thornbury Castle (1514–22) [94] there are six containing the Stafford knot and royal badges in the great hall, and another fireplace has armorial badges also studding the outer moulding.

The most sumptuous surviving fireplace of this date in England belongs to the abbot's parlour at Muchelney (Pl. XIII B). [93] The four quatrefoils are not only sub-cusped but have foliage in the foils as well, and above there is a frieze of vine ornament, with further decoration in the cavetto of the moulded cornice. This is terminated by coupled octagonal capitals, of which the roll-like shafts confine the square moulded fireplace, while above, further roll-mouldings act as a frame to a painting, now destroyed, or to a space for a heraldic tapestry, as possibly at Kenilworth, and with the figure of a lion at each upper angle. Abbot Broke's monogram in the window glass suggests that the room was made *c.* 1509–14,* and indeed the quatrefoils remain popular well into the 16th century, appearing, for instance, in the abbot's hall porch at Cerne Abbas (1497–1509) and the cloister balustrade at Forde Abbey (1521–39), Dorset.†

However, the quatrefoil frieze was not the only ornament used, though it was a very popular one. Sometimes the quatrefoil was combined with other *motifs*. At Salisbury the Church House [65] hall fireplace has shields and merchants' marks between the central and spandrel quatrefoils. Another flat-headed fireplace has a wide lintel on which a great two-centred arch follows the outer line of the jambs, and contains a large quatrefoil centred with a Tudor rose, and with a small one, also in a circle, at each side; the spandrels of this arch have a shield with tracery and there are central and angle shields to the moulded cornice. Indeed a cornice with shields seems to be a late 15th-century and early 16th-century feature. It occurs with a lettered ribbon scroll in the cornice added by Richard Pomeroy in Henry VIII's time above Suger's fireplace, this prior to 1489, in the Vicars' Hall at Wells. [88] A band of six fluted shields with a mid-rib, like an opened book, in square panels, half restored, has been reset over a fireplace at Bindon House. [73]

---

* The contemporary benches may be compared with the late mediaeval settle once at Combe St Nicholas (Pl. 32 B).
† R.C.H.M. *Dorset*, I, pls. 105, 185.

The ornamental arch is also found in a fireplace now in Taunton Museum. [66] It was used at Kingston Seymour, *c.* 1470-80 (Fig. 40, p. 106). In the Bishop's Palace at Wells (Pl. 21 c),[67] two kite-shaped panels, with a shield between, follow the lines of the four-centred arch. There is leaf carving in the spandrels so formed, below a frieze of quatrefoils set diagonally. The polygonal sides of the fireplace have tall trefoil-headed panels, and there is a crested cornice with tablet flower over a string of running ornament, foliage and fruit, similar to that of the fireplace arch.

A shield set against an octafoil, that is a quatrefoil with angle lobes in addition, was

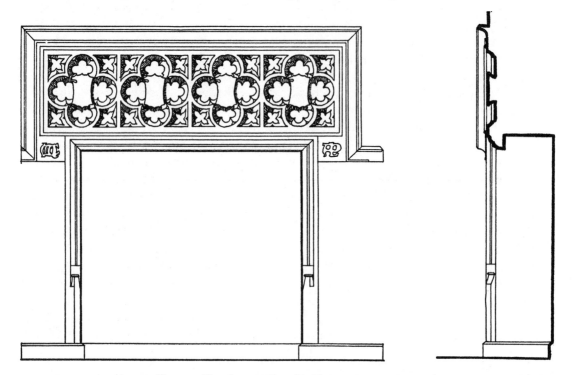

Fig. 79. Fireplace at Cannington Court, *c.* 1475.

another favourite panel treatment. There are three over a square fireplace recently discovered in the abbot's chamber at Meare. Another, now in Church House, Salisbury,[65] has four with a rectangular central figure, and a narrow trefoiled panel terminating the frieze. At West Coker Manor [55] the figure is heavily sub-cusped, the two central panels containing shields, the end ones elaborately traceried, and there are small quatrefoils in the spandrels of the four-centred fireplace arch. At Cannington Court,[74] also in Somerset, a fireplace has four square panels, each containing a fluted shield with spear rest, set in a cusped quatrefoil; there is a square label with out-turned ends and a monogram on each jamb (Fig. 79). In Lyddington Bede House [83] there is a frieze of five panels, three with plain shields in a quatrefoil set diagonally in a circle, and a wheel-traceried panel in between. At Carew Castle, Pembrokeshire,[84] a superb fireplace serves an upper chamber in the eastern range (Pl. XLIII B). This was inserted by Rhys ap Thomas, a great Welsh land-owner and supporter of Henry VII, and who bought the castle in 1480, holding a magnificent tournament there in 1507. The central panel contains the royal arms,* flanked by two rows of cinquefoiled panels, over a rectangular opening and under a cresting of tablet flower.

The fireplace as a vehicle for heraldic display is seen to perfection in the elaborate late example at Fawsley Manor.[100] Above a four-centred arch with splayed trefoiled panelled jambs there is a frieze of seven traceried panels, three of sub-cusped quatrefoils set diagonally and containing shields, the others slightly varied with square floral centres, and with a different design at the ends. Above is a string-course of running ornament, with an em-battled cornice of small trefoil-headed panels with miniature shields, and central and terminal projections, panelled and crenellated. Elsewhere many shields, now plain, were once painted.

Several magnificent fireplaces remain of the last years of our period. One of the finest is closely dated, being inserted in his palace at Exeter † by Bishop Peter Courtenay (1478–1487) [85] and bearing his arms (Pl. XLIII D). The opening is square-headed with tablet flowers in the cavetto, and the initials T between them in the head, T (*tau*) being the badge of the Hospital of St Anthony in London, of which Courtenay was Master. The roll-mouldings terminate in bases, the outer forming a tall shaft with capital, above which stands a shorter column with a rose-bush finial. Springing from the capital of the taller shaft is an elaborate curved frame forming a central ogee-headed panel, and three square ones below. The curves are adorned with tablet flowers, and the Tudor portcullis in the cavetto with a cresting of the former. They support a central corbel carved with rose-bush and portcullis, which bears the Royal Arms in a Garter, with arched crown and grey-hound supporters. The latter, a favourite device of Henry VII, and also associated with his queen, Elizabeth of York, together with the roses and portcullis badges, suggest a date for the fireplace of after 1485 and before 1487, when Courtenay was promoted to Win-chester, and probably 1486, the year of the royal marriage. The three square panels contain in a circle, from left to right, the arms of Courtenay on a fluted shield supported by collared swans; those of the see of Exeter impaling Courtenay within a circle of three dolphins; and Courtenay impaling Hungerford (his mother's family) with boar supporters. In the spandrels are the three-sickle device of the Hungerfords and the garb (corn sheaf) of the Peverells (to whom they were related). The upper ogee-headed panel includes the mitre and sword and keys of the bishopric.

Also closely related is another elaborate Exeter fireplace, given by John Coombe, pro-bably in 1496–9, to the Precentor's house, and now in the Deanery hall (Pl. XLIII C).[89] It has a shouldered head with two slender trefoil-headed panels on each splayed jamb. Above is a wide traceried lintel including two star-like patterns, each the backing for a painted shield. The central part, also cusped, is narrower, without a shield, and plain trefoil-headed panels flank the three divisions. The framing column on each side has a capital continued as a string-course with angel carvings. Above is a cresting of tablet flowers, with

* The same arms appear in three panels over the hall porch.
† A copy is in Powderham Castle, seat of the Courtenays, Earls of Devon.

crocketed spirelets over the columns. This fireplace is said to resemble that, almost completely destroyed, from the Hall of the Vicars Choral, also in Exeter, which was given by John Rise, precentor, in 1518, the ornament including his rebus, a 'birchy broom'.

This frame of mantel and jambs as apart from the chimney, the fireplace surrounds, was known as the *parel* (*pareille* or *enparell*). There is a reference to 'chemeneyes et pareys' (probably 'parels') at Hertford Castle in 1380; 'one enparell of Reigate stone' for Havering in 1440, 'parelles of chymneys redy wroght' for Hunsdon House in 1528, and at Westminster in 1532, 'viij parellis of chymneys' each contained 5 feet of stone.*

In the 16th century the actual fireplaces tend to become plainer, with more and more emphasis on the overmantel, which becomes a great vehicle for heraldic and other ornament, in stone or very often in wood, when it became an important feature of the panelled room so popular in the reigns of Elizabeth I and James I. The mediaeval type of cornice is thus replaced by a larger composition, and in time the Renaissance elements in the latter, particularly the heavy German and Flemish figures, translations of the classical caryatid, are continued down to the jambs of the fireplace also. However, the four-centred moulded arch, a convenient form, persists into the 17th century, now with mouldings stopped some half way up the jamb, and decoration of mediaeval type contained in the spandrels. Wolsey's fireplaces at Hampton Court [97] and others at Thame Park [98] (*c.* 1529–39) are examples, while at St James's Palace [99] a chimney-piece with the initials of Henry VIII and Anne Boleyn (*c.* 1533) still has a frieze of eight panels with quatrefoils set diagonally.

Kitchen Fireplaces

The earliest kitchen fireplace was probably a central hearth with iron grate (*caminum ferreum*), fireback (*reredos*) and louver, possibly with plaster hood, above. This is suggested by documentary evidence, and by the fact that the earliest surviving kitchens are square or hexagonal in plan. Actually a central fire must have been the safest position in a timber building. It may have been supplemented, and later replaced, by fireplaces in the angles or against the side walls of the building, and built against a stone reredos where the kitchen was of timber. This would be more convenient for service traffic, and the louver could become a ventilator. At Stanton Harcourt the 15th-century kitchen has screen walls dividing such fireplaces, but usually, where the kitchen, as here, was of stone, the fires would be placed in the wall thickness, and provided with arch and flue, as in the living-rooms of the house.

Such kitchen fireplaces seem to have been a plainer and wider version of those used in hall and chamber, the width necessary to catch the smoke. But there are few survivals of kitchen fireplace arches before the 14th century. The segmental arch, chamfered, is used at Haddon Hall,[103] Raby Castle,[107] Canford [109] and the probable kitchen fireplaces at Meare and in the Angel and Royal at Grantham; [105] the segmental-pointed arch with scroll-moulding is found in the abbot's kitchen at Glastonbury.[106] The Durham monastic

* References in Salzman (1952), 460, 101.

Plate XLI. Fireplaces.

A. King John's House, Southampton, *c.* 1150.
B. Boothby Pagnell, *c.* 1200.
C. The Undercroft, Southampton, *c.* 1320.
D. Conisborough Castle, *c.* 1190.
E. Prior Crauden's fireplace, Ely, *c.* 1325.
F. Meare Manor House, *c.* 1322–35, with lamp bracket.

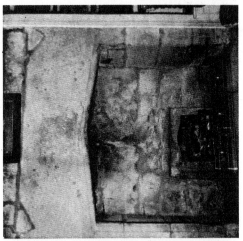

Plate XLII. 15th-century Fireplaces.

A. Red Lion House, Burford, after *c.* 1466. B. The Chantry, Ilminster, hall, *c.* 1480. C. Tickenham Court, parlour. D. Red Lion House, Burford, after *c.* 1466. E. Hall of John Hall Salisbury, *c.* 1470+. F. Bindon House, Axmouth.

kitchen fireplaces [108] (1366–71) have flat chamfered arches. At Shute Barton [110] there is a tremendous cambered arch 18 feet wide, 8 feet high and 6 feet 6 inches deep.

In the 15th century the four-centred arch is usual. There is a good example at South Wingfield,[111] adjoining a flat-arched fireplace, both of which have triangular relieving arches. The arch is segmental in the abbot's kitchen at Battle,[112] 10 feet wide, as is the four-centred fireplace, again with relieving arch, in the little attached kitchen at Martock.[114] At Bowhill [113] the arch, 11 feet 6 inches wide, has joggled voussoirs. There is a tendency to flatness, as in the kitchen fireplaces at Ashby de la Zouch.[115] The brick kitchen fireplaces (1494–1501) at Durham Castle [116] have a crenellated breastwork.

The four-centred arch continued into the 16th century, and there are splendid examples in the great kitchens of Hampton Court.[117]

FIREPLACE EXAMPLES

11TH CENTURY		
		References (mostly with illustrations)
(1) *c.* 1090+	Colchester Castle, Ess., keep	Toy (1953 b), 161, pl. 150 b (plan & section).
12TH CENTURY		
(2) 1126–39	Rochester Castle, Kent, keep	Lloyd (1931), fig. 761.
(3) *c.* 1130	Castle Hedingham, Ess., keep	R.C.H.M. *Essex*, I, 7; Shuffrey (1912), fig. 14.
(4) *c.* 1150	King John's House, Southampton, Hants	Wood (1935), pl. VIII A.
(5) *c.* 1150	Hemingford Grey Manor House, Hunts.	
(6) end C 12th	Rievaulx Abbey, Yorks., warming-house. 2	
(7) *c.* 1185–90	Conisborough Castle, Yorks., keep. 2	Shuffrey (1912), fig. 15.
13TH CENTURY		
(8) *c.* 1200	Boothby Pagnell Manor House, Lincs.	Wood (1935), pl. VIII B; Lloyd (1931), fig. 762.
(9) early C 13th	Lodsworth Manor Farm, Suss.	
(10) *c.* 1230–40	Salt Tower, Tower of London	Godfrey (1962), fig. 20.
(11)	Luddesdown Court, Kent	Wood (1950), pl. X c; Lloyd (1931), fig. 764.
(12) *c.* 1240+	St Briavels Castle, Glos.	*Archaeologia Cambrensis* (1858), 3rd S. IV, 386; A. Clark (1949), *The Castle of St Briavel's*, 11–12.
(13) 1245–62+	Clifford's Tower, York	
(14) *c.* 1250–60	Bennett's Hall (the Old Mint) behind 2 Pride Hill, Shrewsbury	R.C.H.M. (1963), *Monuments Threatened or Destroyed*, 55 (illus.).
(15) *c.* 1260	Abingdon Abbey, Berks., The Checker	Lloyd (1931), fig. 765; Shuffrey (1912), fig. 18.
(16) *c.* 1260	Netley Abbey, Hants., Infirmary	Shuffrey (1912), fig. 20.
(17) *c.* 1270–80	West Dean Rectory, Suss.	G. M. Cooper (1850). On an ancient Rectory House in the parish of West Dean. *Sussex Archaeological Collections*, III, 14.
(18) *c.* 1279	Byward Tower, Tower of London	Godfrey (1962), fig. 26.
(19) *c.* 1280	Charney Basset Manor House, Berks.	Wood (1950), pl. X B.
(20) *c.* 1280	Aydon Castle, Northumb. 3	Turner (1851), 148.

		References (mostly with illustrations)
(59) c. 1466	Crosby Hall, Bishopsgate, London (now at Chelsea)	Godfrey (1962), fig. 31.
(60) 1469–78	Sudeley Castle, Glos., hall	
(61) c. 1470+	Hall of John Halle, Salisbury	
(62) c. 1474	Ashby de la Zouch Castle, Hastings Tower	
(63)	Bird Cage Inn, Thame, Oxon., 2	
(64)	Parliament House, Gloucester	
(65)	Church House, Salisbury, hall, and several from elsewhere	R.C.H.M. Wilts; Shuffrey (1912), fig. 44.
(66)	Fireplace in Taunton Museum	
(67) late C 15th	Bishop's Palace, Wells	Garner & Stratton (1929), pl. CXCIX: Pugin (1839), 47, pl. 58.
(68) 2nd half C 15th	Acacia House, Putson, near Hereford	
(69)	Red Lion House, Burford, Oxon., 2	
(70)	Crypt House, Burford, 2	
(71)	House at Standlake, Oxon.	Long (1938), pl. III.
(72)	(East) Hendred House, Berks.	
(73)	Bindon House, Axmouth, Devon, 3	
(74) c. 1475	Cannington Court, Som.	Vivian-Neal (1959–60), 75, pl. 1.
(75) late C 15th	Vale Crucis Abbey, Denbighs., Abbot's hall and camera	
(76) late C 15th	Abingdon Abbey, Berks., long gallery, 2	Shuffrey (1912), fig. 21.
(77) late C 15th	Ludlow Castle, room over great chamber	Shuffrey (1912), fig. 49.
(78)	Cobham College, Kent, hall	Shuffrey (1912), fig. 32.
(79)	Taunton Castle, Som., gatehouse range	
(80) c. 1480	Greyfriars, Worcester	
(81) c. 1480	The Chantry, Ilminster, Som.	
(82) after 1480	Gifford's Hall, Wickhambrook, Suff.	Garner & Stratton (1929), 204, pl. CLXX.
(83) c. 1480–96	Bede House, Lyddington, Rut., 2	Shuffrey (1912), figs. 42, 43.
(84) 1480–1507	Carew Castle, Pembs.	
(85) c. 1486	Bishop's Palace, Exeter, Courtenay fireplace	
(86) c. 1488	Ashbury Manor, Berks.	
(87) late C 15th	26 East St Helen's, Abingdon, Berks.	Spokes (1960), 4, pl. II.
(88) 1489	Vicars' Close, Wells, Som., in hall	
(89) 1496–9	Deanery Hall, Exeter (from Precentor's House)	

16TH CENTURY

(90) c. 1500	The Chantry, Trent, Dor.	R.C.H.M. Dorset, I, pl. 46.
(91)	Hooke Court, Dor.	R.C.H.M. Dorset, I, pl. 46.
(92)	The Almonry, Evesham	
(93) c. 1509–14	Muchelney Abbey, Som., 2	
(94) c. 1514–22	Thornbury Castle, Glos., 2	Pugin (1839), 37, pls. 35, 42.
(95) early C 16th	Priest's House, Muchelney, Som.	Shuffrey (1912), fig. 75.
(96) early C 16th	The Tribunal, Glastonbury, Som.	
(97) c. 1525	Hampton Court, Middx, Wolsey's closet	Lloyd (1931), fig. 612.
(98) c. 1529–39	Thame Park, Abbot's Lodging	Lloyd (1931), fig. 613.
(99) c. 1533	St James's Palace, London	Garner & Stratton (1929), pl. CC.
(100) c. 1537–42	Fawsley Manor, Northants.	
(101) after 1570	Marcham Priory, Berks.	Spokes & Jope (1959), 91, pls. II, III.
(102) 1576–80	Plas Mawr, Conway, Caer.	R.C.H.M. Caernarvonshire, I, pls. 82–3.

KITCHEN FIREPLACES

		References (mostly with illustrations)
(103)	Haddon Hall, Derbys.	Country Life (10), 1744.
(104)	Markenfield Hall, Yorks.	
(105)	Angel and Royal Hotel, Grantham, Lincs.	
(106) c. 1320	Abbot's Kitchen, Glastonbury, Som.	Lloyd (1931), fig. 766.
(107)	Raby Castle, Dur.	
(108) 1366–71	Durham, monastic kitchen	Parker (1853), 120.
(109)	Canford Manor (School), Dor.	
(110)	Shute Barton, Devon	Country Life (25), 400.
(111)	South Wingfield Manor, Derbys., 2	
(112)	Battle Abbey, Suss.	Brakspear (1933 a), 160–1, fig. 7.
(113)	Bowhill, Exeter	
(114)	The Treasurer's House, Martock, Som.	
(115)	Ashby de la Zouch Castle, Leics.	
(116) 1494–1501	Durham Castle	
(117) early C 16th	Hampton Court, Middx	R.C.H.M. Middlesex, pls. 118–19.

20

The Louver

THE louver (from the French: *l'ouvert*) or smoke turret was a lantern-like structure placed on the roof over the central hearth, with side openings for the escape of smoke (Pl. XL D). Usually the apertures had louver boards, sloping slats to exclude rain and snow. These could be regulated, like our venetian blinds, and louver strings are mentioned in the documents: 'cord for the louver' at Marlborough (1238), Gloucester (1280) and Hadleigh Castle (1363), while 'louerstrynges for the kitchen' were bought for Clipstone in 1370. In the 14th century some louvers could revolve, in the manner of cowls, according to the direction of the wind. A building account of 1365 for Moor End contains the purchase of a block (*massa*) of bronze 'on which the louver of the hall may be turned round'; and another at Westminster records the payment (2s. 4d.) 'for a morteys of bronze weighing seven pounds for the louver of the small hall'.*

Lesser houses would have to be content with a simpler arrangement, a barrel with the ends knocked out, improvement on a mere hole in the roof. 'Barrell pro lovers' were bought at Hedon (Yorkshire) in 1443 and 1481, and at Cambridge a cask (*cado*) was purchased for a louver (*fumerale*) in 1415.†

There are many references to louvers in Henry III's palaces, with various Latinized forms of the word, many based on *fumus* (smoke). The correct term *lodium* was occasionally used. In September 1243 the keeper of the manor of Woodstock is ordered to make a great louver over the hearth in the chamber over the wine cellar, and 'two greater louvers [*lovaria*] in the queen's chamber' there. At Windsor Godfrey de Lister is told to have a louver (*fumatorium*) 'made in the hall to carry off the smoke' (July 1251), while that December the sheriff of Nottingham is commanded to 'make a certain great louver [*fumerium*] on the same hall and cover it with lead'. In April 1253 at Havering a louver (*fumerillum*) is to be made in the house of the king's chaplains.‡

---

* References in Salzman (1952), 220.
† Salzman (1952), 221.
‡ Liberate Roll, 32, 35, 36, 37 Henry III; Turner (1851), 217 (Woodstock), 231 (Windsor), 235 (Nottingham), 244 (Havering).

In 1292 at Langley Henry de Bouindon, carpenter, was paid twenty shillings *pro carpentria y fumerariorum in summitate aule*, and at Portchester lead from the Mendips was brought 'for covering the hall and kitchen and the two new louvers [*femerallorum*] over them'.* Other versions of the term are *fumerale* and *femural* (1363) and *femerelle* (c. 1470).

These projections gave an interesting profile to the roof for, as in other mediaeval necessities, trouble was taken to make them attractive. Thirteenth-century louvers are known

Fig. 80. Reconstruction of the timber louver at the Old Deanery, Salisbury.

from manuscript illustrations. A document of c. 1250 † shows one with two round-headed vents, and sheltered by a small roof with overhanging eaves. In the Old Deanery at Salisbury there is evidence in the roof of the louver position, and Mr Drinkwater of the Royal Commission has designed an attractive timber-framed louver based on one, of which pictures remain, at the Old Hall in the same city. It is four-sided and set square to the ridge, and has horizontal slats and a small roof (Fig. 80).

An octagonal plan was also convenient, as in chimneys. The Penshurst louver (c. 1341–9), now removed, was of this shape and had a trefoiled ogee-headed light with tracery on each face, and concave pyramidal capping or spirelet. The surviving louver at Lincoln College, Oxford (1437), is similar.‡

The present louver at Westminster Hall, copied exactly according to Parker, has a hexagonal plan. It is an elaborate structure resembling a tower, with crocketed spire and buttresses. There are two storeys of 'windows', each of two cinquefoil-headed lights with a lobed trefoil in a two-centred head, the upper storey having in addition a similar light below a transom, and a crocketed ogee head with finial (Pl. 21 A).§

Henry VIII's louver at Hampton Court has gone, but judging from the accounts it was a superb example, adorning the Great Hall and adding to its magnificence. The *fumerell* was hexagonal, of three storeys divided by 'courbes', having windows in each face, three lights on the first, two on the second level. Already its secondary function as a lantern was stressed, for of the eighteen lights on the lowest storey twelve were glazed. There was a domed top, and the exterior was lead covered, surrounded by four lions, four dragons and four greyhounds, carrying vanes, 'the great pryncipall vane baryng the close crowne' held by a great lion, crowned. Inside, Richard Rydge carved a crowned rose in the vault, and four pendants at its junction with the roof, which it matched in its decoration. All was painted and gilded outside and within.‖

* References in Salzman (1952), 221.
† Pierpoint Morgan MS. Facsimiles, reproduced in D. Hartley and M. M. Elliot (1925), *Life and Work of the People of England*, I, pl. 27. Batsford.
‡ The lights are cinquefoiled in the close-up drawing in Parker (1869), 143, but trefoiled in Shuffrey's illustration (1912, fig. 4), and according to the R.C.H.M. *Oxford*, 66. Can it be that the lower cusps have worn off ?
§ Parker (1853), 39.
‖ Salzman (1952), 219; Exchequer Treasury of Receipt, Miscellaneous Books, Hampton Court Accounts, Vol. 238, 160–2; E. Law (1929), *A Short History of Hampton Court*, I, Appendix C. Bell.

An idea of this magnificent erection may be obtained from Grimm's drawing of 1781, showing the almost contemporary hall at Cowdray with its louver. Here there were windows in four stages, a domed cap, and what appear to be heraldic beasts around, carrying gilded vanes, very much in the manner of Hampton Court.*

When their original use for a central hearth was no longer needed these roof embellishments were retained as lanterns, and fulfilled a definite need in a lofty hall with open roof. That at Horham Hall (c. 1502) is hexagonal with two tiers of four-centred lights, leaden spirelet and finial.†

Sometimes the lower frame of the louver remains, and is visible within. At Westminster the Abbot's Hall retains most of the framework, rectangular in plan with trefoil-headed openings, eight on the east and west, six cambered to north and south, below a gabled roof (Pl. 21 B).‡ At Eltham Palace (c. 1479–80) there is just the frame, elongated hexagonal, and at Exeter the Law Library roof retains an octagonal opening, now ceiled, which has all the appearance of an original louver; it now adjoins a partition wall.

Mr Dunning § has found examples of pottery louvers for fixing over the hole in the roof above a central hearth. One type is like a beehive some 14 to 20 inches in diameter, and some 12 to 16 inches high, with two rows of large holes, circular, triangular or rectangular, some with rims or flanges to serve as baffle plates. A good late 13th-century specimen has been found, with others, on the mediaeval town site of Stonar near Sandwich, and portions of an example, closely dated c. 1370–80, with triangular apertures and smoke stain, in the excavations at the More in Hertfordshire. The latter had trellis pattern ornament, and green glaze seems to have been usual. Another variety is taller and conical, of two stages, as found at Winchester.

These form a separate structure from the ridge tiles, and are made to fit on to them. But a second type is constructed in one piece with the ridge tile and is smaller, conical or ovoid, some 8 to 10 inches in diameter and 12 to 15 inches high (above the ridge). A remarkable example (c. 1300) of this second type was found in the 1961 excavations at Goosegate, Nottingham (Fig. 81). It is like a pagoda in green glaze, with three tiers of apertures having flanges and canopies to keep out the rain and deflect the wind. The canopies in the upper rows join to form a scalloped hood, and above three small columns once supported a three-lobed

Fig. 81. Pottery louver, c. 1300, from Goosegate, Nottingham.

* Garner & Stratton (1929), fig. 76.
† Garner & Stratton (1929), pl. LXXII.
‡ Parker (1859), 49.
§ I am greatly indebted to Mr G. C. Dunning, B.Sc., F.S.A., for the kind loan of this material, not yet published, part of his paper to the Society of Antiquaries on 15 January 1959.

cover which has been restored, together with a terminal spike, on the evidence of a louver found at Coventry.* Such pottery louvers seem to have appeared, in southern England, in the late 13th century, to become elaborated in the 14th century.

In 1363 four earthen pots were purchased for the *fumerell* of a barn at Hadleigh (Essex), and four for that of the king's hall at Rayleigh Park.†

* Dunning (1962).
† Salzman (1952), 100.

21

Chimneys

THE word chimney * (*caminum*) in mediaeval documents meant the whole heating structure including the fireplace. Here, however, we are concerned with 'chimney' in its modern sense of the flue outlet or shaft alone.

The earliest type of Norman chimney surviving is found in early 12th-century keeps. Here the smoke outlets are contrived in the side of a shallow buttress by means of oblong vents. At Castle Hedingham (*c.* 1130) the south buttress contains flues for fireplaces at two levels, and the contemporary keep at Rochester has a similar arrangement, as also London, Colchester and Canterbury earlier. The presence of two vents, one each side of a flat buttress, would enable the windward vent to be closed in heavy weather, the leeward one being thus assisted through the protection of the buttress to draw more efficiently. Only in later 12th-century keeps, such as Scarborough (1158–64), do the flues ascend vertically through the wall.† In houses they probably discharged under the eaves.

Circular draught holes running obliquely through the back wall are found in 12th-century fireplaces at the keeps of Tretower (Breconshire) and Ogmore in Glamorgan. At Ogmore the series of holes at the back of the flue are about a foot above the level of the chimney breast.‡ In the keep at Portchester (built *c.* 1135), on the first floor the north fireplace has a flue rising some 10 feet up the wall to a domed vault, and narrow slits in the wall let out the smoke.§ The angle kitchen at Castle Rising has a similar dome to a circular flue 5 feet 6 inches in diameter, and loophole vents.‖ This is like the larger one 8 feet 10 inches in diameter at Canterbury, rising 20 feet up, with loop outlets for the flues in the angle with the buttress.¶

By the middle of the 12th century the cylindrical chimney had appeared, and may have

---

* Or *cheminée* 'for the whole fireplace, hearth, mantel, flue and chimney, or any of its parts'. Salzman (1952), 98.
† Braun (1936), 29. See Toy (1953 b), 161, for plan and section at Colchester.
‡ M.O.W. Guide (31), 7.
§ M.O.W. Guide (34), 8; Toy (1953 b), 86.
‖ Toy (1953 b), 84. The flue over the dome is probably later.
¶ Toy (1953 b), 73–4 (plan).

281

been common in stone houses. The earliest surviving examples yet known are at Framlingham Castle [2] (Pl. XLIV B and C). Two chimneys serving the hall block of *c.* 1150–60 are incorporated in the late 12th-century curtain wall, and have round-headed lancet vents, Tudor brick extensions probably replacing a conical cap. At Christchurch Castle [3]

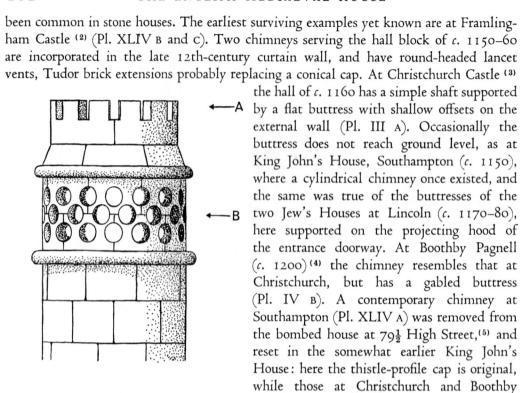

the hall of *c.* 1160 has a simple shaft supported by a flat buttress with shallow offsets on the external wall (Pl. III A). Occasionally the buttress does not reach ground level, as at King John's House, Southampton (*c.* 1150), where a cylindrical chimney once existed, and the same was true of the buttresses of the two Jew's Houses at Lincoln (*c.* 1170–80), here supported on the projecting hood of the entrance doorway. At Boothby Pagnell (*c.* 1200) [4] the chimney resembles that at Christchurch, but has a gabled buttress (Pl. IV B). A contemporary chimney at Southampton (Pl. XLIV A) was removed from the bombed house at 79½ High Street,[5] and reset in the somewhat earlier King John's House: here the thistle-profile cap is original, while those at Christchurch and Boothby Pagnell may be somewhat restored.

At the present stage of our knowledge we shall assume two types of 12th-century chimney shaft—the cylindrical chimney with open top, and that with side vents and conical capping.

It might be argued that the first type is a vestigial example of the second which has lost its conical cap. The edging at Christchurch may be restored, and this can be visualized with a lantern stage and conical cap as in the remarkable shaft called *La Lanterne des Morts* at Bayeux (Pl. I D). The same may have occurred at Boothby Pagnell, but at Southampton the High Street chimney preserves its original

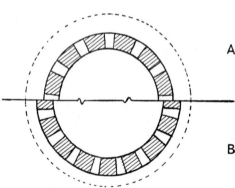

Fig. 82. Chimney at Skenfrith, probably of the second quarter of the 13th-century, a reconstruction.

thistle-like cap, splayed out over a waist-moulding, which makes a lantern cone unlikely here. At Framlingham we seem on firmer ground, with the four lancet vents in the circumference, and there is a striking resemblance to the late 13th-century chimney remaining at Aydon Castle [8] (Pl. XLIV G). Although the Aydon chimney is partly attached to a contemporary wall, it has similar vents above a string-course, though here the lancets, being later, are pointed, and there are only two, while above is a conical cap, as must have existed once at Framlingham.

At Old Sarum [1] there is definite evidence, for parts of a large stone cylindrical chimney *
were found having one or two courses of circular smoke-holes below a chevron string-course,
and confined by a band of scroll-pattern below (Pl. XLIV E); similar vents were pierced
in the sloping stones apparently of a conical cap in the Bayeux manner. The French chimney,
however, has a loftier cone or steeple with room for some ten rows of smoke-holes in its
height.

In the castles under its care the Ministry of Works has found evidence of several interesting 13th-century chimneys, which throw light on the immense variety which must once
have existed. Mr A. J. Taylor's drawing (Fig. 82) reconstructs a chimney probably of the
second quarter of the 13th century at Skenfrith (Monmouthshire). It was circular with
open top, embattled, slightly narrower than the shaft, to which it was splayed to join,
between roll-mouldings, a band of three courses, arranged alternately, of circular vents.
These are reminiscent of those at Old Sarum but used without
a cap. †

On the other hand, a 13th-century chimney from Sherborne
Abbey,[6] now destroyed, may have resembled the Old Sarum
example in shape, having a square conical cap, though without
circular vents, topped by a trefoil finial. Below were three
lancet vents, again reminiscent of Aydon though possibly
earlier, but trefoil-headed with individual gables, and alternating with cusped openings in two rows, a quatrefoil above, a
trefoil below. This suggests a development of the 'window'
feature first seen at Framlingham.

Fig. 83. 13th-century
chimney at Kingham.

A low stone chimney at Kingham, Oxfordshire [10] (Fig. 83),
comes next in the typological, though not necessarily
chronological, sequence, but probably still from the 13th
century. The holes do not appear at all, being replaced by
more trefoil-headed window-vents, six in all. These have
gables, which are however divided off by a string-course to
form a 'fool's cap' round the cone, which has a further string
and flat circular finial. The large ridge-tile under the chimney
also remains.‡ Very similar to this, but octagonal in plan, is
the chimney at Murton Hall, Westmorland,[17] assigned by the
Royal Commission to the 14th century. But here the trefoiled
vents are not divided from their gables.

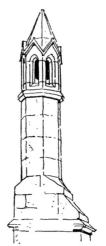

For these capped chimneys the polygonal plan seems to
have supplanted the circular form. It was more convenient
for the window-vent arrangement, providing one opening
in each facet of wall. In the late 13th-century chimney at

Fig. 84. Chimney at Bredon,
probably late 13th century.

---

* Now in the museum at Salisbury.

† I am greatly indebted to the Ministry of Works and Mr A. J. Taylor, F.S.A., for most generously allowing me to
reproduce his drawings, not yet published (Figs. 82 & 85).

‡ This chimney still exists, though rebuilt; it was located for me through the research of Mr A. W. Everett, F.S.A.
A simple conical example with trefoiled vents and scrolled finial is re-used at Woodlands Manor, Mere. It came from
a cottage at Norton St Philip.

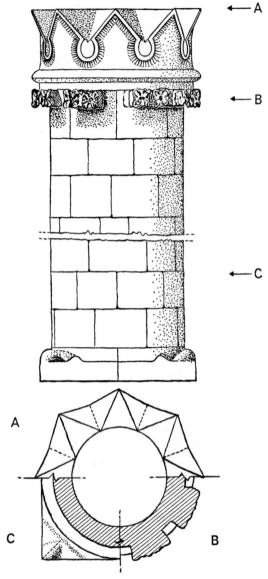

Fig. 85. Late 13th-century chimney at
Conway Castle.

Woodstock [11] (Pl. 22 A) there is still a conical cap, pierced, unlike that at Kingham, with circular vents, and with a small ball finial; there is a ring of gables above the cornice, but these contain triangular openings. The shaft however is octagonal in plan, with oblong vents on each face; it is also set on its own ridge-tile. The chimney is, unfortunately, much worn, but a 19th-century drawing clarifies the arrangement.

At Bredon (Gloucestershire) [12] (Fig. 84) the whole chimney is hexagonal, the lancets having individual gables against the six-sided cap above, producing a particularly attractive design. On Lincoln Cathedral the lavatorium chimney is octagonal, though attached at an angle, and has gabled vents against a polygonal cone terminating in a ball, while at Motcombe in Dorset [13] (Pl. 22 D) the octagonal chimney has lancet vents, ungabled, below a concave cap with stiff-leafed finial.

Open cylindrical chimneys, however, remained fashionable and were used in the royal castles of the late 13th century. At Criccieth (c. 1285) one had a slightly narrowed top, scroll and bead moulded, splayed to a roll-moulding above the shaft, which had angle spurs to the square base. In Conway (Fig. 85), of similar date, fragments of elaborate chimneys have been found in a well, sufficient to allow a reconstruction. They had decorated spurs at the foot of the round section, and at the top a floral circlet below a scrolled collar surmounted by an ornate gabled cresting with curved 'embrasures'. By the first quarter of the 14th century the octagonal plan was in vogue, and the lower portion of such a shaft, with broaches to a square chamfered base, remains on the Chamberlain Tower at Caernarvon Castle.

The type with gabled lancets like Bredon continued into the early 14th century. In the west there are two hexagonal chimneys almost certainly connected in date and design. At St Briavels Castle [18] (Pl. 22 E) the trefoil heads have crocketed gables and the short spire is crowned by the Constable's Horn as finial. At Grosmont Castle [19] (Pl. XLIV D) the alterations of *c.* 1330 provided a chimney with similar arrangement without the moulded string-course, but the spire is truncated and finished by a circlet giving almost a crenellated effect. This chimney has a moulded base. St Briavels was a royal castle, and Grosmont was held in the 14th century by the Dukes of Lancaster, relations of the king, and the same craftsman may have been employed.

Sometimes the chimney gables contained a two-light window pattern. At Harringworth in Northamptonshire [32] each face of the octagon has a small gable containing two lancets with circle above; there are four minute gables on the cone (not octagonal), which is crowned by an annulet and finial. This may be later than the well-known Checker chimney (*c.* 1260) at Abingdon Abbey [7] (Pl. XLIV F), where the lofty stack is oblong in plan with a gable on each face, those of the longer north and south sides being west of the centre of the face. On three sides the gable contains a 'window' of three graduated lancets, but there is a simpler oblong opening on the east. These lancets do not open direct on to the cylindrical flue, there being a larger two-centred arch behind each triplet. The chimney, now disappeared, from Chepstow Castle, [16] illustrated in Parker (1869) (Pl. 22 B), and there dated *c.* 1320, may have had a similar arrangement. The rectangular stack has offsets sloping back to what seems to have been a miniature house complete with angle buttresses, trefoil-headed loops, trefoils in the gables and large quatrefoil below, with even a minute dormer in the angle of the roofs.

The 13th-century chimney with its conical, or spirelet, cap is an attractive feature perhaps akin to the use of spires in ecclesiastical buildings. Indeed the unique spire at Lostwithiel in Cornwall is like an enlarged mediaeval chimney of the gabled type. In France, although surviving or recorded chimneys suggest the same popularity of the spire, the storey below was not a series of gabled windows but rather a continuous arcade forming a lantern. Indeed the Bayeux chimney is called *La Lanterne des Morts* because of the legend that in times past a light was shown there at the decease of any occupant of the town.

At Bayeux the cylindrical column is divided from the lofty perforated spire by an arcade of some sixteen openings, while another 12th-century chimney, at Puy-en-Velay, has a lantern of six trefoil-headed openings, ungabled, beneath an elegant cone and finial.* A 13th-century example at the Abbaye de St Lô is octagonal, with two stages of colonnade, the upper with double number of shafts (sixteen) forming the open lantern below a ribbed pyramidal spire.† Although survivals are not numerous they do suggest that the conical chimneys of England and France shared a common origin, but diverged, the one having a lantern of gabled windows, the other of a continuous arcade.

The conical chimney persists into the 14th century, with larger traceried vents. There was a charming little example of that date at the Bull Inn, Burford, [20] fortunately recorded. It was short, hexagonal, set on its own ridge stone at the gable end. Each face had a 'window' of two pointed trefoiled lights with quatrefoil below an ogee arch, crocketed, as was the spirelet above. A similar little chimney pinnacle, but square in plan, remains at Hanwell

* Viollet-le-Duc (1859), III, 209.
† Ibid. 210.

Church, also in Oxfordshire. The lantern lights are now much larger, and it may be that the smaller openings, especially the earlier holes in the cone, were discarded as being easily choked with soot and awkward to clean. Wood was at that time used as fuel, and its soot is tarry and more difficult to remove than that of coal.

In the mid and late 14th century gables to the lantern seem to have gone out of fashion,

Fig. 86. Chimney of c. 1360 at the Archbishop's Palace, Southwell.

and the spire also, though at Southwell Palace there is a chimney of c. 1360 [24] (Fig. 86) which combines the remains of a spire together with a new feature, the crenellated top. Indeed the illustration of this chimney in Parker (it has now lost its spire) teaches a cautionary lesson, for other embattled chimneys may also once have had spires. The octagonal steeple illustrated has the point broken off, but there are still two courses left, the lower with lancets between miniature buttresses, the upper with gabled lancets on alternating faces.

These spire openings would seem to be an anachronism in the 14th century, when even the side vents are not usually present, though the traceried quatrefoils and wheels at Child's Wickham (Northamptonshire) [21] are an exception. The fine chimney at Northborough, [22] c. 1340 (Pl. 22 B), is significant. It is hexagonal with an embattled top and ball-flower cornice, below which each face has a gable with crockets and finial, the trefoil cusping beneath seemingly vestigial of the window vent fashion. There is no gabled decoration on a chimney at Maxstoke Castle (c. 1348) [23] but the moulded and crenellated cap has a further extension, also embattled. Indeed most chimneys now become plainer, the battlemented top serving with other mouldings as the capital of a shaft, as at Chipping Norton,[30] or rather simpler, as at Exton (Rutland),[28] and sometimes, as at Lincoln (Pottergate),[29] there is not even an annulet below. The short chimney on the battlements at Longthorpe (c. 1310) [14] shows how the octagonal exterior encloses a cylindrical flue. There are other examples at Bodiam (1385).[26] This plain type, as we shall see, continued into the 15th century and later, allowing for a divergence in the wealth of the builders.

With the increase of fireplaces twin chimneys appear. At Stokesay Castle [9] two pairs date from the late 13th century, two octagonal in the North Tower, two cylindrical in the South Tower, both with moulded open tops. At Harlech Castle (1286–9) a quadruple stack, of which part remains, served four fireplaces in the southern half of the gatehouse and there was originally a second stack serving the four northern ones.*

However, fireplaces shared chimneys as early as the 13th century. In December 1251 the sheriff of Nottingham was ordered at Clipstone 'to make a chimney in the king's wardrobe, through a mantel [hood], and through another mantel in the queen's wardrobe by one and the same flue [*per unum et idem tuellum*]'.† These fireplaces were doubtless back to back. Sometimes the smoke emerges from the weathered top of a buttress, as at Donnington Castle (1386), resembling the treatment at Aslackby (Lincolnshire),[27] though here the chimney is corbelled and has a pointed side vent.

But in the late 14th and 15th centuries the lantern form of chimney persists, and is regarded ‡ as akin to the timber louvers or *fumerells*, lead-covered, which must have existed in great numbers over the central hearths of mediaeval halls. They resemble even more, perhaps, the stone louvers set over great kitchens such as that of the 14th-century abbots at Glastonbury, with its two stages of window vents below a conical cap, and might be miniature versions of these. Indeed it is significant that in at least three cases—Tisbury (Wiltshire), Preston Plucknett and West Coker in Somerset—the stack served what was definitely the original kitchen. This may also have been the case at Twywell (Northamptonshire) and at Harringworth in the same county, and at Child's Wickham, already described. Probably the earlier turret type of chimney with side vents was retained for the larger kitchen fireplaces when it had gone out of use for the smaller ones.

Fig. 87. Chimney at Twywell.

Individual gables to the window vents now seem less common. This is suggested by surviving examples, though at Twywell [31] the octagonal stack has triangular openings in two tiers, all separately gabled (Fig. 87). It is like an elaborate version of the Bredon chimney, and might be of similar date or a survival, this being also borne out by the moulded cap of the sturdy cylindrical shaft. There is, however, no spire, only the base of a finial.

Harringworth, [32] also probably early, has a spire, and there is a concave one in the re-used octagonal chimney at Fonmon Castle (Glamorgan).[33] This is topped by a large feather or foliated crest above the annulet, and attached by a band of out-turned crenellation, below which there is a trefoil head to each light which might be as early as the mid 14th century.§ Similar lights are used in the octagonal turret chimney at Southwick Manor, Northamptonshire (*c.* 1350–80),[25] and also at West Coker Manor,[39] which dates from the 15th century (Pl. XLIV H). The latter has a low truncated cap crowned with an annulet and perhaps once with a finial as well. At Place Farm, Tisbury,[40] the

* Information from Mr A. J. Taylor, F.S.A.
† Liberate Roll, 36 Henry III; Turner (1851), 235.
‡ Garner & Stratton (1929), 186.
§ Said to have come from East Orchard, the old manor house of the Berkerolles, dismantled *c.* 1785. A. Oswald, *Country Life* (18 March 1949), 609. G. T. Clark (1869), *Archaeologia Cambrensis*, 3rd S., XV, 65, states that it was a bell-cote for the west gable of the chapel.

octagonal chimney is dated to the late 15th century. It has a conical spire with keyhole vents, now covered over, and a foliated or crocketed finial; the broad lantern has two pointed vents set high on each face. But usually the spires are only represented by low caps as at Wells (Vicars' Close), Child's Wickham or Preston Plucknett.[38] At Wells the vicars' chimneys [37] had a lantern of two trefoiled lights to each face below an embattled cornice surrounding the cap, and a lower stage of two narrower lights set on a plinth. These appear to date from the first half of the 15th century; the gable chimneys of the George Inn at Norton St Philip, also in Somerset, are similar in type.

However, the familiar type of 15th-century chimney is an octagonal shaft, often long and slender, without side vents, and apparently open from the start. The cap was first crenellated but later moulded. The embattled top may have supported, or even been partly derived from, the crown of iron spikes of which there is evidence in many 14th- and 15th-century chimneys in France, and a survival in the Château de Sully-sur-Loire, where the chimney has been disused since the 16th century.* These spikes were intended to break up the cross-currents of wind, and allow the chimney to smoke properly. The out-turned crenella-tions of the chimney at Croscombe (Somerset) [44] might well be compared with the arrangement at Sully-sur-Loire. There is a good example, now detached, at East Meon,[45] and another at Abingdon,[46] which is the model of recent copies there.

There is often a double annulet below the crenellation, as in the small chimney at Red Lion House, Burford,[34] and the very short one on Rushden Manor House, Northampton-shire.[35] Gradually the battlements become conventionalized and developed into a frilled upper moulding as at the Hospital of St Cross at Winchester.[41] In the lofty early 15th-century example at Southwell, [36] the crenellations are still just noticeable, but by the second half of the century many chimneys have a moulded cap, like the fine shaft at the Chantry at Ilminster.[42] The lower part is commonly splayed to rest on a plinth supported on the cross- or end-wall of the building, or on lateral fireplace buttresses, and is often shaped like the base of a column. As early as c. 1330 the Grosmont chimney had a base of this type with two annulets above the slope; the Ilminster example is not unlike it, with a single ring, and the Southwell chimney has a double plinth.

Besides the octagonal chimney the square type appears, and at South Wingfield they are side by side. There is a square crenellated example at Great Chalfield, and at Wells Cathedral is one oblong in plan, which has two courses of trefoil-headed panels, four at the sides, two at the ends. At Castle Cottage, Great Bedwyn in Wiltshire,[43] a great stone stack remains with a cylindrical chimney of Norman type, but dated from its mouldings on cap and plinth to the 15th century. It must be a survival from a great house, now vanished, and was used in the 16th century to serve a house of timber-framing. Some original features can be seen within, at first-floor level.

Brick chimneys are found in 15th-century buildings such as Tattershall.[47] Those highly decorated with spirals and other ornament belong to the reign of Henry VIII (1509–47). There are magnificent examples at Thornbury Castle,[48] Layer Marney [49] and East Barsham.[50] They had become plainer by the reign of his daughter Elizabeth (1558–1603).

* Viollet-le-Duc (1859), 214, fig. 19.

Plate XLIII. Fireplaces.

A. South Wingfield, solar block, *c.* 1440–58.
B. Carew Castle, upper fireplace in east range, *c.* 1485–1507, with arms of Henry VII.
C. Deanery Hall, Exeter, 1496–9.
D. Bishop Courtenay's fireplace, *c.* 1486, Exeter Palace.

Plate XLIV. Chimneys.

A. Chimney from 79¼ High Street, Southampton, c. 1200, now in King John's House. B. and C. Framlingham Castle hall, c. 1150–60, with Tudor brick extensions. D. Grosmont Castle, c. 1330. E. Chimney from Old Sarum, c. 1130+, reassembled in Salisbury Museum. F. The Checker, Abingdon Abbey, c. 1260. G. Aydon Castle, c. 1280. H. West Coker Manor, mid 15th century, turret chimney to kitchen.

PLASTER AND WICKER CHIMNEYS

There must have been many chimneys of flimsy material in the Middle Ages. Even Henry III had some of plaster. At Windsor Castle in 1236 he arranged for *uno camino de plastro* to be made in his wardrobe,* this no doubt including the fireplace hood as well. The 14th-century London Ordinances laid down that chimneys were no longer to be of wood, but of stone, tiles or plaster,† apparently referring, at least in part, to the arrangement over a reredos or central hearth. When the fireplace was built against a wall the flue would run up on its internal face. In 1317 the Earl of Richmond's hall in London was to have its walls plastered, and also the *tewels* (flues) to the summit;‡ while in 1368 four 'pipes' of the two fireplaces in Edward III's chamber at Shene were to be made with plaster of Paris.§ In the same year two chimneys at Clipstone were renewed in plaster after being blown down by the wind, and such external projections may be envisaged as the 'chalk whyt chymnees' on the castle roof described in *Gawayn and the Green Knight*.

Wicker and thatch chimneys survive in Carmarthenshire, and Lloyd illustrates two gable examples, one showing the framework, the other completed after thatching.‖ Later chimneys of timber have also been found in Westmorland, Cambridgeshire, Huntingdonshire and Lancashire.

Other methods of ventilation have been recognized. Mr J. T. Smith has discovered smoke vents in the gables of timber houses such as Fyfield Hall and Stanton's Farm, Black Notley, both in Essex,¶ and this may be the origin of the gabled hip so often met in timber-framed houses of the south-eastern region, the form continuing long after its original purpose had been superseded.

At Minster Lovell Hall, unusually lofty, instead of a louver there were openings at the top of the gable walls, providing a cross-draught to withdraw the smoke; these three apertures are still visible at the east end. At Clevedon Court [15] until lately there was a small chimney on the hall gable, here of stone, its square opening, soot-stained, still visible in the soffit of the great window at the eastern end (Pl. XL c). In Bolton Castle there are also smoke outlets in the soffit of the side windows of the hall, and when visiting the castle *c.* 1535 Leland speaks of 'tunnills' by which 'the smoke of the harthe is wonder strangely conveyed'.** This may have been a development of the possibly earlier method of leaving the traceried head of a two-light window open. Shuffrey believed that this was the method of ventilation at Stokesay.

---

* Pipe Rolls, 20 Henry III; Turner (1851), 84.
† *Liber Albus* (ed. H. T. Riley), 288; Salzman (1952), 99.
‡ Guildhall Muniments, Letter Book E, f. 61, translated in Riley (1868), 125; Salzman (1952), 99.
§ Exchequer, King's Remembrancer Accounts, 493, 29; Salzman (1952), 99.
‖ Lloyd (1931), figs. 560–1.
¶ Smith (1955), 79–81, figs. 2 and 3.
** *Itinerary*.

CHIMNEY EXAMPLES

12TH CENTURY

		References (mostly with illustrations)
(1) *c.* 1130+	Old Sarum, Wilts., evidence	
(2) *c.* 1150–60	Framlingham Castle, Suff., hall, 2	
(3) *c.* 1160	Christchurch Castle, hall	Wood (1963), 18, pl. II.
(4) *c.* 1200	Boothby Pagnell Manor House, Lincs.	Wood (1935), 198, pl. III B.
(5) *c.* 1200	79½ High St, Southampton	Wood (1963), 18, pl. VI.

13TH CENTURY

(6) C 13th	Sherborne Abbey, Dor., recorded	Shuffrey (1912), fig. 23.
(7) *c.* 1260	The Checker, Abingdon Abbey, Berks.	Lloyd (1931), fig. 552.
(8) *c.* 1280	Aydon Castle, Northumb., hall	Wood (1950), 53, pl. XII c.
(9) *c.* 1285–1305	Stokesay Castle, 2 pairs	
(10) C 13th	House at Kingham, Oxon.	H. J. Massingham (2nd ed. 1941–2), *Cotswold Country*, 13 (Batsford).
(11) *c.* 1290	House at Woodstock, Oxon.	Parker (1853), 90.
(12) ? late C 13th	House at Bredon, Glos.	H. J. Massingham (2nd ed. 1941–2), *Cotswold Country*, 13 (Batsford).
(13) late C 13th	House at Motcombe, Dor.	Parker (1853), 91.

14TH CENTURY

(14) *c.* 1310	Longthorpe Tower	
(15) *c.* 1320	Clevedon Court, Som., recorded	*Country Life* (6), 1674.
(16) *c.* 1320	Chepstow Castle, Mon., recorded	Parker (1869), 63.
(17)	Murton Hall, West.	R.C.H.M. records.
(18)	St Briavels Castle, Glos.	G. T. Clark (1858), *Archaeologia Cambrensis*, 3rd S., IV, 386.
(19) *c.* 1330	Grosmont Castle, Mon.	Parker (1853), 90; Lloyd (1931), fig. 556.
(20)	Bull Inn, Burford, Oxon., recorded	Shuffrey (1912), fig. 34; Parker (1853), 88.
(21)	House at Child's Wickham, Northants.	Shuffrey (1912), fig. 37.
(22) *c.* 1340	Northborough Manor House, Northants.	Shuffrey (1912), fig. 33; Parker (1853), 91.
(23) *c.* 1348	Maxstoke Castle, War.	Parker (1859), 120
(24) *c.* 1360	Southwell Palace, Notts.	Parker (1853), 90.
(25) *c.* 1350–80	Southwick Manor, Northants.	*Country Life* (26), 1298–9.
(26) *c.* 1385	Bodiam Castle, Suss., several	Lloyd (1931), fig. 555.
(27)	House at Aslackby, Lincs.	Parker (1859), 120.
(28)	House at Exton, Rut.	Parker (1853), 91.
(29)	Pottergate, Lincoln	Parker (1853), 91.
(30)	House at Chipping Norton, Oxon.	Garner & Stratton (1929), pl. CLV.
(31)	House at Twywell, Northants.	Garner & Stratton (1929), fig. 323.
(32)	House at Harringworth, Northants.	Shuffrey (1912), fig. 35.
(33)	Fonmon Castle, Glam.	

15TH CENTURY

References (mostly with illustrations)

(34)	Red Lion House, Burford	
(35)	Rushden Manor House, Northants.	
(36) early C 15th	Southwell Palace, Notts.	
(37)	Vicars' Close, Wells, Som.	Pugin (1840), pl. 4.
(38) 1st half C 15th	Manor Farm, Preston Plucknett, Som.	Garner & Stratton (1929), pl. CLIV.
(39) mid C 15th	West Coker Manor House, Som.	
(40) late C 15th	Place Farm, Tisbury, Wilts.	Dufty (1947), 168–9, pl. XVIII.
(41)	Hospital of St Cross, Winchester, several	Lloyd (1931), fig. 90.
(42) *c.* 1480	The Chantry, Ilminster, Som.	Pantin (1959), 231–2, pl. XXI E.
(43)	Castle Cottage, Great Bedwyn, Wilts.	
(44)	House at Croscombe, Som.	Lloyd (1931), fig. 557.
(45)	Court House, East Meon, Hants	
(46)	Abingdon Abbey, Berks.	
(47) 1433–43	Tattershall Castle, Lincs.	

16TH CENTURY

(48) *c.* 1511–21	Thornbury Castle	Garner & Stratton (1929), pl. CLIV; Parker (1859), 120.
(49) *c.* 1520	Layer Marney Towers, Ess.	Parker (1859), 180.
(50) *c.* 1523–35	East Barsham Manor, Norf.	Garner & Stratton (1929), pl. CLIV.

22

Roof Covering

SINCE no early roofs survive externally, we must rely on documentary evidence and archaeological finds in destroyed houses, such as roof covering lying in the debris on the floor.

In many cases, however, the roofing material would be unlikely to survive at all, being of thatch, a covering of straw or reed. But remains of burnt thatch have been found in some excavations, such as the homestead of Dean Moor in South Devon.* Thatch must have been the normal type of roof in early times, for as Mr Salzman † has shown, 'thack' (Old English *þæc*) originally meant the outer layer of a roof, and as so many buildings were covered in this way the word 'thatch' acquired the restricted meaning in use today.

These thatched roofs in towns were doubtless a prime cause of the many devastating fires of the early mediaeval period, in London in 1077, 1087, 1135–6 and 1161, Winchester in 1161 and 1180, Canterbury and Exeter in 1161, Glastonbury in 1184, Chichester in 1187, Worcester in 1202 and Chester in 1140, 1180 and 1278. To combat these the London authorities not only encouraged the building of stone houses, or at least of stone party walls, but also laid down conditions of roofing in the city. In the London Assize of 1212, 'whosoever wishes to build, let him take care, as he loveth himself and his goods, that he roof not with reed, nor rush, straw nor stubble, but with tile only, or shingle or boards, or, if it may be, with lead or plastered straw [*estra detorchiato*] within the City and Portsoken. Also that all houses which till now are covered with reed or rush, which can be plastered, let them be plastered within eight days, and let those which shall not be so plastered within the term be demolished by the alderman and lawful men of the venue'.‡ This does not seem to have been enforced completely, but thatch seems to have given way, in the better buildings, to more fireproof material. Yet the royal hunting lodge 'King John's Palace' at Writtle was thatched, over timber walls. At Kennington in 1237 a royal chapel was still roofed with thatch.§ In the late 12th-century manor house excavated at Wharram

---

* A. Fox (1958), 145.
† Salzman (1952), 223.
‡ Turner (1851), 282 and 23, gives the Latin original and translation; Salzman (1952), 223.
§ Liberate Roll, 21 Henry III; Turner (1851), 185.

Percy, tiles seem to have been used round the chimney, thatch elsewhere.* This may have been a usual practice. Often early churches are found close by a river, a safeguard in case of fire to a thatched building.

Shingles (oak tiles) were early in common use, and flat square boards appear in illustrations of Saxon houses (*c.* 1000),† also oval shingles as in the Bayeux Tapestry (*c.* 1077–82),‡ resembling Norman scale ornament as used in the treforium of Christchurch Priory, Hampshire. Shingles were used in the chief hall of Brionne Castle in Normandy, which was set alight by red-hot darts projected on to its roof,§ as later Simon de Montfort was said to have contemplated freeing cocks with flaming brands on their feet over the roofs of London, which was apparently still thatched in the mid 13th century.‖

Some of Henry III's buildings were roofed in this way. In June 1233 the king ordered the sheriff of Oxford 'to cause the aisles [*alas*] of the great hall at Woodstock to be unroofed, and re-covered with shingles'. In April 1239 Walter de Burgh was 'to roof our chamber at Kennington and the chamber of our queen there with shingles', this being repeated in April 1246. The constable of Marlborough Castle, in May 1260, is ordered 'to remove the shingles from the roof of the king's great kitchen and cover it with stone . . . to take the thatch off the outer chamber in the high tower, and cover it with the shingles of the said kitchen and to crest it with lead'. We thus see how the more inflammable material is being replaced. At Winchester in January 1241 the great wardrobe with its penthouses was to be roofed with shingle, but the queen's chapel with lead, as was the wardrobe at Nottingham in July 1244. Later, shingles seem to have been used by Henry III only for less important buildings like his privy chamber at Clipstone (January 1252), where indeed even the hall and kitchen were of wood, his mews at Geddington (January 1252), and stables at Havering (April 1254). However, as early as March 1241 the queen's new stable at Woodstock was to be roofed with slate.¶

The rectangular type of shingle in the 13th century is suggested by the reference of 1259 at Woodstock, where men were 'sawing blocks of wood [*gobones*] to make therefrom shingles [*cendulas*] for the covering of buildings'.** The Otford seal of *c.* 1273 depicts a timber-framed house with a shingled hipped roof having a central chimney and finials at each end of the ridge.†† But the price of shingles was going up in the 14th century: whereas a hundred cost 2*d.* in 1238 (Marlborough), they rose from 4*d.* in 1316 (Clarendon), 11*d.* per hundred 'shyngle' in 1329 (Westminster from Croydon), 12*d.* in 1365 (Dover) to 16*d.* in 1386 ('scindul' to Westminster from Croydon).‡‡ This restricted their use. Even in 1314 stone slates or earthen tiles were cheaper, and Queen Margaret's manors were re-roofed that way.§§

* Hurst (1958), 206.
† British Museum, Harley MS. No. 603, fol. 57; reproduced in Lloyd (1931), 4.
‡ Turner (1851), 8 for drawings from Caedman's Paraphrase MS. (*c.* 1000), British Museum, Cottonian MS. Nero CIV (*c.* 1125) and Bayeux Tapestry.
§ *Ordericus Vitalis: Historia Ecclesiastica* (ed. A. le Prevost 1838–55), VIII, 13, quoted in Thompson (1912), 56.
‖ Salzman (1952), 223.
¶ Liberate Roll, 17, 23, 30, 44, 25, 28, 36, 28, 36, 38, 25 Henry III; Turner (1851), 183 (Woodstock), 190 and 211 (Kennington), 250–1 (Marlborough), 199 (Winchester), 205 (Nottingham), 236 and 205 (Clipstone), 238 (Geddington), 244 (Havering), 199 (Woodstock).
** Exchequer, King's Remembrancer Accounts, 497, 21, quoted in Salzman (1952), 228.
†† Illustrated in Turner (1851), 71.
‡‡ Salzman (1952), 228, which gives references per thousand, etc.
§§ Salzman (1952), 228–9.

Weather-boarding may also have been used for roofing. Mr Rigold suggests that it was an alternative to shingles as early as the 13th century, when many documents refer to a roof as just *cooperta cum bordes*.

In 12th-century illustrations of churches the roofs are often covered with curved *tiles* resembling the Roman *imbrices*, and in the earlier Harley MSS., Saxon houses of *c.* 1000, portrayed as combining various forms of roofing, also show these semicircular tiles; * so does the Bayeux Tapestry in the late 11th century. Tiles were certainly in use for houses by 1212, as they are given as one of the alternatives to thatch in the London Assize. They are mentioned, together with thatch, shingles, lead and slate, in the Liberate Rolls of Henry III, but not a great deal, possibly because tile was assumed.† In August 1237 Walter de Burgh is ordered 'to unroof the king's chamber at Kennington and afterwards to recover it with good tile', and in April 1240 the said Walter 'the keeper of our demesnes' is reimbursed 3s. 1½d. 'for tile bought to cover our hall at Kennington'. By October 1260 even the rebuilt gardener's house at Windsor is to be covered with tile.‡

Their cost was 3s. a thousand in 1237 at Marlborough (where next year a thousand shingles cost 2s.), in 1258 and 1278 in London, and 2s. in 1291 at Guildford. The price was fixed at the maximum of 5s. per thousand in London in 1350, the Black Death causing a rise in prices, but the usual cost in the second half of the 14th century was from 4s. to 5s. 6d. In the 15th century size and quality varied so much that an Act was passed in 1477 regulating the process, manufacture and size of tiles. The standard flat tile was to be 10½ × 6¼ inches and at least ⅝ inch in thickness.§

Much research needs to be done on mediaeval roofing tiles, fostered by excavation. At the Manor of the More in Hertfordshire red tiles striped with white were used on the hall ridge *c.* 1380.

Stone slates called *stone tiles* were much in use. They are called 'sclatestone' in 1286 at Cambridge Castle, and 'thakestone' at Clipstone in 1368. The most famous quarries, at Collyweston in Northamptonshire, provided 9,500 stone slates for Rockingham Castle in 1375 at 8s. per thousand and 4,500 'sclastones' in 1390, costing 6s. 8d. (with carriage extra), and for Oakham Castle 5,000 'sklat' were provided in 1383.‖ Later Henry VII's mother, Lady Margaret Beaufort, Countess of Richmond, owned the manor of Collyweston.

Possibly stone slates were those used at Bury St Edmunds in the late 12th century. Jocelin de Brakelond relates how Abbot Samson (1182–1212) 'ordered that the stables and offices in and around the court, which had previously been covered with reeds, should be covered with new roofs, made of slates . . . that so all fear might be removed and all danger of fire'.¶

Slate is not among the fireproof roofing materials laid down in the Assize of 1212. But in April 1237 Henry III ordered the house 'erected in the middle of the castle' (Winchester) to be roofed with slate, and at Woodstock in March 1241 'a new stable for the use of our

---

* Reproduced in Lloyd (1931), 4. For another example, see F. Wormald (1952), *English Drawings of the Tenth and Eleventh Centuries*, pl. 25 a. Faber.
† Salzman (1952), 229.
‡ Liberate Roll, 21, 24, 44 Henry III; Turner (1851), 187, 195 (Kennington), 252 (Windsor).
§ Salzman (1952), 229–31.
‖ References in Salzman (1952), 232.
¶ *Chronicle of Jocelin de Brakelond, Monk of St Edmundsbury* (trans. L. C. Jane, 1932), 151.

queen' is to be roofed with slate, 'and another house for the use of our salter, likewise roofed with slate'. Walter de Tywe is also to 'cover with slate all the houses of each court which are not slated'. These may have been stone slates, for around Woodstock there is laminated stone suitable for splitting.*

Recent research, however, by Messrs Jope and Dunning, has revealed the early use of *blue slate* roofing in this country.† These blue schist slates were imported all over southern England by means of a flourishing coastal trade from Devon and Cornwall. Blue slate can be split much thinner than the stone slates found in fissile beds in limestone and sandstones, or the Horsham 'slates' from the clays of the weald. They are usually less than $\frac{1}{4}$ inch thick, compared with the $\frac{1}{2}$ to 1 inch of Cotswold 'slates' and others, and thus give a much lighter roof. They are used even in districts where, as at Corfe, the local stone beds provide the normal roofing material.

As early as the late 12th century, as we know from the Pipe Rolls, thousands of slates were being shipped from the Devon ports of Dartmouth, Totnes and Plympton to the great one at Southampton. Over 800,000 slates were imported for the king's buildings at Winchester, 1171/2–1186/7, and Southampton 1186/7. In 1180/1 100,000 slates came from Totnes to Portchester Castle, and examples have been found in excavations there by the Ministry of Works.

The trade seems to have been intensified in the 13th century. At Taunton Castle, the work of Peter des Roches (1208+) was roofed with tiles, probably from Devon, and other excavated examples come from Corfe and Sherborne Castles, Winchester, the kitchen foundations of Netley Abbey, among many others.

Dorset and Cornwall also exported slates, rather later than Devon. At Winchester in 1314 buildings 'covered with Cornwall stone called Esclate' suffered damage from storms,‡ and in 1363, 2,000 'sclat de Cornwayll' were purchased for 10s. for a house in the New Forest.§ Slates were bought in 1325–6 for the Pilgrims' Hall at Winchester, which, like a contemporary building excavated at Bishops Waltham,‖ had a roof of this kind.

Much remains to be discovered concerning this English blue slate trade. Did it increase or grow less in the 15th century? Cases are known of slates imported from Brittany and Belgium. But in 1436 Thomas Wylby of Southampton was allowed to buy 'a hundred thousands of the slates called sclat' in Devon, and convey them to the Abbey of Mont St Michel for the ransom of William Jacob of Southampton, who was imprisoned there. At Windsor in 1481, 'tiles called sklates of blue colour' are mentioned.¶

Welsh slates as yet did not penetrate beyond Chester and the border.

Most of the slates found are rectangular, the most usual size being *c.* $7 \times 3\frac{1}{2}$ or 4 inches. Three larger ones, $9\frac{1}{4} \times 5\frac{1}{2}$, $6\frac{1}{2}$, and $7\frac{1}{4}$ inches, have been found at Totnes Castle, and one $10 \times 4\frac{3}{4}$ inches at Dover. The slates have a hole for fixing, and were hung on wooden pegs, one of pine still remaining in a 13th-century example excavated by Mr Rigold at Totnes.

Lead roofs, so much associated with the low-pitched 15th-century churches and the flats

* Liberate Roll, 21, 25 Henry III; Turner (1851), 185 (Winchester), 199 (Woodstock); Salzman (1952), 232.
† Jope & Dunning (1954).
‡ Calendar of Miscellaneous Inquisitions, No. 179; Jope & Dunning (1954), 216.
§ Exchequer, King's Remembrancer Accounts, 476, 20; Salzman (1952), 233.
‖ *Medieval Archaeology* (1957), I, 152, 154.
¶ Salzman (1952), 233.

of castle towers, are also mentioned in the buildings of Henry III. Certainly, except for a chapel (in the queen's chamber) at Nottingham and a new hall and chamber at Newcastle,* lead seems to have been used for the lesser structures such as wardrobes, penthouses and (external) staircases.

Roof Ornament

The roof line of a mediaeval house was more elaborate than that normal today (except in some Victorian Gothic buildings). The Bayeux Tapestry, which is now considered to be southern English work of *c.* 1077–82, shows roofs of that period with finials at the gable ends, including knobs, spurs and foliated scrolls.† More evidence is provided a century later in the buildings depicted in the *Life of St Guthlac* of Croyland, where spurs with scroll and foliated finials appear.‡ Finials in the form of animals are seen in the mid 12th-century drawing of Christchurch Priory at Canterbury, where a lion appears on the roof of the north hall and a wyvern (dragon with two legs) on the reredorter gable. All these finials were doubtless of wood, but among existing Norman houses Saltford Manor has a stone lion on one gable, and Oakham Castle Hall has Samson and the Lion on one terminal and a centaur on the other. There are also stone finials of bears on the late 12th-century transept of Southwell Minster. Animal heads appear too as gable crests on the metal house-shaped caskets and reliquaries of the period. All seem to derive from the barbaric dragons and other beast-heads used on Viking buildings, and which can be seen on certain stave churches in Norway, mostly restored.§

Mr Dunning has found examples of these zoomorphic finials in pottery excavated on 13th-century sites. A horse decorated the ridge of a merchant's house in the once important port of Stonar in Kent, there was a bear on the hall of Miserden Castle near Stroud, an eagle at Whichford Castle, Warwickshire, and a lion at Henblas in Flintshire. The dragon (*c.* 1300) at Stoke Bardolph, Nottinghamshire, seems to hark back to the Vikings. A stylized horse's head found at Oxford was originally gilded.‖

In Henry III's buildings the ridge was treated decoratively though no details are normally mentioned. The usual order is for the houses to be 'roofed and crested', as at Clarendon in 1237. Sometimes lead is specified for the cresting: in December 1247 'the sheriff of Wiltshire is ordered to crest with lead all the passages [*aleyas*] at Clarendon, between the king's hall and chamber, and the chamber and wardrobe, and the chamber of the king and queen; and likewise to crest with lead all the king's houses at Clarendon'. A cresting of lead is used over shingles at Marlborough Castle (May 1260). There is an interesting reference to Clarendon in 1250, where the sheriff is 'to cover the chamber outside the chamber of

---

* Liberate Roll, 28, 21 Henry III; Turner (1851), 205 (Nottingham), 186 (Newcastle).

† Stenton (1957), pls. 30, 32, 47 and 52.

‡ G. F. Warner (1928), *The Guthlac Roll* (Roxburghe Club), pls. I, III, V, VI, VII and XII (scroll finials), pls. X, XI, XIII, XVI and XVII (foliated); G. C. Dunning in Biddle *et al.* (1959), 175.

§ They are original at Lomchurch (mid 12th century). A. Bugge (1953), *Norwegian Stave Churches*, pls. 1, 4, 18, 37 and 110.

‖ I am greatly indebted to Mr G. C. Dunning, F.S.A., for the use of material not yet published, the subject of his paper to the Society of Antiquaries of London on 15 January 1959.

Alexander with shingle and chevron it [*keveronari facias*]'.* A clue to this chevroning is provided by ridge tiles (containing finials) discovered at Old Sarum and Portsmouth and dating from the late 13th century. The cresting was cut by a knife into sharp peaks, following on an earlier 13th-century type in which the peaks were lower, moulded by hand, as shown in examples from Winchester, Southampton and Cirencester.† There are two probably 14th-century crested tiles on 39–43 the Causeway, Steventon. The mitres and crosses

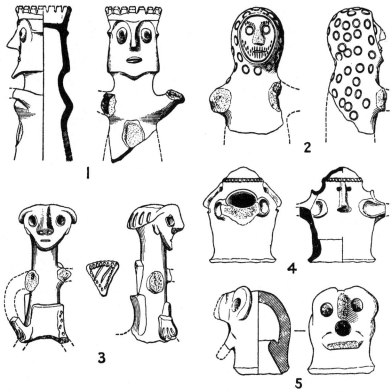

KEY: 1. Noble in coronet, from London (Fitzwilliam Museum, Cambridge). 2. Mounted knight clad in mail, from Cambridge (Fitzwilliam Museum). 3. Tonsured priest on saddle, from Stamford (Lincoln City Museum). 4 and 5. Crude heads from King's Lynn (King's Lynn Museum).

Fig. 88. Pottery roof finials.

still seen on the kitchen wing of Little Chesterford Manor Farm, and elsewhere, may be derived from this mediaeval 'cresting'.

The finials which form part of these serrated roof tiles seem to be decorative derivatives from pottery ventilators, of which Mr Dunning has discovered and reconstructed a number dating from the 13th and 14th centuries. They throw a new light on the picturesque side of mediaeval building (Fig. 88).

---

* Liberate Roll, 22 and 32, 44, 35 Henry III; Turner (1851), 187–8 and 215 (Clarendon), 251 (Marlborough), 227 (Clarendon).
† These are respectively in Salisbury Museum; Cumberland House Museum, Southsea; Winchester City Museum; Bargate Museum, Southampton; and Corinum Museum, Cirencester.

These ventilators are a revelation of the mediaeval sense of humour, childlike yet some-times grim, of people used to seeing the heads of traitors displayed on public buildings. There is a king's head so designed that smoke came out of eyes, mouth and crown; a student of Oxford with his tongue out at authority (mid 13th century); a head with two faces sharing a conical cap; and another with outlets for smoke in his eyes, ears, mouth and the top of his head.*

A moulded face may be applied to the opposite side of a hollow globular finial, such as the Nottingham example, in the manner of the pottery face jugs of this region; dating from the first half of the 14th century, it is 13 inches high, and the smoke came out of a hole in the top. Another, from Coventry, had two rows of holes on the inverted pear-like surface, a tubular top, and was 19½ inches high. Another type terminated in a long spike, vents provided only by holes made in the globular body of the finial, which may have one or more frilled collars. This kind is found in Hereford, the Marches and South Wales,† and seems to be the earliest, dating, as at White Castle, from the first half of the 13th century, and from which the others were derived. This kind was made to fit into a socket on the ridge tile, whereas later, especially in the south by the middle of the 13th century, finial and socket were made in one piece. Such ventilators have been found at Sherborne Castle and Cirencester.

But gradually the finials became purely decorative, without vents, and their ridge tile was completed with a floor across the finial base. In the complete mid 13th-century example found at Winchester the smoke could get into the finial (discolouring the inside) but not escape from it.

Mounted knights in pottery must have been a popular embellishment of roofs, as they were on the jugs, aquamaniles, of the time. Examples have been found at Cambridge, and in the excavations of the hall of Pachesham Manor near Leatherhead, built c. 1290 by Sir Eustache de Haache. These are fragmentary but confirmed by a grant of 1373 relating to Banstead Manor, where 2s. were paid 'to John Pottere of Chayham for two crests made in the fashion of mounted knights', bought for the hall.‡ Sometimes a king or a tonsured priest was depicted, or just a doubled face attached to the ridge tile, as at Lincoln (Pl. XL E), where the masks are bearded and share a round cap with apical tuft; the fact that the cresting was originally on both sides shows that the tile was placed along the roof and not at the extreme end. This may date from the 14th century.§

The picturesque element continued in roofs of the 14th century and later. Fifty-two expensive earthenware crests (crestis luteis) were bought in 1353, 30 crestes de figulo for the ridge of hall and chamber in 1366, and 36 'krestys of tyyl' in 1432.‖

Excavations at the Manor of the More have revealed details of a roof of c. 1380. It had ridge tiles of red with white stripes and spur finials at the ends, as well as a louver also gaily coloured set midway along the crest. Mr Dunning considers that these late 14th-century spur finials 'represent, in a reduced and simplified form, the wooden scroll-

* Respectively in the Colchester Museum, Ashmolean Museum, King's Lynn Museum and Reading Museum.
† Respectively in Nottingham Museum, Coventry Museum, Hereford Museum.
‡ Exchequer, King's Remembrancer Accounts, 494, 18; Salzman (1952), 231.
§ G. C. Dunning (1946), Archaeological Journal, CIII, 167, pl. XXV.
‖ Salzman (1952), 231.

ended finials of the Norman period. In the 13th and 14th centuries the wooden prototypes were translated into baked clay'.*

The louvers, whether of pottery or wood, over the central hearth provided another feature of interest.

The stone finials on 12th-century houses also had descendants, and the crest of the owner of the hall was doubtless used to decorate the gable end. At Penshurst the great hall built by Sir John de Pulteney (c. 1341–9) retains on its gables the cognizances of a later owner, Henry V's brother John, Duke of Bedford, a falcon and an ibex. At Great Chalfield figures of men in armour surmount three of the larger gables, and griffins † holding the Tropenell arms the two smaller ones.

Gutters

Leaden gutters are often mentioned in the Liberate Rolls. In 1240 at the Tower of London they are to be carried down to the ground to prevent injury by rainwater to the newly whitewashed walls, and at Woodstock (1249) 'leaden spouts' are to be made 'about the alures' of the chamber of Prince Edward.‡ Such projecting spouts survive at Aydon and Little Wenham Halls.

There is more decoration to these in the 14th century. At Haddon Hall half-length figures project above the drains from the wall-walk (alure) over the buttery,§ and at Abbot's Grange there is a crouching figure on top of a chute at the angle between chapel and solar. At Donnington (c. 1386) the grotesque gargoyle is in evidence, familiar in churches of the 15th century. South Wraxall (c. 1435) preserves some fearsome examples, one barbarous head having a child in its mouth.‖

---

* Biddle, Barfield & Millard (1959), 174–6.
† A heraldic creature with the head, breast, foreclaws and wings of an eagle, the hind quarters and tail of a lion. Pugin (1840), 19, pl. 30.
‡ Liberate Rolls, 25, 33 Henry III; Turner (1851), 197 (London), 219 (Woodstock).
§ *Country Life* (10), 1746, pl. 12.
‖ Pugin (1840), pls. 64 (frontispiece) and 70.

23

Roofs

MEDIAEVAL roofs in churches, especially in East Anglia and the south-west of England, are often of consummate craftsmanship, the result of experiment throughout many centuries. In houses, more susceptible to change and destruction, fewer examples of course survive. Those which remain are on the whole less elaborate, but can be of the greatest interest. Very often they are concealed by later ceilings and a rich harvest may await the attic explorer.

The cruck truss (see Fig. 89) is a primitive survival, though it persisted to the 14th and 15th centuries. Over four hundred examples have been found in England and Wales, and a recent map shows a distribution west of a line stretching from the Humber to Southampton Water, and including Yorkshire, the upper Thames valley, Berkshire and Hampshire. This distribution, as Mr J. T. Smith has shown, closely conforms with that of British names,* which suggests a pre-Saxon origin. East of this line is the lowland zone of England, mostly below 250 feet, which Professor Cordingley called the homeland of the box frame carpentry system, also of remote origin, in which the tie-beams form a skeletal box with the side walls in wholly wooden buildings (see Fig. 90). He believed that the homeland of the cruck frame is the highland zone (above 500 feet) of northern England (but excluding east Yorkshire and south Lancashire) and of Wales. The rest of the western region he divided into intermediate zones with both types, but with the cruck frame dominant in east Yorkshire, south Lancashire, Cheshire and the Midlands north of the Cotswolds, and the box frame dominant in Wessex (i.e. the central south and south-west of England) and in Buckinghamshire.†

The box frame became general with regard to the body of the building, but in the roof constructional details show its derivation. Particularly characteristic is the treatment of the side purlin (a longitudinal beam supporting the common rafters). In a box frame roof it is received on the sides of the principal rafters, and is called a 'butt' purlin; in a cruck

* Smith (1958 a), 146, fig. 16.
† Cordingley (1961). A classification of roof types, the outcome of discussions of the Vernacular Architecture Group, of which Mr J. T. Smith is also a prominent member.

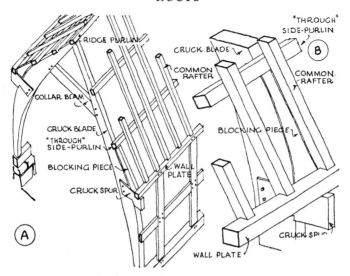

Fig. 89. Cruck truss construction.
A, 'Open' cruck truss. B, Detail showing 'through' purlin

or cruck-derived frame it is carried, in one piece where possible, on the backs of the inclined cruck blades, or principals.

It is thus apparent how important is the study of the structural details of mediaeval roofs, a work also being carried out by Mr C. A. Hewett in Essex, where his research on the dovetail (believed to date from 1275–1300) and earlier joints is producing a revolution in the dating of early buildings.*

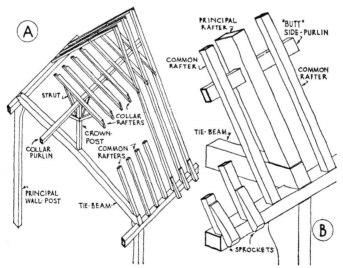

Fig. 90. Box frame construction.
A, Crown-post rafter roof. B, Detail showing 'butt' purlin

* Hewett (1961, 1962 a, 1962 b, 1962–3).

In the cruck frame each pair of curved principals, halved or attached by a 'saddle' at the apex, supports the ridge of the roof. The feet of the crucks, which may be narrow, are tenoned into a sill, which can be set on a stone plinth. Some one-third to half way up the blades are connected by a tie-beam, halved into them, forming together a large letter A. The tie-beam, however, projects a foot or so beyond, and on its ends supports another horizontal, passing at right angles—the wall plate. In an 'open cruck truss', in the centre of the house, to give head room the tie-beam is replaced by 'cruck spurs', shorter timbers supporting or anchoring the wall plate. Indeed the presence of a cruck truss in a house may be detected, in the lateral wall, by the fact that the wall plate rests on the end of a tie-beam or spur, notched into a stud. This has been called 'the outward and visible sign of internal cruck construction'.* In other (box framed) types of roof the tie-beam is *above* the wall plate. A collar beam, some half way up towards the apex, ties together the blades carrying the purlins, and some primitive examples show it projecting to support a purlin on each side.† Base crucks (sawn-off crucks) are a development, as are upper crucks, in the apex, and sometimes there is a combination of both.

There is another ancient roof, of box frame type, occurring in the cruck-frame homeland of the north-west: the king-post and ridge roof, with massive timbers. Its distribution points, on place-name evidence,‡ to a Scandinavian origin. This portion of the highland zone received the latest Viking invasions of the early 10th century, and through its remote position was not influenced by the Norman invasions which no doubt displaced the type elsewhere. However, the Normans, of Norse descent themselves, may have had the same roof originally, until influenced by lighter, more scientific, roofs of probably French origin. Indeed, the heavy king-post and ridge construction may have been widespread in Scandinavia and north Germany, and the vanished roofs of Anglo-Saxon, Danish and even Norman England were doubtless of this kind. The king-post is supported on the tie-beam and is thus in compression, unlike the modern type in which the king-post holds up the tie-beam and is in tension. It may derive from the central post in primitive houses, originally standing on the ground and later raised to roof level. This north-west type seen in some Westmorland houses is quite distinct from the tie-beam, king-post and ridge roofs found in many late mediaeval churches, notably in Somerset, where the tie-beam was found eminently suited for the flatter lead-covered roofs of the 15th century, its absence of thrust permitting the thinner walls and large clerestory windows of the period, its weight concentrated at points between the latter. The low-pitched triangle in the apex was filled with a short king-post and tracery. There also developed the still flatter firred-beam roof, without king-post but with tapering firred pieces laid on top of the tie-beam, and the cambered roof where the purlins rested directly upon it.

Recent discoveries show that a number of 13th-century domestic roofs remain, usually fairly steep, as we also know from the gable evidence of Norman ones. A most interesting roof, believed to be of *c.* 1280, survives at Donington-le-Heath,[4] with tie-beam, angle struts and collar, and in the closed truss at the end of the hall a set of vertical struts tenoned

---

* Fox & Raglan (1951), 21.
† See Webster (1954), fig. 2, etc,; Walton (1948 b); and Morgan (1938).
‡ Smith (1958 a), 146, figs. 15 and 20.

centrally into the tie-beam, collar and intermediate horizontal, giving the effect of a king-post, or rather king-strut, as the upper only touches the underside of the inclined principals at the apex, for there was no ridge originally. The purlins are butted into the principals, a usual box frame feature.

But most 13th-century examples in the south-eastern half of England are of trussed rafter type, like those at Bisham Abbey hall [5] (restored) and the chapel at Thame Prebendal. It is a single-framed roof, each rafter being separately treated, without the principal truss or triangular framework at bay intervals, linked by purlins supporting the common rafters, which is characteristic of the double-framed roof. In the trussed rafter roof there is no ridge; each pair of rafters is halved at the apex and joined some two-thirds up their height by a collar beam; each rafter has a straight brace to the collar, and another vertically

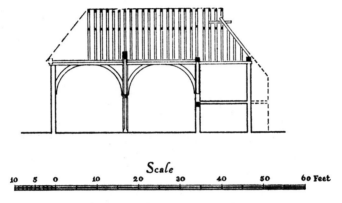

Fig. 91. Stanton's Farm, Black Notley, early 14th century,
longitudinal section.

(the ashlar piece) to the wall plate, on the inner side of the wall, producing a polygonal profile, which made it a useful type under a pointed vault in churches. In this roof, of lighter, more scientific construction, timbers of small scantling (similar in breadth and depth) could be used, which made for economy but needed careful jointing. Where a wider span was needed the roof line was extended down to form an aisle, divided from the main portion by a longitudinal arcade, or series of posts which were kept steady by a tie-beam across the nave. Stanton's Farm, Black Notley [15] is an early 14th-century example (Fig. 91).

It will be appreciated how these slight timbers above the tie-beam contrast with the heavy ones in crucks and north-western roofs, and Mr Smith has recognized in them a uniform scantling school of roof carpentry, prevalent in south-eastern England, the evidence suggesting that it was an importation from France brought in by the Norman invasion. Examples have been found in France from the mid 11th century.*

The scissors truss is a variety of this, in which two struts connect the opposite rafters like a St Andrew's cross, halved into each other and the collar, which is often present. It occurs from the 13th century, as found at Kersey [1] (c. 1200) and Great Bricett [2]

* Smith (1958 a), 116, 118.

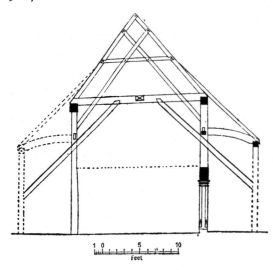

Fig. 92. Fyfield Hall, *c.* 1300, suggested reconstruction of main truss.

(1250–60) Priories in Suffolk,* and may have been common. A spectacular ecclesiastical example dating, it is believed, † from *c.* 1245 exists above the painted ceiling of 1849 over the nave of Ely Cathedral. Here no fewer than eighty-one scissor braces are present, without a single longitudinal member, over a length of some 200 feet. They have the early feature of notched laps and lap-dovetailed joints.

In such roofs of uniform scantling, timbers were duplicated when strengthening was necessary. At Fyfield Hall [14] (*c.* 1300) (Fig. 92) the tie- and collar-beams were originally fastened to long timbers parallel to the rafters, rising from arcade posts and crossing above the collar. From the tie-beam another long brace, almost parallel, passed across each arcade post to end some half way down the aisle wall. A scissor-beam arrangement was thus produced, with parallel braces below. Another experiment with such long lattice braces has been found at Edgar's Farm, Stowmarket, in Suffolk [28] (*c.* 1330) (Fig. 93), the braces rising from the aisle walls and crossing arcade posts and tie-beam to form an inverted V, a subsidiary 'ridge', just above the collar, which is here supported by a collar

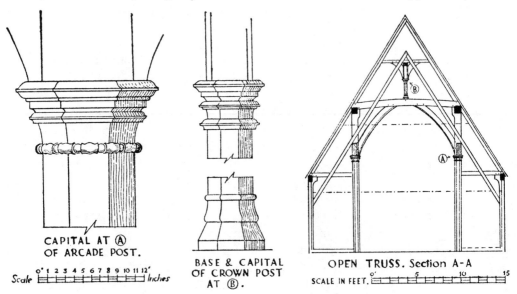

CAPITAL AT Ⓐ
OF ARCADE POST.

Scale

BASE & CAPITAL
OF CROWN POST
AT Ⓑ.

OPEN TRUSS. Section A-A

SCALE IN FEET.

Fig. 93. Edgar's Farm, Stowmarket, *c.* 1330.

* To be published by Mr P. G. M. Dickinson, F.S.A.
† In a recent survey by Dr J. M. Fletcher and Mr P. S. Spokes.

B

A

Plate XLV. Roofs.
A. Charney Basset Manor House, solar, *c.* 1280. B. Old Parsonage, Marlow, great hall, *c.* 1340.

Plate XLVI. Roofs.

A. Ightham Mote, hall, *c.* 1325.
B. Hall of John Halle, Salisbury, cusped wind-braces, *c.* 1470.
C. Ashbury Manor, cornice to great chamber, *c.* 1488.

purlin. Scissor braces and a profusion of such lattice-work with a crown post are found above the (once arch-braced) tie-beam in the hall at Hampton Court, King's Lynn,[58] said to date from the late 14th century.

The great defect of the trussed rafter roof was the lack of lengthwise stiffening, and if a joint decayed the weight of the roof covering might force the rafters to lean out of line. This was remedied by the insertion of a longitudinal beam under the collar, the central or collar purlin, which was supported from a tie-beam by a king-post with four-way struts, two tenoned to the collar purlin, two to the rafters or the rafter braces. This is now called a crown-post roof, a term coined by Professor Cordingley denoting a king-post which carries a central purlin and does not, like the true king-post, rise to support the ridge.

The crown-posts, at first plain, become shaped like a small column with moulded capital and base, and octagonal shafts. In their survey * Dr Fletcher and Mr Spokes distinguish three phases of English crown-post roofs:

1. c. 1220–80. The crown-post is square or chamfered, with straight struts, and the tie-beams uncambered, almost square in section.

2. c. 1280–1300. The crown-post is long and octagonal, with moulded capital and base, the tie-beam having a slight camber and roll-mouldings.

3. c. 1315–60. The short crown-post has curved struts and the tie-beam is well cambered, with divided baulks.

The short examples usually date from the 14th century; in the 13th and 15th centuries they tend to be tall and slim below the struts. The solar roofs at Charney Basset [6] (c. 1280) (Pl. XLV A) and Old Soar [7] (c. 1290, of almost identical span) show this combination of the tall crown-post (Pl. VII C), tie-beam and trussed rafter, and are very similar to that of Sutton Courtenay 'Abbey' [30] (Pl. 23 A), which the window tracery places in the early 14th century. In the 13th-century examples the transverse struts off the crown-post are straight and support the rafter braces; at Sutton Courtenay they do the same but are curved, as they are in the 14th-century aisled hall of Lampetts, Fyfield, [37] where they stiffen the rafters direct. Here the tie-beam is definitely cambered (Fig. 94).

Sometimes the rafter braces were curved to give a rounded instead of polygonal profile

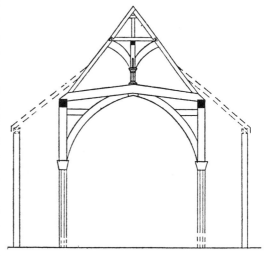

Fig. 94. Lampetts, section of truss.

to the roof, an arch below the collar. In Devonshire roofs of the 15th century the rafters were boarded to produce the typical wagon or barrel roof of that region, like a covered wagon or inverted ship, often with subsidiary timbers to form a panelled effect. Indeed the trussed rafters may have been intended to be concealed from the beginning. This may

* Fletcher & Spokes (1964).

have been the case as early as *c.* 1318 at Camoise Court, Chislehampton (Oxfordshire),[21] where such a curved roof, of three bays, is combined with the tie-beams and crown-posts, and the barrel shape appears though the semicircular braces forming it, from tie to collar, are concealed by plaster. Between the ties the braces appear to rest on wooden corbels projecting from the wall, but these are concealed by the later attic floor at tie-beam level. Turner refers to such as 'a kind of short hammer beam',* but there are no brackets. The closest analogy seems to have been the roof over the Master's House, now destroyed, but illustrated by Turner, at St John's Hospital, Northampton.[8] At Camoise Court there are roll-mouldings on the four-way struts (Pl. VII F), the wall plates and the under edge of the tie-beams.

A remarkable early 14th-century roof, contemporary with Camoise Court, survives from the refectory of Bradenstoke Priory, Wiltshire,[22] though it has been removed to St Donat's Castle, Glamorgan. Here there is no tie-beam, and the barrel below the collar is formed by a semicircular arch enriched with ball-flower ornament. There are square-set purlins, and above the collar a crown-post with moulded cap and base and curved struts; an 'upper cruck' gives additional support. An 'upper cruck', here without crown-post, is used above the collar of the magnificent arch-braced roof over the 14th-century barn at Bradford-on-Avon,[23] and is a local feature in Wiltshire.

Posts or columns impeded the floor space, and the late 13th-century carpenters were already experimenting in methods of spanning a wide hall without the use of these. A successful attempt has been discovered in the Old Deanery at Salisbury,[3] which is dated *c.* 1258–74 (*see* Fig. 19, p. 50). Raking principals in lieu of posts support the aisle plates, which in turn carry the tie-beams and trussed rafters. Two of the chamfered crown-posts had scissor-braces and the original presence of a chamfered collar purlin is firmly established.† The original crucks (*c.* 1285) at Stokesay show another experiment to avoid an aisled arrangement.‡

A further advance is shown at West Bromwich [12] (Pl. VI), the hall being an aisled derivative, with arcade posts used only in the spere truss. The main truss has a cambered collar beneath which is a moulded wooden arch rising from wall posts; this is formed by a chief member parallel to the collar, with its curve continued by braces tenoned and pinned into it and the inclined principals ('base crucks') on the walls. Above is a plain crown-post with longitudinal struts flanked by cross-braces. The experimental aspect of this roof fits with a date *c.* 1290–1310, and the scalloped decoration on the wall-post capitals is similar to that of the crown-post at Halesowen Abbot's Lodging,[11] which dates from the late 13th century. The same detail is found on crown-post capitals at Wasperton Manor,[13] and Mr S. R. Jones considers that this roof may have come from the same carpenter's yard as West Bromwich, *c.* 1300 (Figs. 50, 51, 95). The Wasperton roof was very similar. There are also crossed struts, here with one arm acting as a strut to the crown-post on either side, somewhat more advanced, and the main truss still shows a doubled collar-beam which suggests an arched arrangement like that of the Staffordshire house. Wasperton retains

---

* Turner (1851), 156.
  † Information kindly given me by Mr Norman Drinkwater, A.R.I.B.A., F.S.A., of the Royal Commission on Historical Monuments.
  ‡ Survey by Professor R. A. Cordingley (1962).

cross-braces at the screens, and had curved parallel braces to the spere truss and to the arcade posts laterally, as at West Bromwich. These duplicated braces are a feature of the late 13th-century aisled hall of St Mary's Hospital, Chichester, [9] and in the early 14th-century (or earlier) barn at Great Coxwell, Berkshire,[16] where the parallel braces, here straight, connect the nave posts to tie-beam and arcade plate. Creslow Manor House, Buckinghamshire [29] (c. 1330), has two sets of collar beams and moulded purlins, the lower collars

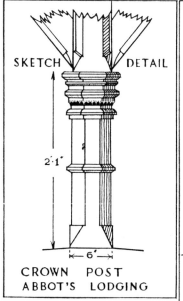

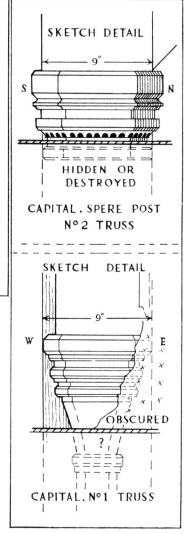

Fig. 95. Detail of crown-posts, Halesowen Abbey (above), and Wasperton Manor, c. 1300.

heavily moulded and cambered, the upper close to these with their arched brackets repeated in subsidiary trusses. There are no crown-posts.

A truncated cruck-truss (base crucks) is used in the early 14th-century hall, an aisled derivative, at Tickerage, West Hoathly.[19] The inclined principal has an arch brace butted on to it, and the collar these support is formed by two cambered portions, with crown-post and collar-purlin above. In a barn formerly at Dorchester (Oxfordshire),[17] base crucks with curved braces and double collars alternated with arcade posts in the old fashion, these backed by further curved timbers across the aisle. By the time the earlier part (c. 1343) of the Leicester Guildhall [41] was built, it was realized that the double collar was unnecessary. A further combination of cruck and arched brace is found at Amberley Court,[20] where the base crucks are integrated with the timber walls (see Fig. 18, p. 43).

At Mancetter Manor House,[31] c. 1330–40, the inclined principals are cusped to form a great trefoiled arch in the central truss, while the spere and end trusses, still of aisled form, have narrower trefoils over the 'nave' portion. The large cusps of the central arch, 3 feet 6 inches across at their maximum, support foiled braces which rise to the square-set purlin or arcade plate; this truss has a crown-post over the steeply cambered tie-beam. It may be compared to the later, less strong, trefoiled roof at Athelhampton Hall.[101]

There is a remarkable roof at Gate House Farm, Felsted (Essex),[39] where the aisled arrangement is again raised to roof level, here the arcade posts represented by columned queen-posts, standing on a tie-beam of unusual double curvature, with curved braces below taking the thrust at the change of direction. There are ogee braces from the ends of the tie to the top of the queen-posts. This has been compared to one dated 1299–1300 in the accounts of Merton College, Oxford, in the Warden's Lodging,[10] where three cambered tie-beam trusses have queen-posts with, standing on the lower collar, a crown-post as well (Fig. 96). The Merton roof might be the arrangement at Lampetts raised on a tie-beam, for Lampetts is an aisled hall, and Merton's might be called an aisled roof. Church Farm, Fressingfield, in Suffolk,[38] shows a further development on Merton, with a central post in the lower tier, thus three below and one crown-post above.

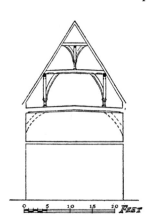

Fig. 96. Merton College, Oxford, section of truss.

One of the most magnificent roofs surviving is over the great hall at Penshurst,[40] dating from c. 1341–9. It was probably designed by the King's Carpenter William Hurley * and is 39 feet in span. The trussed rafter roof might be said to be aisled, divided by a square-set purlin as heavily moulded as the wall plate. From the latter there rise curved principals forming a four-centred arch. At their springing there are now full-length 14th-century figures, apparently replaced; certainly they do not appear in the Blore drawing of c. 1853. The great arches support a crown-post with moulded cap and base and curved four-way struts to the upper collar and purlin. Crouched figures of stone are used as corbels to the arched principals over the Guest Hall at Ely.

The arch-braced collar-beam roof was very popular, especially in the 14th century, except in the extreme north-west and south-east; in Kent a tie-beam roof was preferred. It may have been influenced by the primitive cruck construction, as suggested by the 14th-century examples of base crucks with the arch-braced collar. Another derivation, perhaps, which in turn may have been due to cruck influence, lies in the curved braces from posts to tie-beam, forming an arch over the nave of an aisled hall. When posts, cumbering the floor space, could be cleared, owing to more scientific roof construction, the arches were sprung from the side walls, as indeed must have occurred earlier in halls of smaller span. Arch-braces sometimes supported the tie-beam, as in the aisled hall, but were more usually raised to the collar, to give an impression of height and unhampered space. Without a tie-beam, however, the roof became a thrusting type, though in some halls, like Mayfield,[25] great transverse stone arches, buttressed externally, took the thrust. In others the thrust was carried down the arch braces on to wall posts securely fastened to the wall, either supported on stone or wooden corbels, or resting on a horizontal timber (template), or partially embedded in the walls. Occasionally the wall post is formed into an attached shaft with the brace resting on its capital. Sometimes the arch-brace and wall post, really a base cruck, were in one piece, as we have noted, and there is a wide variety

* Harvey (1954), 143.

in the height of the wall posts; these may continue almost to ground level like the base crucks, but be curved at the head and tenoned into the principal rafter (a 'scarfed cruck').

In the hall at Sutton Courtenay 'Abbey' [30] (Pl. 23 B), an aisled derivative, the central truss has a fine moulded two-centred arch, the lower part as a wall post resting on stone corbels a few feet up from the ground. It supports a cambered collar, in the position of a tie-beam had the hall been aisled, the low crown-post having curved four-way struts to collar purlin and the braces of a trussed rafter roof (Fig. 97).

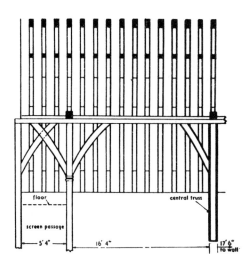

It is interesting to compare the hall at Sutton Courtenay with a true aisled hall of similar date, a magnificent structure of which part remains, disguised, at Nurstead Court [36] (Pl. 2). Here wooden columns, closely resembling those of stone, support a pointed arch, moulded, like that at Sutton Courtenay, but here over the nave alone. Again its apex cuts into the cambered beam above, and here the crown-post is a definite octagonal shaft with moulded capital and base, and of its curved four-way struts, the transverse ones rise to the upper collar direct, and not to the braces (as at Sutton Courtenay), which are fastened into them. The arcade plate is moulded, with enriched terminals; at Sutton Courtenay it is becoming a purlin.

Fig. 97. Sutton Courtenay 'Abbey', longitudinal section of hall, c. 1330.

There are certain resemblances to another early 14th-century hall, that of Ightham Mote[26] (c. 1325) (Pl. XLVI A). Again the roof is of trussed rafter type, but the central pointed arch is of moulded stone, copied in timber on the end walls, and rising from corbels, of stone or wood, at a much higher level than at Sutton Courtenay. The timber arches have a carved boss at the apex. This roof has strong affinities with that once over the great hall at Mayfield Palace,[25] (Pl. 24) spanned by great stone arches, and may have had the same designer; it is now re-roofed as a convent chapel.* Corbels for a similar arrangement, in wood, can be seen at the slightly earlier Charing Palace, another residence of the archbishops of Canterbury. Stone arches had already been used in the 12th-century keep at Hedingham, at hall and entrance levels, but here to shorten the span and support the joists of the floor above. At Chepstow Castle in the hall, 'Great Tower', refashioned in the mid 13th century, the springers remain of a richly moulded transverse arch, built to carry a cross wall for the great chamber above (Pl. III c). In the hall at Conway [42] there were eight stone transverse arches (one is left), but these replaced in 1346–7 a wooden arched roof of 1284–1286 of which evidence remains,† and which seems to prove that the stone-arched roof developed from the wooden-arched one, and not *vice versa*.

* These arches inspired the new roof to the Guildhall in London.

† Remains of the original stone corbel, and the lower part of the seating for a wall post of the earlier wooden arched roof can be seen below the springing of the surviving arch (A. J. Taylor).

One of the most beautiful examples of the arch-braced collar-beam roof can be seen in the still open hall of the Old Parsonage at Marlow [34] (Pl. XLV B). This dates from the mid 14th century, judging from the net tracery of two surviving windows. The crown-posts (one concealed) have square bevelled abaci, hollow-chamfered below, and bases with double chamfer and square plinth with broach stops. The collar is cambered and the great chamfered arch braces are supported on wooden corbels, roll and cavetto moulded, set high at the top of the flint walls. The purlins are square-set, vestigial arcade plates, and there are angle braces; a spere truss remains in part. Here the rafters are no longer trussed.

Often the space above the collar- or tie-beam was fitted with tracery, formed by cusping the upper side of the beam and the raking struts. It is found in most of the many surviving domestic roofs of the 14th and 15th centuries in Herefordshire, and might be considered a local style. However, this county, which has escaped industrialism and has been most carefully studied by the Royal Commission, preserves many original roofs of types which may have existed elsewhere but have now been lost, or not discovered. Traceried roofs have also been found at West Bromwich and in Worcestershire, and this certainly appears to be a west country type, although not common in churches.

Amberley Court [20] preserves a fine early 14th-century example. The main truss is arch-braced with a central quatrefoil and flanking trefoils, the tracery of the spere truss being similar; the intermediate trusses have a higher foiled collar, and the rafters are cusped below. Many other 14th-century roofs in Herefordshire show this bold foiling above the collar, and it may also be used over a tie-beam. At Middle Hill Farm, Hope-under-Dinmore,[48] the cusped openings are formed by collar-beam, struts and the blades of a cruck. Roof tracery is also associated with crucks at Pencombe, Lower Marston,[50] and Court Farm, Preston Wynne.[49] Weobley [51] preserves roofs with foiled openings over collar-beams, tie-beams, sometimes in the same roof as a foiled collar, and also combined with crucks.

Worcester has sustained a great loss in the disappearance of its Guesten Hall [24] (c. 1320) (Fig. 98), south of the cathedral, with its elaborate windows, though the roof has been re-used over Trinity Church there. It was arch-braced with ogee-pointed quatrefoil and trefoils over the collar, moulded purlins and cusped wind-bracing. An absolute loss is another Guesten Hall, at Great Malvern Priory,[32] demolished in 1841, but fortunately detailed drawings were made by Blore (Pl. 25 A). This was a wooden hall with traceried windows. The roof had alternate tie- and collar-beam trusses, both with elaborate cusping, that over the tie in two tiers of openings. The ogee arch with apex cut into the collar is reminiscent of the early 14th-century roof of Baguley Hall, Cheshire,[18] although the braces there rest not on the wall plate, but on posts.

Dorset provides two notable examples of cusped roofs, but varying from the usual west country type. Behind the Elizabethan house of Tyneham, its mid 14th-century predecessor [45] remains with a portion of the original hall roof. This had a cusped or scalloped arch-brace, with a quatrefoil over the collar. The wind-braces are also cusped, but not to the extent of the remarkable roof at Fiddleford Manor,[46] where there are not only wind-braces with ogee trefoils and traceried spandrels, but scalloped wheels set horizontally between the

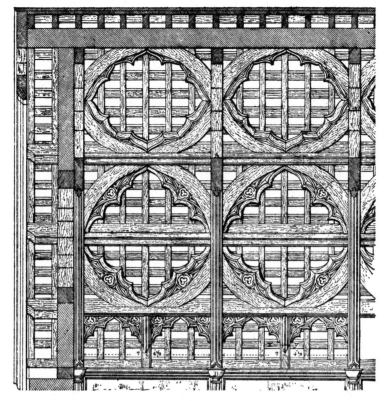

Fig. 98. The Guesten Hall, Worcester, c. 1320, wind-braces.

collars and upper purlins (Pl. XLIX A). This delicate elaboration probably dates from c. 1370, or between 1355, when William Latimer married Margaret, heiress of John Maury of Fiddleford, and 1382, after which Latimer is no longer in evidence, having been active in the county as a king's commissioner and sheriff. The property was apparently held of the Abbot of Glastonbury. The solar, with original window, has a roof of the same type and detail, but the hall roof must have been taken down and re-erected when the hall was reconstructed c. 1500, the date of the windows and screens doorways.

The arch-braced collar-beam roof continues as a popular form into the 15th century, and intermediate trusses with smaller arches develop, as at Woodlands [66] (Pl. XI) and Ashbury [99] Manors. Bold foiling is found in the west country; an elaborately cusped example existed till 1937 in the hall of the merchant William Canynge's House at Bristol.[70] Elsewhere the roofs tend to be plainer, although cusped wind-braces are still in fashion alongside the simpler curved forms. The crown-post is now normally absent and the space above the collar often free of timbers. The arch-braces are chamfered at Tickenham,[62] as they once were at Kingston Seymour; [94] at Martock [68] they are moulded with roll and fillet of the slender ogee-curved type of the 15th century. The destroyed roof of the Fish House at Meare,[67] in the same county, was very similar, and possibly also a 15th-century renovation, though Parker considered it contemporary with the house. Moulding is also used in the main arches of the superb roof of Woodlands Manor, Mere, their cambered collars set high with two raking struts, absent in the intermediate trusses. At Wenlock the prior's hall [98] has richly moulded arches with carved bosses half way up and at the apex, where a trefoil is cut above. Lytes Cary [76] has a carved pendant.

The arch braces may have their ends sunk into the walls, or springing from the wall plate. The moulded arches rise directly from stone corbels at St Cross, [61] and from wooden ones in the late 15th-century halls of Gainsborough [95] and Cothay Manor. [96] In Devon, where a number of such roofs remain, the wall posts may come within a foot of the ground in some houses and in others be not more than 4 feet in length. They are set on a template, either square or 4 to 5 feet long. Mr Everett has found such an arrangement at Trayhill, [87] and at Gorwyn Farm near Cheriton Bishop, [86] where there is an attached shaft with capital.

These shafts are often set on stone corbels, as in the hall at Lincoln College, Oxford, [73] where there are moulded bases to the posts. At Wanswell Court [75] there are separate attached columns with capitals and bases, standing on corbel heads of which the head-dresses, like those on the stops of the parlour windows, suggest a date c. 1450–60. Octagonal posts with elaborate capitals and bases stand on moulded corbels in the hall of Prior Singer at Wenlock. [98] At Ashbury Manor the shafts are short, with base and corbel combined.

There is a neat arrangement at Bewley Court, Lacock. [91] Here the arch-brace rests on a stone corbel, semi-octagonal, embattled like the wall plate and carried on a small shaft which joins a string-course dividing the wall surface horizontally some 8 feet from the ground. Near the oriel arch this string turns down to form the inner order of a moulded jamb, of which the outer order is carried upwards and returned as a cornice below the wall plate.

There are some fine 14th-century examples of the tie-beam roof, and one of great magnificence in the first-floor hall (c. 1340) (frontispiece) of Brinsop Court [33] with crown-posts having cusped four-way struts, trussed rafters between the principals, and moulded beams and wall plates. Part of another remains to the solar wing at 54–56 Church Street, Chesham (Buckinghamshire); [35] a larger arched chamfered tie-beam with curved wall brackets and crown-post; the net tracery of the window suggests a mid 14th-century date. At Staick House, Eardisland (Herefordshire), [52] there is a carved *patera* at the apex of the arch-braced tie-beam, and at 20 Swan Street, Kingsclere (Hampshire), [53] a carved head in 'mason's cap' * (Pl. VIII F and G). Here the arch-braces have gone, but their sockets remain, and the apex is cut in the tie-beam itself, as at Hampton Court, King's Lynn. [58] There is no crown-post, but a braced collar above; a late 14th-century date is suggested by the ogee-mouldings of the posts. The carved head and all signs of an early hall were disguised until Mr A. R. Florance bought the property in 1951 and uncovered the timbering.

The tie-beam crown-post roof was especially popular in the south-east, probably because of its association with the aisled hall which survived longer here than in the west and Midlands. There are a number in Essex. In Kent especially the Wealden House, replacing

* A linen coif.

the aisled hall, was already developing in the late 14th century, and at Wardes, Otham,[57] there is a notable early example of arch-braced tie-beam roof with crown-post and collar purlin. But the majority date from *c.* 1450 to *c.* 1530. Sussex roofs are of similar character. At 4 High Street, East Grinstead, Mr R. T. Mason has found a 15th-century crown-post very similar to that at Charney Basset. There is a fine roof of this kind, still open, in the Pilgrims' Rest at Battle,[77] with moulded capital and base to the crown-post and four-way struts as usual.

At East Meon the Court House [69] probably dates from the first half of the 15th century, and has a trussed rafter roof with, at intervals, a cambered tie-beam with the heads of kings and bishops. In Queens' College, Cambridge,[74] the hall roof was designed by Thomas Sturgeon, an Essex carpenter, in 1449. It combines tie-beams and arch-braced collars; angels hold shields charged with the initials of the Foundresses, Queen Margaret of Anjou (1448), followed by Queen Elizabeth Woodville (1465). The 15th-century colouring has been restored, the gilded lead stars being original.

An unusual roof once existed at Little Mytton, Lancashire,[79] its form remaining to us in J. C. Buckler's drawing (Pl. XXIV c). The tie-beam is steeply cambered, with curved braces forming a wide pointed arch below, and having traceried and carved spandrels. The arch-braces rest on corbels on one side, and on shafts, with capitals, to floor level on the outer wall. Above the tie there is latticed strutting, moulded. Another truss in the hall is of arch-braced collar type.

A sturdier type of roof seems to have been usual in the north, to combat the snow and strong winds of the upland region. The lighter south-eastern roof of equal scantling, the trussed rafter, is almost unknown, though one example has been found at Sowerby Bridge,[54] near Halifax. However, this lacks the usual crown-post and collar purlin. There is no ridge piece, the pairs of rafters being halved at the apex and connected by a collar and occasional tie-beam. It is suggested that the south-eastern type of roof came northwards in the 14th century, but was swamped by the local type, which is not found in the south or even the Midlands. It is used in the other Halifax aisled halls discovered recently, such as Towngate, Sowerby,[55] and High Bentley, Shelf.[56] This is a heavier, double-framed roof with a ridge-piece set square and carried by a central post, the principal rafters meeting the sides of the latter near the apex. The heavy king-post supporting the ridge seems also to have occurred in Westmorland, as in the west wing of Preston Patrick.

The low-pitched roof with a short king-post and the purlins laid direct on the cambered tie-beam occurs late in the 14th century at Westminster. In the Abbot's Hall,[47] glazed 1375–6, the end trusses are original, with trefoil and other tracery in the spandrels, and the roof was probably the work of Hugh Herland himself. The curved braces rest on stone corbels carved with angels, each holding his shield in a different manner. The adjoining solar, the Jerusalem Chamber, is of similar date and type, but with elaborate ornament. In the recent restoration this was repainted in the original colours, blue, gold, green and red.

The hammer-beam roof was evolved to strengthen the arch-braced roof over a wide hall, and solved the problem of covering a span of over 30 feet. The old idea of development from a curtailed tie-beam is incorrect, for the hammer-beam is an elongated sole-piece, which is the horizontal timber set at right angles to the wall plate, and where there were two wall plates, as later, it connects the inner to the outer plate. The hammer-beam tied the principals more firmly to the wall. If the horizontal sole-piece was extended into the room as a hammer-beam, the arch-brace could be embedded in its inner end, the rafter foot in its outer end, this providing a cantilever, and a curved brace supporting the hammer-beam from the wall post would bring the thrust further down the wall. Later

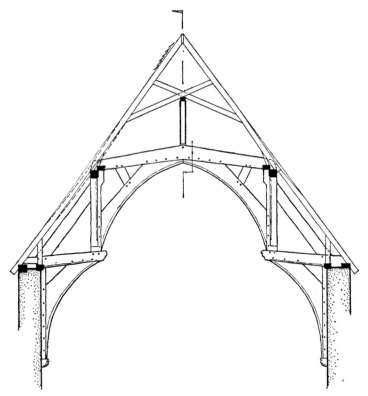

Fig. 99. Pilgrims' (Strangers') Hall, Winchester, section of truss.

this process was repeated with a second hammer-beam, as in East Anglia, especially famous for roofs of this type. Indeed it is believed that some of the Norfolk hammer-beams were developed to strengthen the point of junction of the two parts of an arch-brace in a 'couple' roof (one without tie-beam or collar). It was then realized that there need not be the same curve above as below the hammer-beam, hence a less steep arch could be used above, providing a wider span to the building.* The hammer-beam projected more and more, and with the upper arch springing from its inner end, formed as it were the cusp of a trefoiled roof section, often with angel or other carved projection.

The hammer-beam appears as early as *c.* 1240 in the sketch-book of the French architect, Villard de Honnecourt, 'a good light roof' to use over a stone vault,† but does not seem

* Howard and Crossley (1933), 99.
† Harvey (1947), 51–2, with illustration.

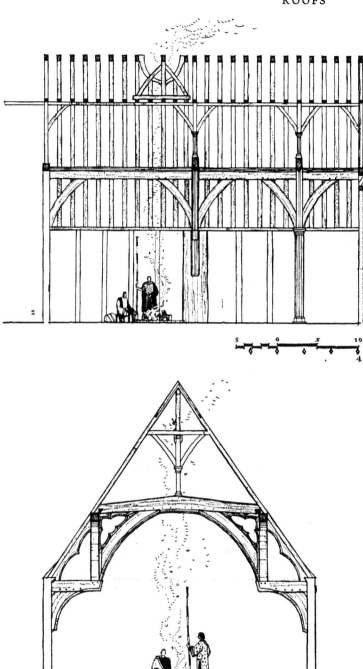

Fig. 100. Tiptofts, Wimbish, *c.* 1348–67, longitudinal and transverse sections (principal truss).

to have developed in France. In England the earliest known example is in the Pilgrims' Hall at Winchester,[27] 1325–6 (Fig. 99), with heads of kings and bishops carved at the ends of the hammer-beams, and scissor-braces above the crown-post. The roof at Tiptofts at Wimbish [43] (Figs. 100 and 101) has been dated *c.* 1348–1367, and is slightly more ad-vanced, for the strut fastening hammer-beam to post is now nearer the slope of the roof; the collar and curved braces are wave-moulded and have cusping in the spandrels.

At Market Deeping Rectory in Lincolnshire [44] there is an incipient hammer-beam with-out post, a carved (lion) corbel, which projects from the wall plate to support a pointed arch, also moulded, to the collar-beam; this truss alter-nates with tie-beam trusses. In the early 15th-century hall at South Wraxall [72] there are other lion corbels, here supporting a four-centred arch, but they rest on traceried stone brackets with shafts having moulded bases. At Great Dixter, Northiam (*c.* 1465–75),[80] the hammer-truss is again alternated with a tie-beam and crown-post, here to give stability to the timber walls. The arch-braces are sometimes set nearer the wall plate than the inner end of the hammer-beam. Such incipient hammer-trusses, with elaborate angel terminals and corbels, occur in the refectory at Cleeve Abbey.

Hugh Herland's superb roof of 1395–9, spanning 67 feet 6 inches, at Westminster Hall [60] is the finest piece of carpentry in Europe. It is a combination of arch-brace and hammer-beam. The great two-centred arches rise from stone corbels, and intersect the

Fig. 101. Tiptofts, Wimbish, c. 1348–67, reconstruction of hall.

stiffening hammer-beams and posts to meet a cambered collar. From the hammer-posts subsidiary braces rise to the apex of the main arch, forming, with the curved braces of the hammers, a trefoiled profile, with horizontal angels acting as cusps; from embattled pilasters on the posts there spring lateral four-centred arches to uphold the main purlin at collar level. There is pierced tracery in all the spandrels, the larger having rows of trefoiled ogee-headed panels. The beautiful angels were carved by Robert Brusyndon; they rise from clouds and hold shields of the royal arms of Richard II.

The roof of the Law Library at Exeter (8 The Close) [63] (Fig. 102; Pl. XLVII B) is a smaller copy of this, with certain modifications. It has the same main arch, hammers and trefoiled profile, together with trefoiled ogee-headed panels in the spandrels. However, instead of the tracery above the collar, there is a semicircular coving with central boss, and another local feature is found in the shallow curved intermediate principals, fronted at the wall plate with a lion *séjant*, which connect the purlins and the apex of the lateral arch, which is nearly semicircular. There is a carved head at the springing of the upper cove, and a large boss at the central purlin, from which straight wind-braces are set diagonally to end in a curve near their junction with the main trusses. It is difficult to date this roof,

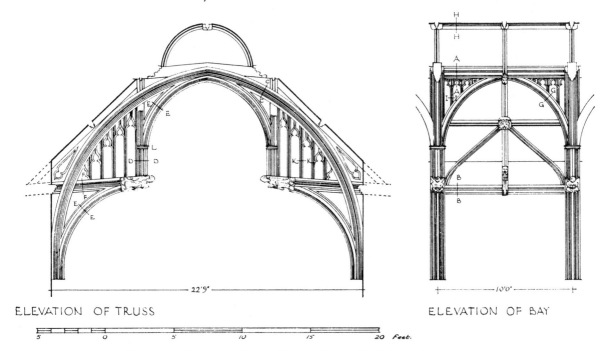

ELEVATION OF TRUSS

ELEVATION OF BAY

Fig. 102. The Law Library, Exeter, first half of the 15th century.

which in itself suggests the early 15th century. But the hall doorways seem quite late in type, and the windows are not symmetrical with the roof, or even opposite. The hammer angels with their long robes and cloud terminals are a cruder representation of those at Westminster. They carry shields or open books, and their longer hair might place them in the later 15th century. The cloud terminals were copied elsewhere, as in the angel decoration above the arcades of Broadclyst Church (Devon) of *c*. 1500.

Certain features of the Law Library roof are common to a group of five roofs in Exeter and its neighbourhood, the product no doubt of the same carpenter or yard, within perhaps a period of thirty years.* The others are at Bowhill, the Guildhall and Deanery, all in Exeter, and Cadhay Manor at Ottery St Mary, twelve miles away. The common feature lies not only in the upper coving, in the manner of the south-western barrel roofs, also found at Athelhampton, but in the treatment of the intermediate trusses.

* A. W. Everett.

The nearest to the Law Library is found at Cadhay,[85] where the hall roof has lost its hammers, but part of their arch below the main truss, and also evidence of an intermediate truss similar in form, remain.

At Bowhill [64] (Fig. 103) the hall roof is of simple arch-braced construction, but with the same upper coving. A roof over the east (solar) wing has an intermediate member with boss and shallow curve reminiscent of the lesser truss at Cadhay, the lower cusp here retaining its leaf ornament, in the position of the lion *séjant* at the Law Library.

Very like the Bowhill solar is the roof over the Deanery at Exeter,[83] where the arch-braces, delicately moulded, rise from stone corbels, and the intermediate trusses have the shallow curve and foliage cusp. The Guildhall roof [84] of *c.* 1465 is very similar, and must

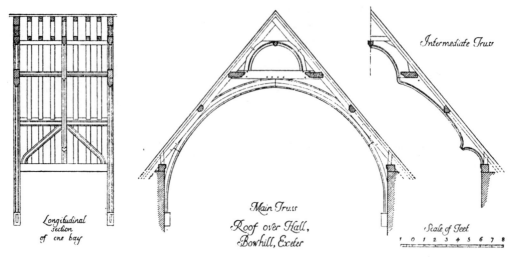

Fig. 103. Bowhill, Exeter, first half of the 15th century.

be close in date. Here the corbels are of carved wood and the intermediate trusses retain their bosses and foliage cusps, with straight wind-braces, like those of the Law Library and Cadhay, but here repeated in the upper tier also.

It is interesting to speculate how the Westminster design came to be adopted so far away in Devonshire. The link may have been provided by Hugh Herland's presence at Darting-ton [59] to design the roof of the hall of Richard II's half-brother, John Holland, Duke of Exeter, built 1388–1400. The King's Carpenter would probably have been consulted for such a roof, of 38 foot span, and we know that the result was a hammer-beam construction of similar proportions to the larger one at Westminster, but without the arch-rib. It has been copied in the modern roof by William Weir.

Over Beddington Hall in Surrey [107] there is a beautiful roof of *c.* 1500 which might be an adaptation of that at Westminster to suit a four-centred arch. Again the arch-rib inter-sects hammer-post and beam, and springs, as does the curved brace of the hammer, from a moulded corbel with a band of quatrefoils and cresting. The hammer-beams terminate in octagonal cappings, with short pendant. From them springs the central arch, also four-centred, of the trefoiled profile, and which is set in a square frame with traceried spandrels and collar, all the timber being heavily moulded. A second collar divides two tiers of pointed cinquefoil-headed panels.

Typologically later, at least, is Edward IV's magnificent roof to his great hall at Eltham [93] (Pl. XLVII A), designed by his chief carpenter Edmund Graveley, 1479–80. Indeed, from its close resemblance to Beddington, Graveley may have designed both. The arch-rib has gone, but there is the same square frame with bevelled angles for the central four-centred arch, stone corbels, and two rows of cinquefoiled panels above the collars. Again heavy mouldings give a most decorative effect, and are very similar in section. This has been called a 'false hammer-beam roof', because the posts with their slender shafts do not stand upon the hammer-beams but are mortised into them. Here the octagonal cappings are bolder, and the pendants lengthened by the inclusion of traceried 'lanterns', now restored from one surviving original. The hall was framed beside the palace gateway; it was restored in 1933–5 through the munificence of Mr Stephen Courtauld.

It is interesting to compare the Eltham roof with that of one of Edward IV's rich subjects. Moulded hammer-beams are used in the Hall of John Halle [92] (Pl. XLVI B), and the long wall posts, with moulded caps and bases, are supported on stone heads; the intermediate arches terminate in carved angels holding scrolls. The hall roof of Colston's House, [88] home of a Bristol merchant, is known to us from a drawing of 1821. Here rows of trefoiled panels adorned the spandrels of the great arch-braces. How these panels were formed is shown in a 15th-century roof discovered by Mr Everett at Yard Farm, Rose Ash in Devon. [89] Here the carving was done on the roof in position, for the decorative arcading of the truss was left unfinished (Pl. XLVII C). First a row of holes was bored with an auger to form the head of each panel, then the body cut out with a chisel, and the heads roughed out with a gouge. At Cochwillam, Llanllechid [82] (c. 1450–80), the moulded hammer-beams are embattled, and once carried heraldic shields of which the pin-holes remain. The curved braces have foliated spandrels, and the wall posts, again shafted, rest on stone head corbels; there is west country foiling above the collar.

Perhaps the most remarkable roof for ornament is that over Weare Giffard Hall in North Devon. [100] A great arch-brace cut in one piece with the collar is trefoiled and sub-cusped, with finial-pendants and tracery. It rests on moulded hammer-beams faced with seated animal figures, the braces also cusped and traceried, supported on corbels. The whole surface of the roof is traceried, and no doubt was once picked out in colour (Pl. XLVIII B).

The Commandery at Worcester [102] once had hammer-beams, but now these are connected by a similarly moulded tie for strengthening. The central arch is nearly semi-circular, with a carved boss at the apex and traceried spandrels below a straight collar. At the sides and above the collar are three tiers of traceried panels, with similar decoration in the brackets, supported on slender shafted wall posts down to floor level.

The central arch is again semicircular at Rufford Old Hall, [105] with a boss at the apex, but here the collar is cambered, with foiling above, and crenellated, as are the hammer-beams. These have angels carrying shields, and traceried braces. Adlington Hall [106] is very similar, with the main arch embattled as well as moulded.

The four-centred arch of Eltham and suites of horizontal mouldings are adopted, and the composition improved, in the true hammer-beam roofs designed by Humphrey Coke at

Oxford, those of Corpus Christi College and Christ Church. At Corpus Christi (1512–1517) [108] the collar is cambered and has curved braces, and no tracery above. Again there are stone corbels for the wall posts, and the hammers have octagonal terminals, their pendants here carved.

Christ Church (c. 1529) [112] has more elaboration, with traceried spandrels to the four-centred arch, a carved boss at the apex, and cinquefoiled panels flanking the king-post

Fig. 104. Crosby Hall, ceiling of 1466+.

above the collar. There is a band of quatrefoils with badges to the hammer-beams, a continuation of the wall-plate frieze. Here is renewed the feature of four-centred lateral arches springing from the ends of the hammer-beams. This appears at Westminster Hall and the Law Library, but not at Beddington and Eltham.

These lateral arches are developed into hammer-beam trusses with additional pendants in the great hall roof at Hampton Court [113] (Pl. XLVIII A). This was designed by Coke's successor (1531) as King's Chief Carpenter, James Nedeham, who became Surveyor General of the royal works (1532–44) and was aided by Coke's son-in-law John Russell, who succeeded him in the earlier post.* The tradition of Coke's Christ Church roof continues, with elaborated detail, every surface decorated with blind tracery, as in the spandrels of the four-centred arches, which here are loftier and have four-light tracery above, on either

* Harvey (1954), 191.

A

B

C

Plate XLVII. 15th-century Roofs.

A. Eltham Palace, hall, *c.* 1479–80.
B. Law Library, Exeter.
C. Yard Farm, Rose Ash, Devon, showing uncompleted pattern.

B

A

Plate XLVIII. Roofs.

A. Hampton Court, hall. *c.* 1530–5.
B. Weare Giffard, later 15th century.

side of a columned crown-post. Renaissance decoration is now added to Gothic, such as the foliage combined with the arms of Henry VIII and Anne Boleyn used in the spandrels of the hammer-braces, which rest as usual on stone corbels.

John Nedeham may also have been responsible for the roof of the hall at Cowdray,* [110] perhaps built *c.* 1540 for the Earl of Southampton. Burnt down in 1793, it is, however, known to us from Grimm's drawing of 1782. It had much open tracery in the spandrels and above the collar, but no lateral hammer-beam trusses.

The hammer-beam roof continued to develop throughout the 16th century, and the double hammer-beam became popular. It is used at Gifford's Hall, Stoke-by-Nayland. [114]

This went concurrently with the preference for concealing the roof timbers. Crosby Hall [81] (*c.* 1466) (Fig. 104) represents the transition from the open roof to a decorated ceiling. This unique roof has been called a fan-vaulted ceiling because of its hosts of elaborate pendants, four in each truss, each having four curved braces with traceried spandrels, forming arches lengthways and across, the resultant compartments further divided by moulded ribs with bosses at the intersections. The result might be called a cusped wagon roof, a highly decorative ceiling hung from simple structural timbers, a depressed four-centred arch with scissor truss above.†

Wind-braces

Wind-braces have an interesting development. They seem to derive, at least in part, from the braces forming the arcade of an aisled hall. When the floor was cleared of posts the arcade plate became a purlin, at first square set as before, and part of the actual roof. The arch-braces were then transformed into wind-braces, to give lateral stability. The roof from Bradenstoke Priory shows this development.

However, the aisled hall at Fyfield has straight wind-braces, and in an aisled hall derivative, such as Amberley Court, there is often an upper tier of wind-braces as well as the vestigial arch-braces to a square-set purlin.

As might be expected from their origin, the 14th-century wind-braces were usually curved, as at Creslow Manor, forming an arch against the rafters. Sometimes they appear to have been decorated with geometric ornament, like the circles containing stars and flowing tracery at Bewley Court.

With the growth of roof cusping in the west, the curved wind-braces tended to be foiled as well. This is found in most of the Herefordshire roofs of the 14th century. Trefoiled arches are found at Amberley Court and the March at Eyton, and with pierced spandrels at Eaton Hall, Leominster. At Burton Court, Eardisland, there are two tiers of cinquefoiled arches. Tyneham (Dorset) has ogee arches, the lower tier scalloped, and at Fiddleford they are scalloped with pierced trefoil ornament in the spandrels, like the great horizontal wheel-braces at collar level (Pl. XLIX A).

Cusping continued into the 15th century, the cinquefoiled arch being especially fashionable, as at Gothelney, [71] where the upper (third) tier, over the hall, is reversed. They are sub-cusped in four tiers at the Hall of John Halle. At Woodlands Manor the cinquefoiled arches alternate in each tier, the apex of one forming the springing of the next in height (Pl. XLIX c). Here some of the foliated points remain to the cusps, as in the upper two tiers of the fine early 15th-century roof of Chapel Farm, Wigmore, Herefordshire [65] (Fig. 105). Again the three tiers are arranged to form a pattern; the lowest has pierced trefoiled arches; in the next stage these are placed alternately and with other arches back to back, to form, in between, a lozenge cusped to a quatrefoil; the uppermost tier has

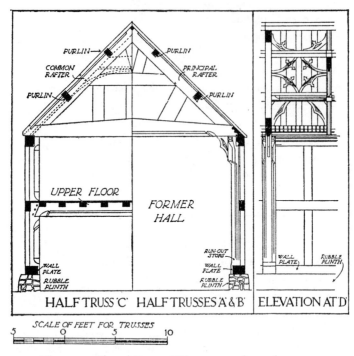

Fig. 105. Chapel Farm, Wigmore, early 15th century.

trefoiled arches again, but upside-down. Such foliated cusps may have been present in other roofs, but are now lost.

Indeed wind-braces could provide an admirable vehicle for the display of Gothic tracery. At Eltham Palace (Pl. 25 b) the pattern is somewhat akin to that at Wigmore but with ogee arches cusped on both sides in top and bottom tiers, combined in the central tier to form an ogee-curved lozenge, or vesica, trefoiled at either end, laid horizontally.

Earlier, at South Wraxall, the central vesica is set vertically, quatrefoiled with traceried spandrels, two in each bay divided by the intermediate truss; there is a trefoiled arch below each, reversed in the upper tier. Quatrefoils were used in two main stages at Vaughan's Place, Shrewsbury,[90] a roof now existing only in Buckler's drawing, and at Rufford Hall angle cusping forms a quatrefoil in each of the three tiers. In Lancashire cusped angle-braces had already appeared in the 14th-century Smithells Hall. They are small in the 15th-century Cochwillam in North Wales, and at Denton Hall [78] they are cut to form an elaborate figure at the junction of truss and purlin.

The cusping can be fragile, almost ribbon-like, as in the seven-foiled wind-braces in three tiers at Lytes Cary. The cusping of Ashbury Manor is similar, but here the lowest tier is cinquefoiled, the next alternated, and the narrow topmost stage retains one of a band of pointed quatrefoils set diagonally (Pl. XLIX B).

In the ornate roof at Weare Giffard the wind-braces are crossed and cusped. Sometimes the arches are arranged to form two-light tracery. In the late 15th-century Abbot's Hall at Milton Abbas (Dorset) [104] there are two cinquefoiled pointed 'lights' having a central cusped bar, the intermediate truss forming the mullion, arranged in four tiers. The wind-braces at Hampton Court (1530–5) are further elaborated with tracery behind the lateral arches and subsidiary hammer-beam. These roofs were probably once gay with colour. In one of the most splendid, at Wenlock, the wind-braces form with the purlins a broad band of flowing trefoil ornament.

The simple curved wind-braces occurring in the 14th century were a popular form in the 15th century, as at Church House, Salisbury, and Gainsborough Old Hall. The Fish House, Meare, had two tiers of such arches, and there are three tiers at Wanswell Court (Pl. 5 B) and Lincoln College, with four at Little Sodbury. [97] These wind-braces are arranged with the arches parallel. At Martock there are two arches in each bay of the lowest and upper-most tiers, and one large one in the central stage. Sometimes the arches are alternated, the apex in one tier against the springing of the row above. This is found in the hall at St Cross, but here the lowest tier has merely curved angle-braces. In the hall at Cothay the wind-braces are set in curved V formation, in parallel tiers, but there is the normal arrangement in the solar. At Cotehele (before 1520) [109] the hall roof has four tiers of moulded wind-braces, the usual arch and the V intersecting in each bay, a method already elaborated with cusping into the 'two-light' form at Milton.

At Beddington there are two stages of ogee arches, and at Great Chalfield four-centred wind-braces above the contemporary hall ceiling (Pl. 26).

Simple curved, rather than cusped, wind-braces continue into the 16th century, as at Brasenose and Corpus Christi Colleges, Oxford.

The Cornice

The wall plate was moulded as early as the 14th century. In the 15th century a crenellated member was added, as at Gothelney and Wenlock Priory. Elaboration into a cornice seems to have been a feature of the 15th century. At Winchester the hall roof of St Cross has a band of trefoiled panels reminiscent of the stone frieze above the nave arches in the cathedral. This is used in the Exchequer of the Vicars' Close at Wells, also early in the century.

A frieze of running ornament is more common, such as the band of pierced flowing tracery between two moulded members at Cochwillam Hall, here embattled. This is more delicate than the somewhat similar work at the Hall of John Halle, and the uncusped tracery of the solar cornice at Ashbury Manor (Pl. XLVI c). At Weare Giffard the ornament is more naturalistic, and there is a crest of tablet flower above the upper moulding. Cleeve Abbey refectory has a frieze of leaf designs and crenellation, while running ornament combined with quatrefoils is used in the pierced traceried frieze at Lytes Cary. At Crosby Hall a band of quatrefoils is a dominant feature, with embattled cornice, and some quatrefoils remain of a frieze in the porch chamber roof at Ashbury (Pl. VIII E). This type continued to be popular in the early 16th century. At Oxford the hall roofs at Corpus Christi and Christ Church have a frieze of quatrefoiled panels carved with Tudor badges, and the Abbot's Hall (*c.* 1528) at Forde [111] has a band of diagonally set quatrefoils enclosing *paterae*, above an embattled wall plate. At Hampton Court there is elaborate blind tracery over the moulded wall plate, as in the other lateral surfaces of the hall roof.

In Lyddington Bede House (Rutland) [103] at the end of the 15th century, the ribbed ceiling has an elaborate coved and traceried cornice, with fan vaulting over a frieze of running ornament. It is similar to that of a rood-screen gallery in a church of this period.

ROOF EXAMPLES

		References (most with illustrations)
(1) *c.* 1200	Kersey Priory, Suff.	Dickinson (in press).
(2) *c.* 1250–60	Great Bricett Priory, Suff.	Dickinson (in press).
(3) *c.* 1258–74	The Old Deanery, Salisbury	Drinkwater (1964).
(4) *c.* 1280	Donington-le-Heath Manor House Farm, Leics.	Marsden (1962), 33–42.
(5) *c.* 1280	Bisham Abbey, Berks., hall	*Country Life* (3), 320–4.
(6) *c.* 1280	Charney Basset Manor House, Berks., solar	Turner (1851), 153–5; Wood (1950), 8–10.
(7) *c.* 1290	Old Soar, Plaxtol, Kent, solar	Wood (1950), 36–8; M.O.W. Guide (33).
(8) end C 13th	Master's House, St John's Hospital, Northampton, evidence	Turner (1851), 156.
(9) *c.* 1290	St Mary's Hospital, Chichester	Smith (1958 a), 115–16.
(10) 1299–1300	Merton College, Oxford, Warden's Lodging	Smith (1955), 88.
(11) last quarter C 13th	Abbot's Lodging, Halesowen, Worcs.	Jones & Smith (1958), 25.
(12) *c.* 1290–13'0	West Bromwich Old Hall, Staffs.	Smith (1958 a), 140–1.
(13) *c.* 1300	Wasperton Manor Farm, War.	Jones & Smith (1958).
(14) *c.* 1300	Fyfield Hall, Ess.	Smith (1955), 91–2; Smith (1958 a), 119.
(15) early C 14th	Stanton's Farm, Black Notley, Ess.	Smith (1955), 81–3.
(16) early C 14th–	Great Coxwell Barn, Berks.	Horn (1958), 11; Horn & Born (1965).
(17) early C 14th	Barn at Dorchester, Oxon., evidence	Smith (1958 a), 140, pl. XVII (Buckler drawing).
(18) early C 14th	Baguley Hall, Ches.	Smith & Stell (1960), pls. XXV–XXVII; Crossley (1951), 127–8, pl. 138.
(19) early C 14th	Tickerage, West Hoathly, Suss.	Mason (1957), 82–5.
(20) 1st half C 14th	Amberley Court, Marden, Heref.	R.C.H.M. *Herefordshire*, II, 137–8; Crossley (1951), 133.
(21) 1318	Camoise Court, Chislehampton, Oxon.	*V.C.H. Oxfordshire*, VII.
(22) early C 14th	Bradenstoke Priory, Wilts., refectory, now at St Donat's Castle, Glam.	Smith (1955), 89–90, pl. XIII.
(23) C 14th	Barn at Bradford-on-Avon, Wilts.	M.O.W. Guide (5).
(24) *c.* 1320	The Guesten Hall, Worcester; evidence	Fletcher (1946), 432.
(25) *c.* 1325	Mayfield Palace, Suss.	Parker (1853), 292.
(26) *c.* 1325	Ightham Mote, Kent	
(27) 1325–6	Pilgrims' Hall, Winchester	Nisbett (1894–7); Smith (1958 a), 123; *Medieval Archaeology* (1957), I, 152.

		References (most with illustrations)
(28) *c.* 1330	Edgar's Farm, Stowmarket, Suff.	Smith (1958 b), 54–61.
(29) *c.* 1330	Creslow Manor House, Bucks.	R.C.H.M. *Bucks.*, II, 97; R.C.H.M., MS. sketch.
(30) *c.* 1330	'The Abbey', Sutton Courtenay, Berks., hall solar	Parker (1853), 32. Parker (1853), 87.
(31) *c.* 1330–40	Mancetter Manor House, War.	Smith (1955), 80, 89, 90; *V.C.H. Warwickshire*, IV, 117–19.
(32) *c.* 1340	The Guesten Hall, Great Malvern Priory, Worcs., evidence	Parker (1853), 35, 258.
(33) *c.* 1340	Brinsop Court, Heref.	R.C.H.M. *Herefordshire*, II, 31, pl. 102; *Country* *Life* (5), 745–6, 649.
(34) *c.* 1340	The Old Parsonage, Marlow, Bucks.	Wood (1949), pl. XIII.
(35) mid C 14th	54–56 Church St, Chesham, Bucks.	R.C.H.M. *Bucks.*, I, 95.
(36) mid C 14th	Nurstead Court, Kent	Parker (1853), 282 (Blore's drawing); Smith (1955), 84–6, fig. 3.
(37) *c.* 1340–50	Lampetts, Fyfield, Ess.	Smith (1955), 84, 87–9.
(38) C 14th	Church Farm, Fressingfield, Suff.	Smith (1958 a), 121–2.
(39) C 14th	Gate House Farm, Felsted, Ess.	R.C.H.M. *Essex*, II, 76; Smith (1955), 87–9; Smith (1958 a), 121.
(40) *c.* 1341–9	Penshurst, Kent	Parker (1853), frontispiece; *Country Life* (23), 844–54, 894–902.
(41) *c.* 1343	The Guildhall, Leicester	Smith (1955), 90–1; *Country Life*, 2 Oct 1958, 719.
(42) 1346–7 & 1284–6	Conway Castle, Caern., hall	M.O.W. Guide (12), 17–18.
(43) *c.* 1348–67	Tiptofts, Wimbish, Ess.	Smith (1955), 90, fig. 5; Smith (1958 a), 123.
(44) mid C 14th	Market Deeping Rectory, Lincs.	Parker (1853), 242–3.
(45) mid C 14th	Tyneham, Dor.	Oswald (1935), 33.
(46) *c.* 1355–82	Fiddleford Manor, Dor.	N. Teulon-Porter (1955), *Somerset & Dorset* *Notes and Queries*, XXVII, pt. CCLIX, 1–4.
(47) *c.* 1375–6	Abbot's Hall, Westminster	R.C.H.M. *London*, I, 86–8, pl. 170.
(48) C 14th	Middle Hill Farm, Hope-under-Dinmore, Heref.	R.C.H.M. *Herefordshire*, III, 71, pl. 39.
(49) C 14th	Court Farm, Preston Wynne, Heref.	R.C.H.M. *Herefordshire*, II, 155, p!. 39.
(50) late C 14th	Pencombe, Lower Marston, Heref.	R.C.H.M. *Herefordshire*, II, 151.
(51) C 14th	Houses at Weobley, Heref.	R.C.H.M. *Herefordshire*, III, 196, 197, 199, 201, pl. 38.
(52) late C 14th	Staick House, Eardisland, Heref.	R.C.H.M. *Herefordshire*, III, 47–8.
(53) late C 14th	20 Swan St, Kingsclere, Hants	
(54) late C 14th	Lower Bentley Royd, Sowerby Bridge, near Halifax, Yorks.	Atkinson & McDowall (in press).
(55) late C 14th	Towngate, Sowerby, near Halifax, Yorks.	Atkinson & McDowall (in press).
(56) late C 14th	High Bentley, Shelf, near Halifax, Yorks.	Atkinson & McDowall (in press).
(57) late C 14th	Wardes, Otham, Kent	Oswald (1933), 21–7.
(58) late C 14th	Hampton Court, King's Lynn, Norf.	Pantin (1963), 447–9, 453.
(59) *c.* 1388–1400	Dartington Hall, Devon.	Emery (1958), 194–6, pl. XXII.
(60) 1394–1402	Westminster Hall, remodelled	R.C.H.M. *London*, II, 121–2, pls. 176, 178, 180; Crossley (1951), 138–9, pl. 166.
(61) late C 14th– early C 15th	Hospital of St Cross, Winchester, hall	Crossley (1951), fig. 160.
(62) *c.* 1400	Tickenham Court, Som.	Smith (1958 a), 131; British Museum Add. *MS.*, 36436, f. 396.
(63) 1st half C 15th	Law Library, 8 The Close, Exeter	*Archaeological Journal* (1957), CXIV, 138–9, pl. XXVII.
(64) 1st half C 15th	Bowhill, Exeter	Everett (1958 b).

References (most with illustrations)

(65) early C 15th	Chapel Farm, Wigmore, Heref.	R.C.H.M. *Herefordshire*, III, 209, pls. 35, 184.
(66) 1st half C 15th	Woodlands Manor, Mere, Wilts.	*Country Life* (31), (10 May 1924), figs. 7, 8, 10; (17 May 1924), fig. 2.
(67) C 15th	Fish House, Meare, Som.	Parker (1853), 300.
(68) C 15th	Treasurer's House, Martock, Som.	
(69) 1st half C 15th	Court House, East Meon, Hants	
(70) 1st half C 15th	Canynge's House, Redcliff St, Bristol, evidence	Pantin (1963), 470–2, pl. XXIII.
(71) 1st half C 15th	Gothelney Manor, Som.	Research by W. A. Pantin, F.S.A.
(72) *c.* 1435	South Wraxall Manor House, Wilts., hall	Pugin (1840), pls. 68, 69.
(73) *c.* 1436–7	Lincoln College, Oxford, hall	R.C.H.M. *Oxford*, pl. 119.
(74) 1449	Queens' College, Cambridge, hall	R.C.H.M. *Cambs*, 172, pl. 226.
(75) 1450–60	Wanswell Court, Glos.	Parker (1859), 78; *Country Life* (28), 896.
(76) *c.* 1453	Lytes Cary, Som., hall	National Trust Guide, (4).
(77) C 15th	The Pilgrims' Rest, Battle, Suss.	
(78) C 15th	Denton Hall, Lancs.	H. Taylor (1884), pls. XXV, XXXI.
(79) C 15th	Little Mytton Hall, Lancs.	
(80) *c.* 1465–75	Great Dixter, Northiam, Suss.	Lloyd (1931), 362.
(81) 1466+	Crosby Hall, London	Garner & Stratton (1929), 213.
(82) 1450–80	Cochwillam, Llanllechid, Caer.	R.C.H.M. *Caernarvonshire*, I, 134–6, pls. 86, 87, 91.
(83) mid C 15th	The Deanery, Exeter	Research by A. W. Everett, F.S.A.
(84) 1465	The Guildhall, Exeter	Research by A. W. Everett, F.S.A.
(85) later C 15th	Cadhay, Ottery St Mary, Devon	M. Baldwin & S. D. T. Spittle (1957), *Archaeological Journal*, CXIV, 161–2.
(86) C 15th	Gorwyn Farm, Cheriton Bishop, Devon	Research by A. W. Everett, F.S.A.
(87) C 15th	Trayhill, Thorverton, Devon	Research by A. W. Everett, F.S.A.
(88) C 15th	Colston's House, Small Street, Bristol, evidence	Pantin (1963), 476–7, pl. XXIII.
(89) late C 15th	Yard Farm, Rose Ash, Devon.	Research by A. W. Everett, F.S.A.
(90) C 15th	Vaughan's Place, Shrewsbury (Salop), evidence	Smith (1958 a), 143, pl. XIX (Buckler drawing).
(91) C14th & late C 15th	Bewley Court, Lacock, Wilts.	Brakspear (1912), 390, 395.
(92) 1470–83	Hall of John Halle, Salisbury	R.C.H.M. *Wilts* (in preparation).
(93) *c.* 1479–80	Eltham Palace, Kent	Pugin (1838), pls. 46, 47, 49; Garner & Stratton (1929), 212.
(94) *c.* 1470–80	Kingston Seymour Manor House, Som., evidence	Smith (1958 a), 131, pl. XVII A (Buckler drawing).
(95) *c.* 1470–84	Gainsborough Old Hall, Lincs.	*Country Life* (8), 912.
(96) *c.* 1480	Cothay Manor, Som., hall	Lloyd (1931), 363; Garner & Stratton (1929), pl. CLXXX.
	solar	Lloyd (1931), 365; Garner & Stratton (1929), pl. CLXXX.
(97) *c.* 1485	Little Sodbury Manor, Glos.	Braun (1940), fig. 22.
(98) *c.* 1486–1521	Prior's House, Wenlock, Salop	*Country Life* (29), 1433, (Buckler drawing *c.* 1850); Parker (1859), 369.
(99) *c.* 1488	Ashbury Manor, Berks.	
(100) later C 15th	Weare Giffard, Devon	Garner & Stratton (1929), 213, 215, pl. CLXXXII.
(101) *c.* 1495–1500	Athelhampton Hall, Dor.	Fletcher (1946), 405; *Country Life* (2 b), 837.
(102) *c.* 1484–1503	The Commandery, Worcester	Dollman & Jobbins (1863), pls. 36, 37.
(103) 1496–1514	Bede House, Lyddington, Rut.	Lloyd (1931), 369.
(104) *c.* 1498	Milton Abbas, Dor., Abbot's Hall	R.C.H.M. *Dorset*, II (in preparation); *Country Life* (18).

			References (most with illustrations)
(105)	1500	Rufford Old Hall, Lancs.	Crossley (1951), figs. 141, 153; Garner & Stratton (1929), pl. CLXXXII.
(106)	*c.* 1500	Adlington Hall, Ches.	Crossley (1951), 131, figs. 142, 143.
(107)	*c.* 1500	Beddington Hall, Sy.	Garner & Stratton (1929), pl. CLXXXI.
(108)	1512–17	Corpus Christi College, Oxford	R.C.H.M. *Oxford*, 51, pl. 110.
(109)	before 1520	Cotehele House, Calstock, Corn.	Garner & Stratton (1929), 40 (Buckler drawing *c.* 1835); National Trust Guide (3).
(110)	*c.* 1520–40	Cowdray Park, Suss.	Garner & Stratton (1929), 52 (Grimm drawing).
(111)	*c.* 1528	Forde Abbey, Dor., hall	R.C.H.M. *Dorset*, I, pl. 188.
(112)	*c.* 1529	Christ Church, Oxford, hall	R.C.H.M. *Oxford*, 34, pls. 81, 85.
(113)	*c.* 1530–5	Hampton Court, Middx, hall	R.C.H.M. *Middlesex*, 34, pls. 79, 80, 85.
(114)	*c.* 1538	Gifford's Hall, Stoke-by-Nayland, Suff.	Crossley (1951), fig. 161; Garner & Stratton (1929), pl. CI.

24

Staircases,

Corridors and Pentices

STAIRCASES were usual, although, judging from documentary evidence, the ladder and trapdoor were frequently used in the earlier part of the period, and doubtless continued till the end of it in the houses of poorer people. Even in the palace at Clarendon a *trapa descendens* led from the king's chamber to his chapel, but in 1244 the sheriff was ordered to replace it by a staircase, no doubt a spiral, in the angle of the building. *

The normal staircase mentioned in the Rolls is the external flight, probably of wood, protected by a penthouse roof. In June 1237 the staircase of the king's great chamber at Clarendon is to be repaired and roofed with lead, and in 1244 the outer stairs of the queen's chamber are to be removed and replaced by a staircase in the angle to ascend into her oriel. In 1250 the keeper of the manor of Feckenham is told 'to repair the porch before the door of the king's chamber there, and to make a certain penthouse over the stair descending from that porch'. At Rochester in 1256 the king ordered an outer staircase to be made 'so that strangers and others might enter that chapel without passing through the middle of the king's chamber as they used to do'.† This remark brings Henry III very close to us, although seven hundred years have passed, and it also shows why a similar outer staircase once served the first-floor chapel doorway at Old Soar.

What remains of the external staircases of the 12th and 13th centuries? There is a remarkable Norman survival to the Almonry, Great Guesthouse of the Poor, at Canterbury.‡ This ascends at right angles to the building, the sides with open arcading, the bases of the shafts mounting with the stair, their arches level with the horizontal roof; in treatment this resembles a refectory pulpit. At the bottom are four cylindrical piers with

---

* Liberate Roll, 28 Henry III; Turner (1851), 203.
† Liberate Roll, 21, 28, 34, 40 Henry III; Turner (1851), 184, 203 (Clarendon), 226 (Feckenham), 246 (Rochester).
‡ Lloyd (1931), fig. 362.

fluted capitals and large square abaci, supporting round arches with chevron ornament. The lower stairs now turn at a right angle, but in the 18th century a roadway ran between two arches, from north to south, parallel with the almonry. Rowlandson's water-colour * shows a portcullis in the northern arch, and the east end of the staircase, now free, seems to have been attached to a building containing a two-light window of late 13th-century appearance.

A covered staircase open at one side is suggested at Durham Castle, where the entrance arch to the hall is especially elaborate and well preserved.

The base of a columned respond once at the foot of a staircase to the hall has been found at the 'Music House', Norwich (*c.* 1175). Here, as at Eynsford, however, the staircase must have been enclosed in a forebuilding on the lines of those to the great 12th-century keeps. At Castle Rising (*c.* 1140) a notable stairway mounts parallel to the east wall of the keep, to serve the main entrance at an upper level on that side, here reached through a projecting guardroom; three doorways defend the steps. Maurice the Engineer's great towers at Newcastle (1171–5) and Dover (1180–6) have a similar staircase forebuilding to serve a second-floor entrance, with intermediate defensive gates; at Newcastle the steps make a right-angled turn at the top; at Dover there is an upper vestibule to the main entrance to the keep and a lower vestibule making a right-angled entry to the forebuilding. It will be noticed that the forebuilding is often set on the east, or towards that direction, to allow a chapel (two at Dover) to be accommodated. Similar stairways of approach once existed in the keeps at Hedingham (*c.* 1130), Scarborough (1158–64, south side) and Middleham (*c.* 1170, east).

At Rochester (*c.* 1130) the steps mounted along two sides, the west and north with a gate (destroyed) and a drawbridge in front of the existing forebuilding porch with chapel above. Henry III's order of 1240 for renovation and the building of a penthouse over applied to the part of this staircase below the gate. †

There are some remains of the stairway up to the vestibule of the hall and adjoining room built by King John at Corfe (1201), ‡ and Manorbier Castle retains outer staircases to both hall and chapel (Pl. L B). Otherwise, with the possible exception of Aydon, external staircases of the 13th century seem

Fig. 106. Aydon Castle, external staircase to hall.

* Reproduced in W. Townsend (1950), *Canterbury,* pl. 36. Batsford.
† Liberate Roll, 24 Henry III; Turner (1851), 196.
‡ Faulkner (1958), 167–8; Toy (1929), 96, pl. XXXVII.

Fig. 107. The Archbishop's Palace, Maidstone,
external stairs.

to have been replaced. But evidence of their position remains in the weathering of their penthouse roof at Grosmont, Netley and Aydon halls (Fig. 106), and Stokesay (solar) (Pl. L A), with, in the last three, signs of a porch roof above the entrances, apparently a form of oriel. Such steps, as at Manorbier, usually run parallel with the wall, an economical layout enabling them to be flanked by the hall windows. At the Abingdon Checker, however, they appear to have mounted at right angles, as did those of Harold's hall at Bisham, depicted in the Bayeux Tapestry, like the steps up to a motte, or the present ones at Boothby Pagnell. Steps of the latter type, resembling a ladder that could be drawn up when necessary, remind us that in some houses wooden steps may have been used, which could be removed within in case of danger. There might even have been a type of drawbridge, as has been suggested between the solar and south tower at Stokesay. Of existing stairs, no wooden ones remain of early date, except for some oak treads at Stokesay, set obliquely on a plain string and with a moulded handrail. These served doorways on two floors at the lower end of the hall, inside but rather on the lines of an external staircase.

At Great Yarmouth an early municipal building of great interest, the Tolhouse, contains a forebuilding, possibly of the late 13th century, heavily restored, over an outer stairway. The latter is renewed, but ascends to an original first-floor entrance dating from c. 1230–1240. Like the rest of the structure the forebuilding is of flint with stone dressings; above the segmental pointed arch to the basement is a row of moulded corbels carrying trefoil arcading, and over this is a two-light window with cinquefoiled heads, opposite the hall entrance. There is a straight joint between this forebuilding and the earlier remains of a staircase turret which projects slightly at the north-east angle, and has two small loops and a chamfered plinth which continues along the north wall.

A simpler covering to the stairs is provided by the solar lean-to at West Tarring, also built in flint, but the steps were removed and the projection made into a porch in the 16th century. There was a similar staircase at the Old Deanery, Salisbury (1258–74), the stairs mounting up the hall wall to a solar entrance near the angle. A right-angled turn occurred at Northborough (c. 1350), where the solar staircase occupied an 'oriel chamber' off the hall. At Maidstone, in the Archbishop's Palace,* an external staircase survives, with its corbelled stone parapet, perhaps 15th century in date but of a type which must have been general in the Middle Ages (Fig. 107).

* Garner & Stratton (1929), fig. 8.

In the bishop's castle at Llawhaden in Pembrokeshire the early 14th-century hall was entered from a staircase with wooden porch, of which the roof corbels remain. The steps were carried on blocks of masonry linked by arches, and rose parallel to the wall, as at Lamphey, but were later altered to run in two right-angled stages when the bakehouse wing was added. Indeed after the 13th century many important staircases rise at right angles rather than parallel to the hall to allow a more impressive porch. Perhaps this was as early as *c.* 1292 at Ludlow Castle, where the hall steps remain as a rubble ramp rising at right angles, but parallel to the projecting earlier solar block, which is also given access from the landing opposite the hall entrance. These stairs may have been covered by a porch, as they are in part at Bishop Gower's hall (1327–47) at St David's. The grand stair at Kenilworth was no doubt thus protected, as were the entrance steps to Richard II's hall at Portchester Castle, of which the porch remains. Little Sodbury Manor, in the late 15th century, has steps in an entrance porch, again at right angles to the main building. There is also a covered staircase up to the hall doorway at Hampton Court (*c.* 1535). This flight rises from the northern jamb of Anne Boleyn's Gateway, as did once the Norman staircase from a vanished gate at Canterbury.

At Hexham Priory the dormitory staircase is remarkable and dates from the 14th century if not earlier. It uses one wall of the transept; on the other side the stepped parapet is probably similar to the arrangement in external stairways which are also parallel to a wall. Here too arches lead below the steps to the ground-floor rooms beyond.

Straight staircases internally, between parallel walls, are found occasionally. An early 14th-century one leads up to the chapel at Broughton Castle, and there is a fine enclosed flight up to the Vicars' Hall at Wells, this being one of the improvements of Bishop Beckington (1443–65) or his executors. At Wells also, in the Deanery, John Gunthorpe (Dean, 1472–98) built an ingenious entrance to his suite in the northern range. At the west end a straight staircase in stone leads up to the vestibule of his great chamber. Across the western part of the vestibule a stone arch carries an enclosed gallery, reached by a newel staircase, which leads to three guest rooms on the second floor and rises in a tower; there is a closet north of this staircase.* Another straight staircase of great interest ascends from a side arch of the oriel at Bewley Court near Lacock; its outer wall is common with that of the oriel, and it mounts to the room over a projecting porch giving access to the great chamber beyond (Fig. 108). At Muchelney a stone staircase leads up to the Abbot's Parlour or chamber (*c.* 1500); this has winders at the top. There is another in the private apartments at Horham Hall (*c.* 1502). A straight flight, well-used, with handrail, gives access to Ewelme Church for the almspeople in the hospital cloister.

A narrower internal staircase may ascend from a doorway off the screens passage. At Chepstow Castle, with its double floor service (*c.* 1280), the central opening, usually a passage, has this stairway, as is now the case at Clevedon Court. The fourth service doorway at Haddon Hall gives access to a solar staircase of this kind, as does a similar opening at Yardley Hastings, with a companion doorway near the back end of the passage, leading to the cellar steps. The first step often forms the threshold as in staircase doorways opening from outside; Marshall Farm at Ide, near Exeter, and a house at Exminster provide examples.

* Godfrey (1950), 110–12 (plan); Parker (1866), 18, pl. XX.

A straight staircase may be contrived in the thickness of the wall, as in castles. This is found in semi-military examples, such as the south tower at Stokesay, a defensive solar. Here a narrow stairway, with small loop windows and a pointed barrel vault, runs up

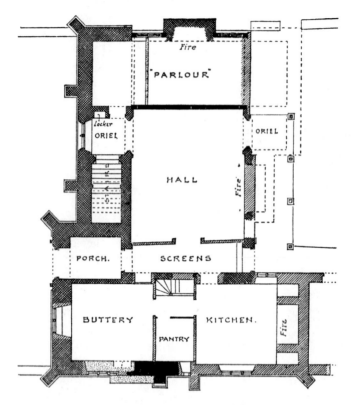

Fig. 108. Bewley Court, ground-floor plan.

KEY: Black, 14th-century work   Cross-hatching, 15th-century work
Single hatching, 17th-century work   Dotting, later and modern

three walls of this polygonal 'keep'. It begins at basement level through a segmental-pointed doorway in the north (right-hand) jamb of the entrance, entering the first floor on the eastern jamb of the entry there, and proceeds to the second floor through a similar opening in the opposite jamb in the thickness of the north-west wall, coming out facing a garderobe in the embrasure of the upper doorway. Meanwhile a similar wall staircase starts from the western jamb of the north-east window on this second floor and gives access to the leads. It may be compared with the narrow wall passages, with shouldered arch roofs, in the towers at Caernarvon Castle, or those from the solar to the garderobe at Manorbier. Fourteenth-century examples of a wall staircase are found at Longthorpe Tower, Preston Patrick, Beetham and Kirby Thore Halls in Westmorland,* and

* See plans in R.C.H.M. *Westmorland*, 196, 41, 148.

Nunney Castle, Somerset,* where it starts, like Stokesay, in the jamb of the basement entrance.

Many 15th-century buildings show the staircase housed in a lateral projection. This seems to be a union of the wall thickness and newel types. It is found in the priests' houses of south-west England, such as Congresbury and Dunchideock. Rising from the hall or parlour, the staircase turns at right angles to rise parallel to the side wall, emerging by another turn into the upper room. The ascent is often by a left turn (anti-clockwise) but is to the right in the lay houses, Yard in Rose Ash, and Ashbury Manor, Berkshire, the latter having a similar type of staircase but with a further room, which it also serves, beyond.†

Newel or spiral staircases, or vices,‡ are a particular feature of mediaeval architecture. The form must have come in with the Normans, for it is a stone method of construction, though much later, in Elizabethan times, it was copied with wooden steps. The chief use of these staircases was to give internal access between the floors, and they seldom opened from outside. The spiral mode of construction enabled them to take up little space, and to be built in the thickness of a Norman wall, or in a corner turret or slight projection. They were thus eminently suitable for the angles of great towers. Being narrow they were also defensive, and in the 12th century normally designed to mount clockwise, thus allowing the defender greater room for his sword arm, the newel column and narrow end of the step being on his left. This arrangement is general in the keeps,§ and also in the domestic halls of the 12th century, Christchurch, Burton Agnes and Eynsford.

At first the steps were laid on a spiral vault round a newel made by a series of circular stones, each with a projection forming the narrow end stone of the wedge-shaped steps. This is the system in keeps such as Hedingham ‖ and Dover, and allowed for a wide staircase; the circumference at these is 13 feet. Rochester has another good example.¶

Speed was an important factor in military building, and a quicker, more satisfactory method, though necessitating a narrower staircase, was to form the whole wedge-shaped step and slice of newel in one stone, each step forming the support of the next, no vaulting being necessary. This came into use at the end of the 12th century.

In the 13th century the newel staircases mostly rise clockwise, but the reverse is some-times used for convenience, chiefly in examples near the end of the century. Burnell's palace at Wells and the castles of Caernarvon, Conway and Beaumaris have both types, though the clockwise staircases are still in the majority. In White Castle (Monmouthshire) one tower of the gatehouse has a clockwise staircase, the other an anti-clockwise. Good domestic examples are found at West Dean, Little Wenham and Old Soar.

The turret staircase in an angle of Burnell's hall at Wells (1275–92) shows the polygonal exterior coming into fashion.

Fourteenth-century staircases also rise clockwise in the main, especially in domestic

---

* M.O.W. Guide (30), plan.
† See plans in Pantin (1957).
‡ From the French *vis* (screw) from the Latin *vitis* (vine).
§ Rochester and Hedingham (*c.* 1130), Scarborough (1158–64), Portchester (*c.* 1160), Middleham (*c.* 1170), Newcastle (1172–7), Dover (1181–8) and others.
‖ Godfrey (1911), fig. 4.
¶ Lloyd (1931), fig. 815.

examples, but there are some castles with both, like Bolton; the anti-clockwise type is found in Chipchase Castle (c. 1340),* and some later 14th-century castles such as Donnington and Kenilworth, though Bodiam and Caesar's Tower at Warwick have the reverse. Markenfield and Clevedon show particularly good (clockwise) staircases of this kind. The polygonal shape (externally), chiefly octagonal, is now usual.

Clockwise newels remain popular in 15th-century houses, but there are more anticlockwise examples than before, and in the early 16th century the latter are more usual. South Wingfield (c. 1440–59) and Sandford Orcas Manor have both types. Instances of clockwise staircases remain at Minster Lovell and Walton Old Rectory, and anti-clockwise at Cothay, Gothelney and Mells. The octagonal plan is general, as at Sudeley Castle. In this period the brick staircase becomes important, and vaulting is again necessary to support the treads, which are no longer in one piece. There are fine examples at Nether Hall (c. 1470) and Faulkbourne Hall in Essex (c. 1494) † and Kirby Muxloe (1480–3). A spiral handrail was now provided, either of brick or of stone set into the brick, as at Tattershall. A stone one serves the stone newel staircase at Lincoln Palace (Bishop Alnwick's Tower) and Raglan Castle.

Besides their familiar corner position, as in 12th-century and later building, these little staircases were often fitted into the re-entrant angle between two blocks, such as that of hall and chapel at Little Wenham, giving access to both. The newel may be set in the angle between porch and service, as at Clevedon, which has another spiral between the back porch and hall. At Dartington and Holcombe Court, both in Devon, the newel rises as a higher turret next to the porch, and at South Wingfield it is in the angle between the 'portal' or garden porch and the solar-service block. There is a turret staircase in the angle between hall and solar at Beetham Hall, Westmorland. The staircase adjoins the oriel at Aston Eyre, and at Penshurst (Pl. L c) occupies it.

The turret may project off a lateral wall. At Tickenham Court, early 15th century, it is attached to the outer wall of the private wing, against the junction of two rooms, but opens out of the projecting parlour, and only serves the chamber above this, coming out in the cross wall, which is thickened at this end at the expense of the other chamber. The latter and the room below it are reached through doorways in this cross wall.

The entrance is usually internal, but at Walton Old Rectory the staircase is entered from outside to give access to upper hall and solar, and is set in the angle of junction. Some gatehouse turrets have doorways from the courtyard: this is the case at Thornton Abbey.

In Old Soar the steps end in the floor of the solar. But generally the staircase in its turret continues further, giving access to the leads and to serve as a look-out. At Little Wenham it rises above the hall and the tower roof as well. In these cases it would be crenellated with the rest, but sometimes the newel is completed with a conical cap, as at Markenfield and Spofforth Castle, both in Yorkshire.

In some northern examples the top of the staircase is finished with an umbrella vault, the ribs radiating out from the newel. Belsay, Alnwick and Warkworth have examples, all of 14th-century date.‡ This could have been the result of French influence. There is a

---

* Toy (1953 b), 193.   † Lloyd (1931), fig. 820.   ‡ Toy (1953 b), 254.

fine example of early 16th-century date at Linlithgow Palace; * here the newel has a moulded capital and semicircular arches, connected by lierne ribs, springing from it and the elaborate corbels on the circumference. At Thornton Abbey Gatehouse (c. 1382) there is a remarkable stone roof to the newel. Supported on the circumference by moulded corbels with carved ornament, there rise eight four-centred arches, cusped, with quatrefoiled spandrels, to meet in a central boss, now gone, without attachment to the newel.†

French newels show a further development: elaborate spirals with open balustrade, their polygonal turrets highly embellished, a chief feature of the courtyard. There are three in the house of the rich merchant Jacques Cœur at Bourges, begun in 1443,‡ and other magnificent 15th-century examples in noble houses such as Châteaudun and Lavardin, while at Blois the staircase tower may have been built for Francis I by Leonardo da Vinci, who died in 1519 at Amboise.§ At Chambord the château (1526) also contains a double spiral staircase by which persons could ascend and descend simultaneously unseen by the others; this is sited at the junction of four vaulted halls on each floor.‖

In England the open balustrade apparently did not come into use until later, but there is an unusual survival of a wooden balustrade, with trefoiled openings, to a straight staircase at Downholland Hall near Ormskirk.¶

Sometimes in the early 16th century, as at Lytes Cary and Sandford Orcas, the top of the newel is of wood, with stone below. In the second half of this century the circular staircase, now often with wooden steps and newel, was being replaced by a new form, which might be called the Elizabethan staircase, of lighter construction. Instead of solid steps, as at Hampton Court, thin boards, 'treads' and 'risers', were set into sloping 'strings' framed into newel posts, the flights passing round an open well, or doubled back on the previous one to form a 'dog-legged' stair. With this arrangement of lighter steps the second parallel wall was not needed—only a handrail and balustrade between the newels for safety.

CORRIDORS AND PENTICES

The small staircases, taking the minimum of space, were of great service in days when there were few if any internal corridors, and a single newel could serve pairs of rooms on several floors. Otherwise interior communication seems to have been from room to room, except for the screens passage or entry, and the passage to the kitchen. There are, however, examples of vaulted corridors between stone walls in the solar basement at Swalcliffe and Broughton Castle, in the early 14th century. Akin to these are some curious passages at ground level in this wing at Nassington; the southern has a right-angled turn, and is entered through a chamfered doorway. Evidence is given by the absence of windows on a basement wall, as on the bailey side of Christchurch Castle hall, and especially by the presence of the corbels and weathering of a vanished pentice roof, as remains on the east side, towards the courtyard, of the hall at Goodrich Castle (c. 1300), and along two sides of Vicars' Court at Lincoln (c. 1310).

* Godfrey (1911), fig. 5.   † Parker (1859), 231.
‡ Evans (1948), 169–71, pls. 157, 158.   § Fletcher (1946), 681, 697.
‖ Fletcher (1946), 682, 697.   ¶ Godfrey (1911), pl. II.

The external corridor, or pentice (penthouse, *apenticium*), must have been common. It gave access from one house to another in the assortment of buildings that formed a 13th-century palace, and it was an easy way of linking up extra buildings. There are frequent references in the Liberate Rolls, the most celebrated being the order to make an aisle between Queen Eleanor's new chapel and chamber at Woodstock 'so that she may go to and return from that chapel with a dry foot' (March 1239). Pentices led from Henry III's hall to the chapel at Rochester Castle; the queen's chamber to her wardrobe beneath the new chapel at Clarendon; and from the hall doorway to the kitchen at Woodstock.* Such vanished timber excrescences were a feature of lesser buildings as well. Evidence is given by the absence of windows on a basement wall, as on the bailey side of Christchurch Castle hall, and especially by the presence of the corbels and weathering of a vanished pentice roof, as remains on the east side, towards the courtyard, of the hall at Goodrich Castle (*c.* 1300), and along two sides of Vicars' Court at Lincoln (*c.* 1310).

There were also covered alleys (*aleiae*), or passage-ways with open or built-up sides. Such must have been the pentice from hall to kitchen excavated at Weoley Castle, and a similar one, built in 1289, found by Mrs O'Neil † at Prestbury Moat in Gloucestershire. At Havering, from the porch of 'the chamber of Edward, the king's son', there was to be made a passage (*alea*) to the alley between Henry III's chamber and the hall, and 'a certain passage from the same porch to the knight's chambers' (1251). Sometimes the sides were wainscoted as was 'the long alley from the chapel into our chamber at Winchester' in 1239, and glass windows were fitted at Woodstock, where in November 1240 the king ordered 'the apertures of the two penthouses between our hall and the queen's chamber, and our chapel, towards the herbary, to be boarded [*bordari*] and two white glass windows to be made in the same boards [*borduris*]'. A fireplace might be provided. In 1237 Henry told Walter de Burgh, 'We command you to make a certain penthouse, with a chimney [fireplace] at the head of our hall at Brill, in the manner in which our reeve shall tell you on our behalf'; this suggests a lean-to type of pentice, as at Guildford where the sheriff of Surrey and Sussex is to make, in 1246, 'under the wall towards the east, opposite the east part of the king's hall, a certain penthouse which, although narrow, shall be competently long, with a chimney and privy chamber, for the queen's wardrobe'.‡

Occasionally the penthouse is two-storeyed. In 1245 the constable of Marlborough Castle is ordered to make 'an alley of two storeys between the king's chamber and the chamber of the queen'.§

These covered passages were also arranged as a cloister round an open space or garth. In 1244 the keepers of the works at Woodstock were commanded 'to cause the cloisters round the fountains at Evereswell [Oxfordshire] to be well paved and to wainscote the said cloisters'; and the sheriff at Guildford in 1256 is 'to make a certain new cloister with marble columns in the king's garden', which in 1260 is to be paved and have two doors and a bench. This may be compared to the walks with arcaded and shafted sides in a

---

* Liberate Roll, 23, 24, 21, 28 Henry III; Turner (1851), 190 (Woodstock), 196 (Rochester), 184 and 186 (Clarendon), 201 (Woodstock).
† (1956), 9, 17–18, fig. 2.
‡ Liberate Roll, 23, 36, 35, 23, 25, 21, 30 Henry III; Turner (1851), 190 (Clarendon), 234 (Woodstock), 232 (Havering), 191 (Winchester), 197 (Woodstock), 186 (Brill), 208 (Guildford).
§ Liberate Roll, 29 Henry III; Turner (1851), 206.

monastic garth of the period. Whether the domestic quadrangle was always complete is doubtful, for at Silverstone the sheriff of Northampton is 'to make a certain cloister from the door of our chamber to the other cloister going toward the queen's chapel' (1252).* Ockwells (1465) retains a cloister of this sort, a most valuable survival, timber-framed with brick-noggings, and the cloisters at Eton (c. 1440) and once at Herstmonceux may be compared with this, as can Wolsey's brick cloister along two sides of the Round Kitchen Court which remains at Hampton Court. Similar evidence has been found at the King's Lynn building of the same name.

Other corridors in the form of galleries, extended landings of external staircases, were doubtless common. A timber gallery, partly renewed, can be seen at Kirkham House, Paignton (c. 1400). It served two upper rooms, each once reached by a staircase, only one of which has been restored.† One of 15th-century date survives, renewed, at Tretower Court (Brecon.), giving access to first-floor rooms on the north, and originally west, range, with steps at the end.‡ Scaplen's Court, Poole, had a similar gallery.§ This arrangement resembles that of a mediaeval inn, like the New Inn at Gloucester (1450) or the George at Dorchester (Oxfordshire, c. 1500).‖ In the 15th century this corridor tended to be incorporated under the main roof of the building. This is suggested by two late examples, one in timber, the second of stone, at Abingdon Abbey and Wenlock Priory.

The 'Long Gallery' at Abingdon has been so called since the Tudor period. It may have been built as an administrative department of the abbey, adjoining the 13th-century Checker, or as an additional guest house. It is a long range of ten (originally twelve) bays, built of stone on the south, of brick with timber above it on the north. The latter shows the built-in wooden corridor at first-floor level, with a range of windows, never glazed. This corridor was originally divided from the rooms by a partition, of which the posts and horizontal beam with traces of doorways survive. There were two large rooms, each of three bays, in the centre of the block, equipped with a shouldered fireplace (one now remains below) and two-light window on the south. Flanking these rooms were smaller apartments of one bay each, three on the west, and probably the same on the east, but of which one is left. The ground floor has been considerably altered.

The Prior's House at Wenlock ¶ shows a double gallery, in stone, also built at the end of the 15th or early in the 16th century, and an impressive exterior is produced by the twin ranges of trefoiled windows. Again the gallery windows were not glazed originally but partly protected by the overhanging eaves. The corridors serve four rooms at each level, with good moulded entrances in the internal wall, which is here of stone. A newel staircase at the north end gives intercommunication, and there are smaller staircases between the rooms, serving the two sections, the infirmarer's and prior's apartments, of the range.

But communicating rooms remained general until after the Elizabethan period, hence the privacy of curtained beds, which were also draught-proof. When the corridor came in, the little projecting newel staircases went out, though there was still one at the end of the gallery at Wenlock. Their absence made for a flatter façade, with less vertical interest, but allowed an uninterrupted range of windows.

* Liberate Roll, 28, 40 and 44, 36 Henry III; Turner (1851), 201 (Evereswell), 246 and 252 (Guildford), 238 (Silverstone).
† M.O.W. Guide (25).　　‡ M.O.W Guide (41), 6, 12 and plan.　　§ Pantin (1962–3 a), 210, 213.
‖ Pantin (1961), 169–73, 184–5.　　¶ Country Life (29), 1283, 1434 (plan).

25

Doorways

Late Eleventh and Twelfth Centuries

LATE 11th- and 12th-century doorways are normally round-headed, though the segmental arch occurs occasionally, chiefly in the inner or rear arch, which is often higher than the other. Sometimes there is a projecting impost, as at Saltford Manor (*c.* 1150), where there are several segmental arches. The arches are joggled in the entrances (inner face) to Aaron's House, Lincoln (*c.* 1170–80) and Boothby Pagnell cellar (*c.* 1200). The last has, like that to the solar basement, a corbelled lintel externally, the shoulder being convex. Similar corbels with a round arch are used in the doorway from hall to solar. The pointed arch appears in transitional form in the inner order of the gateway into St Mary's Guild at Lincoln (Pl. LI A).

The jambs are straight or slightly splayed. Beyond the rebate (door check) the doorway can be divided into recessed orders with shafts in the angles. Two orders are usual, with one shaft a side, as at the Jew's House, Lincoln (Pl. I B). More elaborately shafted doorways, however, like the many surviving in churches, once existed in more palatial buildings, as witnessed by the magnificent shafted entrance with three larger and two smaller orders in Bishop Pudsey's Hall at Durham Castle. Simpler doorways without shafts are often finished with a chamfer (bevel) or a roll-moulding; and a hood with stops, like the entrance to the hall at Boothby Pagnell. The north doorway at Sutton Courtenay has an attached shaft or roll with a capital.

A strong bar was used to secure the door, and holes for it in each jamb, on one side several feet long to house the bar when not in use, survive in some houses, notably Scolland's Hall at Richmond Castle. Bar-holes were of course absent in service doorways opening from the screens end of the hall to pantry, buttery and kitchen passage. But here the door-check would be on the hall side.

THIRTEENTH CENTURY

In 13th-century doorways the outer arch is usually pointed (two-centred) as at Netley. It may be segmental-pointed, as at Old Soar and Bisham Abbey (Pl. LI c), where the entrance arch is stilted; but the Norman round arch persists, being found in several of the earlier houses such as Appleton Manor (Pl. XXIII A). The segmental arch is not usual externally. Cusped doorways exist but are not at all general. There are a rounded trefoil at the Bridge House cellar, Chester; a pointed trefoil at Godlingston (Dorset), and an elaborate double form at Lambeth Palace Chapel, with a quatrefoil in a round-headed tympanum, resembling the entrance to a chapter house. Cinquefoiled doorways are found at Rockbourne Manor (Hampshire) and at Wells Palace, where the western doorway to the chapel has a trefoiled outer arch, and cinquefoiled rear arch, both with semicircular hoodmoulds.

The shouldered lintel (Caernarvon arch) is found in the second half of the century, and must not be confused with the corbelled lintel, found earlier at Boothby Pagnell (Pl. LI D). It is very popular at Stokesay Castle, in the solar and north tower.

The opening is usually chamfered, occasionally hollow-chamfered, but often moulded in one or more orders. Simple doorways have a roll-moulded head, and the roll may have a keel-mould, this being an earlier type; others are more elaborately treated with deep roll-mouldings, keel and rolls, and roll and fillet, the last sometimes enriched, as in earlier houses like the Tolhouse, Great Yarmouth (c. 1230–40), with the fashionable dog-tooth ornament. A late form of chevron is used, with roll-mouldings, in a particularly fine doorway (c. 1224–44) at Exeter Palace (Pl. LI B).

The hood (or 'label' when rectangular) follows the line of the round or two-centred arch, but seems less frequent with the segmental-pointed, occurring however at Winchester Castle (1222–35). It may be chamfered, of roll section (an early type), as in the Appleton service doorways, where it is used as a finish, not for its original purpose of throwing off the rain-water externally. Another profile has a convex surface above, concave below, and the scroll-mould is fashionable in later examples, used with hollow and bead, or with bead moulding alone, as at Little Wenham Hall (c. 1270–80). Often the hood has out-turned ends, with square masks, carved head or foliage stops.

Jamb-shafts are less often used than in Norman houses, but they occur in earlier examples and in buildings of special decoration, where there are two or more shafted orders externally. Two on each jamb are found at Lincoln Palace (c. 1224) and Bisham Abbey, three at Exeter Palace and four at Appleton Manor. At Temple Manor, Strood, the jamb-shafts are flanked by hollow chamfer with leaf and fillet stops. Internal shafts are rare, except when the doorway opens outwards, but the south doorway at Winchester Castle has shafts to the rear arch as well. Sometimes the capital mouldings are continued as an impost. The service doorways (c. 1225) at Little Chesterford show no sign of bases and the capitals seem to have had tongued terminations rather than shafts, a feature appearing in vaulting responds at Netley (c. 1250–60) and elsewhere. In many doorways the jamb-shaft has developed into an uninterrupted roll- or keel-moulding continuous with the head.

Rear arches are segmental or segmental-pointed. Occasionally they are stilted, like a doorway at Winchester Castle hall, an ungraceful feature also found in some 13th-century windows. A shouldered lintel may be seen. These arches are normally chamfered and are sometimes extremely tall.

Several late 13th-century doorways, when near an angle, are provided with a recess in the adjoining wall, into which the open door can be set back. This is so at Little Wenham, West Dean, Old Soar and Charney Basset.

FOURTEENTH CENTURY

The 14th-century outer arch is still usually two-centred, and in the last quarter of the century it may be placed in a square frame. The segmental arch seems to have died out, and the segmental-pointed is apparently more prevalent in the first than the second half of the period. However, it is used over the hall staircase at Winchester College (1387–94). At Goodrich (c. 1300) the doorways, like the windows, have triangular heads. Sometimes the arch has an elliptical form, as at Donnington Castle gatehouse (back c. 1386) and the two hall entrances at Norrington Manor (c. 1377). Trefoiled and cinquefoiled doorways are replaced by the ogee arch, introduced in the early 14th century, which is used in both wood and stone. It can be seen in two service doorways at Abbot's Grange, Broadway (c. 1320), a wooden door frame from Prior Crauden's study (c. 1324–5) at Ely, in Bishop de Gower's porch (c. 1327–47) at St David's (Pl. XXVII c) and (trefoiled) in the hall doorway (c. 1340) at Brinsop Court (Pl. V b). The shouldered arch occurs at Southwick (Northamptonshire, c. 1330), Preston Patrick Hall (late 14th century) and several other examples in Westmorland; at Uffkin's Café, Burford, it is wave-moulded. From c. 1386 the four-centred arch, at first somewhat steep, comes into occasional use, exampled at Winchester College and Donnington Castle.

The square frame is another late mediaeval feature, of the Perpendicular style. In houses it appears in the last thirty years of the 14th century, made fashionable possibly by Henry Yevele, who used it in the London Charterhouse as early as 1371. Here the arch within is two-centred, as also at Arundel College (c. 1381) (Pl. LII E), where his style has been recognized. This is also the shape in an earlier example (c. 1348–67) at Tiptofts Manor in Essex. The latter, however, is in a timber house, where a wooden frame would be the natural accompaniment to the pointed arch. At Brinsop Court there is a square frame to an ogee doorway of c. 1340. Soon the arch became four-centred, and Yevele's colleague, William of Wynford, used it framed in his hall entrance at New College, Oxford (1380–1386) with a quatrefoil in the spandrels, an obvious place for shields, foliage or other ornament. However, the two-centred arch was still used in the square frame, as late as 1396–9, by Yevele's deputy Walter Walton for the king in the porch of Portchester Castle hall (Pl. LVII 1). Here it is interesting to find in the spandrels a variety of lobed trefoil with the extra leaf, found in the vaulting panels of Donnington Castle gatehouse and Wynford's chantry of Bishop William of Wykeham at Winchester.

In some early examples the jambs are shafted, at Mayfield (c. 1325) with carved capitals,

A

B

C

Plate XLIX. Wind-braces.

A. Fiddleford Manor, *c.* 1355–82.
B. Ashbury Manor, *c.* 1488.
C. Woodlands Manor, Mere, first half
of the 15th century.

Plate L. **Staircases.** A. Stokesay Castle, *c.* 1285; south side of hall, with evidence of roof to solar staircase. B. Manorbier Castle, external steps to chapel, *c.* 1260. c. Penshurst Place, oriel staircase, *c.* 1341–1349. D. Ashbury Manor, wooden **vault** over staircase, *c.* 1488.

these moulded at Battle Abbey gatehouse (*c.* 1338) and Penshurst (1341–9), but more often the arch mouldings are continuous (Pls. LII A and B).

For most of the 14th century the chamfer is still the natural treatment for a simple doorway; it is sometimes of two orders with a moulded hood or label. The hollow chamfer also occurs, and the sunk chamfer occasionally. In some houses the corner is rounded instead of bevelled, and this may occur with a scroll-moulded hood.

A very common treatment of the early to mid 14th-century arch is the wave-moulding; possibly derived from the convex 'ovolo' or wide roll-moulding found in some early examples, such as the service doorways at the Provost's (Prebendal) House at Edgmond in Shropshire. The introduction of the ogee or double curve, so popular in the early 14th century, would soften the sides of the roll into a wave, just as it undulated the lower part of the scroll-moulding. The wave could be used in one order instead of a chamfer (e.g. 'Prior's Manse', Broadway) or appear in two orders with scroll-moulded hood as at Clevedon Court (*c.* 1320); it has ball-flower decoration at Fyfield Manor (Berkshire, *c.* 1335–40) (Pl. XXVIII A).

The roll-and-fillet moulding persists in early examples, such as the Bull Cottage at Burford, associated here with the wave and ball-flower ornament. A late type is in the porch at Mayfield. Here the rolls are fat and the fillet is wide, while the Clevedon entrance shows this softened by the ogee curve into a double wave-moulding.

In the second half of the century the roll-moulding returns to fashion, boldly cut and flanked by hollow chamfers. It is favoured by Wynford and used by him in the doorways of both Winchester and New College, Oxford. There is a good example at Wardour Castle (1393) (Pl. LII C). It appears with hollow chamfer and ogee at Dartington Hall (*c.* 1388–1400) and Chorley Hall, Cheshire, probably earlier.

The hall entrance at Penshurst is notable for the band of quatrefoils round the whole arch, very similar to the doorway of the Infirmary Chapel at Westminster Abbey (1371–2), both possibly the work of royal craftsmen.* Kenilworth retains evidence of an elaborate entrance to the hall.

The hoodmould follows the curve of the arch, but sometimes ends, with its carved stops, short of the springing, as in the porch entrance at Edgmond (Pl. LI E). The scroll mould of the late 13th century continues, often softened with an ogee under-curve, and is often found in the earlier part of the 14th century. The 13th-century roll-and-fillet hood persists at Markenfield (*c.* 1310) and another early type has a chamfer below the upper curve.

Rear arches are normally plain and chamfered, segmental, segmental-pointed, four-centred, or a cambered or flat four-centred type which is common in the 15th century.

FIFTEENTH CENTURY

The two-centred arch remains popular in the 15th century, being found in many examples. The four-centred form tends to supplant it in the later years, and was used earlier particularly in larger openings such as gateways. Sometimes, as at Crosby Hall (1466+),

* William Ramsey may have advised at Penshurst; Harvey (1954), 217.

they occur together. In Athelhampton, a late example, the arch is nearly semicircular, while it is entirely so at Yanwath Hall (Westmorland).

Not many ogee-headed doorways remain, but, as survivors are of wood, no doubt more once existed. There is an entrance of this shape at Kirkham House, Paignton, and another at Priesthill, Kentisbeare, also in Devon. The service doorways at West Bromwich are similar and may be of this century.

The four-centred arch was useful in providing a wider entrance and, when set in a square frame, gave opportunity for the display of the owner's arms, merchant marks and, later, initials in the spandrels. South Wraxall porch shows the earlier rather steep variety (Pl. XXVIII c).

The square frame was also used with the pointed arch, the Norrington porch (Pl. XXVIII b) being an example. At Preston Plucknett the arch has no separate hood, but is merged into the roll-moulded frame, and has a shield and carved foliage in each spandrel (Pl. LII d). A similar design of shield, foliage and frame is found with a four-centred arch at Norton St Philip, and with two-centred arch and heavy hoodmould at Croydon Palace. At Thame the Prebendal porch has a shield in circle in each spandrel, as earlier at Arundel College, and a square label, but the arch is still two-centred. A similar fine entrance to the Old Palace at Salisbury has the arms of Henry VI in a panel above (Pl. LII F). These may be compared with those of Henry VIII at Compton Wynyates (Pl. XIX E). In Ashbury Manor the hall entrance is four-centred, in a square frame, the circles containing quatre-foils. With a square label this would be typical of the late 15th and 16th centuries.

Simpler doorways are still chamfered. At Woodlands Manor the porch entrance has an outer chamfered order, with the inner arch dying into the jambs (Pl. LII B). But a moulded form is usual, as at Cochwillam (North Wales). Here the main entrance is moulded, while the back door has chamfers with long broach stops.

Although the ogee arch is much less often found, this double curve was extensively used in the mouldings of jambs and head. Also popular was the roll-moulding, revived at the end of the 14th century, the hollow chamfer and the cavetto, a deeper hollow, earlier almost a circle like a roll in reverse, and shallower in later and 16th-century examples. These mouldings were used in various combinations, the ogee with hollow chamfer (Bowhill and Nettlestead Place) and with the roll-moulding added to these (Ilminster Chantry) and to the cavetto also (South Petherton).

The ogee was often doubled to form a bracket profile, as somewhat earlier in the hall doorway at St Cross and now the Beaufort Tower there. A cavetto between such 'ogee brackets' is a popular treatment, used in the entrance to the Vicars' Hall at Chichester (after 1397) and the doorways of the chapel at Rycote (1449).

The 14th-century wave-moulding is found in some, mostly earlier, examples. It is used in the lower end hall doorways at Minster Lovell (c. 1431–42), in the doorway in the oriel at Gainsborough, while at Preston Plucknett (c. 1425–30) it is combined with roll and hollow chamfer in the entrance to the porch.

Occasionally the entrances were shafted, as at Lincoln College, Oxford (1436–7), and Great Chalfield (c. 1480). But more often such shafts were in the form of a roll moulding, triple in the porch at South Wraxall, sometimes given a capital as at Norrington (porch) and the 'portal' at South Wingfield. More delicate rolls are combined with quirk and ogee in several doorways at Tickenham Court.

In 15th-century hoodmoulds the typical profile consists of a straight upper slope, with hollowed under-surface and bead moulding. This is found in arched hoods or square labels. The upper surface may be curved, and earlier hoods tend to be more heavily moulded, as in the porch at Norrington. There the hood forms the square outer frame of the doorway, but usually there are 'stops', the mouldings terminating in a curl (Grevil's House, Chipping Campden, *c.* 1400+), a square (Ashleworth Court), a diamond (Great Chalfield), or having out-turned ends as at South Wraxall porch.

Occasionally there is carved decoration to the arch. The porch doorway at South Wingfield has *paterae* in the cavetto moulding. Panelled reveals embellish the porch entrances to the King's House at Salisbury, also dating from the mid 15th century.

Rear arches are usually plain, segmental, segmental-pointed, four-centred, or the cambered or flat four-centred type met with also in windows, as at Tickenham Court. Usually there is a chamfer, but a four-centred arch in a square frame, both roll-moulded, is found in the oriel doorway at Eltham Palace.

Some examples of traceried doorways in wood remain, such as one from the Rectory at Pyrton (Oxfordshire).

EXAMPLES OF DOORWAYS

late C 11th	Scolland's Hall, Richmond Castle, Yorks.	*c.* 1230–40	King John's Hunting Box, Romsey, Hants, two
c. 1150	Saltford Manor House, Som., several	*c.* 1230–40	The Tolhouse, Great Yarmouth, Norf.
c. 1150	Hemingford Grey Manor House, Hunts.	*c.* 1230–50	Bishop Jocelyn's Palace, Wells
c. 1160	Christchurch Castle, Hants, hall	? 1st half C13th	Rockbourne, manorial chapel
c. 1170	Pudsey's Hall, Durham Castle	*c.* 1250	Temple Manor, Strood, Kent
c. 1170–80	Jew's House, Lincoln, several	*c.* 1250–60	Abbot's House, Netley, Hants
c. 1170–80	Aaron the Jew's House, Lincoln, several	*c.* 1258–74	The Old Deanery, Salisbury
c. 1190	'Norman Hall', Sutton Courtenay, Berks., two	*c.* 1270–80	Little Wenham Hall, Suff., several
		c. 1270–80	Moigne Court, Ower Moigne, Dor.
c. 1200	Boothby Pagnell Manor House, Lincs., several	*c.* 1270–80	West Dean Rectory, near Seaford, Suss., several
c. 1210	Appleton Manor, Berks.	*c.* 1280	Bisham Abbey, Berks.
1st half C13th	The Prebendal Manor House, Nassington, Northants.	*c.* 1280	Charney Basset Manor House, Berks., several
c. 1224	Lincoln Palace, several	*c.* 1280	Aydon Castle, Northumb.
c. 1225	Little Chesterford Manor Farm, Ess., several	*c.* 1283–92	Ludlow Castle, Salop
1222–35	Winchester Castle, hall	*c.* 1285– 1305	Stokesay Castle, Salop, several
c. 1224–44	Exeter Palace	*c.* 1290	Old Soar, Plaxtol, Kent

c. 1290   Godlingston Manor, Dor.

c. 1300   Haddon Hall, Derbys.

c. 1310   Markenfield Hall, near Ripon, Yorks.

c. 1315   Bull Cottage, Burford, Oxon.

c. 1320   Clevedon Court, Som.

?*c.* 1320–30   Winchester House, Southwark

early C 14th   Provost's (Prebendal) House, Edgmond, Salop

c. 1325   Mayfield Palace, Suss.

c. 1327–47   Bishop's Palace, St David's, Pembs.

c. 1330   'The Abbey', Sutton Courtenay, Berks.

earlier
 C14th   Prior's Manse, Broadway, Worcs.

c. 1335–40   Fyfield Manor, Berks.

c. 1340   Brinsop Court, Heref.

c. 1340   Old Parsonage, Marlow, Bucks.

c. 1340   Northborough Manor House, Northants., several

c. 1341–9   Penshurst Place, Kent

mid C 14th   Yardley Hastings, Manor House, Northants., ruins, several

c. 1348–67   Tiptofts Manor House, Wimbish, Ess.

c. 1377   Amberley Castle, Suss., several

c. 1377   Norrington Manor House, Wilts., two

c. 1381   Arundel College, Suss.

c. 1380–6   New College, Oxford

c. 1386   Donnington Castle, Berks., several

1387–94   Winchester College, several

1393   Wardour Castle, Wilts.

1388–1400   Dartington Hall, Devon, several

1390–3   Kenilworth Castle, War., hall

1396–9   Portchester Castle, Hants, hall
                Tickenham Court, Som., several

1397+   Vicars' Hall, Chichester, Suss.

c. 1400   The Chantry, Bridport, Dor.

?*c.* 1400   Littlehempston Old Manor, Devon

early
 C 15th   Norrington Manor House, Wilts., porch

c. 1420   Bradley Manor, Newton Abbot, Devon

1st half
 C 15th   Preston Plucknett Abbey Farm, Som.

1st half
 C 15th   Bowhill, Exeter

1st half
 C 15th   Woodlands Manor, Mere, Wilts.

1st half
 C 15th   Prebendal House, Thame, Oxon.

1st half   Court House, East Meon, Hants,
 C 15th   several

c. 1435   South Wraxall Manor, Wilts.

c. 1436–7   Lincoln College, Oxford

c. 1431–42   Minster Lovell Hall, Oxon.

c. 1440–59   South Wingfield Manor, Derbys.

1443–52   Croydon Palace, Sy.

c. 1450   Old Bishop's Palace, Salisbury

mid C 15th   The King's House, Salisbury

before 1463   Ashleworth Court, Glos.

1466   Crosby Hall, London

1450–80   Cochwillam, Llanllechid, Caer.

c. 1479–80   Eltham Palace, Kent

between
 1470 &
 1484   Gainsborough Old Hall, Lincs.

c. 1480   Great Chalfield Manor, Wilts.

c. 1480   The Chantry, Ilminster, Som.

c. 1488   Ashbury Manor, Berks.

c. 1495–
 1500   Athelhampton Hall, Dor.

late C 15th   Yanwath Hall, West.

26

Windows

TWELFTH CENTURY

WINDOWS in Norman houses were of two main kinds: narrow loops in the basement and two-lights in the hall above. We have less evidence for those in the ground-floor type of hall: here they were probably of one light with semicircular head, as in Norman churches, set high in the walls. This is on the analogy of the refectory windows in 12th-century monasteries, such as those remaining at Dover Priory, but it must be remembered that these were bound to be placed high on one side, to give light above the adjoining cloister walk. Yet the defensive element was also important. In the aisled hall, however, because of the roof arrangement, the side windows would have to be lower. At Oakham, late in the century, they are even quite large, of twin-light type, but the castle hall stood in a protected court.

Loops were of defensive character, and indeed the basement (ground floor), largely used for storage and servants' sleeping accommodation, did not require very good lighting. However, the narrow windows were widely splayed internally, in jambs and head, to make the most of the light that entered. The loops might have round heads, as at St Mary's Guild, Lincoln (Pl. II A), or be a completely oblong chamfered light, as at Christchurch Castle (Pl. III A); occasionally they were recessed into the wall. The rear arch was commonly semicircular.

In the hall above, the two-light was normal, with a mid-shaft dividing the twin openings. Frequently there were jamb-shafts in one or more recessed orders.

The one-shaft window seems the earliest type, met with in houses up to *c.* 1150, such as at Portslade Manor (ruins) in Sussex, and King John's House, Southampton. It has a mid-shaft only, and no covering arch, the two lights being flush with the outer wall.

The next stage, the three-shaft window, is found in the mid 12th century. Here, in addition to the mid-shaft, there is one jamb-shaft a side, supporting an enclosing arch, of which the impost is sometimes extended to the shaftless inner order. The type occurs

predominantly in the florid middle period of English Romanesque, and both orders and
hood are often richly decorated, especially, as at Christchurch, with chevron or zigzag
ornament (Pl. LIII A and B).

The five-shaft window is also of two orders, but now has jamb-shafts to the lights as
well, where they serve to balance the mid-shaft, there being a common impost in each
jamb. It is an elaboration of the three-shaft type, but not due to greater wealth, as many of
the former are richer in detail. Rather does it seem a natural development, for most of the
five-shaft examples are later in date, c. 1170–80. Already the jamb had imposts to match
the abacus of the mid-shaft, thus the addition of inner shafts and capitals should follow.
Indeed the triple-shafted window at Saltford (c. 1150) contains the germ of the later type
in its attached half-shafts, a development from the rolls of earlier windows. The chevron
now seems less popular, although it appears luxuriantly at Pudsey's Hall, Durham Castle,
c. 1170, perhaps the earliest of our surviving examples (Pl. LIII C). The window at Charleston Manor, Sussex, has a plain covering arch although the capitals are foliated, while
Aaron's House at Lincoln has rolls and hollows in the arch, these being enriched in the
other Jew's House there by ball-and-acanthus ornament.

Sometimes instead of a mid-shaft there was a mullion, and this came to supplant the
other as being more convenient; for it could continue the mouldings of the lights and,
being rebated on the inside, form an easier support for the fastening of shutters into it. At
King John's House holes are found at the back of the mid-shaft through which pegs were
inserted to fasten the shutters, and Christchurch has a semicircular swelling with bar-
hole. At Hemingford Grey (Huntingdonshire), c. 1150, there are unusual lobes protruding
from the soffit of the lights. These were probably to help to keep the shutters in place,
and may even be the origin of the cusped heads of 13th-century windows.

The late 12th century shows the Transitional style from Norman to 'Early English'.
There is a return to simplicity, with fewer jamb-shafts and sometimes only a mid-shaft
or mullion. The straight head occurs at Moyses Hall, Bury St Edmunds. But sometimes
there are internal jamb-shafts, as earlier at Christchurch and at 'Canute's Palace' (the
Long House), Southampton, c. 1180. Here the south window is a single light, as at West
Malling in Kent, but since they are in a bad condition it is not impossible that they are
mutilated two-lights. However, at Sherborne Old Castle earlier (c. 1130), the one-light
form is certain, in two good windows on the first floor, one having rich chevron decoration
and jamb-shafts to the outer order.

At the end of the century, also, the tympanum over the lights may be pierced, as at
Merton Hall, Cambridge (c. 1200), the first step towards Gothic tracery. The rear arch
was usually semicircular, as in the window revealed in Stonegate, York. At Christchurch (north window) it is roll-and-quirk moulded supported on internal jamb-shafts
with scalloped capitals. But the example at 'Canute's Palace' shows a segmental head.

Circular windows are used in gable walls, and there is evidence of these at Chepstow
Castle hall (c. 1090) (Pl. III C), Christchurch and the guest houses at Fountains
Abbey.

Stone window seats and a raised foot-rest remain in two houses. At Moyses Hall the
seats are parallel with the splayed jambs, at Boothby Pagnell they are at right angles to the

wall (Pl. LIII D). It may be mere chance that surviving Norman examples are late, but the possibility that window seats are a late 12th-century development is supported by the fact that they continued, hardly altered, into the 13th and 14th centuries.

THIRTEENTH CENTURY

Thirteenth-century windows continue the general line of the Norman, with loops for the storage basement and the two-light most popular in hall and solar. The single light is common as well. Perhaps the main difference, already marked in the late 12th century, is the decline of the external jamb-shaft. The latter certainly occurs in the early example at Winchester Castle, and rather later at Godmersham in Kent (Pl. LIV A), but in most houses the lights are not deeply recessed, and the jambs of the lights and covering arch, where one exists, are simply moulded or chamfered.

Internal jamb-shafts, however, were popular. Already used in late 12th-century houses, they remained in fashion for over a century. Good examples of *c.* 1260 remain at Chepstow Castle hall, and of *c.* 1270–80 at Owen Moigne. In early houses the shafts may be pointed (keeled), and occasionally they are coupled, as at Winchester Hall.

The mid-shaft remained in fashion, and to Henry III the two-light pillared window (*fenestra columpnata*) was an obvious favourite. In the chapel at Gillingham six windows were to be made, 'with columns in the middle',* while at Clarendon the old hall, now made into a chamber, was to have 'one pillared window and the chimney [fireplace] on one side', and in the opposite wall 'two decently pillared windows and one window in the gable without a pillar, to be made as high as possible'†.

In existing examples the mid-shaft is found at Aydon Castle, Little Wenham and other houses, but the mullion has become more prevalent. It is often chamfered, sometimes hollow chamfered, and at Cogges Manor (Oxfordshire) one mullion has a keel, the other a roll-moulding following the design of the window heads. This feeling for continuity probably explains why the mid-shaft was supplanted by the mullion.

The individual lights vary in shape. The narrow loops to the basement are frequently oblong with mitred angles. Such chamfered lights occur at Millichope (Shropshire) and the Old Deanery at Salisbury. At Hambledon and Donington-le-Heath they are found on both floors. In the garderobe at Old Soar (*c.* 1290) the loops are cruciform, like arrow-slits, giving a horizontal view of the field (Pl. LIX B). This is probably a late 13th-century development, and occurs tentatively at Godlingston, and more adroitly at Acton Burnell. The pointed loop, or small lancet, is found in the basements of Crowhurst and Little Wenham, while at West Dean the ground floor has unusual windows of corbelled lintel form.

The single light also occurs in living-rooms. The lancet is still round-headed at the Chantry, Chichester, but the usual form is pointed, which is very popular in chapels, the length naturally varying according to the height of the wall. At Stokesay (South Tower) each one has a hoodmould. Lancets may be hollow chamfered, double-chamfered, or roll-moulded. The trefoiled single light is used at Donington-le-Heath, while at Old Soar

* Liberate Roll, 34 Henry III (July 1250); Turner (1851), 224.
† Liberate Roll, 28 Henry III (March 1244); Turner (1851), 202.

the shouldered lintel appears: this is more usually a 14th-century feature, as at Chepstow and Aydon Castles.

Circular windows were used in the gables. At Swanborough Manor (Sussex) this is a true circle, as in 12th-century examples. But cusping soon became general, first with 'soffit cusps', which may have fallen out in some cases, and later with the more stable

Fig. 109. The Bishop's Palace, Wells, north window
of Bishop Jocelyn's solar, c. 1230–40.

'chamfer' variety. There is a sexfoil in the Strangers' Hall at Winchester, a quatrefoil at Rockbourne and at the Chantry in Chichester, where it is arranged over two separate lancets, suggesting a development towards the traceried two-light window. This treatment, however, is followed in the elaborate north window (c. 1230–40) at Wells Palace, the quatrefoil here designed over a pair of two-light windows, each with a quatrefoil in the heads as well (Fig. 109, Pl. LIII E).

In a two-light window the heads may be pointed, but trefoiled heads are usual. The plain pointed or lancet lights, being simpler, might be regarded as the earlier type. Nevertheless they occur in the same wall at Cogges (c. 1250) with a window having trefoiled

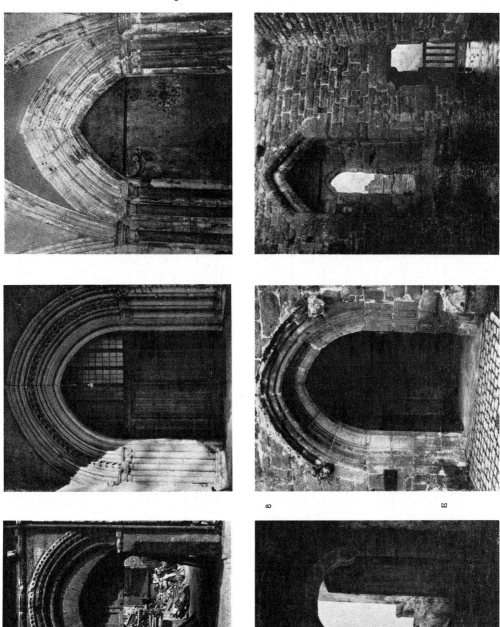

Plate LI. Doorways.

A. St Mary's Guild, Lincoln, gateway, *c.* 1190. B. Bishop's Palace, Exeter, hall entrance, *c.* 1224–44. C. Bisham Abbey, hall entrance, within porch, *c.* 1280. D. Boothby Pagnell, hall to solar, *c.* 1200. E. Provost's House, Edgmond, porch, early 14th century. F. Goodrich Castle, chamber in gate tower, *c.* 1300.

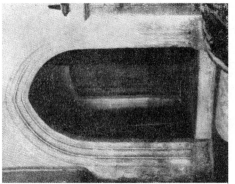

Plate LII. Doorways.

A. Meare Manor House, doorway in outbuilding, *c.* 1322–35. B. Woodlands Manor, Mere, mid 14th-century doorway to chapel staircase. C. Old Wardour Castle, 1393, interior of entrance passage. D. Preston Plucknett Abbey Farm, porch, first half of the 15th century. E. Arundel College, *c.* 1381. F. Old Bishop's Palace, Salisbury, with arms of Henry VI, *c.* 1450.

heads, and are also found later in the century. The rounded trefoil, however, may be an earlier form, and is used in Henry III's hall at Winchester Castle, dated 1222–35 (a rebuild of a late 11th-century structure), and Bishop Jocelyn's hall at Wells (*c.* 1230–40). Indeed the windows in these two buildings are very similar, each having two rounded trefoil heads with a quatrefoil above in plate tracery, though the king's have two-centred hoods, and the bishop's trefoiled hoods and the elaborate cusped rear arches of the west of England. The mouldings are also akin, and it may be significant that there is a link between the two buildings in the person of Master Elias of Dereham. He was in charge of the works at Winchester (but was not the designer of the hall), and in 1229 steward to Bishop Jocelyn at Wells. He was also a canon of Salisbury, and director of the new cathedral fabric from 1220 until his death in 1245; * his house, Leadenhall, still stands, much altered, in the Close with one window of this type remaining.

The round-headed trefoil was much used at Salisbury too, and seems to have been a general form in the earlier 13th century, being more akin to the semicircular arch, now superseded by the pointed. It could also be employed for a hoodmould, as at Wells, at 'King John's Hunting Box' at Romsey (*c.* 1240), which may have been the work of a Salisbury mason, and in pointed form at the demolished Godmersham Court Lodge in Kent, which had the rounded trefoil hood internally. This house belonged to the priors of Canterbury and may have been built by a cathedral mason; the detail suggested a date *c.* 1250.

The earlier wing at Martock (*c.* 1250–60) has rounded trefoil-headed lights with quatrefoil above, and a pointed trefoiled rear arch; originally there was a rounded trefoil hood externally, of which the shape remains (Pl. XVI c). It was built for the treasurer of Wells Cathedral perhaps by the architect of Bishop Jocelyn's Palace. Poyntington Court, Dorset, has been considered late 14th century, but could be a hundred years earlier. A late 13th-century date is suggested by the rounded trefoil rear arch, chamfered, and the similar shape of a destroyed hood can be traced outside above two lancet lights with quatrefoil.

The pointed trefoil head to the lights is much more common, perhaps because the greater number of surviving houses date from the second half of the 13th century. At Stokesay the hall windows have soffit cusps, but cusps built as part of the chamfer of the lights are usual in that period.

Some two-light windows have no covering arch, the heads being cut out of a single stone; others have a covering hoodmould only. But it is common to have both external arch and hood, and occasionally the lights have individual hoods.

Already in the late 12th century some windows had the tympanum pierced above the lights. Now this earlier form, or plate tracery, was developed, the first stage being sunk decoration, such as the quatrefoil at Cogges and the man's head, perhaps reworked later, carved in a quatrefoil at Aydon Castle. A pierced trefoil or quatrefoil followed, and finally the head was completely filled with bar tracery, in which the shapes were not cut out of the solid as before, but made up of stone strips or bars. The change seems to have occurred at Wells during the last work at Jocelyn's Palace perhaps *c.* 1240, for the north windows to the solar are similar to those in the other parts of the building, but with bar not plate

* A. H. Thompson (1941); Harvey (1954), 84–5.

tracery as before. At Ludlow Castle hall (Pl. III B) and Charney Basset (c. 1280) the bar tracery forms plain kite-shaped openings, a type which continued into the 14th century; but other windows are more elaborate, with geometric cusping. The Stokesay hall windows have a plain circle in the head, and it is unlikely that soffit cusps to form a cinquefoil have fallen out, because these remain in the trefoiled lights, and at Swainston (Isle of Wight), the east window has three circles without any evidence of cusping. The chamfer cusps at Little Wenham form trefoils in the east and west hall windows, a quatrefoil to north and south, and the latter occurs with greater elegance at Ower Moigne (c. 1270-80) (Pl. LIII F), where the quatrefoil is almost cruciform, resembling the rather later tracery at Spofforth Castle (Yorkshire). At Chepstow the quatrefoil is the looser type, normally later. Indeed the typical later 13th-century window is of two pointed trefoil-headed lights with a quatrefoil above. Sometimes the latter is placed horizontally, like a St Andrew's Cross, as at the 'Moot Hall' at Dewsbury. At the end of the century there are the elaborate windows of Bishop Burnell's palaces: at Wells (c. 1285-90) a sexfoil over lobed trefoils above the pointed trefoil lights in the hall; at Acton Burnell (c. 1284-92+) a sexfoil triangulated above pointed cinquefoil-heads (Pl. 27 A). This type of geometric tracery continued into the early years of the 14th century.

Tall windows with a transom occur early in the King's hall at Winchester, and at Wells (Burnell's hall) the transoms are cusped with trefoiled heads. In the second half of the century transoms appear in first-floor halls, such as Chepstow and Acton Burnell. At Chepstow the upper end of the hall is lit by a composite window of unusual design. It consists of a pair of two-light windows similar to those in the body of the hall (with trefoiled transomed lights and quatrefoil), each in a larger trefoiled light, placed together with a quatrefoil in plate tracery above, the whole enclosed in a two-centred arch.

The three-light window is suitable for a gable end. A triplet of graduated (the heads of the lights stepped up to the central one) lancets was very popular for the east end of chapels, and was used in the great hall of the Knights Templar at Bisham Abbey. The lancets are each splayed to a rear arch, chamfered or moulded, often supported on shafts, as in the beautiful example at Thame Prebendal (Oxfordshire), where a moulded hood encloses the whole design internally (Pl. XXXVI c). At Swainston the three lancets have three plain circles in the head, and this developed into geometric tracery, like the quatrefoils over three trefoiled lights in the restored chapel window at Little Wenham.

The five-light window with graduated cinquefoiled lancets is used in Burnell's chapel at Wells, and there is an earlier design of five separate graduated lancets in the end window of Lambeth Palace chapel, which has a triplet in each of the lateral bays.

The outer arch is usually two-centred, straight or hollow chamfered or moulded, and in early houses the Norman round arch persists. The hoods are of similar shape and treatment, sometimes with mask terminals, head or foliage stops. The trefoil hood is less usual, but occurs in rounded form at Wells and Romsey, with the pointed form at Godmersham, which like Poyntington had the rounded trefoil hood internally.

In a ground-floor hall the walling over the windows could be carried up into gables, each with a separate roof, giving a dormer effect. This was once the case at Winchester Hall, and at Woodstock King Henry ordered three windows of the hall 'to be raised with masonry in the fashion of a porch'.* It was doubtless a usual 13th-century fashion, and an example of *c.* 1250 existed until 1955 at Godmersham (Pl. LIV A). The gables in the hall at Stokesay, and those restored at the Old Deanery, Salisbury, can still be seen; there the end gable with the entrance is carried down to the eaves of the roof. The device continued into the 14th century.

The rear arch varies in form, being two-centred, segmental or segmental-pointed, and usually chamfered. The segmental type, with a curved, almost stilted springing, is an early 13th-century feature found in the solar at West Tarring, like the doorways at Winchester Hall. Segmental-pointed is probably more common. Sometimes the rear arch projects downwards as a chamfered rib, as at Netley, and occasionally there is an internal hood, chamfered or moulded, as at Ower Moigne. At Chepstow Castle hall the windows are especially elaborate with richly moulded rear arch and scrolled hoods with head stops. At Romsey there remains an example with dog-tooth ornament. Besides the rounded trefoils at Godmersham and Poyntington and the pointed one at Martock, the foliated rear arch of the west appears, both trefoiled and cinquefoiled, in Bishop Jocelyn's work at Wells.

The internal jambs are invariably splayed in the basement to give the maximum of light from a narrow opening. They are usually splayed in two-light windows, and occasionally a double splayed opening occurs, for example at Tollard Royal (basement) and Netley (first floor).

Often there were seats, and a foot-rest in the window embrasures, forming the 'sitting windows' mentioned in Henry III's instructions. At Marlborough the queen's chamber is to have four great 'well-sitting windows with pillars',† and this contrasts with the 'standing' and 'upright' (*stantinas*) windows mentioned elsewhere.‡ The seats may be placed at right angles to the wall, or parallel to the splayed jambs. The cappings of the seats are usually straight or hollow chamfered but are sometimes moulded, with roll or scroll and bead. Window seats occur even in vaulted basements, like that below the chapel at Lambeth, but this is not usual.

Most windows are rebated for shutters, and at Old Soar the solar east window has a pointed recess for one in the jamb. The mullion is often swollen internally to provide bar or bolt holes to secure the shutters. These perforated knobs had appeared as early as *c.* 1160 at Christchurch, *c.* 1180 at Conisborough Keep, and one projection occurs at Cogges, Upper Millichope, Cottisford, and in a more refined roll-and-fillet form in the solar windows at Martock. The mullions at Chepstow are scalloped in a somewhat similar manner.

Window glass is known to have existed in Roman and Saxon times, and examples remain from the Norman period in Canterbury Cathedral, but in 13th-century England it was still the prerogative of the rich. No doubt the quatrefoil in the head of a window would first be glazed if funds allowed, otherwise filled with horn, with shutters below. But the use of glass seems to have become more prevalent in the period,§ and this is suggested by Henry III's ordering even the king's and queen's privy chambers to be glazed at Clipstone.

* Liberate Roll, 28 Henry III; Turner (1851), 201.
† Liberate Roll, 29 Henry III; Turner (1851), 206.
‡ Liberate Roll, 28, 35, 36 Henry III; Turner (1851), 204, 227, 238–9.
§ At Eynsford after the fire *c.* 1250 at least the south-east hall window was glazed, for pieces of *grisaille* glass (with a black linear design) have been discovered. This is one of the earliest known examples of the glazed window in houses. (M.O.W. Guide (16).)

There are constant references to white glass lights and 'glass windows' (*verrinae*), as when 'the glass of the window of the hall at Winchester over the great doorways' has to be repaired (December 1237). This is in contrast to 'wooden windows' or shutters, *fenestrae ligneae* or *bordeae*, of fir bound with iron made to fit internally (over the glass windows at Guildford). Sometimes only the upper part of a transomed window was glazed, with shutters below. At Geddington the sheriff is ordered to make, in the gable, 'a white glass window with the image of a king in the middle, and likewise put white glass windows in the two small round windows which are above the windows in the hall' (as at Winchester originally). At Guildford 'an upper window in the king's hall towards the west nigh the dais is to be filled with white glass lights so that in one half of that glass window there be made a certain king sitting on a throne, and in the other half a certain queen likewise sitting on a throne'. Heraldic glass is mentioned at Havering, where the chapel windows were to have the shields of Provence, in honour of Queen Eleanor. The gable windows at Rochester hall had the shield of the king and that 'of the late Count of Provence', the side windows each having the figure of a king.*

Glass windows were now made to open and shut. At Guildford the glass windows between the pillars had panels (*panellis*), and at Clarendon two windows in the Queen's Chapel were to be 'cleft through the middle, that they may be shut or opened when necessary', as also at Sherborne. At the Oxford hall two fair upright windows with white glass casements are to do the same.†

At Windsor a double window is suggested. King Henry ordered a white glass window in each gable of the (high) chamber, outside the interior window, 'so that when the inner window shall be closed, these glass windows may appear outside'.‡ But the inner window may have been of wood.

Windows, whether glazed or not, seem to have been 'well barred with iron'.§ The holes of such grilles may be seen at Conway and elsewhere.

FOURTEENTH CENTURY

The last years of the 13th and beginning of the 14th centuries are akin in window tracery, which has geometric figures, cusped circles, trefoils and quatrefoils in the head above the lights. The sexfoil (hexafoil), and what may be called elongated or lobed trefoils, steeply pointed, which can usually be dated *c.* 1290–1310, become popular. A good example of the latter form over trefoiled lights may be seen at 3 Vicars' Court, Lincoln (*c.* 1310), with ribbon-like tracery, perhaps a northern feature, occurring also at the Dewsbury 'Moot Hall' (*c.* 1290). The sexfoil, used in Bishop Burnell's palaces, appears, as does the seven-foiled circle, over cinquefoiled lights in the solar windows at Broughton Castle, which might be a little earlier than the date 1306 usually given. In the chapel

* See translations of Liberate Rolls in Turner (1851), 236 (Clipstone), 188 (Winchester), 191, 205 (glass windows), 225 (shutters), 182 (fir bound with iron), 209 (Guildford), 226 (glass in upper part), 204 (Geddington), 209 (Guildford), 243 (Havering), 214 (Rochester).
† Turner (1851), 209 (Guildford), 224 (Clarendon), 225 (Sherborne), 200 (Oxford).
‡ Turner (1851), 260 (Close Roll, 28 Henry III).
§ Turner (1851), 191, 199, 206, 208.

there the east window is a fine example of geometric tracery, having three cinquefoil-headed lights, the side ones with a rounded trefoil above, the central with a large circle containing three smaller ones cinquefoiled (Pl. 17 B). A large sexfoil flanked by lobed trefoils is used, over three trefoiled lights, in the magnificent window of what was once the chapel at Membury Court in Devon (Pl. XXXVI D).

At Broughton only a hint remains of the hall window tracery, which probably contained a large quatrefoil over two pointed trefoil-headed lights. Indeed, an outsize geometrical figure in the head seems to have been fashionable in the transomed windows of early 14th-century ground-floor halls. There are three survivals in Kent and Sussex, which are possibly akin: the archbishop's palaces at Charing and Mayfield, and the hall at Ightham Mote. The hall at Charing dates from the first years of the century, probably built for Archbishop Robert Winchelsea (1294–1313). One window remains, though partly blocked, sufficient to denote the pattern of all the rest: a tall opening of two lights, trefoiled above and below the transom, with an octafoil in the head (Pl. LIV B). Roof

Fig. 110. The Archbishop's Palace, Mayfield, windows in the great hall, *c.* 1325.

evidence links Charing with Mayfield, some twenty to thirty years later, where the windows are much more perfect (Fig. 110). Here the lower lights are cinquefoiled, the upper trefoiled, and in the head there is a large sub-cusped trefoil with roses on the inner points. Ightham Mote preserves a great roof arch similarly moulded to those at Mayfield, and seems the work of the same architect. An original window remaining on the north has in the head an octafoil as at Charing, but over two cinquefoiled lights with plain moulded transom. Flowing tracery over two rounded trefoiled transomed lights occurs in a window (*c.* 1320) at Hill House, Burford, but this is unusual, like the elaborate tracery of Prior Crauden's chapel at Ely (*c.* 1325–35).

But the normal type of domestic window in the 14th, as in the late 13th century, was one of two trefoil-headed lights with a quatrefoil in a two-centred head, and it is interesting to trace its development for the next hundred years. The 13th-century quatrefoil had rounded leaves, and this persists into the early 14th century at Haddon Hall and Markenfield (1310 licence), although at Haddon the lowest leaf has a point following the curves of the lights. Soon the upper leaf shows a similar point, forming what may be called a 'lobed quatrefoil', which became a very popular 14th-century feature. It developed in association with the ogee arch, and when repeated in larger windows led to the net or reticulated tracery so much favoured from the second quarter of the 14th century onwards. An early example of the 'lobed quatrefoil' is found at Bampton Castle (Pl. LV A) (now Ham Court), Oxfordshire, licensed in 1315. Here the lights, though still trefoiled, have an ogee curve, a chief feature of the 'Decorated Style', and an early form of this also can be seen in the chapel of 'Abbot's Grange', Broadway (*c.* 1320) (Pl. LIV F). These may be compared with the early type of trefoiled head, nearer the 13th century, as seen in the two-light (from hall to chapel) at Clevedon Court. At Meare Manor House (Pl. V A) the ogee heads to the lights are cinquefoiled, in a steeper form than was usual in the next century (Fig. 111).

Fig. 111. Meare Manor House, hall window, *c.* 1322–35.

The Fish House at Meare has similar windows; it was likewise built by Adam of Sodbury, Abbot of Glastonbury 1322–35. Tall cinquefoiled lights, again, appear at the Treasurer's House at Martock, also in Somerset, probably built *c.* 1330 (Pl. LIV D), but here the quatrefoil above, where it is used, has the earlier rounded leaves. At Brinsop Court the hall (*c.* 1340) has the fully developed 14th-century window with ogee-pointed upper and lower leaves to the quatrefoil, over two trefoiled ogee lights (frontispiece and Pl. V B). This ogee framework, if continued, would form a piece of net tracery, similar to the reticulated windows in the chapels at Clevedon Court (Pl. XXXVII D) and Woodlands Manor (Pl. XXXVIII C), and the hall (*c.* 1340) of the Old Parsonage at Marlow (Pls. LIV E, LV E).

Penshurst (1341–9) is akin to the earlier hall at Mayfield in its general arrangement, with large two-light transomed windows placed under wide arches to carry the thickened wall and parapet. The lower lights have trefoiled ogee heads similar to those above, but with a crenellated transom. In the head is a quatrefoil set diagonally in a vesica. The porch window has two quatrefoils set crosswise; here the arch is not two-centred but flat with angular hoodmould.

The cinquefoiled ogee head to the lights grew very popular in the mid 14th century. Apart from the early somewhat steep version at Meare Manor (*c.* 1322–35), there is a good example of *c.* 1330 at Southfleet Old Rectory in Kent. The ogee is more definite at Battle Abbey, where Abbot Adam de Katling (1324–51) added chambers over the porch in his house, and of which one good window survives (Pl. 27 C). As at Meare, the lights below the transom are also cinquefoiled, and the upper leaves of the quatrefoil still rounded. Very similar are the windows in the Vicars' Hall at Wells (*c.* 1350–60), though here the transom is moulded only and the quatrefoil set in a longer vesica frame. The Abbot's Kitchen at Glastonbury has been dated late in the century by Pugin, but from moulding and window evidence the lower portion seems earlier. A window with lobed quatrefoil over two cinquefoiled ogee lights bears a strong resemblance to those at Battle and Wells, suggesting a mid 14th-century date: it could have been the work of the designer of Meare Manor, which belonged to Glastonbury Abbey. The same type of window occurs in the hall of Tickenham Court (Pl. LV G), also in Somerset, which might be somewhat later, perhaps *c.* 1370, judging from the more pointed cusping and the flatter rear arch; the quatrefoil is set in a shorter kite-like frame as at Battle, and there is the same type of hood. But it is possible that these windows are the survival of an earlier fashion since the mouldings of all the hall doorways seem of 15th-century date.

It will be seen how the ogee arches of the lights continue their sinuous curve as a lateral frame to the quatrefoil until the junction with the outer arch. At the end of the century this frame stiffens into a vertical line flanking the quatrefoil and initiates the so-called Perpendicular tracery. This will be noted in comparing the Tickenham windows with those in the hall at St Cross, Winchester, possibly resulting from repairs of *c.* 1383 onwards. The quatrefoil is the same, but now there is a vertical line above each of the cinquefoiled lights, which are confined not in an ogee but in a two-centred arch like the normal type of the 15th century. These small Perpendicular bars are seen above trefoiled lights in the hall windows (*c.* 1377) at Norrington Manor (Pl. LV F), the lobed quatrefoil now somewhat flattened. The porch chamber window at Preston Plucknett is similar, and the cinquefoiled transomed lights to the hall have the same vertical bars in the head, showing that the type continued into the early 15th century; the oriel at West Coker has the same (Pl. LIV G). Still later, before 1463, Ashleworth Court has these bars and quatrefoil over trefoil-headed lights (Pl. XIX B).

It is noticeable that the Perpendicular bars occur in windows associated with the architect Henry Yevele, who flourished from 1353 until his death, at about eighty, in 1400, and his friend William of Wynford, working 1360–1403, who were responsible for much of the best work in south-east and south-west England in the second half of the 14th century. At Westminster, Yevele probably designed the Abbot's Hall (1372–6) and gave the windows a novel form, 'blunted cinquefoil' heads to the lights, and above, between the Perpendicular bars, a cross made up of four lobed quatrefoils. He may have built Nunney Castle in Somerset, licensed in 1373, and here we get the simpler form of tracery, very like the hall windows, already mentioned, at Norrington Manor, a work notable enough to have Yevele or Wynford as designer.

Later the quatrefoil became broader, with the side foils smaller than the wide ogee leaves to top and bottom, and this appears, with lights cinquefoiled as is usual with Yevele, in his windows at Westminster Hall (1394–1400), and those he added, similar but with an added transom, to the Water Tower at Canterbury. Mr Harvey considers that Yevele influenced the windows in Wynford's hall at New College, Oxford (1380–6), which again have a late quatrefoil over cinquefoil transomed lights. The chapel windows, however, are an enlarged form of Wynford's hall windows at Winchester College (1387–1394), where the hexagon between the bars is subdivided, forming two narrow trefoiled lights, and this probably also occurred at Wardour Castle (licensed 1393), which seems to be in his style.* The trefoiled panel was a favourite device of his, as on the internal walls of Winchester Cathedral, and this seems also typical of the heads of his tracery. At Donnington Castle the remaining tracery of the gatehouse window (1386) shows evidence of a cusped hexagon over trefoil-headed lights; or else a quatrefoil with large side leaves, or only the top of the panel cusped, as in the south transept at Alton (Hants).

Of John of Gaunt's princely hall at Kenilworth, built by Robert Skillyngton in 1391–1393, enough remains of the magnificent traceried windows to allow a reconstruction. They combine elements of both Wynford and Yevele, cinquefoiled and trefoiled heads, with lobed quatrefoils, sometimes set in a lozenge; they are lofty with two sets of transoms, and the upper part is subdivided into a double two-light window elaborately cusped (Pl. 28).

Cinquefoil-headed lights, so popular in the 15th, began in the 14th century, in a steeper form at first; as we have noted, at Meare and Martock the earliest had the upper leaf pointed or of ogee form. At Beverston Castle, perhaps as early, the chapel windows, though cinquefoiled, are very steep indeed, with trefoiled kite-shaped tracery above. The pointed upper leaf persists in Yevele's beautiful windows, now unblocked, in the Parlour at Westminster (c. 1362), and he used a peculiar blunted cinquefoil in the Abbot's Hall. But he normally employed the rounded leaf, the topmost sometimes a little larger and with a slight point. Wynford's cinquefoiled heads are similar and often used for a single light, as at Winchester College gateway, and in the lofty openings to the kitchen at Wardour Castle. These tall cinquefoiled windows were popular with John Lewyn, the great northern architect of the time (1364–c. 1398), and used in the hall at Bolton Castle (1378), and at Lumley Castle (c. 1392), also probably his work.

The square-headed window is often chosen for a side wall, as at Martock. The ogee heads of the lights rise to the frame, and form tracery with it. At Southfleet (c. 1330) there is a hexafoil in the head, but the usual treatment is to reverse the treatment of the lights, like the Bellhouse window at Wilton (Pl. LV c). This type is particularly suited to reticulated tracery, as in the chapel at Lytes Cary (1343) (Pl. LV d) and the hall at Marlow. Plainer windows of this form were used at Winchester College, a moulded label with head stops serving either single or coupled trefoiled lights.

The shouldered arch (really lintel) is a feature especially of the earlier 14th century in windows, and is much used in the c. 1305 additions at Aydon Castle. In a transomed window it may appear in the lower lights, as at Berkeley Castle hall (c. 1340), and (from evidence) in the restored hall at Compton Castle (c. 1329). At Market Deeping Rectory,

---

* Harvey (1954), 310.

Lincolnshire, the upper lights are shouldered also, with tracery to match, forming an unusual pattern (Pl. 27 B).*

Gabled windows continue in the first half of the 14th century. There were admirable examples at Nurstead Court shown in Edward Blore's engraving of *c.* 1837.† The Abbey at Sutton Courtenay had this arrangement originally, akin to those once existing at Cumnor Place, also in Berkshire, *c.* 1330–40 (Fig. 21).‡ At Cumnor the larger gable of the solar continued down to the main eaves at the end of the building, like the 13th-century entrance gable in the Old Deanery at Salisbury. At Marlow two opposite windows of this type remain at the Old Parsonage, though the actual gables may have been rebuilt.

Fig. 112. Window in Bishop Gower's hall, St David's, *c.* 1327–47.

This gable fashion for windows probably died out before the end of the century, except for oriel projections. Winchester Castle hall was transformed in the reign of Richard II; the windows lost their gables, of which the roundels were re-used internally, and the hall eaves were made a uniform height.

Circular windows of great beauty survive from the first half of this century. In Bishop Gower's great hall (*c.* 1327–47) at St David's (Fig. 112) the east end is embellished by a wheel window with trefoiled spokes radiating from a central quatrefoil. About the same date is the magnificent window some 12 feet in diameter, now bricked up, in the hall of

Fig. 113. Window in the hall, Winchester Palace, Southwark, dating from the first half of the 14th century.

Winchester Palace at Southwark, now a warehouse, which was surveyed in 1944 by Mr Sidney Toy (Fig. 113). It is even more elaborate. From a central carved boss trefoiled spokes of alternate sizes form a hexagon; this is surrounded by cusped triangles within an encircling keel and roll-moulded frame. These are a variant from the three-light window treatment of a gable, as exemplified by the hall (*c.* 1320) at Clevedon Court, which has a five-light, now blocked, below (Pl. XL C).

The two-centred rear arch is still a common form. The segmental arch is found occasionally, but more often the segmental-pointed; at Goodrich (*c.* 1300) the arch is triangular (Pl. LI F). There is, however, a growing tendency towards the four-centred

* Illustrated in Parker (1853), 242.
† Illustrated in Parker (1853), 281.
‡ Illustrated in N. Whittock's *Microcosm of Oxford* (1830) (reproduced in *History Today*, April 1956, 254). See also D. & S. Lysons (1813), *Magna Britannia*, I, part II, 213.

form, convenient as giving width yet being not too high for the average wall. Sometimes it rises steeply as at Kenilworth, and it becomes flat towards the end of the century, as at Tickenham, resembling the 15th-century type, and especially where a low ceiling was desired. The shouldered or 'Caernarvon' arch occurs in the north, and with a double shoulder at Brinsop Court. The foliated arches of pointed cinquefoil type are found in the south-west, at Meare Manor House (Fig. 111) and Martock (Pl. LIV c), and the Vicars' Hall, Exeter.

The rear arch is commonly chamfered or hollow chamfered, the latter becoming more usual in this century. It often projects downwards as a rib from the edge of the soffit, chamfered or often hollow chamfered on both sides; or there may be a hollow chamfer towards the lights, with the internal head moulded. Internal jamb-shafts have gone out of fashion, but sometimes the roll-moulding of the arch is continued downwards and provided with moulded bases, as in two late examples, Kenilworth and Westminster Halls.

FIFTEENTH CENTURY

By the 15th century glass had become rather less expensive, though still it could be afforded only by the nobility, gentry and the growing number of well-to-do merchants. Glass windows were regarded as luxuries, movable property until the reign of Henry VIII, when they were judged to be fixtures. The glass was set in rectangular casements secured by iron bars or bolts, of which the holes remain, and protected by an iron grille. They were removed and the shutters closed when the owner was away,* perhaps travelling in his baggage to the next of his houses to be visited.

Large windows were the vogue in great halls, though in some, and especially where a bay window was provided, a range of shorter untransomed windows was used, set high to allow tapestry and benches below. This tends to be a rather later 15th-century development, as is the bay window on the whole; however, the late 14th-century hall at Wardour had transomed windows over a cornice.

Glass was often used as a vehicle for heraldry, showing the connections and allegiance of the owner, and adding greatly to the richness and display. At West Bower the windows still contain quarries painted with flowering plants and the initials M and A, probably for the heiress Margaret Coker and her first husband Sir Alexander Hody, who was executed in 1461 on a charge of treason. Heraldic medallions are recorded in the hall windows of Minster Lovell, and we have a fortunate survival at Ockwells Manor in Berkshire. Here Sir John Norreys embellished his hall with the arms of his king, family and associates. He was Esquire of the Body to Henry VI and Edward IV, and Master of the Wardrobe to the former. But the emphasis of his glass is Lancastrian rather than Yorkist, and probably it was made between 1455 and 1460 by John Grayland or John Prudde, the King's Chief Glazier, who worked at Eton a few miles away.† The arms of Henry VI and Queen Margaret of Anjou are given prominence, and those of Sir John's associates include Henry

---

* The Earl of Northumberland's windows at Alnwick and elsewhere were taken out and carefully laid by during his absence, because of possible damage by heavy winds. Clarkson's *Survey of Alnwick Castle* (1556), quoted by Parker (1859), 122.
    † *Country Life* (22).

Beauchamp, sixth earl and first and last Duke of Warwick, Hereditary Pantler to the king, who died in 1445 and was succeeded (1449) as earl by his brother-in-law the Kingmaker; Edmund Beauchamp, Duke of Somerset, Constable of England, killed at St Albans (1455); Sir John Wenlock, Chamberlain to Queen Margaret, whom Norreys appointed supervisor of his will (dated 1465); * and the same queen's Keeper of the Wardrobe, Richard Bulstrode, nephew to Norreys, who became Comptroller of the Household to Edward IV. The presence of the coat of Richard Beauchamp, who was Bishop of Salisbury from 1451 to 1481, gives a date *postquam* for the glass, and the other limiting date is provided by that of James Butler, Earl of Wiltshire, attainted and executed in 1462, and by the fall of Henry VI in 1461. The arms of Sir John Norreys himself (d. 1467) are supplemented by his motto 'Feyth fully Serve' and the badge of the Wardrobe, three golden distaffs.

Whether long or short, the window of two cinquefoiled lights is the main type of the 15th century, the upper leaf now also rounded, in a less pointed arch, though after *c.* 1480 the lights tend to be four-centred and uncusped. The square frame and label (hoodmould) are general.

Four such tall windows, of two cinquefoiled transomed lights with square label, remain on one side of the hall of Bishop's Waltham Palace. At Bowhill, Exeter, there are two on each side with cinquefoils also below the transom, and similar windows are found in the hall of the Prebendal House at Thame. At Woodlands Manor (Pl. LVI G), as at East Meon Court House, the windows have cinquefoils to the upper lights alone. (The hall at East Meon probably dates from before the 1461 incident when Bishop Wayntlete was rescued from his irate tenants.) In Wanswell Court (*c.* 1450–60) the second lateral window is narrower, with a trefoil, not cinquefoil, to the lights, to allow it to be placed between the entrance door and fireplace.† Further tall cinquefoiled windows are found in the two merchants' houses at Salisbury: the arms of Edward IV occur in the glass of John Halle. Both tall and short four-light windows, all cinquefoiled, are used in the 'Banqueting Hall' (*c.* 1469–78) at Sudeley Castle (Pl. LVI A), associated with Richard, Duke of Gloucester (later king); the long ones have two transoms, and come nearly to floor level, one set out slightly as a bay; an end window, set high, contains eight similar lights under a wide three-centred arch.

In the Old Palace, West Tarring (Sussex), new windows were inserted *c.* 1400 in the hall. These have not the usual square label, but a straight segmental-pointed or four-centred outer arch above the cinquefoiled heads. In the earlier wing there is a similar window, placed in the 13th-century opening of which the early jamb-shafts are visible inside. This type of arch also occurs over cinquefoiled lights (*c.* 1420) at Nettlestead Place, together with others under square labels. Sometimes the cinquefoiled lights share a low arch which allows a small kite-shaped aperture, which may be cusped, between the heads. At Crosby Hall a range of such windows has a continuous hood, but at Eltham each pair is divided by a buttress. In Lincoln College, Oxford, there is a square frame and hood in addition

---

* The house was not quite complete in 1465, for in the will he bequeaths 'to the full building and making uppe of the chapell, with the chamber adjoyning within my mannor of Okholt, in the parish of Bray, not yet finished xl. li'. (Lysons (1813), *Magna Britannia*, I, part II, 449, and coloured drawings of the glass, 247).
† In S. Lysons's *Gloucestershire Antiquities* it is incorrectly drawn as resembling the other cinquefoiled two-light. See *Country Life* (28), 896.

to the arch. Triangular arches to the head and upper trefoiled lights are a feature in Prior Singer's windows (c. 1486–1521) at Wenlock.

Windows of three cinquefoiled heads were inserted at Martock when the 13th-century undercroft became a parlour in the 15th century (Pl. XVI c). They share a square label with out-turned ends, as does a similar three-light in the gatehouse at Ightham Mote.

The cinquefoiled ogee was also popular throughout the 15th century, the upper leaf being pointed. The ogee head allows for slight tracery between the lights and square head, as in the inserted early 15th-century windows at Woodsford Castle, Dorset, where the lower lights are shouldered below the transom. In the added wing at Tickenham Court of similar date, the mullion is carried up to the square head, and the lower lights have the normal rounded cinquefoil (Pl. LVI F).

Sometimes the ogee lights are trefoiled, as at Tretower Court, Brecon. (c. 1450), and (East) Coker Court in Somerset. A later type of trefoil has the upper leaf practically a full circle, as in some of the smaller windows at Tattershall (Pl. LIV H), or with a very slight point, rather than the ogee as before. This is shown in the range of wooden windows at 26 East St Helen's, Abingdon, an unusual survival (Pl. XXIX c).

A favourite treatment is to place a quatrefoil in each spandrel of the ogee arch, as in the lower lights of the north-west chamber window at Minster Lovell (Pl. LVI B, C) (probably c. 1431–42). In the upper lights there is evidence of cusped panels in a square head, reminiscent of the treatment (c. 1450–69) at Raglan Castle; * the label has head stops, perhaps portraits of William, seventh Lord Lovell (d. 1455), and his wife, while at Raglan there were figurines. Buck's drawing of 1729 † shows similar windows in the great chamber at Minster Lovell, with the same oblong frame externally, but with the quatrefoils here in the upper lights. The windows (c. 1495) of Bradley Manor have this decoration, also the Abbot's Parlour windows at Muchelney (c. 1508) and the inserted window in the Priest's House there. A small lobed trefoil is a variant in the wooden cinquefoiled lights of the Bird Cage Inn at Thame (Pls. XXXV A, LVI E).

A late 15th-century type used the cinquefoiled cusping in a very flat ogee. This is seen to perfection at Ashbury Manor (c. 1488) (Pls. XXXV c and D, LVI H), with square-framed two-light windows to the upper rooms and similar but longer windows, with moulded transom, to the hall below. The spandrels are merely pierced. In the George Inn at Glastonbury, another building of Abbot Selwood, the four-centred arch is cinquefoiled, as well as the ogee. The trefoil is similarly flattened at Wenlock.

By now the four-centred light was popular, and at Athelhampton (c. 1495–1500) we find such hall windows combined with uncusped ogee heads in the oriel lights. There are still cinquefoils to the ogee heads in the oriel (c. 1535) of the Strangers' Hall, Norwich, but the growth in simplicity is seen in the plain uncusped tracery above.

The window tracery continued the late 14th-century development, with more and more emphasis on vertical lines in the head, until the rather dull 'Perpendicular' grid is usual. The quatrefoil between parallel bars remains in earlier or remote examples, such as

---

* Pugin (1839), Pl. 27.

† See illustration in M.O.W. Guide (28). However, Buck should not be trusted implicitly, for he gives the hall windows trefoil heads on the north, whereas those remaining are cinquefoiled.

Plate LIII. Windows.

A and B. Christchurch Castle Hall, north window, interior and exterior, *c.* 1160. C. Durham Castle, Pudsey's Hall, *c.* 1170. D. Boothby Pagnell, with window seat, *c.* 1200. E. Wells Palace, Bishop Jocelyn's solar, *c.* 1230–40. F. Ower Moigne, Dorset, *c.* 1270–80.

Plate LIV. Windows. A. Godmersham Court Lodge, hall, c. 1250; demolished 1955. B. Charing Palace, hall, c. 1294–1313. C and D. Treasurer's House, Martock, hall, interior and exterior, c. 1330. E. The Old Parsonage, Marlow, c. 1340, interior of east window of hall. F. Abbot's Grange, Broadway, c. 1320, interior of chapel window. G. West Coker Manor House, oriel window interior, mid 15th century. H. Tattershall Castle, turret chamber, 1445–6 +.

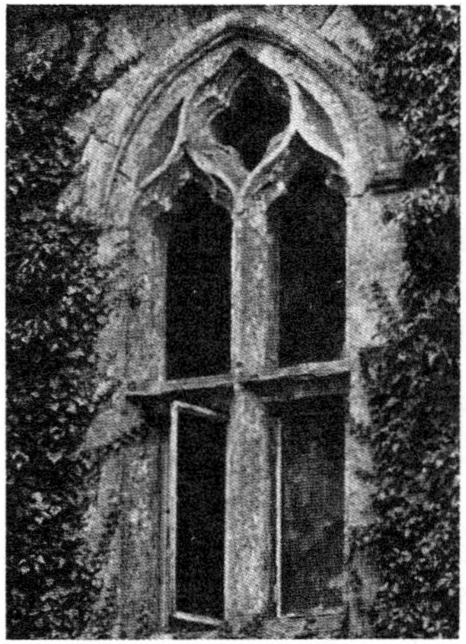
A

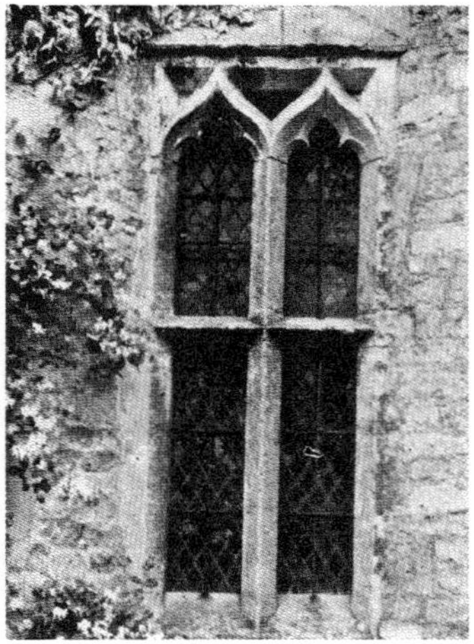
B

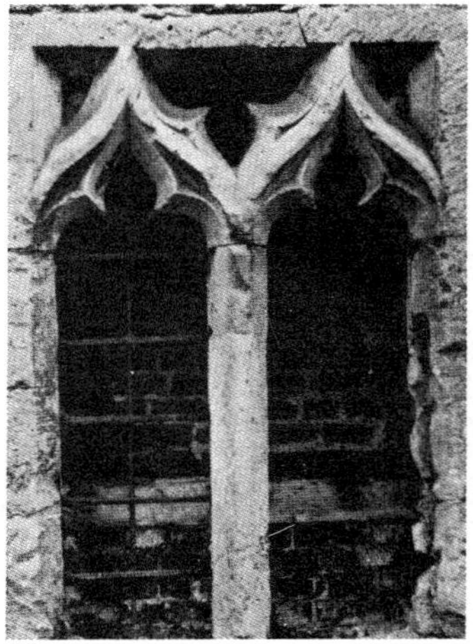
C

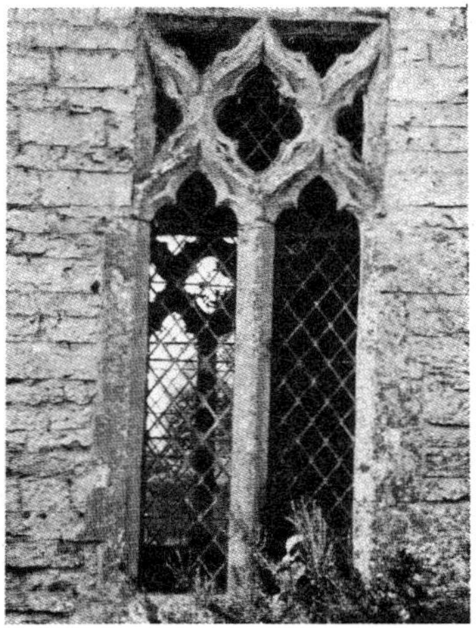
D

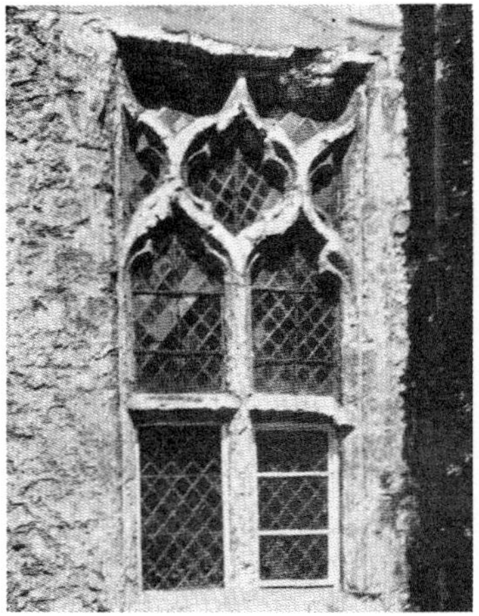
E

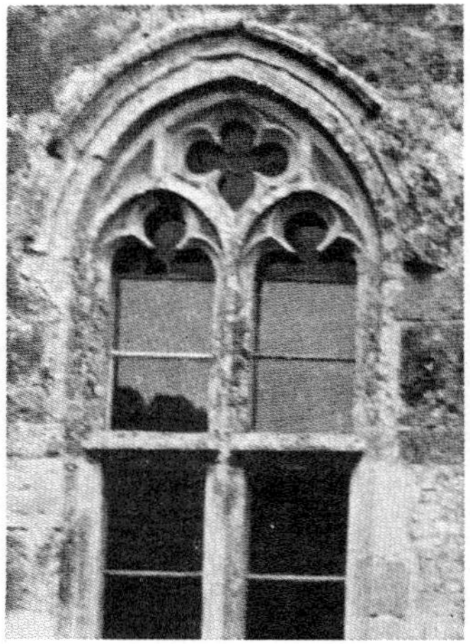
F

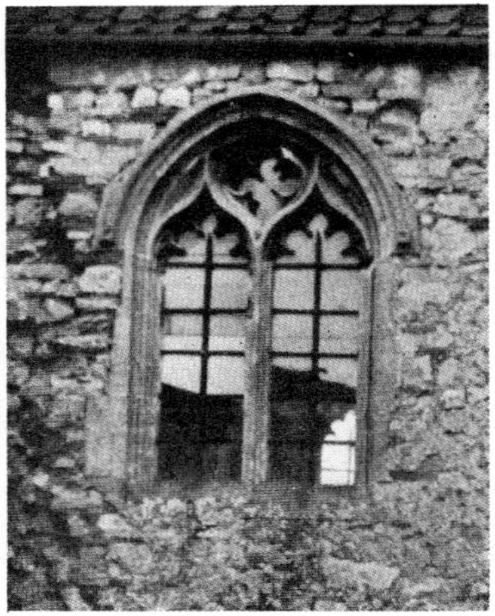
G

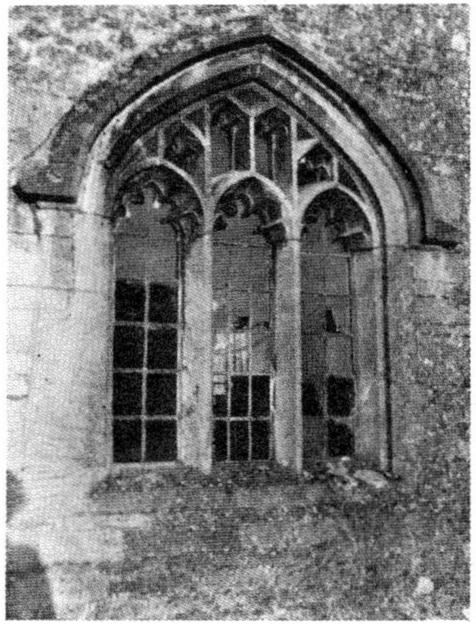
H

Plate LV. Windows. A. Bampton Castle, 1315, gatehouse range. B. Abbot's Grange, Broadway, *c.* 1320, window in hall next to oriel chamber, set obliquely. C. The Bellhouse, Wilton House, mid 14th century. D. Lytes Cary, chapel, 1343. E. The Old Parsonage, Marlow, *c.* 1340, east window of hall. F. Norrington Manor, *c.* 1377. G. Tickenham Court, hall, *c.* 1370–1400. H. South Wraxall Manor, *c.* 1435, window in oriel chamber.

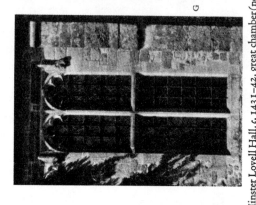

Plate LVI. 15th-century Windows. A. Sudeley Castle, hall, c. 1469–78. B and C. Minster Lovell Hall, c. 1431–42, great chamber (north-west), interior and exterior. D. Minster Lovell Hall, withdrawing-room. E. Bird Cage Inn, Thame, oriel interior. F. Tickenham Court, solar wing, 15th century. G. Woodlands Manor, Mere, hall, first half of 15th century. H. Ashbury Manor, c. 1488.

Ashleworth Court (before 1463), over trefoiled heads, the West Coker oriel, and the east window of Naish Priory, which has a quatrefoil over two cinquefoiled transomed lights. In West Bower Farm, Durleigh, also in Somerset, the turret windows contain a shield or carved ornament on both sides, instead of an opening in the head; there is a continuous hoodmould (Pl. XXIX B). At (East) Coker Court the flowing lines of similar trefoiled ogee lights are continued to form a curved hexagon containing two lobed quatrefoils (Pl. XXI A). These, if elongated, would form a figure trefoiled at either end, as in the attractive panels in the chapel tracery at Bradley Manor (1428) (Pl. XXXVIII B). Here the east window has three cinquefoiled ogee lights, hence two panelled hexagons in the head, with a cruciform quatrefoil or cusped lozenge between them in the apex. This may be compared to the 15th-century tracery inserted into an earlier arch in the east window of the chapel at Woodlands Manor. Now the two hexagons are simpler, the panel heads alone trefoiled like small versions of the lights, and again there is an apex quatrefoil.

This subdivision of the main pattern of the head into two panels, instead of one cusped figure, we have seen to be characteristic of William of Wynford's tracery, as in the hall windows at Winchester College, and it lends itself to the general fashion for verticality. At South Wraxall the porch window still has a lobed quatrefoil over cinquefoiled lights, but the hall windows have two trefoiled panels in the head, and the oriel chamber has a three-light more 'Perpendicular' still, each mullion carried up to the main four-centred arch, with parallel bars rising from the apex of each cinquefoiled light (Pl. LV H); the panels so formed have trefoiled heads; above this a two-light to the closet has a square head with similar tracery on a smaller scale.

At Tattershall (1433–46) the great tower has large traceried windows at all four levels (Pl. XXXI D). They are of two cinquefoiled lights, each with a small two-light (cinquefoiled or trefoiled) with quatrefoil above; these miniatures are arranged over each of the main ones, like the South Wraxall oriel, and not between them as at the Bradley and Woodlands chapels.

Already at Tattershall on two storeys a horizontal bar or subsidiary transom divides the main lights from the miniature windows in the tracery. At South Wingfield (c. 1440–59) the Great Chamber has a magnificent window of two tiers of four cinquefoiled lights. Those above the transom are stepped, the two central higher, but all have this bar and miniatures of two trefoiled lights above. A segmental arch and ogee hood with finial complete the composition (Pl. XXVII B).

In Devon, Compton Castle chapel has two windows of vertical tracery over four cinquefoiled lights. The central mullion branches out to form two separate parts, with a miniature of two trefoiled lights over each pair. The lozenge in the head, now larger, contains further trefoiled panels divided by a small horizontal bar. This type is familiar in many 15th-century churches.

The two-centred rear arch is now displaced by much flatter types, segmental-pointed, four-centred and later elliptical being typical of the 15th century. Sometimes a straight-sided or flat triangular arch is employed. A late type, used especially in the early 16th century, is the elliptical arch, as in the Abbot's Parlour at Muchelney and Horham Hall in Essex, and the four-centred rear arch is general in this period.

The rear arch may be chamfered, but is often moulded. *Paterae* decorated the hollow chamfer at Gothelney and in the Law Library at Exeter. Internal jamb-shafts are used again, now tall and slender like those at South Wraxall. At Raglan Castle these support a four-centred moulded arch with carved foliage in the spandrels (*c.* 1450–69).* Sometimes the spandrels are pierced, either left plain or filled with tracery. A quatrefoil is a favourite device, as in the withdrawing room below the chapel at Minster Lovell (Pl. LVI D), and in another important apartment below the hall at Sudeley Castle. In the great hall at Forde Abbey (*c.* 1528) between the windows there are grouped shafts with moulded bases set on angel corbels. A fashion in later houses was to treat the soffit and reveals with stone panelling akin to the decoration of an oriel arch. There is elaborate tracery in the soffit of the great window of the state bedroom (*c.* 1450–69) at Raglan, where small fluted shields *à bouche* are set in a panelled framework (Pl. 29),† and in the Deanery at Wells a pair of first-floor windows on the north front share a panelled and traceried soffit.‡ There are two rows of plain trefoiled panels in the soffits of Prior Singer's windows at Wenlock; and at Horham Hall (1502–5) these continue, trefoiled at either end, down the jambs as well.

* Illustrated in Pugin (1839), pl. 27.   † Illustrated in Pugin (1839), pls. 25, 26.   ‡ Illustrated in Pugin (1839), pl. 52.

WINDOW EXAMPLES

The examples are placed in what appears to be chronological order, the dates given if known

12TH CENTURY (AND EARLIER)

BASEMENT LOOPS.
Round-headed:
St Mary's Guild, Lincoln, *c.* 1180–90
Chamfered oblong:
Christchurch Castle, Hants, hall, *c.* 1160

ONE-LIGHT WINDOWS.
Sherborne Old Castle, *c.* 1130, with chevron ornament

TWO-LIGHT WINDOWS.
One shaft:
Scolland's Hall, Richmond Castle, Yorks., late C 11th
Portslade Manor ruins, Suss., *c.* 1150
King John's House, Southampton, *c.* 1150
Three shafts:
Christchurch Castle, Hants, hall, *c.* 1160
Five shafts:
Saltford Manor, Som., *c.* 1150, incipient inner shafts
Pudsey's hall, Durham Castle, *c.* 1170.
Jew's House, Lincoln, *c.* 1170–80
Aaron's House, Lincoln, *c.* 1170–80
Charleston Manor, Suss., *c.* 1180

Mullion:
Hemingford Grey Manor House, Hunts., *c.* 1150

INTERNAL JAMB-SHAFTS.
'Canute's Palace' (The Long House), Southampton, *c.* 1180

CIRCULAR WINDOWS (in gables).
Chepstow Castle, Mon., hall, late C 11th
Fountains Abbey, Yorks., guest houses, after 1147
Christchurch Castle, Hants, hall, *c.* 1160

13TH CENTURY

BASEMENT LOOPS.
Chamfered oblong:
The Old Deanery, Salisbury, *c.* 1258–74
Aydon Castle, Northumb., *c.* 1280
Cruciform:
Old Soar, Plaxtol, Kent, *c.* 1290
Pointed head (small lancet):
Crowhurst Manor ruins, Suss. *c.* 1250
Little Wenham Hall, Suff. *c.* 1270–80
Corbelled lintel:
West Dean Rectory, Suss.

ONE-LIGHT WINDOWS.

Round-headed lancet:

The Chantry, Chichester, Suss., early C 13th

Pointed lancet:

Little Wenham Hall, Suff., *c.* 1270–80

Trefoiled lancet:

Donington-le-Heath, Leics., *c.* 1280

TWO-LIGHT WINDOWS.

Lancet lights:

Cogges Manor, Oxon., *c.* 1250
Aydon Castle, Northumb., *c.* 1280
Charney Basset Manor, Berks., *c.* 1280

Rounded trefoil lights with quatrefoil in head:

Leadenhall, Salisbury, *c.* 1220
Winchester Castle, hall, 1222–35
Wells Palace, Bishop Jocelyn's hall, *c.* 1230–1240
Treasurer's House, Martock, Som., 1250–1260 block

Pointed trefoiled lights with quatrefoil in head:

Godmersham Court Lodge, Kent, *c.* 1250, destroyed 1955
Cogges Manor, Oxon., *c.* 1250
Barneston Manor, Dor., *c.* 1260
Chepstow Castle, hall, *c.* 1260
Little Wenham Hall, Suff., *c.* 1270–80 (also trefoil)
Ower Moigne, Dor., *c.* 1270–80

CIRCULAR WINDOWS (in gables).

Sexfoil:

Strangers' Hall, Winchester

Quatrefoil:

The Chantry, Chichester, early C 13th
Wells Palace, Bishop Jocelyn's north window, *c.* 1230–40

14TH CENTURY

One trefoiled light:

Meare Manor, Som., 1322–35
Beverston Castle, Glos.
Old Hall Farm, Warsop, Notts.
Winchester College, 1387–94

One cinquefoiled light:

Bolton Castle, Yorks., hall, 1378
Lumley Castle, Yorks., *c.* 1392
Wardour Castle, Wilts., kitchen, 1393

Two trefoiled lights with quatrefoil in a two-centred head:

Haddon Hall, Derbys., *c.* 1300
Markenfield Hall, Yorks., 1310
Bampton Castle (Ham Court), Oxon., 1315
Abbot's Grange, Broadway, Worcs., *c.* 1320
Brinsop Court, Heref., hall, *c.* 1340
Penshurst Place, Kent, 1341–9
Nunney Castle, Som., 1373
Norrington Manor House, Alvediston, Wilts., *c.* 1377

Two cinquefoiled lights with quatrefoil in a two-centred head:

Meare Manor House, Som., 1322–35 *
The Fish House, Meare, Som., 1322–35
Treasurer's House, Martock, Som., *c.* 1330
Glastonbury, Som., Abbot's Kitchen
Battle Abbey, Suss., Abbot Adam de Katling's work, 1324–51 *
Vicars' Hall, Wells, *c.* 1350–60
Tickenham Court, Som., *c.* 1370 type
Hospital of St Cross, Winchester, hall, ? *c.* 1383 +
New College, Oxford, hall, 1380–6
Westminster Hall, 1394–1400
The Water Tower, Canterbury

Two trefoiled lights in square head:

Abbot's Grange, Broadway, Worcs., *c.* 1320
Brinsop Court, Heref., *c.* 1340
Wilton, Wilts., bellhouse
Winchester College, Hants, 1387–94
Vicars' Hall, Chichester, Suss., 1397 +

Two cinquefoiled lights in a square head:

Treasurers' House, Martock, Som., *c.* 1330
Southfleet Old Rectory, Kent, *c.* 1330

Reticulated (net) tracery:

Clevedon Court, Som., chapel, *c.* 1320
Lytes Cary, Som., chapel, 1343
Woodlands Manor, Mere, Wilts., chapel
Old Parsonage, Marlow, Bucks., *c.* 1340

Elaborate tracery:

Mayfield Palace, Suss., *c.* 1325 *
Kenilworth Castle, War., hall, 1391–3

* Also cinquefoiled below the transom.

CIRCULAR WINDOWS (in gables).

Wheel:

Bishop Gower's Hall, St David's, Pembs.,
(*c.* 1327–47)

Winchester Palace Hall, Southwark, first
half C 14th

15TH CENTURY

---

*Two cinquefoiled transomed lights with square
label:*

Bishop's Waltham Palace, Hants, hall *

Bowhill, Exeter *

Prebendal House, Thame, Oxon., hall

Court House, East Meon, Hants

Woodlands Manor, Mere, Wilts.

Wanswell Court, Glos., also with trefoiled
heads

Sudeley Castle, Glos., hall, probably
c. 1469–78

Hall of John Halle, Salisbury, *c.* 1470–83

Church House (hall of John Webbe),
Salisbury

Ashbury Manor, Berks., *c.* 1488

*Two cinquefoiled ogee transomed lights with square
label:*

Woodsford Castle, Dor., inserted windows
with shouldered lights below the transom

Tickenham Court, Som., solar wing *

*Two trefoiled ogee transomed lights with square
label:*

Tretower Court, Brecon., *c.* 1450

Quatrefoils in spandrels of ogee arch to the lights:

Minster Lovell Hall, Oxon., probably
c. 1431–42

Bradley Manor, Devon, *c.* 1495

Muchelney, Som., Abbot's Parlour, *c.* 1508

Priest's House, Muchelney, inserted window

Two cinquefoiled lights in low arched head:

Nettlestead Place, Kent, *c.* 1420

Crosby Hall, London, 1466+

Eltham Palace, Kent, *c.* 1479–80

Perpendicular tracery:

Bradley Manor, Devon, chapel, 1428

South Wraxall Manor, Wilts., hall, *c.* 1435

Tattershall Castle, Lincs., 1433–46

South Wingfield Manor, Derbys., great
chamber, *c.* 1440–59

Compton Castle, Devon, chapel, *c.* 1450

Rear arches with decorated spandrels:

Minster Lovell Hall, Oxon., probably
c. 1431–42

Raglan Castle, Mon., Fountain Court,
c. 1450–69

Sudeley Castle, Glos., probably *c.* 1469–78

Stone panelling to soffit and reveals:

Raglan Castle, Mon., state bedroom,
c. 1450–69

The Deanery, Wells

Prior's House, Wenlock, Salop, *c.* 1486–
1521

Horham Hall, Ess., 1502–5

---

* Also cinquefoiled below the transom.

27

Squints; Lighting

VISUAL access by squints or miniature windows is found in a number of houses, and there must have been many more such apertures now concealed. Look-outs from the solar down into the hall allowed the owner to maintain control there after retiring to his private chamber adjoining. This was necessary where no doorway gave direct access by means of a stairway into the hall itself. At Stokesay two oblong chamfered windows serve as peep-holes from the solar, and there is a similar look-out at Penshurst. In the later 15th-century manor house of Kingston Seymour, Buckler's drawing shows a small canopied opening at solar level, near the angle next to the oriel.*

At Dartington Hall a small opening, now blocked, overlooks the hall, but at the service end and at second-floor level, the hall being particularly high. Possibly this was in the steward's room. At Great Chalfield a mask head is found at the level of the gallery at the service end, as well as two others, with perforated eyes and ears, one over the arch to each oriel, being a look-out from the closet over the latter which had access from the great chamber at this upper end of the hall (Pl. 31 A). This is the position for mediaeval squints when oriel chambers are present. There is an early example at Clevedon Court (c. 1320), a window of two trefoiled lights, looking down from the chapel into the hall (Pl. LVII c), and another trefoil-headed opening, of the 15th century, at West Coker, in the same position, but here contrived in a cell in the thickness of the wall. At Little Sodbury Manor the squint over the oriel arch is of mask type like those at Great Chalfield.

Squints are used giving visual access to the chapel from adjoining rooms. At Broughton Castle there is not only a two-light opening from the solar, looking down into the chapel from the west, but, also at an upper level, a squint of five small graduated lancets from the chamber adjoining it on the south; while at Beverston Castle the oratory on the second floor is overlooked from the rooms on either side by means of two parallel squints, set diagonally (Pl. 30).

In the 15th-century Chantry at Ilminster an original timber-framed partition has been uncovered in the room next to the chapel on the first floor; in one of the lower panels, at eye level when kneeling, a pierced quatrefoil was revealed (Pl. LVII A). The chapel screen

* Reproduced in *Archaeological Journal* (1958), CXV, pl. XVII.

at the Chancery in Lincoln is probably of similar date; in the wall parallel to it, that of a chamber divided from the chapel by a staircase, is a small squint lancet, allowing the occupant to see across the steps through the screen into the chapel itself (Pl. LVII B).

Look-outs commanding the entrance are quite common. One of the most interesting is at Nassington Prebendal House, where an oblique squint is set in the side of the projecting bay at the upper end of the hall, perhaps a prototype of the side lights of the later bay windows, which also had a view, along the lateral wall, of the entrance doorway. A miniature two-light window is sometimes found for this purpose, as at Wanswell Court, where it is of two trefoiled and transomed lights, here on the side of a projecting parlour wing (Pl. 31 B). This is still *in situ*, but often these small windows are re-used elsewhere, as in several houses at Burford. Squints overlooking the gate exist in the porch, and the chamber over it at Little Sodbury Manor.

At Winchester oral access seems to have been obtained from the king's solar to the great hall of the Castle. In the west wall a 'speaking-tube', 'the king's ear', has been found, a channel set askew in the wall with an outlet over the dais. At Bindon there is a similar curious aperture near the position of an original entrance.

LIGHTING

There remains occasionally in a mediaeval hall, between the windows, a moulded or traceried bracket. In some cases this supported a wall post of the roof, as it still does at Crosby Hall, but a corbel similar in design might have been used for another purpose. What that was is revealed by a valuable survival at Norrington Manor (*c.* 1377), where on top of the moulded bracket there are still two of the iron spikes on which candles were once fixed (Pl. LVII G). A similar bracket, also moulded, but now without the spikes, can be seen in the Vicars' Hall (1397+) at Chichester. Sometimes the shelves were more elaborate. That at Tickenham Court, not far off in date, has tablet flowers in the hollow chamfer below the moulding * and, above, a frieze of quatrefoils set diagonally (Pl. LVII F). This greatly resembles two brackets in the hall at Martock and another by the solar window, also of 15th-century workmanship and even more ornate. These have a shield with foliage on the chamfer, elaborated quatrefoils in the frieze, and a crenellated cornice; the corbels are rectangular, otherwise they bear a close resemblance to the polygonal supports for the roof at Crosby Hall and Christ Church, Oxford.

Perhaps these were a development from iron rings to support flares, and later examples of the *tabulatus* ordered by Henry III, in December 1252, to be placed 'on the walls of the chambers of Edward the king's son, and the king's brothers, to which lights [*luminaria*] may be fastened' at Clarendon. In the same month herces (*herciae*), wooden beams with prickets, 'on which the wax tapers should be placed', were to be repaired in the king's chapel at Winchester Castle.† Henry also is known to have ordered iron branches as candelabra to be attached to the pillars of his halls at Oxford and Winchester. He had a candlestick in his own chamber.‡

---

* This appears to be a scroll which suggests the 14th century.   † Liberate Roll, 37 Henry III; Turner (1851), 242.
‡ Turner (1851), 101.

Candles were used from the Roman period onwards. The clock candles of King Alfred in Saxon times are famous, and we are told by William of Malmesbury that Ethelred the Unready, as a child of ten, 'so irritated his furious mother by his weeping that, not having a whip at hand, she beat the little innocent with some candles she had snatched up. . . . On this account he dreaded candles during the rest of his life'.

The best candles, for churches and great houses, were of wax; the more usual type were of tallow, made from melted down animal fat. Rushlights (rush candles), made by dipping the pith of a reed in grease, were used in cottages as lately as the mid 19th century. Many rushlight holders can be seen in our folk museums, with a top to be adjusted as the taper declined.

Candlesticks have, of course, an equally long history, and Roman examples have been found in London. The mediaeval candlestick was either of pricket type, in which the candle end is impaled on a vertical spike, thus a real candle stick, or made with a loop gripping the candle, this being better for candles of poorer quality. The pricket type, made of iron usually set upon a tripod base, seems the earlier. A fine 14th-century example from the collection of the late F. W. Robins, F.S.A., of Bournemouth is illustrated in Pl. LVII E. Another iron candlestick of mediaeval date for the table, in the form of a Viking ship, for three candles, from Dale church in Norway, can be seen in the Historical Museum at Bergen University. The socketed form, which became general, was also known in the 14th century.*

Our modern match was represented by the striking of flint against steel, which ignited 'tinder' (inflammable material, often charred linen); and indeed 'tinder boxes' were in use until the mid 19th century. But as early as the 14th century small wooden sticks, one end dipped in sulphur, were used to obtain a light more quickly than this.†

Cresset lamps with oil and a floating wick were used. These could be like a bowl placed on a stand, or shaped like a funnel with a downward projection. The funnel type could be set in a ring for suspension, as shown in illuminated manuscripts of the 12th and 13th centuries. It is clearly depicted in the *Psalter of Queen Ingeburge of Denmark* at Chantilly, c. 1200.‡ The tapering part could also be set in a bracket, or even be carried. A glass lamp of this shape was excavated at Winchester in 1959, and, now restored, may be seen in the City Museum.

Lamp niches are known from Saxon times. There are a number in the crypts at Hexham and Ripon (c. 675) attributed to St Wilfred. At Hexham, two at the east end are arranged so as to throw light especially on to this end wall. There is a 15th-century lamp recess in the Abbot's (now Church) House at Gloucester (Pl. LVII H), and another, of early 16th-century date, in the lobby outside the Jerusalem Chamber at Westminster. The latter has trefoiled and sub-cusped head, and moulded cornice with cresting.

At Portchester Castle, in the hall which was completed in 1399, the porch doorway is provided with brackets for lanterns, one terminating the square label on either side (Pl. LVII I).

---

* Victoria and Albert Museum (1959), *Norwegian Art Treasures*, pl. 33.
† British Museum (1924), *Guide to Mediaeval Antiquities*, 96.
‡ Reproduced in *Archaeological Journal* (1935), XCII, pls. VII, VIII.

28

The Piscina and Laver;
Baths; Water Supply

BUILT-IN stone washing-basins are a feature of mediaeval houses, as they are in churches for the washing of the chalice, where they are given the name of piscina. When they serve for domestic purposes the term laver will be used. Piscina derives from the Latin *piscis* (fish) and was first used for a fish-pond. Laver comes from the Latin *lavare* (to wash).

Piscinae were usual in domestic chapels, and are found arched or cusped like contemporary windows. In 13th-century examples the head may be two-centred, sometimes moulded; it is trefoiled at Charney Basset, and has a shouldered lintel in the Prebendal House at Thame. At Little Wenham the piscina is irregular in plan with two trefoil-headed arches with shafts and an eight-petalled drain; one arch is set along the eastern jamb of the southern window.

An elaborate example, of 14th-century date, can be seen at Markenfield, the ogee arch embellished with finial and crockets and having a decorative vault; the projection has the shield of the Markenfields and other ornament. At Clevedon Court there is a trefoiled ogee head to the niche, while in the Lincoln Chancery the upper ogee arched leaf of the trefoil is enlarged, giving a keyhole effect, the whole moulded with roll and fillet. A steeper trefoiled head is found at Woodsford Castle (*c.* 1337) with a shelf, another at Goodrich (Pl. LVIII c, B), and also, well moulded, in the chapel at Beverston Castle, here sited on the south-eastern angle of the nave (Pl. LVIII D). At Old Soar the piscina (Pl. LVIII A), possibly refashioned in the early 14th century, has a cinquefoiled head with triangular canopy containing a lobed trefoil, and adorned with crockets; the sexfoil drain may be earlier.

Fifteenth-century examples include the moulded two-centred arch at the Ilminster

Chantry, and there is a piscina crested with flanking finials, part of an elaborate composition in the early 16th-century chapel at Bindon.

In mediaeval behaviour much emphasis was laid on the cleanliness of the hands. Forks were a rarity during our period, although Piers Gaveston in the early 14th century had some silver ones 'for eating pears'. At meals each person had a knife and spoon, and fingers did the rest, with the aid of crusts of bread. Also, one platter was often shared by two people. Thus strict cleanliness was urged by the 14th-century *Boke of Curtasye*, and no dog or cat was to be stroked beneath the table during meals. Sticky fingers are also most uncomfortable, and pictures in manuscripts often show a page with ewer and basin, a towel over his shoulder, giving opportunity for the guests to wash their hands after eating. Thus the domestic piscina or laver would be in use before and after meals, like the monastic lavatory near the frater doorway.

It seems to have been the custom to wash the hands on entering the hall for meals. Describing the feast given in Paris to Queen Isabella in 1389, Froissart says that after washing their hands (presumably in the entry), the king and queen and all the court entered the hall (apparently through the speres).* Thus a laver is often found in the entrance passage, like the late 13th-century example at Flore's Hall, Oakham; one is close to the screen at Battle Hall (*c.* 1330), near the entrance at Dacre Castle, and opposite it in the Hall of the Vicars at Chichester (1397+). In the suite built by Dean Gunthorpe (1472–98) in the Deanery at Wells, a canopied wash-basin is provided in the vestibule.†

Such lavers were general for domestic use. At Woodsford Castle there is a four-centred recess with moulded shelf in the solar, probably once a laver, as well as a round-headed niche with polygonal ledge, the drain now served by a modern tap, in the garderobe tower. Indeed, a laver was a suitable provision for a dressing-room with privy. There was a drain in the low window-sill of a trefoiled lancet in a closet of the Master's House at St John's Hospital, Northampton,‡ and the garderobe at Cottisford Manor Farm in Oxfordshire has a projecting semicircular trough with drain, also below a window.§

A less elaborate type of drain is found in service quarters. At Aydon Castle (*c.* 1280) the buttery, west of the hall, has a chamfered sink with square recess splayed to a small opening on to the external gutter,‖ and there is a projecting trough below a loop window in the cellar scullery at Warwick Castle (14th century).¶ Other examples include those in the kitchen and south-east tower of Compton Castle. At the Moat House, Appleby (Leicestershire), a plain square stone block has a basin hollowed out, and a pipe from it. ** Simple recesses of this kind, with semi-octagonal basin within, are found in two of the principal rooms of the late 15th-century Prior's House at Wenlock, the water passing through the wall into a projecting gutter, and so out of the mouth of a lion in one case

---

* *The Chronicles of Froissart* (translated by Baron Berners, 1913 edition), 386; also quoted by Parker (1853), 45–6.
† Parker (1866), pl. XX.
‡ Illustrated in Turner (1851), 156.
§ Turner (1851), 162.
‖ Turner (1851), 149 (illus.).
¶ Parker (1859), 130 (illus.).
** Parker (1859), 73 (illus.).

and of a man in the other.* From the same period dates the laver with four-centred arch found in the students' room recently restored at Magdalene College, Cambridge. Such a recess must have been, by now, a normal domestic feature; it is sited between the fireplace and garderobe doorway, the drain passing through the thickness of the wall. A more elaborate contemporary example, with cinquefoiled head and decorated basin, is provided near the fireplace in the Exchequer chamber over the great staircase to the Vicars' Hall at Wells.† The later type of trefoiled laver is found, also near the fireplace, at 4–6 Cross Street, Barnstaple in Devon (c. 1530).

Water was laid on by means of a lead pipe in the head of the recess, communicating with a cistern, and carried away by another pipe from the sink below. At Flore's House, Oakham, a pipe and leaden cistern were discovered in the back wall of the recess, which has a two-centred arch and projecting sink on which the rose and square flower decoration in hollow chamfer resembles the 13th-century detail in a fireplace at Aydon Castle. In the sink four drain holes flank a horizontal head carving, much worn.‡

At Westminster in 1275 Master Robert the Goldsmith was paid for work in the laver in the bathroom (domo balnei) and 26s. 8d. 'for 4 keys of gilt bronze and 4 heads made in the shape of leopards' for the baynes. These seem to be the equivalent of our tap with spout. In 1288 he was paid 40s. 'for the working of five heads of copper, gilded, for the laver of the small hall', and 25s. 'for the images of the said laver, and for whitening the laver and gilding the hoops' (circulis).§ This document is made clearer by the fortunate survival at Battle Hall near Leeds, Kent, of the hall laver, which still retains a cistern (Pl. 31 C), formed like the twin rounded towers of a castle, moulded and battlemented, each with a leonine head as spout, probably equivalent of the Westminster leopards.‖ This is a magnificent specimen, in a hall built c. 1330, perhaps by the king's mason Thomas de la Bataile, who built the Despenser's hall at Caerphilly Castle.¶ The moulded ogee arch is cinquefoiled, richly sub-cusped, supported on shafts; there is a finial and crockets terminating in carved heads, of which one remains. The projecting sink is moulded. **

At Dacre Castle a domestic piscina with trefoiled head and hood is identical with those found in churches and has a shelf and twelve-petalled drain (Pl. 31 D). Larger and more elaborate is the recess in the Hall of the Vicars at Chichester. This has a moulded ogee arch with finial supported by carved corbels of priests; the trough is upheld by the figure of a hooded man; it faced the entrance doorway (Pl. LVIII F and G).

There were two of these domestic piscinae at Kirkham House at Paignton, which dates from the early 15th century; but, mistakenly believed to have been removed from the parish church at the Reformation, they were taken out, and the hall one was used for the vicar's vestry at the church (Pl. LVIII E), the parlour one set in the chancel at Goodrington, where they can still be seen. The hall piscina is slightly larger. Both have an ogee-trefoiled arch

* Parker (1859), 129 (illus.).
† Pugin (1840), pl. 25.
‡ Turner (1851), 178–80 (illus.).
§ Exchequer, King's Remembrancer Accounts, 467, 6 and 467, 17; Salzman 1952), 276, 275.
‖ In ancient heraldry a leopard meant a lion facing the spectator.
¶ Harvey (1954), 27.
** Parker (1853), 46 (illus.).

decorated with four-petalled flowers; the hall laver has a domed head with central mask formed of the joined upper halves of two faces with open mouth common to both, for the lead pipe; the parlour piscina has vaulting ribs springing from bosses of foliage, rising to a central boss with hole for the supply pipe. Each has a quatrefoil in the basin, with the drain below a knot of foliage. Some of the lead pipe remains to the parlour drain.*

At Little Wenham, on the south (lower) end of the hall, there is an early 15th-century laver with a drain in the back wall. It has a sub-cusped cinquefoiled ogee arch with traceried panels in a square frame; the cornice has square flowers and battlements. From the head there hangs a slender iron bar which ends in a double circular twist (Pl. 32 A). It has been suggested that this was to suspend a towel, but more likely it was to act as a support or strengthener to a lead pipe from an overhead tank.

A laver was provided in the prior's solar added to Castle Acre at the end of the 15th century. It has a trefoil head and shelf for a small cistern.

BATHS

The bath was used in the Middle Ages, being usually the literal bath tub, a cask or barrel filled with water. Illustrations in manuscripts show these in use, such as the 13th-century picture of Bathsheba in her tub in an upper room, while her maid hastens with a cauldron of hot water, and King David observes from a balcony near by.† Sometimes there is a conversation piece, with persons gossiping in adjoining tubs (Fig. 114).‡ As usual, a tent-like arrangement or canopy, supported on a pole, is provided, and a stool was no doubt supplied for comfort; in view of the trouble of filling and emptying the tub, the water must have been shared by members of the family in turn. In some illustrations, however, larger receptacles are shown to accommodate several people at once. Mr Lawrence Wright's engaging study § shows a variety of these. One of the tubs has a waste-pipe, others had to be baled out, and the baling instrument is shown. A reference of 1403 describes the purchase by Princess Margaret of Flanders of sixty-four ells of common cloth to pad two

Fig. 114. Mediaeval bath tubs.

* Everett (1958 a) (illus.).
† Pierpoint Morgan Library, M 638, fol. 41 v; Holmes (1953), 98, 19 (illus.).
‡ British Museum, Sloane MS. 2435, fol. 8 b; Holmes (1953), 166, 115 (illus.).
§ Wright (1960), 40–6, etc.

bath tubs, as well as red Malines cloth for a canopy.* Bath tubs are also shown in use in the garden, in a wattle enclosure but not screened.

The provision of a bath was an act of hospitality to an important guest, travel weary, or to a knight returning from the joust. It is often referred to in mediaeval romances, and the illustrations suggest a bathroom in important houses.† Certainly royalty had more elaborate arrangements in the form of bathrooms akin to those in use today, with water laid on, according to the documentary evidence found by Mr Salzman.

Henry III was particular about cleanliness, and organized a vast drainage system at Westminster, influenced by monastic example. We also know that he had a 'wardrobe where the king is wont to wash his head', the room in 1256 being adorned with a picture by 'Master William the monk of Westminster, lately ordained and provided at Winchester', 'of the king who was rescued by his dogs from the sedition plotted against the same king by his subjects'.‡

Thus we should expect King Henry to be foremost in the matter of baths, even more than his father, King John, who had his bath tub and William the bathman travelling with him.§ But it is in 1275, three years after his death, that we get definite reference to water being laid on to a bath at Westminster. Robert the Goldsmith was paid 14s. for a metal key (tap) to the laver in the bathroom (*domo balnei*), 26s. 8d. for four keys of gilt bronze and four heads made in the shape of leopards for the *baynes*, 20s. for making four large keys of *latun* for the *baynes*, and 10s. for making a water pipe (*spurgelli*) and four keys to it.‖

In 1351 Edward III had a bath (hot and cold) at Westminster, for Robert Foundour was paid 56s. 8d. for two large bronze keys (taps) for the king's bath tub (*cuua balnei*) for carrying (*conducend*) hot and cold water into the baths. This is the only definite mention Mr Salzman ¶ has found for hot water being laid on to the bath-house, or stews, though at Langley, another royal residence, the 'square lead for heating water for the stues' may have meant that the hot water was piped there direct.

But many more references are found relating to pots for hot water either filled from the leads or heated in a special furnace. In 1344 at Bardfield Park forty-one earthen pots (*olla*) were bought for the *stues* and cost 18d; and in 1366, 125 costing 8d. each, *pour les stewes* at Windsor, where in 1391, 'the furnace of the King's *stywes*' was remade, and John Brown, carter, was employed 'for 2 days carrying with his carts 229 earthen pots from Farnborough to the Castle for the use of the *stywes*'. At Eltham in 1364, John Jury, potter, supplied 120 *pottes pro styuez* and Thomas Mason received £4 'for making the walls and setting 2 leads called *fournaysez* and 120 pottes of the *stuuy* house', which suggests that the pots were heated *in situ* and not just filled.

* Wright (1960), 42.
† Salzman (1929), 106; Holmes (1953), 166.
‡ Close Roll, 40 Henry III; Turner (1851), 262.
§ W. L. Warren (1961), *King John*, 136–7.
‖ Exchequer, King's Remembrancer Accounts, 467, 6; Salzman (1952), 276.
¶ Exchequer, King's Remembrancer Accounts, 466, 4; Salzman (1952), 276.

A valuable description is given of Edward II's bathroom at Westminster in the 1325 accounts:

William de Wynchelse for 3 boards called righok for crests and filetts of the bathing tub,—18*d*. For 3 oak boards called clouenbord for making the covering [i.e. canopy] of the said tub, 6 ft long and 2½ ft broad,—3*s*. . . . for 100 fagett for heating and drying the stuwes—3*s*. For a small barrell [*cumelino*], 2 bokettes and a bowl [*boll*] for carrying water to the stuwes . . . carpenters working on the covering of the bathing tub and the partition [*interclaus*] in front of the said tub —For 6 pieces of Reigate stone for making a slabbing [*tabliamentum*] in front of the partition of the said tub in the King's ground-floor [*bassa*] chamber. . . . For 2250 pauintil for the said chamber . . . for 24 mattis, at 2*d*. each, to put on the flore and pavement of the King's chamber on account of the cold.*

It will be seen that the bath had an oblong canopy, was partitioned off, had a paved floor in front, and was placed with tiled floor at ground level where removal of water would be easier. Mats were also provided.

Richard II had a tiled bathroom at Shene Palace, for in the royal accounts of 1385, 15*s*. was paid to Katherine Lightfote, later Yevele's second wife, 'for 2000 painted tiles for the room set apart for the king's bath'.†

An illustration of *c*. 1415 shows a long bath resembling the modern shape draped with fabric, with a tiled base, set on a tiled floor. There is a tent-like canopy. The occupant, wearing a crown, is being assassinated by three men in armour.‡

Public baths are known as early as the 12th century, and the street cries of Paris included '*Li bain sont chaut*'.§

However, the official religious view of the bath was not encouraging. Memories of the luxurious bathing practices of the Romans influenced the monastic attitude towards it. Cleanliness of the body was not regarded as next to godliness—rather the reverse. A bath should be taken for reasons of sickness, not enjoyment. As the Benedictine Rule laid down:

The use of the bath shall be offered to the sick as often as it is necessary: to the healthy, and especially to youths, it shall not be so readily conceded.‖

The Augustine Rule, as practised at Barnwell, enlarges on this theme:

A bath should be by no means refused to a body when compelled thereto by the needs of ill health. Let it be taken without grumbling when ordered by a physician, so that, even though a brother be unwilling, that which ought to be done for health may be done at the order of him who is set over you. Should he wish for one, however, when not advantageous, his desire is not to be gratified. Sometimes, what gives pleasure is thought to do good, even though it may harm.¶

---

* Exchequer, King's Remembrancer Accounts, 469, 6; Salzman (1952), 276-7.
† Exchequer, King's Remembrancer Accounts, 473, 2; Salzman (1952), 146.
‡ Bibliothèque de l'Arsenal, Paris, MS. 5193; reproduced in Salzman (1929), 107.
§ Holmes (1953), 133.
‖ D. H. S. Cranage (1934), *The Home of the Monk*, 59. Cambridge University Press.
¶ Ibid. 60.

In the early 14th century it is remarked that in St Augustine's Abbey at Canterbury (Benedictine), where formerly four baths a year were allowed, only two were now permitted.*

However, at Barnwell the Chamberlain who is 'to provide warm water for the shaving of the convent, and soap for washing their heads' is 'to provide soap for the baths of the brethren, if it be asked for'. At Canterbury the *balnearium* (bath-house) was sited some way east of the cloister, and the great 12th-century water supply which served it also provided, among other places, water for the prior's water tub. Prior Thomas Chillenden's works of 1390+ there include 'another chamber downstairs [*inferius*] with a chamber and a decent bath'†. A possible fixed monastic bath (*c.* 4 feet 7 inches × 4 feet 3 inches originally, and at least 5 feet 6 inches deep) of 13th-century date has been excavated at Kirkstall Abbey in Yorkshire. It is supplied with a lead pipe and has a removable stone 'plug'.‡ There is a large stone cistern, perhaps for the storage of water, in the warming-house of Lacock Abbey.

WATER SUPPLY

There had been schemes of water supply in Roman Britain, with the use of long-distance pipes and aqueducts, for instance at Lincoln, where more evidence has recently come to light.§ After the Dark Ages a revival seems to have come, as in other elements of civilization, *via* the church, and good drainage systems are found in early mediaeval monastic establishments. At Canterbury a plan of 1165 still exists, showing the tanks and reservoirs. These served all portions of the monastery, with a raised cistern with basin below in the infirmary cloister, and another laver in the main cloister where the water tower still stands, the lower portion of contemporary date, with later windows inserted above. A practical note is struck by the notice on the plan, in the infirmary court. Here, besides the well, there stands a hollow column on the main pipe, with the explanation: 'If the [supply from the] aqueduct fails, water can be drawn from the well and being poured into the column will be supplied to all the offices.'‖

The Water Tower at Canterbury resembled that at Durham, in the same position, where we are told: 'Within the Cloyster garth, over against the Frater House dour, was a fair Laver or Counditt for the Monncks to washe ther hands and faces at, being maid in forme round, covered with lead, and all of marble, saving the verie uttermost walls; within the which walls you may walke round about the Laver of marble, having many little cunditts or spouts of brass, with xxiiij cockes of brass, round about yt.' ¶ The fine *lavatorium* at Wenlock comes into this category.** The London Charterhouse also had a conduit house in the Great Cloister, illustrated in the 'Watercourse Parchment' of *c.* 1430.††

Waverley Abbey (Surrey) possessed a water supply in 1179, but this failed, and a new

*Cranage, op. cit., 61.
† *Literae Cantuarienses*, III, 114–20; Salzman (1952), 397.
‡ Wright (1960), 29.
§ F. H. Thompson (1954). The Roman Aqueduct at Lincoln. *Archaeological Journal*, CXI, 106–28. Indeed there was water sanitation as early as 2500–1500 B.C. in the Indus civilization.
‖ Salzman (1952), 268; J. Willis (1869), *Architectural History of the Conventual Buildings of Christ Church in Canterbury*, 159–90.
¶ *Rites of Durham* (Surtees Society), quoted by Salzman (1952), 268. Plan reproduced in Wright (1960), 26, 27.
** See Godfrey (1952); also reconstruction by A. E. Henderson in *Country Life* (29), 1494.
†† Plan in Wright (1960), 28.

system was arranged in 1215, underground pipes covering a distance of 570 yards.* At Bury St Edmunds the Abbey water supply in *c.* 1200 came in lead pipes for two miles.

More evidence is coming to light concerning the water supply in castles, this being of vital importance, especially in time of siege. At Newcastle there is proof of water having been raised by wall pipes to the various floors of the Keep (1171–5). We know that Dover Keep (1180–6) was designed by the same Maurice the Engineer, and in 1920 Major Macpherson discovered there a similar arrangement, the water passing through lead piping in at least two directions from a small tank, of which traces remain, in a recess adjoining the high well-head on the second floor of the keep. This 'Harold's Well' is upwards of 242 feet in depth, stone lined for 172 feet of it, after which it narrows from 3 feet 3 inches to 2 feet 9 inches in diameter. There is, also on the second floor, a circular storage tank, 3 feet 6 inches across and 2 feet 6 inches deep, probably to collect rain-water. The lead pipes (3½ inches in diameter) are contemporary with the keep, being laid in the thickness of the wall in special arched conduits.†

Henry III seems to have inaugurated a good water supply at Westminster Palace, following the example of the 12th- and 13th-century abbeys, such as Netley which he founded (1251). In 1234 Master William the conduit-maker (*conductarius*) was 'to bring water to our court of Westminster in accordance with what we have told him'.‡ In June 1260 payment was made for 'repairing the conduit of water which is carried underground to the king's lavatory and to other places there' as well as 'making a certain conduit through which the refuse of the king's kitchens at Westminster flows into the Thames; which conduit the king ordered to be made on account of the stink of the dirty water which was carried through his halls, which was wont to affect the health of the people frequenting the same halls'.§

The king's lavatory (*lotoris*) seems to have resembled the monastic arrangement, as at Canterbury or Wenlock. In 1244 it is called 'the round lavatory in the king's court at Westminster', sited between the new porch to the smaller hall and the kitchens.‖

More and more evidence is accumulating with regard to a good water supply and drainage arrangement in the large houses of the later Middle Ages. At the Manor of the More, Rickmansworth, the fourth period house (1426+) had a water supply carried in a wooden pipe from the gateway and presumably across the moat from a source on the hillside. It was replaced by a brick and tile conduit also running from the gatehouse and carrying lead pipes, the plumbers 'forcing of the pipes across the moat'. Trenches remain for the lead pipes, which converged on what must have been the conduit-head in the courtyard. These works seem to have been due to George Neville, Archbishop of York (1465–76), a brother of Warwick the Kingmaker. He bought the manor in 1460 and had alterations carried out before 1470 (when we know he was in residence), and he entertained John Paston there at Christmas 1471; he made great preparations for a visit of Edward IV in

---

* Brakspear (1905), 89–90.
† *Archaeological Journal* (1929), LXXXVI, 253–4.
‡ Close Roll, 18 Henry III; Salzman (1952), 275.
§ Liberate Roll, 44 Henry III; Turner (1851), 251.
‖ Close Roll, 29 Henry III; Turner (1851), 260.

1472 but was arrested by the latter at Windsor, and his manor was seized by the king. A later Archbishop of York, Cardinal Wolsey, made further improvements.*

Wolsey also arranged for an excellent water supply when he built Hampton Court. Three conduit houses were built round the springs at Coombe Hill 3½ miles away, and pure water brought that distance by means of a double set of lead pipes 2½ inches in diameter. The pipes run from Coombe to Surbiton, under the Hogsmith River, and under the Thames above Kingston Bridge, thence through the Home Park to the palace. There were 'tamkins', small brick buildings at intervals, access points for plugging-off sections of the pipe for repairs.†

* Biddle, Barfield & Millard (1959), 139, 151, 154, 156 (plan).
† Lindus Forge (1959) (fully illustrated).

29

Garderobes

PRIVIES or garderobes were more numerous and better planned in the Middle Ages than is generally supposed. These are even cases of water having been 'laid on', where rain-water or kitchen drainage was diverted for flushing, this being more frequently done by the mere emptying of the washing-tub contents down the privy shaft.

The term 'garderobe', although in general use, is misleading. It is the polite version of 'latrine', and may be confused with the mediaeval wardrobe (French *garderobe*), which was then not a piece of furniture but an important storage chamber for the dress materials acquired at the great fairs, clothing and valuables, a room with a fireplace, and in which dressmaking and similar work was done. It was also a royal finance department, with its documents and accounts, and by the 13th century was becoming an organized office of government, always following the king. 'The king's wardrobe' and 'the queen's wardrobe' will be familiar to readers of Henry III's Liberate Rolls. To these rooms, in which they would also dress, a privy chamber was a customary adjunct. In 1239 the king ordered 'a wardrobe and a privy chamber to the same wardrobe at Brill for the use of our queen',* and the enlargement of the privy chamber to the wardrobe at Clarendon; † while at Feckenham, in November 1251, the bailiff was ordered to make 'a wardrobe great and good, and a privy-chamber to the same'.‡

However, the word 'garderobe' was used in the privy sense as early as the 14th century. A document of 1314, relating to the remaking of the Earl's *latrinam* at Kenilworth is glossed in the margin *custus garderobe domini Comitis*; and at York Castle (*temp.* Edward III) payment of ten shillings was given 'for making the pit of the garderobe of the Exchequer'.§ The term may be compared to the cloakroom of double meaning today.

'Privy' is however the more appropriate mediaeval term, and there are constant references to privy chambers (*camerae privatae*) in the Liberate Rolls. They were attached to other

* Liberate Roll, 23 Henry III; Turner (1851), 190.
† Liberate Roll, 23 Henry III; Turner (1851), 193.
‡ Liberate Roll, 36 Henry III; Turner (1851), 234.
§ Salzman (1952), 281.

rooms: in fact a chamber with a chimney (fireplace) and a privy chamber was the usual combination. In 1238 the sheriff of Southampton was ordered 'to make in our castle of Winchester, behind the chapel of St Thomas the Martyr, a certain chamber for the use of the bishops, and a chimney and a certain privy chamber to the same'.* The great chamber of Edward the king's son, at Ludgershall (1251) was even to have two chimneys and two privy chambers.† Sometimes the privies were added outside the wall, as at Clarendon,‡ or in the moat of the tower at Marlborough Castle,§ and one for the household at Clarendon was built at the end of the penthouse for litter.‖

The term *longaigne* (a far-off place) is used for privy in Old French documents.¶ But a distant site from the chamber was not convenient. So where practicable the garderobe was situated at the end of a passage contrived in the thickness of the wall, with access from the chamber by means of a right-angled turn. It was thus as far away as possible. Small door-ways leading to such wall passages with garderobe at the end are noticeable in the corners of rooms, such as the Checker chamber at Abingdon Abbey. Henry III, always particular, ordered double doors at Woodstock.** The thick walls of 12th-century keeps were especially useful for garderobe construction. At Canterbury one is constructed in the angle which is thickened by pilaster buttresses, and there are twin garderobes to an intermediate buttress at Castle Rising (Pl. LIX A). At Dover the garderobe passages run under the wide window embrasures.

Where the chamber walls were less thick other means were adopted. Sometimes the garderobe was corbelled out from the outside wall, like an external buttress. The same principle was used in the machicolations of military architecture, in which an overhanging gallery had apertures in the floor through which missiles or boiling water †† could be thrown on to an enemy attacking the base of the wall. At Compton Castle such balcony-like pro-jections, here less continuous, would appear to be garderobes, if the latter were not provided at the further end of the same room. There is a 13th-century example of the corbelled garderobe on the north tower at Stokesay, and another off the corridor connecting solar and south tower. Fourteenth-century ones can be seen at Broughton Castle; and at Long-thorpe Tower two large corbels still project, though the original wooden covering is gone; the stone seat, however, is preserved inside (Pl. LIX D). Corbelled-out garderobes are still seen in some villages in France. In Boccaccio's *Decameron* there is the story of such an outer platform (over an open court) which collapsed under the occupant. ‡‡ One illustration shows a 15th-century garderobe, with seat, built like a gallery between two projecting wings, with a partial brick screen below.§§

In a mediaeval town there must have been a constant struggle by the authorities to keep the streets clean. When there was any public procession or festivity exceptional efforts

* Liberate Roll, 23 Henry III; Turner (1851), 189.
† Liberate Roll, 35 Henry III; Turner (1851), 230.
‡ Liberate Roll, 21 Henry III; Turner (1851), 184.
§ Liberate Roll, 34 Henry III; Turner (1851), 223.
‖ Liberate Roll, 23 Henry III; Turner (1851), 190.
¶ Holmes (1953), 96, 188–9.
** Liberate Roll, 25 Henry III; Turner (1851), 199.
†† Not lead—too rare and expensive to be so used.
‡‡ II, Novella 5; Holmes (1953), 96.
§§ Illustrated in Wright 1960), 61.

were made. It is a human failing to throw litter outside, and the corbelled-out garderobes provided an extreme case. For instance, in 1321 there were complaints that Ebbegate, a lane in London, was blocked through these overhanging latrines *quarum putredo cadit super capita hominum transeuntium.* *

This open arrangement was obviously insanitary, except where there was a stream or river below, as at Chepstow Castle above the Wye. At Conway a number of these corbelled projections overhang the rocks lining the river Gryffin, one beside each southern tower. On the northern, more accessible, side of the castle, the garderobes were provided with a long shaft reaching nearly to the ground. This improvement, however, might prove dangerous in time of siege. Richard I's seemingly impregnable Château Gaillard had already, in 1204, been taken by this means, entry being made by intruders climbing up the privy shafts. As a precaution against this, at Conway the outfall of each northern shoot was covered by a semicircular wall of masonry. At Beaumaris such entry would be difficult, two of the garderobes here discharging into the moat by means of a shoot ending in a grotesque face with open mouth.† The garderobe with covering shaft was obviously more hygienic, and at Harlech these masonry screens were later added to garderobes of the corbelled type. At the Tower of London we are told that in 1313 Sir William de Norwico ordered a wall to be built to hide the discharge from the garderobe shoots (*tuell*).‡

It was early recognized that grouping of the sanitary arrangements into one tower was the most convenient. At Richmond Castle (Gold Hole Tower) there remains the lower part of a late 11th-century example, including the pit and part of an arch spanning it. Where possible the garderobe tower was sited near a stream or on an arch over it, and usually at the angle of the hall or solar. There are two excellent Norman examples in the little guest houses built after 1147 at Fountains Abbey. In the eastern house the garderobe projects off the south-west angle with an arch over the stream. It is two-storeyed and is subdivided, the western portion serving the undercroft, whence it is reached by a doorway at the end of the west wall, the eastern containing the shaft for the privy of the hall above. In the western guest house the garderobe tower retains a vaulted chamber on the ground floor, with access from the undercroft, and east of it in the wall thickness is the shaft of the upper privy off the hall. The stream runs through the basement.

The added garderobe tower at Christchurch Castle with its remaining round arches over the mill stream was a 13th-century improvement. Also at the angle was the turret of which the ruins remain at King John's House, Tollard Royal (*c.* 1240–50). At Netley the Abbot's House has a garderobe block, the pit remaining, projecting at right angles off the solar. These may have resembled one ordered by Henry III at Clipstone in October 1251, when the sheriff was 'ordered to break without delay, the wall at the foot of the king's bed in the king's chamber . . . and to make a certain privy chamber for the king's use, and cover it with shingles'.§ This command was repeated in January 1252.||

The privy was sometimes vaulted, judging from the evidence at Fountains and at

---

* *Liber Custumarum*, 449, quoted in Salzman (1952), 283.
† R.C.H.M. *Anglesey*, pl. 79.
‡ Exchequer, King's Remembrancer Accounts, 489, 16; Salzman (1952), 283.
§ Close Roll, 36 Henry III; Turner (1851), 262.
|| Liberate Roll, 36 Henry III; Turner (1851), 236.

Winchester, where Henry III ordered one to be built 'in the fashion of a turret' with double vaulting (*duplice vousura*) and a chimney.* Could the latter have meant a fireplace as usual, or a ventilation shaft? Some idea of this arrangement is still given at Wells, where the south-west turret of Burnell's solar (*c.* 1280) retains an octagonal chamber, with ribbed vault, central drain and a staircase to the battlements.†

Sometimes there was a larger annexe in the same relative position to the solar, and containing a garderobe pit at the further end. This was probably a bedroom or a wardrobe with privy like those mentioned in the documents. At Old Soar (*c.* 1290) this room lies off the north angle of the solar, at the opposite end from the chapel, and is reached by a diagonal passage slightly corbelled out; it is lighted only by cross-loops, and the basement has an external doorway as well as a clearance arch to the garderobe pit, once partitioned off (Pl. LIX B and C). At Aydon (*c.* 1280) the wing (25 feet × 10 feet 8 inches) is off the end wall of the solar, and contains the garderobe pit in a great hollow buttress off the south-east angle, with a drain discharging eastwards down the precipice. This provides definite evidence that, although correctly orientated, this building was not a chapel. There are loop windows on both floors, and on the upper a recess (not sedilia) on the south wall, a sink (not piscina) on the east, with a wall cupboard on the north. An earlier 13th-century garderobe, also once believed to be a chapel because of its orientation, lies off the east wall of Bishop Jocelyn's solar at Wells, having a pit below the modern oriel. There are other wings containing a garderobe at the Palaces of Lamphey and St Davids.

Fourteenth-century examples show similar types of plan. At Markenfield (*c.* 1310) an annexe projects off the north end of the solar, its east wall almost in line with the buttresses of the latter (Pl. LIX G). As at Old Soar the pit, with clearance opening, is walled off from a larger ground-floor apartment with loop window, reached by a curved passage, possibly later, from the solar undercroft. The upper room has loop windows, and there is a lean-to roof.

Markenfield also retains the ingenious contrivance of a garderobe-buttress. The south-west angle buttress of the hall is thickened at ground-level floor to contain a small privy, reached by a vaulted wall passage through a narrow pointed doorway just within the entrance to the undercroft. Another irregular buttress at Mayfield (*c.* 1325) housed a small garderobe off the high table end of the Palace hall. This reminds us of Henry III's privy chamber at the head of the hall at Clipstone.‡

At Camoise Court, Chislehampton (*c.* 1318) there is an annexe placed so much in the position of that at Old Soar as to suggest that it also contained a garderobe (Pl. LIX F). A chamfered doorway gives access from the solar.

In No. 3 Vicars' Court, Lincoln (*c.* 1310), each lodging was provided with a privy chamber, and two great buttress-like towers serve two storeys § and have drainage arches in the basement. The eastern projection was double as it served two pairs of rooms, being divided by a stone wall at ground level, and (originally) a timber partition above. From their size—12 feet × 13 feet 6 inches (east) and 14 feet × 6 feet 6 inches (west)—each chamber was probably in the nature of a 'wardrobe' with a privy at the south end, where

* Liberate Roll, 53 Henry III; Turner (1851), 256.
† Pugin (1839), 45, pls. 55–6.
‡ Liberate Roll, 36 Henry III; Turner (1851), 235.
§ There are two storeys on the north, three on the south (garderobe) side of the building owing to the slope of the ground.

one lofty trefoil surviving at first-floor level serves for ventilation, there being lancet windows in the other walls. The clearance arches are also near this end in the basement. At Amberley Castle the lodgings against the curtain wall (1377) have similar pairs of garderobe doorways at two levels, though the tower projection is smaller (Pl. LIX I). The ventilation roundels on the first floor resemble gunports and could have served as such. The side walls have, on each stage, a demi-cross loop at the angle with the curtain.

In Tretower Court, Breconshire, a turret projects off the south-west angle of the north range, and contains two garderobes on each floor. Instead of the arrangement, which became usual later, whereby the shafts of the upper privies descended beyond those of the lower, here the four shafts are arranged in a row, the two inner ones serving the upper compartments, of which the seats are placed at right angles to the others, in a thickened dividing wall. On the north wall of the range the eastern garderobe is single, serving two floors, the seats hidden at right angles to the entrance. Indeed, by the 14th century the garderobe tower had reached a high standard of development, and survivals show excellent planning. Often there was a lobby between the solar and the garderobe proper to give the farthest distance possible (*longaigne*) with easy access from a chamber which was also a sitting-room. This could have been used as a wardrobe, dressing-room, or subsidiary bedroom, perhaps for the owner's children or body servants.

At Ludlow the early 14th-century double garderobe tower survives to the full height of four storeys over a plinth containing the shoot apertures, two on each face (Pl. LIX H). It obviously contained bedrooms, the garderobes being contrived in the thickness of their walls, and accessible by means of an 'elbow' passage from each room. The two lower floors were subdivided, each apartment reached from the great chamber block or the living-room adjoining, on the ground floor by doors and a passage in the thick wall between these; on great chamber level by doorways in the extreme corners of these rooms. On the second floor the tower room was one comfortable apartment with space for a fireplace between the windows; it is reached by a passage from both 'the ladies' solar' and the adjoining apartment. On the third floor there is another large room with fireplace and long transomed windows, which make it a good look-out chamber for some important official, who had access to it from a newel staircase off the hall dais. His privy was possibly a small one, now blocked, its trefoiled window showing on the west wall near its junction with the curtain. The other garderobes are complete save for their seats. They are lit by square-headed loops, those to the better rooms being trefoiled,* and are roofed with corbelled slabs; some are reached by ascending steps. They are arranged so that their shoots pass separately down each wall, six outlets all told, with shouldered heads like those of the doorways.

At about the same period a new tower was added to the west curtain at Middleham Castle, Yorkshire. This too has three storeys of privies, with access from adjoining rooms, and also by a gallery or bridge from the great chamber in the keep, apparently supplementary to or displacing a 12th-century double garderobe tower off the west wall of the latter. The 'litill tower' with three garderobe shoots on the north wall is also of the 14th century (Pl. LIX E).

---

* It is strange that the ladies' floor has square-headed windows to the bedroom, trefoiled heads to the privies.

Fig. 115. Garderobe tower at Langley Castle, end of the 14th century.

There is accommodation for no fewer than twelve privies in the south-east tower of Langley Castle, built towards the end of the 14th century (Fig. 115). They are arranged in tiers: a row of four on each floor, so that the shafts could discharge parallel inside the walls to a pit below, through which a stream of water was turned.* Each privy has an individual recess with pointed arch, and corbels to take the seats remain in some cases. The third-floor privies being nearest to the outside, the rest of the tower space forms a larger lobby at this level. On the ground floor a wall conceals the shafts from the rest of the room, which has wall passages flanking them on two sides, and an entrance from the main part of the castle.

At Southwell Palace there is a garderobe tower (c. 1360) of great ingenuity, built well away from the house, at the south-east angle of the garden wall. It was probably for the general use of the household. Circular in plan, it has a central pillar from which diverge apsidal closets with a passage round and loop windows (Fig. 116).†

Less spectacular examples are left of 15th-century date, but the evidence suggests that privies were normally built to every chamber. This is the case at Raglan, where two garderobe towers of c. 1450–69 remain, one of three storeys, off the south-west range, with a vaulted ground floor and cross slits, and even gunports below in the side of the pit. Compton Castle was provided with garderobes in most of its towers, including a large one in the 'Watch Tower' on the south-eastern angle of the curtain wall.

Lodgings, such as vicars' closes, were usually well provided, as in the houses at Wells, each originally with a garderobe at the back. The 14th-century twin arrangement at Lincoln, but with smaller projections, appears in Cardinal Beaufort's buildings at the Hospital of St Cross. Lodgings for retainers in the great houses were planned in similar fashion. At Dartington Hall (c. 1388–1400) the garderobes are also placed in pairs, on each floor, opposite the twin entrances at the front. Indeed it seems to have been a common practice to have such a pair serving adjoining rooms also divided by a timber partition. There is a later mediaeval example at Leigh Barton near Kingsbridge

* Parker (1853), 113–14 (elevation and section), 332 (plan). But his south-west tower is really south-east.
† Parker (1853), 114 (illustration and plan).

in Devon, and at Boycombe, Farway, near Honiton, the projection is unusually large, containing not only the twin garderobes but a newel staircase as well. Coupled privies, here opposite the staircase, occur in the late 15th-century apartments for officials at Haddon Hall, in the west range of the lower court, with a single privy at the back of a single room, perhaps for the steward, at the end, again like Vicars' Court, Lincoln, but smaller. Those at Thornbury Castle, early in the next century, were also planned in pairs.

Students' rooms seem less well served with private garderobes,* but there are some for the Fellows at Winchester College. In the east range of Chamber Court (*c.* 1387–1400)

Fig. 116. Garderobe tower, *c.* 1360, at the Archbishop's Palace, Southwell.

one large projection served two rooms accommodating three persons in each. Though little evidence remains at Oxford, there is more at Cambridge, where the monastic students at Magdalene College were most comfortably housed, and a garderobe next to the laver and fireplace was provided for the four occupants of the room.

In the priests' houses a privy was a normal adjunct, as shown by survivals at Combe Raleigh Chantry and Dunchideock. A corner projection off the back angle of the parlour-chamber end seems to have been the rule, as earlier. At Ilminster Chantry the north-west projection containing a possible laver recess may have been a wardrobe with garderobe, of which there is evidence in the gable end of the kitchen below, next to the chimney stack.†

Ashbury Manor (*c.* 1488) retained until recently a remarkable survival, the original moulded seat in position.‡ It was sited in a wardrobe projection which forms an L-plan with the hall, beyond a staircase. This may be compared with the plank-like seat, once

* Pantin (1959), 257.
† Pantin (1959), 233, fig. 83.
‡ Preserved in Oxford. The recess is now used in a modern setting.

slotted into the wall, found in the excavations at Bungay Castle,* and with the stone seat at Longthorpe Tower.

There were public lavatories in London even in the 12th century. In 1237 there is reference to the 'necessary house built at Queenhithe at London by Maud, formerly Queen of England [i.e. of Henry I], for the common use of the citizens'. When the quay was enlarged this had to be extended too, to give access to the Thames as before.†

A notable late 13th-century example is visible today on the town wall at Conway, a 'battery of little garderobes' constructed for the use of the King's Wardrobe, as Mr A. J. Taylor's researches have shown.‡

In London, again, there was a common latrine at 'The Moor' (near Moorgate) which in 1415 had become offensive and was ordered to be removed to the Walbrook, where it could be cleansed by a water gate called a *scluys* or a *speye* (? penstock).§

The privies were always provided with a small window or some other form of ventilation. The windows were narrow loops splayed internally, as in the 12th-century guest houses at Fountains, the 14th-century examples at Markenfield and the 15th-century Skelsmergh Hall in Westmorland. Sometimes the slits were given trefoiled heads, like Ludlow in the 14th century and Ashbury Manor (*c.* 1488). Cross-slits occur at Old Soar, Amberley and the 15th-century examples at Raglan Castle. We know that Henry III's privies at Clipstone even had glass windows.

Sometimes little cusped ventilators were used, like the trefoils high up in the walls at Vicars' Court, Lincoln, and the two small quatrefoiled openings at Yardley Hastings, also dating from the 14th century. We have already noted the circular openings like gunports at Amberley.

Ventilators in the roof also occur, like a small louver, possibly the case at Cottisford Manor, Oxfordshire, where there is a 14th-century chimney without an obvious fireplace remaining.

The shafts could also be ventilated. At Conway Castle (North West Tower) the shoot is aired through a rectangular opening, with triangular capping, in its sloping roof.‖ There is a narrow slit for this purpose at Yardley Hastings.

The window-sill would serve as a place on which to put a light, unless a corbel was provided, as possibly at Aydon. Jocelin de Brakelond relates how Abbot Samson of St Edmundbury (1182–1212) narrowly escaped death. He was 'journeying through the lands of St Edmund' inspecting 'his manors and ours'. 'But when he came to Warkton and was at night sleeping, a voice came to him saying, "Samson, arise up quickly", and again, "Rise, thou tarriest too long". So he arose half dazed, and looking round about him saw in a necessary place [*necessarium*] a light; a candle which Reiner the monk had left there through carelessness, and which was about to fall on the straw.¶ And when the Abbot had put it out, he went through the house and found the door—for there was but one—so fastened that it could only be opened with a key, and the windows barred. Wherefore, had the fire grown,

* Hugh Braun, *Proceedings of the Suffolk Institute of Archaeology and Natural History* (1934–6), XXII, 118, 207, fig. IX.
† Salzman (1952), 282.
‡ M.O.W. Guide (12), 45.
§ Riley (1868), 615; quoted by Salzman (1952), 282.
‖ Section in Toy (1937), 180.
¶ Doubtless 'hay' was meant, the mediaeval equivalent of our toilet paper.

A. Squint from priest's room to chapel in the Chantry, Ilminster, *c.* 1480. B. Squint in the Chancery, Lincoln, 15th century. *c.* Squint from chapel down into the hall at Clevedon Court, *c.* 1320. D. Bracket in chapel at the Chantry, Ilminster, *c.* 1480. E. 14th-century candlestick.

F. Light bracket in hall, Tickenham Court, *c.* 1400. G. Light bracket with remains of spikes for candles at Norrington Manor, *c.* 1377. H. Lamp recess at Church House, Gloucester, 15th century. I. Portchester Castle hall, porch doorway with lantern brackets, 1398.

Plate LVII.

A

B

C

Piscinae in chapels. A. Old Soar, early 14th century. B. Goodrich Castle, *c.* 1300. C. Woodsford Castle, *c.* 1337.

D

E

F

G

D. Piscina in chapel at Beverston Castle, *c.* 1356–61. E. Laver from hall of Kirkham House, Paignton, early 15th century (now in the Church). F. and G. Laver in Vicars' Hall, Chichester, 1399 +.

Plate LVIII

both he and all they who were sleeping in that building would have perished. For there was no way by which they might have gone out or escaped.' *

This window could also give light for reading, and the *Life of St Gregory* (Pope, 590–604) recommends the privy as a retiring-place where tablets could be read without disturbance.†
Indeed the privy was well named, since it was often the only private place in the early Middle Ages.

Garderobe pits occur in the earliest mediaeval buildings. At Old Sarum there are 12th-century examples of great size, one being 11 feet square and 42 feet deep, and depth was regarded as of special importance (the idea of the 'far-off place' again), this being stressed in Henry III's instructions. Great ingenuity was displayed in the 13th and 14th centuries in the grouping of garderobes, designed so that the shafts from several floors could use a common cesspit, as at Beaumaris and Langley castles. In the Prison Tower at Denbigh there are five shoots at different levels.

In towns the siting of the garderobe was a special problem. As early as 1189 the 'London Assize' stipulated that 'Garderobe pits, not walled, must be dug three and a half feet away from a neighbour's boundary; if walled, the pit can be only two and a half feet'. ‡ But the pits seem often to have been part of the house. In a contract of 1370 for the building of eighteen shops in London, the foundations were to include '10 stone pits for *prevez*, of which pits 8 shall be double [i.e. serve two houses], and each in depth 10 feet, and in breadth 11 feet'.§ This may be compared to an order, in 1425, for a twelve-foot-deep pit for a new latrine at Eltham.‖

Where the base of the pit was accessible, clearance was arranged through an external arch. At Old Soar the clearance arch has been reopened in the Ministry of Works restoration, and similar examples can be seen in each of the great garderobe projections at Allington Castle, Kent, and Vicars' Court at Lincoln. A small arch survives in the gatehouse at Donnington Castle (1386) near ground level on the north side. This gives access to a wide pit serving a garderobe, staggered off the turret passage, on the first and second floors. At Ashby de la Zouch there is a sloping ramp from the courtyard to such an opening, in a pit to one of the privies of the late 15th-century 'Priests' Rooms'.

These garderobes needed constant attention which they did not always get. In 1282 thirteen men worked for five days clearing the accumulated soil in the cesspit at Newgate Prison.¶ Beaumaris Castle was made defensible by 1298, but as early as 1306 there were complaints about the 'little houses' of which the shaft-exits were choked. Indeed two of these shoots still end in a grotesque head with open mouth, which would need frequent clearance.

Who were the people who had this disagreeable work of cleaning out cesspits? The documents show that they were rightly very highly paid. There are a number of references to these specialists. In 1406 a *mundator latrinarum*, Thomas Watergate, was paid 40s. for 'cleaning out and cleansing a latrine under the chamber of the Keeper of the King's Privy

---

* *Chronicle of Jocelin de Brakelond*, trans. L. C. Jane (1931), 49.
† *Vie de Saint Grégoire*, vv. 1302–51, *via* Holmes (1953), 96.
‡ Translation in Turner (1851), 20, with Latin original, 277.
§ St Paul's MSS. No. 1074; Salzman (1952), 284, 443–4.
‖ Exchequer, King's Remembrancer Accounts, 496–7; Salzman (1952), 284.
¶ Exchequer, King's Remembrancer Accounts, 467, 11; Salzman (1952), 284.

Seal, and for clearing out two drains leading from the King's cellar to the Thames'.*
By 1500 they were known as 'gong fermers', from one of the terms for latrine, others
being 'withdraught' or 'draught', and 'jakes'; and in this year the accounts of St John's
College, Cambridge, refer to payment 'to the gong fermer for the feying [cleansing] of xij
draughts' at Collyweston, while in 1532 at Westminster 'Philip Longe, gong fermer'
was paid 'for the clensyng of certain jakes'.†

The mediaeval king was continually on the move, travelling about his dominions. In
England it was his custom, in the 11th and 12th centuries, to spend Christmas at Westminster, Easter at Winchester and Whitsun at Gloucester. This was for political reasons,
to show himself to his subjects, hear legal cases (King John being particularly good in this)
and also, in days of poor transport, to consume on the spot the produce of his various
estates. The lesser lords did the same, literally eating their way across the country, for
their lands were often scattered, through the deliberate policy of the first Norman king, who,
except in special regions of external danger, the palatines of Durham and Chester and the
Marches of Wales, discouraged large accumulations of territory in a single hand. Such
progresses made easier the problem of sanitation, for after a period of intensive use the
great houses were abandoned temporarily by all but a retaining staff, the place left to air,
and, we trust, to be spring-cleaned, and the garderobes cleansed ready for the next visit
of the master with his family and large train of attendants.

The Liberate Rolls show Henry III visiting his residences in turn, and leaving instructions
for improvements to be made before his next coming to them. He was very particular
about sanitation, influenced perhaps by his queen, Eleanor of Provence, who came from
a country of higher civilization. In 1246 he sent an urgent order to Edward Fitz-Otho:
'Since the privy chamber of our wardrobe in London is situated in an undue and improper
place, wherefore it smells badly, we command you on the faith and love by which you are
bounden to us, that you in no wise omit to cause another privy chamber to be made in the
same wardrobe in such more fitting and proper place that you may select there, even though
it should cost a hundred pounds, so that it may be made before the feast of the Translation
of St Edward, before we come thither.' ‡

Henry was not averse from arranging for his convenience in a house belonging to another.
Before going to York in 1251 for the marriage of his daughter Margaret to Alexander III
of Scotland, he ordered a privy chamber, twenty feet long 'with a deep pit' to be constructed
next to his room in the Archbishop's Palace.§

Henry was influenced by the monks, who were pioneers in sanitary arrangement. The
reredorter of the monastery was extremely well planned. This was a privy wing at the end
of the *dorter* (dormitory), often at right angles to it, sited where possible over or near a
stream. Fountains Abbey has a good 12th-century example. Here it serves the lay brothers'
infirmary as well as their dorter, and is a long range, built over a stream, divided longitudinally by a parallel wall. In the southern portion the cubicles are arranged at infirmary
level, whereas the northern part has a similar range on the first floor to serve the

* Exchequer, King's Remembrancer Accounts, 502, 26; Salzman (1952), 284.
† Salzman (1952), 281–2.
‡ Liberate Roll, 30 Henry III; Turner (1851), 261.
§ Close Roll, 35 Henry III; Turner (1851), 261–2.

dorter.* The monk's reredorter is further east, served, like the guest houses, by the same river (Skell). It is at right angles to the dorter, like the 13th-century example at Netley Abbey. In both the drainage portion, flushed by a stream, is divided from a ground-floor room, perhaps the day-room of the novices at Fountains, apparently the infirmary, vaulted with a hooded fireplace, at Netley. At Canterbury the waste from the Prior's water tub (*cupa*) meets that from the bath-house and flushes the reredorter.

In houses the privies were doubtless frequently cleansed, to a certain extent, by the emptying of washing-basins of water down the shoot. There is, however, evidence, of which more may come to light, of a deliberate arrangement to flush the garderobes by the diversion of rain-water from the gutters, or collected in a cistern. At Caernarvon a stone water channel, lined with lead, has been discovered running all round the Eagle Tower (completed in 1317) about 3 feet 6 inches from the inner wall face. It is carried to the garderobe shaft, its lead lining continuing some distance down the latter. The channel perhaps collected the rain-water from an earlier roof.† It has heavy cover stones and is now buried in the walls.

At another Edwardian castle, Denbigh, in the Prison and Bardnes Towers, the rain-water was conducted from the roof to the garderobe pit by a curving pipe in the wall thickness.‡ In Warkworth Keep, at the end of the 14th century, there was a complicated system by which the garderobe shafts were flushed from a cistern filled with rain-water collected from near the light well in the centre of the building.§

At Kirby Muxloe drains were arranged to carry the water used for swilling the old kitchen floor (14th-century) across to the garderobes on the east side of the south tower, and from the 14th-century hall to those on the north-west side of the eastern tower. These late 15th-century garderobes, though placed near the moat, were designed not to discharge into it, but into vaulted chambers which could be cleared.‖ This is unlike the earlier arrangement, as at Fountains and Langley, where a stream flushed the base of the shafts.

In Bull Hill, a house near the church at Pilton in Devon, Messrs Everett and Grimmett have found evidence of water flushing in the base of a garderobe turret, a stone box-drain, 14×18 inches, six feet below ground level. Through this water had been conveyed, presumably from the river Yeo, a mile or more away. The house was perhaps connected with the Priory.

Cardinal Wolsey, who held the More at Rickmansworth from 1522 to 1530, modernized the sanitation there, constructing in the west a brick-lined garderobe with drainage outlets on three sides. Henry VIII made further improvements in the east, a garderobe pit having a vaulted drain.¶ At Hampton Court Wolsey's sanitation also was most efficient and not superseded till 1871; brick sewers 5 feet high and 3 feet wide carried the sewage into the Thames.**

After the Middle Ages there seems to have been a tendency for the privies to become

---

* At Furness Abbey, Lancashire, there is a double row of seats, back to back.
† M.O.W. Guide (7), 27.
‡ M.O.W. Guide (13), 17, 18.
§ M.O.W. Guide (43), 18.
‖ M.O.W. Guide (24), 16, 19.
¶ Biddle, Barfield & Millard (1959), 157, 159, pls XX A and D.
** E. Law (1929), *A Short History of Hampton Court*, 25. Bell.

separate from the house, perhaps due to the neglect of cleaning treatment most essential in the other kind. This was in spite of the invention, premature by many years, of the water closet by Sir John Harrington, ingenious godson of Elizabeth I. Close stools were used in important bedrooms, made comfortable with padded seats, and Henry VIII's, made in 1547, was portable with a separate case for a cistern.* The royal close stool, *c.* 1600, at Hampton Court, is covered with crimson velvet, with lace and gilt nails, and handles for carrying.†

Houses of the late 16th century often contain closets, used as secret hiding-places, and vaulted cellars and tunnels connected with the sewage. At Baddesley Clinton (Warwickshire) there is a tunnel some 30 inches wide passing below the west wing, constructed as a sewer to receive, through slots in its roof, the drainage of the house. The level of the moat was raised at intervals to clean it, and steps at one end allowed access for a servant to brush it out. During the times of religious persecution it was transformed into a hide for Catholic priests by that specialist Nicholas Owen. The steps and loop windows were blocked, a secret portcullis arrangement made at the exit, escape shafts into it organized and the moat level raised. All this was done, probably, under cover of building a new garderobe projection.‡ In his memoirs Father Gerard describes standing with his feet in water in this hide for four hours, while the pursuivants (priest-hunters) were searching the house.

Garderobe shoots were also utilized as means of escape. There is a famous one at Ufton Court in Berkshire. But perhaps the most notable is at Harvington Hall in Worcestershire, probably later than Nicholas Owen's time but following on his methods. There is secret access *via* a garderobe to a shaft concealed by a false wall, and which contains the oak pulley by which the spit of the adjoining kitchen was worked, a mechanism operated by gravity which came into use at the end of the 16th century. The pulley wheel could also be used for escape, and in the floor of the shaft was access to a lower chamber with its exit on the edge of the moat.§

In the 17th century we read of pewter chamber-pots melted down for ammunition in the Civil War, and those in silver formed part of the Georgian civic regalia shown in York and elsewhere. 'Little houses' up the garden were regarded as more sanitary in the 18th century, and this system remains in some places even today. At Marlow, when Jerome K. Jerome lived at the 'Fisherman's Retreat' (now modernized), a flag was hoisted on the garden house as a sign of occupation.

* Wright (1960), 70.
† Wright (1960), 70 (illustration).
‡ Granville Squiers (1934), *Secret Hiding Places*, 29–33 (illustration). Paul.
§ Squiers (1934), 77–9, 113 (illustration); C. Hussey (1953), *Harvington Hall*, reprinted from *Country Life* (11) (illustrated).

30

Floors

A SECTION on floors must be included, but this is in the nature of an interim report, to be revised when more is known from further excavation of mediaeval buildings; for in many houses still standing the flooring has been renewed. However, in empty stone houses, as in castles, the stone floor seems original, as in the hall at Boothby Pagnell. In the undercroft at Old Soar great blocks of stone support the chapel above, and the gallery floor is of stone at Nassington, also of 13th-century date.

At the Old Deanery, Salisbury (1258–74), the hall floor was found to be of tamped (hard-beaten) chalk, and this may have been common. Rammed earth seems to have been used on the ground floor of early houses, such as Pallingham Manor, Sussex, now a barn. This would be expected; it is more surprising to find beaten earth used on top of wooden flooring. A number of such examples have been discovered in the documents. Even in a royal chapel, in 1260, Henry III instructed the bailiff 'to well earth the flooring [*planchicium*] at Havering'.* There are many instances as late as the 15th century. At the Queen's Manor of Pleasaunce at Greenwich in 1447, twenty loads of mud (*luti*) were used '*in teryng* [earthing] *diversorum florys*', and in 1453 at New College, Oxford 'a cartload of red earth for earthing [*terand*] the flore' was used on a chamber floor which was boarded first.†

The excavation of deserted villages, revealing the kind of house in which the mediaeval peasant lived, is a source of information on the type of flooring used, here unaltered in modern times. In the 13th-century settlement at Beere, North Tawton in Devon, one house had a floor of small pebbly gravel in the living-room, distinct from the earthen floor of a byre under the same roof. But at Riseholme in Lincolnshire, dating from the first half of the same century, the byre had a floor of stone slabs, the dwelling part a mortar floor. A paved area inside the entrance occurs in similar houses of early date.‡

The undercroft of the late 12th-century manor house at Wharram Percy (Yorkshire)

* Liberate Roll, 44 Henry III; Turner (1851), 251.
† Salzman (1952), 147.
‡ Jope & Threlfall (1958), 119–21 (Beere); F. H. Thompson (1960), 101–4 (Riseholme); Biddle (1961–2), and in *Medieval Archaeology*, IV, 159–60; A. Fox (1958).

was set in natural chalk. In the late 13th- or 14th-century hall on the moated site at Harlington (Bedfordshire), puddled chalk 6 inches thick was used for the floor. At the lost village of Riplingham in Yorkshire the 14th-century floors were of clay and marl, replaced much later by cobbles.* The latter, now concealed, were used for the kitchen of the 16th-century Hobletts Manor at Hemel Hempstead. Cobbled ways, as excavated (patterned) at the 15th-century Minster Lovell Hall, must have been quite common.

The Manor of the More at Rickmansworth, excavated 1952–5,† covers some four hundred years of occupation, c. 1250–1650, and eight periods of building. It thus throws valuable light on our subject. The kitchen building with its three ovens, of Period II (c. 1300–50) shows successive floors of clay, or yellow clay and gravel, but our most useful evidence comes from the elaborate timber hall of Period III (c. 1350 (or 1366)–1426). Here again there were several phases, the second producing a floor of thick clay combined with a fine hearth, the third one of white mortar and clay containing on it pottery of the last half of the 14th century. It was apparently not until its supplanting by the great brick house of c. 1426 that the (new) hall had a tiled floor, of which the mortar spread remains. Of the actual tiles found, one indeed comes from the second period of occupation of the house, but most from the period after 1426, especially the early 16th century.

Floors of plaster were also used, but do not occur so frequently in the documents as those of beaten earth.‡ In July 1269, Henry III instructed the sheriff 'to plaster the floor [area] of the queen's chamber' at Winchester Castle.§

Tiled floors are those which he normally ordered. Their introduction into his houses seems to date from after his marriage to Eleanor of Provence in 1236, which suggests the influence of higher living standards from France. In February 1237 three chapels at Westminster Palace were to be tiled. St Stephen's chapel and a new one for the queen were to have marble altar steps, 'and if that marble should not be sufficient for both works, then to cause those steps [of the queen's chapel] to be made of painted tile'. The king's treasurer, Henry de Pateshull, is 'likewise to cause the small chapel at Westminster to be decently paved with painted tile'.‖ At Clarendon, in March 1244, the sheriff of Wiltshire was ordered 'to make a pavement of tiles in the kings demesne [dominica] chapel and in that oriel'. This, the king's chapel, was on the first floor over two rooms, the eastern being the queen's wardrobe, which in 1251 were made one and became known as the Antioch Chamber from its painted decoration. The research of Mrs Eames has revealed, from the fallen tiles, that the chapel pavement had a circular design, with ten lines of plain green tile alternating with nine decorative rings, one with an inscription, the others with fleur-de-lis and kindred foliated motifs, inlaid in white on red clay and treated with a clear lead glaze.¶ The tiles were made in a kiln some hundred yards away, but the designer was probably familiar with French examples such as that in the abbey church of Cunault

---

* Hurst (1957), 206 (Wharram Percy); *Medieval Archaeology* (1959), III, 314–15 (Harlington); *Medieval Archaeology* (1957), I, 166 (Riplingham).
† By the Merchant Taylors' School Archaeological Society. See Biddle, Barfield & Millard (1959), 136–99.
‡ Salzman (1952), 147.
§ Liberate Roll, 53 Henry III; Turner (1851), 256.
‖ Close Roll, 22 Henry III; Turner (1851), 258.
¶ A segment of the circular pavement has been re-assembled in the British Museum. The plain green tiles have assembly marks on their under or outer sides. See *Journal of the British Archaeological Association* (1963), 3rd S., XXVI, 40–50.

(Maine-et-Loire). One other English pavement of circular design was uncovered at Muchelney Abbey and relaid in the parish church there. But it was not only chapels which were so treated. Already in January 1241 Henry had ordered Paulin Peyvere and his colleague to 'pave the whole of our hall' at Winchester Castle, where, in November 1256, the sheriff was 'to make a pavement of tiles on the upper step of the king's hall towards the east'; doubtless those on the dais would be decorated tiles like the floors of the Westminster chapels. At Winchester also, in December 1250, the sheriff was not only 'to cause the king's new chapel to be paved with tiles', but 'to pave the king's chamber and the queen's chamber with tiles' as well; and in December 1252 'to pave the chamber of Edward the king's son with flat tile.' *

At Clarendon Palace, which was Henry's favourite residence, other elaborate pavements have been uncovered which supplement the documentary information. In December 1249 the king commanded the sheriff of Wiltshire to 'pave our chamber with plain tile [*plana tegula*]', and in July 1250 'let the chamber of our queen there be decently [or suitably] paved', in July 1251 'to make two screens [*sporos*] in the Queen's high chamber and pave it', and in July 1252 'to pave the Queen's chamber at Clarendon and the chamber under the same queen's chapel', which chapel itself was paved when it was newly painted in 1260.† The queen's apartment at Clarendon occupied a range running north-west to south-east, east of and at right angles to those of the king, and consisted of three rooms, the southernmost having a chapel on the east. The paving of these, ordered in 1250–2, seems to have been completed and paid for by Michaelmas 1252.‡ In the most northerly of these apartments part of an elaborate tile pavement was found *in situ* during the excavations of 1935. This has now been raised, and exhibited in the British Museum, an important example earlier than the famous tiled pavement still in use in the Chapter House at Westminster, and which was completed between 1253 and 1259.§ The Clarendon pavement is arranged in six long panels, the first two bearing quartets of heraldic tiles, lions and griffins, each in a circle with trefoils in the corners of the square tile, and borders of dark oblong tiles. In the next panel these green tiles form a lattice-work enclosing square tiles set diagonally, each containing a foliated cross, also in a circle. The main part of the floor is made up of geometric pattern, interlacing circles forming quatrefoils. Then follows a narrow panel with plain yellow squares set diagonally in a green border, and finally a wider green lattice-work containing squares of four tiles, set diagonally, each set forming a large foliated cross with quatrefoil. The colours are red, golden brown, yellow and olive green. Two fine early 14th-century pavements have been discovered in Clifton House, King's Lynn.

In the documents Mr Salzman has found useful evidence concerning prices. At Westminster in 1274, 'paving tiles cost 5s. per 1,000, and in 1289 11,500 *de tegulis subtilibus* (ornamental tiles) were bought at the same rate to pave Edward I's stone chamber and the new chamber with the oriel towards the garden. In 1324 ordinary paving tiles cost 10s. per 1,000 there. At Westminster Palace also, in 1365, Henry Yevele supplied "8,000

* Liberate Roll, 28, 25, 41, 37 Henry III; Turner (1851), 203 (Clarendon), 199, 248, 228, 243 (Winchester).
† Liberate Roll, 34, 34, 35, 36, 44, Henry III; Turner (1851), 221, 224, 230, 240, 252.
‡ Eames (1957–8), 97–8.
§ Close Roll, 43 Henry III (22 April).

tiles of Flanders for the paving of floors (*arearum*) and other work" at 6*s.* 8*d.* per 1,000, and in 1368 he provided 1,000 "tiles called valthill" (surely special wall tiles or bricks, costing 16*s.* 6*d.*) to pave the wardrobe at Eltham'. *

In 1385 at Shene 1,000 'tiles called pennetyl, painted, used for paving' are mentioned, and 2,000 'painted tiles' for Richard II's bathroom.† The tile industry at Penn and Tyler's Green (hence the name) in Buckinghamshire flourished in the 14th century,‡ documents citing manufacture there by 1332 at least. Many of its products were found by Group Captain Knocker when he excavated the Black Prince's Manor and stud farm, the Mount at Princes Risborough in the same county, the decorated ones mainly from the solar block.§ Two Penn tiles were also found at the More in 14th- and 15th-century associations. These are printed tiles as distinct from the earlier inlaid tiles, less durable but cheaper and so more prevalent.

For inlaid tiles a wooden stamp of the pattern was pressed into a square of clay, then pipeclay was spread into the hollows thus formed. In printed tiles there was only one operation, the pipeclay being spread on to the raised parts of the stamp, and pressed directly into the clay (like an inked wood block in printing on paper). The inlaid tiles have the clearer cut design, for pipeclay, unless very carefully applied on the stamp, may spread and smudge the pattern. However, to a casual glance, the finished tile looks much the same in either case.‖ Yellow against red is the normal colouring.

Apart from these glazed tiles, there is evidence that sometimes the tiles were coloured with ordinary paint. For instance, Hugh le Peyntour and Peter the Pavier were employed for 28 days 'making and painting the pavement at Westminster' in 1308.¶

Other printed tiles were made in Warwickshire and London. Except for the tiles manufactured at Great Malvern and in Wessex, the late mediaeval printed tiles were of little merit, which may explain the importation of Flemish printed tiles in the late 15th and early 16th centuries into fashionable buildings mostly in and around London.

These Flemish tiles were found at the More, probably of the period when Wolsey held the manor as Abbot of St Albans (1521–30). But the most famous can be seen in the Chapel of the Vyne, which was built by Sir William, later Lord, Sandys, who was Treasurer of Calais. The tiles are said to have been brought by him from Boulogne, and were once believed to be Italian, but are now regarded as having been made at Antwerp by potters of Italian descent.** 'Flemyshe pavyng tyll of grene and jowllo' (yellow), at 5*s.* the 100, were bought in 1535 for Hampton Court.††

Some halls, even at this date, were floored with earth, with rushes strewn to keep down the dust, and in some cases inadequately changed, so as to merit the frank criticism of the Dutch humanist Erasmus, who wrote (prior to 1530) in a letter to Francis, physician to

* Salzman (1952), 145–6 (from Exchequer, King's Remembrancer Accounts).
† Salzman (1952), 146.
‡ Hohler (1941–2); Rouse & Broadbent (1951–2).
§ Pavry & Knocker (1957–8), 173–4.
‖ The two processes are described in London Museum (1940), *Medieval Catalogue*, 231; *see also* p. 235.
¶ Salzman (1952), 146.
** Biddle, Barfield & Millard (1959), 186.
†† Salzman (1952), 146.

Cardinal Wolsey, of English houses: 'The floors are commonly of clay, strewed with rushes, under which lies unmolested an ancient collection of beer, grease, fragments, bones, spittle, excrements of dogs and cats, and everything that is nasty.' *

No wonder the head of the household preferred his parlour. But earlier, when the family dined in hall, they were provided with a raised dais of wood or stone, which could be kept clean. A stone dais has been uncovered at the Old Deanery, Salisbury, and portions remain at Old Soar. Henry III certainly had one at Winchester and Clarendon,† and there seems to be no reference to rushes in his Liberate Rolls. He would not have tolerated the state of affairs criticized by Erasmus three centuries later.

Rushes were not the only floor covering. Wolsey impregnated with saffron the rushes on the floors of his apartments at Hampton Court.‡ The clippings of pungent shrubs from the knot gardens were also used. Thomas Tusser, in *Points of Good Husbandry* published in 1557, lists twenty-one herbs suitable for 'strewing', and this must have applied to previous centuries. They are:

'Basil, baulm, camomile, costmary, cowslip and paggles, daisies of all sorts, sweet fennell, germander, hysop, lavender, lavender spike, lavender cotten, marjoram, mandeline, pennyroyal, roses of all sorts, red mints, sage, tansey, violets and winter savory.'

Carpets were not used until quite late, and at first only to cover tables. They seem to have been introduced by Edward I's wife Eleanor of Castile in 1255. Matthew Paris said the Londoners were shocked to see the very floors covered with costly carpets by the Spaniards. When the future queen came to Westminster she found her apartments 'carpeted'—after the Spanish fashion? § Earlier, in December 1246, Henry III ordered 'mats [*natas*] to put upon the forms and under foot in the king's chapel of Winchester'.‖

* A mild translation of the Latin original, both given in Lloyd (1931), 80.
† Liberate Roll, 28 Henry III; Turner (1851), 203.
‡ R. Dutton (1937), *The English Garden*, 32.
§ Paris, *Chronica Majora* ('Rolls Series'), V, 513; Turner (1851), 98.
‖ Liberate Roll, 31 Henry III; Turner (1851), 212.

31

Interior Decoration

THE inside of a mediaeval house was much brighter than would appear today. The stone-work would not show but be white- or colour-washed, or else covered up with hangings or wainscot. Indeed it is a mistake on the part of a restorer to let the stone show internally. Buildings even of good masonry seem to have been whitewashed outside as well, this being supposed to feed the stonework. Hence derives the 'White Tower' of London, where in December 1240 the keepers of the works were ordered 'to cause all the leaden gutters . . . to be carried down to the ground; so that the wall of the said Tower, which has been newly whitewashed, may be in no wise injured, by the dropping of rain-water, nor be easily weakened'.* In the previous July Henry III had commanded the constable to have the keep at Rochester 'whitewashed in those places where it was not whitewashed before', and in 1244 the great tower at Corfe was likewise to be whitewashed externally.†

At the Tower of London in December 1240 the whole chapel of St John was ordered to be whitewashed, and the great hall at Clarendon in February 1249. In May 1256 the sheriff 'is ordered to whitewash the king's hall at Guildford within and without . . . to whitewash within and without the king's chapel, the queen's chapel and chamber and the queen's great wardrobe'‡. Westminster Hall was whitewashed for the coronation in 1274 of Edward I.

Besides whitewash (whiting = powdered chalk and water), and sometimes with it, plaster was used, this being a mixture of lime, sand and hair. Especially fine white plaster was made by burning gypsum, which was found in quantity near Montmartre, hence the name 'plaster of Paris'. Matthew Paris notes that on Henry III's visit to that city in 1254, 'he took note of the elegance of the houses, which are made of gypsum, that is to say plaster'.§ King Henry was always eager for the latest improvements; already in 1251

---

* Liberate Roll, 25 Henry III; Turner (1851), 197.
† Liberate Roll, 24 and 28 Henry III; Turner (1851), 196, 202.
‡ Liberate Roll, 25, 33, 40 Henry III; Turner (1851), 198 (London), 218 (Clarendon), 246 (Guildford).
§ *Chronica Majora* ('Rolls Series'), V, 481; Salzman (1952), 155.

he had told the sheriff of Nottingham to make, or rather finish, the wooden dais in the Castle hall with French plaster (*franco plastro*).*

Gypsum deposits were also present in England, and it was probably 'plastre de Nower' (Nore Down) not Paris which was brought from Purbeck for use at Clarendon in 1288; in 1362 'plaster of Corfe' was employed at Windsor, and 'burnt plaster of Purbyk' at Porchester in 1397. But the French name continued to be used (as indeed it still is); at Ludgershall in 1342, payment is made 'for digging white stone called chalk at Shudebury for making the walls of the chapel and chamber of plaster of Paris'.†

Like whitewash, plaster was used to cover stonework; the new freestone windows at Newgate, inserted in 1282, were covered at once in plaster of Paris 'in the chamber where the justices sit'.

A favourite decoration was to mark the whitewashed or plastered wall with lines, usually of red paint, forming blocks to represent masonry. Such sham pointing can still be seen on the plaster of 13th-century houses: King John's Hunting Box at Romsey, Luddesdown Court, and Temple Manor, Strood. In the dais end wall of the Old Deanery at Salisbury, traces of painted line-ashlar work were found together with a short length of marginal frieze containing stiff leaf foliage decoration. In 1251 at Nottingham Castle, Henry III ordered the sheriff to have whitewashed 'the queen's chamber, wardrobe and chapel on every side and point them lineally',‡ while in May 1256 the sheriff is ordered 'to whitewash and quarry [*quarellari*]' § the king's chamber at Guildford.

Within the blocks of this painted 'masoning', ornament might be added in the shape of a device such as a flower. At the Tower of London in November 1238 the constable is 'to cause the walls of the queen's chamber, which is within our chamber . . . to be whitewashed and pointed, and within those pointings to be painted with flowers', ‖ while in February 1240 'the chamber of our queen in the aforesaid Tower [is to] be wainscoted without delay, and to be thoroughly whitened internally, and newly painted with roses'. Could this have been the same room? If so the new work at so short an interval seems extravagant. At the same time 'our great chamber in the same tower [is] to be entirely whitewashed and newly painted'.¶ Peter the Painter did the work for Henry at Marlborough, 'whitening and lining [*lineand*] the hall behind the chapel', and 'whitening and lining three windows and round the windows, where the wall was broken and painting roses [*rosand*]'.** Window splays, similarly decorated, may be seen in 13th-century churches.

Wainscot was normal in the great houses of the 13th century, judging from its use in the royal palaces. The wood employed was often fir, which is softer and more easily worked than oak, and was imported from Norway. In November 1252 the king orders his bailiff 'to buy in our town of Southampton, for our use, two hundred Norway boards [*bordos de*

---

* Liberate Roll, 36 Henry III; Turner (1851), 235.
† Salzman (1952), 156, for references.
‡ '*linealiter pertractari facias*'. Liberate Roll, 36 Henry III; Turner (1851), 235.
§ Mark out in squares. Liberate Roll, 40 Henry III; Turner (1851), 246.
‖ Liberate Roll, 23 Henry III; Turner (1851), 189.
¶ Liberate Roll, 24 Henry III; Turner (1851), 194.
** Exchequer, King's Remembrancer Accounts, 476, 3; Salzman (1952), 158.

Norwagia] of fir [*sapio*] and deliver them without delay to our sheriff of Southampton, to wainscote therewith the chamber of our beloved son Edward, in our castle of Winchester'.*
This panelling was probably of the simplest kind, vertical boards, meant to be painted. One exception only has been found, where there was an attempt at patterning: in 1243 'the keepers of the works at Windsor are directed to cause the high chamber, on the wall of the castle beside the king's chapel, in the upper bailey of the castle, to be wainscoted by day and night, so that it may be ready and becomingly wainscoted by Friday, when the king shall come there, with radiated and coloured boards, and that nothing be found reprehensible in that wainscot'.†

There is thus frequent mention of wainscoting in Henry III's instructions regarding his houses. The bailiff of Windsor in 1239 is commanded to 'wainscote the chamber of Edward our son'. In 1244 at Ludgershall the king's chamber and the queen's chamber are both to be wainscoted, 'the king's great chamber' at Nottingham Castle and the chamber of the queen, at Bristol the wardrobe under 'our chamber', and chapels at Woodstock and Oxford.‡ By 1261 wainscoting was usual in many of the rooms: 'Aymon Thurumbert is commanded to wainscot the new chamber contiguous to the queen's chamber in Windsor Castle, like the king's other chambers there are wainscoted.' §

Besides certain chapels, where only the chancel or 'behind the chancel altar' are to be wainscoted, there are several other examples of rooms lined with wainscot only in part. At Cliff (Northamptonshire) in 1239 Walter de Burgh was to 'wainscote our great chamber beyond our bed', and the same appears at Geddington. The dais end of the great hall was similarly treated.‖

The wainscot was normally painted in the more important rooms. Walter de Burgh had also 'to cause the chamber of our queen' (at Cliff) 'to be wainscoted and painted with a "history" [*subject picture*]', while in 1252 the bailiff of Gillingham was commanded to wainscot and illuminate the king's chapel and chamber, also those of the queen, and 'to wainscote, whitewash and illuminate the chamber of Edward the king's son'. Green seems to have been fashionable in the 13th century, but was probably the most expensive paint. It was certainly the favourite colour of Henry III. This is obvious from his instructions in the Liberate Rolls. In 1233, the wainscoting of the king's great chamber at Woodstock is to be painted green, and at Winchester Castle, the 'king's painted chamber' is to have the wainscot 'painted with green colour'. Green and gold are often combined: 'Green colour scintillated with gold' in 'our queen's chapel' at Geddington and 'our chamber', also two other chapels there (1252). Even the queen's wardrobe at Winchester Castle is to have 'green paint and golden stars' in 1252, as was the new chamber next to hers at Windsor in 1261. 'Green with golden spots' adorned the king's chamber at Geddington in 1250, and in his chamber at Guildford, with its whitewashed 'quarried' walls, the ceiling was painted 'of a green colour becomingly spangled [*extencellari*] with gold and

* Liberate Roll, 37 Henry III; Turner (1851), 240–1.
† Close Roll, 28 Henry III; Turner (1851), 259–60.
‡ Liberate Roll, 23, 28, 28, 34, 23, 28 Henry III; Turner (1851), 191 (Windsor), 204 (Ludgershall), 205 (Nottingham), 225 (Bristol), 190 (Woodstock), 200 (Oxford).
§ Liberate Roll, 46 Henry III; Turner (1851), 253.
‖ Liberate Roll, 23, 34 Henry III; Turner (1851), 192 (Cliff), 222 (Geddington).

silver' (1256). Green bordered with red is found once, in the queen's chamber at Woodstock (1252).*

Green starred with gold was a suitable ground for the paintings of 'histories' from the Old and New Testament in circles on the wainscot, as was ordered by Henry for the chamber at Winchester in 1237. Was this the same room, the king's wainscoted chamber, which the sheriff of Southampton in 1233 had to have 'painted with the same "histories" and pictures with which it was before painted'? † We know that the king's chamber here was already painted in the 12th century. Giraldus Cambrensis refers to its being decorated with various paintings and colours, with one space left blank by command of Henry II, which was afterwards painted on his instructions with an eagle being attacked by his four offspring, just as Henry himself, as he remarked, was harried by his warring sons. The year 1182 is the date which fits their aggression, and it is also the year mentioned in the Pipe Rolls for paintings being carried out in the king's chamber.‡

At Clarendon, in Henry III's lower chamber, the green wainscot was to have a border painted with the heads of kings and queens; his upper chamber was to have paintings of St Margaret and the Four Evangelists as well as, probably above, wainscot painted 'of a green colour, spotted with gold [*auro deguttari*]', and painted on it 'heads of men and women', all to be done with 'good and exquisite colours' (1246). One is reminded of an illuminated manuscript, and perhaps one of these served as pattern. Indeed Clarendon Palace seems to have had a wealth of painted chambers. In the king's chamber under his chapel, the 'history' of Antioch and the combat of King Richard were to be painted, apparently above or against the 'wainscote of a green colour with golden stars [*scintillis*]',§ and small gilded lead stars and crescents were found in the excavations.‖ So many of King Henry's apartments were of green scintillated with gold. Surviving wall paintings at Westminster Abbey give an idea of the splendour of these vanished rooms.

Tapestry does not seem to have been in use until the 14th century, though possibly introduced, as a Spanish fashion, by Eleanor of Castile, wife of the Lord Edward, who arrived in England in 1255. It is not mentioned in the Rolls, though no doubt curtains were used as partitions and over doorways to keep out the draught. There is, however, constant mention of wainscot and even the dais, where especially wall hangings might have been expected, was generally wainscoted and painted. At Winchester the dais in the king's great hall had painted and gilded heads upon it. This upper and principal part of the hall was wainscoted, 'to the extent of five couples [*copulae*] beyond the king's seat' at Oxford (1244), and 'beyond the dais for the space of five couples' in the same year at Clarendon. The rest of the hall was apparently whitewashed, like those of Guildford and Westminster. But there might be a great painting on the end wall, as in 1246 at Ludgershall where a picture of Dives and Lazarus adorned the gable facing the dais. This subject Henry also

---

* Liberate Roll, 23, 37, 17, 17, 36, 37, 46, 34, 40, 36 Henry III; Turner (1851), 191 (Cliff), 242 (Gillingham), 182 (Woodstock), 183 (Winchester), 237-8 (Geddington), 242 (Winchester), 253 (Windsor), 222 (Geddington), 246 (Guildford), 234 (Woodstock).

† Liberate Roll, 22, 17 Henry III; Turner (1851), 188, 183.

‡ Pipe Roll, 28, 29 Henry II; G. Henderson, *Archaeological Journal* (1961), CXVIII, 175-9.

§ Liberate Roll, 30, 35 Henry III; Turner (1851), 211, 229.

‖ *Journal of the British Archaeological Association* (1963), 3rd S., XXVI, 40, n. 4.

used in his halls at Guildford and Northampton. At Winchester a map of the world was to be painted in the hall in 1239, perhaps the predecessor to the 'Round Table', ancient in the time of Henry VIII, which still hangs there; a *Mappa Mundi* also figures by 1250 in Henry III's Painted Chamber at Westminster. There was a Wheel of Fortune in the king's hall at Clarendon, and the Twelve Labours of the Months at the queen's hall there. In 1243 Dublin Castle hall was to have in paint 'over the same dais a king and queen sitting with their baronage'. At Ludgershall the piers of the aisled hall were painted a marble colour, and at Clarendon the piers (*postes*) and timbers were also ordered to be painted.*

Other rooms were painted as well, and 'Alexander's chamber' must refer to the 'histories' depicted on its walls, as in the next century Charles V of France had a 'Chamber of Charlemagne' in his Hôtel Saint-Pol.† Henry III had even his washing-room painted. We may imagine such walls as enlarged versions of pictures found in such manuscripts as the *Douce Apocalypse* (*c.* 1270), in the Bodleian Library, Oxford.

The famous Painted Chamber in the Palace of Westminster has gone, destroyed in the fire of 1834 which burned the Houses of Parliament. But fortunately copies were taken of the paintings when they were uncovered in 1819, by Crofton Croker and Stothard, those of the former more complete, the latter being probably the more accurate. Croker's water-colour copies are in the Ashmolean and Victoria and Albert Museums, those of Stothard in the library of the Society of Antiquaries. Professor Tristram's reconstructions, based on both, are in the House of Lords. From these we can get an idea of the magnificence of this painted room, the combined audience and bed chamber of Henry III's chief palace.

There were several periods of painting here, great activity in 1236–7 at the time of the king's marriage, repainting after a fire of 1262, and emendations and additions 1265–72, with further expenditure recorded in 1289–94, and until 1307.‡

The paintings known from the 19th-century copies included six superimposed horizontal bands, with inscriptions, of Old Testament illustrations. These included the Miracles of Elisha and the story of Hezekiah; there was also a battle scene from the Acts of Judas Maccabaeus in the Apocrypha. There were two pairs of Virtues and Vices (not earlier than 1262), and St Edward with the Pilgrim on the splays of the three side windows, the Coronation of the Confessor, added in 1266–7, over the bed and doorway to the chapel, and Soldier Guardians on each side of the royal bed. We know also from the records that there was a Bestiary beneath the *Magna Historia*; this was discontinued in 1237. That May, Henry de Pateshull, the king's treasurer, was 'ordered to cause the king's great chamber at Westminster to be painted of a good green colour, in the fashion of a curtain and to paint in the great gable of the same chamber that verse,

"Ke ne dune, ke ne tune, ne prent ke desire"'.§

---

* Liberate Roll, 30, 28, 28, 40, 30, 23 Henry III; Close Roll, 27 Henry III; Liberate Roll, 30, 34 Henry III; Turner (1851), 210 (Winchester), 200 (Oxford), 203 (Clarendon), 246 (Guildford), 210 (Ludgershall), 191 (Winchester), 259 (Dublin), 210 (Ludgershall), 221 (Clarendon).
† Evans (1948), 180.
‡ See Tudor-Craig (1957), 92–105, for the most recent discussion.
§ Anglo-Norman: 'Who does not give, who does not storm, does not get what he desires.'

However, in August 1237 we read that 'Odo the goldsmith is ordered to displace without delay the painting which was commenced in the king's great chamber at Westminster, under the great history [*magna historia*] of the same chamber, with panels containing the species and figures of lions, birds and other beasts, and to paint it of a green colour in the fashion of a curtain, so that the great history may be preserved unhurt'.*

There was also a Calendar round the mouldings of the fireplace, probably renewed in 1259, a Jesse-Tree over the fireplace (probably on the hood), a *Mappa Mundi* mentioned by Matthew Paris, 1250–5, and the Four Evangelists, each on a lion, one on each wall, added in 1243.

Now what was the *Magna Historia* mentioned in 1237? Was it the Old Testament scenes of the 19th-century copies, or did these replace it in 1262–5 after the fire? From internal evidence, especially the architectural details, Mrs Tudor-Craig believes that they did, and that Henry was influenced by the revival of Old Testament subjects in Parisian art, seen on his visit to Saint Louis (IX) in 1254. The *Magna Historia* may well have been what it says—a long series of historical scenes, and grown shabby after some twenty-five years.

We are becoming more and more familiar with the presence of wall paintings in mediaeval churches. Through a series of fortunate survivals and discoveries, and the work of Professor Tristram, Mr E. Clive Rouse and Mr and Mrs Baker, an idea of a mediaeval church interior can be achieved. An increasing number of murals are being discovered throughout the country, and many more must await careful uncovering below successive coats of white-wash.† Of the decoration of houses we were ignorant, except for documentary evidence and the copies of the Westminster paintings. Then came the remarkable discovery of the Painted Chamber at Longthorpe Tower. This was a revelation: we could now enter a mediaeval room and see it as it once was in the early 14th century (Pl. LX).

The Painted Chamber, a room some 16 feet square, comprises the first floor of the solar tower, added *c*. 1300 as a new apartment for the owner. The entire room was painted, but the decoration completely hidden under coats of limewash and distemper until 1945. Then, the tower being evacuated by the Home Guard, the tenant, Mr Hugh Horrell, preparing to redecorate, found evidence of painting and wisely called in expert advice. Now the Painted Chamber has been recovered, preserved and recorded by Mr Clive Rouse, and is under the care of the Ministry of Works. But for Mr Horrell's wisdom the entire scheme would have been lost, as must have happened in so many other cases.

We will now see the painted room with the eyes of Robert de Thorpe, who commissioned the work, entering his room, as he did, from the south-west angle. Facing him on the north wall above the window arch the Nativity is painted, and over that the Seven Ages of Man (Infant, Boy, Youth, Manhood with hawk and lure, Middle Age, Old Age and Decrepitude with crutches); these are set in an arc, and pairs of Apostles below continue as a frieze round this half of the room, with a dado beneath of Fenland birds, exceptionally well portrayed. The western window recess is divided into upper and lower parts; in the large space south of the trefoiled loop there are two seated figures engaged in a discussion. Above them in this inner arch is a hermit with birds and rabbits behind him; he stands

* Close Roll, 20, 21 Henry III; Turner (1851), 257.
† See G. H. Cook (1955), *The English Mediaeval Parish Church*, 195–202, for an excellent summary. Phoenix House.

in an attitude of prayer below a vision of Christ, whose head and shoulders are seen, in clouds, in the apex. The hermit may represent St Anthony, the Hermit *par excellence* of the Middle Ages, who was the patron saint of basket-makers, one of whom is depicted with him. The outer arch on this (western) side showed the Labours of the Months, January to April and December remaining. The eastern wall has an original fireplace opening, and above it is a splendid composition in which a king is rotating a large Wheel of Five Senses, these represented on it by a monkey (taste), a vulture (smell), spider's web (touch), boar (hearing) and cock (sight). Above, a fashionable young man is followed by his dog, but of his companion only a leg and foot remain. The embrasure north of the fireplace (and now the public entrance) shows the morality of *Les Trois Vifs et les Trois Morts*, so often used in churches of the 14th century, in which three living kings meet three skeletons, who teach the futility of earthly greatness. The south wall is secular and heraldic: below there is a diaper pattern of lozenges including the arms of Thorpe, and the hunting of an unpleasant creature called the Bonnacon over two doorways near the south-west angle. Above are two seated figures conversing, the one on the left a king, either Edward II or III with the royal arms of three leopards, thus before 1340, when Edward III combined them with the fleurs-de-lis of France. The other figure must, from the evidence of his shield, be Edmund, Duke of Kent, brother to Edward II, the greatest tenant of the Abbey of Peterborough, (of which two Roberts de Thorpe in turn were Steward), whose tragic fate at the hands of Roger Mortimer in 1329 caused him to be regarded as a martyr. Thus either as great tenant or martyr Kent was depicted at Longthorpe, where the evidence suggests a date of *c.* 1330 for the paintings.

The hanging of painted shields following that of real ones, as wall decorations, seems to have been customary by the late 13th century. They are found (paint on stone) in the east end of the nave at Westminster, and at his own Abbey of Peterborough Robert de Thorpe must have seen the arms of the Knights of the Barony decorating the sanctuary walls. He would thus place those of his co-tenants with his own, on the walls of his Painted Chamber.

The paintings once covered the vault as well. Parts of the Four Evangelists, each in a barbed quatrefoil, can be seen, and better preserved figures of musicians, one with organ, two with viol or gittern, another with bagpipes, King David playing his harp and King Saul or Solomon his psaltery.

The colour scheme, now of warm red and yellow ochres, on a biscuit ground, was once enriched with gold and a wider colour range. But there is now no sign of green or blue. Black was used as undercoat for the flesh tints of the faces, much of which has worn off giving a curious effect. Vermilion seems to have been used as a base for gold, and is now the tint of the leopards in the royal shield. The general theme of the paintings seems to point a moral, the contrast between the worldly and the spiritual life, 'the pitfalls, dangers and transience of the one, and the teaching, aspirations and rewards of the other'.*

The paintings have similarities to manuscripts like the Queen Mary's Psalter, probably dating from the first quarter of the 14th century, and especially the Peterborough Psalter, executed between 1299 and 1321 when Hugh de Stiuecle was prior. The south wall closely

* Rouse & Baker (1955) (fully illustrated); M.O.W. Guide (27).

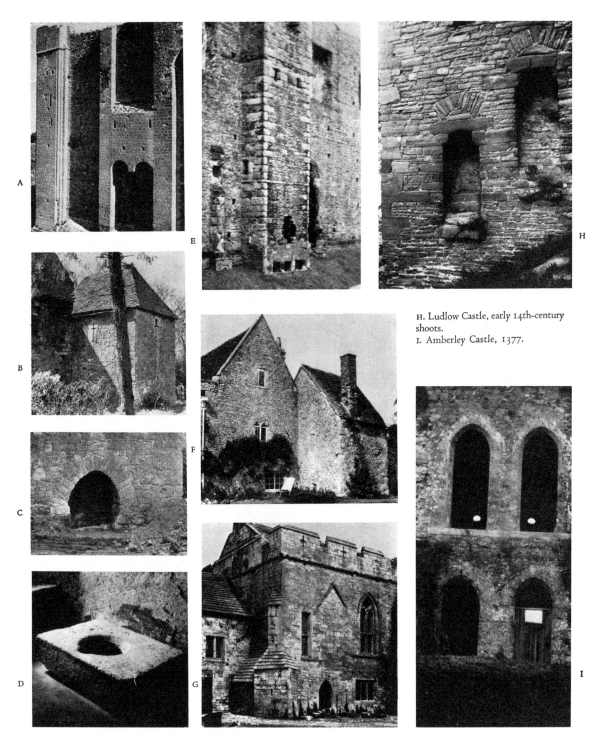

H. Ludlow Castle, early 14th-century shoots.
I. Amberley Castle, 1377.

Plate LIX. Garderobes. A. Castle Rising, *c.* 1141–76, twin privies in the intermediate buttress; kitchen buttress at angle *(left)*.
B. Old Soar, *c.* 1290, annexe 'wardrobe' with garderobe. C. Old Soar, drainage arch. D. Seat at Longthorpe Tower, *c.* 1300 +.
E. Middleham Castle, 14th century. F. Camoise Court, Chislehampton, *c.* 1318; garderobe annexe *(right)*. G. Markenfield Hall,
1310, garderobe buttress at angle of hall.

Plate LX. Wall paintings of *c.* 1330 at Longthorpe Tower.
A. West wall: St Anthony and the basket-maker (*above*), philosopher and pupil (*below*). B. South wall:
A king, possibly Edward III. C. North-east corner: (*left*), the Seven Ages of Man; the Nativity; part
of the Apostles' Creed; Fenland birds; (*right*), the Wheel of the Five Senses.

resembles a miniature in the Treatise of Walter de Milimete (1326–7). The Longthorpe paintings have likeness (for birds and heraldry) to the Luttrell Psalter (*c.* 1340) but are far superior to that work, which is coarser. They were probably executed by a skilled artist from the Scriptorium of the Abbey which produced such fine manuscripts and of which the tenant of Longthorpe was steward.

Perhaps the most interesting point about this painted room, remarkable in our eyes, is that it may have been a normal feature of a 14th-century house. For the owner was not a man of great importance, a nobleman or great lord, though he had a certain local standing in being Steward to the Liberty of the great Abbey of Peterborough. His family had only recently risen from servitude. His great-grandfather Thurstan had been a villein on the manor of Thorpe and manumitted (freed) at the beginning of the 13th century. His son William was confirmed in his holding of land in Thorpe, and the latter's son Sir William had licence in 1263 to rebuild Longthorpe Chapel, the church which still stands. He also probably built the house, to which his son Robert seems to have added the tower. This Robert became Steward of the Abbey in 1310, and was not finally released from villein service until 1324. In 1330 he was succeeded as steward by his son Robert, who was holding Thorpe in 1346, and probably commissioned the paintings. Possibly it was one of his sons, Sir Robert, who became Chancellor to Edward III, and another, Sir William, who became Lord Chief Justice.

Thus two Roberts de Thorpe, in turn Stewards of the Abbey, 1310 and 1330, had their solar in Longthorpe Tower, and the second man commissioned the wall paintings, it is believed, from the internal evidence of the decoration, and also of the structure. Apparently there was some settlement in the north wall of the tower, and to give stability the original wide recess in this wall was partially blocked. The paintings continue over this blocking, and must be subsequent to the building of the tower by a period sufficient to allow the defect to develop and be rectified.

The Painted Chamber at Longthorpe has been described in detail, because of its supreme importance. Mr Clive Rouse calls it 'by far the most impressive piece of mediaeval secular mural decoration in the country', and which in 'not a particularly large or important dwelling, suggests that mural painting of a hitherto unimagined richness and elaboration must have been usual in the castles and great houses of the English nobility during the mediaeval period'.

For France, Dr Joan Evans has found records of sumptuous painted rooms. The accounts of Matilde (Mahaut), Countess of Artois, are a 14th-century rival to the Liberate Rolls of Henry III. They reveal ceilings of blue or green with metal stars, coloured vaulting-ribs, painted wainscot and sham masonry and curtains.* The nobles often ordered their walls to be decorated with scenes from their favourite romances, sometimes including part of the text, as in the *Salle aux chansons* of the Counts of Artois at Hesdin. In England this must also have been the vogue, and we know that the *Morte d'Arthur* was depicted at Tamworth Castle, with huge figures of Sir Lancelot and Sir Tarquin painted on the wall of the hall.†

* Evans (1948), 179–81.
† Parker (1859), 67.

Historical events were also portrayed. The coronation, marriage, wars and funeral of Edward I were painted on the walls of the bishop's palace at Lichfield,* and after 1356 the Countess of Artois employed a Paris artist to embellish the gallery at Conflans with the battle feats of her father—the strictest accuracy to be shown.

Indee battle pictures, whether historical, from the Old Testament, Apocrypha or the romances, were particularly suited to mediaeval society. Feats of arms were of the highest interest to the upper classes, for whom such painted rooms were made. These battles were represented in their tapestries also. But quieter subjects were in vogue as well. Like the leafy decoration of rooms in spring and summer, gardens and country scenes were also depicted on the walls. In 1335 at Saint-Pol Charles V of France had his long gallery painted like a great wood, including fruit trees, and with lilies and roses underneath.†

Yet religious subjects continued to be painted, such as those revealed in what was probably a hospice or pilgrims' hostel at Piccotts End, Hemel Hempstead. These include an impressive Christ in Majesty flanked by his Baptism and a Pietà, with other panels showing St Peter in papal tiara, St Clement, St Catherine with her wheel and St Margaret with the dragon. From costume evidence these seem to date from the end of the 15th century.

A woollen hanging on the wall made for comfort and warmth. As early as Saxon times wall clothes are mentioned, and in *Beowulf* ‡ even wall coverings embroidered with gold. The Bayeux 'Tapestry' (c. 1077), however, was rather embroidery, consisting of pictures stitched in wool on a strip of linen 230 feet long by 22 inches wide.§

The use of woven hangings seems to have begun at the upper end of the hall, to make the dais more comfortable. To lessen draught the high table was given a backing of fabric, as shown in the Luttrell Psalter, and soon in great houses combined a higher portion with canopy over the chair of the owner, emblazoned with his 'cloth of estate'. Comfort and decoration always started at this end of the building.

Painted cloths were certainly in use in the 14th century. They appear in the inventory in 1360 of the late Queen Isabella, mother of Edward III, and include a dorsal and banker (hangings for back and bench) of worsted painted with the Nativity, and a wall hanging painted with the Apocalypse for the hall, while at Salisbury in 1376 Richard Gilbert had 'stained cloths' in both his hall and parlour, the first having the story of Solomon on it.‖ These pictorial hangings were used instead of the pictures on the plaster, or perhaps these were combined, with the lower portion of the walls hung with worsted or coloured canvas, and the upper left uncovered but painted. 'Steyned cloths' continued in use in the 15th century, as the less expensive form of wall covering, while tapestry would be used by the well-to-do. In 1463 the nieces of John Baret of Bury inherited 'the steyned cloth of the Coronacion of Oure Lady' and another depicting the Seven Ages of Man, but a wealthy man like Sir John Fastolf (d. 1459) had only 'Arras'.¶

* Wall (1914), 96.
† Evans (1948), 180.
‡ lines 994–5.
§ Stenton (1957).
‖ Evans (1949), 137–8.
¶ Evans (1949), 138.

By the late 14th and 15th centuries, in a great house, tapestry (*Tapisserye*) was the rule for hall and chamber. Instead of being painted on plaster, canvas or other hanging, the picture was now stitched and woven into fabric itself. The fashion seems to have derived from the courts of France and Burgundy, and the great centre of manufacture, until 1477, was Arras in the province of Artois, with Flanders part of the domains of the Dukes of Burgundy, from which the best-known tapestry derives its name, with which readers of Shakespeare are familiar.* It was known as such as early as 1376, when the Black Prince's will speaks of his *Sale d'Arras du pas de Saladyn.*†

Many of these sumptuous hangings must have come to England as a result of the French Wars, either as loot or received as gifts. Philippe 'le Hardi', Duke of Burgundy, in 1393 presented Henry of Derby (later Lancaster) with tapestries depicting King Clovis, Pharaoh and Moses, and others, including the life of the Virgin, to the Duke of Gloucester, and in 1394 a life of Saint Ursin to Richard II, and later virtues and vices accompanied by kings and emperors.‡

Some tapestry, however, was made in London, where the Ordinances of the trade of Tapiciers are dated 1331, and one of them accompanied Chaucer to Canterbury. But they had powerful rivals in the 'trade of Alien Weavers' from Flanders. Already in 1317–18 Edward II's wardrobe accounts had included: 'To Thomas de Hebenhith, mercer of London, for a great hanging of wool wove with figures of the king and earl upon it, for the king's service in his hall on solemn occasions, 30.l.'; and Thomas de Varley was paid six shillings and three pence for making and sewing a border of green cloth round it, to save damage in fixing it up.§ These figures might resemble the king and Duke of Kent depicted at Longthorpe Tower. Edward III created the office of 'The King's Tapestry Maker', and in 1348 his daughter, Princess Joan, had one 'halling' hanging of worsted, worked with popinjays, and another with roses ‖ while his son Edward the Black Prince bequeathed Richard II hangings for a hall embroidered with swans having ladies' heads and ostrich feathers, and to his wife Joan, the Fair Maid of Kent, one embroidered with eagles and griffins.¶ These may not have been London work, but the will of Richard FitzAlan, sixth Earl of Arundel, in 1392 records a halling of blue with red roses and coats of arms 'lately made in London'.** At Bolton Castle Sir Richard, later Lord, Scrope had 'for the hall there' (probably behind the dais) 'my green tapestry woven with griffins with my Arms worked in metal'.†† This is an item of his will of 1400, which mentions arras work in the chambers. To Roger his son he leaves 'one bed of embroidered velvet, with 4 sides of arras work, and 4 tapestries of the same colour as the said bed. . . .' ‡‡ In the latter part of the 14th century Norwich also became important for woollen hangings; in fact 'worsted' was called after a Norfolk village of that name.

---

* In 1477 at the death of Charles the Bold the prosperity of Arras was extinguished by Louis XI's eviction of its inhabitants, who were replaced by Frenchmen; the town's fame was inherited by Brussels.
† J. Nichols (1780), *A collection of all the Wills . . . of the Kings and Queens of England.*
‡ Evans (1949), 93.
§ T. Stapleton (1836), *Archaeologia*, XXVI, 342; Parker (1853), 49.
‖ Sir N. Nicolas (1848), *Archaeologia*, XXXI, 78; Parker (1853), 49.
¶ J. Nichols (1780), op. cit. 73; Parker (1853), 49.
** *Testamenta Vetusta*, I, 130; Parker (1853), 50.
†† Azure, a bend or, the subject of a Court of Chivalry case between Sir Richard le Scrope and Sir Robert Grosvenor in 1385–90. *Boutell's Heraldry*, ed. C. W. Scott-Giles (1950), 106–7, pl. II.
‡‡ Jackson (1956), 20, 12.

Such wall hangings soon made habitable the rooms in great houses which were visited at certain seasons by the owners and their train of attendants. They provided a feeling of comfort and concealed cold walls or shabby painted plaster. Such tapestries were relatively easy to pack and transport, and this portion of the owner's luggage was sent on ahead to be set up in readiness for his arrival. Pegs for such hangings remained, at least until recently, at Sudeley Castle, the Prior's House at Wenlock, South Wingfield Manor and Wolfhall in Wiltshire. In a large room the tapestries would extend some 8 to 10 feet up the wall (perhaps painted above), hence the loftier position of the windows in 15th-century and early 16th-century halls. These hangings transformed and made comfortable a temporary building or one improvised, as those on the marshes of Calais for Cardinal Beaufort's peace negotiations of 1439.[*]

The tapestry was often made in sets to match and referred to as a 'hall', a 'chamber' or a 'bed'. In 1398 the Duke of Orleans purchased a portable chamber: '*une chambre portative*', comprising a seler (canopy), dosser (back-cloth), curtains and counterpoint (coverlet).[†]

A wealthy noble might have several sets for use at different seasons; hence doubtless the popular hunting and hawking scenes for autumn and spring, and shepherds for summer. These, however, were items of luxury; ordinary folk would be glad to have even a set of painted cloths.

Like those of the wall paintings, the subjects of the tapestries were varied, and based on these at first. They included, besides the all important heraldry, biblical scenes from both Old and New Testaments, events in history and romances, allegories and pictures of hunting and the countryside.

When the rich Sir John Fastolf died at Caister in 1459 the inventory of his goods included pieces of arras depicting the Assumption of the Virgin, the Siege of Falaise, the Nine Paladins, as well as scenes of hunting, hawking and shepherds, and a 'gentlewoman harping by a castle'.[‡] Among the twenty pieces of arras which Edward IV purchased in 1480 were representations of the Passion, the history of 'Nabugodonoser' and of Alexander.[§] Henry VII made equally large purchases and had some magnificently furnished rooms at Windsor. In 1509 William Makefyr wrote of his welcome there to Philip the Fair, King of Castile. 'Then the King's grace offered to take him by the arm, and so went to the King of Castile's chamber, which is the richestly hanged that ever I saw; several chambers together, hanged with cloth of Arras wrought with gold as thick as could be . . .[||]

Unfortunately few of these beautiful hangings survive. Those that remain, particularly in France, suggest, as do the documents, the glories of those which have disappeared. Particularly lovely is the tapestry of *c.* 1400, with figures of the Duke and Duchess of Orleans, standing in a flowery field, just emerged from their pavilion of which the curtains are held back by angels. The Duchess, Valentine de Milan, is watering her flowers.[¶] These figures of great charm, undoubtedly portraits, could represent the owners of the

---

[*] Parker (1853), 63–6.
[†] Parker (1853), 62 n.
[‡] Evans (1949), 138.
[§] Parker (1859), 63.
[||] *The Paston Letters*, 248–9.
[¶] Now in the Musée des Arts décoratifs in Paris; Evans (1948), 184, pl. 170.

great houses of 15th-century England, whose portraits are now unknown. Another tapestry with portrait figures of his courtiers, made for Charles VII of France, shows the costume of c. 1430. The courtiers walk against a background of wide green and white stripes, the king's colours, against which is his rose spray device.* This may be compared with the four Hunting Tapestries from Chatsworth, now in the Victoria and Albert Museum. These show ladies and gentlemen in similar apparel and look rather earlier than the suggested association with the marriage of Henry VI and Margaret of Anjou (1445), one lady's horse having the letter 'M' on its trappings. They were most probably woven at Tournai, which by 1450 rivalled Arras in importance.

The battle scene, used in Henry III's painted walls, is a favourite subject in the hangings, and such a view, of great vigour and movement, can be seen in a 15th-century tapestry at Brussels, from *Le Chanson de Roland*.† Another, woven at Tournai, in silk and wool, shows Ajax, Pyrrhus and Agamemnon in their tent, the Trojan War waging dramatically outside, the heroes depicted in great detail, with the armour of c. 1470.‡ Tournaments also were a subject for tapestries in the 14th and 15th centuries, judging from the documents.

Heraldic tapestry was extremely popular, particularly for the 'cloth of state' behind the high table. One placed on the dais wall at Haddon is thought to have been given to a Vernon by Henry VIII, but has been dated earlier to c. 1460–70, partly from the shape of the five shields. These contain the royal arms (England quartering France) within the Garter, the central having the lion crowned as crest; there is a background of *millefleure*. The heraldic beasts of Charles VII of France (1422–61) are seen in a tapestry at Rouen. These are winged stags, one carrying the royal banner, the others gorged with a crown and the fleur-de-lis shield of France; they stand in a flowery meadow, with lions rampant beyond a wattle hedge; above them are banderoles (ribbon-like scrolls with inscription) and in the background castle towers and the sea.§

The background detail is often delightful, especially in the six tapestries known as 'La Dame à la Licorne', probably woven in the Loire district between 1509 and 1513. This lady with her attendant, and a lion and unicorn, share a green carpet full of flowers with dogs, rabbits and a monkey, while there are other small animals strewn with myriad blossoms against a background of a deep and particularly attractive shade of pink.‖

Made about the same time, but in Flanders, are two pieces of tapestry, part of one subject, preserved in the Founder's Tower at Magdalen College, Oxford. They show a crowd of courtiers in magnificent garments, and are said to represent the betrothal of Prince Arthur, elder brother of Henry, to Katherine of Aragon (1501).¶

Although linenfold panelling came into vogue for smaller rooms in the early 16th century, often, as at Thame Park, combined with carved portraits in medallions, tapestry was still in demand for the great hall and state apartments. At Hampton Court in the Great

* Now in the Metropolitan Museum, New York; Evans (1948), pl. 169.
† Musée de Cinquantenaire, Brussels; Evans (1948), pl. 168.
‡ Victoria and Albert Museum (1930), *100 Masterpieces* (Publication No. 191), pl. 84.
§ Evans (1948), 186, pl. 171.
‖ Victoria and Albert Exhibition (1947), *Masterpieces of French Tapestry*, pls. 17 and 18 (in colour). The tapestries are now in the Musée de Cluny, Paris.
¶ R.C.H.M. *Oxford*, 75, pl. 136.

Watching Chamber, four tapestries depict the Conflict of the Virtues and Vices; they were woven in Flanders in 1500, and were perhaps some of those which Wolsey bought in 1522 from Richard Gresham. In the same room are three early 16th-century tapestries, also Flemish, showing the Triumphs of Petrarch, Death over Chastity, Fame over Death and Time over Fame; others show the arms and badges of Henry VIII. Another in the Horn Room, adjoining, shows Avarice riding on a Griffin. The tapestries in the Great Hall date from c. 1540; they are seven of a set of ten, made in Brussels by Wilhelm Pannemaker, and show scenes from the Life of Abraham.* Above the screen are five strips of early 16th-century heraldic tapestry including the royal Tudor arms and badges, and those of Wolsey and the See of York.

These survivals give an idea of the superb hangings now known only from their titles in the documents.

* R.C.H.M. *Middlesex*, 35, pls. 80, 83.

COMPARATIVE MOULDINGS
Key to locations of examples on facing page

1. St Mary's Guild, Lincoln; c. 1190.
2. Winchester Castle hall; 1222–35.
3. Ower Moigne; c. 1270–80.
4. Little Wenham; c. 1270–80.
5. Markenfield; c. 1310.
6. Northborough; c. 1340.
7. Winchester College; c. 1387–9.
8. Preston Plucknett; first half 15th century.
9. Bowhill; first half 15th century.
10. Minster Lovell; c. 1431–42.
11. South Wingfield; c. 1440–59.
12. Stanton Harcourt kitchen; c. 1460–83.
13. Christchurch Castle hall; c. 1160.
14. Little Chesterford; c. 1225.
15. Crowhurst; c. 1250.
16. Sutton Courtenay 'Norman Hall'; c. 1190.
17. Netley Abbot's House; c. 1250–60.
18. Bull Cottage, Burford; c. 1315.
19. Fyfield Manor, Berks; c. 1335–40.
20. New College, Oxford, and Winchester College; c. 1380–9.
21. Dartington Hall; c. 1390–9.
22. Vicars' Hall, Chichester (very similar to entrance at Dartington); 1397+.
23. Tickenham Court; c. 1400.
24. Tattershall Castle and Gothelney; c. 1433–43.
25. Preston Plucknett; before 1438.
26. West Coker; after 1457.
27. Ilminster; c. 1480.
28. Great Chalfield; c. 1480.
29. Muchelney Abbot's Parlour; c. 1509–14.
30. Music House, Norwich; c. 1175.
31. Chantry, Chichester; early 13th century.
32. Little Wenham; c. 1270–80.
33. Beaulieu, Great Gatehouse; c. 1325.
34. Dartington Hall; c. 1390–9.
35. South Wingfield; c. 1440–59.
36. Tickenham Court; c. 1400.
37. South Wraxall; c. 1435.
38. Great Chalfield; c. 1480.
39. Lytes Cary; c. 1530.
40. Dartington Hall; c. 1390–9.
41. Preston Plucknett solar; before 1438.
42. Tattershall; c. 1433–43.
43. South Wingfield; c. 1440–59.
44. Crypt House, Burford; later 15th century.
45. Abingdon Abbey; later 15th century.
46. Ilminster; c. 1480.
47. Ashbury Manor; c. 1488.
48. Lytes Cary parlour; 1583.

1 to 12, Hood moulds and abaci; 13 to 15, Internal window jambs; 16 to 29, Doorways; 30 to 35, Vaulting ribs; 36 to 39, Oriel arches; 40 to 48, Doorways.

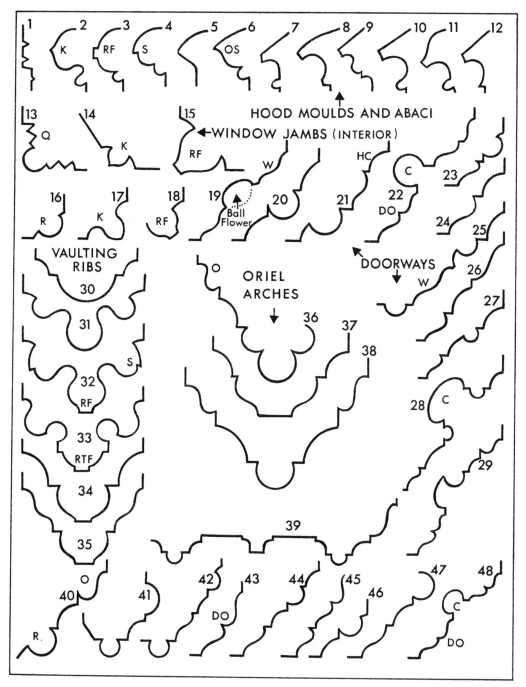

Fig. 117. Comparative mouldings. (*For locations see numbered list opposite.*)

KEY TO TYPES:
- C cavetto
- DO double ogee or bracket
- HC hollow chamfer
- K keel
- O ogee
- OS ogee scroll
- Q quirk
- R roll
- RF roll and fillet
- RTF roll and triple fillet
- S scroll
- W wave

GLOSSARY

Abacus, flat upper member of a capital.

Acanthus, plant of which the leaves are represented in a classical capital of the Corinthian order.

Alure, wall walk.

Apse, semicircular or polygonal end to a building.

Arcade, a range of arches supported on piers or columns. Hence *Arcade posts* if of timber.

Arcade-plate, longitudinal horizontal beam carried on the arcade posts of an aisled hall to support the rafters of nave and aisle. Square-set, then developed into a PURLIN.

Arch:

Caernarvon. See ARCH, SHOULDERED.

Depressed, flattened elliptical, or straight head with only the angles rounded.

Drop. See ARCH, POINTED.

Elliptical. See ARCH, THREE-CENTRED.

Equilateral, pointed arch formed on an equilateral triangle, i.e. the radii equal to the span.

Four-centred or Tudor, arch with curves struck from four centres, the two outer (lower) arcs struck from the springing line, the two inner (upper) from below the springing line. In later work the two upper arcs are represented by straight lines.

Lancet, pointed arch formed on an acute-angled triangle, the radii greater than the span.

Ogee, pointed arch of double curved sides, the upper arcs convex, the lower concave.

Pointed, Two-centred, or Drop, arch struck from centres on the springing line.

Relieving, arch, often rough, placed in the wall over an opening to relieve it of superincumbent weight.

Round. See ARCH, SEMICIRCULAR.

Segmental, a single arc struck from a centre below the springing line.

Segmental-pointed, a pointed arch struck from two centres below the springing line.

Semicircular, a single arc, forming half of a circle from the springing line. Common in the 11th and 12th centuries.

Shouldered, lintel on corbels which are concave on the under side. Sometimes called *Caernarvon arch* because of its prevalence in that castle, and found in the late 13th and 14th centuries. A late 12th-century type (e.g. Boothby Pagnell) has the corbels convex to the opening.

Skew, arch not at right angles to its jambs.

Stilted, arch with springing line raised above the level of the imposts—i.e. with upright masonry between the imposts and feet of the arch.

Three-centred, Elliptical, arch formed by three arcs, the middle (uppermost) struck from a centre below the springing line.

Two-centred. See ARCH, POINTED.

Arch-brace, a curved timber across the angle between principals, etc., and tie- or collar-beam, two forming an arch below the latter.

Argent, white or silver (heraldic).

Ashlar, worked stone, masonry or squared stones in regular courses.

Ashlar-piece, a short timber rising vertically from the inner end of the sole-piece to the underside of the common rafter.

Aumbry, cupboard.

Azure, blue (heraldic).

Bailey, ward, courtyard of a castle.

Ball-flower, ornament resembling a ball enclosed in a globular three-petalled flower; characteristic of the first quarter of the 14th century.

Baluster, a small column supporting a hand-rail.

Balustrade, a series of balusters.

Barbican, outwork to a gateway.

Barrel roof, like a covered wagon, or inverted ship.

Barrel vault. See VAULTING.

Bartizan, overhanging battlemented corner turret, corbelled out; common in French and Scottish military architecture.

Base crucks. See CRUCKS.

Batter, lower sloping surface of a wall linking a wide base to a narrower upper structure.

Battlements, indented parapet for defence (*see also* CRENELLATION, EMBRASURE).

Bay, compartment into which a building is divided by roof principals, vaulting piers, etc.

Bay window, projecting window usually at ground level. *See* ORIEL.

Bead, a small round moulding.

Blade. See CRUCKS.

Bond, arrangement of bricks in courses. *See* BRICKWORK.

Boss (Fr. *bosse* = lump or knot). Projecting ornament concealing intersection of vaulting ribs, etc.

Brace, subsidiary timber of a roof, inserted to strengthen the framing.

Brattishing, ornamental cresting on screen, cornice, etc.

Bressumer, beam supporting an upper wall of timber framing.

Brickwork:

   English bond, alternate courses of *Headers* and *Stretchers.*

   Flemish bond, alternate *Headers* and *Stretchers* in the same course.

   Header, brick with end showing on wall face.

   Header bond, bricks laid so that only ends show on wall face.

   Stretcher, brick with side showing on wall face.

Broach-stop, a half pyramid against a chamfer to bring the edge to a right angle, often short with deep hollow chamfer in the 13th century, long with very shallow hollow chamfer in the 15th century.

Buttress, projection from a wall for additional support.

   Angle buttresses, a pair meeting (or nearly) at right angles on the corner of a building.

   Diagonal buttress, one set on the angle of a building, diagonally to each wall.

Cambered (*beam*), with slight curve, the centre higher than the ends.

Camera, chamber, private bed-sittingroom.

Canopy, suspended covering over high table, roof-like projection over a niche, etc.

Casement moulding, a wide hollow.

Catslide, long slope of roof continued over a lean-to, e.g. aisle or outshut.

Cavetto (Latin *cavus* = hollow). Concave or hollow moulding.

Cellar, room, often for storage, on ground floor or partly underground. Basement.

Centering, temporary framework to support arch or vault during construction.

Chamfer, bevel, plane formed by cut-off angle.

   Hollow chamfer, concave rounded chamfer.

   Sunk chamfer, plane of chamfer sunk below its edges.

Chamfer cusp, cusps springing from the chamfered side or edge of an arched head (not the soffit, for which see SOFFIT CUSP).

Checker, accounts department.

Chevron (Fr. = rafter). Zigzag ornamental moulding of the 12th century.

Cinquefoil (Latin *quinque folium*; Fr. *cinque feuilles*). Five-leaved; *see* FOIL.

Clapboarding, a series of vertical boards set up on a sill, each tongued on one edge, grooved on the other, to fit into its neighbour. A term still used in the U.S.A., but the boards are there set horizontally.

Clerestorey, upper storey pierced by windows rising clear above adjoining parts (e.g. aisles) of a building.

Cloister, covered way round open space or garth; quadrangle.

Close-studding, walling of timber posts set little more than their own width apart, with plastered panels between.

Clunch, hard chalk used for building.

Cob, wall made of unburnt clay mixed with straw.

Collar-beam, horizontal beam tying together a pair of truss blades, or rafters, usually at or about half way up their length. There may be one to three collars to each pair.

Collar purlin, horizontal longitudinal beam supporting collar.

Column (Latin *columna* = post). Vertical support to arch, consisting of base, circular or octagonal shaft, and capital.

Common rafters. See RAFTERS.

Corbel, projection from wall to support a weight.

Cornice, horizontal moulded projection uppermost on a wall, fireplace, etc.

Cove, coving, concave under-surface.

Crenel, open space in embattled parapet, for shooting through.

Crenellate, furnish with battlements.

   Licence to, royal permit to furnish with battlements, i.e. to fortify.

Crenellation, battlemented parapet, sign of fortification.

Crest, heraldic device worn on helm.

Cresting, ornamental finish surmounting screen, battlements, etc.

Crockets (Fr. *croc* = hook). Projecting carved leaves or flowers decorating spires, pinnacles, hoodmoulds, etc., tending to curl downwards in the 13th century, to rise upwards in the 14th and 15th centuries.

Crown-post, post standing on a tie-beam to support the collar purlin and usually with four-way struts to it and the collar or its braces. Often shaped like a small column, the short examples usually dating from the 14th century, the tall and slim ones from the 13th and 15th centuries.

Crucks, primitive truss formed by two main timbers, usually curved, set up as arch or inverted V. Each cruck is called a blade, and a pair may be cut from the same tree.

   Base crucks, crucks truncated by a collar-beam.

Cruck-spur, small timber projecting from the outer edge of a cruck blade to support or anchor the wall plate, used in an open cruck truss without a tie-beam.

Curtain, outer wall of a castle, between towers.

Cushion capital, cubical (square) capital, with lower angles rounded off to fit the circular shaft.

Cusp (Latin *cuspis* = point). Point separating the foils (small arcs) in tracery.

Cusp-point, end of cusp sometimes ornamented with leaves, flowers, etc.

Dado, decorative or protective treatment of the lower part of a wall to a height of 3 to 4 feet.

Dado-rail, moulding on top of the dado.

Dais, raised platform for high table.

Dexter, heraldic: on right hand of shield, i.e. on the spectator's left.

Diaper, all-over decoration of surfaces with small pattern such as flowers in squares, lozenges, etc. Carved examples characteristic of the 13th and 14th centuries; in the 15th century used for painted ornament. Perhaps derived from patterned cloth from Ypres in Belgium (Dyaper, i.e. D'Ypres).

Dog-legged staircase, staircase going backwards and forwards without a well-hole.

Dog-tooth ornament, a late 12th- and early 13th-century development from the nail-head, in which the pyramids are cut into four-petalled flowers; used on hollow mouldings.

Dormer window, vertical window with own gable and individual roof, in the slope of a roof; usually lighting a sleeping apartment, hence the name.

Dorser, cushion or hanging for the back of a seat.

Dorter, monastic dormitory.

Double-ogee moulding, two ogees meeting at the convex ends.

Dovetail, tenon shaped like a dove's spread tail or reversed wedge, fitting into corresponding mortice and forming a joint.

Dragon-beam, horizontal timber bisecting the angle of a floor, receiving the shortened joists on both sides, these being at right angles to each other.

Drawbar, long bar to secure the door, fitted into a socket in one jamb, and slid back when not in use into a long channel in the other.

Dressings, worked stones at angle, openings, etc.

Drum tower, low, squat circular tower.

Eaves, overhanging edge of roof.

Embrasure, opening in battlemented parapet, recess for window or doorway.

'End-hall house', hall at free end of house (P. A. Faulkner).

Fan-vaulting. See VAULTING.

Farmery, monastic infirmary.

Fenestration, window arrangement.

Fillet, a flat thin band used to separate mouldings.

Finial (Latin finis = end). Terminal ornament, such as a bunch of foliage to a pinnacle.

Flemish bond. See BRICKWORK.

Foil (Latin folium = leaf). Each of small arc openings in tracery, separated by cusps.

Foliated (Latin folium = leaf). Carved with leaf ornament.

Forebuilding, additional building against a keep, containing the entrance staircase, and sometimes a chapel.

Frater, monastic refectory.

Frieze, horizontal band of decoration, immediately below the cornice.

Gable, triangular upper part of the wall at end of a ridged roof.

Gabled hip, hipped roof with small gable above.

Garderobe, privy or latrine.

Great chamber, solar, owner's bed-sittingroom, master bedroom.

Groin, the edge formed by intersecting vaults.

Hall, principal room in a house. Open hall, one on ground floor open to the roof. Upper end, high table end, furthest from entrance. Lower end, adjacent to entrance and service department.

Hammer-beam, roof bracket projecting at wall-plate level; a pair resemble a tie-beam with its centre omitted; there may be a second (and third) series of these above.

Hammer-post, short vertical post rising from the inner end of a hammer-beam to the principal rafter.

Hipped gable, gable with small hipped end above.

Hipped roof, one with sloped, not vertical, end(s).

Hoards (Hourds, Brattices), covered wooden galleries supported on brackets at the top of a castle wall, to defend its base through openings in the gallery floor.

Hood, canopy of stone or timber and plaster over the fireplace to collect and conduct smoke to its flue.

Hoodmould (Label, Dripstone), projecting moulding on the wall face over a window or doorway, either following the shape of the arch, or square in outline.

Hotel, at first denoted the town house of a nobleman.

Impost, upper course of pilaster, pillar or pier, from which an arch springs.

Jamb, side of doorway, window, fireplace, etc.

Jetty, overhanging upper storey.

Joist, one of parallel timbers stretched from wall to wall, to support the floor-boards. Laid flat earlier, from the later 17th century laid on edge.

Joggling, stepping (or scalloping, etc.), of adjoining stones to prevent slipping.

Jowl, the enlarged head or foot of a timber, usually a vertical post, frequently used where two members, e.g. top-plate and tie-beam, were to be joined to the post.

Keel, roll-moulding with sharp edge.

Keep, Great Tower or Donjon of a castle, usually of late 11th and 12th centuries.

Hall keep, earlier, with hall beside chamber in a large lower building, e.g. London, Colchester, Corfe, Canterbury, Rising, Middleham.

Tower keep, later 12th-century with chamber above the hall in narrower, taller and probably less expensive and more defensive building, e.g. Hedingham, Guildford, Goodrich and Brougham. Portchester was transformed from one to the other. (See Braun (1936), 40 et seq.)

King-post, a vertical post extending from a tie-beam to the apex of the roof, usually supporting a RIDGE PURLIN.

Label. See HOODMOULD.

Lancet, long narrow window with pointed head, characteristic of the 13th century.

Lap, a timber of diminished thickness which overlaps another.

Laver (Latin *lavare* = to wash). Stone washing-basin.

Lierne vault. See VAULTING.

Linenfold panelling (Latin *Lignum undulatum* = wavy woodwork). Decoration with appearance of a fold of linen, derived from a moulded rib multiplied and stopped.

Lintel, a horizontal beam or stone over a doorway, window or fireplace.

Long house, vernacular building of long rectangular plan with living-room(s) and byre under one roof, with common entrance.

Loop, small narrow window with its head rounded (12th century), pointed (13th century) or square (12th, 13th and 14th centuries).

Louver (Louvre) (Fr. *l'ouvert*). Smoke turret; lantern-like structure placed on the roof over the central hearth, with side openings for the escape of smoke.

Lozenge, diamond figure.

Machicolation, opening in floor of projecting parapet of a castle between supporting corbels, through which missiles could be dropped on to assailants at base of wall. Translation of hoards into stone.

Mask stop, stop at the end of a hoodmould, with distant resemblance to the human face.

Merlon, solid part of embattled parapet between embrasures, sometimes pierced with slit.

Mitre, junction of two timbers at an angle of 45 degrees.

Mortice, cavity cut in the end of a timber to receive the tenon.

Motte, artificial steep circular mound for a castle.

Moulding, ornamental outline of capitals, cornice, etc.

Mullion, vertical bar dividing the lights of a window.

Muntin, intermediate upright in panelling.

Nail-head, 12th-century ornament like a small pyramid.

Newel, central pillar round which wind the steps of a circular (newel or turnpike) staircase or vice, made up of the rounded projection of each step; also the principal post at the angles of a dog-legged or wall staircase, into which the handrail is framed.

Notch, V-shaped indentation in an edge or across a surface.

Ogee, double continuous curve, convex passing into concave.

Or, gold (heraldic).

Oriel, originally a projection or built-out gallery, often a porch outside an upper entrance reached by an external staircase, later a projection usually containing a window. Now chiefly used for a window corbelled out from an upper storey. *See* BAY WINDOW.

Outshut, Outshot, lean-to extension.

Parchemin, parchment panel, kindred to linenfold. Here the central rib branches to the four corners, stopped by ogival curves.

Parlour, private sitting-room on ground floor, often under the solar, in the later Middle Ages.

Patera (pl. *Paterae*), flat ornament, usually a square four-petalled flower, or four-lobed leaf, used in cornice, frieze and mouldings.

Pediment, triangular low-pitched gable over a classical portico, or over doorways, windows, etc.

Pentice, Pentise, Penthouse, lean-to building or covered passage or gallery.

Pier (Latin *petra* = rock). Mass of masonry, as distinct from a column, from which an arch springs. Also used, less correctly, for pillar or column in Gothic architecture.

Pilaster, shallow rectangular pier attached to wall.

Pillar. See COLUMN.

Piscina, built-in stone basin near altar for washing the chalice. Derives from Latin *piscis* = fish, and first used for a fish-pond.

Plank-and-muntin, a partition of vertical posts (muntins) tenoned into sill and moulded beam, forming a framework into which long panels were set, their edge tapered to fit into a groove (or rebate) in the muntin.

Plinth, projecting base of a wall or columns.

Portcullis (Fr. *porte coulis* = sliding door). Iron-shod wooden grating, a movable gate for defence, rising or falling in vertical grooves in the jambs of a gateway.

Postern, back door.

Principal rafters, the pair of inclined timbers that also serve as enlarged common rafters (box frame derivation.)

Principals, the main inclined timbers of a roof truss on which rest the purlins which support the common rafters (cruck frame carpentry).

Purlin, longitudinal horizontal beam.

> *Butt purlin*, one interrupted by trusses at bay intervals, received on the sides of the principal rafters (box frame carpentry system).

> *Collar purlin*, one supporting a collar, or collars.

> *Side purlin*, one supporting the common rafters, part way up the slope of a pitched roof and carried by roof-trusses, partitions and end walls.

> *Through purlin*, one running uninterruptedly from end to end of building, carried on the backs of the principals (cruck frame derivation).

Quadripartite, consisting of four parts (*see* VAULTING).

Quatrefoil, four-leaved (*see* FOIL).

Queen-post, pair of vertical posts standing on the tie-beam and supporting the side-purlins.

Quirk, sharp V-shaped incision in moulding.

Quoin (Fr. *coin* = angle). Dressed corner-stones of building.

Rafters, common, the regularly spaced inclined timbers which support the roof covering. *See also* PRINCIPAL RAFTERS.

Rear arch, internal arch over door or window opening.

Rear-vault, space between rear arch and outer stonework of window.

Rebate, rectangular recess or groove cut longitudinally to receive a(nother) timber; e.g. recess in door jamb into which door fits.

Reredorter, monastic latrine building.

Respond, half pillar or half pier attached to the wall to support an arch.

Ridge purlin, longitudinal timber at the apex of a roof, against which rest the upper ends of the rafters.

Roll-moulding, moulding of rounded section.

Rubble, rough walling of unsquared stone or flint.

> *Coursed rubble*, with stones very roughly dressed and levelled.

Scallop, shellfish, common in heraldry.

Scalloped capital, development of cushion capital in which the cushion is elaborated into a series of truncated cones.

Scantling, dimensions of a piece of timber in breadth and thickness, but not including length.

Scarfed joint, one in which two pieces of timber are bevelled or notched so that they overlap without increase of thickness, and are then pegged.

Scissor-braces, crossed timbers usually halved at the crossing, bracing the rafters, in the form of a St Andrew's Cross.

Screens, wooden partitions at lower end of hall, separating the latter from the entry or service *screens passage*, a cross-passage which has hall entrances and doorways to pantry, buttery and kitchen passages.

Sexpartite, consisting of six parts. *See* VAULTING.

Shaft, slender column.

Shafted Jambs, jambs with one or more shafts engaged or detached, at the angle with the wall.

Shingle, wooden roofing tile, of cleft oak.

Sinister, heraldic; on left side of shield, i.e. on spectator's right.

Slit, narrow window for defence, deeply splayed within, to get maximum light. *See* LOOP.

Soffit, under-surface of arch, lintel, canopy, etc.

Soffit cusp, cusp springing from the flat soffit of an arched head, not from the chamfered side or edge (CHAMFER CUSP).

Solar (Fr. *sol* = floor, *solive* = beam). Private room always on upper level, often the private bed-sittingroom of the owner and his family (great chamber).

Sole-piece, short horizontal timber lying across the wall-top, forming base of small triangle sustaining the foot of a common rafter.

Span, breadth of opening between imposts of arch, walls of room, etc.

Spandrel, triangular space between the shoulder of an arch and its rectangular frame, or between a curved brace and tie-beam, etc.

Spere, barrier; short wooden screen projecting at side of doorway.

Spere-truss, the side-posts of the spere forming part of a roof truss, the middle part being commonly closed by a movable screen.

Squinch, arch across an interior angle, e.g. of square tower as support for side of octagon.

Squint, opening in wall affording view into adjoining apartment.

Stanchion, upright iron bar between mullions of window, screen, etc.

Stop, ornamental termination to a moulding or chamfer.

String-course, projecting horizontal band, usually moulded.

Strut, sloping timber supporting a beam, etc.

Studs, intermediate posts between the main ones of a timber frame.

Sub-cusp, secondary cusp.

Template:

(1) Wooden or metal pattern for cutting mouldings.

(2) Horizontal wall timber, square and 4 to 5 feet long to distribute weight of wall post and roof.

Tenon, projection at the end of a timber to fit into the mortice of the next.

Tie-beam, transverse horizontal beam at or near wall-top level, tying together the feet of the rafters and preventing their spread. It is above the wall plate in box-framed types of roof, below it in cruck construction.

Timber-framed, constructed of a wooden skeleton with filling of wattle-and-daub, brick, etc.

Tracery, stone openwork pattern in head of Gothic window, screen, etc.

Bar tracery, made up of moulded bars forming geometrical figures, etc.

Plate tracery, cut out of a solid surface.

Transom, horizontal bar of wood or stone in window.

Trefoil, three-leaved. *See* FOIL.

Truss, triangular framework within roof, to be self-supporting and carry other timbers, purlins, etc. These divide the building into bays.

Tympanum, triangular space in the pediment of a classical building, semicircular solid space between the arch and lintel of a Gothic doorway or between the covering arch and lights of a window.

Undercroft, basement, cellar.

Vaulting, arched ceiling or roof in stone or brick, or imitated in wood and plaster.

Barrel vault, continuous arched vault, semi-circular, segmental or segmental-pointed, plain or with transverse ribs.

Fan vault, vault with numerous ribs springing in equal curves, to give fan-like effect; 15th and 16th centuries.

Groined vault, cross vaulting, formed by inter-section of simple vaulting surfaces.

Lierne vault, vault with short intermediate ribs not rising from the springing.

Quadripartite vault, vault of four compartments divided by ribs.

Ribbed vault, framework of arched ribs sup-porting vaulting cells covering the spaces between them.

Sexpartite vault, ribbed vault of six compart-ments.

Vaulting rib, arch supporting vault, arch or raised moulding on groin.

Vesica, pointed oval.

Vert, green (heraldic).

Vice (Fr. *vis* = screw, Latin *vitis* = vine). Spiral staircase. *See also* NEWEL.

Voussoirs, wedge-shaped stones forming an arch.

Wagon roof. See BARREL ROOF.

Wall arcade, series of arches, blind or with win-dow apertures, on a wall face.

Wall plate, horizontal timber along wall top to receive ends of the common rafters, etc. In timber-framing, the studs are tenoned into it.

Ward, bailey, courtyard of castle.

Wattle-and-daub, hurdlework of vertical stakes, interwoven with mixture of clay strengthened with straw, cow-hair, etc., and finished with plaster.

Wave-moulding, slight convex curve between two concave curves (hollows) typical of mid 14th century.

Wealden house, now known to be of wider distribution than Kent. A house with open hall between two-storeyed blocks, the roof with continuous eaves, the deeper projection over the hall being supported by curved braces from the jettied end chambers.

Weather-boarding, a series of horizontal boards set up on a sill, each overlapping the next, to throw off rain. The boards are wedge-shaped in section, the upper edge being the thinner.

Weathering, sloping surface (to buttresses, hood-moulds, etc.) to throw off rain.

Wind-brace, subsidiary timber inserted between purlins and principals to resist lateral thrust and wind pressure. May be straight, curved or cusped. Two tiers or three usual.

Winder, step that changes direction at bend.

Yale, a heraldic composite animal, like a spotted deer with swivelling horns.

BIBLIOGRAPHY

ADDY, S. O. (1933). *The Evolution of the English House*. Ed. J. Summerson. London: Allen & Unwin.

ANDREWS, W. J. & ATKINSON, T. D. (1929). *King John's House at Romsey*.

ATKINSON, F. & McDOWALL, R. W. (1967). Aisled Houses in the Halifax area. *Antiquaries' Journal*, XLVII, 77–94. London.

ATKINSON, T. D. (1933). *The Architectural History of the Benedictine Monastery of Saint Etheldreda at Ely*. Cambridge University Press.

BAILLIE REYNOLDS, P. K. *See under* Ministry of Works Guides (8, 17, 23, 40).

BARLEY, M. V. (1961). *The English Farmhouse and Cottage*. London: Routledge.

BIDDLE, M. (1961–2). The deserted medieval village of Seacourt, Berkshire. *Oxoniensia*, XXVI/XXVII, 70–201. Oxford.

BIDDLE, M., BARFIELD, L. & MILLARD, A. (1959). The Excavation of the Manor of the More, Rickmansworth, Hertfordshire. *Archaeological Journal*, CXVI, 136–99. London.

BORENIUS, T. & CHARLTON, J. (1936). Clarendon Palace: An Interim Report. *Antiquaries' Journal*, XVI, 55–84. London.

BORENIUS, T. & TRISTRAM, E. W. (1927). *English Medieval Painting*. Paris: Pegasus Press.

BRACE, H. W. (1954). *Gainsborough Old Hall*, guide.

BRAKSPEAR, SIR H. (1905). *Waverley Abbey*. Surrey Archaeological Society.

(1912). Bewley Court, Lacock. *Wiltshire Archaeological and Natural History Magazine*, CXVII, 391–399. Devizes.

(1916). The Bishop's Palace, Sonning. *Berkshire, Buckinghamshire and Oxfordshire Archaeological Journal*, XXII, 9–21.

(1933 a). The Abbot's House at Battle. *Archaeologia*, LXXXIII, 139–66. London.

(1933 b). Wigmore Abbey. *Archaeological Journal*, XC, 36–9. London.

BRAUN, H. (1936). *The English Castle*. London: Batsford.

(1940). *The Story of the English House*. London: Batsford.

(1951). *An Introduction to English Mediaeval Architecture*, 155–85, 237 *et seq.* London: Faber & Faber.

BROWN, R. A. (1954). *English Mediaeval Castles*. London: Batsford.

CHADWICK, S. J. (1911). The Moot Hall, Dewsbury. *Yorkshire Archaeological and Topographical Journal*, XXI, 345–51.

CHAMBERS, G. E. (1937). The French Bastides and the Town Plan of Winchelsea. *Archaeological Journal*, XCIV, 177–206. London.

CHARLES, F. W. B. (1967). *Mediaeval Cruck-Building and its derivatives*. Society for Medieval Archaeology, Monograph No. 2.

CHATWIN, P. B. & HARCOURT, E. G. (1941–2). The Bishop Vesey houses and other old buildings in Sutton Coldfield. *Transactions of the Birmingham Archaeological Society*, LXIV, 1–19.

CLAPHAM, A. W. (1923). Diagrams of house types in Royal Commission on Historical Monuments *Essex*, IV, xxxv.

(1930). *English Romanesque Architecture before the Conquest*. Oxford University Press.

(1934). *English Romanesque Architecture after the Conquest*. Oxford University Press.

(1948). Tour of Southampton (research paper).

See also under Ministry of Works Guides (40).

CLAPHAM, A. W. & GODFREY, W. H. (1913). *Some Famous Buildings and their Story*. Technical Journals.

COLVIN, H. M. (1958). Domestic Architecture and Town Planning. In A. Lane-Poole (ed.) *Mediaeval England*, I, 38–97. Oxford University Press.

CORDINGLEY, R. A. (1961). British Historical Roof-Types and their Members: A classification. *Transactions of the Ancient Monuments Society*, N.S., IX, 73–118. London.

(1963). Stokesay Castle, Shropshire: the chronology of its buildings. *The Art Bulletin*, XLV, 91–107. College Art Association of America.

CORDINGLEY, R. A. & WOOD-JONES, R. B. (1959). Chorley Hall, Cheshire. *Transactions of the Ancient Monuments Society*, N.S., VII, 61–86. London.

Country Life:

(1) *Alston Court, Nayland, Suffolk* (C. Hussey). 19 July 1924, 100–3.

(2a) *Appleton Manor, Berkshire*. 11 May 1929, 670–7.

(2b) *Athelhampton Hall, Dorset*. 2 June 1906, 786–94; 9 June 1906, 834–42; 23 June 1906, 906–12.

(3) *Bisham Abbey, Berkshire* (E. T. Long). 12 April 1941, 320–4; 19 April 1941, 342–6; 26 April 1941, 364–8.

(4) *Bradley Manor, Devon* (D. Woolner). 1 Sept. 1944, 378–9.

(5) *Brinsop Court, Herefordshire*. 22 May 1909, 738–46; 7 Nov. 1914, 614–22; 14 Nov. 1914, 647–52.

(6) *Clevedon Court, Somerset* (A. Oswald). 30 June 1955, 1672–5; 7 July 1955, 16–19.

(7a) *Coker Court, Somerset*. 2 Jan. 1909, 18–25.

(7b) *Manor Farm, Frampton-on-Severn, Gloucestershire* (C. Hussey). 19 Nov. 1927, 736–42.

(8) *Saving an Historic Building (Gainsborough Old Hall)* (M. U. Jones). 16 Sept. 1954, 910–12.

(9) *The Old Deanery, Gloucester* (A. Oswald). 13 April 1951, 1102–6.

(10) *Haddon Hall, Derbyshire* (C. Hussey). 2 Dec. 1949, 1651–6; 9 Dec. 1949, 1742–6; 16 Dec. 1949, 1814–18; 23 Dec. 1949, 1884–8.

(11) *Harvington Hall, Worcestershire* (C. Hussey). 4 Aug. 1944, 200–3; 11 Aug. 1944, 244–7; 18 Aug. 1944, 288–91.

(12) *Little Sodbury Manor House, Gloucestershire* (C. Hussey). 7 Oct. 1922, 40–7.

(13) *Lytes Cary Manor House, Somerset* (C. Hussey). 18 July 1947, 128–31; 25 July 1947, 178–81; 1 Aug. 1947, 228–31.

(14) *Monks at a Cambridge College. A 15th-century room at Magdalene restored* (A. Oswald). 7 Nov. 1952, 1486–7.

(15) *Manorbier Castle, Pembrokeshire* (C. Hussey). 23 Sept. 1939, 308–12.

(16) *Markenfield Hall*. 10 Feb. 1912, 206–12; 28 Dec. 1940, 566–70.

(17) *Mells, Somerset* (C. Hussey). 30 April 1943, 792–5.

(18) *Milton Abbas, Dorset* (M. Conway). 29 May 1915, 734–41; 5 June 1915, 770–5.

(19) *Nettlestead Place, Kent* (A. Oswald). 16 Oct. 1958, 832–5; 23 Oct. 1958, 886–9.

(20) *The Norman House in Norwich and the 'Music House'* (W. Buston). 21 Aug. 1942, 360–1.

(21) *Nunney Castle, Somerset* (C. Hussey). 29 Jan. 1943, 218–21; 5 Feb. 1943, 264–7.

(22) *Ockwells Manor, Bray*. 2 April 1904, 486–95.

(23) *Penshurst Place, Kent*. 2 Dec. 1911, 844–54; 9 Dec. 1911, 894–902.

(24) *Saltford Manor House, Somerset* (Bryan Little). 24 July 1958, 178–81.

(25) *Shute Barton, Devon* (C. Hussey). 2 Feb. 1951, 326–30; 9 Feb. 1951, 398–401.

(26) *Southwick Hall, Northamptonshire* (A. Oswald). 24 May 1962, 1236–40; 31 May 1962, 1298–1301.

(27) *Thame Park, Oxfordshire* (A. Oswald). 21 Nov. 1957, 1092–5, 28 Nov. 1957; 1148–51.

(28) *Wanswell Court, Gloucestershire* (A. Oswald). 16 Sept. 1954, 894–7.

(29) *Wenlock Abbey, Shropshire* (C. Hussey). 1 Dec. 1960, 1282–5; 8 Dec. 1960, 1432–5; 15 Dec. 1960, 1492–5.

(30) *West Coker Manor, Somerset* (C. Hussey). 14 Oct. 1922, 470–4.

(31) *Woodlands Manor, Mere* (F. Meyrick Jones). 10 May 1924, 732–8; 17 May 1924, 776–83.

(32) *Wortham Manor, Devon* (A. Oswald). 31 May 1956, 1174–7; 7 June 1956, 1228–31.

(33) *Restoration of York Guildhall* (G. B. Wood). 16 Nov. 1961, 1190–1.

COUNCIL FOR BRITISH ARCHAEOLOGY (1955). Research Report 3, *The Investigation of Smaller Domestic Buildings.* (Reprinted from *Archaeologia Cambrensis,* CIV.)

CRAMP, R. (1957). Beowulf and Archaeology. *Medieval Archaeology,* I, 57–77, especially 68 *et seq.*

CROSSLEY, F. H. (1935). *The English Abbey.*

(1951). *Timber Building in England.* London: Batsford.

DAVIS, H. W. C. (ed.) (1924). *Mediaeval England.*

DICKINSON, P. G. M. (1946). *Historic Hemingford Grey,* 28–35.

(in press). Early 13th-century roofs in Suffolk. *Proceedings of the Suffolk Institute of Archaeology and Natural History* (forthcoming).

DOLLMAN, F. T. & JOBBINS, J. R. (1861, 1863). *An Analysis of Ancient Domestic Architecture,* I (1861); II (1863).

DRINKWATER, N. (1964). The Old Deanery, Salisbury. *Antiquaries' Journal,* XLIV, 41–59. London. Norrington Manor House (forthcoming).

DUFTY, A. R. (1947). Place Farm, Tisbury. *Archaeological Journal,* CIV, 168–9. London.

DUNNING, G. C. (1961). Medieval Chimney Pots. In *Studies in Building History,* ed. E. M. Jope, 78–93.

(1962). The Pottery Louver from Goosegate, Nottingham. *Transactions of the Thoroton Society of Nottinghamshire,* LXVI, 20–3.

EAMES, E. S. (1957–8). A tile pavement from the Queen's Chamber, Clarendon Palace, dated 1250–2. *Journal of the British Archaeological Association,* 3rd Series, XX–XXI, 95–106. London.

(1963). A thirteenth-century tile pavement from the King's Chapel, Clarendon Palace. *Journal of the British Archaeological Association,* 3rd series, XXVI, 40–50. London.

EMERY, A. (1958). Dartington Hall. *Archaeological Journal,* CXV, 184–202. London.

ENGLEFIELD, H. C. (1801 and 1805). *A Walk through Southampton* (1st & 2nd edns).

(1808). Account of an Ancient Building in Southampton. *Archaeologia,* XIV, 84.

EVANS, J. (1948). *Art in Mediaeval France.* Oxford University Press.

(1949). *English Art.* Oxford University Press.

EVERETT, A. W. (1934). St Katherine's Priory (Polsloe) Exeter. *Proceedings of the Devon Archaeological Exploration Society,* II. Exeter.

(1937). Leigh. *Buckfast Abbey Chronicle,* VII, No. 3, 148–57.

(1956). *The Rebuilding of the Hall of Compton Castle.*

(1958 a). Domestic Piscinas in Devon. *Transactions of the Devon Association,* XC, 126–8.

(1958 b). A note on·Bowhill, Exeter. *Archaeological Journal*, CXV, 203–6. London.

   See also under National Trust Guides (2).

FAULKNER, P. A. (1958). Domestic Planning from the Twelfth to the Fourteenth Centuries. *Archaeological Journal*, CXV, 150–84. London.

   (1961). Haddon Hall and Bolsover Castle. *Archaeological Journal*, CXVIII, 188–205. London.

   (1962–3). A model of Castle Acre Priory. *Medieval Archaeology*, VI-VII, 300–3. London.

   (1963). Castle Planning in the Fourteenth Century (re Goodrich, Bolton and Bodiam). *Archaeological Journal*, CXX, 215–35. London.

   (1966). Medieval Undercrofts and Town Houses. *Archaeological Journal*, CXXIII, 120–35. London.

FERRY, E. B. (1870). *South Winfield Manor.*

FLETCHER, SIR BANISTER (1946). *A History of Architecture on the Comparative Method* (13th edn.). London: Batsford.

FLETCHER, J. M. (1961). Master John atte Halle, John de Harewell. *Harlequin*, Summer number. Harwell: Atomic Energy Research Establishment.

   (1961–2). Cruck Cottage in Church Lane, Harwell. *Oxoniensia*, XXVI/XXVII, 207–14.

   (1962). Middle Farm, Harwell. *Harlequin*, Spring number, 50–5. Harwell: Atomic Energy Research Establishment.

   (1963). Radiocarbon dating of Cruck Cottages and Barns. *Transactions of Newbury District Field Club*, XI, No. 2, 94–7.

   (1965–6). Three Medieval Farmhouses in Harwell. *Berkshire Archaeological Journal*, LXII, 45–69.

FLETCHER, J. M. & SPOKES, P. S. (1964). The Origin and Development of Crown-Post Roofs. *Medieval Archaeology*, VI. London.

FLOYER, J. KESTELL (1905). Warton Old Rectory, Lancashire. *Transactions of Lancashire and Cheshire Historical Society*, N.S., XXI, 28–47.

FORREST, H. E. (1935). *The Old Houses of Shrewsbury.* London: Wilding.

FORRESTER, H. (1959). *The Timber-framed Houses of Essex.*

FOSTER, I. LL. & ALCOCK, L. (eds.) (1963). *Culture and Environment: Essays in Honour of Sir Cyril Fox.* London: Routledge.

FOX, A. (1958). A monastic homestead on Dean Moor, south Devon. *Medieval Archaeology*, II, 141–57. London.

FOX, SIR CYRIL (1932). *The Personality of Britain.* Cardiff: The National Museum of Wales.

FOX, SIR CYRIL & RAGLAN, LORD (1951). *Monmouthshire Houses*, I. Cardiff: The National Museum of Wales.

FOX, L. (1944). *Leicester Castle.*

GARNER, T. & STRATTON, A. (1929). *Domestic Architecture of England during the Tudor Period* (2nd edn). London: Batsford.

GEE, E. A. (1958). Some Dating Criteria. *Vernacular Architecture Group Occasional Paper*, No. 1.

GILYARD-BEER, R. A. (1958). *Abbeys.*

GODFREY, W. H. (1911). *The English Staircase.*

   (1926). Michelham Priory. *Sussex Archaeological Collections*, LXVII, 1–24. Lewes.

   (1928). *The Story of Architecture in England*, I. London: Batsford.

   (1929). Thame Park. *Archaeological Journal*, LXXXVI, 59–68. London.

   (1931). A Fourteenth Century Hall at Hamsey. *Sussex Notes and Queries*, III, No. 5, 133–6. Lewes.

   (1932). Charleston Manor House. *Sussex Notes and Queries*, IV, No. 2. Lewes.

(1936). Swanborough Manor House. *Sussex Archaeological Collections*, LXXVII, 3–14. Lewes.

(1947). St Mary's and Priory Cottage, Bramber. *Sussex Archaeological Collections*, LXXXVI, 102–17.

(1950). The Deanery, Wells. *Archaeological Journal*, CVII, 110–12. London.

(1952). English cloister lavatories as independent structures. *Archaeological Journal*, CVI, supplement, 91–7. London.

(1955). *The English Almshouse*. London: Faber & Faber.

(1962). *A History of Architecture In and Around London* (2nd edn). London: Phoenix House.

GOTCH, J. A. (1909). *Growth of the English House*. London: Batsford.

GROSE, F. (1774, 1777). *Antiquities of England and Wales*, II (1774); V (1777).

HAMILTON, J. R. C. (1956). *Excavations of Jarlshof, Shetland. See also under* Ministry of Works Guides (21).

HANNAH, I. C. (1927). Houses in the Close at Chichester. *Sussex Archaeological Collections*, LXVIII, 143–8. Lewes.

HARVEY, J. H. (1946). *Henry Yevele: the Life of An English Architect*. London: Batsford.

(1947). *Gothic England, a Survey of National Culture 1300–1550*. London: Batsford.

(1954). *English Mediaeval Architects*. London: Batsford.

HEARNSHAW, F. J. C. & LUCAS, R. MACDONALD (1932). *Description and History of Tudor House, and the Norman House traditionally known as 'King John's Palace'* (19th edn) (obtainable at the Tudor House Museum, Southampton).

HEMP, W. J. (1942–3). Early timber work at Henblas, Llandderfel and Pengarth Fawr Llanarmon. *Archaeologia Cambrensis*, XCVII, 67–76. Cardiff. *See also under* Ministry of Works Guides (13).

HEWETT, C. A. (1961). Timber buildings in Essex: some evidence for the possible origins of the Lap Dovetail. *Transactions of the Ancient Monuments Society*, N.S., IX, 33–56.

(1962 a). Giant Barns of an Essex Farm (Cressing Temple near Witham). *Country Life Annual*, 147–150. London: *Country Life*.

(1962 b). The Timber Belfries of Essex: their Significance in the Development of English Carpentry. *Archaeological Journal*, CXIX, 225–44. London.

(1962–3). Structural carpentry in medieval Essex. *Medieval Archaeology*, VI–VII, 240–71. London.

HILL, J. W. F. (1948). *Medieval Lincoln*. Cambridge University Press.

HILL, J. W. F. & PANTIN, W. A. (1953). *The Cardinal's Hat, 286 High Street, Lincoln*.

HODGSON, J. F. (1896). The chapel of Auckland Castle. *Archaeologia Aeliana*, 2nd. S., XVIII, 113–240. Newcastle-upon-Tyne.

HOHLER, C. (1941–2). Medieval Paving-tiles in Buckinghamshire. *Records of Bucks.*, XIV, 1–49. Aylesbury.

HOLMES, U. T., Jnr (1953). *Daily Living in the Twelfth Century*. Madison: the University of Wisconsin Press.

(1959). Houses of the Bayeux Tapestry. *Speculum*, XXXIV, 179–83.

HOMAN, W. MACLEAN (Unpublished). Plans and sections of Winchelsea cellars, deposited in the Sussex Record Office at Chichester; available to students.

HOPE, W. H. ST JOHN (1900). Fountains Abbey. *Yorkshire Archaeological Journal*, XV, 120–5. Leeds.

(1908). Ludlow Castle. *Archaeologia*, LXI, 276–325. London.

(1919). *Cowdray and Eastbourne Priory*.

HOPE-TAYLOR, B. K. (1950). The Excavation of a Motte at Abinger in Surrey. *Archaeological Journal*, CVII, 15–43. London.

(in press). *The Saxon Palace at Yeavering*. London: Ministry of Works.

HORN, W. (1958). On the Origins of the Mediaeval Bay System. *Journal of the Society of Architectural Historians*, XVIII, No. 2, 2–23.

  (1963). The Great Tithe Barn of Cholsey, Berkshire. *Journal of the Society of Architectural Historians*, XXII, No. 1, 13–23.

HORN, W. & BORN, C. (1965). *The Barns of the Abbey of Beaulieu at its Granges of Great Coxwell and Beaulieu-St Leonards*. University of California Press.

HOWARD, F. E. & CROSSLEY, F. H. (1933). *English Church Woodwork and Furniture*. London: Batsford.

HURST, J. G. (1957, 1958, 1960). Wharram Percy, Yorkshire. *Medieval Archaeology*, I, 166–8; II, 205–7; IV, 164. London.

  (1961). The kitchen area of Northolt Manor, Middlesex. *Medieval Archaeology*, V, 211–99.

HUSSEY, C. (1951). *English Country Houses open to the Public*. London: Country Life.

See also under Country Life (1, 7 b, 10, 11, 12, 13, 15, 17, 21, 25, 29, 30).

JACKSON, G. (1956). *The Story of Bolton Castle*.

JONES, S. R. & SMITH, J. T. (1958). Wasperton Manor Farm, Warwickshire. *Transactions of the Birmingham Archaeological Society*, LXXVI, 19–28.

  (1960). The great hall of the bishop's palace at Hereford. *Medieval Archaeology*, IV, 69–80.

JOPE, E. M. (1961). Cornish Houses 1400–1700. *Studies in Building History, Essays in recognition of the work of B. H. St J. O'Neil* (ed. Jope), 192–220. London: Odhams Press.

JOPE, E. M. & DUNNING, G. C. (1954). The Use of Blue Slate for Roofing in Medieval England. *Antiquaries' Journal*, XXXIV, 209–17. London.

JOPE, E. M. & THRELFALL, R. I. (1958). Excavation of a medieval settlement at Beere, North Tawton, Devon. *Medieval Archaeology*, II, 112–40. London.

KENT, E. A. (1945). Isaac's Hall, or the Music House, Norwich. *Norfolk Archaeology*, XXVIII, 28–38. Norwich.

KING, D. J. C. & PERKS, J. C. (1962). Carew Castle, Pembrokeshire. *Archaeological Journal*, CXIX, 270–307. London.

KIPPS, P. K. (1933). The Palace of the Archbishops of Canterbury at Charing, Kent. *Archaeological Journal*, XC, 78–97. London.

  (1935). The chapel of the Knights Hospitallers at Sutton-at-Hone. *Archaeologia Cantiana*, XLVII, 205–10. London.

KNOWLES, W. H. (1898). The Camera of Adam of Jesmond, popularly called King John's Palace. *Archaeologia Aeliana*, 2nd S., XIX, 29–38. Newcastle-upon-Tyne.

  (1899). Aydon Castle. *Archaeologia*, LVI, 71–88. London.

LAWSON, P. H. & SMITH, J. T. (1958). The Rows of Chester, two interpretations. *Chester Archaeological Society Journal*, XLV, 1–42.

LINDUS FORGE, J. W. (1959). Coombe Hill Conduit House, and the water supply of Hampton Court Palace. *Surrey Archaeological Collections*, LVI, 3–14.

LLOYD, N. (1931). *A History of the English House*. London: Architectural Press.

  (1934). *A History of English Brickwork*. Montgomery.

LONG, E. T. (1938, 1939 a). Medieval Domestic Architecture in Oxfordshire. *Oxfordshire Archaeological Society Reports*, LXXXIV, 45–56; LXXXV, 97.

  (1939 b, 1940, 1941). Medieval Domestic Architecture in Berkshire. *Berkshire Archaeological*

Journal, XLIII, 101–5; XLIV, 39–48, 101–13; XLV, 28–36. Datchet.

See also under Country Life (3).

MARKHAM, C. A. (1903–4). The Manor House of Yardley Hastings. *Associated Archaeological Societies Reports*, XXVII, 401–7.

MARSDEN, T. L. (1962). Donington-le-Heath Manor House Farm, Leicestershire. *Transactions of the Ancient Monuments Society*, N.S., X, 33–42.

MASON, R. T. (1957). Fourteenth-Century Halls in Sussex. *Sussex Archaeological Collections*, XCV, 71–93. Lewes.

(1958). Four Single-Bay Halls. *Sussex Archaeological Collections*, XCVI, 9–16. Lewes.

(1960). Dunster's Mill House, Ticehurst. *Sussex Archaeological Collections*, XCVIII, 150–5. Lewes.

(1964). *Framed Buildings of the Weald.* Handcross: R. T. Mason.

MINISTRY OF WORKS GUIDES:

(1) *Acton Burnell Castle, Shropshire* (C. A. Ralegh Radford), 1957.

(2) *Ashby de la Zouch Castle, Leicestershire* (T. L. Jones), 1953.

(3) *The Early Christian & Norse Settlements at Birsay, Orkney* (C. A. Ralegh Radford), 1959.

(4) *Bishop's Waltham Palace, Hampshire* (in preparation).

(5) *The Mediaeval Tithe Barn, Bradford-on-Avon, Wiltshire*, 1953.

(6) *Burton Agnes Old Manor House, Yorkshire* (M. E. Wood), 1956.

(7) *Caernarvon Castle* (Sir C. Peers), 1933.

(8) *Castle Acre Priory, Norfolk* (P. K. Baillie Reynolds), 1952.

(9) *Chepstow Castle, Monmouthshire* (J. C. Perks), 1955 & 1962.

(10) *Christchurch Castle Hall, Hampshire* (M. E. Wood), 1956.

(11) *Clifford's Tower, York* (B. H. St J. O'Neil), 1960.

(12) *Conway Castle & Town Walls, Caernarvonshire* (A. J. Taylor), 1956.

(13) *Denbigh Castle and Town Walls* (W. J. Hemp & C. A. Ralegh Radford), 1935.

(14) *Donnington Castle, Berkshire* (M. E. Wood), 1964.

(15) *Eltham Palace, Kent* (D. L. Strong), 1958.

(16) *Eynsford Castle, Kent* (S. E. Rigold), 1963.

(17) *Framlingham Castle, Suffolk* (F. J. E. Raby & P. K. Baillie Reynolds), 1946.

(18) *Goodrich Castle, Herefordshire* (C. A. Ralegh Radford), 1960.

(19) *Grosmont Castle, Monmouthshire* (C. A. Ralegh Radford), 1956.

(20) *Hampton Court Palace* (G. H. Chettle), 1946.

(21) *Jarlshof, Shetland* (J. R. C. Hamilton), 1957.

(22) *Jewel Tower, Westminster* (A. J. Taylor), 1956.

(23) *Kenilworth Castle, Warwickshire* (P. K. Baillie Reynolds), 1948.

(24) *Kirby Muxloe Castle, Leicestershire* (C. R. Peers), 1917.

(25) *Kirkham House, Paignton, Devon* (S. E. Rigold), 1963.

(26) *The Bishop's Palace, Lamphey, Pembrokeshire* (C. A. Ralegh Radford), 1959.

(27) *Longthorpe Tower, Northamptonshire* (E. Clive Rouse), 1949, 1957.

(28) *Minster Lovell Hall, Oxfordshire* (A. J. Taylor), 1958.

(29) *Netley Abbey, Hampshire* (A. Hamilton Thompson), 1937.

(30) *Nunney Castle, Somerset* (S. E. Rigold), 1956.

(31) *Ogmore Castle, Glamorgan* (C. A. Ralegh Radford), 1956.

(32) *Old Sarum, Wiltshire*, 1950, 1961.

MINISTRY OF WORKS GUIDES—*continued*

 (33) *Old Soar, Plaxtol, Kent* (M. E. Wood), 1953, 1961.

 (34) *Portchester Castle, Hampshire* (Sir C. Peers), 1957.

 (35) *Raglan Castle, Monmouthshire* (A. J. Taylor), 1950.

 (36) *Richmond Castle, Yorkshire* (C. R. Peers), 1926.

 (37) *The Bishop's Palace, St David's, Pembrokeshire* (C. A. Ralegh Radford), 1953.

 (38) *Sherborne Old Castle, Dorset* (to be published).

 (39) *Temple Manor, Strood, Rochester, Kent* (S. E. Rigold), 1962.

 (40) *Thornton Abbey, Lincolnshire* (A. W. Clapham & P. K. Baillie Reynolds), 1958.

 (41) *Tretower Court, Breconshire* (C. A. Ralegh Radford), 1948, etc.

 (42) *The Tribunal, Glastonbury, Somerset* (C. A. Ralegh Radford), 1953, 1956, etc.

 (43) *Warkworth Castle, Northumberland* (C. H. Hunter Blair & H. L. Honeyman), 1955.

 (1963) *The History of the King's Works* (R. Allen Brown, H. M. Colvin, A. J. Taylor). (Published after most of my MS. was complete.)

MOORE, MATLEY (1951). *The Greyfriars, Worcester.*

MORGAN, F. C. (1938). The Cruck Buildings of Herefordshire. *Woolhope Naturalists' Field Club Papers*, 99–119.

 (1953). Domestic Architecture of Herefordshire. *Transactions of the Ancient Monuments Society*, N.S., I, 58–73.

MYERS, A. R. (1959). *The Household of Edward IV.* Manchester University Press.

MYRES, J. N. L. (1934). Butley Priory, Suffolk. *Archaeological Journal*, XC, 177. London.

NATIONAL TRUST GUIDES:

 (1) *Bradley Manor, Devon* (D. Woolner), 1955.

 (2) *Compton Castle, Devon* (A. W. Everett), 1957.

 (3) *Cotehele, Cornwall* (J. Lees-Milne), 1956.

 (4) *Lytes Cary, Somerset* (M. Kearney), 1950.

 (5) *Tattershall Castle, Lincolnshire* (A. H. Thompson), 1937.

 (6) *The Vyne, Hampshire* (J. Lees-Milne), 1959.

NICHOLS, J. F. (1931). Southchurch Hall. *Journal of the British Archaeological Association*, N.S., XXXVII, 101. London.

NISBETT, N. C. H. (1894–7). Notes on the Roof of the Pilgrims' Hall, Winchester. *Proceedings of the Hampshire Field Club and Archaeological Society*, III, 71–7; Wolvesey Castle in the 12th century. Ibid. 207.

 (1906). Notes on a ruined building in Warnford Park. *Proceedings of the Hampshire Field Club and Archaeological Society*, V, 299–307.

NORMAN, P. & CAROE, W. D. (1908). *Crosby Place*; with plans, etc., by W. H. Godfrey.

OAKESHOTT, W. F. & HARVEY, J. H. (1955). *Winchester College.*

O'NEIL, H. E. (1956). Prestbury Moat, a Manor House of the Bishops of Hereford in Gloucestershire. *Transactions of the Bristol and Gloucestershire Archaeological Society*, LXXV, 5–34.

OSWALD, ADRIAN (1962–3). Excavation of a thirteenth-century wooden building at Weoley Castle, Birmingham, 1960–61. An interim report. *Medieval Archaeology*, VI–VII, 109–34.

OSWALD, ARTHUR (1933). *Country Houses of Kent.* London: *Country Life*.

(1935). *Country Houses of Dorset*. London: *Country Life.*

See also under Country Life (6, 9, 14, 26, 27, 28, 32).

PACKHAM, A. B. (1923). The Old Palace at West Tarring. *Sussex Archaeological Collections*, LXIV, 140–79. Lewes.

(1924). The Marlepins, New Shoreham. *Sussex Archaeological Collections*, LXV, 158–97. Lewes.

(1934). Portslade Manor House. *Sussex Archaeological Collections*, LXXV, 1–18. Lewes.

PANTIN, W. A. (1947). The Development of Domestic Architecture in Oxford. *Antiquaries' Journal*, XXVII, 120–50. London.

(ed.) (1948). *Durham Cathedral*. London: Lund, Humphries.

(1957). Medieval Priests' Houses in south-west England. *Medieval Archaeology*, I, 118–46. London.

(1959). Chantry Priests' Houses and other Medieval Lodgings. *Medieval Archaeology*, III, 216–58.

(1961). Medieval Inns. In *Studies in Building History*, ed. E. M. Jope, 166–91.

(1962–3 a). Medieval English town-house plans. *Medieval Archaeology*, VI-VII, 202–39. London.

(1962–3 b). The merchants' houses and warehouses of King's Lynn. *Medieval Archaeology*, VI-VII, 173–81. London.

(1963). Some Medieval English Town Houses, a study in adaptation. In *Culture and Environment*, ed. I. LL. Foster & L. Alcock, 445–78. London: Routledge.

(in press). Upper and Lower Halls in Priests' and some Lay Houses in Somerset and Devon.

PANTIN, W. A. & ROUSE, E. CLIVE (1955). The Golden Cross, Oxford. *Oxoniensia*, XX, 46–89. Oxford.

PARKER, J. H. (1853, 1859). *Some Account of Domestic Architecture in England*, II, from Edward I to Richard II (1853); III, pts I & II, from Richard II to Henry VIII (1859). (*See also* Turner.)

(1866). *Architectural Antiquities of the City of Wells.*

(1869). *A Concise Glossary of Architecture.*

Paston Letters, The. Ed. J. Warrington. Everyman's Library edition, 1956. London: J. M. Dent.

PAVRY, F. H. & KNOCKER, G. M. (1957–8). The Mount, Princes Risborough. *Records of Bucks.*, XVI, Part 3, 131–78. Aylesbury.

PEAKE, W. B. (1920). *Luddesdown Court, Kent.*

PECKHAM, W. D. (1921). The architectural history of Amberley Castle. *Sussex Archaeological Collections*, LXII, 21–63. Lewes.

(1939). The House of William Ryman. *Sussex Archaeological Collections*, CLXXX, 148–64. Lewes.

PEERS, (SIR) CHARLES. *See under* Ministry of Works Guides (7, 24, 34, 36).

PEVSNER, N. 'Buildings of England' Series. Harmondsworth: Penguin Books.

(1951). *Nottinghamshire.*

(1952 a). *North Devon.*

(1952 b). *South Devon.*

(1957). *Northumberland.*

(1958 a). *Shropshire.*

(1958 b). *North Somerset & Bristol.*

(1958 c). *South & West Somerset.*

(1961). *Northamptonshire.*

(1966). *Berkshire.*

PITT-RIVERS, A. H. (1890). *King John's House, Tollard Royal, Wiltshire.*

PLATT, C. (1962). Excavations at Dartington Hall, 1962. *Archaeological Journal*, CXIX, 208–24.

PORTMAN, D. (1958). Cruck Houses in Long Wittenham. *Berkshire Archaeological Journal*, LVI, 35–45.

POWER, E. (1925). *Medieval People*. London: Methuen.

POWICKE, F. M. (1947). *King Henry III and the Lord Edward*. Oxford University Press.

PUGIN, A. & A. W. (1838–40). *Examples of Gothic Architecture*, I (1838); II (1839); III (1840).

RADFORD, C. A. RALEGH (1957). The Saxon house, a review and some parallels. *Medieval Archaeology*, I, 30–3, 68–9, 94–103. London.
  (1960). Tretower: The Castle and the Court. *Brecknock Society, Brycheiniog*, VI, 1–50.
  (1962). Acton Burnell Castle. In *Studies in Building History* (ed. E. M. Jope), 94–103.
  See also under Ministry of Works Guides (1, 3, 13, 18, 19, 26, 31, 37, 41, 42).

RAHTZ, P. A. (1957). King John's Palace, Clipstone, Notts. *Medieval Archaeology*, I, 162–3. London.
  (1958). King John's Hunting Lodge, Writtle, Essex. *Medieval Archaeology*, II, 202–4. London.
  (1962–3). The Saxon and medieval palaces at Cheddar, Somerset—an interim report of excavations in 1960–2. *Medieval Archaeology*, VI–VII, 53–66. London.

RANSON, F. LINGARD (1937). *Lavenham, Suffolk*.

RIGOLD, S. E. (1958). The timber-framed buildings of Steventon and their regional significance. *Transactions of the Newbury District Field Club*, X, No. 4, 4–13.
  See also under Ministry of Works Guides (16, 25, 30, 39).

RILEY, H. T. (1868). *Memorials of London and London Life in the 13th, 14th and 15th Centuries*.

ROUSE, E. CLIVE (1927–33). Some recent discoveries at King John's Lodge, Wraysbury. *Records of Bucks.*, XII, 157–64. Aylesbury,
  See also under Ministry of Works Guides (27).

ROUSE, E. CLIVE & BAKER, A. (1955). Longthorpe Tower. *Archaeologia*, XCVI, 1–34. London.

ROUSE, E. CLIVE & BROADBENT, J. D. (1951–2). Further discoveries of tile fragments and wasters in connection with the fourteenth-century paving-tile and roof-tile kilns at Penn. *Records of Bucks.*, XV, 314–18. Aylesbury.

ROYAL COMMISSION ON HISTORICAL MONUMENTS:
  Anglesey (1937; reprinted 1960).
  Buckinghamshire, I (1912); II (1913).
  Caernarvonshire, I (1956).
  Cambridge, 2 vols. (1959).
  Dorset, I (1952); II (forthcoming).
  Essex, I (1916); II (1921); III (1922); IV (1923).
  Herefordshire, I (1931); II (1932); III (1934).
  Hertfordshire (1910).
  Huntingdonshire (1926).
  London, I (Westminster Abbey) (1924); II (West London) (1925); IV (The City) (1929); V (East London) (1930).
  Middlesex (1937).
  Oxford (1939).
  Westmorland (1936).
  (1963). *Monuments Threatened or Destroyed*.

SALZMAN, L. F. (1929). *English Life in the Middle Ages.* Oxford University Press.
  (1952). *Building in England down to 1540.* Oxford University Press.

SHUFFREY, L. A. (1912). *The English Fireplace.*

SIMPSON, W. DOUGLAS (1935). The Affinities of Lord Cromwell's Tower-house at Tattershall. *Journal of British Archaeological Association,* N.S., XL, 177–92. London.
  (1937). Buckden Palace. *Journal of the British Archaeological Association,* 3rd S., II, 121–32. London.
  (1938). Warkworth, Castle of Livery and Maintenance. *Archaeologia Aeliana,* 4th Series, XV, 115–36. Newcastle-upon-Tyne.
  (1939). The Castles of Dudley and Ashby de la Zouch. *Archaeological Journal,* XCVI, 142–58. London.
  (1940). Belsay Castle and the Scottish Tower Houses. *Archaeologia Aeliana,* 4th Series, XVII, 75–84. Newcastle-upon-Tyne.
  (1941). The Warkworth Donjon and its Architect. *Archaeologia Aeliana,* 4th Series, XIX, 93–103. Newcastle-upon-Tyne.
  (1942). Herstmonceux Castle. *Archaeological Journal,* XCIX, 110–22. London.
  (1946). Bastard Feudalism and the Later Castles. *Antiquaries' Journal,* XXVI, 145–71. London.

SIMPSON, W. DOUGLAS & BARNES, H. D. (1951). Caister Castle. *Norfolk Archaeology,* XXX, 178–88.
  (1952). Caister Castle. *Antiquaries' Journal,* XXXII, 35–51.

SMITH, J. T. (1955). Medieval Aisled Halls and their Derivatives. *Archaeological Journal,* CXII, 76–94. London.
  (1956). Stokesay Castle. *Archaeological Journal,* CXIII, 211–14. London.
  (1958 a). Medieval Roofs: A Classification. *Archaeological Journal,* CXV, 111–49. London.
  (1958 b). A 14th-Century Aisled House, Edgar's Farm, Stowmarket. *Proceedings of the Suffolk Institute of Archaeology and Natural History,* XXVII, 54–61.
  (1964). Cruck Construction: a survey of the problems. *Medieval Archaeology,* VIII, 119–51. London.
  (1965). Timber-framed building in England: its development and regional differences. *Archaeological Journal,* CXXII, 133–58. London.

SMITH, J. T. & STELL, C. F. (1960). Baguley Hall: the Survival of Pre-Conquest Building Traditions in the Fourteenth Century. *Antiquaries' Journal,* XL, 131–51. London.

SOUTHAMPTON MUSEUMS PUBLICATIONS (1959). No. 5: *Historic Buildings of Southampton.*

SPOKES, P. S. (1960). Some Notes on the Domestic Architecture of Abingdon. *Berkshire Archaeological Journal,* LVIII, 1–19.

SPOKES, P. S. & JOPE, E. M. (1959). The Priory, Marcham; a small 16th-century house. *Berkshire Archaeological Journal,* LVII, 86–97.

STEER, F. W. (1958). *The Vicars' Hall at Chichester and its Undercroft.*

STENTON, SIR F. (ed.) (1957). *The Bayeux Tapestry.* London: Phaidon Press.

STONE, P. G. (1891). *Architectural Antiquities of the Isle of Wight.*

STOW, J. (1598). *Survey of London.* Ed. C. L. Kingsford, 1908.

TANNER, L. & MOTTISTONE, LORD (1954). The Abbot's House and Deanery of Westminster Abbey. *Transactions of the Ancient Monuments Society,* N.S., II, 71–86.

TAYLOR, A. J. *See under* Ministry of Works Guides (12, 22, 28, 35).

TAYLOR, H. (1884). *The Old Halls of Lancashire and Cheshire.*

THOMPSON, A. HAMILTON (1912). *Military Architecture in England during the Middle Ages.* Oxford University Press.

  (1936). *The English House.* Historical Association, Pamphlet No. 105. London.

  (1941). Master Elias of Dereham and the King's Works. *Archaeological Journal*, XCVIII, 1–35. London.

  See also under Ministry of Works Guides (29), National Trust Guides (5).

THOMPSON, A. HAMILTON & FARNHAM, G. F. (1923–4). The Manor, House, and Church of Holt. *Transactions of the Leicestershire Archaeological Society*, XIII, 200–44.

THOMPSON, F. H. (1960). The deserted medieval village of Riseholme near Lincoln. *Medieval Archaeology*, IV, 95–108. London.

TIPPING, H. AVRAY (1921). *English Homes*, Periods I & II. London: *Country Life.*

TOY, S. (1929). Corfe Castle. *Archaeologia*, LXXIX, 88, 96. London.

  (1937). The Town and Castle of Conway. *Archaeologia*, LXXXVI, 163–92. London.

  (1946). Winchester House, Southwark. *Surrey Archaeological Collections*, XLIX, 75–81.

  (1953 a). Langney Grange, Westham. *Sussex Archaeological Collections*, XCI, 125–33. Lewes.

  (1953 b). *Castles of Great Britain.* London: Heinemann.

TREVELYAN, G. M. (1945). *English Social History.* London: Longmans.

TROTTER, T. (1934). *Cowdray.*

TUDOR-CRAIG, P. (1957). The Painted Chamber at Westminster. *Archaeological Journal*, CXIV, 92–105. London.

TURNER, T. HUDSON (1851). *Some Account of Domestic Architecture in England,* I, from the Conquest to the end of the thirteenth century. Oxford: J. H. Parker.

  For vols. II & III *see* Parker, J. H.

URRY, W. (1953). *The House of Jacob the Jew.* (Notes on the history of the County Hotel, Canterbury.)

VERDIER, A. & CATTOIS, F. (1855). *Architecture civile et domestique au moyen-âge et à la Renaissance.* Paris: Librairie archeologique de Didron.

VICTORIA COUNTY HISTORIES, especially:

  Berkshire, III (1914, pub. 1923).

  Cambridgeshire, IV (1953).

  Essex, IV (1956).

  Hampshire, III (1908); IV (1911); V (1912).

  Lancashire, VIII (1914).

  Northamptonshire, II (1906); IV (1937).

  Oxfordshire, VII (1962).

  Surrey, II (1911).

  Sussex, III (1935); IX (1937).

  Warwickshire, III (1945); IV (1947).

  Worcestershire, III (1913); IV (1914, pub. 1924).

  Yorkshire, I, North Riding (1914).

VIOLLET-LE-DUC, E. E. (1859). *Dictionnaire raisonné de l'architecture française du XIe au XVIe siècle.* Paris.

VIVIAN-NEAL, A. W. (1959–60). Cannington Court. *Proceedings of Somerset Archaeological and Natural History Society*, CIV, 62–86. Taunton.

WADMORE, J. F. (1897). The Knights Hospitallers in Kent. *Archaeologia Cantiana*, XXII, 232–74. London.

WALL, J. C. (1914). *Medieval Wall-paintings*.

WATKINS, W. (1913). St Mary's Guild, Lincoln. *Journal of the Royal Institute of British Architects*, 3rd Series, XX. London.

WALTON, J. (1948 a). The Development of the Cruck Framework. *Antiquity*, XXII, 179–89. Newbury.
  (1948 b). Cruck-framed buildings in Yorkshire. *Yorkshire Archaeological Journal*, CXLV, 49–66. Leeds.
  (1954). Hogback tombstones and the Anglo-Danish house. *Antiquity*, XXVIII, 68–77. Newbury.

WEBSTER, V. R. (1954). Cruck-framed buildings of Leicestershire. *Transactions of Leicestershire Archaeological Society*, XXX, 26–58. Leicester.

WOOD, M. E. (1935). Norman Domestic Architecture. *Archaeological Journal*, XCII, 167–242. London.
  (1937). A Late Fifteenth-Century House in George St, St Albans. *Transactions of St Albans and Hertfordshire Architectural and Archaeological Society*, 99–104.
  (1949). A Fourteenth-Century House at Marlow, Bucks. *Journal of British Archaeological Association*, 3rd Series, XII, 54–6. London.
  (1950). Thirteenth-Century Domestic Architecture in England. *Archaeological Journal*, CV, Supplement. London.
  (1951 a). Measuring a Medieval House. *Lincolnshire Historian*, No. 7, 273–7. Lincoln.
  (1951 b). The Bishop's Palace, Lincoln. *Lincolnshire Historian*, No. 7, 278–80. Lincoln.
  (1951 c). Number 3 Vicars' Court, Lincoln. *Lincolnshire Historian*, No. 7, 281–6. Lincoln.
  (1952). Deloraine Court, Lincoln. *Lincolnshire Historian*, No. 10, 356–8. Lincoln.
  (1963). Norman Domestic Architecture. *Transactions of the Newbury District Field Club*, XI, No. 2, 5–40.
  See also under Ministry of Works Guides (6, 10, 14, 33).

WOOD, M. E. & SALMON, J. (1949). An Early House at Upper Millichope. *Transactions of the Shropshire Archaeological Society*, LIII, 61–7.

WOOD-JONES, R. B. (1956). The Banbury Region, Minor Domestic Architecture before 1600. *Transactions of the Ancient Monuments Society*, N.S., IV, 133–46.

WORDSWORTH, C. (1915–17). Elias de Dereham's Leadenhall in Salisbury Close. *Wiltshire Archaeological Magazine*, XXXIX, 433–44. Devizes.

WRIGHT, L. (1960). *Clean and Decent: The Fascinating History of the Bathroom and the Water Closet*. London: Routledge.

WYNDHAM, W. P. (1779). Observations on an Ancient Building at Warnford. *Archaeologia*, V, 357–366. London.

Photographs: National Buildings Record, Fielden House, 10 Great College Street, London, S.W.1.

Index

N.B. Houses described are placed under localities, except where otherwise indicated. The colleges of Oxford and Cambridge appear under their respective names. Roman numerals refer to half-tone illustrations, and bold arabic numerals to engravings.

Aaron (of Canterbury), 5

Aaron (of Lincoln), 2–4

Abberbury, Sir Richard, 157

Abingdon, Berks.: Great St Helen's Church, 44; fireplace and windows at 26 East St Helen's, 268, 360, XXIX C

Abingdon Abbey, Berks., 55, 67; the Checker, 92; Checker vault, 92, fig. 36 (plan, p. 92); lodgings, 185; fireplace, 266; Checker chimney, 285, XLIV F; another chimney, 288; Checker staircase, 330; Long Gallery, 337; garderobe, 378

Abinger, Surrey, Norman watch tower excavated at, 215

Acton Burnell Castle, Salop, 167; XXXI B; staff lodgings, 180; window, 347, 350, 27 A

Adam, mayor of Lincoln, 7

Adam de Port, 11

Adam of Jesmond, 12

Adam of Sodbury, Abbot of Glastonbury, 29, 265, 354

Adderbury Chuch, Oxon., 112

Addyman, P. V., 210

Adlington Hall, Cheshire: hall, 43; tester over high table, 134; spere truss, 142; roof, 319

Æthelfrith, King of Northumbria, 209

Agecroft Hall, Lancs. (now in Richmond, W. Virginia): oriel, 116, 10 A

Aisled derivative (or spere truss) hall, 42–3

Alexander III, of Scotland, 386

Alexander, Abbot, of Peterborough, 84

Alfred, King, 210, 212, 367

All Souls College, Oxford: gatehouse, 159; ground floor plan, fig. 58 (p. 181); service lodgings, 183

Allington Castle, Kent: garderobe, 385

Alnwick Castle, Northumberland, 157; staircase, 334

Alresford, Hants: Angel Inn, 192, 220

Alton Church, Hants: window, 356

Amberley Castle, Sussex, 183; service doorways, 128; service lodgings, 182; fireplace, 265; garderobes, 381, 384, LIX I

Amberley Court, Herefordshire, 214; wind-braces, 321

Amboise, France: staircase, 335

Andover, Hants, 192, 220

Andrews, W. J., 11, 12

Angle brackets, 263–72

Anglo-Saxon Chronicle, 17

Anglo-Saxon houses, 208–9

Appleby, Leics.: laver in Moat House, 369

Appleton Manor, Berks.: plan, fig. 43 (p. 124); doorways, 124, 339, XXIII A

Apuldram, Sussex: Rymans: solar, 78; solar tower, 174

Archaic framing, 222, 223

Archambaud de Saint Antonin, 8

Arch-braced collar-beam roof, 308–12

Arch-braced framing, 222, 223–4

Ardres, Flanders: tower house, 214, 215

Arnold, lord of Ardres, 214, 217

Arras, 403

Arthur, Prince, 405

Artois, Matilde (Mahaut), Countess of, 401, 402

Arundel, Richard FitzAlan, 6th Earl of, 183, 403

Arundel College, Sussex: service lodgings, 183; doorway, 340, 342, LII E

Ashbury Manor, Berks., 197, 200, XXXV C, D; plans, fig. 60 a, b (pp. 194–5); staircase, 91, 333, L D; chapel screen, 145; internal partitions, 146; porch, 152; double hall, 196; chapel,

239; kitchen, 252; fireplace, 267; roof, 311, 312, XLVI C; wind-braces, 323, XLIX B; cornice, 323, XLVI C; frieze in porch chamber roof, 324, VIII E; doorway, 342; windows, 360, XXXV C, D, LVI H; garderobe, 383, 384

Ashby de la Zouch Castle, Leics.: hall, fig. 12 (plan, p. 36); solar, 71, 72, 78; Hastings Tower, 173, 252; chapel, 237; chapel windows, 242; kitchen, 252, 255; Hastings Tower fireplace, 268; solar fireplace, 269; kitchen fireplaces, 273; garderobe, 385

Ashleworth Court, Glos., 216, XXVI A; oriel chamber, 104, XIX B; doorways, 343; windows, 355, 360

Aslackby, Lincs., chimney on house at, 287

Aston Eyre Manor House, Salop: solar, 77–8; oriel chamber, 104; oriel arch, 110; private doorways, 132; plans, fig. 48 (p. 133); staircase, 334

Athelhampton Hall, Dorset: hall, 56, 60, XX A; oriel, 104, 108, 112, 114, XXII A; porch, 153; roof, 307, 317; doorway, 342; hall windows, 360

Athelstan, King of the English, 210

Aydon Castle, Northumberland, 9; hall, 22; solar, 72, 75, 76; oriel, 99; private doorway, 130; hall porch, 150; service lodgings, 180; kitchen, 252; fireplaces, 263, 370, 20 B; gutters, 299; staircases, 329, 330, fig. 106 (p. 329); windows, 347, 348, 349, 356; laver, 369; garderobe, 380, 384

Ayscough, William, Bishop of Salisbury, 156

Baddesley Clinton, Warwickshire, 388

Baguley Hall, Cheshire, 213–14; hall,